TRIAL

ADVOCACY BEFORE JUDGES, JURORS, AND ARBITRATORS

Fifth Edition

■ ■ ■

by

Roger Haydock

Professor of Law, William Mitchell College of Law
Member, Minnesota, South Dakota, and Federal Bars
Director, FORUM International
Founder, ABA LSD Arbitration Competition
Board Member, Academy of Court-Appointed Masters

John Sonsteng

Professor of Law, William Mitchell College of Law
Member, Minnesota and Federal Bars
Regional Director, National Institute for Trial Advocacy
Director, William Mitchell Summer International Program

AMERICAN CASEBOOK SERIES®

WEST
ACADEMIC
PUBLISHING

American Casebook Series is a trademark registered in the U.S. Patent and Trademark Office.

© 1990 West Publishing Company
© 1999 West Group
© 2004 West, a Thomson business
© 2011 Thomson Reuters
© 2015 LEG, Inc. d/b/a West Academic
     444 Cedar Street, Suite 700
     St. Paul, MN 55101
     1-877-888-1330

West, West Academic Publishing, and West Academic are trademarks of West Publishing Corporation, used under license.

Printed in the United States of America

ISBN: 978-1-63459-278-9

To the Next Generation:
Mallory, Megan, Brady, Blake,
Chase, Will, Brooks, Emma, Olivia, Cole, and Kelsey

To Diane, Michael, David, Molly, and Sam

PREFACE

Welcome to the real world of advocacy.

This book explains the fundamental advocacy skills and explores the theories, tactics, and techniques involved in preparing and presenting a case to a judge, jury, arbitrator, and administrative judge. The goal of this book is to help you learn how to prepare and present a case in a judicial, arbitral, and administrative forum. Much of this text also applies to other professional work involving transactional lawyering, in house counsel, government lawyers, non-advocacy attorneys, and lawyer presentations before public and private organizations including executive boards, legislative bodies, and other professional decision makers.

Your clients will want you to be an effective, skilled, and trained advocate. They will and should expect you to successfully prepare and present their case to a decision maker. This book provides you with what you need to know to meet your clients' expectations and goals.

Chapters 1, 2, and 3 explain considerations involving the advocate, the planning and preparation of a case, and trial and hearing procedures and motions. Chapter 4 covers evidentiary objections and summarizes the law of evidence. Chapter 5 explains the jury selection process. Chapter 6 describes opening statements. Chapters 7, 9, and 10 cover witness examinations including direct examinations, cross-examinations, and experts. Chapter 8 explores real and demonstrative exhibits and visual aids and the foundation for exhibits including traditional and modern exhibits. Chapter 11 describes final argument and summation. Chapter 12 concludes this book with an explanation of verdicts and post-trial and post-hearing proceedings.

This Fifth Edition continues to reflect the evolutionary changes in advocacy. Cases are being presented in ever more efficient and effective ways. All chapters have been updated to explain how advocates can better try a case before a judge or jury. Additional materials have also been added that explain how advocates can best prepare and present cases before arbitrators and administrative judges.

This book blends traditional advocacy approaches with the latest contemporary methods. There are advocacy advancements interwoven throughout the chapters that combine the best of the past and present. New and innovative materials include the following additions.

Modern technology, computerized systems, and social media communications provide new approaches to advocacy planning and presentations. This Edition includes revised sections and examples explaining these advances. Chapter 4 explains how to successfully introduce electronically stored information and social network and digital evidence. Chapters 6 and 9 include new examples for direct and cross-examination. Chapter 8 includes innovative and novel computer and electronic exhibits. Chapters 6 and 11 describe additional winning examples for openings and closings.

The primary focus of this book continues to be what advocates can say or do to win by successfully influencing decision makers and fact finders. New approaches to gain favorable judgments, awards, and verdicts are described that go beyond the facts and law. Augmented sections discuss how influential factors such as normative values, balanced fairness, and proportional justice can be effectively presented.

Modified subsections highlight modern advocacy insights and developments. Contemporary notions regarding the abilities of witnesses to accurately recall events modify direct and cross-examination strategies and tactics. Scientific developments involving various forms of evidence including DNA revise the presentation of relevant evidence and related expert testimony.

Advocacy practice includes professional relationships lawyers maintain with clients, colleagues, staff, advisors, consultants, experts, and other attorneys. Case preparation and planning also involve cooperation among and collaboration with these various individuals. Advocacy work today entails more teamwork than in the past, and descriptions of these working relationships appear in this text.

Transformative changes are underway affecting the practice of law, including advocacy. Explanatory materials describe those changes and how they influence the work of current advocates. A new section summarizes what experts and commentators predict what may happen to advocacy practice in the near future.

This book recognizes that the traditional notions of justice occurring in a physical and face-to-face place such as a courtroom or hearing room are being modernized. Justice is a service to disputing parties that can take place in virtual hearings, telecommunications, and online formats. New materials explain how advocates can operate effectively in these modern forums.

Contemporary sources of available information provide new sources of facts and law for advocates. Internet search engines and a large variety of private and public websites are productive resources for evidence and legal research. Case preparation sections describe these novel ways to develop information.

Judges, arbitrators, and jurors expect advocates to present information and evidence that reflect modern developments, methods, and sources. This book covers and includes these current approaches to improve your advocacy skills for the future. You will learn the latest and most effective ways to successfully advocate cases.

The analyses contained in these chapters explain the whys and why nots and the shoulds and should nots of advocacy and trial practice. Learning about advocacy also requires reading about how lawyers actually try cases. This book presents numerous examples and illustrations of lawyers making statements, examining witnesses, introducing exhibits, and presenting arguments.

These examples reflect the broad range of civil and criminal cases and demonstrate trial, arbitration, and administrative processes. The illustrations presented are based on real and fictional events from the world of history, literature, business, science, art, and contemporary events. We selected parties and witnesses that relate to the topic or skills being explained. Hopefully these illustrations will make interesting, memorable, and entertaining reading. You, as the advocate, need to determine the appropriate approach to employ in the context of each case you try.

Another innovative learning method that accompanies this Edition is the *Supplement to Trial Advocacy Before Judges, Jurors, and Arbitrators,* available in book form or online from West Academic. A highly effective way to learn how to be an advocate is to read, review, and analyze the work of successful advocates. Three transcripts—a jury trial, an arbitration, and an administrative hearing—provide you with a firsthand opportunity to study the presentation of complete cases in those three distinct forums. You may obtain a print or electronic version of the *Supplement* from store.westacademic.com. No other law school text offers this extraordinarily helpful resource and experience.

You can learn much by studying the individual chapters in this book. You can learn more from reading these case transcripts with commentary. The *Supplement* also includes the Federal Rules of Evidence and selected federal civil procedure rules for your handy and ready reference. Future revisions to the *Supplement* will add additional resources including demonstration lawyering skills presentations.

Current professional videos of lawyers demonstrating effective lawyering skills freely appear at http://software.westacademic.com/lawyering-skills/. This site contains two videos, one a bench trial and one an arbitration. Both videos illustrate how lawyers successfully try cases, how various stages of a case interrelate, how evidence is introduced, how case theories are crafted, and how arguments are presented. The advocacy strategies, tactics, and techniques explained in this book are brought to video life in these lawyering skills demonstrations.

The *Darren Lamar v. Naomi Cullen* video illustrates a bench trial including opening statements, direct and cross-examinations, exhibit introductions, objections, and closing arguments. The Plaintiff Lessee is suing for breach of a commercial lease and for personal injury damages suffered by him on the premises. The Defendant Lessor defends on the grounds that the Plaintiff breached the lease and Plaintiff caused his own injuries. A companion Manual contains the transcript with commentary: Lawyering Skills: Depositions and Trial by P. Knapp, A. Juergens, & R. Haydock (West Academic).

The *Bingham v. Ecotronics* video arbitration also demonstrates experienced lawyers effectively trying a case. This dispute involves claims of age discrimination and breach of employment brought by Lester Bingham against his former employer. Ecotronics asserts that Les Bingham was an at will employee and was terminated because of poor performance and because his position was eliminated. The arbitration depicts lawyers performing openings, witness examinations, and closings and the arbitrator conducting the case. A companion Manual contains the transcript with commentary: Lawyering Skills: Mediation and Arbitration by P. Knapp, A. Juergens, & R. Haydock (West Academic).

Other sources of learning beyond the scope of this book are also available to you. CLE programs in your community often involve lawyers demonstrating and discussing advocacy skills. Professional websites and video sharing sites produce various types of advocacy events. Arbitration based reality television shows adjudicate disputes in simulated court proceedings. Some of these events are educational, some entertaining, and some both.

Courtrooms and hearing rooms are obviously real places to observe actual cases. Many judges, arbitrators, law clerks, and administrators are very willing and eager to help you learn and can provide you with hearing and trial schedules and educational experiences. These efforts may lead you to develop an advocacy internship or law school externship.

We hope you will find or have discovered the adventure and excitement that accompanies the practice of advocacy. We encourage you to send us comments, suggestions, stories, anecdotes, and examples that we can include in our next edition. We wish you the best at becoming and being an advocate now and throughout your practice in the future.

ROGER HAYDOCK
JOHN SONSTENG

William Mitchell College of Law
875 Summit Avenue
St. Paul, MN 55101
Roger.Haydock@wmitchell.edu
John.Sonsteng@wmitchell.edu

May 1, 2015

ACKNOWLEDGMENTS

Many persons contributed to the making of this book. We received substantial support and assistance from our marvelous families, friends, and colleagues. We thank them all and greatly appreciate their being an extraordinary part of our lives.

The special individuals whose contributions we acknowledged in the first, second, third, and fourth editions deserve continuing recognition for their part in the development of this book. Without them, this edition would not be. We also want to thank other individuals who have made this Fifth Edition a reality.

All the members of our immediate loving and caring families allowed us the opportunity to work on this book: Roger thanks Elaine, Marni, Marci, Jeffrey, Chuck, Gabe, Dan, and all 11 grandchildren named in the Dedication. John again thanks Diane, Michael, David, Molly, and Sam.

The very talented students at the William Mitchell College of Law, whom we have had the privilege and honor of teaching, deserve our special appreciation. All of them are above average. Our many clients also deserve our particular thanks for permitting us to represent them. They patiently allowed us to develop and improve as advocates.

The exceptional and wonderful staff at William Mitchell with whom we joyfully work helped make our ideas appear in print. Jennifer Miller and Sue McKenzie edited and proofed this Edition. Jean Backes and Linda Thorstad also assist us in teaching advocacy. Kaela McConnon helped with our research efforts.

Our outstanding and gifted colleagues, especially Professors Peter Knapp, Ann Juergens, Carolyn Grose, and Brad Colbert, provided us with inspiration and encouragement. Deans Eric Janus, Mehmet Konar-Steenberg, and Mary Pat Byrn supported our writing efforts. Dean Mark Gordon continues that great support.

Other excellent lawyers and very good friends, including David Herr, Lucinda Jesson, Edward Anderson, Catherine Anderson, Thomas Harvick, Libby Joyce, Morgan Wood, John Wood, Joyce Wharton, Richard Wharton, and Hon. Michael Davis also provided us with ideas. The terrific staffs at Forthright Solutions and The Forum further supported our work.

Dianna Case, Connect Litigation, and Litigation Insights very ably assisted with the content and design of the demonstrative exhibits in Chapter 8. The law firm of Robins Kaplan had provided some of the original exhibits.

Our supportive and brilliant publisher and editors at West Academic deserve our deep appreciation and thanks.

We further acknowledge you who will be reading and using this book. We have written this book for you, for the clients you will represent, and for the justice system you will serve.

SUMMARY OF CONTENTS

———————

TABLE OF CONTENTS

TABLE OF FORMS

——————

TABLE OF FEDERAL RULES

TRIAL

ADVOCACY BEFORE JUDGES, JURORS, AND ARBITRATORS

Fifth Edition

CHAPTER 1

THE ADVOCATE

• • •

1.1   Introduction
    A.   This Advocacy Book
    B.   Advocacy Sources and Resources
    C.   Future Advocacy Services
1.2   The Advocate
    A.   The Goal of the Advocate
    B.   Roles of Advocates
    C.   Character Traits
    D.   Balanced Approach
    E.   Client Relationships
    F.   Collaborative Relationships
1.3   Dispute Resolution Systems
    A.   Litigation
    B.   Arbitration
    C.   Administrative Hearings
    D.   Online Advocacy Resolution
1.4   Alternatives to a Trial or Hearing
    A.   Negotiated Settlements and Plea Bargains
    B.   Mediation
    C.   Fact/Issue Finding
    D.   Mini-Trial
    E.   Summary Jury Trial
    F.   Moderated Settlement Conference
    G.   Collaborative Law
    H   Private Judging
    I.   Special Masters
    J.   Court Mandated or Consensual Procedures
1.5   Storytelling Techniques
    A.   Use Primacy and Recency
    B.   Reasonably Repeat Information
    C.   Use the Rule of Three
    D.   Establish Realism
    E.   Develop Interest
    F.   Employ Visual Senses
    G.   Use Impact Words
    H.   Create Images
    I.   Remember What Is Presumed
    J.   Enhance Imagination
    K.   Employ Understandable Language
    L.   Develop Emotions and Reactions
    M.   Be Reasonably Brief

REFLECTING ON ADVOCACY

Justice cannot be for one side alone, but must be for both. . . .

—ELEANOR ROOSEVELT

Oh, do not ask, "What is it?"
Let us go and make our visit.

—T.S. ELIOT

THE LOVE SONG OF
J. ALFRED PRUFROCK

§ 1.1   INTRODUCTION

Welcome to advocacy. You will learn how to efficiently prepare and effectively try a case. You will discover what to do, when to do it, where to do it, and why to do it.

A.   THIS ADVOCACY BOOK

This text explains civil and criminal trial practice in the federal and state court systems, arbitration procedures and hearings, and administrative law processes. Our dispute resolution system includes three primary forums: judicial, arbitral, and administrative. This book thoroughly covers strategies and tactics applicable in these forums.

Many of the skills covered in this text are useful in other types of practice including transactional lawyering and other non-advocacy legal work. Lawyers in many types of professional roles need to persuade others, evaluate the strengths and weaknesses of cases, and understand how disputes can be most effectively resolved. These important skills are essential for lawyers to develop in crafting deals, or in resolving disputes, or in whatever professional work they do.

This book prepares you to be a highly professional, responsible, and competent advocate. You will face times of success (!), failure (#%?), excitement (yea!), weariness (sigh), fun (yes!), anxiety (oh, no), satisfaction (ahhh), frustration (ah, me) and peace (it's over). This book is designed to provide you with the theories, knowledge, procedures, skills, and techniques to guide you through these advocacy experiences.

The sources of trial "law" include rules of procedure, statutes, case law, constitutional provisions, local court rules, judges' orders and rulings, as well as customs and traditions. The sources of arbitration procedures also include the agreement of the parties and the applicable code of rules in addition to the law. The sources of administrative procedural law include statutes, regulations, and administrative and judicial opinions.

What occurs during trials and hearings follows common rules and procedures. A case tried in one jurisdiction is tried similarly in another jurisdiction. This book explains these common practices, as well as dissimilar practices.

Further, these materials analyze systems and strategies used by successful lawyers in planning cases. Attorneys learn from each other and adopt and adapt successful tactics and techniques. We look to the past to decide what to do presently and for the future.

This text describes alternative trial and hearing tactics and approaches applicable in current as well as evolving forums. There is no single or singular way to try a case. Much of what occurs during a trial and hearing is determined by the advocate's choice of strategies. The illustrations and examples of tactics and techniques presented will assist you in making well-reasoned judgments and informed decisions useful for all types of cases and tribunals, now and in the future.

Judgments and decisions advocates must make—from the planning of what to do to the presentation of a case—are based on analytical legal reasoning and incisive judgments. This process is a primary focus of this book. Both the theory and practice of why and how advocates effectively think and reason are analyzed.

The psychological and emotional dimensions involved in advocacy are also explored throughout this text. Trying a case can be a trying experience. The information presented in this book is designed to assist you in developing the level of confidence necessary to try a case well.

Advocates make mistakes in every case, and problems commonly occur during cases. The key is not letting the mistakes and problems overwhelm or negate the presentation. Many problems can be anticipated and many mistakes can be eliminated through preparation and an understanding of available solutions described in these materials.

Ethical issues arise during the preparation and presentation of a case. An underlying premise of this book is that advocates must hold themselves to high ethical standards. An understanding of professional rules and guidelines assists in identifying ethical concerns, resolving problems, and becoming a responsible advocate.

The legal profession is a helping profession. The mission of advocates, like all lawyers, is to help their clients. This humanistic dimension of advocacy shapes and influences the work of the advocate. The situations and problems presented in this book involve and affect the lives of clients, parties, lawyers, and others. We encourage you to bring to life what you read so you also can experience this human dimension of advocacy.

B. ADVOCACY SOURCES AND RESOURCES

Sources of advocacy law and dispute resolution solutions continue to evolve. The *Supplement to Trial Advocacy Before Judges, Jurors, and Arbitrators* is a companion source of materials to this book. The *Supplement* contains three complete transcripts of a jury trial, an administrative hearing, and an arbitration, accompanied by commentary explaining the advocacy tactics and techniques. The *Supplement* also includes the Federal Rules of Evidence and selected Federal Rules of Civil Procedure. Future revisions and updates to the *Supplement* will include additional and new informational sources including demonstration advocacy presentations. See store.westacademic.com.

Clients and parties may search for advocacy information online through a variety of legal resource websites ranging from Wikipedia to proprietary sites to the Legal Information Institute. They may explore dispute resolution websites about mediation (Mediate.com), arbitration (ADRForum.com), and administrative cases (state agencies). And they may learn about federal court procedures and how to try a federal lawsuit from United States district court websites. As a result, they will find some answers and also have questions about their options and need wise lawyers to advise and represent them.

Lawyers can review any number of books, websites, and blogs that explain advocacy developments and describe successful strategies and tactics. Legal publishers have an array of specialized civil and criminal advocacy texts. There are a variety of commentators and bloggers who post periodic legal updates, case opinions, and dispute resolution results. These and other easy to access sources are readily available to you.

Advocates can also learn advocacy skills from watching videos of lawyers trying lawsuits, administrative trials, and arbitrations. Professional videos provide educational demonstrations of a wide variety of lawyering skills including openings, direct and cross-examinations, and summations. These can be found online, in law libraries, and in legal publishing catalogs. The Preface to this book includes references to effective and excellent demonstration advocacy skills videos.

Cameras in the courtrooms provide another venue to view cases. Some appellate courts record their oral arguments, and some trial courts may record motions, hearings, and trials. And, ubiquitous video sharing and other social media websites provide even more opportunities to view reality, of some sort.

Observing real lawyers try actual cases is another valuable resource for educational experiences. Courtrooms in your locale provide a wide variety of civil and criminal cases. Court administrators can provide schedules of trials. Law clerks are receptive to helping law students attend trials. Trial lawyers will typically make themselves available to answer questions and explain what is happening. And judges commonly and graciously welcome advocates-to-be to their courtroom and chambers.

Administrative hearings and arbitrations may likewise be useful resources for observing these types of cases. Administrative staff can provide schedules for public hearings. Arbitration administrators and arbitrators may allow observations with the parties' consent.

Seeing, hearing, and experiencing the real thing provides ideal educational training. Law clinics, internships, externships, and practicum courses likely have some of these experiences available. Pro bono opportunities during and after law school are another worthwhile source of advocacy practice and provide invaluable community legal services.

Movies, television, and the theater may replicate historic or fictional trials. The upside is that these experiences can be entertaining and occasionally educational. The downside is that so much of what is portrayed is unrealistic, poorly done, or just plain wrong. There are also reality court shows that resolve disputes. Overall, it can be quite difficult to discern from these observations what might apply to real cases.

As you read and analyze the textual materials and examples in this book and other resources, you will become knowledgeable, curious, wiser, surprised, pleased, and perhaps shocked. Not everything in the real world of advocacy will conform to your expectations and your experiences with the adversary process, the legal profession, and our system of justice. We present the way things are, the way we believe them to be, and the way they should be. Your task as an advocate is to bring this all together, for yourself and your clients and for fact finders and decision makers.

C. FUTURE ADVOCACY SERVICES

Evolutionary changes in advocacy forums provide new and innovative approaches to dispute resolution. Some types of cases are being handled through virtual hearings (interactive video motions) and online exchanges of evidence and decisions (domain name dispute resolutions). Other innovative methods are forthcoming that provide fair and affordable justice, as discussed in later sections of this book.

Our traditional notions of justice view dispute resolution as an event that occurs in a place, such as a courthouse or an arbitration or administrative hearing room. Another view is that dispute resolution is a *service*—without boundaries. This notion provides additional opportunities for advocacy-trained lawyers to serve clients.

There will always be a need for advocates to conduct direct and cross-examinations representing clients before judges, jurors, and arbitrators. And there will be new and evolving opportunities to offer legal services to clients before, during, and after disputes arise, including the following.

Wise counselor. The value added benefits advocates can provide their clients are their insights, acumen, and judgment. Clients look to us for legal wisdom.

Risk manager. We can help clients avoid legal disputes. We know what may cause disputes, and we can predict how and when they may occur. Smart clients may retain us to prevent disputes and not just to resolve problems after they arise.

Hybrid Professional. Advocates may have other skill sets to offer clients. They may have expertise in technology, business, accounting, or other professions that combined with their knowledge of advocacy provide clients with multi-talented advocates.

Advocacy Adviser. Because of the multiple options clients will have regarding pre-dispute, ongoing dispute, and post-dispute choices and decisions, advocates can guide them through these processes. The value of the advocacy adviser is reflected in saving clients money and time and avoiding worries and disruptions to their business or personal lives.

Project and Process Manager. Advocates can readily manage and monitor available dispute resolution processes. A holistic dispute process can be subdivided into various components with specific tasks performed by a variety of professionals managed by the advocate.

Online Dispute Expert. Dispute resolution services will continue to evolve beyond physical locations, virtual hearings, teleconferences, and video hearings to online submissions. See Section 1.3(D).

§ 1.2   THE ADVOCATE

A.   THE GOAL OF THE ADVOCATE

The goal is to win. A case is tried because other alternative efforts at resolving the dispute—negotiation and mediation—have been unsuccessful. The client obviously expects to win, and counsel must make every reasonable effort to win. However, this goal of winning must be kept in perspective, for this end does not justify all means; and ethical rules and norms must be maintained.

The advocate uses all reasonable approaches to present a case to secure a favorable outcome. An all-out effort is governed by rules, ethics, and common sense. A process that involves acrimony or unreasonable approaches does not serve the client's interests or the system of justice. The effective advocate must be firm, persistent, and compassionate.

B.   ROLES OF ADVOCATES

The most obvious role of an advocate is to prepare and present the best possible case for a client. Another major role is as a risk assessor and dispute manager. Lawyers who are not advocates also have these roles. In house lawyers, transaction attorneys, legal consultants, and of counsel consultants advise clients about prospective legal risks. They often consult with advocates to determine the prospects for potential disputes, and they also frequently manage advocates. These lawyers need to understand the various roles advocates play including:

- A learned counselor who provides sound advice to clients,

- An officer of the court who follows ethical norms,

- An investigator who gathers and preserves information,

- A facilitator who promotes alternative resolution methods,

- A negotiator who makes good faith efforts to settle cases,
- A litigator who drafts pleadings and conducts discovery,
- A planner who prepares and argues motions,
- A manager who supervises support staff,
- A collaborator who works with other professionals,
- A storyteller who crafts a persuasive, compelling narrative, and
- An appellate lawyer who brings or defends an appeal.

The advocate may also perform other professional roles:

- An artistic lawyer who is creative and imaginative,
- A scientific based attorney who is rational and logical,
- A lawyer psychologist who understands behaviors,
- A legal historian who recreates time past, and
- An advocacy director who directs a dispute resolution play where the court or hearing room is the theater, the witnesses are actors, the exhibits are props, and the decision maker is the audience.

C. CHARACTER TRAITS

Our personality and character traits influence our professional approach and behavior. All effective advocates possess integrity, honesty, fairness, sensitivity, and respect for others. Trustworthiness is our goal.

Decision makers must be able to trust attorneys. They rely upon the attorney's word and explanations. An untrustworthy advocate is an ineffective advocate. The attorney must also display a sincere belief in the merits of the client's case. The lack of sincerity may cause the decision makers to conclude that the attorney does not believe in or care about the case. And, lawyers who take unfair advantage of situations or who are disreputable will not be perceived as fair.

Additionally, advocates encounter a full range of personality temperaments in dealing with opposing attorneys, witnesses, arbitrators, judges, and jurors. These individuals may be courteous or rude, cooperative or hostile, friendly or arrogant, pleasant or intimidating, trustworthy or untrustworthy. The advocate must adopt various approaches to deal with this broad spectrum of personalities.

D. BALANCED APPROACH

Advocates suffer stress due to: the pressure to win, unrealistic expectations, fear of failure, insufficient fee payments, excessive expenses, ego, physical discomfort, fatigue, anxieties, tension, peer pressure, neglect of personal and family matters, emotional withdrawal, and preoccupation with a case. Attorneys may take cases for financial rewards but may also take them to accept a difficult challenge, work with a specific client, obtain publicity, achieve fame, satisfy a legal fantasy, change the law, protect a client's rights, or promote justice.

A number of ways advocates can deal with stress and maintain a balanced life include:

- Before accepting a case, reflect on the reasons why you are taking the case and your expectations.

- Maintain a proper relationship with the client. Involve the client in making decisions and avoid being too controlling.

- Do not worry about events or matters that cannot be altered. Learn to let go and accept what cannot be changed.

- Assess your legal fees. You need to be fairly and timely compensated for your work, unless you are working pro bono.

- Monitor advocacy expenses. Clients are responsible for litigation costs and need to be informed of expenses as the case progresses.

- Expect that relationships with family, friends, and colleagues will be disrupted. Advise them problems may arise and offer solutions.

- Discuss your feelings and attitudes with family members and other caring listeners.

- Monitor your workload to avoid becoming overworked. Delegate appropriate responsibilities and tasks to support staff. Learn not to interfere unnecessarily and second-guess decisions.

- Exercise your body as well as your mind.

- Avoid alcohol, drugs, tobacco, and other harmful escapes.

- Afterwards, discuss the case with your client and colleagues.

- Celebrate the experience, whether you win or lose.

- Take a break and enjoy some rest and relaxation.

E. CLIENT RELATIONSHIPS

Clients place their legal fate in the hands of advocates. This reliance places enormous responsibility on the advocate to justify the client's trust. The exact relationship between the client and the attorney varies depending upon the needs of the client, the client's familiarity with the legal system, and the client's and attorney's views of the appropriate relationship. The key to effective client/attorney relationships is communication and the continuing involvement of the client in the preparation and presentation of the case.

The client and the attorney in consultation with each other can identify the interests of the client, consider potential ways to compromise or win the dispute, and select a course of action to succeed. Clients may best determine what their needs are with the advice of counsel. The more a decision has a substantial legal or non-legal impact on a client, the more crucial it is to have the client involved in making that decision. The more a decision involves professional expertise and skills, the more likely it is the attorney can wisely make the decision.

Clients' expectations of their lawyers evolve. The more knowledgeable and sophisticated they are, the more demands they may place on their attorneys. In house counsel, executives with law degrees, and parties with previous experience with litigation may expect high levels of efficiencies, alternative fee arrangements, cooperative relationships, and perhaps even more work and lower fees.

Many clients recognize that law practice, including litigation work, can be a very inefficient, laborious, and painful process, especially if advocates are paid by the hour. There can be inherent tensions between what is the best course of action for a client and what is in the best financial interests of a lawyer. Ongoing and open discussions between clients and lawyers regarding these and related issues help create trusting and collaborative relationships.

F. COLLABORATIVE RELATIONSHIPS

Advocates engage in a variety of collaborative relationships. There are simple cases that may only require the skills of one advocate to resolve, or clients may only have the resources to retain a single advocate. More complicated cases involve advocates managing a support staff of paralegals, law clerks, experts, and other professionals. Complex and multi-district litigation cases require teams of lawyers to work together for one or a group of clients.

Lawyers need to develop skills of cooperation and collaboration to succeed in these types of cases. Clients may retain several law firms in complex cases, one to handle discovery, another to work on potential settlement options, and still another to try the case. The changing practice of advocacy law has some clients dividing advocacy tasks into components and out-sourcing these jobs among lawyers, document review companies, financial experts, legal audit consultants, and other professionals.

§ 1.3   DISPUTE RESOLUTION SYSTEMS

A. LITIGATION

Lawsuits may be brought in federal or state court, whichever has proper jurisdiction. Federal courts resolve disputes involving federal statutes and the federal constitution, disputes between citizens of different states in excess of $75,000, and special cases such as patent disputes and bankruptcy. State courts are courts with general jurisdiction and hear the vast majority of judicial disputes.

A plaintiff begins a lawsuit by serving a summons and complaint on the defendant who can reply with an answer. Litigation proceeds with the parties conducting discovery and bringing motions eventually resulting in a jury or bench trial. Federal and state constitutional and statutory provisions provide parties with the right to a jury trial in most civil cases, particularly those involving money damages. Other cases, including injunctive relief cases, are tried to a judge. Any party with grounds may appeal to an appellate court.

Litigation is often the remedy available to the parties if they are unable to agree to another dispute resolution method. Litigation may be the last resort parties rely on to have their dispute resolved because the trial process can be very expensive, time consuming, and painful.

B. ARBITRATION

There are two primary types of arbitration. One is a contractual process where a neutral arbitrator (usually an experienced lawyer or a retired judge) conducts a hearing and issues a final, binding award. Procedural rules govern the case, such as The Forum Code of Procedure, which provide for discovery and motions. This system is widely used in numerous types of disputes and is becoming the preferred way businesses, individuals, companies, and employees resolve their differences. Arbitration clauses appear in all types of agreements and relationships, including commercial contracts, financial documents, employment relationships, adhesion contracts, health care transactions, insurance contracts, and business agreements. Arbitration is typically much more affordable, a lot faster, and as fair as a trial.

The other is a non-binding process (often called court-annexed arbitration) that is mandatory in some jurisdictions. In this non-binding pretrial proceeding, the arbitrator, who is usually an attorney randomly selected from a panel of arbitrators, hears evidence and arguments and renders a decision. If the decision is acceptable to both parties, the lawsuit is dismissed. If the decision is unacceptable, the case goes to trial.

C. ADMINISTRATIVE HEARINGS

Administrative hearings typically resolve disputes involving government benefits or statutory remedies. A party may file a petition with an administrative tribunal, and an administrative judge holds a hearing and decides the case. Administrative proceedings are similar to bench trials. The availability of discovery and motions may be limited.

Controversies resolved through federal and state administrative hearings include workers' compensation claims, unemployment compensation claims, tax claims, social security claims, welfare claims, and other rule based claims. Administrative claims may also involve regulatory procedures. Parties involved in a dispute regarding the enactment or enforcement of government regulations may also appear before administrative bodies to present their case. Examples include utility rate setting cases and environmental cases.

D. ONLINE ADVOCACY RESOLUTION

The three traditional forums involve disputing parties appearing before judges, arbitrators, administrative judges or jurors presenting and pleading their case. An evolving modern system involves a blend of traditional and new methods to resolve disputes. Parties with the assistance of lawyers or on their own may use electronic and computer assisted systems to obtain a resolution. Claimants may submit their claims online with respondents filing their defenses online. The participants may present their evidence through online submissions. Judges or arbitrators may review these submissions online and issue electronic orders or rulings resolving the dispute.

Not all future disputes may be resolved through our traditional notions of due process and in-person hearings and trials. As other professions, business, and government agencies develop online systems to conduct their work, dispute resolution forums may adapt their procedures to adopt similar methods providing fair, accessible, and affordable justice.

§ 1.4   ALTERNATIVES TO A TRIAL OR HEARING

Before placing their fate in the hands of a judge, arbitrator, or jury, clients and advocates need to consider how else the dispute may be resolved. Parties may be more likely satisfied if they control their fate through a settlement or other alternative dispute resolution (ADR) process. These include traditional methods involving face to face interactions as well as on line video and email exchanges. Major dispute resolution methods are discussed below.

A. NEGOTIATED SETTLEMENTS AND PLEA BARGAINS

Negotiated settlements are an essential part of the dispute resolution process. The large majority of civil and criminal cases are settled or plea-bargained. Various factors influence the results of negotiation practice, including the willingness of the parties to go to trial and the experience and ability of the attorneys to try cases.

Judges often take an active role in negotiations by encouraging and becoming directly involved in settlement conferences. Judicial approval or consent is not normally required for settlement of civil litigation unless the case involves a class action or an injury to a minor. Many judges require the parties to use a mediator. Arbitrators and administrative judges tend not to become involved in settlement talks as their role is to conduct a hearing and decide the case.

The type of settlement agreement depends upon the nature and circumstances of the civil case. One universal settlement document is a dismissal with prejudice that disposes of the case. The dismissal may be a stipulation signed by the attorneys that dismisses the case, or it may be an order signed by the decision maker based on a stipulation by the parties. The dismissal should specify whether the costs are to be borne by each of the parties or are to be paid by one of the parties. Federal Rule of Civil Procedure 41, similar state court provisions, arbitration rules, and administrative procedures commonly regulate these dismissals.

In criminal cases, the judge usually needs to approve the plea bargain entered into by the prosecutor and defendant. The plea bargain may consist of a guilty plea, a plea to a less serious offense, nolo contendere, or another plea authorized in the jurisdiction, and may also include conditions of probation and sentencing. Pleas of guilty are taken in open court. The defense counsel, prosecutor, and judge all have an obligation to make sure that the defendant understands what is happening and that the plea is complete and legally sufficient to support a conviction.

B. MEDIATION

Mediation is an informal process where a neutral professional assists the parties in reaching a mutually acceptable agreement. The mediator's primary role is to facilitate a negotiated settlement between the parties. The mediator does not decide any issues or make any decisions but may offer opinions and predict likely outcomes. In some jurisdictions, mediation is compulsory, and the parties must attempt to mediate a settlement in good faith before proceeding to trial. A related process is known as a med-arb proceeding. The parties first attempt to mediate, and if that fails, they arbitrate the dispute.

C. FACT/ISSUE FINDING

Fact/issue finding is an informal process in which a neutral third party selected by the parties or the court reviews the case and submits a written or oral report that identifies and evaluates disputed facts and issues. This process is useful in resolving complex scientific, technical, business, or economic issues where the presentation of proof is extremely difficult, expensive, and time-consuming. The use of a highly experienced neutral assists the parties in reaching agreement on the undisputed and disputed matters. The neutral professional may be appointed by the court under Federal Rule of Evidence 706 or similar state rules.

D. MINI-TRIAL

A mini-trial is a private, consensual proceeding where counsel for each party makes a short presentation before a panel consisting of a representative of each of the parties and a neutral third person. This process, with the assistance and perspective of the neutral panel member, assists the parties in understanding both sides of the case in an effort to reach a mutually acceptable agreement.

E. SUMMARY JURY TRIAL

A summary jury trial takes place in a courtroom with a judge, magistrate, or special master and a mock jury selected from the regular jury list, sometimes with the assistance of a private consultant. Counsel for each party makes a presentation consisting of a brief opening statement, the summary introduction of key evidence, and a closing argument. The jury deliberates and renders an advisory verdict or verdicts, which provide the parties with a reliable basis to predict what jurors would do after a complete trial. One party may unilaterally conduct this summary trial privately seeking the help of mock jurors as a focus group to evaluate the case. These methods are primarily used in major cases where other ADR methods have been unsuccessful.

F. MODERATED SETTLEMENT CONFERENCE

A moderated settlement conference is a forum for case evaluation and structured settlement negotiations between the parties and their attorneys. The advocates present their cases before an impartial professional or a panel of impartial third parties who evaluate the case and render an advisory non-binding opinion for use by the parties in settlement negotiations. This method may be used in non-jury cases.

G. COLLABORATIVE LAW

A balanced approach to resolving disputes is known as the collaborative law approach. The parties with the help of a professional versed in dispute resolution agree on their own process to settle their dispute and then proceed to follow the process to a resolution. The professional seeks to involve the parties in a mutually cooperative approach and result, which can be very effective in family law cases.

H. PRIVATE JUDGING

Parties to a dispute may agree or be ordered by the court to submit their dispute to a private (usually former or retired) judge for resolution. Parties may prefer a private judge (or arbitrator) because the private judge may have experience resolving the type of dispute and the trial may be able to be scheduled much more quickly than a public trial and conducted more privately. In some states, the decision by the private judge (special magistrate or referee) can be enforced as if it were a civil judgment or reviewed by a public judge who converts it into a judgment.

I. SPECIAL MASTERS

Experienced and expert professionals may serve as masters to assist the parties, lawyers, and court in resolving disputes. Federal Rule of Civil Procedure 53 permits these masters to serve a variety of roles that will help the case move forward and result in settlement. Similar state court rules allow for the appointment of judicial adjuncts to serve these roles. More information can be obtained at www.courtappointedmasters.org.

J. COURT MANDATED OR CONSENSUAL PROCEDURES

A growing number of jurisdictions are mandating the use of one or more of these alternatives to resolve disputes prior to trial. Some states require the parties to attempt an ADR method (usually mediation) before a case may proceed to trial. Other decision makers by statute or rule have discretion to require parties to submit to a dispute resolution procedure.

Parties may also agree to use one or more ADR methods instead of relying on the court system to solve their problems. Some parties believe the judicial system is too costly, too slow, and too unpredictable. They may well prefer and choose private mediation and binding arbitration to resolve their problems.

§ 1.5   STORYTELLING TECHNIQUES

Advocates are storytellers, and effective storytelling techniques are adaptable to advocacy. Advocates use language, images, words, pictures, and other devices to tell a compelling, interesting, and persuasive story. Good storytellers immediately draw the reader into the story and maintain the reader's attention throughout. Playwrights establish the circumstances of time and place, introduce the protagonists, develop a conflict, and then present solutions to the conflict. Advocates can look to these and other approaches in crafting a story.

There are a variety of professions beyond the legal profession that focus and rely on storytelling as part of their success. Ingredients basic to all effective stories include narrative theory and story construction. Narrative theory provides the basis to understand the possible contents of what constitutes an effective story. Story construction is an essential step in case planning, before the case has to be performed and presented.

Advocates need to make choices in creating story lines. They review and shape what happened and why, what really matters, what are the plot lines, who are the main characters and other actors, and what are the crucial factual issues and legal elements. The ending of the story concludes with the best way to resolve what happened—a choice ultimately to be made by the decision maker.

Advocates have alternative ways to tell their stories. There are critical decisions to be made regarding what is included in the story and what is left out, what is emphasized and what is minimized, and what solutions are available to resolve the dispute. That's why it's vital for clients to be involved in deciding what story is best told. They can and should influence their lawyers. Parties want to be proud and pleased with the story being told by their lawyers and they need to make their preferences known. The facts, the law, and client goals largely shape these choices.

A variety of other factors discussed below and in subsequent chapters influence the final decisions and the final story to be told.

A. USE PRIMACY AND RECENCY

People remember best that which they hear first and last. The doctrines of primacy—what a person hears first—and recency—what a person hears last—may dictate when evidence and statements ought to be introduced during a case. These doctrines apply to the case as a whole as well as to each stage of the trial or hearing, including the opening statement, witness examinations, and the closing argument.

B. REASONABLY REPEAT INFORMATION

The more times individuals perceive something the more likely they will believe it and remember it. Evidence can be referred to a reasonable number of times to increase the chances that the fact finders will recall and believe it. What is reasonable depends on the circumstances of the case, how long it lasts, and how the matter is repeated.

C.　USE THE RULE OF THREE

Advocates: explain what happened (opening statement), detail what happened through witnesses and documents (evidence), and summarize what happened (summation). This format follows a rule of persuasion: "Tell them what you are going to tell them, tell them, and tell them what you have told them."

D.　ESTABLISH REALISM

A successful play or movie captures the audience so they forget they are at a play or watching a movie. A poorly presented dramatic act makes the audience aware of what they are watching and anxious for the end of the make-believe story. The advocate, paralleling the goal of the playwright, wants the fact finders to forget they are decision makers at a trial or hearing, but instead believe they are observers at an event unfolding before them.

E.　DEVELOP INTEREST

Advocates need to make all cases as interesting as possible to hold the attention of decision makers and influence the final decision. Some cases are interesting by their very nature. For example, a wrongful death or murder case is usually dramatic. Other cases, such as those involving commercial litigation and real estate, are not nearly as exciting, but need to be made interesting.

For example, every commercial case is about people making business decisions. The advocate must present these people and these decisions in as stimulating a way as possible. As another example, every real estate case involves a unique piece of property. The advocate might be able to establish the special value or historical nature of this property to increase the interest level of the case. Even with seemingly mundane facts, the advocate must create and develop as much interest as possible so the fact finder will be more likely to understand and remember the events.

F.　EMPLOY VISUAL SENSES

Studies and experience indicate that individuals remember a much larger percent of what they both see and hear compared to what they just hear. And, modern educational and entertainment approaches are designed to involve and influence multiple senses. The use of visual aids and documentary and computer exhibits in advocacy cases increases the likelihood that the fact finder will recall and understand specific evidence and presentations. Chapter 8 describes the use of effective exhibits.

G. USE IMPACT WORDS

Individuals react to words that are used to describe an event. Descriptive words emphasizing specific facts of a case create more vivid images of an event than nondescriptive words. Descriptive language includes impact words that graphically describe a situation, such as "smashed" instead of "hit," "huge" instead of "large," and "shrieked" instead of "yelled." These impact words affect the fact finder's perception of what happened and are more easily remembered by the fact finder.

Impact words should be factually specific to accurately convey what happened and not exaggerated conclusions unsupported by the evidence. Thesauruses, dictionaries, and works of literature may serve as sources of such words and phrases. For example, in an automobile accident case, when the accident is described merely as an "incident" this neutral term will not create a specific image of the accident. When the accident is described as a "collision" or "violent crash," a more graphic image of the accident is portrayed.

H. CREATE IMAGES

Individuals learn and understand by forming images in their minds. When fact finders hear a word or listen to a description of an event, they visualize images based on what they have heard from a lawyer or witness.

For example, when an attorney says the word "chair" to a fact finder, each decision maker draws a mental image of a chair. That image might be of a wooden chair, a padded chair, a rocking chair, a desk chair, or a plastic chair. The advocate must make certain that the actual chair involved in the case is the image the fact finders picture in their minds. The more vital the details of this chair are to the case, the more precise the attorney must be in presenting details that give an accurate picture.

As another example, when an attorney asks jurors to assess damages for pain and suffering, the attorney must use words that make the jurors feel the pain and suffering. Injured parties need to describe what the injury really felt like. Witnesses should not merely say they had a headache, but that it felt as if someone was inside their head pounding with a hammer. Witnesses should not merely say that their leg was cut by a saw, but that they felt an intense, burning pain of hot metal slicing through their flesh.

I. REMEMBER WHAT IS PRESUMED

There is not enough time in a trial or hearing to introduce everything that could or even should be introduced to help the fact finder understand all the facts and circumstances of a case. Evidence law limits facts to those that are relevant; common sense presumes the fact finder knows a lot about some things in a case based on information that is not introduced as evidence. There are many factual details that are never even mentioned that everyone presumes we all understand sufficiently.

For example, in an automobile accident case, it is presumed that fact finders realize that cars have four wheels and the steering wheel is used to turn the car and brakes are used to stop it. Unless one of these issues is a major issue in a case, there are no facts introduced to explain what a wheel looks like or how brakes operate. To do so, would likely insult the fact finder. Advocates need to be aware of the background or detailed facts that are presumed to be known to determine if they need to explain or augment any of those facts.

J. ENHANCE IMAGINATION

The images created in the fact finders' minds may be clear or hazy, complete or incomplete. An ideally communicated image should involve the senses and should focus on all details of an event. This, however, is impossible because everything cannot be recreated. The advocate must make the critical images as realistic as possible to enable the fact finder to imagine the event vividly and accurately. For example, an advocate may need to decide whether to introduce a photo or a graphic image of a chair or rely on the fact finder to imagine that chair.

K. EMPLOY UNDERSTANDABLE LANGUAGE

Clarity of expression is critical. Simple and clear language is preferable to complex legalese. Large words used only to show off vocabulary skills turn off the decision maker, while overly simplistic words and explanations sound condescending. The attorney needs to select language appropriate to the background and experience of the decision maker.

L. DEVELOP EMOTIONS AND REACTIONS

An advocate may be able to use the emotions inherent in a case as an actor relies on the emotions inherent in a play. An actor does not become the source of an emotional catharsis; it is the reenactment of an event that creates cathartic reactions in the audience. A good actor leads the audience to the threshold of emotion, and the culmination of that emotion is felt by the audience. An advocate tries to create an atmosphere in which the decision maker is affected by emotions at the right time. In a wrongful death case, the plaintiff's lawyer wants the jurors to feel grief in such a way that their compassion favorably affects their judgment during deliberations.

M. BE REASONABLY BRIEF

Audiences, including judges, arbitrators, and jurors, have limited attention spans, which can be maximized if the presentation is interesting, dramatic, reasonably paced, and otherwise well presented. The length of a presentation must be based not only on what must be said, but also on the fact finder's likely attention span. The advocate needs to observe the decision makers and tailor a presentation to make certain they are paying sufficient attention.

§ 1.6   FUNDAMENTAL APPROACHES OF PERSUASION

This section explains established methods of persuasion that significantly influence the presentation of a case and that apply to all phases of a case.

A. RELY ON VALUES AND PRINCIPLES

Decision makers often interpret facts, apply the law, and make decisions based on their values, norms, principles, and beliefs. A primary task of an advocate is to attempt to identify these values and predict how a decision maker will make a decision consistent with these principles. Subsequent sections of this text will explore how advocates can best accomplish this critical task.

B. ACTIVELY INVOLVE THE FACT FINDER

A fact finder who becomes mentally and emotionally involved in a case is more likely to be interested in the case and more likely to believe and remember evidence. The goal is to present the events in such a way that the fact finders think they are a part of the case, perceive they are observing what actually happened in the past, and feel the emotions of the situation. In a robbery case, the prosecutor may design questions that invite the fact finder to view the crime as if they were there in the moment instead of considering it from a distance as a past event. For example, questions such as the following may engage the fact finder to be at the scene: "As you walked that first block from the bus stop, tell the jurors what you saw. . . . And as you walked the second block, describe what you heard. . . . And as you crossed to the third block, describe what you felt. . . ."

C. FOCUS ON RESPONSIBILITY

Most disputes involve issues of *responsibility*—and irresponsibility—and *accountability*—and the failure to be held accountable. Plaintiffs portray defendants as having breached their contract duties or tort responsibilities. Defendants assert that plaintiffs refuse to be held accountable for mistakes they made in breaching a contract or causing an accident.

These dual themes often determine who wins the case. The goal of the plaintiff is to establish that the defendant ought to be held more accountable for their conduct; and the goal of the defendant is to show the plaintiff is more irresponsible than the defendant and ought to lose. The reality is that both parties to a civil dispute usually acted in some irresponsible way and that both should be held accountable for their mistakes and errors. Whichever party convinces the decision maker that the opposing party is *more irresponsible* will usually win. Whichever party the decision maker believes ought to be held *more accountable* will typically lose.

D. IDENTIFY INCONSISTENCIES

Disputes obviously involve differences of facts, opinions, memories, and perceptions. In determining which side is right and which is wrong, the decision maker will need to understand the scope and degree of these inconsistent positions. The advocate can identify and emphasize the sources and reasons behind these differing viewpoints or positions. Once identified and understood, advocates can then provide evidentiary answers regarding why their client is right or why the opponent is wrong.

E. PRESENT ALTERNATIVES

The advocate must obviously avoid presenting mutually contradictory positions. Some situations require a presentation of alternative explanations. These presentations are most effective if they are described as alternative and not contradictory positions by avoiding the use of the terms "but" or "however." It is better to affirmatively state a position and then add another explanation, using such terms as "moreover" or "further."

For example, in an automobile accident case, the plaintiff may contend that she was hit in the crosswalk while the defendant contends that she was hit outside the crosswalk. Plaintiff's counsel could argue that plaintiff was in the crosswalk when she was hit, or even if she wasn't in the crosswalk, she was hit negligently by the defendant outside the crosswalk. A more effective explanation to avoid this contradictory statement is: "The defendant negligently struck plaintiff where she was walking; moreover, we will prove that she was walking in the crosswalk."

F. MAKE SIMPLE EXPLANATIONS

The more straightforward and less convoluted an explanation, the more likely it will be understood. The advocate should provide the fact finder with as simple and credible an explanation of what happened as possible. This type of presentation fulfills the need of many decision makers looking for a reasonable, straightforward answer to explain a conflict, even when the case is difficult and complex.

Unfortunately, lawyers are not always trained to develop simple explanations, but are often taught in law school to present complicated explanations of both sides of a case. For example, in analyzing a criminal case, a criminal defense lawyer could argue that the defendant was not present at the armed robbery, or if the defendant was present, the defendant was not holding a gun, or if the defendant was holding a gun, it was used in self-defense. These possible explanations may generate a high grade in a law school exam, but will only convince a fact finder of the defendant's guilt.

G. IDENTIFY WITH THE DECISION MAKER

Decision makers are more likely to believe a witness or favor a party if they can identify with that individual. Perceiving similarities between themselves and the witness or party helps form this identification. Fact finders may not consciously disbelieve a witness because they do not identify with that witness, but usually the more a witness or party has in common with a fact finder, the more likely the fact finder will identify with and believe that person.

Background information that establishes similarities between the witness and the fact finders should be emphasized. Specific examples of similarities can be described during the direct examination of the witness. The questions should not be so numerous or obvious, however, that the fact finders perceive that the witness is being portrayed to be like them.

§ 1.7   ELEMENTS OF ADVOCACY

There are a variety of approaches to trying a case. These variations reflect the difference in opinions among advocates. This section describes alternative approaches to case presentation.

A. THE PERSUASIVE ADVOCATE

Many lawyers believe that advocacy requires them to convince the decision maker of the correctness and righteousness of their client's position by attempting to "sell" the position to the decision maker. Typically, these advocates ask the decision maker to find "in favor of" or "for" or "on behalf of" their client. The underlying premise is that the advocate's client deserves a certain result because the advocate has convinced the decision maker the client is entitled to win.

Another view is that the advocate provides the decision maker with information which would lead reasonable people to come to but one conclusion. This approach does not require that the attorney usurp the decision maker's function. The responsibility remains on the decision maker to reach a decision based on the facts, the law, and justice. Rather than attempt to cajole, sell, or otherwise convince the fact finders, the attorney simply says "here are the facts, here is the law, and the result you should reach is clear."

An approach that combines the benefits of both approaches may be most effective. The benefit of the first adversarial approach is that it can result in a very persuasive and compelling presentation, while a disadvantage is that the advocate may appear to be inappropriately partisan and manipulative. The benefit of the second approach is that the fact finders reach their own conclusion based on the information the attorney presents to them, while the disadvantage is that the attorney may appear to be uncertain or unconvincing.

B.   INVOLVEMENT OF ADVOCATE

The degree to which advocates should involve themselves in cases is a matter of disagreement among advocates. Some argue that attorneys should not emphasize their professional beliefs during the case, while others argue that it is critical to establish their professional belief. By professional belief, we mean it appears to the decision maker that the advocate believes in the client's cause. This is distinguished from the advocate's personal belief that cannot or need not be expressed.

Advocates who suggest that the display of involvement is necessary say things like "I will prove to you" and "I will introduce evidence to convince you of these facts." Advocates who suggest that their involvement should be diminished use phrases during the case such as "You will hear evidence and you will conclude. . . ." These two positions do share common principles and may differ only in the emphasis placed upon them. The decision maker must be given the impression that the advocate believes in the client and the case presented. The fact finder is unlikely to find in favor of a client whose lawyer expresses doubts about whether that client should win.

C.   THE OBJECTIVE PARTISAN

The advocate has a dual role that needs to be balanced: being both a partisan and an objective participant. The attorney as partisan needs to present selective evidence to the fact finder and zealously argue for the client's position. The attorney as objective participant must appear to present evidence in an objective way and provide reasonable explanations. If the decision makers perceive that lawyers are too partisan, they will be less likely to believe the lawyers. Likewise, if the decision makers perceive that a lawyer is too objective, then they may be less influenced because the lawyer does not appear to advocate a position.

D. OPEN-MINDEDNESS OF DECISION MAKER

It is difficult, if not impossible, for the decision maker to have a completely open mind before or during a trial or hearing. Many advocates believe that no decision maker ever has a completely open mind and present their case based on this premise. They believe that all fact finders have some biases and prejudices, and some decision makers may be partial to one side or the other. They recognize that decision-making processes in cases may parallel other life experiences.

At the early stages of a case, the decision maker may begin to form impressions about the case, the attorneys, and the parties. The notion that decision makers impartially absorb information during a trial or hearing and wait to decide a case can be inaccurate. Some fact finders, especially jurors, selectively listen for evidence that supports their initial inclination or position. Evidence that does not support their position is rejected, disbelieved, rationalized, forgotten, or not even heard. Some decision makers make up their minds well before the closing argument.

The lack of open-mindedness on the part of the fact finders affects the way an advocate presents a case. The goal of the advocate is to provide the information and reasons sufficient for the decision maker to want to find for the advocate's client early in a case, and then to continue to provide information and reasons to support that decision during the trial or hearing. It is much more difficult to change someone's mind once it is made up or to alter an opinion once it is formed. The case presentation may need to be tailored to provide additional evidence and creative reasons to overcome perceived or real biases and prejudices.

E. MEMORIES OF WITNESSES

In preparing a case, an advocate must determine the degree to which each witness has an accurate recollection of an event. There exists a range of opinions among lawyers regarding a witness' ability to remember. Some advocates suggest that witnesses remember very little, if anything at all. These advocates believe that witnesses draw on the few recollections they have, collect evidence from other sources (such as other individuals or documents) and use the law of probability to form a recollection. Other lawyers believe that witnesses are able to draw upon the resources of their memory and accurately (or fairly accurately) recall things that happened in the past. The right belief depends upon the ability of that individual to perceive and remember the event, the impact the event had upon the witness, and whether the witness had any reason or expectation to perceive or recall the event.

Cases which arise from situations that the parties did not anticipate may result in less complete and accurate recollections. For example, in a typical automobile accident case, the parties do not anticipate they will be involved in an accident and have no reason to focus on the events that occur before an accident. There is little reason for them to concentrate on remembering their speed, distances, or the traffic situation. After the accident, however, witnesses to the event may pay close attention to what is said or how people act because they may expect to be called on to give a statement. It is more likely that the later part of their stories will be more complete and accurate. For another example, in a criminal case the victim may or may not have good reasons to be able to identify the defendant. Some victims are so scared or frightened during the crime that they are unable to look at the criminal, while other victims may want to get a good look so they can later help catch the criminal.

Psychology surveys show that most witnesses add details that they did not perceive and that they do not actually recall. This "filling in the details" phenomenon is often done unconsciously and without the witness intending to exaggerate or lie. Some witnesses, however, intentionally exaggerate or lie. Recent studies regarding the problems inherent with eyewitness testimony raise questions about the accuracy and credibility of eyewitnesses. Advocates must address these concerns in presenting direct examination testimony and in challenging questionable testimony on cross-examination.

F.　DISPLAYING A RELATIONSHIP WITH A CLIENT

The nature of the case and the kind of client dictate what relationship should be displayed between an attorney and client. If the fact finder is likely to perceive the client as a credible or a good person, the advocate should display a close relationship with the client by talking with the client and appearing to like the client. In cases in which the fact finder may not identify with or like a client, lawyers disagree as to the relationship they should establish in front of the decision maker. Some lawyers believe that they should distance themselves from this kind of client as much as possible, fearing that the appearance of a close relationship with such a client will hurt the attorney's standing in the eyes of the fact finder. Other lawyers believe that such a client needs visible support from the attorney. They fear the opposite reaction from the decision maker who may not support the client because it appears that the client's own attorney wants little to do with the client.

G. PERSONAL EMBARRASSMENTS

Inevitably, advocates make mistakes and errors of judgment. The attorney's reaction to these situations increases or decreases the chances of winning. When we make mistakes, we may be naturally inclined to think about ourselves first and what the decision maker will think about us and then find a scapegoat for our errors. When we learn about some surprise information at the beginning of a trial, we may want to blame our client for not telling us about this information rather than ourselves for not properly discovering it. When we ask an awkward question during jury selection, we may want to blame the judge for refusing to ask such a question instead of blaming ourselves for not properly asking it. When the witness makes a misstatement on the stand, we may be inclined to shift the blame to the witness rather than have the decision maker think we did not properly prepare the witness. These reactions are natural and normal, but they must be avoided by the professional advocate.

There is no place for an advocate to be concerned about personal embarrassments during a case. The advocate should not embarrass the client or undercut the client's position. Advocates may assume responsibility for mistakes even if not theirs and accept the blame.

§ 1.8   METHODS OF EFFECTIVE PRESENTATION

All advocates have some talent and capabilities that they can develop and enhance to make them effective advocates. Methodical planning, thorough preparation, and intense practice can make most any lawyer a competent and skilled advocate. This section describes some general principles of effective communication skills. Subsequent chapters contain additional techniques applicable to specific advocacy skills.

A. A GOOD PERSON

Be good. A principle of rhetoric is that an effective orator is a "good person who speaks well." Be an advocate who displays good will and character and who presents the case well.

B. CONFIDENCE

Appear confident and in control of the case. Thorough preparation develops the necessary confidence, and an effective presentation allows the attorney to remain in control. Successful advocates view the forum as "their" courtroom or hearing room, where they present their clients' cases.

C. FOCUSING

Focus on the ideas. In preparing a speech, effective speakers do not focus on the specific words they are to deliver but on the concepts and images they wish to express and evoke. A speech that is simply read from a prepared text is rarely interesting. Similarly, a memorized speech where the speaker merely recites words is also unpersuasive. Focus on the ideas that need to be expressed and explained, practice out loud, and then present the ideas using specific words when needed for impact.

D.　EYE CONTACT

Maintain appropriate eye contact. It is critical to establishing credibility and persuasion. The lack of eye contact causes decision makers to doubt the attorney's sincerity or lose interest in what is being said.

Advocates must speak with their heads up and avoid the extensive use of notes that prevent them from maintaining sufficient eye contact. Some advocates get nervous and lose their concentration while looking a decision maker directly in the eyes. An effective way to look at someone is to focus on the bridge of the person's nose rather than the pupils of the person's eyes. The speaker avoids the intensity of eye contact, while the listener perceives that the speaker is looking at the listener.

E.　BODY LANGUAGE

Be natural. Body language is a significant part of the advocate's communication process. The key is congruence, that is, the body language of the attorney should be consistent with the abilities of the lawyer and the message the advocate seeks to communicate. A lawyer whose body language lacks confidence or certainty is unable to be persuasive. An attorney who appears indifferent or uncaring may display an inattentive and insensitive attitude. Advocates are regularly on view in front of the decision maker, and inappropriate body language interferes with communication.

F.　GESTURES

Act natural. Good speakers employ natural gestures to make a presentation more effective, and an advocate should incorporate appropriate gestures into a presentation.

G.　APPEARANCE

Appear natural. A speaker's appearance often affects the listener's perceptions of that person. An attorney who is well groomed usually appears more professional and credible. The attorney's appearance should be consistent with the personality and approach of the attorney.

Counsel should dress comfortably, in a manner that suits their taste and that conforms to the customs or rules of decorum established or promulgated in a jurisdiction. Many attorneys dress according to a standard they believe is expected of them by the decision maker. Some attorneys prefer to wear a distinctive piece of clothing during a trial to help the jurors remember and identify the attorney.

The dress of an attorney should not become an issue that detracts attention from the client's case. Attorneys may have to put aside personal tastes and conform their dress to the standards of a community or decision maker so as to safeguard and promote the client's best interests.

H. VOCAL TONE AND PACE

Use variety. The tone, volume, modulation, and pace of an attorney's delivery affect the listening capabilities of the decision maker. A dull, monotone presentation is as ineffective as a loud, boisterous approach. A balanced and well-modulated approach is usually most effective. Sometimes silence is the best thing that can be used. Silence can be an effective way to highlight a point, gain attention, or create a transition.

§ 1.9   ETHICS

The process of becoming an advocate includes an understanding of and adherence to ethical norms and standards. Advocates must reflect on, wrestle with, and come to an understanding about the values, norms, and ethics that should be preserved and that shape the judgment and conduct of the advocate. Attorneys are members of a community consisting of clients, colleagues, opponents, judicial officers, and the public. Each advocate is not only a lawyer but also a person, guided not only by professional or legal ethics but also by individual and community concerns and values. This section specifically describes the shaping of ethical guidelines formed by decision makers within the adversary system, constraints within the system, and professional rules of conduct and behavior.

A. SOURCES OF DECISION-MAKING POWER

Attorneys do not have power to control the fates of parties, but attorneys can influence the source of this power. It is the ability of the attorney to convince the decision maker to right a wrong that activates the power within the adversary system. Attorneys influence the results of a case by selecting the theories to be advanced, the evidence to be introduced, and the law to be applied.

B. CONSTRAINTS

Clients have limited resources. The lack of sufficient funds makes it impossible to do everything that could be done in a case. Many cases do not justify significant monetary expenditures. The advocate must work within these restrictions to do the best possible job.

Lawyers have only limited available time. The time that an attorney can devote to a case is limited by the fee charged, professional hours available, and the lawyer's life outside the practice of law.

C. PROFESSIONAL RULES OF CONDUCT

The rules of professional responsibility and state ethical rules provide both a set of disciplinary rules and guidelines for advocates. Some of the rules deal with the external, objective conduct of an attorney. Many rules deal with internal, subjective thinking of the lawyer. It is often difficult to apply these rules and guidelines to cases where there are two or more versions of what happened, two opponents who may dislike each other, and two advocates who are skilled at creating plausible explanations and portraying questionable behavior as legitimate. Attorneys must develop an internal code of ethics and constantly monitor their own conduct to determine whether it complies with the norms of the profession and their own ethical norms.

Every state has rules that establish standards and impose restraints on a lawyer's behavior. The Rules of Professional Conduct have been adopted with various modifications by the states. These rules codify norms that reflect the collective views and values of lawyers. State rules of procedure, case law, and local customs and traditions also regulate the conduct of advocates. The remainder of this section summarizes ethical rules based on the Model Rules of Professional Conduct that specifically apply to advocates.

1. Abide by Client's Decisions

Model Rule 1.2(a) states:

[A] lawyer shall abide by a client's decisions concerning the objectives of representation . . . and shall consult with the client as to the means by which they are to be pursued. . . . In a criminal case, the lawyer shall abide by the client's decision, after consultation with the lawyer, as to the plea to be entered, whether to waive jury trial and whether the client will testify.

The United States Supreme Court has approved this rule and the following standard:

The decisions on what, when, whether, and how to conduct cross examination, what jurors to accept or strike, what trial motion should be made, and all the strategic and tactical decisions are the exclusive providence of the lawyer after consultation with the client. Jones v. Barnes, 463 U.S. 745, 753 N. 6 (1983).

The advocate has an obligation to discuss the objectives of the case and the strategies that are to be pursued with the client. The attorney must consult with the client in making decisions regarding the objectives of the representation and alternative ways these objectives can be achieved. It is up to the attorney to implement these decisions.

2. Competent Representation

The advocate must provide competent representation and act with reasonable promptness and diligence. Competent representation minimally consists of legal knowledge, thorough preparation, and effective case presentation. The lawyer must render candid advice to the client and exercise independent, professional judgment. Model Rule 1.1.

3. Confidentiality

What a client tells a lawyer and the advice a lawyer renders to a client is confidential and may not be revealed unless the client consents, or certain situations permit or require disclosure. The factual story a client tells an attorney is disclosed when the client testifies at a deposition, a hearing, or at trial. The legal theories discussed between the client and the attorney often form the basis for the theory of the case which is presented at the trial or hearing. Model Rule 1.6.

4. Conflict of Interest

A lawyer may not represent a client if that representation will compromise or be compromised by the lawyer's responsibilities to another client or to a third person. Similarly, if the lawyer's own interests conflict, the case should be referred elsewhere. A client, after being fully informed by the attorney, may willingly waive the conflict and agree to be represented. Model Rule 1.7.

5. Good Faith

Model Rule 3.1 states:

A lawyer shall not bring or defend a proceeding, or assert or controvert an issue therein, unless there is a basis in law and fact for doing so that is not frivolous, which includes a good faith argument for an extension, modification, or reversal of existing law. A lawyer for a defendant in a criminal proceeding or the respondent in a proceeding that could result in incarceration may nevertheless so defend the proceeding as to require that every element of the case be established.

Federal Rule of Civil Procedure 11, similar state rules, and related arbitration and administrative provisions contain a similar standard. These rules prohibit an attorney from presenting any claim or defense unless to the best of that attorney's knowledge, information, and belief formed after reasonable investigation and research, it is well grounded in fact and is warranted by existing law or a good faith argument for the development of new law.

These rules establish an objective standard of conduct as distinguished from a subjective belief. An attorney who has a personal belief that a claim or defense is valid does not meet the standard. The attorney must have an objective basis in law and fact to support the claim or defense. It is insufficient for an attorney to merely have a "pure heart" in asserting a claim or defense. These rules require that an attorney have a "good legal head" and factual and legal support for a claim or defense.

6.   Expediting the Case

A lawyer must make reasonable efforts, consistent with the legitimate interests of a client, to expedite a trial or hearing and not delay proceedings for improper reasons. It is inappropriate for an attorney to engage in time-consuming discovery and motion practice if these strategies are not legitimately employed to promote a client's case. It is unethical for an attorney to employ delaying tactics that are used for the primary purpose of causing the opposing party to expend unnecessary resources or for unreasonably extending the time before the case is brought to a final resolution. Model Rule 3.2.

7.   Evidence

Model Rule 3.3(a)(3) states:

A lawyer shall not knowingly . . . offer evidence that the lawyer knows to be false. If a lawyer . . . has offered material evidence and comes to know of its falsity, the lawyer shall take reasonable remedial measures, including, if necessary, disclosure to the tribunal. A lawyer may refuse to offer evidence, other than the testimony of a defendant in a criminal matter, that the lawyer reasonably believes is false.

Model Rule 3.4(e) further states that:

Lawyers shall not . . . allude to any matter that the lawyer does not reasonably believe is relevant or that will not be supported by admissible evidence.

A lawyer may not unlawfully obstruct another party's access to evidence or alter, destroy or conceal a document or other material having potential evidentiary value. The obviously despicable nature of this conduct should not require a rule to prevent it.

8. Disclosing Controlling Authority

Model Rule 3.3(a)(2) states:

A lawyer shall not knowingly fail to disclose to the tribunal legal authority in the controlling jurisdiction known to the lawyer to be directly adverse to the position of the client and not disclosed by opposing counsel.

A lawyer must disclose all controlling authority—supportive or adverse—but is not obligated to disclose legal authority if it is not controlling. Precedent from another jurisdiction that does not bind the decision maker need not be disclosed. The attorney may rely upon the law from other jurisdictions and argue that this law ought to apply, requiring the opposing attorney to argue against the application of this analogous law even though it is not controlling.

9. Influence

A lawyer may not seek to influence a judge, arbitrator, or juror by means prohibited by law and may not communicate ex parte with such persons unless permitted by law. An advocate should communicate with the decision maker about a matter in a case only if the opposing lawyer is present or involved. Model Rule 3.5.

10. Complying with Rulings

Model Rule 3.4(c) states:

A lawyer shall not . . . knowingly disobey an obligation under the rules of the tribunal except for an open refusal based on an assertion that no valid obligation exists.

A lawyer must comply with the rulings and orders of the decision maker except in extraordinarily unusual situations in which an attorney would decide to face a contempt citation and be penalized for disobeying.

D. ATTORNEY MISCONDUCT

A review of attorney disciplinary cases reveals that common reasons for lawyer malfeasance result from greed, alcohol or drug abuse, laziness, and legal incompetence. Many lawyers who operate dysfunctionally will do so until they are caught, and do not stop because of a code of external or internal ethics. A client, colleague, partner, friend, or family member may be the person or persons who get them help.

A review of complaints filed with licensing boards by clients against lawyers reveals that common complaints involve the lack of sufficient or ongoing communications and inappropriate fees. Lawyers can substantially reduce potential client problems by maintaining sufficient, regular communications and explaining the fees charged.

E.   CLIENT DEMANDS AND SATISFACTION

Clients expect their lawyers to be knowledgeable and wise and also responsive and available. Smart phones, texts, emails, and other social media methods make it easy to both send and expect prompt messages. Some clients will anticipate that their lawyers will be available when they want and need an answer or an update of what is, or what is not, happening in their case. Other clients may expect service at most anytime during the week and on weekends. Lawyers learn to discuss these anticipations with their clients to reach a mutual understanding of reasonable expectations.

Periodic and timely efforts by advocates to update their clients are reasonable expectations. A common concern and complaint clients have is the failure of their lawyers to communicate. Sometimes clients will need a prompt answer; other times they need to know their lawyers are working on their case; and other times they need an empathetic response.

Advocates may also feel pressure from their clients to win, sometimes at all costs, and sometimes by using inappropriate approaches. They obviously need to avoid submitting to this pressure and explain why they cannot act accordingly, or withdraw from the representation. The demands of clients and the lawyer's need to satisfy their interests must be properly balanced with doing what is ethical and proper.

F.   THE CONSEQUENCES OF MISCONDUCT

The most egregious misconduct by an advocate will be handled by the court or arbitrator through a contempt citation or a motion and order for a new trial or hearing, and by the appellate court through a reversal. Lesser misconduct will usually prompt a reprimand by the court or a professional responsibility board or office. Other sanctions may be imposed by state or local ethics committees for misconduct, but this may not occur in a timely or sufficient manner to deter such conduct.

The lack of prompt and stern external sanctions should not be taken as a license to engage in questionable conduct that may win the case. The primary protection against abuses by advocates lies within each lawyer. The true sanctions are personal and professional, such as the loss of self-esteem, respect, credibility, and ultimately, cases and clients. It is critical for the advocate to develop and maintain a reputation as an honest, trustworthy, and ethical professional.

———

Trial Advocacy Supplement

Examples of the skills described in this book appear in the *Supplement to Trial Advocacy Before Judges, Jurors, and Arbitrators*. This *Supplement* also contains the Federal Rules of Evidence and selected Federal Rules of Civil Procedure applicable to advocacy. Students may obtain a print or electronic version of the *Supplement* from store.westacademic.com.

Transcripts appear in the *Supplement* with commentary and include three cases:

A jury trial, *Rita Riley v. Garfield House Apartments*

An arbitration, *Bingham v. Ecotronics*

An administrative law proceeding, *Mr. Scratch v. Jabez Stone*

These cases demonstrate the strategies, tactics, and techniques that are explained in this text. The transcripts reflect how an entire case is tried before a jury, an arbitrator, and an administrative law judge and supplement the individualized examples appearing throughout this book.

CHAPTER 2

PLANNING AND PREPARATION

■ ■ ■

REFLECTING ON ADVOCACY

Few things are brought to a successful issue by impetuous desire, but most by calm and prudent forethought.

—THUCYDIDES

Life can only be understood backwards; but it must be lived forwards.

—SOREN KIERKEGAARD

§ 2.1 INTRODUCTION

Before trying a case, the advocate must effectively plan and properly prepare the case. Experienced advocates share similar approaches to case planning. This chapter explains the preparation process and describes effective planning methods. The following sections cover the stages of a case, the planning process, the selection of case theories, the analysis of evidence, and the submission of jury instructions and verdict forms in a jury trial. Chapter 3 describes additional case procedures including pretrial and prehearing conferences and motions.

§ 2.2 STAGES OF A CASE

A. CIVIL JURY TRIAL

The trial lawyer must review each stage of a trial and prepare an integrated plan for the presentation of a case. The stages of a civil trial, after the pretrial litigation process of pleading, discovery, and motion practice has been completed, include the following:

- Pretrial conference.

- Chambers discussion immediately preceding the beginning of the trial.

- Jury selection, with the plaintiff proceeding first, followed by the defendant (in some jurisdictions defendant proceeds first).

- Opening statement by the plaintiff, followed by the defendant's opening unless reserved until commencement of the defendant's case.

- Plaintiff's case, including the introduction of evidence and direct examinations by plaintiff, cross-examinations by defendant, and redirect and recross examinations.

- Defendant's motion for directed verdict.

- Defendant's case, including the introduction of evidence and direct examinations by defendant, cross-examinations by plaintiff, and redirect and recross.

- Rebuttal (if necessary), with the plaintiff introducing rebuttal evidence followed by any rebuttal by defendant.

- Motion for judgment as a matter of law or for a directed verdict, which can be brought by both the plaintiff and defendant.

- Final selection of jury instructions by judge.

- Closing argument by plaintiff, followed by defendant's summation, followed by plaintiff's rebuttal; or, in some jurisdictions, closing argument by defendant, followed by plaintiff's summation.

- Charge to the jury (in some jurisdictions the judge instructs the jurors before summation).

- Jury deliberations.

- Verdict.

- Post-trial motions, including a motion for a new trial and a motion for judgment as a matter of law or a judgment notwithstanding the verdict.

- Notice of appeal.

B. CRIMINAL JURY TRIAL

The stages of a criminal trial after a defendant has been arrested and arraigned and after preliminary hearings have been completed are:

- Pretrial conference.

- Chambers discussion immediately before the start of the trial.

- Jury selection, usually with the defendant proceeding first, followed by the prosecutor (in some jurisdictions the prosecution proceeds first).

- Opening statement by the prosecutor, followed by the defendant's opening unless reserved until the commencement of the defendant's case.

- Prosecution's case, including the introduction of evidence and direct examinations by the prosecutor, cross-examinations by defendant, and redirect and recross examinations.

- Defendant's motion to dismiss or for acquittal.

- Defendant's case (unless defendant declines to introduce evidence), including direct examinations by defendant, cross-examinations by prosecutor, and redirect and recross.

- Rebuttal (if necessary), with prosecutor introducing rebuttal evidence followed by rebuttal evidence introduced by defendant.

- Renewal of defendant's motion for acquittal.

- Final selection of jury instructions by judge.

- Closing argument by prosecution, followed by the defendant's summation, with many jurisdictions permitting rebuttal by prosecutor, and a few jurisdictions allowing defendant to close last (or in even fewer jurisdictions the defense goes first followed by prosecution with no rebuttals).

- Charge to the jury (in some jurisdictions instructions are given before closing arguments).

- Jury deliberations.

- Verdict.

- Post-trial motions, including defense motion for judgment of acquittal and motion for new trial.

- Notice of appeal.

C. BENCH TRIAL

The stages of civil and criminal bench trials are the same as jury trials, except that there obviously is no jury selection, jury instructions, jury deliberation or verdict. Instead, there are findings of fact, conclusions of law, and an order for judgment entered by the judge. See Section 2.11.

D. ADMINISTRATIVE HEARING

The type of an administrative hearing determines its procedures and stages. Many administrative hearings are identical or similar to a bench trial. The process includes all stages of a bench trial (sometimes without opening statements) and concludes with a written opinion by the administrative judge that explains the decision. An example of this type of hearing is a worker's compensation trial.

Another administrative hearing format involves the administrative judge as an active participant in the presentation of the case. The judge may initially question the witnesses before the parties have an opportunity to conduct witness examinations. The administrative judge may ask questions that consist of direct and cross-examination questions. Closing statements may be made by the parties with the judge asking questions or phrasing issues. This type of hearing is common in situations where the parties do not have attorneys representing them, for example, in unemployment compensation hearings.

Other administrative hearings involve regulatory law. The administrative body may receive evidence in different ways. The role of the administrative officers may be to present and submit evidence as well as to consider it. Parties who are directly affected by a potential regulatory ruling may cross-examine witnesses and may present their own evidence. Parties who are permitted to intervene in a case may present evidence or arguments in a limited role. The staff of the administrative body may act as advocates for specific regulations. Examples of these hearings include utility and environmental cases.

E. ARBITRATION

The stages of an arbitration process include:

- Filing and serving of the arbitration claim and response.
- Selection of an arbitrator.
- Exchange of discoverable information before the hearing.
- Prehearing procedures and issue resolution.
- The hearing.
- The award.

Arbitration procedures appear in a set of rules established by the arbitration organization, (e.g., Forum Code of Procedure).

Parties agree to use arbitration by including a pre-dispute arbitration clause in their agreement or transaction or by agreeing to arbitration after a dispute arises. A claimant may file a claim with the arbitration administrator (e.g., The Forum or the American Arbitration Association or JAMS) to initiate the arbitration process. The claim consists of a detailed explanation of the facts and law supporting the claim, documents which contain relevant information, and the filing fee. The respondent has to respond in writing with a detailed explanation of defenses and available counter-claims, accompanied by supporting documents. After the parties have completed their submissions, a neutral and experienced arbitrator is selected, usually from a panel of arbitrators. The arbitration forum may appoint an arbitrator or three arbitrators whom the parties may challenge, or may submit a list of potential arbitrators and the parties may remove one or more of the arbitrators.

Parties may exchange discoverable information, and may obtain from each other relevant and reliable documents. Discovery may range from a limited number of depositions to all the discovery methods available under the federal rules. The arbitrator resolves any discovery disputes between the parties.

The arbitration organization administers the arbitration proceeding. The parties exchange a list of witnesses and exhibits a reasonable time before the hearing. Arbitrators have subpoena power and can require individuals to appear at arbitration hearings if the parties request.

There are two major types of arbitration proceedings: document hearings and participatory hearings. In a document hearing, the parties submit their case in writing or via computer to the arbitrator. Parties may submit documents, exhibits, affidavits, memorandums, and any writings or electronically stored information for consideration by the arbitrator. The arbitrator issues an award after reviewing the submissions. Parties do not appear at a document hearing. This hearing is especially useful for document cases decided without oral testimony.

A participatory hearing resembles a bench trial. Parties attend that hearing and present their evidence through witnesses and exhibits. Parties may represent themselves or choose to have an attorney represent them. The stages of a participatory hearing include an opening statement, direct and cross-examinations, and summation. Parties may have witnesses appear in person or by a deposition transcript, testify over the telephone, or through video transmission. The arbitrator conducts the hearing and admits all relevant and reliable evidence. The case is concluded when the arbitrator issues the award. Parties may also submit additional information or legal memorandums after the hearing. The decision of an arbitrator in a binding arbitration is final and enforceable.

A variation of these two common types of hearings is an online hearing which may consist of a variety of communication modes: the lawyers and witnesses who are in different locations may appear using video conferencing programs; the arbitrator may ask questions or seek information using a computer chat program; documents may be submitted electronically to all the participants. The ongoing development of technological communication methods will provide additional modes for distant hearings conducted via video and computers with software. Arbitration hearings can be readily adapted to provide participants with this flexibility and accessibility.

§ 2.3   CASE NOTEBOOK

In order to prepare efficiently, the advocate must develop a systematic approach to each case. The approach can be consistent among cases yet flexible enough to deal with the particular circumstances of a distinct case. Forms and charts in this and subsequent chapters provide examples of a systematic approach to case preparation. See Form 2.1.

Preparation for a trial, arbitration, or administrative proceeding includes the creation of a case notebook. It can be crafted on a laptop using computer software and electronic files or on paper placed in a ring binder or accordion file. A useful notebook organizes the material needed for trial or hearing, permits new material to be added during case preparation, establishes an orderly approach to each stage of the case, and permits ready access to case material. The notebook should contain separate files or sections for each stage of the case, including:

- Summary of case theory, including legal theories and factual summaries.

- Calendar of deadlines, cut-off dates, and significant times and days.

- List of all lawyers involved and their contact information.

- Discovery and other pretrial plans and orders.

- Applicable substantive law, including cases and statutes.

- Applicable procedural rules, including court rules, arbitration code of procedure, and administrative regulations.

- Pleadings, including a list of admitted allegations.

- Discovery, including discovery responses, witness statements, and deposition testimony that will be introduced as evidence or available for impeachment.

- Summary of documents, electronically stored information, and digital evidence.

- Motions or requests, including pretrial motions, in limine motions, trial motions, and post-trial motions.

- Pretrial or prehearing conference information, including a list of things to be discussed with the judge or arbitrator.

- Case brief, see Section 3.4(E).

- Orders issued by judge affecting trial.

- Objections and applicable rules of evidence and case law decisions to support anticipated evidentiary positions.

- Jury selection, including questions for prospective jurors, the law relating to jury selection, and charts or forms to be used during jury selection.

- List of visual aids to be created and used during opening and summation.

- Opening statement, including an outline and visual aid list.

- Witnesses, including a list of witnesses and the order they will be called.

- Exhibits, including a list of exhibits to be introduced and a chart describing the exhibits, the marking number or letter, the witnesses through whom the exhibits will be introduced, and whether the exhibits have been offered and received.

- Exhibit preparation, detailing where exhibits are located, what needs to be done for their proper introduction and use, a log of their status, and how many duplicate copies are needed for judge, opposing counsel, jurors, and witnesses.

- Direct examination, including a list of topics or questions for each witness and exhibits that will be used with each witness.

- Cross-examination, including a list of topics or questions for each witness, prior statements from depositions or hearings, and any exhibits to be used.

- Information needed for expert testimony, including expert reports and resumes.

- Statements of judicially noticed evidence.

- Stipulations of fact and other agreed upon stipulations.

- Equipment, materials, and supplies needed to present evidence, including video sources, computer laptop and monitor, document cameras, display machines, electronic devices, and power cords.

- Jury instructions and verdict forms, including proposed general and specific instructions and interrogatory questions to be used.

- Closing argument, including an outline or text of summation and a list of exhibits and visual aids to be used.

- Expenses, including costs, bills, attorney fees, and time logs.

- Proposed bench trial findings of fact, conclusions of law, and order.

- Errors, including a list of prejudicial errors occurring during the trial to support a motion for a new trial and for appeal.

- Log of evidence when introduced and recorded as part of transcript or other recording and parts of record for appeal.

The development of a case notebook is a team effort. Advocates work closely together with lawyers, paralegals, law clerks, experts, and other professionals to prepare for many trials and hearings. Attorneys may also join forces with other law firms in representing a client and divide the work because that is what the client prefers or because of the differing talents of the different attorneys. These relationships require the advocate to be a manager and an administrator and to work cooperatively and collaboratively with others.

Private vendors have available efficient and economical software that help create and maintain case notebooks, trial materials, and litigation support. Technology provides easy to use programs and devices that maintain the various components of case files outlined above. These sources can be found on the internet and can greatly assist advocates in both planning and presenting a case.

§ 2.4   PLANNING OBJECTIVES

The initial planning for a trial or hearing actually begins with the first client interview. Before a trial or hearing gets underway the lawyers have: counseled clients, gathered facts, issued litigation holds for possible evidence, researched the law, drafted pleadings, preserved documents and electronically stored information, completed discovery, reviewed evidence, and resolved motions.

The planning process is critical for several reasons:

- Effective preparation develops successful strategies, tactics, and techniques.

- Planning allows for the creation and completion of a case notebook.

- Preparation helps identify and anticipate problems that may occur and creates responses to those problems.

- Planning builds confidence and reduces anxiety, uncertainties, and surprises.

- Thorough preparation substantially offsets the disadvantage of inexperience.

A. BEGINNING AT THE END

Begin at the end. The summation is the final destination of the case, and its composition is the first step of case preparation. The outline and content of the closing argument provides a form and structure for the presentation of the case.

This initial summation contains an outline of the theory of the case, facts, law, inferences, reasons, and arguments that support a winning decision. This summary forms the basis for the subsequent selection of case theories, what forum or decision maker should be selected, how the opening should be presented, what evidence should be preserved and introduced, and how the case can best be won. If a fact must be established to support a statement made during the closing argument, the attorney can plan to gather and introduce that evidence through direct or cross-examination. If an issue will be part of the summation, information about that issue can be developed. A summation developed early will undoubtedly undergo change as the case progresses.

B. OBJECTIVE ANALYSIS BY ATTORNEY

Analyze the facts and the law objectively. As an advocate, it can be difficult to be objective when reviewing the strengths and weaknesses of a client's case. Lawyers must put themselves in the place of the decision maker in assessing the facts, determining the credibility of witnesses, drawing inferences, and accepting arguments.

C. ANALYZING THE OPPONENT

Assess the opponent. The assets and liabilities of an opponent affect the presentation of an attorney's case. These factors include: the degree of experience, skill level, ability to use modern technology, demeanor, reputation, habits, relationship with the tribunal, and how the decision maker will perceive and evaluate the lawyer. Information about an opposing lawyer can be obtained from colleagues, attorneys from other firms, websites, internet searches, and individuals who know the lawyer.

D. ANALYZING THE JUDGE/ARBITRATOR

Assess the decision maker. As explained previously and as expanded on in subsequent sections, an essential approach to succeeding at advocacy is for the advocate to ascertain and predict the values, norms, principles, and beliefs that will influence a decision maker. This analysis will help in selecting evidence and arguments that reflect these values and resonate with these principles. It will be far easier and much more likely for a decision maker to find for a party if the case presented supports the underlying norms and beliefs of the decision maker.

Familiarity with the strengths and weaknesses of trial and administrative law judges and arbitrators also require process assessment. These factors include:

- How are proceedings handled?

- How are rulings made?

- What are the demands or expectations of advocates?

- How are the rules of evidence applied?

- How familiar is the decision maker with computer and electronic case presentations?

- What is the educational and professional background of this decision maker?

Information about a judge or arbitrator may be obtained by talking with colleagues, lawyer friends, and others who know the professional. It is improper for an attorney to contact a decision maker ex parte about a case. Information can also be obtained from internet searches and available listings of cases, data, articles, resumes, education, and background and other public or published information.

§ 2.5 SELECTING A THEORY OF THE CASE

The "theory of the case" provides the decision maker with a summary of the reasons why a client is entitled to win. An effective theory of the case is concise and compelling. When communicated, the decision maker will *want* the client to win. It is a vital part of case planning.

A theory of the case can be short and summarized in a few sentences; or a theory may need a longer paragraph. While it is called a theory, the concept blends compelling facts and instructive law into a persuasive practical statement.

An effective case theory has to work for the client, advocate, and decision maker. The client has to accept the explanation. The lawyer has to be able to rely on a recognizable legal claim or defense and be able to prove the supporting facts. And, the values and principles advanced in the theory need to reflect the norms and beliefs of the decision maker.

A theory of the case is presented and repeated throughout the trial or hearing. The use of themes, words, phrases, and images contained in the case theory are described in the opening statement, introduced through witnesses and exhibits, and explained in the closing argument.

The issues in a case determine available approaches to crafting a theory. As described previously, civil cases typically involve responsible or irresponsible conduct. Tort law calls this negligence, and contract law calls this breach of contract. A common civil case theory revolves around who is more or less accountable for the accident or breach. A case theory can also blend legal doctrines with critical facts to create a compelling explanation. The following examples demonstrate case theories.

Criminal Prosecution Example:

This case involves a brutal assault. Polly Pozdol was savagely beaten by that man (pointing to defendant). She had locked him out of her home telling him he was no longer welcome. He left angry and later came back with a plan to beat her. He smashed his way in and pummeled Polly again and again with this bat (holding bat). She suffered severe injuries as shown here (showing photo). She deserves justice, and he deserves to be found guilty of criminal assault.

Criminal Defense Example:

This is a case of mistaken identity. The lone witness, Michael Lanyard, saw his assailant for a few seconds, in the dark, after a long, tiring day. He mistakenly identified the wrong person.

Tort Case Example:

For the Plaintiff

This case involves the irresponsible conduct of the defendant Country Club that invited a lot of members to a party and then made a lot of money by selling them a lot of drinks. But the club did not give them a lot of room to enjoy themselves. The plaintiff, while dancing to a hired band near a very slippery and very crowded pool area, was uncontrollably pushed by the crowd into the pool severely injuring his head and back. The club—that knew about these dangerous conditions—must be held accountable for its blatant irresponsibility.

For the Defendant

This case is about unwise choices and deliberate irresponsibility. The plaintiff, Francis Ouimet, chose to come to a party for club members and decided to drink so many drinks that he got drunk. That was his choice. He paid for his drinks. No one once forced him to drink more. And instead of going home, he chose to stay and found himself a slippery spot to dance on, right next to the pool. His falling into that pool was his fault, and not the drinks, not other members, and not the Club.

Products Liability Case Example:

For the Plaintiff

The Garbomatic Company negligently designed, manufactured, and sold the Spinchop garbage disposal to the plaintiff. That disposal was defective when it was designed, defective when it was manufactured, and defective when it was sold. These defects caused the disposal to explode. The metal pieces that exploded out of that Spinchop destroyed Alex Wojcik's eye. The Garbomatic Company was negligent and is responsible for what happened. It must be held accountable because its defective machine caused Mr. Wojcik's severe and permanent injuries.

For the Defendant

What happened to Mr. Wojcik is a tragedy. The Spinchop garbage disposal is a safe, well designed, and expertly manufactured consumer product—when it is installed properly and used as intended. The tragedy is that Mr. Wojcik negligently installed the disposal himself and then negligently used it. He knew he was supposed to install the switch within easy reach of the disposal. He did not, knowing better. He also knew he should not start the disposal if there was silverware in it. But he did, knowing better. Unfortunately, he is responsible for his own injuries, not the local Garbomatic family owned business.

Discrimination Case Example Explained in Summation:

For the Plaintiff Employee

Judith Kincade had a right to be treated as any other law firm attorney. She was judged by the men at Owen, Voss, Raphael, and Marks not as an attorney, but as a woman attorney. She is being punished for the very same behavior for which male associates have been rewarded. They were assertive, she was abrasive. They showed leadership, she was bossy. They were businesslike, she was cold.

Nobody told her when she first interviewed with the firm that she would be judged not only by how hard she worked, but by how much fun she was to be around. Nobody told her that her failure to smile or her lack of interest in sports would represent an insurmountable obstacle to advancement. And the reason nobody told her was that the men who interviewed her wanted her to work for them. They knew that this was a bright, driven attorney who could be depended upon to work as hard as possible. They knew it would be six or seven years before they would have to tell her she was not going to make partner. They knew what a good deal they had here.

She now rightfully asks for the good deal they promised her. She lost her job because they discriminated against her, because she was a woman. There is no doubt that the men at Owen, Voss, Raphael, and Marks are somewhat uncomfortable with Judith Kincade. They may be more comfortable having as partners other men that look and act like themselves. They hired Judith Kincade, worked her hard for seven years, and got rid of her without recognition or reward. They now have to pay for their decision and their comfort. We ask you to make them pay.

For the Defendant Employer

Judith Kincade chose to work at the Owen Law Firm. She interviewed with a group of successful, experienced lawyers and decided to join their practice. They allowed her to represent their clients.

What did she have a right to expect? She had a right to expect to be paid fairly, be given the same opportunities as other associates at the firm, and be judged fairly. She was. The firm paid her very generously, provided her with the same opportunities to succeed or fail as other associates, and judged her the way they judged everyone.

What obligations did she have to fulfill? She had responsibilities to work hard, to be productive, and to work well with colleagues. She failed with her responsibilities. Her work was reasonable but not up to the billable hour standards of the firm; her legal production was good but she did not generate sufficient new business for the firm; and her demeanor and willingness to work with others was questionable. Ms. Kincade lost her job because she could not do it well. The firm chose others who they felt were much better qualified. So long as there were legitimate reasons for their decision they were wholly within their rights.

Hard work and talent will result in women taking their rightful place in all strata of our society. In order for that to happen, they must be permitted to fail. All of us who work for a living stand on our own two feet. We are subject to the judgment of others. We get knocked down, we get back up, brush ourselves off, get back to work. We learn from our failures. We learn from our mistakes. Let Judith Kincade learn the very same thing.

---

§ 2.6   CASE ANALYSIS

When planning, the advocate must analyze the:

- Applicable legal claims and defenses,

- Available facts,

- The story that best blends the law and facts,

- Favorable factual issues,

- Persuasive evidence, and

- Effective strategies.

The following sections describe these six critical assessments.

A. SELECTING LEGAL CLAIMS AND DEFENSES

A legal claim or defense is based on an existing law or a good faith argument extending, modifying, or attempting to change existing law. In many cases, the advocate identifies claims and defenses by applying established law. An example is a breach of contract theory for failure to perform an obligation under a written contract. All jurisdictions recognize this claim. In other cases, an attorney advances a claim or defense that expands or modifies existing law. An example is a breach of an implied covenant of good faith and fair dealing in an oral employment contract arrangement. Only a few jurisdictions recognize this legal doctrine.

The law supporting the legal theory is found wherever laws are found: in statutes, case law, constitutional provisions, rules, and regulations. Elements of a legal theory appear in jury instructions which can be found in a text of standard jury instruction guides ("JIGs") or by researching the substantive law of a jurisdiction.

Legal claims for civil plaintiffs and prosecutors correspond to the legal elements of the claim or crime. For example, the legal theory of an arbitration claimant who brings a breach of contract action may be based on the following elements: the existence of a contract, performance by plaintiff of the contract, breach by defendant of the contract, and damages resulting from the breach. The legal theory of a prosecutor who charges the defendant with aggravated assault may be based on these elements:

intent to do bodily harm, possession of a dangerous weapon, and infliction of injuries.

Legal defenses for civil and criminal defendants arise from a number of sources, including the denial of the allegations of the claim or crime, affirmative defenses, counterclaims, third party complaints, and the joinder of related issues and parties. In composing an effective legal claim or defense an advocate should:

- Research all sources of the law,

- Assess the strengths and weaknesses of available doctrines,

- Consider multiple legal doctrines,

- Employ claims or defenses supported by favorable jury instructions or conclusions of law,

- Avoid selecting a legal technicality as a claim or defense,

- Select a doctrine readily supported by the facts, and

- Choose a legal theory that resonates with the values, norms, and beliefs of the decision maker.

B. COMPOSING A FACTUAL SUMMARY

A factual summary consists of a description of what happened and is based upon the evidence that is available and admissible. The story outline consisting of the important facts to be proven and inferences to be drawn is the framework for the factual summary.

A factual summary for a civil plaintiff in an automobile accident case may consist of the following outline:

- The plaintiff was driving home after work.

- The plaintiff stopped the car behind a crosswalk at a stop sign.

- The defendant's car rear-ended the plaintiff's car.

- The defendant was not paying attention.

- The defendant was speeding.

- The plaintiff and the defendant exchanged information.

- The plaintiff suffered injuries, including whiplash.

- The plaintiff paid medical expenses and lost income from work.

- The plaintiff endured pain and suffering.

A factual outline for a prosecutor in a theft case may be:

- The victim was walking down the street to go to the store.
- The crime was committed on the corner.
- The lighting conditions were bright.
- The victim was carrying her purse over her right shoulder.
- The defendant grabbed the purse from behind.
- The victim saw the defendant's face.
- The defendant stole the purse and ran away.
- The value of the contents of the purse amounted to over $1,500.
- The victim gave a description of the defendant to the police.
- The victim identified defendant at a lineup.
- The victim identified defendant in court.

In crafting an effective factual summary an advocate should:

- Construct a factual summary that will survive a motion for summary judgment or motion to dismiss,
- Compose a summary supported by credible and persuasive evidence,
- Avoid creating inconsistent alternative factual stories,
- Create a story that the fact finder wants to believe in, and
- Craft a story that resonates with the values, norms, and beliefs of the fact finder.

C. BLENDING LAW AND FACTS INTO A STORY

An advocate in effectively crafting a story that weaves together the applicable clams and defenses and relevant facts needs to:

1. Assert Affirmative Positions

A story should reflect affirmative, positive positions. Approaches that are purely defensive or negative are usually insufficient. Even a criminal defendant must usually present a story of what happened and not just argue that what the plaintiff/prosecutor says did not happen.

2. Employ an Approach Based on Common Sense

Decision makers may ultimately resolve the disputed law and facts in the case based upon their common sense, and it makes sense to focus on that approach.

3. Have the Fact Finder Identify with the Story

If the fact finders can identify with a position because they or others have experienced something similar in their lives or the story could reasonably have happened to others, it can be more persuasive.

4. Use an Approach That Results in a Fair and Just Decision

If a position results in a determination that is unfair or unreasonable, the decision maker is less likely to accept the position.

5. Avoid Employing a Position That Requires the Fact Finder to Make a Difficult Choice

The less difficult a decision that has to be made, the more likely a favorable decision will be made. If a judge, arbitrator, or juror has to choose to believe something or to reach a conclusion that conflicts with their values and norms, it will be difficult for them to do that.

6. Compare and Contrast a Position with That Likely to Be Taken by the Other Party

A decision maker who has to choose between two versions of events or who has to accept one of two explanations will more likely select the more persuasive, believable, and acceptable version. An advocate who can craft a better story, a more likely scenario, and a version that more closely matches the beliefs and values of the fact finder, has a better chance of success.

7. Test the Approach

The advocate can explain positions to colleagues, relatives, or friends to discover strengths and weaknesses of the position and to obtain their favorable or unfavorable response to the approach. In cases with significant resources, the positions can be presented to a mock jury or a focus group who will give their reactions and evaluations of the position.

D. DETERMINING THE FACTUAL ISSUES

Another stage of the planning process is determining what issues the fact finder must decide in a case to render a favorable decision. Effective advocates put themselves in the place of the fact finder to identify the difficult issues that must be resolved in a case:

Issue: *What story to believe?*

Solution:

- Review the evidence and determine which facts are in dispute.

- Determine why the fact finder would believe the supporting facts.

- Determine why the fact finder would not believe the supporting facts and would believe contrary facts.

- List the reasons why the fact finder should not believe these unfavorable facts.

For example, a corporation may defend a fraud case by arguing that there was no intent to deceive the claimant nor reliance on the part of the claimant. The attorney for the corporation should review the facts that establish no intent and no reliance to determine why the administrative judge would more likely accept the story presented by the corporation.

Issue: *What witness to believe?*

Solution:

- List reasons why your witnesses are credible.

- List reasons why opposing witnesses are not credible.

- List factors that establish credibility or reduce believability.

- List sources of these factors such as the law, common sense, and biases.

For example, a respondent may claim she never made a specific representation or statement as alleged by the claimant. The defense attorney should list all the reasons why the respondent should be believed and all the reasons why opposing witnesses should not be believed to assist the arbitrator in deciding credibility.

Issue: *What favorable inferences can be made from the evidence?*

Solution:

- Identify all favorable inferences and list reasons why these inferences are reasonable.

- Identify all unfavorable inferences and list reasons why these inferences are unreasonable.

- Review the events and happenings from other perspectives and consider whether other inferences may exist.

For example, a plaintiff in an automobile accident case may rely upon circumstantial evidence to prove a defendant was negligent. The attorney for the plaintiff should identify all reasonable circumstantial inferences that can be drawn from the direct evidence to support the plaintiff's case.

<u>Issue</u>: *How should facts be interpreted and applied to the law?*

<u>Solution</u>:

- Create favorable interpretations that support a helpful conclusion.

- Identify unfavorable interpretations to negate the opponent's case.

For example, a defendant in a criminal case may rely upon the prosecutor's failure to prove guilt beyond a reasonable doubt as a defense. Counsel for the defendant must present an interpretation and application of the burden "beyond a reasonable doubt" to the fact finder and present the reasons why the facts in the case support "reasonable doubt."

E. SELECTING EVIDENCE

An essential part of the planning process is the identification of evidence that is admissible. Methods available to introduce evidence are:

- *Testimony* of witnesses, including both lay and expert witnesses. See Chapter 7 on direct examination and Chapter 9 on supportive cross-examination.

- The introduction of *exhibits,* including real evidence. See Chapter 8.

- The availability of electronically stored information and *digital evidence*. See Chapter 8, again.

- The use of *demonstrative evidence,* computer generated graphics, and other displays that explain facts and opinions. See Sections 8.7 and 8.8.

- The availability of *expert evidence* to create and support evidence. See Chapter 10.

- *Stipulations.* The parties can stipulate to the introduction of evidence. See Section 3.6(H).

- *Admissions.* Statements made by an adverse party contained in discovery responses, including interrogatory answers, deposition transcripts, and responses to requests for admissions, may be offered by the opposing party as evidence. See Section 3.6(I).

- *Former testimony.* Witnesses who are unavailable for a trial or hearing and who have previously testified at a deposition or hearing may have their testimony admitted as evidence. See Section 3.6(J).

- *Judicial/Arbitral/Administrative Notice.* A party may ask that a judge or arbitrator take notice of certain facts. See Section 3.6(K).

In addition, a lot of information fact finders need to help them decide a case comes from their own life experiences. In every case, the attorneys presume fact finders understand certain information without having to introduce evidence to explain the obvious. For example, in an automobile accident case, witnesses may testify that a car ran a red light; but, as mentioned earlier, there will not be general testimony regarding what a car is or that it has an engine unless there is a controversy regarding one of these issues. The attorneys presume that the fact finder is familiar with cars and knows how automobiles operate.

In every case, many elemental facts are presumed to be understood by the fact finder, and the attorneys will not present information regarding these common life experiences. To do so would be a waste of time and insult the fact finder. The advocate must make a judgment regarding what facts should be explained by a witness or document and what should be presumed to be known by the fact finder.

F. DEVELOPING A STRATEGY

A case strategy is the overall, grand plan designed to win the case. The strategy consists of the numerous tactics to be used in presenting the case. Tactics are the individual approaches, techniques, and applications of the strategy. The effective case strategist:

- *Views the case as a whole* and is able to integrate the various parts and stages of the case,

- *Identifies the arguments* that will most likely influence the decision maker favorably,

- *Thinks creatively* by brainstorming, generating optional strategies, and evaluating these options,

- *Reviews the available evidence* and considers what else might be found,

- *Identifies real and demonstrative exhibits* that exist or may be created to present facts and opinions,

- *Considers visual aids* that may be helpful in opening and summation,

- *Imagines what modern technology exists* including computer software and hardware, electronic devices, and internet and web based sources of information,

- *Predicts how the decision maker will decide* and fashions a strategy to reflect that process,

- *Identifies weaknesses* and considers ways to reduce or eliminate their impact,

- *Considers risks* attendant with a strategy and attempts to minimize or eliminate those risks,

- *Develops alternative strategies* and tactics as a contingency plan in case the primary strategy fails or falters, and

- *Lists the toughest questions* the decision maker has to make and composes favorable answers to those questions.

The following section demonstrates how a strategy is implemented using supportive tactics and techniques.

FORM 2.1

CASE STRATEGIES WORKSHEET

Selecting Theory of Case

    Available Legal Theories/Elements of Claims or Defenses:

    Factual Summary/Story Outline:

    Significant Issues:

§ 2.7   IMPLEMENTING A CASE THEORY AND STRATEGY

This section demonstrates the implementation of a strategic theory of the case and the use of supporting tactics and techniques. The example involves an automobile accident. The defendant's theory of the case is that a key witness for the plaintiff misperceived what happened. The strategy is to focus the jury's attention on this issue throughout the trial and to convince them the witness is wrong. This approach is initially introduced during jury selection and repeated and reinforced throughout the trial.

Jury Instruction

A preliminary or final jury instruction given by the judge reads:

> You have to determine the credibility of the testimony of the witnesses. You must assess their interest or lack of interest in the outcome of the case; their ability to see what they say they saw; their distance from the accident and how clear their line of vision was; their memory; their frankness and sincerity; and the reasonableness or unreasonableness of the witnesses' testimony in light of all the other evidence in the case.

Jury Selection

The defense attorney asks the jurors:

> Judge Amanda Anderlee will instruct you regarding credibility of witnesses, that is, their ability to see what they tell you they saw. If she tells you that the ability of eyewitnesses to see something depends upon their distance from the event, the direction that they were looking, and their line of sight, would all of you be able to follow that instruction that Judge Anderlee gives you?

Opening Statement

Defense counsel says:

> Members of the Jury, the plaintiff's case rests on the testimony of an eyewitness who was mistaken about what she saw. The plaintiff will rely extensively on the testimony of Alice Kramden, who the facts will show could not have seen what she said she saw. At the time of the accident, she was more than half a block away from the intersection, looking in the opposite direction, and her line of vision was blocked by cars as well as buses.

Cross-Examination

During cross-examination of Alice Kramden the defense attorney asks:

Q: Immediately before the accident, you were at the bus stop?

A: Yes.

Q: The bus stop is located in the middle of the block?

A: Approximately.

Q: You were waiting for a bus?

A: Yep.

Q: You were sitting on the bench at the bus stop?

A: For a while.

Q: You sat there until the bus came to your stop, right?

A: I did.

Q: You were looking down the street for the bus coming to pick you up?

A: Yes.

Q: The bus was coming from the opposite direction of the intersection where the accident happened?

A: Yes.

Q: There were cars parked between where you were sitting and the intersection?

A: There were some cars.

Q: In fact there was a row of cars between where you were and the intersection?

A: There were several cars, maybe more.

Q: Yes. And there was traffic on the street between the bus stop and the intersection?

A: Yea.

Q: By traffic, you mean there were cars driving on both sides of the street?

A: Sure.

Q: And these cars were either heading for or leaving the intersection?

A: Yes.

Direct Examination:

During direct examination of the defendant, the attorney establishes:

Q: Where was the bus stop?

A: In the middle of the block.

Q: In which direction did buses come from to stop there?

A: They came the opposite way from the intersection where the collision took place.

Q: Immediately before the accident, did you see any cars down Main Street?

A: Yes, there were cars parked on both sides of Main Street and there was traffic moving in both directions.

Summation

The defense attorney concludes:

> Members of the Jury, the evidence introduced during this case proves to you that Alice Kramden could not have seen what she says she saw. The facts establish that she is mistaken about what happened. She was too far away to get an accurate look. She was not looking in the direction of the intersection before the accident. She was looking for a bus coming from the opposite direction. When did she first look in the direction of the intersection? After the accident happened. After she heard the noise of the collision. Further, the cars parked along Main Street and the traffic going in both directions along Main Street as shown on this diagram show that she is wrong. This mark, that we have labeled Kramden, is where she told us she was sitting. This mark, labeled Accident, is the accident scene. As I now draw a line between the bus stop bench where Ms. Kramden was sitting and the location in the intersection where the accident occurred, you will conclude that it is not possible for her to see what she says she saw.

Verdict

Judgment for the defendant . . . hopefully.

§ 2.8   SELECTING THE FORUM

A.   SELECTING THE FINDER OF FACT

An advocate may have an opportunity to choose a forum in which a matter will be decided. If there is a choice, the advocate must consider the facts and law of the case, who the fact finder will be, and the advantages and limitations of the different forums. In litigation, one of the initial and critical decisions the advocate must make is whether the case should be tried to a judge or to a jury. Many cases tried are non-jury trials, also called bench trials, and in numerous respects are similar to arbitrations and administrative hearings. In some cases, the parties do not have a right to a jury trial. In other cases, trial attorneys decide to waive the jury trial and try the case before a judge. There are several factors to consider in determining the appropriate forum.

1. The Nature of the Factual Issue

A case primarily involving emotional or sympathy issues or subjective damages may be better tried before a jury than a professional decision maker because judges or arbitrators may be less likely to be swayed by these factors. Conversely, a party opposing these kinds of issues may prefer a non-jury forum.

2. The Type of Client

The personality and nature of a client may be very appealing to a jury of peers while a judge or arbitrator may not be affected by such personal appeal. Also, an experienced decision maker may be less affected than a jury by the traits of a client. For example, while jurors may be unfairly predisposed to favor an individual opposed by a large corporation, a judge may not be unduly influenced by this factor.

3. The Nature of the Legal Theory

If the case involves a legal issue that presents a legal problem, a professional decision maker rather than a jury may be more inclined to provide a recovery. Jurors may be inclined to ignore a point of law if it results in what appears to be an unfair or unjust result.

4. The Complexity of the Case

A jury may or may not be able to understand and decide complex cases as well as a judge. A judicial judge may not have the background or experience to understand complicated cases as well as an experienced arbitrator or a specialized administrative law judge. Other cases may involve extremely difficult factual or legal issues that may take a very long time to try if presented to a jury and may be much more readily presented to and better decided by a judge or arbitrator who has the requisite expertise.

5. The Efficient Presentation of the Case

Trial procedures are lengthier in a jury trial and the rules of evidence excluding or restricting testimony or exhibits are more strictly enforced. See Section 3.11. These factors may suggest that a bench trial, arbitration, or administrative hearing is preferable because it is more efficient and effective.

6.   The Effectiveness of the Advocate

Whether the opposing lawyer will be more effective before a professional or a jury may influence the decision.

7.   Types of Evidence and Manner of Presentation

Both the content of the evidence and the alternative ways it can be introduced may affect the choice of the forum. Documentary evidence that appears in lengthy, difficult to understand documents may be better understood by a professional judge or arbitrator. Testimonial evidence that involves the credibility of witnesses may be better decided by jurors.

8.   Preferences of the Client

The client's wishes should also be considered by the lawyer. The client may prefer a decision reached by a jury, or may prefer an experienced arbitrator who can decide the case much more quickly and affordably.

9.   The Type of Decision Maker

If the judge assigned to a case may be favorably disposed, a jury trial need not be demanded or may be waived. Some judges may be more empathetic and compassionate than a jury. Parties can select an arbitrator mutually acceptable to them. Administrative law judges may not be able to be effectively challenged and removed.

10. Nature of Potential Appeal

Appellate courts are much less likely to overturn the factual findings of a jury than those of a trial judge because the standards of review are higher in a jury case. See Section 12.9. Decisions by administrative law judges who may be given deference are reviewable. Awards issued by arbitrators are reviewable within strict limits by a judge or appellate panel.

11. Familiarity with Counsel

There may be situations where, either in a social or professional context, an attorney and professional decision maker are favorably acquainted with each other. While this in no way should affect the decision maker's objectivity in hearing the case, it does give this attorney a psychological edge over an opposing counsel not known by the judge or arbitrator.

12. Timing of Decision

In litigation, an attorney may initially demand a jury trial regardless of what the previous factors suggest. That demand can later be waived, if, as the case develops, it appears that a bench trial would be better. The demand for a jury trial may increase the chances of an early favorable settlement with an opposing side who may have more to fear from a jury verdict. The timing of the waiver of the jury trial may affect what judge is assigned to hear the case. If an attorney would like to have a certain judge or would like to avoid a certain judge, the timing of the decision to waive may be crucial.

B. JURY TRIAL

In criminal cases and a large variety of civil cases, the parties have a right to a trial by jury. In arbitration, the parties agree to have an arbitrator and not a judge or jurors decide their case. In administrative proceedings, the parties may be required by law to proceed before an administrative judge and not a jury. Many more trials and hearings are conducted by arbitrators, administrative judges, and judicial judges than before juries.

In federal court cases, the Seventh Amendment guarantees a jury trial in all actions triable to a jury at common law, and Federal Rule of Civil Procedure 38 preserves this right. Similar state constitutional provisions or rules guarantee the same right in state cases. Criminal cases that may not require a jury are those in which the possible penalty is not incarceration but only a fine. Civil cases that do not require a jury are actions that are primarily equitable in nature, such as cases that do not involve money damages but seek injunctive relief or actions involving statutory claims that by law have to be decided by a judge.

Jurisdictions vary on how a party may demand a jury trial. In some courts, a party need not do anything affirmatively to obtain a jury. The filing of the action is sufficient to preserve the right to a jury trial. In other jurisdictions, a party must formally request a trial by jury. In these jurisdictions, a rule or statute specifies how a party must notify the court and the opposing party of a demand for a jury trial. These provisions typically require a party to include a demand for a jury in the complaint or to submit a separate jury request.

Federal Rule of Civil Procedure 38(b) states that a party may make a jury demand at any time after commencement of an action and within 14 days after the close of the pleadings. In federal courts and in state courts that impose a time limit for the jury demand, a party waives the right to a jury trial unless the party timely complies with the applicable rule. In these jurisdictions, it is common for the party who wants a jury trial to include such a request in the pleading submitted by that party. If the time period has lapsed, a party may move the court for leave to have the case tried before a jury, which the judge has discretion to grant. Once a jury demand is made by either party, the case will be tried to a jury unless the parties agree to a bench trial, or unless a judge orders a bench trial based on a motion to strike the jury demand brought by an opposing party or the court. See, e.g., Fed.R.Civ.Proc. 39(a).

C. ADVISORY JURY

A judge may empanel an advisory jury to render a verdict in cases that are not triable to a jury by right. See, e.g., Fed.R.Civ.Proc. 39(c). An advisory jury may be used whenever the court believes that jurors can assist the court in finding the facts. The jury verdict is purely advisory, and the judge may ignore it or use it as a guide in making findings. Although not often used, advisory juries may be empanelled in cases where the principal dispute centers on the credibility of witnesses, or where some issues are to be decided by a jury and other issues by the judge. For example, if the plaintiff's case has two causes of action, one of which is a common law claim triable by right to a jury and the other is a statutory claim triable only before a judge, the judge may have the jurors deliberate and render an advisory verdict on the statutory claim along with their verdict on the common law claim.

D. ROLE OF JUDGE AND JURY

In a jury trial, the judge administers the trial, manages the attorneys and the participants, rules on motions and the admissibility of evidence, instructs the jury regarding the law, issues orders and enters judgments. In a non-jury trial, the judge is the finder of fact as well. Judges usually maintain notes or minutes of the trial proceedings. These notes may become part of the official record and may also be used by the judge in making rulings.

In a jury trial, the jury is the fact finder. The jurors apply the law given by the judge to the facts. The jurors must deliberate fairly and impartially to reach a verdict and determine liability and damages, guilt or innocence.

In some jurisdictions, jurors are permitted to ask questions by submitting questions to the judge who reviews, approves, and asks the questions. This role changes the function of the jurors from being passive to being active participants in seeking evidence. Questions that may be appropriately asked are clarification questions seeking admissible evidence. See Section 3.7(D).

E. ROLE OF ADMINISTRATIVE JUDGE

The power and authority of an administrative judge depends upon the type of administrative hearing. Some administrative judges act similarly to judges during bench trials. Other administrative judges have a broader or more restrictive role depending upon the statute and rule that empowers them to decide a case. An advocate may object to an administrative judge exceeding the power and applicable authority.

F. ROLE OF ARBITRATOR

Arbitrators have the power provided them by the agreement of the parties, the rules of the arbitration organization, and the law. An arbitrator commonly has the same power and authority that a judge has in a bench trial. The arbitrator has broad discretion to conduct and control the hearing and usually has the power to issue any legal or equitable relief to which a party is entitled.

G. ROLES OF COURT PERSONNEL

Court personnel assist with and affect the presentation of a case. Court personnel include court clerks, court reporters, law clerks, administrators, assistants, and bailiffs. The court clerk administers the oath to the jurors and witnesses, performs general clerical duties during the trial, and enters orders on the judge's instruction. A court reporter marks exhibits and records the trial proceedings with a stenograph machine or computer or an audio recording system.

A law clerk (an attorney or a law student) researches the law and assists the judge in drafting memoranda and orders. An administrative assistant to the judge performs scheduling and clerical duties. The bailiff or court attendant (often a law enforcement officer) is usually responsible for enforcing order in the courtroom and is responsible for tending to the jury. Some of these functions may be combined so that one person serves as both court clerk and law clerk, or as court clerk and assistant.

These court personnel work closely with the judge and some are available to answer attorneys' questions regarding the judge's procedures and preferences. Trial attorneys should familiarize themselves with the procedures preferred by the court personnel, flexibly adapt to these procedures, and suggest alternative procedures if the best interests of the client are not advanced by the routine procedures. These personnel deserve to be treated with respect, and advocates do well to remember to always interact with them professionally and respectfully.

H. ROLE OF ARBITRATION AND ADMINISTRATIVE LAW PERSONNEL

Arbitration organizations commonly administer arbitration procedures by filing documents, assigning arbitrators, scheduling the hearing, and issuing the final award. Arbitrations can be filed electronically through online transmissions. Arbitration organizations may have a website with filing and communication capabilities. (e.g. www.adrforum.com).

Administrative law personnel process the filing, scheduling, and completion of a case. Clerks and administrators work with the administrative law judges in handling a case. Some administrative proceedings are handled through telephone and computer transmissions.

§ 2.9   JURY INSTRUCTIONS

For jury trials, an essential part of the planning process involves the identification and preparation of jury instructions and verdict forms. Jury instructions are explanations of the law of the case which the judge reads or explains to the jury during or at the end of the trial. Judges may also provide the jurors with a written copy of the instructions during the trial or for use during deliberations.

The instructions describe trial procedures and the legal elements of claims or defenses that need to be proven. Verdict forms contain questions (often called interrogatories) which the jurors must answer or statements they must complete. These forms contain the conclusions the jurors reach during their deliberations.

It is critical that instructions be selected early during trial preparation, even though they need not be submitted until the trial. The instructions contain the legal elements that support the legal theories of the case. A legal claim or defense can only be advanced in the case if it is contained in the jury instruction the court gives to the jury. The jurors only consider the elements of the controlling law submitted to them through instructions. The primary goal in composing and submitting jury instructions is to have the judge instruct the jury regarding a legal claim or defense which, if accepted by the jury, supports a verdict in a client's favor.

A. RIGHT TO JURY INSTRUCTIONS

A party usually has a right to an instruction if evidence has been introduced to support the instruction and if the instruction correctly states the applicable law. Judges will routinely give these instructions. The advocate wants the jury instructions to explain the elements of the law involved, the claims or defenses, and any material issues in a case.

B. SOURCES OF INSTRUCTIONS

Instructions, also called charges, must be based upon the law of the jurisdiction. Case law, statutes, rules, and other legal authorities provide the basis for the content of the instructions. Nearly all jurisdictions have jury instruction guides, "JIGs" or "pattern instructions," which are generally recognized and accepted charges. Many instructions and verdict forms have been approved by appellate courts or adopted by judicial or bar committees.

In determining the applicable instructions and forms, the first source to consider is the set of standard JIGs or pattern instructions used in a jurisdiction. The table of contents or index of the JIG book reveals which instructions are available. Pattern instructions are readily available for common types of cases, such as negligence and criminal cases. Other sources will have to be researched if there are unsatisfactory JIGs or no pattern instructions are available. A second source is the applicable law of the jurisdiction contained in cases, statutes, rules, regulations, or constitutional provisions. A third source is jury instructions used in previous cases in that jurisdiction. A fourth source is the analogous law or jury instructions of another jurisdiction.

Instructions and verdict forms that appear as standard instructions ordinarily reflect current and correct law, but not always. The accuracy and currency of each charge should be verified. Most JIG books and pattern instruction texts are updated periodically. If not, further research may be necessary to confirm that the pattern instruction or JIG is a proper instruction or verdict form.

The instructions submitted to the judge must be complete and correct to avoid creating an appealable issue. The failure to give necessary instructions, or the giving of incomplete or erroneous instructions, presents grounds for a new trial or a reversal of a verdict on appeal.

C. INSTRUCTIONS

There are several types of instructions a judge gives to the jury during a trial to explain trial procedures, describe the duties of the jurors, and explain the law applicable to the case. These include preliminary instructions, periodic instructions, cautionary instructions, curative instructions, and final instructions.

1. Preliminary Procedural Instructions

These are instructions the judge gives the jury at the beginning of the case. Preliminary instructions explain to the jury their responsibilities during the trial and may also include an explanation of the law applicable to the case; these instructions may be similar or identical to the final instructions. Some judges have standard preliminary instructions that they give. The trial lawyer may also ask the judge to give some different or additional instructions.

Example:

Members of the Jury, now that you have been sworn, I will give you some preliminary instructions to guide you through the trial.

First, you must not discuss the case among yourselves or with anyone else. At the end of the trial, you will have as much time as you need to discuss the case, but not during the trial.

Second, do not read or listen to anything regarding this case in any way. If anyone should try to talk to you about it, bring it to the court's attention promptly. And you should not text or email or use any social networks to discuss this case with anyone.

Third, do not try to do any research or make any investigation about the case on your own. This means you are not to use your smart phone, tablet, laptop, or any other device to contact others or to search websites, blogs, or any internet source for general or specific information about any issue or person in this case.

Finally, do not form any opinion until all the evidence is in. Keep an open mind until starting your deliberations at the end of trial.

It will be your duty to find from the evidence what the facts are. You, and you alone, are the judges of the facts. You will then have to apply those facts to the law as explained to you.

---

2.   Preliminary Substantive Instructions

At the beginning of the trial, judges may also inform the jury regarding the elements of the claims or defenses that will be presented and the applicable substantive law. These instructions are identical to what will be explained at the end of case.

3.   Periodic Instructions

In some trials, particularly those where the issues are complex or unusual, jurors may be assisted by instructions concerning the case or the law given to them periodically during the trial. An attorney who believes these periodic instructions to be helpful should explain this need to the judge, because the judge may not initially consider the use of periodic instructions necessary or helpful. A periodic instruction is usually identical to a final instruction, which may be repeated during the final charge in the case.

4.　Cautionary Instructions

Cautionary instructions are given before recesses and adjournments during the trial to remind the jurors to conduct themselves properly.

Example:

Remember that over the lunch hour you are not to talk to anyone including each other about this case and you are not to use your smart phone, tablet, or any internet access device.

5.　Curative Instructions

During the trial, the judge gives curative instructions after an inappropriate event has occurred, after some inadmissible evidence has been improperly referred to, or after trial misconduct.

Example:

I instruct the jury to disregard the last comment about the defendant attending a mosque. That is totally irrelevant to this case and should not be considered by you in any way.

6.　Final Instructions

There are two categories of final instructions: general instructions and specific instructions. General instructions are those charges that apply to all or most cases and involve the conduct of the trial, such as instructions regarding the role of the jurors, burden of proof, circumstantial evidence, and the credibility of witnesses. Specific instructions include those instructions that contain the legal elements of the claims and defenses applicable to a specific case. General instructions are typically found in pattern JIGs. Specific instructions may also be found in pattern JIGs if the case is common. See Section 12.2.

---

§ 2.10　PLANNING AND SUBMITTING JURY INSTRUCTIONS

A.　PLANNING

Jury instructions must be selected and drafted to meet several goals. Jury instructions must:

- Reflect the legal theories and factual summaries of the case.

- Be clear and understandable.

- Withstand legal attacks.

- Comply with ethical rules.

- Be drafted as a complete set.

1.   Reflect Legal Theories and Factual Summaries

The initial draft of jury instructions must contain the legal elements reflected in the legal claims and defenses. See Section 2.9(B). These instructions may be modified as the trial preparation develops and as the trial progresses. Final preparations for trial may require revisions in the selection and wording of the instructions. The opponent's submitted instructions may also necessitate revisions and so might discussions with the judge regarding what the judge thinks to be proper or improper.

Jury instructions must also reflect the factual summary. Instructions must be consistent with the evidence presented during trial so that jurors will conclude that the facts support the legal theories. Factual summaries should be reviewed to make certain that instructions covering all important facts are submitted.

Other instructions also need to be considered. Common instructions regarding the credibility of witnesses should be selected. Special instructions may need to be drafted.

2.   Drafting Clear and Understandable Instructions

Instructions should be drafted to accurately reflect the law and explain legal concepts, and should use words that are understandable to the jurors and support the client's case theory. The extent to which an attorney may submit a modified standard instruction or compose an original instruction depends upon the use of standard instructions in a jurisdiction and how effectively the attorney has edited or created an instruction.

The use of standard instructions may be so firmly entrenched in a jurisdiction that no proposed change will be acceptable to a judge. Other judges may accept changes that make the instruction more accurate and more understandable. There may be little latitude available to revise the instruction if the source of instruction is a specific and understandable statutory provision or case law opinion. If the source is unclear or incomplete, the judge may be flexible and modify the instruction based upon a reasonable interpretation of the source.

Several guidelines should be followed to draft instructions that will be accepted and used by the judge:

A.   The instructions must be legally correct and complete. Only instructions that accurately reflect the law should be submitted.

B.   Instructions should be clear and concise. Instructions must be drafted so that jurors, who have no legal training, can readily understand them. Some standard jury instructions drafted by lawyers and judges erroneously presume that jurors are able to understand certain legal terms. A standard instruction must be reviewed to determine whether it is easily understood, and original instructions should be drafted clearly and concisely.

C.   Jury instructions should be drafted following principles of effective writing. Some of the more important principles include: the use of simple sentences instead of complex sentences, the use of commonly used words instead of confusing legal terms, the use of active voice instead of passive voice, and the use of affirmative statements rather than negative constructions. An instruction likely to be accepted by a judge is one that includes legal terms that appear in standard instructions and adds an explanation of the terms using common language understandable to the jurors. This reduces chances the judge will reject the proposed instruction because required concepts and phrases are excluded.

D.   Instructions should be balanced and not biased in favor of one party. While an instruction should support a party's case theory, it should not do so in an overtly biased way. Judges must give objective and impartial jury instructions, not favoring one side or prejudicing the other. However, if there is a choice available between reasonably supportive and impartial words, then the words that most favor a client's position ought to be selected for proposed instructions.

3.   Instructions Must Be Able to Withstand Challenges

Opposing counsel may challenge proposed instructions by objecting to the use of certain words or phrases. Opposing counsel will argue that their proposed instructions ought to be used by claiming that no evidence supports the use of another instruction or by arguing that any other instruction could be inaccurate or incomplete. The trial judge carefully reviews the submitted instructions to assure they are correct. A ground for reversible error raised in many appeals involves improper jury instructions. Appellate judges review the instructions and decide whether the instructions correctly explained the law to the jurors. By following the suggestions in this section, instructions should be submitted which will survive these challenges.

4.   Instructions Must Comply with Ethical Rules

Ethical rules as well as rules of civil procedure prohibit an attorney from knowingly making a false statement of law to the court and from failing to disclose controlling legal authority adverse to the attorney's position. These rules also require that statements of law be based on existing law or a good faith extension, modification, or reversal of the existing law. Instructions must be drafted to comply with these ethical rules. An attorney who fails to comply with these rules has not only committed an unethical act but may also be sanctioned by the court.

5. Jury Instructions Must Be Viewed as a Complete Set of Instructions

Jury instructions cover all legal and factual issues of the case and must be complete and concise. Each individual instruction is part of a set of instructions, and the length and interrelationship of these jury instructions affects their comprehensibility. A set of instructions that is overly lengthy or presented in an unstructured, disorganized manner may confuse and overwhelm the jury. A set of instructions that is too concise and too short may omit necessary explanations. The goal is to submit a balanced set of instructions with a structure and organization that enhances their meaning.

For example, an automobile accident case may include the following instructions:

- Explanation of duties of jurors,
- Description of claims and defenses,
- Burden of proof,
- Meaning of preponderance of evidence,
- Direct and circumstantial evidence,
- Credibility of witnesses,
- Rulings and objections to evidence,
- Definition of negligence,
- Definition of proximate cause,
- Definition of ordinary care,
- Explanation of comparative fault,
- Violation of applicable statute, ordinance, or regulation,
- Explanation of measure of damages,
- Recoverable injuries,
- Medical expenses,
- Loss of income,
- Pain and suffering,

- Explanation of special interrogatories,

- Selecting foreperson, and

- Concluding instructions.

B. SUBMITTING INSTRUCTIONS

Instructions must be submitted in accord with the applicable rules of procedure which usually require that requests for instructions be submitted to the court no later than at or before the close of evidence. Many courts require and many other judges expect instructions to be provided at the start of the trial to help them understand the issues to be tried. Other courts may accept instructions during the trial at a reasonable time before the charge to the jury. Early preparation by the trial lawyer will ensure that instructions are ready at whatever point the judge requests them. As a practical matter, because substantive instructions contain the elements of the relevant claims or defenses, a trial lawyer has reviewed appropriate instructions at the beginning of the case and has used them to craft the theory of the case and the initial closing argument outline.

Instructions must ordinarily be provided in writing or electronically in a file or as an email attachment. See, e.g., Fed.R.Civ.Proc. 51 and Fed.R.Crim.Proc. 30. Oral requests not made part of the record are ineffective, but some jurisdictions do allow recorded oral requests in place of printed submissions. Some courts require or expect a memorandum of law to be submitted in support of significant instructions. It may be advisable, regardless of the rules or practice of the court, to submit a supporting memo to increase the chances the judge will accept the use of instructions that are not usually used.

There are a variety of ways to submit instructions, depending upon the preference of the judge and the type of instruction. The preferred way to submit important or specific instructions is to submit two sets of instructions. One set includes the text of each instruction on a separately numbered document with a reference to the source or citation for the instruction. The reference to the authority can include an indication whether the instruction is a direct quote from the source or has been edited or revised to reflect the facts of the case. The second set of instructions includes just the text of the instruction with no number or authority. This is a copy the judge can use and give to the jury.

General or less important instructions that appear in the JIG book or pattern instructions may be submitted by providing the judge with a list of the respective numbers from the pattern JIGs. Depending upon the judge and the jurisdiction, this method of submission is often used in simple cases or short trials. The attorney should ask the judge if this method is acceptable or if the judge prefers a set of proposed instructions in print, on an electronic file, or as an email attachment. Regardless of how instructions are submitted, the trial attorney must make certain that the judge clearly understands what instructions have been proposed and that there is a record of the requested instructions.

§ 2.11 VERDICT FORMS AND BENCH TRIAL ORDERS

A. TYPES OF VERDICT FORMS

In jury trials, the jurors are given a verdict form, which they must complete and sign. The form contains the jury's decision. There are three common types of verdict forms.

1. General Verdict

A jury may return a general verdict form, which is signed by the foreperson or by the jurors. In this form, the jury simply finds for or against a party.

Example:

We, the Jury, find for the plaintiff in the sum of $_____.

or

We, the Jury, find the defendant _____ (guilty or not guilty).

---

2. Special Verdict

The judge may submit a special verdict form to a jury that requires the jurors to answer specific questions and make findings of fact on critical factual issues. This form ensures that the jury does not ignore the controlling law, and also makes clear the jury's decision on specific issues.

Example (Product liability case):

(1) Was the product in a defective condition and unreasonably dangerous because of the manufacturing process used to manufacture the product?

Answer: Yes_____ No _____

(2) If your answer to Question No. 1 was "Yes", then answer this question: Was the defective condition caused by the manufacture of the product a direct cause of the plaintiff's injury?

Answer: Yes_____ No_____

(3) If your answer to Question No. 2 was "Yes", then answer this question: Was the defendant manufacturer negligent in the manufacture of the product?

Answer: Yes_____ No_____

(4) If your answer to Question No. 3 was "Yes", then answer this question: Was such negligence a direct cause of the plaintiff's injury?

Answer: Yes_____ No_____

(5) Did the plaintiff fail to exercise reasonable care for her own safety?

Answer: Yes_____ No_____

(6) If your answer to Question No. 5 was "Yes", then answer this question: Was the plaintiff's failure to exercise reasonable care a direct cause of her injury?

Answer: Yes_____ No_____

(7) If you answered "Yes" to Question No. 6, and you also answered "Yes" to Questions Nos. 2 or 4, then answer this question:

Taking all of the fault that directly caused the plaintiff's injury as 100%, what percentage of fault do you attribute to:

Defendant Manufacturer   _____   %

Plaintiff   _____   %

Total   100   %

---

3. General Verdict Form with Interrogatories

The court may submit a general verdict form with written interrogatories. This form combines both a general verdict and special interrogatories. When this type of form is used, the answers to the interrogatories must be consistent with the general verdict. If they are not consistent, the specific answers prevail over the inconsistent general verdict. Similar to the special verdict, this form ensures jurors follow the applicable law.

B. PROPOSING A VERDICT FORM

The type of case and nature of the issues determine which verdict form should be used. In criminal cases, the general verdict form is usually used. In personal injury cases, special interrogatories are typically used. The applicable rules or statutes in a jurisdiction may mandate what form of verdict is to be used.

The general verdict form is simple and only requires the jury to reach a general conclusion. A special verdict requires the jury to decide the facts and requires the judge to apply the law to the facts and enter a judgment. The special verdict form obliges jurors to consider and discuss all the important issues in a case. The use of a general verdict form with written interrogatories combines both the advantages and disadvantages of the two verdict forms. A general verdict form allows jurors to decide a case for whatever reason they wish and, unlike special interrogatories, does not focus the jury's attention on specific factual issues. Special interrogatories, on the other hand, may be improperly or inconsistently answered, and the judge may not be able to readily understand the basis for the jury's determination.

Procedural rules, case law, or statutes establish guidelines or mandates for the use of verdict forms. Federal Rule of Civil Procedure 49 and similar state rules regulate the use of special verdicts and interrogatories. Usually, during closing argument, counsel can suggest to the jury how they should complete the verdict form. Ordinarily, counsel may also advise the jury of the effect of the answers to special interrogatories. In some jurisdictions, however, counsel may be prohibited from so commenting. These considerations help counsel determine what type of verdict form counsel should propose to be used.

C. FINDINGS OF FACT AND CONCLUSIONS OF LAW

In a bench trial and some administrative hearings, the judge must issue findings and conclusions. In some arbitrations, the arbitrator must support an award with findings and conclusions. Advocates may submit proposed findings of fact and conclusions of law to the judge or arbitrator. See Section 3.11(E). The proposed findings should cover all the important facts contained in the factual summary. Similarly, the proposed conclusions should cover all the elements of the legal theories. The guidelines used in drafting proposed findings and conclusions are similar to those followed in drafting jury instructions, as explained previously.

Example:

FINDINGS OF FACT

1. The following events occurred on February 2, 2015, on Grand Avenue, St. Paul, Minnesota.

2. At about noon, plaintiff walked along Grand Avenue. She approached defendant from behind. Defendant was, at that time, carrying a round bakery product with sweet toppings, commonly known as a bagel with cream cheese and jelly.

3. The bagel was made of dense, chewy dough with a browned, crispy exterior.

4. As plaintiff passed defendant on the sidewalk, defendant swung around abruptly and unintentionally hit plaintiff in the face with the bakery product.

5. Plaintiff suffered damage as a result of the incident.

CONCLUSIONS OF LAW

1. The statute that applies in this case is Minnesota Statute Section 112.02, which provides:

   Laws, Section 112.02 Assault with a Roll

   Whoever hits another person with a sweet roll shall be liable to the other person for actual damages and punitive damages not exceeding $1,000.

2. Defendant did not "hit" plaintiff, within the meaning of Section 112.02, because the contact between the two was not intentional.

3. The bakery product involved in this incident was not a sweet roll within the meaning of Section 112.02 because it was not made of soft, flaky dough.

4. Defendant is not liable to plaintiff for damages and is entitled to an order dismissing plaintiff's complaint.

ORDER

1. This court orders that judgment be entered for defendant.

2. The parties are to bear their own costs.

_____

JUDGE

§ 2.12 BURDEN OF PROOF AND PRESUMPTIONS

For each issue within a case, one of the parties has the burden of proof regarding that issue. The concept, "burden of proof," actually includes two different burdens: the burden of production and the burden of persuasion.

A. BURDEN OF PRODUCTION

The term "burden of production" (also known as the burden of going forward) requires that a party produce sufficient evidence so that a reasonable person could find on behalf of that party. The judge determines whether sufficient evidence has been produced to meet this burden of production. In legal terms, the burden of production requires a party to introduce evidence of sufficient quality and weight that reasonable and fair-minded persons in the exercise of impartial judgment might find in favor of that party.

An opposing party challenges the burden of production by bringing a motion for a directed verdict or a motion for a judgment as a matter of law in a jury trial or a motion to dismiss in a bench trial, arbitration, or administrative hearing. These motions require the judge or arbitrator to evaluate the evidence and determine whether the evidence is sufficient to meet the burden of production. If the evidence is sufficient, the motion is denied and the case proceeds. If the evidence is insufficient, the motion is granted. A motion for a judgment as a matter of law or a directed verdict or a motion to dismiss may be brought to resolve an issue, a claim or defense, or the entire case of the opposing party. See Section 3.8(C)(7).

B. BURDEN OF PERSUASION

The burden of persuasion (also known as the risk of non-persuasion) requires a party to introduce evidence sufficient to win. The fact finder weighs this evidence and determines whether the party is entitled to a favorable decision. In legal terms, a party must introduce evidence that convinces the fact finder that the elements of the claim or defense have been proven.

C. TYPES OF BURDENS OF PROOF

There are three common degrees of burdens of proof:

1. Preponderance of the Evidence

This burden applies in civil cases. The burden requires a party, usually the plaintiff or claimant, to prove that it is more probable than not that the party's facts are true. In percentage terms, a party carries this burden and wins the case if its facts exceed 50% probability.

2. Clear and Convincing

This is a standard of proof that applies to some issues in some civil cases that involve a higher burden of proof than that imposed by the preponderance standard. For example, issues of fraud in many jurisdictions are required to be proven by clear and convincing evidence. To satisfy this burden, a party must establish proof greater than the preponderance of evidence. The exact percentage of proof required is unknown, but something more than 50% and less than proof beyond a reasonable doubt is required.

3. Proof Beyond a Reasonable Doubt

This burden applies to criminal cases. It is the highest of the three burdens of proof. In percentage terms, it is a high percentage, but is not expressed in a number. What is a "reasonable doubt" is left to the determination of the fact finder. It is not the absence of all doubt, and not the existence of some doubt. The fact finder decides what is "reasonable" after hearing the facts of the case.

D. ALLOCATION OF BURDENS

The burden of production and the burden of proof for each issue in a case must be allocated between the plaintiff or claimant and defendant or respondent. These two burdens can be allocated in four ways:

- The plaintiff/claimant has both the burden of production and the burden of persuasion.

- The plaintiff/claimant has the burden of production and the defense has the burden of persuasion.

- The defense has the burden of production and the plaintiff/claimant has the burden of persuasion.

- The defendant/respondent has both.

The law of a jurisdiction regarding an issue determines how the burdens are allocated. In many civil cases, the plaintiff/claimant has both the burden of production and the burden of persuasion. In civil cases involving a counterclaim or an affirmative defense, the defendant/respondent has both burdens on the counterclaim and affirmative defense. In criminal cases, the prosecution has both burdens. In criminal cases involving an affirmative defense, the defendant may have the burden of production. The allocation of the burden of persuasion and the burden of proof is critical in determining which party prevails.

E. PRACTICAL IMPLICATIONS OF BURDENS

The legal concepts of burden of proof may be more important to lawyers and judges than to jurors. Regardless of which party has the burden, the jurors want to find on behalf of a party based on truth and justice and not based upon probabilities. Civil attorneys who argue to the jury that they will prove what "probably" happened reduce the persuasive impact of their position. See Section 1.6. This is particularly true in civil cases where the notion is that a party wins even if jurors are only 50.1% sure of what happened. While this may make sense to lawyers and judges, it often leaves some jurors befuddled. Many jurors take the approach that they ought to be able to figure out what happened and which party is rightfully, and not just likely, entitled to a verdict. In close cases or where both parties are substantially at fault, the preponderance burden will favor the party who does not have the burden as jurors can reasonably conclude the probability burden has not been met.

Judges and arbitrators may be more influenced, and properly so, by the effect of the burden. In cases where both parties have presented equally compelling cases, the professional decision maker may decide the case based on which party has the burden of proof. If everything else is equal, the party with the burden will lose. It is the law that the party with the burden has to produce more compelling evidence to win. This concept is more easily understood and accepted by professional decision makers, which is why they can more likely produce a fair result in various cases than jurors could.

The burden of proof has an effective application in criminal cases where the system of justice requires a prosecutor to prove guilt beyond a reasonable doubt and allows the defendant to rely on a presumption of innocence. A criminal defense attorney can explain to the jurors that their role is to render a not guilty verdict if they have a reasonable doubt. Many jurors will nonetheless be skeptical if a defendant does not testify or presents no defense. In these cases the common sense perception of the jurors that an innocent person ought to raise some defense may offset the advantage that the burden of proof provides the defendant.

Another practical problem in relying on the burden of proof is that the jurors may misunderstand or misapply the proper burden. Many jurors have heard the phrase "proof beyond a reasonable doubt" prior to the trial and may improperly rely upon this prior understanding of the burden of proof. They may even apply this criminal standard of proof to a civil case because of their familiarity with the term and their unfamiliarity with the preponderance burden.

The authors have had the opportunity to review hundreds of video recorded jury deliberations of mock trials. During deliberations of criminal trials, many jurors wondered aloud why the defendant did not present a defense unless, of course, the defendant was guilty. On the other hand, other jurors mentioned that they wanted to be "positive" or "sure" before they found the defendant guilty. More often than not during deliberations in civil trials, jurors talked in terms of determining what "actually" happened and not what some lawyer said "probably" occurred. Still other jurors used the phrase "beyond a reasonable doubt" in describing the burden a civil party had. Further, these results reflect what happens in real cases based on remarks made by jurors to judges and trial lawyers after a trial.

These inaccurate statements by jurors may have occurred because neither the trial attorneys nor the judge accurately explained the applicable burden of proof during the trial, or because the jurors misunderstood the burdens. These results, nonetheless, do reflect a preference by jurors to reach a just decision based upon actual facts and not necessarily upon which party has which burden.

F. PRESUMPTIONS

A presumption is the conclusion a fact finder must reach unless contrary evidence of that conclusion has been presented. A presumption requires that a fact finder conclude fact "B" occurred based on the proof of fact "A" unless contrary evidence of "A" or "B" has been introduced. There are hundreds of legal presumptions established by statute or case law in each jurisdiction.

A traditional example of a common presumption is due receipt by postal mail. If there is evidence that a communication was properly addressed and mailed, it is presumed that the addressee received that envelope and its contents, unless evidence is introduced to the contrary. The effect of the due receipt presumption is that the fact finder must find that the communication was received unless sufficient evidence has been introduced showing it was not written or prepared, was not addressed properly, was not mailed, or was not received. In other words, proof that the communication was properly addressed and mailed (fact "A") requires the fact finder to conclude that it was received by the addressee (fact "B") unless evidence has been introduced to rebut either fact "A" or fact "B".

The word "presumption" has different meanings that need to be distinguished for trial purposes. A "trial" presumption is a rebuttable presumption; a "substantive" presumption is irrebuttable. Evidence may be introduced to rebut a "trial" presumption, as in the example of due receipt by postal mail. Evidence may not, however, be introduced to challenge a "substantive" presumption because it is irrebuttable.

For example, most jurisdictions have a substantive rule of law that states that a person under the age of seven (or other specific age) is incapable of committing a crime. Often, these rules of law use the word "presume": a child under the age of seven is "presumed" to be incapable of committing a crime. This presumption is not a trial presumption because neither party can introduce facts to rebut the capacity of the child to commit a crime. Once it is established that a child is seven years or younger, no rebutting evidence is admissible. Substantive presumptions may, however, be subject to constitutional attack—there must be a rational connection between fact "A" (age of seven) and conclusion "B" (incapable of committing a crime).

G. INFERENCES

A presumption has characteristics similar to an inference but its effect is different. Presumptions and inferences employ the same process: from the proof of fact "A" the existence of fact "B" may be presumed or inferred. The difference in their effect is that an inference is permissive and a presumption is mandatory. With an inference, a fact finder *may* infer fact "B" from fact "A". With a presumption, a fact finder *must* conclude fact "B" from fact "A" (unless contrary evidence is introduced).

Common inferences are based on circumstantial evidence. For example, proof of footprints in the sand (fact "A") permits a fact finder to infer that someone walked in the sand (fact "B"), but does not require the fact finder to reach that conclusion. There are many inferences that a fact finder can find in a trial. The law of a jurisdiction determines whether a particular fact leads to an inference or a presumption.

H. BURDEN OF PROOF AND PRESUMPTION RELATIONSHIPS

Presumptions may have an effect on the burden of production and the burden of persuasion. The precise effect depends upon the law of the respective jurisdiction. The following two examples demonstrate the effect presumptions have on the burdens of production and persuasion:

- The presumption may shift the burden of production to the other party. For example, if the plaintiff must prove that the defendant addressee received a letter, the presumption of due receipt may satisfy the plaintiff's burden of production and shift this burden to the defendant to introduce evidence that defendant did not receive the letter. If the defendant fails to introduce contrary evidence to meet this burden, the plaintiff wins because the presumption that the properly addressed and mailed letter was received is sufficient for the fact finder to conclude the letter was received.

- The presumption may have no effect on the burden of proof. The effect of the presumption may vanish if contrary evidence is produced that is sufficiently probative to make it reasonable for the fact finder to find the nonexistence of the presumed fact (also known as the "bursting bubble" presumption). For example, the presumption of due receipt disappears after the defendant introduces reasonable evidence for the fact finder to conclude that the letter was not received. Usually, testimony by the defendant that the defendant did not ever receive the letter is sufficient to rebut the presumption. The plaintiff no longer has the advantage of the effect of the presumption and must now introduce evidence to rebut the evidence introduced by the defendant. Some jurisdictions have modified this effect and require the defendant to introduce "substantial" evidence and not just a reasonable amount of evidence to make the presumption vanish.

The significance of the effects of a presumption relate to the strength of the evidence the defendant must introduce to win. If a defendant introduces no evidence regarding a presumed fact, the defendant loses. If a defendant introduces some evidence, the plaintiff still receives the benefit of the presumption, but may lose. If the defendant introduces contrary credible evidence, the plaintiff loses the benefit of the presumption and the defendant should win, unless the plaintiff introduces further relevant supportive evidence.

I. INSTRUCTIONS ON PRESUMPTIONS/BURDENS

The proper jury instructions to be given in a case depend upon the law of the jurisdiction regarding presumptions and burdens. The impact presumptions and burdens have on jury instructions, findings of fact, and conclusions of law can be substantial. The following alternative instructions, applicable in different jurisdictions, illustrate the differences in the findings the jury may or must make depending upon the facts introduced and how the presumptions and burdens apply in a jurisdiction. This example involves the issue of whether a letter sent by postal mail in an envelope was received.

- You shall find that the letter in question was received by the defendant.

- If from the evidence you believe that the letter in question was regularly addressed and mailed to the defendant, you shall find that it was received.

- You shall find that the letter in question was received, unless from the evidence you believe its non-receipt is more probable than its receipt.

- If from the evidence you believe the letter in question was addressed properly and mailed, then you also shall find it was received, unless you believe its non-receipt is more probable than its receipt.

The overlapping concepts of burdens and presumptions can be confusing unless analyzed in a logical, one-step-at-a-time approach. The primary effect presumptions and burdens of proof have in a trial relate to jury instructions and findings and conclusions. Statutes, court decisions, and standard jury instructions in each jurisdiction usually explain the effects that presumptions and burdens have in a particular case.

The key to understanding presumptions and burdens involves two steps. First, the concepts must be understood. Second, the applicable statute, court decision, evidence rule, procedural rule, or jury instruction that describes the effect of presumptions and burdens applicable in a specific jurisdiction must be found. In many jurisdictions, pattern JIGs provide this information.

———

Trial Advocacy Supplement

Examples of the skills described in this book appear in the *Supplement to Trial Advocacy Before Judges, Jurors, and Arbitrators* in three case transcripts. These cases contain examples of the strategies, tactics, and techniques that are explained in this text. The transcripts reflect how an entire case is tried before a jury, an arbitrator, and an administrative law judge and supplement the specific, individualized examples that appear throughout this book. The *Supplement* is available at store.westacademic.com.

CHAPTER 3

TRIAL PROCEDURES AND MOTIONS

■ ■ ■

REFLECTING ON ADVOCACY

If you're going to play the game properly you'd better know every rule.

—BARBARA JORDAN

Four things belong to a judge: to hear courteously, to answer wisely, to consider soberly, and to decide impartially.

—SOCRATES

§ 3.1   INTRODUCTION

This chapter summarizes various rules and practices that advocates need to know and follow to prepare and present a case effectively.

§ 3.2   CASE PREPARATION

A.   SCHEDULING A TRIAL

The rules of civil procedure that apply in a jurisdiction govern how an attorney places a civil case on the trial calendar. Typically, a written demand or electronic request for a timely trial, sometimes referred to as a note of issue, is required. After the submission has been served upon the parties and filed with the court, the case is placed on the trial calendar. The administrator or clerk of court can provide information regarding when the case will be called to trial. The timing in each jurisdiction varies depending on the calendar system and the number of cases docketed.

Criminal cases are scheduled by the office of the clerk or administrator. Lawyers do not need to file a written request. Statutes, rules, and the defendant's right to a speedy trial govern the scheduling of these cases. Accordingly, criminal cases take priority over the scheduling of civil cases. Some jurisdictions have separate calendars for civil and criminal cases with rotating panels of judges available for these cases.

The assignment of a judge for trial depends upon the type of court calendar used by the court. There are three major types of calendar systems: a master calendar system, an individual calendar system, and a combination of these two systems.

The master calendar system, or special term system, assigns pretrial motion hearings and trials to judges on a rotating basis. When a pretrial motion is filed with the court, a judge is assigned to hear that motion. When the case is ready for trial, a judge, usually not the same judge who ruled on the previous motions, is assigned. The trial judge first learns of the case shortly before the trial, unless that judge heard a prior motion.

The individual calendar system, sometimes referred to as the block system, assigns entire cases to individual judges. The assigned judge handles all proceedings as well as the trial. In the individual calendar system, the judge is familiar with the facts, law, and attorneys by the time the case is ready for trial. This system is used in federal courts. A federal magistrate judge is available to assist with cases by hearing discovery and other non-dispositive motions while the judge hears dispositive motions such as summary judgment and tries the case.

Some courts use a hybrid calendar system, combining both the master and individual assignment systems, depending upon the case backlog and court docket. In all systems, a court administrator or clerk assigns the cases on a random basis depending upon the availability and caseload of judges.

B. SCHEDULING AN ADMINISTRATIVE HEARING

Administrative hearings are typically scheduled by an administrator from the administrative agency. Administrative hearings are commonly set for a specific, limited period of time.

C. SCHEDULING AN ARBITRATION

The arbitration organization typically schedules the arbitration proceedings and hearings, depending upon the availability of the arbitrator. The case coordinator with the arbitration organization contacts and advises the parties when and where the arbitration will occur, depending upon their reasonable availability. Some arbitration organizations have the arbitrators schedule their own hearings. It is typical for the parties to estimate the amount of time required for an arbitration hearing, and for the administrator to set beginning and concluding times.

D. READINESS OF COUNSEL

Attorneys should commence case preparation as soon as possible after the cause of action arises. The facts are fresh in the minds of witnesses, and documents are available for preservation. Often, a litigation hold is required to preserve information and prevent it from being destroyed or deleted. The client's lawyer contacts employees and agents and requires them to retain and identify paper documents, emails, social network communications, files, and other electronically stored information. Sanctions exist for the destruction or spoliation of evidence.

Early discovery is usually more productive than later efforts to gather information. Motions typically must be brought to dismiss claims, add parties, complete discovery, and dispose of issues by summary judgment. The schedule for discovery and motions is influenced by many factors, including how soon the case is to be called for trial.

Federal judges and many state judges control the progress of cases by issuing scheduling orders with "cutoff" dates for discovery and motions and a proposed trial date. The parties may or must submit to the court informational statements, joint or separate, providing stipulated or suggested time periods for stages of the case. It is required in federal cases and common in state cases for the lawyers to confer about a discovery and motion plan to be submitted to the judge.

The attorneys must complete discovery and have all motions resolved before the deadlines ordered by the judge. Some jurisdictions require attorneys to file a certificate of readiness notifying each other and the court when they are prepared for trial. This notification may terminate discovery unless opposed by one of the parties. It also may be a prerequisite to placing the case on the trial calendar.

Arbitration procedures commonly keep counsel on a reasonably fast track to a hearing, reflective of the issues to be resolved. The time deadlines included in arbitration rules tend to be strictly enforced. One of the benefits of arbitration is the prompt way a case proceeds to a hearing, and counsel need to comply with the deadlines and be ready to proceed.

Administrative hearings also often proceed at a faster pace than litigation cases. Rules and regulations of the administrative agency prescribe the timing of procedures. It is the nature of some administrative cases to be scheduled according to firm deadlines, also requiring counsel to be prepared and ready.

E. THE BEGINNING DATE OF A CASE

Jurisdictions schedule specific starting dates for trials in several ways. Some jurisdictions notify counsel of a "date certain" when the trial will begin. Other jurisdictions advise counsel that they should be prepared to go to trial on a specific day or during a specific week, but that the trial date may be delayed depending upon the court calendar. In other jurisdictions, attorneys select a trial date from alternative dates available at the pretrial conference.

The beginning date for trials is often uncertain. This uncertainty of not knowing when a trial will begin can cause problems with preparations for the trial. Witnesses are difficult to subpoena when the attorney is unsure when the trial will begin.

Arbitration organizations or arbitrators schedule the arbitration hearing to begin on a specific date and time. Similarly, administrative law cases typically are scheduled for a date certain and begin at that time.

F. DOCUMENT FILING AND ACCESS

Federal courts and many state courts accept document filings from lawyers electronically, either exclusively or as an alternative to paper document submissions. Case Management/Electronic Case Files (CM/ECM) is the federal court's docket management and electronic case file system. Advocates may file all trial documents over the internet, including pleadings, pretrial statements, motions, briefs, affidavits, and proposed orders. PACER (Public Access to Court Electronic Records) is the federal court's electronic public access service that allows lawyers, the public, and other users to obtain case and docket information online from the courts. Many administrative agencies and arbitration administrators have similar electronic case filing systems.

§ 3.3   ASSIGNMENT OF THE JUDGE/ARBITRATOR

A. ASSIGNMENT OF JUDGE

State and federal courts assign judges to cases on a random basis. In every jurisdiction, judges may be disqualified for several reasons. Federal judges may remove themselves from a case, and lawyers seldom have available reasons to disqualify them. In all state courts, advocates can seek to remove an appointed judge for cause. In some state courts, lawyers can remove the first judge assigned to a case without having to state a reason. Subsequently, a judge may only be removed for cause.

B. DISQUALIFICATION OF A JUDGE

Federal and state codes of judicial conduct determine when a judge must be disqualified. Disqualifying situations include:

- Personal bias or prejudice by the judge toward a party.

- Personal knowledge of disputed evidentiary facts.

- Service as a lawyer representing a party to the case.

- Personal, family, financial, or other interests in the case.

- Relationship within the third degree between the judge and a party or lawyer.

These grounds and others disqualify judges who cannot be impartial. A judge may also be disqualified because of illness or physical disability. Federal Rule of Civil Procedure 63 and similar state rules provide a procedure to replace judges. They have to remove themselves if a conflict of interest, objective appearance of impropriety, or serious illness occurs.

C. REMOVING A JUDGE FOR CAUSE

In cases where judges do not remove themselves, attorneys may request that a judge be removed from a case for cause. An attorney who believes that a judge should be disqualified for cause must bring a motion and establish good cause for removal. Most jurisdictions require that the motion be heard by the judge who is allegedly prejudiced or biased. In some jurisdictions the chief judge appoints another judge to hear such a motion. These situations involving requests do not occur often.

D. REMOVING A JUDGE WITHOUT CAUSE

In states where parties can remove the first judge assigned to a case without cause, attorneys do so in hopes that the second judge will be less biased or more favorable. These rules do not permit a lawyer to select a certain judge, but permit the removal of the first assigned judge. In this procedure, the advocate files a notice of removal or similar document that requests another judge for the case. The notice typically need not state any reason for removal. The court clerk or administrator automatically assigns another judge to hear the case.

In some jurisdictions the removal document is referred to as a certificate or affidavit of prejudice and the attorney may have to include a conclusory statement or some perfunctory facts that suggest why the judge may be prejudiced. The clerk must honor the removal request and appoint another judge, usually on a random basis. These procedures permit an attorney to remove the judge initially assigned to a case, but not subsequently assigned judges. A second judge can be removed only through disqualification or by a showing of cause.

Removal documents must be filed promptly. In cases where an attorney receives notice of the judge assigned, typically several days are allowed to file the document. But in cases where the judge is orally assigned during a trial calendar call, the attorney may have only several minutes to ask for another judge.

The decision by an attorney to file a motion for removal of a judge may be tactically difficult. In some jurisdictions, such requests are routinely made and judges do not know, or may not care, whether a request has been made or which party made the request. In these situations, the strategic decision to file a motion for removal may be easy. In other jurisdictions, such requests are viewed with disapproval by the judges. The advocate must consider whether it's better to offend potential replacement judges or stay with the initial judge to avoid the problem.

E.   ASSIGNMENT OF ARBITRATOR

Parties are typically able to select their own arbitrator if they can mutually agree. Otherwise, the selected arbitration organization will provide a list of available arbitrators from the parties to choose from or assign an arbitrator from a list of experienced, impartial neutrals who have no conflict of interest. Some arbitrations involve three arbitrators, and the administrator would appoint all three neutrals. Some arbitration clauses provide that each party select an arbitrator and these two arbitrators select a third neutral arbitrator.

F.   REMOVING AN ARBITRATOR

Parties ordinarily have an opportunity to remove or challenge an arbitrator. In arbitrations where the organization appoints a specific arbitrator, the parties may request another arbitrator by challenging the originally appointed arbitrator for a conflict of interest or insufficient expertise. In arbitrations where a list of arbitrators is provided, each party may remove one or more of the proposed arbitrators which results in the surviving arbitrator being the presiding arbitrator. The arbitration organization commonly provides the parties with a professional resume of the arbitrators and a list of cases they previously decided.

G. ASSIGNMENT OF ADMINISTRATIVE JUDGE

Administrative agencies commonly assign a judge randomly from a pool of judges. Some agencies have their own panel of specialized judges who are assigned to cases. Other agencies draw judges from a statewide pool of administrative law judges who hear a variety of cases.

H. REMOVING AN ADMINISTRATIVE JUDGE

The procedures for challenging an administrative judge will be established by statute or administrative rules. Some administrative judges may not be removed at the request of a party unless a clear conflict of interest or substantial prejudice or bias exists. Other judges may be removed through a process similar to removing trial judges.

§ 3.4   PRELIMINARY PROCEDURES

A. LITIGATION CONFERENCES AND PLANS

Federal procedural rules and some state court rules mandate that the litigators at the beginning of a case confer and create a discovery and litigation plan to submit to the judge assigned to the case. If the lawyers are unable to agree on all issues, they may submit alternative proposals. The judge may then meet with them or may issue an initial pretrial order governing discovery and motions.

Many jurisdictions allow or require submissions by lawyers to be filed electronically and orders issued by judges issued electronically. These formats permit litigation, hearing, and trial documents to be easily and timely accessible to all participants, and also reduce problems with the submission of lengthy and cumbersome paper documents.

B. PRETRIAL STATEMENTS

Advocates as part of pretrial preparation are typically required to exchange written or electronic pretrial statements that summarize aspects of the case. These statements identify and narrow disputed issues, facilitate settlement discussions, help the court understand the case, and assist the lawyers in preparing the case. Such statements typically include the following information:

- Name and identification of the client.
- Name and identification of the attorney trying the case.
- Identity of any insurance carriers.
- Efforts made to settle the case by negotiations or mediation.
- Summary of the pleadings, issues, claims or defenses.
- Description of completed and uncompleted discovery.

- Status of preserving paper and electronically stored information.

- Location of discovery data placed in a depository.

- List of pretrial motions to be brought.

- Names and addresses of witnesses who will testify at the trial, including expert witnesses and their areas of expertise.

- Concise statement of the party's version of relevant facts.

- List of all exhibits offered as evidence.

- Stipulations the parties have about evidence or procedures.

- Elements of law that must be proved in the case.

- Citations to authoritative statutes, ordinances or cases.

- Itemized list of special damages, if sought.

- Estimated length of the trial.

- Jury instructions in a jury trial.

- Proposed findings and conclusions in a bench trial.

The timing of these submissions depends on the applicable procedural rules. Judges may require more than one pretrial submission, with a shorter one submitted early in a case and a detailed one when the case is ready to proceed to trial.

C. PRETRIAL CONFERENCE

At some reasonable and appropriate time prior to trial, the judge will order, or a party may request, a pretrial conference. See Fed.R.Civ.Proc. 16. A conference permits the judge to:

- Discuss settlement and mediation or other procedures.

- Determine whether settlement possibilities have been exhausted.

- Determine the disputed issues.

- Decide whether any pleadings need amending.

- Review the status of discovery.

- Review preserved discoverable evidence and exhibits.

- Rule on any motions or requests made by counsel.

- Determine whether summary judgment or other motions are to be made.

- Determine whether any motions in limine may be submitted.

- Attempt to simplify issues by inquiring whether:

    — any issues in the case may be eliminated, narrowed or modified by stipulation, motion or dismissal;

    — admissions of facts exist;

    — undisputed facts can be presented by stipulation or in a summary fashion;

    — stipulations regarding the waiver of foundation required for evidence and other agreements regarding certain evidence or exhibits may be reached;

    — procedures regarding the review and admissibility of electronic and digital evidence are being followed;

    — any preliminary motions concerning the admissibility or exclusion of evidence will be made or any major evidentiary problems may arise during the case; or

    — any critical legal or factual issues may arise.

- Determine the advisability of referring issues to a master, referee or magistrate.

- Inquire whether the number of witnesses, including experts, may be reduced.

- Determine the order and sequence of opening and closings, and witness examinations, especially in multi-party cases.

- Determine the time required for the trial.

- Set the hours and days scheduled for the trial.

- Prepare for the marking of exhibits and make special arrangements for the review and use of electronically stored information, diagrams, videos, computer generated presentations, demonstrations, and other exhibits.

- Inquire whether counsel plans to use any visual aids or exhibits during opening statements or final arguments.

- Determine whether sufficient and proper computer laptops and monitors and other equipment needed to try the case are available and work in the courtroom.

- Determine whether any scheduling problems may occur because of other commitments or conflicts that the participants may have.

- Make arrangements for daily transcripts, if needed.

- For a jury trial:

    — Certify that a jury has been demanded or waived.

    — Review procedures for jury selection.

   — Determine the number of alternate jurors.

   — Determine the number of peremptory challenges and process.

   — Determine whether the jurors will need to visit a site.

   — Summarize the introductory statement the judge will make to the jurors explaining the case.

   — Review or consider preliminary and final jury instructions.

Form 3.1 provides a pretrial summary worksheet.

On some matters, the judge makes final rulings during or after the conference that are written or recorded. See Fed.R.Civ.Proc. 16. On other matters, a ruling may be made or reserved until later, in order to consider how the issues are presented or how the evidence is offered. Motions, objections, stipulations, and rulings must be preserved on the record. If a reporter is present during conference discussions, a record is or can be made. If a reporter is not present, a record can be made at the end with a reporter present by summarizing all matters that need to be preserved.

D. PRE-HEARING ADMINISTRATIVE CONFERENCE

The existence and scope of a pre-hearing conference for an administrative proceeding depends upon the type of administrative process. In simple cases, there are no pre-hearing conferences, and the parties can discuss issues with the judge immediately before the hearing. In other cases, a complete pre-hearing conference may be conducted. These pre-hearing conferences may occur by a telephone conference call.

E. PRE-HEARING ARBITRATION PROCEDURES

Arbitration parties often have an opportunity to participate in a pre-hearing conference with the arbitrator. Issues to be discussed may depend upon the specific arbitration and may resemble issues that are resolved at a pretrial hearing. The hearing may occur through phone or video conferencing. Arbitration organizations may have available alternative ways to conduct hearings involving a combination of phone, video, and computer-assisted transmissions.

F. CASE BRIEFS

Many decision makers expect or require attorneys to submit case briefs in support of their case. Typically, these submissions contain a summary of the facts to be proved and key witness testimony, a list of exhibits, an explanation of the relevant law, evidentiary issues, and other useful information, such as the anticipated length of the trial or hearing.

FORM 3.1
PRETRIAL SUMMARY WORKSHEET

Case _____   File _____

1. Summary description of case:

2. Description of discovery that remains to be completed:

3. Reasons why case has not been settled:

4. List of pretrial motions:

5. Description of motions in limine or prospective evidentiary problems:

6. Identity of all trial witnesses, including experts:

7. List of all trial exhibits:

8. Concise statement of party's version of facts:

9. Stipulations of facts or undisputed facts:

10. Concise summary of party's claims or defenses:

11. Elements of law that need to be proved:

12. Citations to specific statutes, case law, jury instructions:

13. Case to be tried by: Judge ( )   Jury ( )
    Number of jurors _____ Number of alternate jurors _____
    Number of peremptory challenges.
    Plaintiff/Prosecutor _____   Defendant_____

14. Estimated time for trial_____

15. Other matters to be considered by trial court:

A case brief may consist of short segments regarding various case issues. These memoranda may be separated from the main brief and submitted individually when needed during the trial. Advocates may submit briefs to persuade the decision maker regarding claims or defenses even when they are not required or requested.

§ 3.5   CONDUCT BY THE ADVOCATE

The attorney's conduct is important during every phase of the case because it affects the way people react both to that attorney and to that attorney's client. Below are guidelines for appropriate attorney conduct.

A.   AVOIDING FAMILIARITY

The advocate should not display or take advantage of any familiarity with the judge, arbitrator, jurors, or other participants, especially if it appears to be improper. The judge and attorneys may engage in social banter in chambers, but in the courtroom the relationship displayed should always be professional. Jurors are instructed that the lawyers cannot talk with them during the trial to avoid inappropriate contacts.

B.   USE OF NAMES

A trial or administrative judge should be addressed as "Your Honor" or "Judge" and never by first name. An arbitrator may be addressed as "Arbitrator Surname" or "Your Honor." Some administrative hearing officers who are not judges may be referred to by surname. It is preferred, and required in some jurisdictions, to address all other participants in a case only by their last names to avoid any suggestion of improper familiarity. Some witnesses, such as children, may be appropriately referred to by their first names and some attorneys may prefer to call witnesses by their first names for strategic reasons. The attorney should seek permission from the court to use first names in formal trial and hearing settings.

C.   INTERRUPTIONS

An attorney should not interrupt an argument, question or response unless it is patently objectionable or prejudicial. Professional courtesy dictates that opposing counsel may speak without interruption.

D.   APPROACHING THE WITNESS/BENCH

An attorney should not wander around the courtroom or hearing room, approach a witness, or approach the bench without first determining whether the judge requires the attorney to request permission to do so. Some judges expect attorneys to make a request the first time they move about; other judges expect lawyers continually to ask permission. Many decision makers do not require such requests.

E. MATTERS TO BE HEARD OUTSIDE THE HEARING OF THE JURY

Several events that occur during a trial should or must occur outside the hearing of the jury to prevent jurors from being influenced or prejudiced. See Fed.R.Evid. 103(c) and 104(c). Significant evidentiary arguments, offers of proof and supporting arguments, offers to stipulate, motions and oral arguments should all be made at a bench conference, in chambers, or in the courtroom only when the jurors are absent. Additional sensitive areas of evidence such as questions, answers, exhibits, or arguments that may be prejudicial, inflammatory, or inadmissible must be addressed outside the hearing of the jurors.

F. BENCH/SIDEBAR CONFERENCES

During a jury trial, the attorney must approach the bench and talk quietly with the judge when the jury must not hear a topic. The judge may ask the attorney to approach the bench, or the judge will usually grant a request made by the attorney to approach the bench.

The design of the courtroom and the location of the jury box determine where the bench conference occurs. In some courtrooms, the attorneys stand in front of the judge at the bench. In other courtrooms, the conference occurs at the end of the judge's bench, opposite the jury box, which is called the sidebar. Wherever the conference occurs, it should be far enough away or conducted in a quiet enough manner so that the jurors will not hear what is said. The court reporter must record the conference and usually sits adjacent to where the conference is held.

Attorneys should use bench conferences sparingly and only when necessary. Trips to the bench slow the pace of the trial and cause jurors to speculate about what is being kept from them. Some jurors react negatively to attorneys who too often request bench conferences.

G. COUNSEL TABLE

In courtrooms, the tables typically face the bench and witness stand. In arbitrations, the tables may face each other or the lawyers will sit on opposite sides of a large table. In administrative hearings, the layout may resemble a courtroom or an arbitration room.

In many courts, custom dictates which table is for plaintiff/prosecutor (often the table nearest the jury box) and which is the defense table. In other forums, the attorney who arrives first selects a table. In arbitration and administrative hearings, the arbitrator or judge may assign placements. Whatever table is used, it is critical that the lawyer appear organized and that the table is kept neat. A cluttered counsel table may cause the decision maker to think the attorney's case is similarly disorganized.

In a jury trial, the advantage in having the table nearest the jury is that the attorney can more easily observe the jurors. The advantage in having the table farthest from the jury is that the attorney can watch the entire courtroom, including opposing counsel. Some trial advocates have strong preferences about which table they prefer while others are flexible.

H. SETTING THE STAGE

Requirements vary regarding whether counsel should stand or sit during parts of a trial or hearing. In trials and formal hearings, counsel typically stand during the opening statement and the closing argument. Where counsel stands in relation to the decision maker, and whether counsel must stand behind a lectern, depends upon local rules and the decision maker's preference. The use of visual aids during these presentations will also affect the location of the lawyer.

Some judges require counsel to stand at counsel table or behind a lectern during witness examination and at counsel table during the making of objections. Other courts allow or require attorneys to be seated for witness examination and objections. In arbitrations and administrative hearings, it is common to sit during the cases, or stand if necessary or preferred for presentations.

Many courts restrict attorneys' movements in the courtroom. Some judges do not allow attorneys to move away from the lectern or counsel table during witness examinations unless they introduce or use an exhibit. Some courts do not permit counsel to move around the courtroom during opening or closing. Arbitrators have similar rules and preferences.

The effective advocate may seek permission from the court to stand, sit or move in order to enhance the persuasiveness of the argument or witness examination. An attorney must become comfortable and familiar with the acoustics, distances, furniture, and physical setting of the courtroom. The layout affects where the attorney stands during opening statement and closing argument and how the attorney presents evidence. It usually is wise for the advocate to spend time rehearsing in the trial or hearing room especially if the lawyer is unfamiliar with the room.

The decision makers need to have an unobstructed view of the advocates, the witnesses, and exhibits. Some courtrooms have inadequate space, poor acoustics, uncomfortable jury chairs, and related problems. Advocates need to be aware where in the courtroom or hearing room they will be most effective in making presentations.

I. ROOM EQUIPMENT

Courtrooms typically include an easel, a white or black board, and may have modern electronic devices such as document cameras, video machines, computer monitors, and related equipment. Some courts also have available electronic writing and display boards, computer ready access, wireless availability, overhead projectors, shadow x-ray boxes, and other presentation equipment. Arbitration rooms and administrative hearing rooms may contain equipment appropriate for the type of case to be heard. In complex or lengthy cases, arrangements must be made to store exhibits. Secured electronic storage devices, file cabinets, boxes, or other equipment may need to be brought in to accommodate these items.

Tribunals are adapting to the growing use of computer and other types of electronic devices and equipment used in the presentation of a case. Recently built or remodeled courtrooms can accommodate this equipment. Arbitral and administrative hearing rooms may also be able to do so. The advocate must determine what is provided and what is needed so that the proper equipment is available. See Section 8.3.

J. CASE MATERIALS

Advocates commonly bring a variety of materials to the trial or hearing, including the case notebook, laptops, deposition or preliminary hearing transcripts, parts of the case file, the rules of evidence and procedure, books, disks, and wireless devices. Additional supplies that many lawyers bring are: computer equipment, markers, highlighters, folders, calculators, paper, tape, scissors, whiteout, and other presentation materials. Experienced advocates maintain a "kit" that contains these commonly used supplies for ready accessibility. Information may be stored in a computer drive or be available online via access to the internet.

K. REQUESTS BY COUNSEL

Requests by counsel to go "off the record," read something into the record, or take a recess should be addressed to the judge or arbitrator and not to the reporter or clerk. Usually the reporter stops recording only if the judge so indicates. Routine requests to mark an exhibit may be directly addressed to the reporter by counsel.

L. DEMEANOR OF COUNSEL

Counsel should act with respect toward all participants at all times. This professional demeanor should not prevent counsel from being assertive or insistent in appropriate situations. However, displays of anger, rudeness or any other inappropriate conduct should be avoided.

Counsel should avoid exaggerated facial expressions, body language, head shaking, gesturing, shouting or other conduct that indicates disagreement or approval of rulings, statements by the judge or arbitrator, or events that happen during the case. While an opposing lawyer makes a presentation or conducts questioning, the attorney should refrain from reacting improperly, either verbally or nonverbally, because the decision makers watch the attorneys and expect professional courtesy from them.

§ 3.6   THE TAKING OF EVIDENCE

A. SCHEDULING WITNESSES

Counsel should attempt to schedule witnesses in an efficient manner to avoid unnecessary delays. Attorneys should exchange good faith estimates regarding the sequence, timing, and length of witness examinations. The examining attorney has the responsibility to make certain that the witness is present when needed. Usually a witness' testimony should be pursued until it is concluded and should not be interrupted by the taking of other evidence. This helps the fact finder minimize confusion about the testimony and is also more convenient for the witness.

B. SUBPOENAING WITNESSES

Counsel should always subpoena their witnesses, including supportive witnesses, to make certain they appear to testify. The subpoena reminds a witness of the date of the testimony and the location. The subpoena document can also identify what documents or other relevant materials the witness is to bring to the trial or hearing. Ordinarily, these documents are obtained before the trial and are already in the room. A subpoenaed witness who fails to appear can be ordered by the judge or arbitrator to appear at a rescheduled time. An unsubpoenaed witness who fails to appear may be precluded from later testifying because the examining attorney did not properly subpoena the witness.

Subpoenas are commonly issued by judges and arbitrators and obtained from a court clerk's office, the arbitration forum or arbitrator, or the administrative law clerk or judge. In some jurisdictions, attorneys may issue subpoenas identifying the forum where the case will be heard. Most jurisdictions and forums require that a witness fee be tendered to the witness along with the subpoena. A statute or rule usually establishes the amount of this fee, which includes reimbursement for mileage and a small payment such as $40. Lay witnesses are not paid for their testimony or reimbursed for lost income. Expert witnesses may be and typically are reimbursed for their time in court by a flat fee or an amount reasonable for their services.

A witness who fails to abide by a subpoena may be subject to a contempt citation and arrest. See Fed.R.Civ.Proc. 45(e). A warrant may be issued if the subpoena service was proper and no reasonable excuse exists for the failure of the witness to attend. The attorney who subpoenaed the witness should make diligent efforts to obtain the witness' appearance.

C. SEQUESTERING WITNESSES

The judge or arbitrator has the power and discretion to sequester— that is, to exclude or separate—witnesses during a case. Before the trial or hearing begins, an attorney may request that witnesses be excluded from the room to prevent them from hearing and being influenced by others' testimony. Parties to a case, including individuals and designated corporate representatives, have a right to be present during trial and ordinarily cannot be excluded. Criminal defendants cannot be excluded, although restraints can reasonably be placed on them if they unreasonably interrupt the trial. The rules of evidence may also affect whether witnesses can be excluded from the trial or hearing. Federal Rule of Evidence 615 and similar state rules prohibit the exclusion of a person whose presence is essential to the case, such as an expert witness.

The granting of a motion to sequester bars witnesses from the courtroom or hearing room except when they testify. A witness remains excluded until testifying, until the party calling the witness has rested, or until rebuttal evidence has been completed. Whether the judge or arbitrator grants the motion depends upon the applicable rules and whether a party has a right to exclude witnesses or whether it is discretionary with the decision maker.

Sequestration orders may or may not serve an effective purpose. On the one hand, witnesses usually know from their preparation by counsel what other witnesses will say and what evidence will be introduced. On the other hand, if they listen to each other's testimony, witnesses may gain valuable information and better present their stories in a consistent way. The effectiveness of a sequestration order depends on how thoroughly the attorney has prepared them, how familiar they are with the stories of other witnesses, and whether the sequestration order prohibits contact among witnesses outside the courtroom or hearing room.

D. VIDEO, COMPUTER, AND ELECTRONIC EVIDENCE

Many cases involve evidence that has been preserved on a video, computer, or other electronic device. The evidence may be testimonial or contained in an exhibit. The testimony of experts and lay witnesses who are unavailable during the trial or hearing is commonly presented by video along with relevant exhibits. They have previously testified and the video of their testimony is shown to the fact finder. The lawyers may have stipulated to these procedures or rules permit their use.

Several matters affect how counsel needs to prepare and present this evidence. The advocate needs to ensure there is working equipment to display the testimony and exhibits. The evidence will need to be previewed by opposing counsel and perhaps the judge to make sure it is what it purports to be and is not objectionable. Unlike testimony that appears on a printed transcript or exhibit, electronic information is not readily apparent. It needs to be shown or displayed before the jury sees and hears it. Counsel must make timely arrangements to have this done to prevent trial delays and to make sure it will be admissible.

These types of evidence also involve issues of authenticity and accuracy and concerns about tampering and distortions. These matters need to be addressed by counsel to avoid objections being sustained to the introduction and use of the evidence. These issues also affect the use of visual aids during opening and summation.

Counsel ought not to display evidence that is likely to draw serious and strenuous objections, and advocates should not attempt to improperly display questionable exhibits or visual aids. These matters can be and usually are taken care of during the pretrial conferences.

E. USE OF INTERPRETERS

A witness or party may need an interpreter in order to testify or understand the case presentation, and courts typically have access to available interpreters. The party calling that witness needs to advise the court in advance of this need. An interpreter provided by the examining attorney may be sufficient if that person is reliable; otherwise, the judge or arbitrator will select an interpreter to ensure that the testimony is interpreted fairly and completely. The interpreter will take an oath to accurately interpret the questions and answers.

F. ORDER OF EXAMINATIONS AND USE OF EXHIBITS

The mechanics of the trial, administrative, and arbitral processes and the method and order of interrogating witnesses and the introduction of exhibits is left to the discretion of the judge and arbitrator. Federal Rule of Evidence 611(a) and similar rules provide that a judge or arbitrator shall exercise reasonable control to make the witness examination and evidence presentation effective for the ascertainment of truth, to avoid needless consumption of time, and to protect witnesses from harassment or undue embarrassment. These rules establish that the judge or arbitrator controls the case and the receipt of evidence.

G. SCOPE OF EXAMINATIONS

1. Direct Examination

A competent witness may testify to any relevant matter unless excluded by a specific rule, statute or case. See Fed.R.Evid. 401 and Section 7.2. The pretrial list of witnesses describes who the witnesses will be and, along with proper trial preparation, usually provides sufficient notice about witnesses who present competency or relevancy problems.

2. Cross-Examination

A witness may be cross-examined regarding any matter covered on the scope of direct examination, or related to credibility or impeachment, or any relevant matter permitted within the discretion of the judge or arbitrator, even if not directly covered on direct examination. See Fed.R.Evid. 611 and Section 9.2(D). Cross-examiners are typically provided wide latitude and substantial leeway to ask questions.

3. Redirect, Recross, and Subsequent Examinations

Redirect examination is confined to new matters brought out on cross-examination and cannot merely repeat matters brought out on direct examination. Recross examination is limited to matters brought out on redirect examination. Subsequent examinations are confined to the scope of matters covered during the previous examination. The judge or arbitrator has discretion to permit questions on matters not covered within the scope of a previous examination. See Fed.R.Evid. 611(b).

4. Rebuttal

After the defense has rested, the plaintiff/claimant/prosecutor may present additional evidence in rebuttal. The scope of this evidence is limited to those material areas covered during the defense case that were not covered during the initial case. Rebuttal is limited to new and significant areas of evidence and cannot be used to repeat evidence.

Rebuttal typically consists of a witness who can deny or contradict what an opposing witness has stated or an exhibit that contains contrary information. Judges and arbitrators have broad discretion in permitting or limiting rebuttal. An attorney offering rebuttal evidence should establish its relevance and how it expressly rebuts contrary evidence. Some judges and arbitrators may deny rebuttal evidence if they believe it should have been introduced during the proponent's case in chief. Others may deny rebuttal to both sides because sufficient evidence has been introduced. Witnesses may be precluded from rebuttal if they had been sequestered but observed the trial or hearing after their testimony.

After the plaintiff/claimant/prosecutor has introduced rebuttal evidence, the defense may offer rebuttal evidence. Following the defense rebuttal evidence, the plaintiff/claimant/prosecutor may offer new rebutting evidence if it is appropriate. Judges and arbitrators reasonably prohibit cumulative or repetitive evidence.

H. STIPULATIONS

Stipulations are a means to present evidence in a case without calling witnesses or having to introduce exhibits. The parties may stipulate to specific facts, authentic exhibits, or witness testimony. A stipulation is reduced to writing and approved by the attorneys or made orally on the record. The stipulated facts are presented to the fact finder at an appropriate time in the case, usually during the case in chief of the offering attorney. A stipulation may be read by one of the attorneys, a witness, the clerk, or by the judge or arbitrator.

Example:

Counsel:

Your Honor, I offer Exhibit No. 23, which we have already marked for identification. It has been provided to the court upon agreement of counsel this morning before we started. This stipulation involves the testimony of A.D. Pythagoras.

Judge:

Is that correct, counsel?

Opposing Counsel:

Yes, your Honor.

Judge:

It is received. You may proceed.

Counsel:

Your Honor, at this time I would like to read to the jury the stipulated testimony.

Judge:

You may, counsel. Members of the Jury, you are to accept these facts you are about to hear as true and undisputed.

Counsel:

Members of the Jury, opposing counsel and I have agreed that were A.D. Pythagoras called to testify, he would tell us that he is the owner of the Pythagoras Accounting Service, and that as the owner of the accounting service, he has checked the books and records of Harvester Corporation. He has learned that the gross sales of farm equipment by the Harvester Corporation in 2013 were $7,355,000,300 and that the gross sales of farm equipment by the Harvester Corporation in 2014 were $825,000,5200.

I. ADMISSIONS

Statements made by an opposing party may be admitted as evidence against that party. Federal Rule of Evidence 801 and similar state rules render admissible out-of-court statements made by an opposing party and out-of-court conduct of that party. In civil cases, admissions occur in documents and discovery responses such as interrogatory answers, deposition answers, and responses to requests for admissions. In criminal cases, admissions made by the defendant may be contained in a confession, which can be introduced through a witness, usually a law enforcement officer who heard the oral or video confession or who can authenticate the written confession.

The party seeking to introduce admissions must affirmatively offer them into evidence. Typically, the offering attorney offers the statement by introducing into evidence the authentic document containing the admission. For example, the offering attorney asks the judge or arbitrator to accept in evidence the relevant statements in the discovery document, marked as an exhibit. The attorney also can call the opposing party as an adverse witness and ask the party to admit such statements. If the opposing party denies making the statements, the statements can then be introduced as an exhibit. The offering attorney should decide whether it is better tactically to have the admission read into evidence or to have the opposing party orally admit the statements.

J. FORMER TESTIMONY

Situations arise where witnesses are unavailable to testify during a case. In civil cases, the previous testimony of a witness who is not available may be presented as substantive evidence. The previous testimony must usually be made under oath, at a deposition or hearing, and the opposing party must have had an opportunity to cross-examine the witness at that time. The witness must be unavailable to testify because of illness or death, or more commonly, because the witness is beyond the subpoena power of the tribunal. Section 7.10(A) explains these situations and procedures in detail. In arbitrations and administrative hearings, witnesses may be able to appear by telephone if they cannot be present in person. In criminal cases, former testimony is usually inadmissible because of the constitutional right of the defendant to confront witnesses at the trial.

K. JUDICIAL/ARBITRAL/ADMINISTRATIVE NOTICE

Facts that are indisputable or highly authoritative and widely accepted may be introduced through judicial, arbitral, or administrative notice. Notice may be taken of facts known as adjudicative facts, which are facts generally known within the territorial jurisdiction of the forum, or those that can be accurately and readily determined by highly reliable sources. See Fed.R.Evid. 201.

Examples:

Geographic and Historical Facts:

Notice may be taken of the location and existence of places, events, and things, such as streets, intersections, and landmarks. For example, The United States Supreme Court Building can be established as being located in Washington D.C.

Accurate and Verifiable Facts:

Notice may be taken of calendars, census findings, weather reports, and almanac information. For example, a day can be noted as a legal holiday (May 25, 2015, Monday, Memorial Day).

Scientific Facts:

Notice may be taken of scientifically verifiable or undisputed facts such as the laws of nature and scientific certainties. For example, the hot air in an average size law school classroom weighs 1,904 avoirdupois pounds.

The party offering evidence by way of notice must supply the information and request that it be admitted into evidence. Decision makers may also take notice on their own initiative. A judge may accept judicially noticed facts at any time during the proceeding and may inform the jury of the facts. In civil cases, judicially noticed evidence is conclusive of the facts and jurors cannot find otherwise. The judge instructs the civil jury that they must find the fact as judicially noticed. The party offering such facts need not introduce any other evidence of the fact. In criminal cases, judicially noticed evidence is not usually conclusive and jurors can find otherwise. The judge instructs the criminal jurors that they need not accept or believe the judicially noticed facts.

L. EVIDENCE SUMMARIES

In lengthy, legally complex, or factually complicated cases, timesaving evidence summaries are typically used. In common, shorter, and two party cases, summaries containing evidence regarding dates, schedules, amounts, and other difficult to recall facts are often prepared. The judge or arbitrator may order, or the parties may stipulate to, various types of summaries, including the testimony of a witness listing injuries, a list of exhibits and their contents, outlines of information or damages, or any other summary that makes oral or documentary evidence more understandable to the fact finder. See Section 8.6(K).

M. PLANNING THE INTRODUCTION OF EVIDENCE

Form 3.2 provides a useful format to identify and select evidence.

§ 3.7   COURT INTERVENTION

A. COURT-APPOINTED EXPERTS

A court may, on its own motion or on the motion of any party, appoint its own expert witness to testify in a case. The rules of civil procedure or evidence in a jurisdiction usually cover the procedures involved in such an appointment. Federal Rule of Evidence 706 and similar state rules govern the appointment of court experts. A judge may perceive the need for an expert to clarify confusing points or assist the fact finder in determining certain issues. This rule is seldom invoked. Arbitrators are unlikely to have this power. Administrative judges may have this power, especially in regulatory proceedings.

FORM 3.2

SELECTING EVIDENCE

Elements of Claim/ Defense	Facts to be Proven	Witness	Exhibit	Stipulation	Admission	Former Testimony	Hearing Testimony	Judicial/ Arbitral/ Administrative Notice	Other

B. COURT WITNESSES

The court may, on its own motion or on the motion of any party, call a witness who has not been called by a party. All parties are entitled to cross-examine the witness. Federal Rule of Evidence 614(a) and similar state rules authorize the court to call any person as a witness, with the exception of a criminal defendant. This rule is rarely invoked. An arbitrator is unlikely to have this power. Administrative judges may have this power if the hearing is one that is not solely adversarial.

C. QUESTIONING BY THE COURT

A judge may question any witness. See Federal Rule of Evidence 614(b) and similar state rules. Questioning by a judge occurs more often in bench trials and rarely in jury trials because the judge is the fact finder in a bench trial. The judge may examine a witness during, or more commonly, after the parties have completed their questioning.

Questioning by judges often depends on how they view their duties and responsibilities. Some judges believe they ought not to ask questions because it is the exclusive role of the lawyers to present evidence. Other judges will ask questions if they perceive they need additional evidence in order to conduct a fair trial and to obtain sufficient information for their findings of fact. Still other judges will ask questions if it is apparent that the advocate for a party is doing a poor job asking questions, while others believe it is wrong to help and favor one party over another. Many judges who do ask questions limit their inquiries to areas that need clarification.

After the judge has finished, the attorneys may further examine the witnesses on matters covered by the judge. Attorneys have a right to object to questions by the judge, and to the court's appointment of an expert, and to the calling of a witness. See Section 4.5(F) and Fed.R.Evid. 614(c).

D. QUESTIONING BY JURORS

In some jurisdictions, jurors are permitted to ask questions of witnesses. Usually the jurors submit written questions to the judge, who reviews the questions and determines if they may be asked. Jurors may be permitted to ask questions orally after the attorneys have completed their questioning, but this opportunity can create problems because the jurors may ask inappropriate questions. If judges permit questions, they prefer to screen them first. The attorneys may object to juror questions.

Traditionally, jurors do not participate in a trial by asking questions of witnesses. That responsibility is to be performed by the lawyers and occasionally by the judge. A growing number of judges and lawyers recognize that permitting jurors to ask questions may assist them in their determination of the facts. Some advocates and judges oppose permitting jurors to ask questions because what they want to know may be prohibited by the rules of evidence and non-answers may prejudice a party. Questions that are appropriate and screened by the judge and lawyers may be helpful to all participants. Such questions may properly identify areas the lawyers didn't cover and issues that concern the jurors.

E. MASTERS AND JUDICIAL ADJUNCTS

In certain cases, a judge may appoint a master, referee, or other judicial adjunct to assist with the factual or legal matters in a case. Federal courts have magistrate judges who assist the district court judge with pretrial matters and, often, settlements. Federal Rule of Civil Procedure 53 permits federal district courts to appoint masters to help with cases involving discovery disputes, complicated issues, multiple parties, class actions, mediation, and complex damages or accounting matters. The fees of the master are commonly paid by the parties, and the judge may allocate the costs among the parties.

Multi-district litigation cases and complex cases often have one or more masters who help the case proceed efficiently and economically. Masters may serve a variety of roles including assessing disputed discoverable information, reviewing electronically stored information, identifying documents that are privileged or discoverable, monitoring depositions, providing technological assistance, assisting parties with pretrial procedures, acting as a mediator, managing lawyer conferences, assisting counsel with proposed orders to be submitted to the judge, conducting hearings and recommending factual findings to the court, monitoring a consent decree, or administering the distribution of a monetary settlement. More information is available at www.court appointedmasters.org.

F. ADMINISTRATIVE PROCEEDINGS

Administrative judges may be very active or passive in a case. In some administrative hearings, it is the role of the judge to present evidence, call witnesses, and raise issues. In other administrative hearings, the judge acts similarly to a trial judge or an arbitrator.

G. ARBITRATION PROCEEDINGS

Arbitrators may ask questions of witnesses to clarify evidence and may ask questions of parties regarding legal issues. Arbitrators typically cannot raise new issues or call their own witnesses, unless permitted by the applicable rules or agreement of the parties.

H. COMPLEX OR MULTIDISTRICT CASES

Cases that are complex, prolonged or geographically located in more than one jurisdiction present problems that require special handling. In federal court, the Manual for Complex Litigation provides procedures applicable to the management and conduct of cases that are complicated or venued in more than one district. The administration of large or multi-jurisdictional cases takes place during the early stages of the case, and matters that affect the trial are usually resolved well before trial.

Complicated or very lengthy cases may involve changes in the stages of the trial and the introduction of evidence. Summation may occur periodically during the trial with the attorney summarizing parts of the evidence as the trial progresses. The background of witnesses and the qualifications of experts may be introduced through printed resumes. Testimony of key witnesses and experts may be presented through edited videos. Numerous documents may be submitted through evidence summaries. See Section 8.6(K). These and other efficient procedures may be used in an effort to reduce the duration of the trial and to prevent an overwhelming amount of evidence.

Federal cases that are filed in different federal districts that have common issues of law and fact may be transferred to one federal judge who administers all discovery and pretrial proceedings. The Federal Multi-District Litigation Panel transfers these cases in accord with the applicable federal MDL statute. Nationwide or multi-state products liability cases and disaster cases are examples of the same or similar case that is filed by individual or class action plaintiffs in numerous districts against the same defendants. Thousands of cases may be filed across the country, and this method helps coordinate proceedings. The transferee judge assigns lead counsel, liaison attorneys, and a plaintiff's steering committee to represent the interests of all plaintiffs. Defense counsel may also join together and more easily defend in this singular proceeding. A master or masters can be appointed to assist with the litigation.

There is no similar procedure to coordinate parallel cases filed in different state courts around the country. State court judges in one state have no power over cases filed in other states, and federal judges likewise cannot control state court cases. The state court plaintiff and defense lawyers can and do cooperate with each other in an effort to avoid unnecessary and duplicative litigation efforts. A master appointed by the courts can help promote collaboration and coordination among the participants.

§ 3.8   MOTIONS

Any request, oral or written, made by an attorney seeking an order or some relief from a judge or arbitrator is a motion. Many requests are often not formally referred to as motions by counsel. More typically, lawyers orally ask the judge or arbitrator that something be done or prohibited. Federal Rule of Civil Procedure 7(b) and similar state rules allow oral motions "during a hearing or trial." These oral motions may be made in the courtroom or in chambers.

Motions are much more frequent in litigation. Motions may also be brought in arbitrations (often called "requests") and administrative hearings (sometimes called "petitions"); but some motions are unnecessary or unavailable in arbitration and administrative cases. For example, summary judgment motions are often inappropriate in these cases because the hearing is promptly scheduled and the parties can more efficiently and effectively present their entire case to the arbitrator or administrative law judge, obviating the need for an early preliminary decision. The frequent use of motions in litigation is one of the reasons why judicial cases are more expensive and take much longer to resolve.

Motions should be brought if the relief sought has a significant impact on the status, progress or outcome of the case. If granting relief through a motion may substantially increase the chance of obtaining a favorable decision, then the motion should be vigorously pursued. If the relief sought has only marginal influence on a favorable decision, then the motion should be reconsidered.

The specific relief sought in any one motion must be considered in the context of the entire case. If motions are brought on overly technical or minor points, or if too many motions clutter the proceedings, they may have an adverse impact on the case of the moving attorney. An advocate's ability is evaluated by the judge or arbitrator in part on how effectively the attorney handles procedural matters such as motions.

A. MOTION DOCUMENTS

Some motions are typically presented in writing, by serving paper or electronic documents on the other parties and filing the documents with the court. A case may have documents maintained on a website, accessible to all. Service may be had by acceptance by the opposing lawyer, by postal mail or by email attachments received by the opposing lawyer. Personal service is usually unnecessary unless an order to show cause or similar relief is involved. Prepared motion documents include:

1. Notice of Motion

The notice of motion advises all parties of the time and place of the motion hearing, and typically identifies the judge who will hear the motion. Anywhere from five to thirty or more days may be required to give timely notice of the hearing depending on the type of motion and applicable rules. Trial motions are commonly heard by the trial judge at the final pretrial conference. Whether a printed notice is required depends on the motion, the relief sought, and the type of motion. Sufficient notice should be given to prevent the opposing party from claiming unfair surprise or prejudice in arguing against the motion. Arbitration rules and administrative law regulations delineate the content, timing, and deadlines of motions.

2. Affidavits

An affidavit is a sworn statement by a person stating facts or opinions. Affidavits are used in motion practice to support or oppose a motion. An affidavit may be from a witness who has personal knowledge of the stated information or knows it based on information and belief. Affidavits are necessary when no facts in the file or record support the motion or if relevant facts are based on the personal knowledge of the moving attorney. An affidavit may be created by having the person assert that the statement is true under penalty of perjury or by having the affiant sign the statement under oath before a notary public.

3. Memorandum of Law

Most forums require and most decision makers expect legal authority supporting or opposing a motion. The submission of a persuasive memorandum of law increases the chances that the motion will be granted—or denied. All those hours spent in legal research and writing may actually pay off after all.

4. Proposed Order

Most jurisdictions require submission of a proposed order by the moving party. The order makes clear what is requested and enables the judge to grant the motion expeditiously. Some judges sign the order if it reflects their decision. Other judges draft their own order, often based on the proposed order. Some orders may need to be independently composed by the judge, especially if they contain factual findings. Proposed orders may also be submitted to an arbitrator and administrative judge.

B. OPPOSING MOTIONS

Generally, there is no need for the opposing attorney to bring a motion seeking to deny the relief requested in the moving party's motion. Orally opposing the motion at the hearing may be sufficient to obtain an order denying the motion. Whether the opposing party should submit any documents depends on the rules of the forum, the timing of the motion, and case strategy. Court rules ordinarily state whether the court requires submission of any opposition documents. A motion submitted on the eve of trial or hearing may not provide sufficient time for the opposing lawyer to reply in writing, making an oral response appropriate and sufficient.

In many situations, it is usually not necessary—although it may be advisable—to submit opposing affidavits. Affidavits may need to be submitted if the facts do not appear in the file or record or if the facts claimed to be accurate by the moving party are not true or complete.

In most situations, an opposing memorandum, however brief, is necessary and advisable. The submission of a memorandum opposing the motion may provide the decision maker with legal authority to deny the motion. See Section 3.9(D). Similarly, the proposed order may help the decision maker understand why the motion ought to be denied.

C. TYPES OF MOTIONS

Many types of motions may be made before or during a trial or hearing. The more common judicial motions include the following:

1. Motion to Amend Pleadings

Procedural rules usually permit amendments of civil pleadings during the preliminary stage of a case and during a trial. The procedure to amend pleadings at the trial stage is commonly known as a motion to amend to conform the pleadings to the evidence. See, e.g., Fed.R.Civ.Proc. 15(b). This amendment is ordinarily allowed if the parties expressly or impliedly consent to the evidence offered during the trial. Express consent means that the parties agree to the introduction of evidence that supports or contradicts a claim or defense not appearing in the original pleadings but presented during the trial. Implied consent occurs if a party submits evidence on an issue not contained in the pleadings and the opposing party does not object to its introduction. The introducing party may then move the court to amend the pleadings because evidence exists to support the claim or defense. The opposing party must make a timely objection to the evidence introduction to oppose the motion successfully.

The requirements of the motion to amend the pleadings ensure that one party does not surprise the other party at the trial or hearing. If a party attempts to introduce some new or undisclosed evidence in support of a new claim or defense, the opposing lawyer is usually able to claim prejudice and the judge usually excludes the evidence. The purpose of the motion is to permit the introduction of evidence that might be barred by an overly technical and formal application of the pleading rules, and to allow the fact finder to consider all evidence that bears on a related issue in a case. A motion to conform the pleadings to the evidence is used infrequently because the situations that require its use seldom arise.

2. Motion in Limine

A motion "in limine" seeks to exclude from the trial, usually a jury trial, the introduction of inadmissible evidence. This motion may be made before the trial begins in anticipation of certain evidence being offered, or during the trial immediately prior to the introduction of such evidence. An in limine motion often requests an advance ruling from the judge to prevent the opposing party from offering objectionable evidence during the trial in the presence of the jury. The motion is meant to prevent the prejudicial effect the mere disclosure of such evidence would have on the jurors. An in limine motion may also ask the court to permit the moving party to introduce evidence during trial without being interrupted by an objection from opposing counsel. Seeking an advance ruling of an in limine motion promotes trial efficiency and permits the judge more time for reflection. Section 4.5(A) explains motions in limine in detail.

3.   Motion for Summary Judgment

A summary judgment motion resolves all or part of the issues in a case and is dispositive because the case, some of the claims, or some of the defenses are resolved by the judge without a full trial or hearing. Rules of procedure and case law establish two grounds for the motion: no disputed issues of material fact exist and as a matter of law a party is entitled to judgment. See Fed.R.Civ.Proc. 56. If there is no controversy regarding the material facts, then there is no need for a jury to determine the facts. The judge may apply the law to the undisputed facts and render judgment. The judge does not decide any facts, but only determines whether or not there are disputed material facts. If there are genuine issues regarding disputed material facts, the case must go to trial.

Typically, a summary judgment motion (called a demurrer in some jurisdictions) is a pretrial motion and is brought before the case has been set for trial, most often after discovery has been completed. This eliminates the need for a trial, or at least reduces the number of triable issues. In some situations, a summary judgment motion may be appropriately made at the final pretrial conference or immediately before the trial begins. If the undisputed facts support the motion, then the motion is timely and proper. Pretrial summary judgment motions are ordinarily supported and opposed by fact affidavits and discovery responses. A case that is ready for trial has all the facts developed making affidavits unnecessary.

In some cases a summary judgment motion is available when there are undisputed facts regarding some of the issues in a case. Summary judgment sought on fewer than all the issues is known as partial summary judgment. For example, in a contract case, facts regarding liability may be undisputed, and summary judgment may be determined by the judge on this issue with the damage claim decided by the jury at trial.

Ordinarily, summary judgment motions are written and noticed for hearing. In many jurisdictions, an oral summary judgment motion may properly be brought before the trial begins. At that stage, the undisputed facts have been established and need not be proven, and all of the disputed facts have been developed. In such cases, there is no need for formal written notice, because neither party can claim prejudice nor legitimately request more time to develop contrary facts. Another alternative motion that may be available at this time is a motion to dismiss or a motion for a judgment as a matter of law, depending on the procedural rules.

Example:

Defendant Grace Hanadarko moves this court pursuant to Federal Rule of Civil Procedure 56 for a summary judgment on the grounds that no disputed issue of material fact exists and that Defendant is entitled to a judgment as a matter of law. Defendant bases this motion on the attached affidavits, Plaintiff's answers to Defendant's interrogatories, pages 61 to 69 of Plaintiff's deposition, Plaintiff's responses to Defendant's requests for admissions, and on the memorandum of law and proposed order.

Arbitration rules may not require summary judgment because there is no need for this motion. The arbitration agreement may include a summary judgment provision permitting its use. Administrative law regulations may permit summary judgment in lengthy or complex cases.

4. Motion to Strike

A motion to strike is made during trial in reaction to some objectionable matter such as an improper question by the attorney, an inadmissible answer from the witness, or some inappropriate behavior. The purpose of the motion is to make clear that the improper statement or conduct is to be ignored by the fact finder.

Nothing is actually ever stricken from the record. The court reporter does not delete anything when the motion is granted. The record contains the objectionable remark, objection, motion to strike, and ruling. Nothing is stricken so a complete record exists for the appellate court.

This type of motion may be anachronistic or unnecessary. The objecting attorney does not want what was objectionable stricken from the record. If the objecting party loses the case, that party will want the appellate court to review the objectionable matter on the record.

In a jury trial, a curative instruction from the judge is necessary and should be requested instead of, or in addition to, the motion to strike. In a bench trial, the motion serves no real purpose because the judge knows that the inadmissible matter cannot be used in the findings of fact. But, even in bench trials, many judges expect to hear such motions and require them to be made. Additionally, for many lawyers the motion to strike is automatic and instinctive, and so they use it in all situations, even if it is practically unnecessary.

5.   Motion for a Curative Instruction

A motion for a curative instruction is a request for the judge to advise the jury to disregard some objectionable matter. The curative instruction is an attempt to repair the harm done by an improper question, inadmissible answer, or inappropriate behavior. The curative instruction is meant to reduce or avoid the influence the statement might have had on the jury. For example, if an attorney during opening or witness during testimony refers to inadmissible evidence, the opposing lawyer should object and request an instruction that the jurors ignore that statement.

The use of the curative instruction has advantages and disadvantages. The request by the attorney for the instruction calls the jury's attention to the harmful matter, and the instruction by the judge may reinforce the jury's memory of it. If an objectionable remark or event is not significant, seeking an instruction may do nothing more than highlight the remark. If the harmful matter is significant, the instruction should be requested because the jury will have taken notice of the matter. They may be influenced by the improper comments but, with a curative instruction, will ordinarily not rely on such information in forming a verdict. If the matter is severely objectionable, a motion for a mistrial should be made. Section 4.5(D) explains the use of curative instructions in detail.

6.   Motion for Involuntary Dismissal

In a bench trial, arbitration, and administrative hearing, after the presentation of evidence by the plaintiff/claimant/prosecutor, the defendant may move for dismissal of the case on the ground that no right to relief has been shown or the asserted claims have not been proven. Usually the motion is made orally after the opposing party rests. In court, this motion is used in bench trials and not jury trials. Fed.R.Civ.Proc. 41(b).

In deciding whether to grant the motion, the judge or arbitrator usually asks the moving attorney to identify what elements or facts supporting the cause of action have not been proven. The ruling on the motion may be made at that time, or reserved until the close of all the evidence. This motion requires a determination regarding whether the evidence is sufficient to present a question of fact for the fact finder. In making this decision, the judge or arbitrator must view all the evidence and draw every reasonable inference in favor of the plaintiff/claimant/

prosecutor. This determination is the same standard applicable to a motion for judgment as a matter of law or directed verdict motion in a jury trial.

The motion for involuntary dismissal is occasionally granted, for all or some of the claims. In a bench trial, the judge, who is also the fact finder, usually decides the case on the merits by weighing the evidence and determining the credibility of the witnesses. A motion to dismiss does not permit the judge to weigh the evidence or assess the credibility of the witnesses. In civil cases, seldom are judges prompted to grant motions to dismiss. Arbitrators and administrative law judges are similarly disinclined to grant the motion unless it is clear there is no need to hear additional evidence. Criminal cases, with their higher burden of proof, may involve insufficient facts to support a judgment and prompt a judge to grant the motion. Some judges prefer to resolve those cases with a judgment on the merits after a full trial and not a motion to dismiss. An order granting the dismissal operates as an adjudication on the merits.

7. Motion for Judgment as a Matter of Law or for Directed Verdict or Motion to Dismiss

In jury trials, a motion to challenge the legal sufficiency of the evidence may be brought at the close of a party's case or after the close of all the evidence. This motion may be called: a motion for a judgment as a matter of law, or for a directed verdict, or for a dismissal for failure to prove a prima facie case, or for a nonsuit, or, in a criminal case, for a judgment of acquittal. The motion asks the court to direct a verdict on the ground that the opposing party has not proven the facts or elements of law supporting the claim or defense and there's no need for a jury verdict.

Any party may bring such a motion. Ordinarily, after the plaintiff rests, the defendant automatically brings this motion. Likewise, after the defendant rests, the plaintiff usually brings a directed verdict motion. After rebuttal, or at the close of the evidence, the defendant renews this motion. In some jurisdictions, a directed verdict motion may be brought after the opponent's opening statement if the opening makes no reference to facts supporting the party's assertions. In making this motion, the attorney usually specifies what elements or facts have not been proven. The other party may then rebut this argument or seek leave of the court to produce additional existing information.

This motion should not be made unless a party has sufficient grounds to support the motion or unless the rules of a jurisdiction require it to be made in order to preserve the opportunity to bring the motion after a verdict is returned later in the case. See Section 12.5(B). A party who brings the motion must state the specific grounds supporting the motion.

The motion creates a question of law regarding whether sufficient evidence exists to support a verdict for the nonmoving party. The precise grounds for granting or denying the motion vary among jurisdictions. Typically, in deciding a motion, the judge cannot weigh the evidence or determine the credibility of the witnesses, but must instead draw all reasonable inferences and view all the facts in the light most favorable to the party opposing the motion. If any evidence exists to support the opposing party's version of the case and if a reasonable person could possibly find in favor of this party, then the judge will deny the motion, even if the judge would find for the moving party.

Judges seldom grant these motions because the losing party is deprived of a jury determination on the merits. A trial court holding will be more likely affirmed by the appellate court if the judge submits the case to the jury and then rules on the sufficiency of the evidence in a motion for judgment as a matter of law or for a judgment notwithstanding the verdict after a jury has returned a verdict. Denying the earlier motion allows the judge, in effect, to defer ruling until the jury decides. If the jury decides in favor of a party which has produced insufficient evidence as a matter of law, then the judge may correct the jury's error and grant the subsequent motion. See Section 12.5(D).

8. Motion for Leave to Reopen a Case

If a motion dismissing the case or granting judgment is granted, the losing attorney may move for leave to reopen the case and present additional evidence, if such evidence exists. Judges and arbitrators usually grant this motion if the evidence is readily available and substantial enough to raise a question of fact sufficient to support a favorable outcome. Tribunals prefer that cases be decided on the merits based on all available evidence and not upon an oversight by counsel.

9. Motion for Mistrial

Incidents may occur during a jury trial that give rise to a motion for a mistrial. Grounds that support a mistrial motion include statements or conduct by counsel, witnesses, jurors, court officials, or the judge that:

- Are substantially and unfairly prejudicial,
- Constitute gross misconduct,
- Intentionally violate a court order,
- Deliberately and unfairly attempt to influence the jury,
- Provide false evidence,
- Improperly and adversely affect the substantial rights of a party,

- Result in substantial irregularities in the trial proceedings, or

- Otherwise make a fair trial impossible.

These and other errors are the same as the grounds for a new trial after a verdict. Examples of errors supporting a motion for mistrial include: opposing counsel intentionally making inflammatory remarks, an adverse witness testifying to inadmissible and unfairly prejudicial evidence, a judge making improper comments manifesting a bias in favor of an opposing party, and juror misconduct.

The grounds for a mistrial must be so severe and uncorrectable that a party is denied a fair trial. The mere occurrence of misconduct is not sufficient to support the granting of the motion. The misconduct must significantly influence the judgment of the jury or judge to a degree that adversely affects the substantial rights of a party. The adverse effect can ordinarily be reduced by providing the jurors with a curative instruction to disregard the misconduct or by admonishing the offending person.

The status of the case influences both an attorney's decision to move for a mistrial and the judge's ruling. If an attorney perceives that the case is going well, moving for a new trial may not be advisable. If the attorney believes the case is not going well, the attorney may want to pursue a mistrial motion. A trial judge is not likely to terminate a lengthy trial because of the time and effort invested. A trial that is just beginning stands a better chance of having a judge grant a mistrial motion.

Few cases result in a mistrial. In a criminal case, the constitutional rights of a defendant coupled with prosecutorial misconduct may justify the granting of a new trial. In civil cases, curative instructions and admonitions usually remedy the damage done. The granting of a mistrial motion results in a new trial.

10. Motion to Reconsider

Once a motion is decided, that ruling is the law of the case for that case, and it cannot be changed by asking the judge to rethink and change the decision. The motion decision is final and controlling. Even if another judge becomes the trial judge, a previous ruling by a different judge is still the law of the case, and a party does not get a second chance to try and win a motion just because there is a different trial judge. Judges ought not to be asked to do things twice, and they may ignore motions to reconsider or may even consider them frivolous and harassing. Even at the trial stage, lawyers may be inclined to bring a motion to reconsider after losing a motion. This tactic—just as in pretrial and post-trial practice—should be resisted unless the very, very narrow grounds for reconsideration are available, which are less likely for trial motions.

The primary ground—and sometimes only legitimate ground—for reconsideration is that the law changed between the time of submission and decision that controls the motion. It is usually not sufficient that the law changed after the decision, unless it is clear that the new law is retroactive. If allowable, many courts require a party to bring a motion requesting the opportunity to bring a motion to reconsider, before actually submitting the reconsideration motion. A party must have existing, legitimate grounds in that jurisdiction to support such a motion.

In summary, judges do not like, do not want to see, and will not review motions to reconsider unless there is clear and evident reason to do so. They view this motion as a party seeking a second chance, which ought not to be available. The losing party naturally believes the judge is wrong, but being wrong in the view of a party—however strongly believed or seemingly supported by the facts or law—is not a sufficient reason.

11. Additional Motions

Many other motions may be made during a case, including:

- Motion for jury or court trial,
- Motion to recuse or disqualify a judge,
- Motion to disqualify counsel,
- Motion for jury selection examination,
- Motion to strike a juror for cause,
- Motion for court reporter to record proceedings,
- Motion to sequester witnesses,
- Motion for recess or adjournment,
- Motion to limit testimony of witness,
- Motion to interrupt order of witnesses because of unavailability,
- Motion to exclude testimony or exhibits,
- Motion to preview video presentations or review digital evidence,
- Motion to make offer of proof,
- Motion to receive testimony or exhibits,
- Motion for judicial notice,
- Motion to instruct jury,
- Motion to sequester jury,
- Motion to discharge jury, and
- Motion to poll jury.

Post-trial motions are explained in Section 12.5 and include:

- Motion for judgment as a matter of law,
- Motion for judgment notwithstanding the verdict (j.n.o.v.),
- Motion for new trial,
- Motion for amended findings of fact, conclusions of law, and order of judgment,
- Motion for additur,
- Motion for remittitur,
- Motion for a stay of entry of judgment,
- Motion for a stay of judgment,
- Motion to enforce judgment,
- Motion for interests and costs, and
- Motion for attorney's fees.

§ 3.9   MOTION ARGUMENT

Some motions include oral argument scheduled at a hearing, while other motions are decided by judges on the briefs presented without oral argument. Some courts have rules that determine what and when motions include oral argument. An advocate who prefers to orally argue a motion may request a hearing.

A. AVAILABLE TIME

Whether a specific time limit is set for a motion argument depends upon the forum, judge, or arbitrator. Some forums schedule motions for a specific and limited amount of time; other forums schedule motions in sequence and allow attorneys a reasonable time for argument. The amount of time allocated depends on the importance of the motion, the length of the case, and how much time can be devoted to the entire case. The attorney must decide how much time is necessary and how the available time should be used. If more time for argument is needed than is allocated by a court, the attorney may request additional time.

B. PREPARATION BY THE JUDGE

An attorney must ascertain whether the judge has read or is familiar with the motion, the case, and the applicable law. Some judges review the file before the hearing; others do not have time to do so. The extent of the judge's familiarity with the motion determines the content of the motion argument. If a judge is not familiar with the motion, then the moving attorney must inform the judge about the motion. Otherwise, the judge may spend the first few minutes looking through the file rather than listening to the beginning of the attorney's argument.

A judge who is familiar with the case may not need much background information about the case. The extent of a judge's preparation may be learned from experience, by contacting the law clerk and inquiring about the judge's knowledge of the case, or by simply (and diplomatically) asking the judge if the judge had sufficient opportunity to review the file and motion. Arbitrators and administrative judges are usually familiar with the motion because they schedule a specific time to hear the motion.

C. SUPPORTING MEMORANDUM

Almost all jurisdictions require that a memorandum of law, a summary brief, or citation of authorities be submitted in support of a motion. Motion memoranda are usually submitted prior to the oral motion argument, but may also be submitted after the argument if some issues were raised during argument that need briefing. An attorney may also suggest that a memorandum and reply be submitted, or a judge or arbitrator may request submissions from the attorneys.

A memorandum should be concise and contain a summary of the vital facts and the legal authorities supporting the motion. A short memo that identifies the issues and supporting legal authorities and citations or highlighted copies of cases or references, or links to judicial opinions, statutes or rules is often sufficient. A lengthy, detailed memo should be reserved for complex, complicated issues. The extent of the memo should be commensurate with the nature of the motion and the case.

D. OPPOSITION MEMORANDUM

Submitting a written memorandum in opposition to a motion is required in many jurisdictions and forums and expected in many others. An opposing memorandum should obviously explain why the motion should be denied. An effective reply memorandum should explain the position of the opponent in a positive way and address and refute arguments made in the opponent's motion memorandum. This refutation should focus on revealing weaknesses and mistakes such as factual misstatements or omissions, legal errors, inadequately supported legal or factual conclusions, inappropriate issues, illogical arguments, inconsistent positions, and concessions. An opposing memo need not always be submitted. Some positions advanced by the other side deserve no rebuttal while others may be rebutted during oral argument.

E. LOCATION OF ARGUMENT

Trial motions are argued in the courtroom or judge's chambers. Most judges prefer the formality of a courtroom. Some judges prefer to discuss the merits of the motion on an informal basis in chambers, where the attorneys and the judge are seated around the judge's desk or a conference table. For presentation of a courtroom motion, the attorney usually stands and argues before the judge, who sits at the bench. If the attorney believes that the presentation or determination of the motion would be enhanced by arguing in either the courtroom or chambers, the attorney should make that request of the judge. Lawyers may appear in person or by telephone or video conferencing if they are distant from the court. It is wise to seek the approval of the court ahead of time to appear other than in person so the judge can make the technical necessary arrangements. Arbitration and administrative proceeding motions are argued in writing, by email, in person, by phone or through video conferencing.

F. SEQUENCE OF ARGUMENT

The moving party usually argues first. Then the opposing attorney is given an opportunity to speak in opposition to the motion. Rebuttal arguments are often permitted by both lawyers as long as the statements are responsive and not repetitious.

G. RECORDING OF ARGUMENT

The practice of recording the oral arguments of attorneys varies among jurisdictions and judges. There may be no reason for the argument to be recorded. In such instances, the attorney need not be concerned with the making of a record. But if the attorney wants a record made, the presence of a court reporter should be requested. Arbitration motion arguments are commonly not recorded. Some administrative motion arguments may be recorded in cases involving significant issues.

The making of a record usually influences the tenor and content of statements made by the attorneys and the judge, and reduces the likelihood that injudicious or extraneous statements will be made. A record preserves everything that is requested and argued by the lawyers and everything that is decided by the judge. Further, a transcript can be used to present grounds for a new motion or an appeal and can be made available for a client who is not present. An alternative to having the reporter present to record the entire argument is to argue the motion off the record and then have the moving attorney summarize the motion and the relief sought and have the judge explain the ruling on the record.

§ 3.10 MOTION ARGUMENT TECHNIQUES

Oral motion argument techniques do not differ significantly from other oral argument situations. A successful presentation in support of or in opposition to a motion must address the following questions:

- What information does the decision maker need to decide the motion in favor of the client?

- What issues need to be discussed in order to succeed?

- What questions may the judge or arbitrator have that need to be answered?

- How can the advocate elicit these questions and encourage the decision maker to ask these key questions?

- Has the relief the party seeks or needs been made clear to the decision maker? How?

After considering effective responses to these questions, the advocate can then plan a presentation.

A. BREVITY

Be brief!

B. CONVERSATIONAL, INTERESTING APPROACH

Many lawyers present motion arguments in a formal manner, as if they were in a debate or making an appellate argument. This approach may not be as effective as a conversational approach in which the attorney converses with the judge or arbitrator and invites questions. To be an effective "conversationalist" in this setting, an attorney must adopt a persuasive style, display familiarity with the facts and the law, demonstrate confidence, and persist when necessary. Rapport, eye contact, voice tone, diction, pace, and gestures are among the many factors which influence the effectiveness of a presentation.

C. PREFACE

The moving attorney who speaks first will usually want to include as a preface a short description of the relief sought, the motion, and its grounds to remind the decision maker about why the attorneys are there. Judges want to know specifically what they are expected to rule on. The moving attorney may also wish to provide some background regarding the case and its procedural history. And, the judge may want to know what efforts the lawyers made to meet or talk to resolve the motion. An opposing lawyer may supplement this information.

An attorney should preface the substance of an argument with a brief outline of what will be covered. An argument is more easily followed when the decision maker is advised what topics will be discussed. The judge or arbitrator may suggest to the attorney certain matters that need not be covered because they are already familiar with them and may even have already resolved them. A judge or arbitrator may be inclined to postpone asking questions until that matter is reached during the argument.

D. STRUCTURE

The argument following the prefatory remarks made by an attorney must be structured in an effective, persuasive manner. The optimum order for an argument depends significantly on the type of motion presented. Any lengthy argument must be carefully structured so that it can be easily followed. The relief stated in the proposed order, the grounds for the motion, issues addressed in the memorandum, statements in affidavits, and the contents of other motion papers may provide an attorney with a thorough outline for structuring the argument. However structured, the advocate needs to address the issues the decision maker deems important and the questions that need to be answered.

E. SUBSTANCE OF ARGUMENT

What relief is requested and what an attorney says obviously depends upon the type of motion presented. The presentation should contain an explanation of the facts and the law mixed with reason, logic, equity, and the human dimensions involved. Considerations that increase the successful planning and presentation of an argument include:

- Is the motion a common, routine request or an unusual request?

- Should the strongest position be asserted first, with the second strongest position last and other, weaker positions explained in between?

- Should key words, phrases, or positions be emphasized throughout the argument?

- Should the circumstances causing the motion to be brought be mentioned?

- Should the failure or refusal of the opposing attorney to cooperate with the moving attorney in resolving or compromising the issues of the motion be mentioned?

F. THE LAW

Legal explanations should be accurate and understandable. Advocates lose their credibility and arguments lose their effectiveness because the applicable law is exaggerated or explained in a confusing way. An attorney should carefully select and describe the legal references.

Leading cases, supporting statutes, and persuasive quotations should be used when necessary. Cases from other jurisdictions and peripheral legal authorities should be avoided, unless there is no supportive precedent in the jurisdiction. Legal matters should be argued if they can be explained more effectively in oral argument than in a brief. Legal matters that may be effectively presented in a memorandum need not be repeated orally, unless the arguments need clarification or emphasis.

References to the law should also be concise. Quotations from cases or statutes should be woven into an argument and should not be read at length. Case quotes and specific citations should be provided in the brief.

G. THE FACTS

Many motions revolve around questions of law, and the facts of the case may not make a significant difference in the outcome of the motion. Other motions depend upon the existence of specific facts. Supportive facts in a motion hearing are often presented by submitting affidavits that contain the relevant and necessary information. Some motion hearings involve the presentation of live or video testimony through witnesses and the introduction of exhibits. Such evidence offered during a motion hearing usually mirrors witness direct and cross-examinations.

H. FACTUAL DESCRIPTIONS

A description of the facts should include a complete and accurate recitation of the relevant evidence. Some attorneys tend to ramble during motion arguments, providing the court with factual information not appearing in an affidavit, in the file, or in the record. An opposing attorney should point out the inadequacy of this information and the inappropriateness of an attorney attempting to testify or provide evidence in an improper manner. Other attorneys may exaggerate or stretch the facts to match a point of law. These tactics backfire because the inherent weaknesses of such positions become apparent to the decision maker.

I. NOTES

Arguments should not be read. Notes outlining the essential points of an argument may be used as a guide during a presentation. The motion and legal memorandum can act an outline of points. A lack of notes may indicate a lack of preparation by an attorney and may make a complete and logical presentation difficult. The use of notes, however, should not detract from the presentation of the argument. Attorneys should be flexible and not "glued" to their notes because they may be interrupted with questions about other issues not anticipated in the prepared notes. The attorney must be so well prepared that interruptions by the judge or arbitrator do not fluster or confuse the attorney.

J. EXHIBITS

Exhibits, including real and demonstrative evidence, or visual aids such as diagrams, charts, graphs, power point presentations, and computer generated exhibits may assist an attorney's presentation, and may help a judge or arbitrator in understanding an argument. Exhibits should be used if they enhance the persuasiveness of an argument.

K. INTERRUPTIONS

An attorney should avoid interrupting an opposing attorney or the judge or arbitrator. Interruptions are unprofessional and discourteous, unless the opponent's statements are unfairly prejudicial or mischaracterize something that requires immediate correction. Attorneys who make unnecessary interruptions are likely to be admonished. A more effective approach is to note any misstatements of fact or law and comment on them after the opposing lawyer has completed an argument.

A lawyer should direct all statements to the judge or arbitrator and should avoid arguing directly with the opposing attorney, however tempting. Some situations may require that a lawyer request that opposing counsel be directed to apologize for a remark or be admonished for making disparaging statements.

L. OPPOSITION WEAKNESSES

An argument should contain references to the weaknesses of the opponent's case or to the inappropriateness of a position taken by the other side. This requires an attorney to anticipate positions taken by an opposing lawyer and counter those points during the argument. If this is not possible or appropriate, rebuttal will afford an opportunity to expose the weakness in the opponent's case. An argument sounds more persuasive if made in a positive, constructive manner. A defensive argument that merely attacks the opposition may appear weak.

M. CANDOR AND COMPROMISE

An attorney must be candid during an argument. If a judge has broad or limited discretion to grant or deny a motion, a moving party should not argue that the judge has no discretion. If the facts and supporting law provide a moving party with a reasonable position, an opposing lawyer should not unnecessarily criticize the position or pretend that precedent mandates the arbitrator to deny the motion.

An attorney may also have to compromise during a motion hearing. Many judges view the hearing as an opportunity for the attorneys to accept a compromise solution or negotiate a resolution to the problem. Attorneys who maintain set positions during a motion hearing must be prepared to propose or accept alternative positions to resolve a matter. A motion hearing may provide a forum for the arbitrator to mediate a solution to a problem the attorneys were unable to resolve on their own.

N. QUESTIONS BY THE JUDGE OR ARBITRATOR

Questions asked by the judge or arbitrator should be answered at the time asked. Decision makers expect questions to be answered when asked. An attorney should answer questions directly and completely. Rarely should answers be postponed or evaded. An attorney should frankly admit to not knowing an answer if that is the case.

Efforts should be made to provide answers in a light most favorable to the client's position. An attorney must be prepared, if necessary, to concede a point in a response to avoid arguing an issue unnecessarily. Any concession should be put in perspective, and the attorney should continue on with another point.

Questions from judges and arbitrators should be encouraged. An attorney may want to ask if the judge or arbitrator has any questions. It is critical for the attorney to ascertain and address the issues the decision maker is considering, and inviting questions is an effective way to do so.

O. INVOLVING THE DECISION MAKER

The attorney should prepare and present an argument in such a way as to involve the decision maker in the motion. Some judges and arbitrators are inclined to be active while others are more inclined to be passive during oral argument. An effective presentation by an attorney often develops an interchange between that attorney and the decision maker. The more the decision maker participates in a motion discussion, the more likely the motion will be understood and rightfully decided.

P. RULINGS

After hearing pretrial motion arguments the judge or arbitrator typically takes the matter under advisement and rules at a later date. For some pretrial motions and many trial motions, the decision maker will rule immediately and orally, on the record, if there is one. If a proposed order has been submitted, the judge or arbitrator may promptly sign that order. The rulings and orders a judge makes during a trial are interlocutory orders and are appealable along with the final judgment entered in the case after the trial. A few rulings or orders, which involve significant issues dispositive of a case, may be immediately appealable. See Section 12.9(F).

The determination whether to grant or deny the motion is not always based solely on the law and the facts of the case. Other considerations may influence a judge's decisions. Some judges believe that a case ought to be settled and realize that if a motion is decided in a certain way, settlement will be more likely to occur. Other judges believe that one party has a much stronger case than the other party and may rule on a motion to increase the chances that the party with the stronger case will prevail. Motions provide an opportunity for a judge to influence the result of a case, and some judges take advantage of this opportunity.

Q. WRITTEN ARGUMENTS

For those motions not allowed by the court to be argued orally, the written brief may need to be composed to reflect the lack of oral argument. The questions that need to be addressed are:

- What would have been stated in oral argument that is not contained in the initial draft of the brief?

- Is there an argument that seems inappropriate for briefing but appropriate for oral argument?

- What, if anything, is being left out of the brief that would have been argued at a motion hearing?

- Might the judge have questions the answers to which are not addressed in the draft brief?

The answers to these questions may require the brief to be redrafted, if it is the sole means an advocate has to present an argument. It may well be that the primary purposes of a motion argument are to allow the judge an opportunity to ask questions and to increase the chances that the judge will fully understand why the motion should be granted or not granted. The revised brief will need to explain what the judge needs to know.

§ 3.11 PREPARATION AND PRESENTATION TO A JUDGE OR ARBITRATOR

This section discusses additional considerations applicable to making a case presentation to a trial or administrative judge or an arbitrator. These decision makers are professional decision makers, having made decisions before in cases. Jurors are usually first time legal decision makers and some advocacy approaches that are effective with them will not be effective before judges and arbitrators, especially if they have heard the same argument before in previous cases. But there are many similarities among all types of decision makers, and experienced judges and arbitrators can be successfully influenced and affected by many of the same approaches that work with jurors.

A. OPENING STATEMENTS

Opening statements should be made unless the decision maker is very familiar with the case. A discussion with the decision maker before the start of the trial or hearing—in which the theory of the case and the significant facts and issues have been discussed—may be a sufficient substitute for an opening statement. If an advocate believes the judge or arbitrator knows enough about the case to proceed to the presentation of evidence, then an opening may be unnecessary. Many advocates prefer to make an opening statement, even a brief one, because of the informative and persuasive impact it has. In some administrative hearings, an opening may not be permitted. And if trial judges or arbitrators insist they do not need to hear openings, it may be a waste of time for advocates to pursue making one. Section 6.1 explains the effective use of openings.

B. EVIDENTIARY RULINGS

The judge or arbitrator who must decide both the facts and the admissibility of evidence may have a difficult time avoiding the influence of inadmissible evidence. When deciding whether to admit or deny the introduction of evidence, a decision maker must understand the evidence. Judges and arbitrators may not rely on inadmissible evidence in reaching their decision, but they may have difficulty disregarding its impact, and they may have to hear an offer of proof. See Section 4.5(B).

Fact finders are more inclined to admit evidence than to exclude it. They may need to know or be curious about the information. Trial and administrative judges realize that appellate courts are more likely to overturn their decision if key evidence is omitted than if it is admitted. Many of the exclusionary rules of evidence, discussed in Chapter 4, are primarily designed to restrict the introduction of evidence in jury trials and not bench trials, arbitrations, or administrative hearings.

C. INTRODUCTION OF EVIDENCE

The presentation of evidence through witnesses and exhibits must be done in as persuasive and effective a way as possible. Some attorneys are less formal and less careful in presenting evidence to an arbitrator or administrative judge, but this approach can result in an inadequate presentation. Professional decision makers need to hear all relevant evidence as well as testimony that establishes the credibility of witnesses.

On direct examination, advocates may tend to ask leading questions to speed the case up or may eliminate foundation questions because the judge or arbitrator has heard similar facts before in previous cases. But it is critical to the determination of witness credibility for the professional decision maker to hear the witness testify and not counsel who asks too many leading questions. And it is vital for judges and arbitrators to hear all compelling evidence, and not just a summary version, to make sure they understand the complete and accurate factual stories.

On cross-examination, some areas of cross may not need to be as thoroughly examined with a judge or arbitrator as they would need to be with a jury. For example, impeachment with a prior inconsistent deposition statement need not include questions that explain deposition procedures. If a judge or arbitrator understands what happened in a specific situation, cross-examination to establish the background of the underlying discrediting facts may be unnecessary.

D. SUMMATION

The attorney needs to craft a closing argument that has a compelling impact on the decision maker. The judge or arbitrator will most likely be leaning in favor of one party and may have already decided the case before closing arguments. A summation must be presented in a way that assists and persuades them to interpret and apply the facts to the legal elements in favor of the advocate's client. Judges and arbitrators may ask questions of the attorneys during summation, usually regarding unresolved matters. It is wise for advocates to be prepared for and invite such questions.

Some closing argument approaches may be inappropriate or ineffective if delivered before a professional. For example, arbitrators usually know the applicable law and there is no need for an attorney to engage in an explanation of its basic elements. Further, an explanation about our legal system, or an overly emotional plea, may have an impact on a jury who are hearing it for the first time, but likely will not have a favorable impact on a judge who has heard the explanation or plea before.

An attorney should not underestimate the persuasive impact of a closing argument before a professional, however. If the advocate can present a compelling reason why the client should win—especially a reason that the decision maker has not thought about before—the chances of succeeding have dramatically increased. If the advocate can explain why a client deserves to win which explanation has to this point in the case eluded the judge or arbitrator, then summation will have served its purpose. If the advocate can craft a novel insight into the facts or law, then it should be proffered. Many judges and arbitrators have decided cases based on arguments made during summation. The closing argument ought to be presented in the most eloquent, interesting, and compelling manner possible.

E. FINDINGS OF FACT, CONCLUSIONS OF LAW, AND ORDERS

In a bench trial, the judge must complete written findings of fact, conclusions of law, and an order for judgment. See, e.g., Fed.R.Civ.Proc. 52. Procedural rules may require attorneys to submit proposed findings, conclusions and an order, or the judge may request that the attorneys do so. Arbitrators who have to render a detailed award and administrative judges who have to issue an explanatory decision may also have to compose findings and conclusions. An example of findings, conclusions, and an order appear in Section 2.11(C). Tactically, it is advisable to submit findings and conclusions because they provide the judge with a summary of the party's case and the specific relief sought, and they may favorably influence or assist the judge in making a decision. Section 12.5(I) describes the use of a post-trial motion to amend findings and conclusions.

§ 3.12 MAKING A RECORD

A. PURPOSE

The primary purpose of making a record is to establish and preserve grounds for appeal. A trial record usually consists of a transcript of the proceedings, exhibits, jury instructions, verdict form, pleadings, motions, memoranda, orders, judgment, notice of appeal, and any other filed documents. See Fed.R.App.P. 10. Final and binding arbitration proceedings may not be recorded because there is no factual appeal. Administrative proceedings that are appealable commonly retain an appropriate record. See Section 3.12(F).

The attorney must continually be aware of the need to make the record complete for possible appellate review. Appellate courts may not consider anything other than the record below when making a review. Appeals can be lost due to faulty or incomplete records.

Most appellate courts require compliance with certain procedures to properly raise an issue for appeal. Typically, the trial record must reflect the following:

- A record of the ruling, order, conduct, or event creating the grounds for appeal;

- An objection by the attorney to an error in the trial;

- If an objection has been sustained, an offer of proof showing what the evidence would have proven;

- A request for a curative instruction by the judge to the jury if the error occurred within the hearing of the jury; and

- The submission of a post-trial motion to the judge, identifying the error and requesting a new trial.

These requirements are intended to prevent appeals unless the attorney has properly objected at the trial level, providing the trial judge an opportunity to correct or reduce the impact of the error. Some issues, such as the sufficiency of the evidence to support the findings, will be appealable even if an objection was not made at trial. If "manifest injustice" could result from the denial of an appeal, some courts allow an appeal where issues have not been properly preserved for appeal.

There are several conditions that must be met for an appellate court to reverse a trial judge's ruling:

- The trial judge must commit an error;
- The error must have been objected to by the advocate;
- The mistake must be preserved in the trial record;
- The error must not have been cured or waived or abandoned; and
- The error must have been unfairly prejudicial.

B. COMPLETE AND ACCURATE RECORD

The advocate must ensure that all written and oral rulings, orders, findings, verdicts, and judgments are entered on the record during all stages of the trial or hearing, including pretrial and post-trial proceedings. Also, advocates may prefer to have the reasoning of the judge reflected in the record. If the judge has adopted the opponent's reasons or if the reasoning is apparent from the situation, there may be no need to have the reason appear on the record. If, however, the reasoning differs from that advanced by either party, or is not apparent from the circumstances, the advocate can ask the judge to state the reasoning on the record for appellate purposes. In some situations the losing party will not want the judge's reasoning to appear on the record, either because a well-reasoned ruling or order may make it more difficult to win on appeal or because the losing party intends to argue that the judge abused discretion or exceeded authority due to the absence of any supportive reasoning. The advocate should review the record periodically throughout the case to make certain that a complete and accurate record is being maintained.

C. COURT REPORTER

The general rule is that if an appealable judicial case is worth trying, all proceedings should be recorded so a transcript will be available. If there is no record, there is no transcript nor recorded grounds supporting an appeal. The presence of a recording also holds judges and lawyers accountable and causes them to be more careful and thoughtful regarding what they say and do.

The trial court supplies the court reporter. In federal courts and most state courts, court reporters are available during all stages of the trial. In some jurisdictions, the court reporter may not routinely be available for pretrial proceedings, and the advocate should contact the court ahead of time to make certain a court reporter is present. Budget constraints in some jurisdictions may affect the availability of a court reporter. In other jurisdictions, the trial advocate may be responsible for making certain a court reporter is available. Some jurisdictions are using audio or video recordings in lieu of a court reporter transcription.

Electronic recordings and computer-assisted transcriptions (CAT) may be available to supplement or supplant the work of a court reporter. Recording systems with voice recognition software may be able to record what is said. A CAT system enables spoken words to be captured by a court reporter and converted into text that instantaneously appears on monitor screens. Evolving technologies may provide alternative methods to record proceedings.

A court reporter or reporting system should be present for all trial proceedings, including everything that occurs in the courtroom and in chambers. Not all judges and jurisdictions follow this general rule. In many jurisdictions, court reporters are present only at the conclusion of discussions or proceedings held in chambers and only transcribe a summary of the motions and rulings. The judge typically makes such a summary, supplemented by comments from the attorneys. The advocate should make certain that any matter that may be an issue for appeal is fully reflected in the summary transcription. In some jurisdictions, a court reporter may not be present during jury selection. Anticipating that something may happen that may need to be preserved for appeal, the advocate should request that a court reporter be present to record all questions and responses and arguments.

If a judge refuses to honor the request that a court reporter be made available, the advocate can ask that an independent court reporter, to be paid by the party, be obtained. If this request is denied, the attorney should make every effort to preserve the judge's ruling regarding the denial of the court reporter. The advocate can ask the trial judge to sign a written order denying the attorney's motion for a court reporter, or when the court reporter is present at the next trial stage, ask the court for permission to summarize on the record the previous motion and ruling.

If the judge refuses to grant the attorney permission to comment on the record (even by threatening contempt if the attorney attempts to place such information on the record), the only available avenue the attorney may have is to compose an affidavit summarizing these events and offer the affidavit into evidence as a trial exhibit. Determining whether to have a court reporter present or to summarize events is a matter of judgment and discretion for the trial attorney.

D. LOG OF TRIAL

A losing attorney may not need or want to pay for the costs of an entire transcript. It is helpful for the advocate to maintain a log of the transcribed proceedings to assist in determining what portions of the transcript should be ordered. This log can identify the stage of the case, the date of the event, the reporter or method of reporting, and a concise explanation of what happened or why a transcript might be needed.

E. ASSISTING THE REPORTER

The reporter is responsible for making sure that a complete and accurate transcript is made. Attorneys can assist the reporter in fulfilling this responsibility by:

- Speaking clearly and making certain the witnesses speak clearly.

- Proceeding at a pace appropriate for the reporter.

- Spelling difficult names and words or providing a written list of them.

- Providing any necessary information to assist the reporter in understanding the nature of the case and the identity of witnesses.

- Not blocking the reporter's view of the witness or anyone else talking in the courtroom.

- Avoiding speaking simultaneously with others.

- Describing all conduct, gestures, inaudible responses, nonverbal behavior, and any other event that may not appear on the record. Many judges expect the attorney to ask permission from the judge to have the record reflect what occurred. For example, the attorney may preface the description with the phrase: "Your Honor, may the record reflect that. . . ." Other judges allow the attorneys to describe on the record whatever occurred without requesting such permission.

- Avoiding superfluous comments (O.K., now, let me ask you this, I see), repeating answers, and making unnecessary comments.

- Properly referring to exhibits by number or letter. Section 8.5 describes in detail the marking and handling of exhibits.

- Making sure that necessary computer and electronic devices are working so the reporter can easily make a record or access an exhibit for inclusion in the record.

The judge controls going on and off the record. If an attorney wishes that something not be on the record, the attorney should ask permission of the court to go off the record. After discussion off the record, either one of the attorneys or the judge may want something that was said off the record summarized on the record. The judge can do this independently, or the attorney may do this by requesting permission of the judge.

F.   ADMINISTRATIVE HEARINGS AND ARBITRATIONS

Administrative hearings that are reviewable are commonly recorded by electronic recording devices operated by the administrative judge, usually an audio or video recording. Some proceedings are recorded by a reporter. The purposes and tactics involved in these recorded cases are similar to the approaches discussed with regard to trial proceedings.

Arbitration awards are reviewable by judicial judges, but the factual determinations of arbitrators are not usually reviewable. And so, there is typically no need for a contemporaneous record in arbitrations. Arbitrators by agreement of the parties or as required by the forum code of procedure may need to rely on applicable substantive law in support of their decisions. This aspect of the award is reviewable de novo by a judge, and a transcript is usually unnecessary for the scope of this legal review.

§ 3.13 TRIAL AND HEARING PROBLEMS

A.   PROBLEM DECISION MAKERS

Judges may do or say things during a trial that constitute misconduct. A judge may make adverse comments about an attorney, improper remarks regarding evidence, or unfair comments regarding the testimony or credibility of a witness. A judge may incorrectly prohibit an attorney from presenting the case or may engage in facial grimaces, body language, or non-verbal conduct that disrupts an attorney's presentation. An advocate can place these occurrences on the record, indicating what has happened and the objections to the behavior that were made. This can be a delicate and difficult task, but may be necessary to correct the judge's adverse behavior. The lawyer can approach the bench initially and, out of the hearing of the jury, request that the judge refrain from such conduct and subsequently place it on the record if it continues. Problems with administrative judges and arbitrators should be similarly handled.

B. PROBLEMS WITH ATTORNEYS

If the opposing counsel creates problems for the attorney by making improper statements, behaving in a distracting manner, or engaging in other inappropriate behavior detrimental to the case, the attorney should object on the record, and the court should be asked to intervene and admonish opposing counsel. An attorney should avoid arguing with or responding directly to the opposing counsel.

Problems may also arise with lawyers from other law firms representing the same or other parties in a case. If a client has retained a number of firms to handle different parts of the litigation (e.g. discovery, settlement, trial work), there may arise differences of opinions and direction regarding what should happen. Cooperative and collaborative skills will be needed to resolve these problems.

C. PROBLEM WITNESSES

An attorney who examines a witness on direct examination must be prepared to direct and control the testimony given. Likewise, a cross-examiner must control the responses of an unfavorable witness. An attorney should initially make one or more attempts to insist on responses before seeking the intervention of a judge or arbitrator. Some decision makers may not intervene and prefer that the attorney control the interrogation. See Section 9.3(D).

D. PROBLEMS WITH EXHIBITS

Some exhibits create problems for opposing counsel. The offering lawyer may attempt to introduce exhibits that are inadmissible or improperly refer to them and then withdraw the reference to them. The content of some exhibits will not be obvious and apparent, and an untrustworthy opponent may unfairly use these opportunities to show the judge, arbitrator, or jury inadmissible evidence. Counsel can take steps to avoid these problems by insisting that purported exhibits be made available a reasonable time before their introduction so that counsel can preview them and make any timely objections. The extent of this preparation may depend upon the degree to which the opposing lawyer is honest and fair.

E. PROBLEMS WITH COLLEAGUES AND STAFF

Many cases involve multiple lawyers and law firm staff working together on a case. Issues regarding leadership, direction, administration, and management can readily arise. One chief advocate or a team of leaders will need to resolve these problems and maintain cooperative and collaborative working relationships.

F. RESPONSES

When facing these and other problems that arise, it is critical for the advocate to consider how the best interests of the client are affected. If adversely, the advocate will need to do something during the presentation of the case to rectify or resolve the problem, so the client has the best chances of succeeding. And later, after the case is over, the aggravating situations may make wonderful stories for the next bar convention.

————

Trial Advocacy Supplement

The applicable Federal Rules of Civil Procedure referred to in this Chapter and other chapters in this book appear in the *Supplement to Trial Advocacy Before Judges, Jurors, and Arbitrators*. This *Supplement* also contains the Federal Rules of Evidence and examples of the skills described in this text. Students may order a print or electronic version of the *Supplement* from store.westacademic.com.

CHAPTER 4

EVIDENCE AND OBJECTIONS

■ ■ ■

Trial Advocacy Supplement
Federal Rules of Evidence

The Federal Rules of Evidence appear in the *Supplement to Trial Advocacy Before Judges, Jurors, and Arbitrators*. References to evidentiary rules in this Chapter refer to the Federal Rules of Evidence. The *Supplement* is available at store.westacademic.com.

The explanations, descriptions, and examples in this Chapter reflect both federal rules and state rules widely adopted in the vast majority of states. The reasons and rationales underlying these rules are applicable to federal and state courts, arbitrations, and administrative hearings.

These evidence rules determine the admissibility of evidence in judicial forums and influence or control the admissibility of relevant and reliable evidence in arbitrations and administrative hearings.

REFLECTING ON ADVOCACY

We arg'ed the thing at breakfast, we arg'ed the thing at tea, and the more we arg'ed the question the more we didn't agree.

—WILL CARLETON

BETSEY AND I ARE OUT

He that wrestles with us strengthens our nerves and sharpens our skill. Our antagonist is our helper.

—EDMUND BURKE

§ 4.1   INTRODUCTION

A.   PURPOSES

An objection is the procedure used to oppose the introduction of inadmissible evidence, to resist the use of improper questions, and to contest inappropriate conduct or improper procedures during a case. Evidentiary objections are used to exclude evidence that should not be considered by the fact finder or to change the form of questions improperly phrased by opposing counsel. Objections also may be used to control the behavior and statements of an opposing attorney, a witness, the judge or arbitrator, or other participants, or to prevent a witness from being harassed.

Objections create a record of the error and preserve that error as a ground for a new trial or an appeal. The failure to make an objection usually waives any error as a ground for a new trial or appeal, unless the error is so unfairly prejudicial and obvious that the substantial rights of a party are adversely affected.

Objections may also accomplish reasonable tactical objectives. Tactical reasons for objecting are only proper if there is a good faith legal basis that supports the objection. Objections with no legal basis made solely to interrupt or bother the opposing lawyer are unethical and violate the rules.

An attorney may tactically object to emphasize an opponent's evidentiary problems, to force the opponent to alter the introduction of evidence, or to alter the presentation of the case. An attorney may also object to help a witness testify. For example, if a witness becomes confused or has difficulty answering questions, a legitimate objection may allow the witness a short break to regain composure and plan a responsive answer.

A proper objection may also be used to interrupt the flow of testimony. When an examination is proceeding very smoothly, an objection may break up its rhythm. An experienced advocate may object to confuse or distract a novice lawyer who may become nervous and ineffectual. These tactical objectives, however, must always be supported by a good faith legal basis and are not to be used unfairly or improperly.

Objections can also create problems of their own. If not used for an obviously proper purpose, the judge, arbitrator, or jurors may find their use inappropriate and bothersome. An attorney who overuses them or appears to object for improper motives may alienate the decision maker.

B. CASE TYPE: JUDICIAL, ARBITRATION, ADMINISTRATIVE

Rules of evidence govern the admissibility of evidence in trials. This chapter explains objections to the introduction of evidence in both trials before a judge and before a jury. Arbitrations and administrative hearings are also governed by rules of evidence that usually are less numerous, more broad, and applied with greater flexibility and discretion. The general rule for arbitrations and administrative hearings is that evidence is admissible if it is *relevant* and *reliable*.

These two benchmarks form the bases for determining whether evidence ought to be introduced and admitted. *Relevancy* includes evidence having the tendency to make consequential facts more probable or less probable. *Reliability* includes substantive evidence, such as dependable hearsay and authentic documents, whose trustworthiness outweighs its untrustworthiness.

The concepts and strategies explained in this chapter apply to arbitrations and administrative hearings as well as court trials. And references to judges generally include arbitrators and administrative hearing officers, except, obviously, in jury trial scenarios.

Proper foundation, reliable testimony, and appropriate question formats make evidence more persuasive in all types of proceedings. When used properly, the rules of evidence are excellent guides to aid in preparing and presenting a case. For example, while hearsay exceptions are not strictly enforced in arbitrations and administrative hearings, the reasons supporting the exceptions aid in determining reliable evidence.

The initial sections of this chapter explain objection procedures, and remaining sections explain substantive evidentiary objections. Objections made during jury selection, opening statement, and summation appear in those respective chapters. Some readers may prefer to first read the substantive rules of evidence explained in Sections 4.6 through 4.9 and then read about objection procedures covered in Sections 4.2 through 4.5.

C. CONSIDERATIONS

Objections should be planned around the following considerations:

The approach of the judge/arbitrator. The judge's knowledge of the rules of evidence and inclination to make rulings is a major factor. Some sustain minor, technically correct objections while others apply a broader approach and overrule such objections. The attorney who interposes too many questionable objections may lose favor with the judge. There may be little advantage in making an objection the judge will overrule. While the mere fact that the judge/arbitrator may disagree with an objection is not a reason to avoid objecting, it is a valid consideration.

The effect of an objection. An objection may call a mistake or an omission to the attention of the opponent who may then correct the error. Objections should be avoided if they help the opponent.

The reaction of the jury. Incessant objections, whether sustained or overruled, may annoy the jury. Jurors may perceive that the objecting attorney is attempting to hide evidence or is acting unfairly by making technical or numerous objections.

The nature of the evidence. A lawyer should consider objecting to evidence that lacks probative value, is unclear or confusing, is collateral to the issues in dispute, or breaches a rule of evidence.

Highlighting specific evidence. An objection tends to highlight the evidence to which it is directed. A lawyer might refrain from objecting, knowing that an objection may emphasize the evidence and increase its weight.

Creation of a clear and complete record. If something objectionable and prejudicial occurs during trial, an objection should be made to make a clear record of the inappropriate evidence or behavior and hold the offending attorney accountable.

Preservation of an error for post-trial motions and appeal. Even if a lawyer anticipates that an objection will be overruled, the objection should be made to preserve the error.

The ability of an opponent. An attorney may have little knowledge of evidence law and may not be able to ask proper questions or lay foundations. Appropriate objections may disrupt the presentation of a poorly prepared or inexperienced advocate.

Strategic impact. A lawyer may make appropriate objections that are sure to be sustained early in the trial. Successful early objections give the lawyer the appearance of being knowledgeable. As a result, the judge will likely pay attention to subsequent objections; opponents will be less inclined to offer inadmissible evidence; witnesses will be easier to control on cross-examination; and a jury might pay more attention to the argument of a confident lawyer who has demonstrated competence and skill.

§ 4.2   PREPARATION

Objections are based on violations of the rules of evidence, statutes, trial practice, civil and criminal procedure, case law, common sense, and fairness. The judge makes the final determination whether grounds for objections exist and are proper. Not all judges recognize all objections. The understanding and interpretation of evidence law varies among judges. An attorney must adapt to the rules as applied by the judge and assert those objections that the judge recognizes. Forms appear at the end of this chapter that provide a method to plan for evidentiary problems.

A. ANTICIPATING EVIDENTIARY PROBLEMS

Anticipating evidentiary problems and planning how to handle them are elements of proper preparation. The goal of an examining attorney is to present evidence that is not objectionable. When preparing and presenting evidence, the attorney must recognize potential objections that may be asserted and structure questions to avoid evidentiary infirmities. The opposing attorney must anticipate potentially inadmissible evidence and prepare objections. A motion in limine may be brought before the trial begins or before a witness testifies to obtain a court ruling on the admissibility of evidence before it is introduced. See Section 3.8(C)(2).

B. ADMISSIBILITY AND WEIGHT

Two questions must be resolved about the introduction of evidence:

1.   Is the evidence *admissible* under the law?
2.   What is the *weight* or probative value of the evidence?

The judge decides the first question, and, in a jury trial, the jury decides the second. Federal Rule of Evidence 104 and similar state rules require the judge to make preliminary decisions regarding the admissibility of evidence. The judge reviews the sufficiency of the initial evidence and then decides whether to allow the introduction of further evidence. In a bench trial or arbitration or administrative hearing, the judge/arbitrator decides the admissibility and weight of the evidence.

For example, in a jury trial, the judge decides whether sufficient evidence has been introduced to establish that a person is qualified to be a witness, that a privilege exists, that a duplicate document is admissible, and that a hearsay statement falls within an exception rendering it admissible. After sufficient evidence has been introduced, the jurors then determine whether they find the admissible evidence probative, credible, and persuasive. In situations when a close question exists regarding the sufficiency of the evidence, most judges are inclined to admit the evidence and let the jurors determine its worth.

C. LEARNING HOW TO MAKE OBJECTIONS

The process of making evidentiary objections includes two separate questions:

- Is there a *legitimate, good faith objection* supported by the law of evidence available?

- Is there an appropriate *strategic or tactical reason* for making the objection?

It is difficult enough to make these decisions in a calm, cool, detached atmosphere, such as while reading this chapter. It is much more difficult to make a quick decision amidst the tension and commotion of a trial or hearing. During the case presentation, an objecting attorney must make split-second judgments while concentrating on all other aspects of what is happening. This skill is enhanced with practice and experience.

There are a number of things that can be done by novice advocates to increase their ability to think quickly, make instant judgments, and assert objections during a case:

- *Become familiar with the types of common objections.* Review a list of available objections and organize the objections in a format that can be easily remembered and applied. Form 4.1 and the list of common objections at the end of this Chapter provide a usable framework that can be modified.

- *Learn to recognize types or patterns of evidence that create objectionable situations.* These include:

  — Lengthy direct examination questions are often objectionable because they are leading.

  — Questions that involve conversations may trigger hearsay objections.

  — Questions calling for the witness' observations require proper foundation and may be objectionable based on lack of foundation.

— Questions calling for a lay witness to give an opinion may support an objection based on an improper opinion.

— Documents must be authenticated, otherwise an objection based on lack of authentication may be appropriate.

— Answers that include prefaces such as "I'm not certain, but . . . " may support an objection based on speculation.

— Responses referring to documentary evidence may violate foundation, authenticity, or original writing rules.

Sections 4.6 through 4.8 explain these and other commonly available objections.

• *Prior to trial or hearing, prepare a list of specific objections to the anticipated evidence.* This planning process will assist in more accurately identifying objections during the case.

• *Concentrate on the evidence being introduced.* Although many things are going on while the evidence is being introduced, focus on the evidence.

• *Listen attentively and watch the examination.* The sound of a question or answer, or the demeanor of the attorney or witness, may be objectionable.

• *Rely on common sense.* Some events occurring during a trial or hearing may be objectionable because they are obviously improper and unfair.

• *Over prepare.* Extra preparation helps in applying the evidentiary rules to the evidence introduced in the case.

• *Be prepared to lose an objection.* Valid objections may be overruled and inadmissible evidence is sometimes admitted.

• *Be willing to make mistakes.* Expect that the judge/arbitrator may disagree with an objection and think it's wrong.

• *Prepare to be surprised.* Sometimes evidence comes in differently than expected, and judges/arbitrators exercise discretion in surprising ways.

• *Observe whether an objection is expected.* The judge/arbitrator may invite an objection by sighing, making faces or by appearing impatient with the testimony. However, an attorney need not object at an apparent invitation. The attorney may misinterpret the behavior, or the attorney may not want to object for tactical reasons.

- *Rehearse making objections to anticipated evidentiary problems.* Imagine how opposing counsel may make evidentiary mistakes and practice making objections.

D. DECIDING WHETHER TO OBJECT

Whether an objection should be made even when there is legal support for the objection depends on the strategic impact the objection has on the admissibility of the evidence. The more critical the evidence, the more likely the objection should be made. There are four basic guidelines determining whether to object to evidence:

- If the evidence is clearly admissible, the opposing attorney should not object. Rather, the attorney should try to minimize the effect of the evidence through cross-examination or rebuttal and then argue its lack of weight in final argument.

- If the offered evidence is clearly inadmissible and harmful, the lawyer should object. The rules of evidence should be used to exclude improper evidence that hurts an objecting party's case. The objecting attorney should try as hard as possible to exclude this evidence and use all available means to do so.

- If the evidence is probably inadmissible but not harmful, the attorney should consider not objecting, or may object but not pursue the issue if the judge/arbitrator overrules the objection. Whatever harm there is may be avoided on cross-exam or explained away in summation.

- If the answer will reveal favorable or neutral information, even if the question is improper, no objection should be made.

Objections should be reserved for situations that meet the considerations listed in Section 4.1(C). In some cases, there may be no need to make objections. Trials and hearings between skilled lawyers may have few objections.

E. ALTERNATIVE OBJECTIONS

There may be more than one objection that can be made to a question or an answer. Part of the planning process is formulating a series of potential objections to anticipated evidence. Objections that may be available to the same piece of evidence include:

- *Improper form of the question.* The question may be leading or otherwise improper.

- *Irrelevant.* The topic may not have any relevance to the case.

- *Cumulative.* The evidence has previously been introduced and this item of evidence is unnecessarily repetitive.

- *Unfairly prejudicial.* Even if the item is relevant, it may be unfairly prejudicial.

- *Lack of foundation.* The witness may not be competent to lay a foundation for the introduction of evidence.

- *Improper opinion.* Witnesses may testify to an unfounded opinion.

- *Hearsay.* The source of the information may be from an inadmissible hearsay source.

- *Original writing (best evidence) required.* Oral testimony is offered to prove the contents of a writing that must be introduced.

F.   EXPLAINING WHY NO OBJECTION IS MADE

In some situations an objection may seem appropriate, but the opposing lawyer does not want to object. In such situations, counsel may want to explain why no objection is being made. Instead of sitting silently in the courtroom or merely saying "Your Honor, we have no objection," the attorney may state: "We have no objection and want this testimony to be heard." Or "We agree that this exhibit should be admitted into evidence."

G.   INVITATION BY JUDGE

Judges occasionally look at opposing counsel when evidence is being introduced and say "Any objection?" Some judges ask these questions neutrally without suggesting that an objection exists. Other judges signal that they will sustain an appropriate objection. Even if the lawyer did not plan to make an objection, the attorney should consider whether to object because the judge is apparently suggesting there is something objectionable. An attorney should not object merely because the judge believes an objection ought to be made, but rather the attorney should consider whether there is a strategic reason for making the objection.

§ 4.3   PRESENTATION

A.   MAKING OBJECTIONS

Whether an attorney should stand or remain seated while objecting depends on the jurisdiction and judge. Most judges require or expect the attorney to stand when addressing the court. The seated attorney may say "Objection, your Honor," and then stand to state the grounds. The extra time gained by standing may help in framing an objection. An attorney may remain seated or request to remain seated, if objections are made quickly, the judge rules immediately, or if there is a series of objections. Most objections and rulings are made in front of the jurors unless an explanation is warranted. See Section 4.3(D). Arbitrators and administrative judges typically allow the objector to remain seated.

B.   TIMING

An objection must be timely made. If a question is improper, the objection must be made before the answer is given. For example, objections to the form of a question must be made immediately after the question and before the answer. If a question is proper but the response is inadmissible, an objection should be made as soon as the inadmissible evidence becomes apparent. For example, if a witness begins to testify to inadmissible hearsay, the opposing attorney should interrupt and make an objection. An objection interjected too late, however meritorious, is ordinarily overruled. Late objections are also ineffective because the inadmissible evidence has been presented. If an objection is made after the evidence is introduced, an error may not be preserved for appeal.

Attorneys should avoid making premature objections. If an objection to the content of a statement is available, the attorney must object to the question that introduces the objectionable content. For example, an objection to the preliminary question, "Do you have an opinion about the defendant's condition?" is premature, but the attorney should object to the follow-up question seeking an improper opinion, "What is that opinion?" Similarly, a hearsay objection to the question, "Did you have a conversation with the witness?" is premature. The proper objection should be made to the next question, "What did the witness say?"

This task is made more difficult by the fact that witnesses often are not prepared to respond to the precise wording of the questions. The question "Do you have an opinion?" often produces the opinion rather than the anticipated "Yes" answer. If the examiner has not adequately prepared the witness, an objection may have to be made to the preliminary question in order to prevent these nonresponsive answers. The judge may, however, overrule the premature objection, and the attorney will need to restate the objection following the next question.

Example (Direct Examination):

Examining Attorney:

Q: Did you and Lady Gaga speak to each other?

Objecting Lawyer:

I object your Honor, that question calls for hearsay.

Judge:

The objection is premature, the witness may answer.

A: Yes, we did.

Examining Attorney:

Q: What did Ms. Gaga say?

Objecting Lawyer:

Objection, hearsay.

Judge:

Sustained.

When the witness responds to a question calling for a yes or no response with a further response, the attorney can object to the answer because it goes beyond the scope of the question.

Example (Direct Examination):

Examining Attorney:

Q: Katniss Everdeen, do you have an opinion regarding the importance of the Hunger Games?

A: Yes, I do. It's very likely that the . . .

Objecting Lawyer:

Your Honor, I object. The question has been answered.

Judge:

Sustained.

The witness should stop answering the question once the objection is made. If the witness continues to answer, the opposing attorney should interrupt and ask the judge to instruct the witness to stop answering. If the examining attorney is asking questions too rapidly, or if the witness is answering questions too quickly, the judge may be asked to instruct the attorney or witness to proceed at a reasonable pace, which provides an opportunity to object before the witness responds.

C. PHRASING AN OBJECTION

The proper way to object in most jurisdictions is to say "objection" and state the specific ground or grounds with a few identifying words. This method is simple, quick, and advises the judge of the ground(s) for the objection. The applicable rules of evidence ordinarily require the objecting attorney to state the specific reason supporting the objection. See, e.g., Fed.R.Evid. 103(a)(1). More than one ground may support an objection, and an attorney should state all applicable grounds. If the attorney does not advance a specific reason and the ground for the objection is apparent from the context of the evidence, an objection may be sustained.

Using the name or title of the rule involved is usually sufficient: "Your Honor, objection, hearsay." Or "We object, your Honor, on the grounds of hearsay." Proper courtroom etiquette may require the attorney to preface an objection with the phrase "Your Honor." Also, the addition of a descriptive term to an objection in a jury trial is advisable so the jury may understand the grounds for the objection: "Objection, unreliable hearsay." Some judges expect attorneys to use specific words in making an objection, requiring the attorneys to be very precise. Other judges require objecting attorneys to refer to specific evidence rule numbers.

D. OUTSIDE THE HEARING OF THE JURY

Trial proceedings should be conducted so that the jury does not hear inadmissible evidence, arguments, and statements. Comments by counsel, arguments, lengthy objections, and offers of proof must be made outside the hearing of the jury. Jurors should not be influenced by inadmissible evidence or the explanations of counsel.

"Speaking objections"—arguments in front of the jury—are rarely appropriate. If an attorney needs to explain an objection, permission to approach the bench should be requested and the arguments made at the bench. If an objecting attorney persists in arguing an objection in front of the jury, the other lawyer should interrupt and request permission to approach the bench. When an attorney argues in a voice loud enough for jurors to hear, the judge should be asked to admonish the attorney and instruct the jury to disregard the argument.

A fine line exists between appropriate, descriptive statements and improper speaking objections. For example, an objection may be stated: "Counsel is attempting to present unreliable and untrustworthy hearsay through this witness." This statement explains the grounds of the objection and helps the jury understand the evidentiary problem. While some judges may allow this, others prohibit this lengthy a statement.

An attorney needs to adapt objection procedures to the judge's preferences. Some judges prefer a lengthier explanation of an objection instead of a few descriptive words, and the attorney should provide the judge with that information. Some judges inappropriately allow "speaking objections" instead of requiring conferences at the bench. This practice results in lawyers making arguments within the hearing of the jury.

E. LEGAL SUPPORT

When an anticipated objection is made to a vital piece of evidence, it is sometimes useful to have a short, one or two page memorandum supporting or opposing the objection. This issue brief provides the judge with precedent, eliminates the need to make an extemporaneous argument, and shows the judge that the attorney is serious about a position. A concise memo may sway the judge regarding a close evidentiary ruling.

F. ATTORNEYS' DEMEANOR

Objections should be made in a firm, clear voice and in a professional and reasonable manner. Objections and responses should always be directed to the judge and not to opposing counsel. Arguing with opposing counsel may draw an admonition from the judge and should be avoided. A calm, low-key approach is usually most effective, unless the situation dictates that an attorney be assertive or talk in a louder voice to interrupt an improper question or response.

Responses to adverse rulings by the judge should also be professional and respectful. Statements of disapproval or nonverbal behavior demonstrating disappointment are usually inappropriate and rarely necessary even to highlight outrageous improper evidence or conduct.

G. RESPONDING TO THE JUDGE

An attorney may need to respond to a judge who attempts to unduly restrict the attorney's ability to make or explain objections on the record. Judges want the case to proceed as quickly as possible, and some judges pressure attorneys not to make objections. Occasionally a judge may make comments in front of the jurors about what the judge perceives to be wasteful and time-consuming objections. The attorney cannot always please the judge or do what the judge prefers. It is the responsibility of the attorney, not the judge, to prevent the opposing attorney from introducing inadmissible evidence and to preserve an appeal record. If the judge improperly interferes with objections, the objecting attorney may make a record that the judge's interference is adversely affecting the case.

H.   CONTINUING OBJECTIONS

If an objection has been overruled and subsequent questions are asked on the same subject, the objecting attorney may consider making a "continuing" objection to subsequent questions and answers on the subject. A continuing objection may eliminate the need for the attorney to repeatedly object after each question or answer. Not all jurisdictions recognize continuing objections. A problem with their use is that there is no specific objection on the record to individual questions or answers, and it may be unclear regarding the matters included in the objection.

The lawyer should define the scope of the continuing objection as precisely as possible. Instead of saying, "I object to this entire line of questioning," the attorney should say, "I object to all the testimony about the witness' identification of Exhibit No. 9 on the ground that. . . ." The lawyer should also be alert to additional grounds that arise during subsequent testimony. If another ground becomes apparent during the line of questioning, that ground should be added to the continuing objection. If the scope or grounds cannot be made clear with a continuing objection, a more effective tactic may be to repeat objections to specific questions and answers. While repetitive objections may be annoying and disruptive, they remove any doubt regarding the ground and scope of the objection and avoid the inadvertent waiver of objections.

I.   RESPONDING TO OBJECTIONS

Usually the examining attorney need not say anything in response to an objection. Sometimes the judge asks the examining attorney to argue against the objection. If the examining attorney wants to make a brief statement in opposition to an objection, it may be stated in front of the jury. If the attorney wants to argue further, the attorney should approach the bench and make the argument there.

J.   PRESENTING CONTRARY EVIDENCE

An objecting attorney may have an opportunity to offer contrary evidence—to show that an objection should be sustained—before a ruling on the objection. These situations arise when a judge must determine whether sufficient evidence exists supporting the admissibility of additional evidence, or if a factual or legal impediment bars further evidence. Section 4.2(B) explained that the judge reviews preliminary evidence to decide whether subsequent evidence is admissible.

There are two ways an opposing attorney may introduce contrary evidence. The first and typical way is by questioning the witness to lay the grounds for an objection. The second way, which is used only in unusual circumstances, is through extrinsic evidence.

1. Questioning the Witness

The most common way for an opposing attorney to introduce contrary evidence is to request permission to interrupt the examination to ask questions of the witness for the purpose of establishing grounds for an objection. The procedure—also known as "voir dire" of a witness—consists of counsel examining the witness, usually through leading questions, to establish facts in support of a ruling by the judge that subsequent evidence is inadmissible. For example, the witness may identify a document that the proponent offers. The opposing attorney may question the witness to show the witness cannot authenticate the document.

Judges permit "voir dire" questioning of a witness if the attorney appears able to establish the inadmissibility of the evidence. Usually the opposing attorney can ask a reasonable number of questions to establish the lack of admissibility. These questions, which interrupt the direct examination, may not develop into broader questions that should be asked on cross-examination. Questioning that extends beyond proper "voir dire" and into cross-examination should be objected to as improper. Some lawyers attempt to use "voir dire" to disrupt the direct examination. This tactic is improper unless there is a good faith basis to establish contrary evidence supporting the objection.

Example (Direct Examination):

Examining Attorney:

Q: Ms. Gaeta, please describe the contents of the frozen pizza you bought.

Objecting Lawyer:

Your Honor, may I voir dire the witness by asking a few questions to lay the foundation for an objection?

Judge:

Yes, you may.

Objecting Lawyer:

Q: You are not a food scientist are you?

A: No.

Q: You didn't test any of the ingredients in the pizza did you?

A: No.

Q: You did not read the label did you?

A: No.

Q: You didn't finish eating all the pizza?

A: I could not.

Q: And by looking at it you couldn't tell what it was made of.

A: That's for sure.

To the Court:

Your Honor, I object to any further testimony by this witness about the contents of the Montecarlo pizza on lack of foundation.

Judge:

Sustained.

---

2.   Extrinsic Evidence

Extrinsic evidence is evidence from a source other than the witness on the stand, such as another witness or document. Extrinsic evidence may be admissible if an opposing attorney challenges the competency of a witness or claims the existence of a privilege. For example, a witness testifies on direct examination that she is not married to the defendant and that she had a conversation with the defendant. The opposing attorney may object on the grounds of marital privilege and offer into evidence a marriage certificate as extrinsic evidence. The primary reason the situations involving the use of extrinsic evidence are rare is that these problems are usually taken care of through a motion in limine before trial or before the witness testifies.

§ 4.4   RULING BY JUDGE/ARBITRATOR

A.   DISCRETION

Judges and arbitrators have broad discretion in ruling on the admissibility of evidence. The standard used to determine the admissibility of evidence is whether there exists "evidence sufficient to support a finding" of the proposition sought to be proven. See Fed.R.Evid. 104(a) and (b). If the support is insufficient, the evidence is inadmissible.

B.   RULING

Ordinarily, the judge or arbitrator rules immediately after an objection and says "sustained" (the objection is valid) or "overruled" (the objection is denied). Usually the judge does not state a reason for the ruling because the reason is the same ground the objecting attorney stated. Most judges do not sustain an objection unless the objecting lawyer correctly states the ground for the objection. The explanatory statement describes the defect in the question or answer. Even if a question or answer is objectionable, many judges do not sustain an objection if the attorney states an incorrect ground. While judges and arbitrators have discretion to exclude inadmissible evidence on their own (in the absence of any objection or absent any supporting grounds), many do not exercise this discretion.

C. PROVISIONAL RULING

In some situations, a judge or arbitrator may make a provisional or conditional ruling that can be reconsidered at a later stage of the case. They reserve the opportunity to change the ruling depending on subsequent events in the case that may affect the admissibility of the evidence. Objections based on irrelevancy, lack of foundation, or improper lay or expert opinion may result in conditional rulings that allow evidence to be admitted subject to reconsideration. For example, a judge may overrule a relevancy objection because the examining lawyer advises the judge that the relevancy of this evidence (Evidence A) depends upon the later admission of related evidence (Evidence B). The judge may overrule the objection and allow Evidence A on the condition that Evidence B is presented. If Evidence B is not subsequently admitted, the objecting attorney may renew the objection to Evidence A and the court will sustain the objection.

Example (Direct Examination):

Examining Attorney to the Judge at the Bench:

Your Honor, at this time we offer Exhibit No. 35. We realize that we need to provide another witness in order to establish the technical foundation for chain of custody. We'll do that through Mr. Hercules, who is available as a witness tomorrow. We ask the court to provisionally admit Exhibit 35 with our assurance that we will connect up the foundation with his testimony.

Judge:

With that assurance I will conditionally accept Exhibit No. 35.

D. INQUIRING ABOUT A RULING

If an objection is sustained or overruled and the reasoning of the judge or arbitrator is unclear, the attorney may ask for an explanation of the ruling. In some jurisdictions, the attorney even has a right to such an explanation. The judge may ask the objecting lawyer to explain the ground for the objection.

If the lawyer believes the judge or arbitrator made an incorrect ruling, the attorney may request that the ruling be reconsidered. Judges do not often change their rulings, and this tactic may waste time. The judge may simply have an understanding of evidence—whether right or wrong—that is different from the lawyer's, and no purpose is served by arguing with the judge. If, for example, the judge sustained a leading objection, the examining lawyer should rephrase the question rather than try to persuade the judge that the situation created an exception to the leading question rule. However, in some situations an explanation of the reasons may be effective. For example, the judge may sustain a relevancy objection because the judge does not see any issue that the evidence supports. An explanation of the issue and its connection with the facts may cause the judge to change the ruling and allow the evidence.

E.　RENEWING AN OBJECTION

In jury trials, if the judge overrules an objection, the objecting lawyer can ask to approach the bench for argument. Judges often refuse this request because they are confident of their decision. A more effective practice for the objecting attorney is to object to the next related question or answer. Perhaps the judge will understand the grounds for the objection as it applies to the subsequent question or answer and sustain it. Counsel should be persistent and respectful in pursuing correct objections.

F.　PURSUING OBJECTIONS

A judge or arbitrator may overrule an objection that is premature, as explained in Section 4.3(B). The attorney should make objections to subsequent questions to make certain the judge rules consistently. For example, an attorney may object to the question "Did you form an opinion after your examination?" anticipating that the witness may give a narrative response. The judge may overrule the objection because this question calls for a permissible yes or no answer. The attorney should then object to subsequent questions regarding the content of the opinion.

G.　OBTAINING A RULING

A judge or arbitrator may fail to make a ruling on an objection, either by mistake or to avoid deciding. Some judges have figured out that if they don't make any ruling they can't be reversed on appeal for making a wrong ruling. Attorneys have a right to a ruling and should insist on one.

Example (Direct Examination):

Examining Attorney:

What did Mr. Morse say about this new invention?

Objecting Lawyer:

Objection, hearsay.

Judge:

All right, go on, continue.

Objecting Lawyer:

Your Honor, before we continue, I objected to the last question on the grounds of hearsay.

Judge:

Overruled.

Witness:

He said, "What hath God wrought?"

Examining Lawyer:

Whom was he quoting?

Objecting Lawyer:

Objection, irrelevant and hearsay.

Judge:

Next question.

Examining Lawyer:

Your Honor, may the witness answer the last question?

Judge:

No, sustained.

---

§ 4.5   OBJECTION PROCEDURES

A. EVIDENTIARY MOTIONS BEFORE TRIAL: MOTIONS IN LIMINE

A motion in limine (meaning at the threshold) seeks an advance ruling from the judge regarding the admissibility or inadmissibility of evidence. In criminal cases, these rulings are commonly sought through suppression motions to attack the admissibility of evidence on the grounds that the evidence violates constitutional rights, statutory provisions, or the rules of evidence. See, e.g., Fed.R.Crim.Proc. 41. Motions in limine are also common in civil cases to obtain an advance evidentiary ruling. Section 3.8(C)(2) introduced motions in limine.

Motions in limine are commonly brought prior to jury trials to avoid the prejudicial impact of inadmissible evidence on the jurors, but they also serve a purpose in non-jury trials. Obtaining an advance ruling makes clear what questionable evidence is or is not admissible in a bench trial or hearing. This ruling assists in determining the most effective theory of the case and what facts the judge or arbitrator will consider.

1. Purposes

Motions in limine may be brought for several purposes:

- *To prohibit opposing counsel from introducing or mentioning objectionable evidence in the presence of the jurors.* A ruling can be sought prohibiting the use of evidence that is barred by any exclusionary rule of evidence, such as unfairly prejudicial or irrelevant evidence and inadmissible hearsay. A favorable ruling prevents the jurors from becoming aware of and being influenced by inadmissible evidence and from suspecting that the objecting attorney is trying to hide evidence from them. Examples of this type of evidence include the questionable admissibility of a prior criminal conviction or of subsequent remedial measures taken by a defendant in a tort case.

- *To require opposing counsel to obtain a ruling on admissibility before evidence is offered.* This motion in limine seeks a ruling from the judge requiring opposing counsel to lay a proper and complete foundation before the evidence will be admitted. Examples of such evidence include the facts to authenticate a document and the foundation required to comply with the original writing (best evidence) rule.

- *To obtain a preliminary ruling by the court that evidence offered by the proponent is admissible.* This motion is made by the proponent of the evidence who seeks an advance ruling by the court that certain evidence will be later admitted. A proponent may have some evidence that the opposing party opposes. The proponent of the evidence may want to know prior to trial or hearing whether the evidence will be admitted in order to effectively prepare and plan the presentation. Examples of this type of evidence include photos that contain relevant but grisly depictions of the evidence or expensive demonstrative evidence. Before parties spend money creating an elaborate computerized chart, a complicated model, or a video recording, they may prefer to obtain a preliminary ruling that the evidence will be admissible.

A motion in limine assumes that the opposing party plans to object to the introduction of the evidence. The advantage of the motion is the certainty obtained by a ruling assuring an attorney that the evidence can be referred to during opening statement. Plans can also then be made to introduce the evidence during the case. The disadvantages are that the importance of certain evidence is highlighted and opposing lawyers may be prompted to object where otherwise they may not have done so.

2.   Motion Procedure

Motions in limine may be made either in writing or orally on the record, depending on the nature of the issue and applicable rules. There is usually no specific limit regarding the number of motions that may be made, but strategy and common sense restrict motions to important evidence. A judge who faces a barrage of motions regarding routine evidentiary issues may be inclined not to consider such motions seriously.

Motions in limine usually require that reasonable, advance notice be given to the opposing attorney. The timing of the notice depends on the nature of the motion, the rules of the jurisdiction, and the evidence in question. Many jurisdictions require that motions in limine be brought in writing a reasonable time prior to trial to provide the opponent with an opportunity to respond. Other courts permit motions in limine to be made orally on the eve of trial and during trial.

If a party plans to offer or seeks to exclude crucial evidence, it is best to submit a written motion with notice to the opposing attorney so that memoranda can be submitted and a full hearing held on the issues. When an attorney seeks to introduce or oppose the introduction of routine real evidence or standard demonstrative evidence, an oral request made on the eve of trial or just before a witness testifies may be sufficient.

A motion in limine should state the specific relief sought and the grounds supporting the motion, along with supporting authorities. An opposing attorney can make clear during argument why an evidentiary motion is brought early rather than later during the trial or hearing. Many judges/arbitrators prefer deferring or denying motions in limine until they see and hear the evidence introduced during the case. A moving attorney has to overcome this predisposition by explaining why a preliminary ruling is necessary.

3.   The Order

The order granting the in limine motion must specify the evidence that is excluded or ruled inadmissible. An order that is overly broad may exclude otherwise admissible evidence and become the ground for a new trial or reversible error. An order that is ambiguous may permit opposing counsel to refer to related evidence while still complying with the order. The order, whether written or recorded orally, must be specific and clear as to what evidence is to be excluded or admitted. If there is doubt about the meaning of an order, counsel should ask to have the order clarified.

A judge or arbitrator has broad discretion and several options when ruling on a motion in limine:

- The judge may refuse to hear the motion because it is untimely. Advance written notice of a motion provided to opposing attorney and the judge prevents the opposing attorney from claiming surprise and prejudice and reduces the likelihood the motion will be refused.

- The judge may defer ruling on the motion until later. The judge may reconsider the motion immediately prior to the time the evidence is offered. The judge may decide it is impossible or difficult to make an advance ruling because it is not clear from the arguments whether the evidence is admissible or inadmissible. The judge may prefer to wait until the evidence is developed during the trial and observe how the evidence is being introduced before making a ruling.

- The judge may deny the motion but permit the moving attorney to bring the motion again for reconsideration during the trial. A judge may do this for the same reasons explained above.

- The judge may grant only part of the relief sought in the motion in limine. If the motion seeks to totally exclude a piece of evidence, the judge may permit a part of the evidence to be introduced. Or, if the motion seeks to exclude evidence that is offered to prove several things, the judge may limit the effect of the evidence to prove only some of those things. See Section 4.5(E) on limited admissibility.

- The judge may enter a conditional order requiring that specific facts be introduced during the trial as a condition for the introduction of the disputed evidence. If the specific facts are not introduced, the conditional ruling takes effect and the evidence is excluded. A conditional order is sometimes entered when the court needs to hear certain facts in order to make a proper evidentiary ruling. The intent of this provisional order is to advise advocates that these facts must be offered before a final ruling can be made. See Section 4.4(C).

- The judge may grant the motion in limine and not permit any reference either directly or indirectly to the inadmissible evidence.

4. Preserving Error

A ruling on a motion in limine usually preserves that evidentiary issue as a ground for a new trial and an appeal. In most jurisdictions, there need not be any further evidentiary offer or objection made during the trial because the previous ruling is on the record. In some jurisdictions, a party who loses a motion in limine may need to take further steps during the trial to preserve the evidentiary issue. In these jurisdictions, if a motion in limine is denied, the losing attorney may need to object to the introduction of the evidence during the trial to preserve the issue properly.

5. Violation of Order

The violation of an order granting a motion in limine may result in reversible error, especially if the judge does not properly instruct the jury to disregard the excluded evidence. The intentional violation of an order may subject the offending attorney to sanctions from the court. Sanctions may include rejection of the evidence, a reprimand, and the imposition of attorney's fees. An inadvertent violation of an order may be excusable if it's not the result of negligence. Attorneys have an obligation to inform their witnesses of the effect of the ruling. If the court excludes evidence, the attorney must advise witnesses not to volunteer such evidence.

Example (Motion In Limine and Order):

Motion in Limine

Defendant Jacqueline Wade moves this court for an order stating that Plaintiff St. Elsewhere Hospital makes no reference to the August 15, 2015 medical malpractice insurance agreement between St. Elsewhere and Dr. Wade on the grounds that it is irrelevant and unfairly prejudicial. Defendant supports this motion with a proposed order and memo.

Order in Limine

This court orders that Defendant Dr. Wade's motion in limine is granted and orders Plaintiff St. Elsewhere Hospital to make no reference during this trial to the medical malpractice insurance agreement between Dr. Wade and St. Elsewhere Hospital dated August 15, 2015.

B. OFFERS OF PROOF

When an objection is sustained and evidence excluded, the examining attorney must make an offer of proof to preserve the error for appellate review. The offer of proof provides a description of the excluded evidence so the appellate court can review the offered evidence and determine the significance of its exclusion. Opposing counsel may make other objections after the offer has been made.

There are three ways to make an offer of proof, each of which occurs on the record. All these involve an explanation to the judge or arbitrator of the anticipated testimony and the grounds of its admissibility.

1. The Examining Attorney May Summarize the Evidence

This is the most common way of making an offer of proof.

Example (Direct Examination):

Examining Attorney:

Q: During that afternoon conversation, what was the first thing Carl Spackler said to you?

Objecting Lawyer:

Objection, hearsay.

Judge:

Sustained.

Examining Attorney:

Your Honor, may I make an offer of proof at the bench?

Judge:

Yes, approach the bench.

Examining Attorney:

Judge, the evidence will demonstrate that the witness had knowledge of the defect before the accident. The witness will testify that Mr. Spackler told her that he had known that the repairs on the golf cart were not completed on September 1.

---

2. Counsel May Ask the Witness to State What the Testimony Would Be in a Question/Answer Format

The examining lawyer asks questions which reveal the specific evidence in issue, outside the hearing of the jury in a jury trial. This method is the most time consuming but is also the most accurate. This format reflects the exact questions and answers and not just a summary.

3. The Offering Attorney May Submit a Written Statement of the Proffered Testimony

The written statement is similar to the oral summary described in the first method. The first and third methods are usually adequate to create a sufficient record. The second method is used primarily in situations where an exact transcript of the precise evidence is preferred.

The offer of proof provides an opportunity for the judge to reconsider the original ruling. Sometimes, after hearing the proposed evidence, the judge understands why it is not objectionable and overrules the objection. The offer of proof also provides an opportunity for the examining lawyer to explain why the evidence is admissible. This argument, coupled with proposed evidence, may convince the judge to admit the evidence.

Example (Continued):

Examining Attorney:

Further your Honor, at the time Mr. Spackler made the statement about the golf cart repairs he was still an employee of the defendant, and the statement is an admissible party admission.

Objecting Lawyer:

Judge, but he didn't have personal knowledge of the repairs.

Judge:

An employee need not have personal knowledge if the statement refers to matters within the scope of employment. I'll change my ruling and overrule the objection.

C. MOTION TO STRIKE

A motion to strike usually occurs after a witness has made an improper statement, an objection has been made, and the court has sustained the objection. The purpose of the motion is to make clear that the improper statement or inadmissible evidence is not to be considered by the fact finder. Section 3.8(C)(4) explained the procedure for making motions to strike. Although a motion to strike may clarify the scope and extent of the excluded evidence, a motion to strike should not be made unless it serves a valid purpose, or unless making such a motion is a common practice in the jurisdiction.

D. REQUEST FOR CURATIVE INSTRUCTION

A motion for a curative instruction attempts to repair the harm done by an improper question or inadmissible answer. After an objection has been sustained, the attorney may immediately ask the judge to instruct the jurors that they must disregard what they heard. While completely ignoring some facts may be difficult, jurors usually follow the judge's admonition. If told they cannot consider some inadmissible evidence, they usually will comply, particularly if the party causing the error appears to be acting unfairly. The disadvantage of a curative instruction is that the jury is reminded of the evidence and may remember and understand it better than if it was ignored.

Example:

Objecting Lawyer:

Objection, your Honor. The response is inadmissible hearsay and I ask that the jury be instructed to disregard that answer.

Judge:

Members of the Jury, you are to disregard the testimony about the conversation between this witness and Saint Therese.

E. LIMITED ADMISSIBILITY

Evidence which is admissible for one purpose but not for another may be admitted for a limited purpose when requested by counsel. See Fed.R.Evid. 105. For example, a repair bill may be admissible to prove it was paid but inadmissible hearsay to prove that actual repairs were done. The bill can be received for the limited purpose of proving payment.

A judge in a jury trial has several options in determining what to do with evidence that is admissible to prove some facts but not other facts:

- The judge could admit the evidence and instruct the jury regarding its import.

- The judge could admit the evidence without comment.

- The judge could exclude the evidence if it is unfairly prejudicial and the impact outweighs the probative value of the evidence.

- Separate trials could be held regarding severed issues or claims if overlapping evidence would affect the outcome.

The first option is probably the most common solution. The judge admits the evidence but limits its scope.

Example:

Judge:

Members of the Jury, evidence in this case regarding GIFs is being introduced for a limited purpose. When you see this evidence now, and when you consider it during your deliberations, you are to use it only for (state proper purpose). You are not to use it for any other purpose. You are not to use it for (state prohibited purpose). You are only to use it (repeat proper purpose).

The judge may repeat the limiting instruction after the evidence has been received or a line of questioning completed, depending upon the nature and impact of the evidence. The judge may repeat the limiting instruction during final jury instructions at the end of the case.

Limiting instructions have limits. The jurors who hear the evidence may disregard the limiting instructions and use the evidence broadly to prove other matters. For example, if a repair bill is received with a limiting instruction, the jurors may nonetheless infer that the repairs were properly completed because the bill would not have likely been paid.

F. QUESTIONING OF WITNESSES BY THE JUDGE OR ARBITRATOR

All jurisdictions permit a judge to ask questions of witnesses in a bench trial and arbitrators to ask questions in an arbitration. Most jurisdictions, including federal courts, provide the judge with discretion to ask questions of a witness in a jury trial. Many judges do not ask any questions of witnesses because they do not believe it is their role to do so. Some judges will occasionally ask questions to clarify an important matter, and others may periodically ask questions to supplement the questions asked by the attorneys. A judge may not take over the questioning of a witness, unnecessarily interfere in witness examinations, or unduly influence a jury by questioning witnesses.

In some administrative hearings, the judge will initiate the questioning of each witness and ask many questions allowing the attorneys to ask follow-up and further questions. In arbitrations, the arbitrator may ask clarifying questions but not questions about issues not presented.

An attorney may object to any improper question asked by a judge, administrative judge, or arbitrator that violates a rule of evidence and may ask for a ruling. This objection is difficult to make because counsel is challenging the propriety of the question and may alienate the decision maker. If the question is inappropriate, the objection should be made and hopefully sustained. Counsel should object to exclude inadmissible evidence and to make a record for appeal.

Example:

The family of a mentally impaired patient sues the state for causing his injuries. The plaintiff is called as a witness. The judge has trouble understanding him, interrupts and asks questions:

Judge:

Q: You said your nurse hit you, Mr. Solitano. When?

A: Whenever I started to dance.

Q: And she hit you every time you danced?

A: Every time.

Q: Why do you think she did something as cruel as that?

Objecting Lawyer:

I object. Your Honor, your questions are leading and improper.

Most state court systems prohibit a trial judge from commenting on or expressing opinions about the evidence in a jury trial. State judges usually adhere to this policy and do not comment on the evidence.

The federal court system permits judges to comment on the evidence and express opinions on the weight or sufficiency of the evidence and the credibility of witnesses. Federal judges may make such comments at the time they instruct the jurors. If a federal judge comments on the evidence to the jury, the judge must also advise the jury that they are the sole finders of fact and they may reach a conclusion contrary to the judge's comments. If a judge improperly refers to the evidence, the attorney should make an appropriate objection to such a misstatement.

Example:

Objecting Lawyer:

Objection, Judge Harm. We respectfully submit that your Honor has (improperly commented on the evidence, improperly expressed an opinion regarding the weight of the evidence, improperly made remarks concerning the credibility of witnesses, or otherwise made an improper statement).

G. PRESERVING THE EVIDENTIARY ERROR

An evidentiary error is properly preserved if steps are taken to make a record of the error and to provide the judge with notice and an opportunity to correct the error or reduce its prejudicial impact. Section 3.12(A) explained this process. To preserve an evidentiary error for appeal in most jurisdictions, counsel must:

- Timely object on the record.

- Specifically state all available grounds. The failure to state a ground usually waives the omitted ground, unless it is readily apparent from the context.

- Include the evidentiary error in a motion for a new trial.

- Raise the specific evidentiary issue on appeal.

If the error occurs as a result of the introduction of inadmissible evidence, the opposing attorney may request a curative or limiting instruction, and make a motion to strike, if appropriate. If the objection is sustained, the examining attorney must make an offer of proof.

H. MOTION FOR MISTRIAL

Inadmissible evidence that has been improperly admitted may be a ground for a mistrial. See Section 3.8(C)(9). The inadmissible evidence must be so unfairly prejudicial that a party is denied a fair trial because of its adverse impact. In jury trials, a curative instruction is usually sufficient to reduce the harmful effect of inadmissible evidence. If the unfair impact cannot be cured by an instruction, a mistrial may be granted.

Example:

Objecting Lawyer:

Objection, your Honor. Counsel has explicitly referred to evidence that your Honor previously ruled inadmissible. I now move for a mistrial on the grounds that this misconduct is so unfairly prejudicial that my client is denied a fair trial. A curative instruction will not remove from the minds of the jurors what they have heard. This inadmissible and highly prejudicial information counsel has presented prevents the jurors from considering the evidence in a fair and impartial manner. Furthermore, I ask that you admonish Arthur Kirkland for his gross misconduct.

I. PREJUDICIAL ERROR

In order for an evidentiary error to be a prejudicial (reversible) error, the error must adversely affect a substantial right of a party. Section 12.5(F) describes the requirement of prejudicial error to support the granting of a new trial. An unfair prejudicial error may involve a significant evidentiary fact or may be based on numerous errors that cumulatively violate a party's right to a fair trial.

Many evidentiary rulings are incorrect, but only amount to "harmless error." Harmless error is a mistake that does not substantially prejudice a party. Most evidentiary mistakes during a trial are harmless and not sufficiently prejudicial to warrant a new trial or reversal. An appellate court does not often order a new trial solely based on evidentiary error.

An error of great magnitude may occur during the conduct of the trial, and the appellant's attorney may fail to timely and properly object. The "plain error" doctrine permits the appellate court to reverse a decision based on an error that is obvious and that adversely affects substantial rights of a party, even though the error was not properly preserved. See Section 12.9(D)(1)(c). This reversal seldom occurs.

J. APPELLATE REVIEW

Appellate courts allow judges wide latitude in deciding whether to admit or exclude evidence. This latitude affects the judgment of trial judges in making evidentiary rulings. Many judges are inclined to admit questionable evidence and overrule objections that seek to exclude borderline evidence. These judges reason that jurors can assess the weight afforded such evidence and base their verdict on reliable evidence.

An appellate court is more likely to reverse an evidentiary ruling if a judge excludes evidence, than when the judge admits the evidence. The appellate courts reason that the exclusion of this evidence from consideration by the fact finder may deny a party a substantial right to a trial based on complete evidence. Consequently, judges, in ruling on close evidentiary issues, are more inclined to admit rather than exclude evidence. Similarly, arbitrators tend to accept evidence because one of the few grounds to challenge an award is improper evidence exclusion.

The standard of review an appellate court employs depends on the evidentiary error the judge has made. Section 12.9(G) explains the various standards of review, which also apply to evidentiary rulings.

§ 4.6   OBJECTIONS TO DIRECT EXAMINATION QUESTIONS

This section explains common objections to the improper form of questions asked on direct examination. The cross-examiner can use these objections to force the direct examiner to ask proper questions. Some of these objections may also apply to questions asked on cross-examination.

A. LEADING

Generally, asking leading questions during direct examination is improper. Fed.R.Evid. 611(c). Leading questions are questions that contain and suggest the answer. The problem with leading questions is that the counsel in effect testifies instead of the witness. Leading questions are permitted in limited situations during direct examination. See Section 7.7(B). Leading questions are readily permitted on cross-examination, unless, in some jurisdictions, the witness is clearly supportive of the party represented by the cross-examiner.

Example (On Direct Examination):

Examining Attorney:

Q: Ms. Dickens, you were not convinced it was the best of times and the worst of times, were you?

Objecting Lawyer:

Objection, your Honor. Leading question.

Or

Objection, counsel is testifying and leading.

Judge:

Sustained.

Usually a leading question is one that can be answered by a "yes" or "no" or a specific one or two word answer contained in that question. However, not all questions that call for "yes" or "no" or a short specific answer are leading. In order for a question to be leading, it must *suggest* and *contain* the answer. Even if leading questions are asked, there may not be any tactical advantage in objecting to them. Leading questions are often ineffective on direct examination because the fact finder does not hear the witness testify about the facts, since the lawyer is telling the story and the witness is merely affirming the lawyer's testimony.

Responses to a leading objection:

• Rephrase the question and ask a non-leading question.

• Explain that the question falls within one of the permissible uses of leading questions on direct examination. See Section 7.7(B).

- Explain that the case will proceed more efficiently if there are a reasonable number of leading questions. Judges sometimes prefer efficiency over strict adherence to the rules of evidence.

B. NARRATIVE

An objection may be made to a question that calls for a narrative answer or to an answer that turns into a narrative. Fed.R.Evid. 611. Our system involves witnesses telling their story through questions asked by counsel. An improper narrative question allows the witness to tell a long, uncontrolled story. For example, "In your own words, Mr. Jefferson, tell the jury everything that happened to you on July 4."

Narrative questions allow the witness to interject inadmissible testimony without giving the opposing attorney a reasonable opportunity to object in a timely manner. Sometimes a witness will give a narrative response to an otherwise permissible question. A narrative answer may be objected to as being a narrative answer or as being non-responsive. As a tactical consideration, however, the attorney may not want to object to a witness' narrative if the "rambling" testimony tends to make the opponent's direct examination ineffective.

Example:

Examining Attorney:

Q: Ms. Kellogg, what happened as you pushed your shopping cart down the cereal aisle at Ortiz's market?

A: I went to the center left aisle to pick up my six-year-old's favorite cereal. When I reached for a box of Frosted Flakes, my right foot suddenly slid sideways. I kept sliding. I didn't notice the slippery floor. My ankle turned, and I fell down on my right hip. I couldn't move. I felt nauseated. I then saw the wet spots on the floor. Everything went black and white. I closed my eyes. I heard people talking, but I couldn't look up to answer. When I looked up, there was a cast on my right leg and an IV in my arm, and I felt . . .

Objecting Lawyer:

Objection. Improper narration.

Judge:

Sustained.

A narrative answer is improper because our system requires specific answers to questions and not rambling responses to undirected questions. A judge has discretion to sustain or overrule a narrative objection and will consider the scope of the question, its timing, the preparation of the witness, the ability of the witness to be responsive, and the ability of the attorney to control the examination.

Broad questions may well be appropriate. Potentially objectionable narrative questions will be allowed because the judge realizes the witness will only give a brief response and the attorney can control the examination. For example, the attorney may ask the witness "Then what happened?" This question, if literally answered, would permit the witness to provide a lengthy response explaining everything that happened. A well-prepared witness will ordinarily give a short response, and the examining attorney will follow up with a responsive question, such as: "Then what happened after you arrived at the Temple?"

Responses to a narrative objection:

• Politely interrupt the witness and stop the rambling.

• Ask a specific question to maintain control of the direction of the examination.

• Explain to the judge that these open-ended questions save time.

• Explain that the narrative answers cover uncontroverted, or preliminary matters and not significant issues in the case.

• Say to the witness: "I will now ask you some specific questions to which you can give specific answers."

C. NON-RESPONSIVE

A non-responsive or volunteered answer occurs when a witness provides information not required by the question. Any response that extends beyond the specific information required is objectionable. Fed.R.Evid. 611. Some authorities believe that only the examining attorney can make this objection. In practice, however, the vast majority of judges will sustain an opposing lawyer's objection if the witness on direct examination testifies in a non-responsive manner.

Example:

Examining Attorney:

Q: Ms. O'Leary, when did you become a fire fighter?

A: Well, I had three brothers, and I was the only girl in the family. The whole time we were growing up on DeKoven Street, I was competing with the guys and doing what they did. They wanted to fight fires, and so I started . . .

Objecting Lawyer:

Objection. Witness is non-responsive.

Judge:

Sustained. Just answer the question asked of you.

Responses to a non-responsive objection:

• Interrupt the witness politely and stop the non-responsive answer.

• Ask more specific questions which suggest shorter answers.

D. VAGUE AND AMBIGUOUS

A question should be clear and understandable so that the witness can understand what is being asked. Vague and ambiguous questions are improper and disadvantageous. Fed.R.Evid. 611. Questions may be vague regarding time and circumstances of an event, or may be ambiguous in the choice of words used, or may not make reasonable sense.

Example:

Examining Attorney:

Q: Socrates, who attended your class?

Objecting Lawyer:

Objection. Vague and ambiguous. The witness has taught different classes in Athens and Thermopolis.

Judge:

Sustained.

There may not be a tactical advantage to objecting to vague and ambiguous questions asked on direct if the fact finder becomes confused with the line of questioning. An objection to a confusing question may assist the direct examiner in making clear something that is being presented in a puzzling manner. The better tactic may be not to object but to allow the jurors to remain perplexed regarding the other side's story.

Responses to a vague and ambiguous objection:

• Rephrase the question to make it clearer.

• Ask the witness if the question was understood.

• If the objection is overruled, repeat the question or request it be read back to show how clear the question was and how opposing counsel is attempting to interrupt a proper direct examination.

E. CUMULATIVE

Cumulative evidence is repetitious evidence. The judge has the discretion to control cumulative and repetitive evidence. Fed.R.Evid. 403 and 611. Evidence is cumulative when a series of witnesses testify to the same thing or when a series of exhibits provide identical information. If the evidence is important, additional witnesses or exhibits may corroborate the same facts without being cumulative. However, when many witnesses testify to the same event or when many nearly identical exhibits are offered, they serve no useful purpose and are therefore cumulative.

Example:

Examining Attorney:

Q: The defense calls Citizen Kane.

Objecting Lawyer:

May I be heard, your Honor?

Judge:

Approach the bench.

Objecting Lawyer:

Your Honor, I believe that counsel, through Citizen Kane, is trying to introduce more evidence of the plaintiff's alleged bad faith. This evidence is unnecessarily cumulative as this is the fourth witness testifying to the same thing.

Examining Attorney:

Your Honor, we have a right to introduce supportive and persuasive evidence to prove up our counterclaim based on the plaintiff's bad faith in bringing this action.

Judge:

I overrule the objection. The defense may introduce more evidence of the plaintiff's intent to harass the defendant. However, this is the last witness you may call on this point.

Responses to a cumulative objection:

*   Explain that this evidence is not repetitive, but adds important details to evidence already admitted.

- Explain to the judge that the evidence is not improperly cumulative. Rather, the corroborative evidence from additional sources is needed to buttress relevant facts.

- If the objection is sustained, continue on with the questioning and return to the confirming evidence later during the witness' story.

F. MISSTATEMENT OF EVIDENCE

Misstatement or mischaracterization of evidence is objectionable because it inaccurately describes evidence. Fed.R.Evid. 403 and 611. This objection may be used to object to responses by witnesses as well as to questions. A misstatement or mischaracterization of evidence may be made inadvertently or intentionally. An opposing attorney or witness may not remember exactly what was said in previous testimony or the characterization may be a description of a piece of evidence that can be described with more than one term. For example, a letter opener may arguably be referred to as a knife-like object. Whether the problem is caused inadvertently or intentionally, an objection should be asserted and the court should be requested to instruct the opposing attorney or witness to make proper reference to the evidence or testimony.

Example:

Examining Attorney:

Q: Ms. Baudelaire, what kind of meals did Count Olaf serve?

A: They were poisonous, especially the coconut cream cake that was laced with deadly venom from a pet snake . . .

Objecting Lawyer:

Objection. The witness is mischaracterizing the evidence. I ask that the witness be instructed to properly answer the question.

Judge:

Objection sustained. The jury is instructed to disregard that answer. The witness is directed to answer the question and not to add unnecessary descriptions.

Responses to a mischaracterization objection:

- Be more precise and narrow the scope of the question.

- Point out the specific evidence that has already been introduced referring to the question or answer.

- Explain that there is a source of evidence that will be introduced to support this question. Request that the court conditionally accept the answer subject to the introduction of supportive evidence.

- Explain that the characterization in the question or answer is a proper admissible opinion.

- Explain that the characterization by the witness is the way this witness ordinarily talks and expresses facts.

G. ASSUMING FACTS NOT IN EVIDENCE

This objection is used to object to questions that assume facts that have not been introduced in evidence. See Fed.R.Evid. 403 and 611. A direct examiner who faces this objection may revise the question to eliminate the assumption of fact or may tell the judge that the assumed fact will be proven later. If the latter course is taken, the assumed fact must be proven. If that fact is not proven later, the opposing attorney may request that the judge advise the jury to disregard such evidence.

Example:

Examining Attorney:

Q: Ms. Penelope, when did your husband, Mr. Ulysses, begin his search for you?

Objecting Lawyer:

Objection. There is no evidence introduced about any search.

Judge:

Sustained.

Responses to an assuming facts objection:

- Revise the question to bring out the questionable facts.

- If the witness can describe the facts, allow the witness to tell them.

- Make an offer of proof that the evidence will be introduced through another witness.

§ 4.7   OBJECTIONS TO CROSS-EXAMINATION QUESTIONS

This section explains common objections to improper questions asked on cross-examination. The direct examiner can use these objections to protect the witness from being asked objectionable questions.

A. REPETITIOUS

If a question has been asked and answered, an attorney may object to similar questions as repetitious. See Fed.R.Evid. 403 and 611. This objection prevents the opposing attorney from gaining undue advantage by repeating testimony. The form of the questions does not have to be identical in order to raise this objection. If a new question calls for an answer previously given on cross-examination, the question is objectionable as repetitious. This objection is also referred to as "asked and answered."

Example:

Examining Attorney:

Q: Mr. Hur, at the time you purchased this chariot, Ms. Spartacus handed you a written warranty, didn't she?

A: Yes.

Q: You understood the terms of that warranty, right?

A: I did.

Q: And you had an opportunity to read that warranty over, didn't you?

A: Yes.

Q: Ms. Spartacus specifically explained to you the length of that warranty.

A: She did.

Q: So that you understood how long the warranty would run, didn't you?

A: I did.

Q: And the length of the warranty was for XXX years, correct?

A: Yes.

Q: There was no question in your mind that you understood the length of time of that warranty, isn't that true, Mr. Hur?

Q: And so you fully understood that warranty term, isn't that right?

Objecting Lawyer:

Objection, your Honor. Repetitious.

Judge:

The objection is sustained.

Responses to a repetitious objection:

- Explain that the point needs to be emphasized on cross.

- Point out the witness is being evasive, requiring these questions.

- Ask other questions and emphasize this point during summation.

B. MISLEADING OR CONFUSING

A question must be reasonable, clear, and specific so that the witness knows what is being asked. See Fed.R.Evid. 403 and 611.

Example:

Examining Attorney:

Q: Mr. Quixote, since you ran away, you don't know whether Sancho did a good job or not, do you?

Objecting Lawyer:

Objection, your Honor, the words "good job" are vague and ambiguous.

Judge:

The objection is sustained.

Responses to a misleading objection:

- Ask if the witness understands the question.

- Rephrase the question so it's not misleading or confusing.

C. MULTIPLE OR COMPOUND QUESTIONS

A multiple or compound question presents two or more questions within a single question. These types of questions are objectionable because the answer will usually be ambiguous. Fed.R.Evid. 403 and 611. An example of a compound question is, "The defendant was dancing and also wearing tap shoes?" Answers to multiple or compound questions, which sometimes seem straightforward and understandable, can become extremely confusing when reviewing the record.

Example:

Examining Attorney:

Q: On the day of the alleged threat to Caesar's life, you talked to Brutus about Caesar's gladiator training and then you later visited the defendant at his villa to talk about minting new coins, didn't you?

Objecting Lawyer:

Objection, your Honor. Counsel is asking Mr. Augustus two questions at the same time.

Judge:

Sustained.

Response to a multiple question objection:

• Repeat one of the questions and ask the witness to answer that question and then ask the other question.

D. MISCHARACTERIZATION OF EVIDENCE

This objection is often used to object to questions on cross-examination that include facts that are not in evidence or statements that improperly misstate or mischaracterize the evidence. Fed.R.Evid. 403 and 611. The improper or mischaracterized statement may be an attempt to trick or confuse the witness and may also be an argumentative question. The issues for a cross-examiner are similar to those for a direct examiner who misstates or mischaracterizes the facts (see Section 4.6(F)), but a cross-examiner has more latitude to ask questions that fairly test the credibility or memory of a witness.

Example:

Examining Attorney:

Q: Ms. Newton, you saw your husband sitting under a tree contemplating the meaning of life when a kumquat fell on his temporal lobe stimulating his attentional imagination network, correct?

Objecting Lawyer:

Objection. There are no facts supporting these inaccurate and unfounded assumptions.

Judge:

Sustained.

Responses to a mischaracterization of evidence objection:

- Introduce the evidence before asking this question. Laying a foundation makes this objection inappropriate.

- Explain that evidence has been introduced that supports the question and refer to such evidence.

- Explain that such evidence will be introduced at a later stage of the trial, and request this evidence be conditionally admitted pending subsequent proof.

- Argue that cross-examination can test the memory and credibility of a witness and that the witness can deny the asserted facts if the witness disagrees with the assertion.

E. ARGUMENTATIVE

Any question that is essentially an argument is improper. See Fed.R.Evid. 611. The role of the attorney is to question and not to argue. An argumentative question either elicits no new information or harasses the witness. Argumentative questions often assume a sarcastic tenor: "Do you mean to tell me ... " or "Doesn't it seem strange that. . . ." Such statements should be saved for closing arguments.

Example:

Examining Attorney:

Q: Ms. Cruella De Vil, had you been keeping a proper look out, you know you would never have recklessly run over Pongo.

Objecting Lawyer:

I object to counsel arguing his case through this witness.

Judge:

Objection sustained.

Responses to an argumentative objection:

- Re-ask the question and eliminate the objectionable comment.

- Re-ask using a proper tone so the question sounds proper.

F.   IMPROPER IMPEACHMENT

Improper impeachment is an attempt to incorrectly discredit a witness or to refer to a statement someone else said. Fed.R.Evid. 613. Section 9.4(D) explains impeachment in detail. Improper impeachment may occur in a variety of ways. A cross-examiner may attempt to impeach the witness on a collateral, unimportant, or irrelevant matter, or may attempt to impeach the witness with a prior statement that is not materially inconsistent, or may try to impeach with inconsistent statements made by someone else and not this witness. Improper impeachment should be resisted.

Example:

Examining Attorney:

Q: Ms. Daedalus, in a prior statement you said that Icarus was wearing wings made of yellow wax, not golden wax, true?

Objecting Lawyer:

Objection, your Honor. The color of the wax is not inconsistent, and this impeachment effort is improper.

Judge:

Sustained.

Response to an improper impeachment objection:

- Explain how the impeachment is not collateral or is material.

- Ask additional cross-examination questions to establish the relevancy and importance of the impeachment.

G. BEYOND THE SCOPE

Questions that go beyond the permissible scope of an examination are objectionable. Fed.R.Evid. 611(b). Cross-examination is limited to the subject matter of the direct examination and matters relating to the witness' credibility. The credibility standard usually permits a broad range of questions. If the cross-examiner wishes to go beyond the scope of the direct examination, the cross-examiner must usually call the witness and ask leading questions on direct examination. The cross-examiner may raise new matters, however, if the court permits. Many judges view the scope of cross-examination liberally and permit wide-ranging examinations as long as the questions are relevant.

Example:

Examining Attorney:

Q: Ms. Ingalls-Wilder, you later lived in a little house on the prairie, didn't you?

Objecting Lawyer:

Objection, your Honor. The question goes beyond the scope of the direct which was limited to the Crow Peak mountain cabin.

Judge:

Sustained.

Responses to a beyond the scope objection:

- Point out the testimony from direct examination that relates to this question on cross-examination. The attorney may need to refer to the previous question or answer on direct that touched on the subject. If an objection to the scope of cross is anticipated, listen carefully during the direct for a related topic so it can be shown that this topic or a related topic was asked during direct examination.

- Explain that the questions relate to the credibility of the witness or another witness.

- Explain the judge or arbitrator has substantial discretion to allow questions to be asked beyond the scope of direct examination.

- Explain that if these questions are not permitted at this stage of the case, the witness will be recalled at a later stage that will only take more time and cause inconvenience to the witness.

§ 4.8   OBJECTIONS BASED ON THE EXCLUSIONARY RULES OF EVIDENCE

This section explains common objections used to exclude evidence. The judge decides whether an evidence rule requires the exclusion of evidence. The rules can be grouped into several categories with inquiries:

- *Irrelevant evidence.* Does the evidence have probative value?

- *Unfairly prejudicial evidence.* Whether the probative value outweighs its unfairly prejudicial impact?

- *Privileged information.* Is there sufficient evidence to support a finding that a privilege exists?

- *Lack of personal knowledge and improper opinion.* Does a witness have personal knowledge of a fact or a permissible opinion?

- *Lack of foundation for documents and other exhibits.* Is there evidence to support a finding that the exhibit is what it purports to be?

- *Constitutional limitations on evidence in criminal cases.* Is the evidence inadmissible because the defendant's constitutional rights were violated during a seizure or arrest?

- *Hearsay.* Are there sufficient preliminary facts to establish that a statement is not hearsay or falls within a hearsay exception?

Exclusionary rules may not be strictly enforced in a bench trial and even less so in administrative hearings and arbitrations. The major touchstones for admissible evidence in these forums include *relevancy* and *reliability*, as described previously. The exclusionary rules are still useful before these tribunals to evaluate the impact of evidence. The advocate can explain in summation how irrelevant or unreliable evidence is based on rationales underlying the applicable exclusionary rule.

A. IRRELEVANT EVIDENCE

1. Irrelevant (Fed.R.Evid. 401 and 402)

Evidence must be relevant in order to be admissible. Relevant evidence has probative value, which is the tendency to make more or less probable any facts of consequence to the outcome of the case. Relevant evidence is admissible; irrelevant evidence is not.

Relevant evidence may be either direct or circumstantial. Direct evidence is that which is proved by witnesses who testify to what they saw, heard, or experienced, or by physical evidence of the fact itself. Circumstantial evidence is that which can be reasonably inferred from other facts proven in the case. Most relevancy objections involve circumstantial evidence that requires inferences drawn from direct evidence.

Example:

Offer of Proof Evidence:

The defendant, Starlit Bandit, is identified as the robber of a convenience store. The owners have testified that the store was robbed at 9:45 a.m. and that the female robber wore a neon green jogging suit. A resident of an apartment building one block from the store identified the defendant as the person who ran past her building carrying a bag around 9:45 a.m. wearing a neon green running suit and is prepared to so testify.

Objection:

Irrelevant. There is an insufficient connection between these two observations.

Ruling:

Overruled. The close time proximity of the observations is sufficient to support a reasonable inference of fact.

Relevancy depends upon the evidence offered and the issues to be proven. In offering evidence, an attorney must have an explanation for the evidence's admissibility. In planning to introduce evidence, the attorney must be able to identify the specific issue to be proven by the evidence.

After an objection of irrelevancy is made, the judge may ask the examining attorney about the relevancy of the evidence if the relevancy is not apparent from the context of the case. If the attorney can explain a connection between an issue in the case and the evidence offered, the judge will be inclined to overrule the objection. If the offering attorney anticipates that the judge may sustain the objection, the attorney may ask to be heard before the judge rules and explain the relevancy to the judge. If the objection is sustained, the offering attorney should make an offer of proof and explain the relevancy to the judge.

Judges often defer to the judgment of the attorney regarding admissibility if the attorney can articulate a basis for its relevancy. If the attorney can explain reasons supporting the relevancy of the evidence, the objection will more likely be overruled. If a lawyer hesitates or cannot reasonably explain why evidence is relevant, it's more probable that the objection will be sustained.

2.   Immaterial (Fed.R.Evid. 401 and 402)

Evidence is material if it has some logical relationship to the case. Materiality has been subsumed by Federal Rules of Evidence 401 and 402 and similar state rules. The concept of materiality relates to the concept of what is of "consequence" to a case. What is of consequence depends on the scope of the pleadings, the issues of the case, and the substantive law. Materiality is included in an objection based on relevancy, and is no longer recognized as a distinct objection in most jurisdictions because immaterial evidence is almost always irrelevant.

Example:

Evidence:

Plaintiff Cinderella seeks to prove that the defendant's improper maintenance of a stairway also contributed to the falls of two other residents of the defendant's castle. The other accident victims were hurt when they caught their heels in loose carpeting and tripped.

Objection:

Irrelevant.

Ruling:

Overruled.

Admissible if plaintiff shows that all the relevant circumstances were substantially identical to her own accident: the accidents all occurred on the same stairway, the same carpeting was in the same loose condition, the same means of securing the carpeting to the stairs was used, and the lighting conditions and other circumstances were the same.

3.   Conditional Relevancy

The relevance of a specific item of evidence may be conditioned upon the proof of other facts. In these situations, the court may conditionally admit the proffered evidence, subject to the proof of the additional facts. If those additional facts are not proved, the opposing attorney can object to the admissibility of the previous evidence and request that it be stricken. The process is sometimes referred to as "connecting up." If the evidence is not connected up, it becomes inadmissible.

Example:

Objecting Lawyer:

Your Honor, this court allowed into evidence testimony from Zoe Neytiri regarding a telepathic conversation that supposedly took place on January 6. We objected, and counsel for plaintiff said that she would later offer evidence establishing the date of the conversation. Such evidence has never been established, and the previous evidence should be stricken.

Judge:

The previous objection is sustained and the evidence stricken.

4.   Unfairly Prejudicial (Fed.R.Evid. 403)

Relevant evidence is inadmissible when its unfairly prejudicial effect substantially outweighs its probative value. The key to a successful assertion of an objection based on prejudicial evidence is that the evidence is unfairly prejudicial. All evidence is prejudicial in the sense that it hurts one party and helps the other party. Only evidence that is *unfairly* prejudicial may be excluded. This objection may be made against evidence that appeals to the passion or prejudice of the jurors, to exhibits that unnecessarily display gross injuries, or to an event or scene described in overly graphic or gruesome detail.

Inadmissible unfairly prejudicial evidence includes the following categories specifically barred by the Federal Rules of Evidence and similar state rules of evidence.

a.   *Improper Character Evidence (Fed.R.Evid. 404 and 405)*

The general rule is that evidence of a person's character traits are not admissible to prove that the person acted in conformity with those traits on a particular occasion. For example, evidence that a defendant has caused an auto accident in the past should not be allowed to prove that the defendant caused an accident on a later occasion.

Section 7.10(D) explains the situations and methods under which character evidence may be admissible in criminal and civil cases. If character evidence is introduced in situations other than those permitted by the rules, an objection should be made.

Example:

Evidence:

Doctor House is accused of medical malpractice for transplanting plaintiff's brain. Plaintiff's attorney presents evidence that Doctor House is an arrogant, mean, condescending, and rude physician.

Objection:

Unfairly prejudicial. Improper character evidence.

Ruling:

Sustained.

This evidence of the doctor's bad character is not admissible to prove the doctor's negligence. The doctor may be an arrogant and rude physician, but that perspective is unfairly prejudicial because the fact finder may be improperly influenced and find the doctor negligent based on the doctor's bad character.

b.　*Improper Habit Evidence (Fed.R.Evid. 406)*

Improper habit evidence is inadmissible. Section 7.10(E) explains the introduction of proper habit evidence on direct examination. An objection should be made when evidence of improper habits is being introduced. An example of an improper "habit" that is usually excluded involves evidence of intemperance. Evidence of excessive drinking is ordinarily inadmissible to prove drunkenness in accident cases. Similarly, evidence of other assaults is usually inadmissible in a civil assault case, unless the previous assaults are nearly identical. This type of evidence is usually deemed inadmissible because the fact finder may be unfairly inclined to find the party guilty or liable because of past bad conduct.

Example:

Evidence:

Plaintiff testified that the defendant, Cameron, backed his car out of Ferris Bueller's driveway without looking, and ran into Plaintiff's car. Cameron claimed that he didn't see Plaintiff's car before he backed out because Plaintiff was speeding. Cameron's witnesses would testify the defendant periodically drove them to school, and he usually looked both ways before backing up.

Objection:

Improper habit evidence.

Ruling:

Sustained.

This testimony is inadmissible evidence of habit. There is insubstantial evidence from these witnesses who did not have sufficient opportunities with the Defendant to establish that Defendant's looking both ways was a matter of habit.

---

c.　*Subsequent Remedial Measures (Fed.R.Evid. 407)*

The term "subsequent remedial measures" refers to actions taken after an event that, if taken before the event, would have made the event less likely to occur. An example is fixing a car's brakes after an accident caused by faulty brakes. Evidence of subsequent remedial measures is not admissible to prove negligence or fault in a previous event. Such evidence is considered to be misleading because the repairs inaccurately imply a recognition of liability or may divert the fact finder's attention from the real cause of the accident.

For example, evidence that a railroad installed a crossing gate and warning lights after an accident should not be admissible to prove the railroad's negligence because, in hearing the evidence, the fact finder might incorrectly infer that the railroad admitted its fault. If this type of evidence were admissible to prove fault, many repairs would not be made for fear that liability would be imposed on the party making repairs.

The exclusion of subsequent remedial measures does not apply where the issue to be proved involves controverted matters of ownership, control, feasibility of precautionary measures, or impeachment of a witness. These reasons make subsequent remedial measures admissible.

Example:

Evidence:

Plaintiff Rose DeWitt Bukater slipped on ice on the deck of the titanic ship. Defendant knew that this slippery condition was likely to occur but claimed that there was no effective way to make the ship safe. After the accident, Defendant spread de-icer on the deck.

Objection:

Unfairly prejudicial evidence.

Ruling:

Sustained.

If offered to show Defendant's fault, but overruled if introduced to show feasibility of precautionary measures.

---

d. Offers of Compromise (Fed.R.Evid. 408)

Evidence of offers to resolve a dispute or attempts to settle a lawsuit out of court is inadmissible, because the evidence might be misinterpreted as an admission of liability. Parties are encouraged to negotiate and settle cases before trial, and all statements, discussions, and admissions made during settlement talks are excluded from evidence. However, evidence of a compromise offer to prove bias of a witness or to rebut a contention of undue delay may be admitted as an exception to the general rule.

Example:

Evidence:

Mr. Ferrari and Ms. Porsche were involved in an automobile accident where Mr. Ferrari's fender was dented. Each party believed the other was at fault, and an argument ensued. Ms. Porsche didn't want the hassle of going to court and gave Mr. Ferrari some money to fix his car. A few months later Mr. Ferrari developed some health problems that he claims were caused by the accident. Mr. Ferrari sued Ms. Porsche for personal injury, and attempted to present evidence at trial that the defendant paid for the plaintiff's damaged car after the accident.

Objection:

Unfairly prejudicial evidence as an offer of compromise.

Ruling:

Sustained.

The fact finder might interpret the defendant's payment to fix plaintiff's car as an admission of liability for the accident, and for plaintiff's later health problems.

---

e.　Payment of Medical Expenses (Fed.R.Evid. 409)

Evidence of payment, promises to make payment, or offers to make payment for medical expenses by the opposing party may not be offered to prove liability for an injury. However, this evidence may be admissible to prove other issues in a case.

f.　Plea Bargains (Fed.R.Evid. 410)

A person accused of a criminal offense may offer to plead guilty to a lesser offense rather than plead not guilty and go to trial. The person may also decide to plead nolo contendere, which means that the person neither admits nor denies guilt, but agrees that if the case went to trial there would be sufficient evidence for a jury to make a finding of guilt. Offers to plead guilty to a lesser offense and pleas of nolo contendere are not admissions of guilt, and may not be used as evidence against the person in a later action. Once a guilty plea is accepted, a guilty finding becomes admissible under limited circumstances in another case. If a guilty plea is entered and later withdrawn, it becomes inadmissible.

g.　Liability Insurance (Fed.R.Evid. 411)

The existence or nonexistence of insurance is not admissible regarding an issue of negligence or wrongful actions. This is because the fact finder may believe an insured person does not use as much care as an uninsured person or may improperly decide to give insurance company's money to a needy plaintiff. Evidence regarding insurance is admissible if offered to impeach or to prove agency, ownership, control, or bias.

h.　Religious Beliefs or Opinions (Fed.R.Evid. 610)

Evidence of a person's religious beliefs or opinions is not admissible to show that the person is more or less credible.

Example:

Evidence by prosecuting attorney on cross-examination of a witness for the defense:

Q: Are you sure you heard the victim, Sookie Stackhouse, cry out on the night of the accident?

A: Oh, yea. Real clear.

Q: But you also hear voices when you speak in tongues at church, right?

Objection:

Unfairly prejudicial.

Ruling:

Sustained.

Fact finders might adversely rely on the witness' religious beliefs.

B. PRIVILEGED COMMUNICATION (FED.R.EVID. 501)

A privileged communication consists of a communication between persons having a confidential relationship. The policy behind the privilege is to encourage open, honest communication between certain persons. A valid objection based on privilege will bar the underlying statement, writing, email, or other message from being disclosed.

Common privileges include: attorney/client, doctor/patient, spousal communications, clergy/penitent, trade/business secrets, and news sources. State statutes, constitutional provisions, and case law determine available privileges in a jurisdiction. Every privilege has a number of elements that must be proved. The privilege may not be successfully asserted unless evidence is introduced to establish these elements.

1. Attorney/Client Privilege

The establishment of an attorney/client privilege requires:

(a) A professional relationship between an attorney and a client who seeks legal advice, involving

(b) A communication made in confidence

(c) Between an attorney (or agent of the attorney such as a paralegal) and client, who is the holder of the privilege.

2. Doctor/Patient Privilege

The establishment of a doctor/patient privilege requires:

(a) A doctor/patient relationship in which the patient seeks medical assistance, involving

(b) A communication regarding medical information, including examinations, reports, tests, and notes made

(c) Between a doctor (or medical assistant) and a patient, who is the holder of the privilege.

3. Marital Communications Privilege

A limited privilege recognized in most jurisdictions protects confidential communications made between married spouses. Neither spouse can testify, during or after marriage, concerning certain communications made between them while married. Both spouses hold the privilege.

The establishment of a marital communication privilege requires:

(a) A marriage relationship, involving

(b) Confidential, private communications

(c) Made during the marriage.

4. Waiver of Privilege

Any privilege may be waived if:

- The holder of the privilege or the attorney with the consent of the holder knowingly and expressly waives the privilege;

- Voluntary disclosure of the privileged information occurs during discovery or hearing or trial testimony;

- No objection is made to eliciting privileged communications;

- A privileged matter is discussed in the presence of a third person;

- An eavesdropper, without using surreptitious means, overhears a privileged communication; or

- The holder raises a claim or defense that places the privileged matter in issue.

If a privilege has been waived, the communications are admissible.

Example:

Evidence:

In the hallway outside the courtroom, Defendant Christine Vole discusses strategy with her attorney. A witness who plaintiff intends to call to corroborate evidence sits three feet from defendant and defendant's attorney. In direct examination, opposing counsel questions the witness about the substance of what the witness overheard in defendant's communication with her attorney.

Objection:

This information is protected by the attorney/client privilege.

Ruling:

Overruled.

An attorney may assert the privilege for the holder and seek to exclude the confidential communication. However, in this example, the defendant voluntarily communicated within earshot of the witness and this constitutes waiver in most jurisdictions.

C. LACK OF PERSONAL KNOWLEDGE/IMPROPER OPINION (FED.R.EVID. 601 AND 602)

A witness must be competent to testify. Competency embodies four factors: an understanding of the oath or affirmation, the perception of events, the recollection of those events, and the ability to communicate. Section 7.2(A) describes each of these factors.

Generally, a witness is presumed competent to testify unless challenged by the opponent or by a judge or arbitrator (rarely done). Objections to the competency of a witness are usually made before a witness takes the stand. If a witness appears incompetent while testifying, the opposing attorney may object and "voir dire" the witness to establish that the witness is not competent because the witness does not understand the oath, did not perceive a relevant event, does not remember the event, or cannot communicate. Because witnesses are usually minimally competent, opposing lawyers rely on cross-examination to impeach the witnesses' story.

Example:

Evidence:

Witness saw a collision between a meteor and an asteroid.

Examining Attorney:

Q: Ms. Sagan, what was the speed the meteor traveling?

Objecting Lawyer:

Objection. Your Honor, this witness is not competent to testify to the speed of the meteor. She did not see it for a sufficient amount of time before the collision because she was running to a bunker.

Ruling:

Sustained.

Some judges would overrule the objection and allow the witness to testify the meteor was moving "very fast" for what it is worth.

1. Lack of Personal Knowledge (Fed.R.Evid. 602)

A witness may not testify to any matter unless evidence is introduced which is sufficient to support a finding that the witness has personal knowledge of the matter. If the proponent does not establish that the witness has personal knowledge of the matters about which the witness will testify, an objection to the testimony should be made. Whenever a witness is about to testify, the opposing attorney should ask: "How does the witness know this information?" or "What is the source of the information the witness is about to give?" If the opposing attorney knows the witness has firsthand knowledge and the information is reliable, no objection should be made. If the opposing attorney believes the witness does not have firsthand knowledge or that the source of information is unreliable, an objection should be made. The proper objection is either lack of personal knowledge or lack of foundation.

Example:

Examining Attorney:

Q: What happened in the fencing room?

A: I told D'Artagnan and Aramis that I no longer was going to be a Musketeer and then I left the room, and they continued to talk about. . . .

Objecting Lawyer:

Objection. Your Honor, the witness has no personal knowledge of what D'Artagnan and Aramis said after he left the room.

Judge:

Sustained.

---

2.   Lack of Foundation (Fed.R.Evid. 901 and 903)

Foundation is preliminary information that must be established before other evidence is admissible. Section 7.2(C) describes and provides examples of foundations. A lack of foundation objection is used to prevent the introduction of evidence or to compel facts to be established.

Example:

Examining Attorney:

Q: Ms. Toad, what happened to your car on the way home?

A: It broke down.

Q: What caused the car to break down?

Objecting Lawyer:

Objection. There's been no foundation laid for this witness to respond to that question.

Judge:

The objection is sustained.

If the objection does not keep the evidence out but forces the examining attorney to establish the missing element of foundation, it may be strategically inappropriate to object because the additional foundation may make the evidence appear more reliable, especially if the examining attorney can readily supply the missing facts.

Example:

Examining Attorney:

Q: Before your car broke down, Ms. Toad, what did you first notice?

A: I saw black smoke coming out of the engine compartment.

Q: What did you see next?

A: I heard this explosion and the hood of the engine blew off, and I saw it land about a hundred feet to the side of the car.

Q: Then what happened?

A: I saw a huge ball of fire erupt from the engine compartment.

Q: What happened after you heard this explosion and saw this huge ball of fire erupt from the engine compartment?

A: The car broke down.

---

3. Opinion

There are two types of opinion testimony: that given by an expert and that given by a layperson.

a. *Expert Opinion (Fed.R.Evid. 702 to 705)*

Expert opinion is admissible to provide conclusions or inferences beyond the abilities of the fact finder. Experts can give opinion testimony after the judge or arbitrator determines:

- The subject matter of the opinion is based on scientific, technical, or other specialized knowledge and not on common knowledge.

- The area of expertise is well recognized or accepted by other well-recognized experts.

- The opinion will assist the trier of fact to understand evidence or determine a fact in issue.

- The expert, by way of knowledge, skill, experience, training, or education, possesses sufficient expertise to render an opinion.

- The basis of the opinion is reliable and will assist the trier of fact.

Objections should be made if these factors have not been met. Chapter 10 explains the intricacies of expert witness examination.

Example:

Evidence:

Annie Oakley's testimony establishes she is qualified as a ballistics expert and that based on tests conducted on the handgun found in William Cody's possession, it is her opinion, based upon her education, training, and experience in ballistics analysis, that the bullet that killed the buffalo was fired from Mr. Cody's gun.

Objection:

Improper expert opinion.

Ruling:

Overruled.

Ballistics is a widely accepted area of expertise in the courts; the witness is qualified as an expert; and the expert opinion will help the fact finder.

b. Lay Witness Opinion (Fed.R.Evid. 701)

Lay witnesses may render opinions and conclusions if the opinion is based on the perception of the witness and is helpful to a clear understanding or determination of a fact in issue. Lay witnesses can render opinions if they have personal knowledge to support their perceptions and if there is a rational basis for the conclusion. As examples: (1) A witness may not testify to what a person was thinking but may render an opinion regarding the appearance of the person from which the fact finder may infer the person was thinking. (2) A lay witness may not testify that someone had a specific type of fracture but may testify that the person appeared to have a broken arm.

There are many opinions and conclusions a lay witness may render. Permissible lay opinions may be given regarding speed, distance, time, appearances, conditions, emotions, age, health, sobriety, value of personal property, and other rational perceptions. Lay witnesses may testify that a person appeared nervous, happy, sad, scared, excited, or drunk. Inadmissible lay opinions are those that exceed the perception of the witness, are not rationally based, or do not assist the fact finder.

Lay witnesses may testify to a conclusion in some situations even though they are unable to explain specific observations that support the conclusion. The most common example involves the formation of an instantaneous opinion regarding matters that are observed, referred to as the collective facts doctrine. For example, an eyewitness to an accident in which a pedestrian was hit by a car can testify to the conclusion that the car could not have swerved in time to avoid hitting the pedestrian. It would be difficult, if not impossible, for the witness to testify to specific, detailed facts that support the opinion. This type of conclusion assists the jury in determining the facts and is admissible in most jurisdictions.

Example:

Examining Attorney:

Q: What did you see, Ms. Guinness?

A: I saw the defendant holding a can of beer in one hand and staggering as he walked over to me.

Q: What else?

A: His eyes were bloodshot, he smelled like a brewery, and he slurred his words.

Q: Do you have an opinion about his condition?

A: Yes.

Q: What is your opinion?

A: He was drunk.

Q: What else did you conclude?

A: He was negligent when he drove the car while drunk and he caused the accident.

Objecting Lawyer:

Objection. Improper opinion.

Judge:

Sustained.

While the witness may testify that the defendant was drunk when she talked to him, the witness cannot draw the conclusion that the defendant was negligent because she did not perceive the event and the opinion infringes on an ultimate issue of the case.

4. Speculation (Fed.R.Evid. 602 and 701)

A question that asks the witness to guess or engage in conjecture is objectionable. Speculation by a witness about what could have happened is of little probative value. Words like if, should, could, and similar phrases in a question may render a question susceptible to this objection.

Example:

Examining Attorney:

Q: How close were you to Galavant when he was knocked off his horse?

A: About fifteen feet away.

Q: Could Madalena have possibly avoided Galavant if she had been cantering instead of galloping her horse?

Objecting Lawyer:

Objection, the question calls for speculation.

Judge:

Sustained.

D. DOCUMENTS

Four evidence rules determine the admissibility of a document:

- *Relevancy,* explained in Section 4.8(A);

- *Hearsay,* explained in Section 4.8(F);

- *Original writing (best evidence),* explained in this section; and

- *Authentication,* explained in this section and Section 8.6.

Whenever a document is introduced, an opposing attorney should review the document for potential objections and determine whether these objections have been overcome by the attorney offering the document. Parts of a document may also be objectionable, and the attorney should scrutinize the entire document to make sure all the paragraphs, sentences, phrases, and words are admissible. If any one of these evidence rules precludes the introduction of all or part of a document, an objection should be made to exclude the document or its objectionable parts. Section 8.4(F) explains the process of redacting documentary exhibits.

Example:

Examining Attorney:

Your Honor, Ms. Emily Dickinson offers Exhibit No. 640, the poem, as evidence.

Objecting Lawyer:

I object, your Honor, to the admission of a part of this Exhibit. I object to the introduction of the handwritten notes in the margin of this document. There has been no foundation made to authenticate the handwriting, and this handwritten statement constitutes inadmissible hearsay.

Judge:

Sustained. The handwritten notes in the left margin are excluded from evidence and are to be removed. The remainder of Exhibit No. 640 is received in evidence.

---

1. Original Writings (Fed.R.Evid. 1001 to 1007)

The modern "original writings" rule permits originals and duplicate originals to be introduced to prove the contents of a writing, unless a question exists regarding the authenticity of the original or if it would be unfair to introduce a duplicate. This rule is also known as the "best evidence" rule, which is a misleading term. There never has been, and is not now, any requirement that the "best" or most persuasive evidence be introduced. The traditional "best evidence" rule required that the original of the document be introduced to prove its contents, and did not permit copies of the original.

Modern evidence law recognizes that there may be a number of "originals" of a document and that mechanical copy machines, electronically stored information, or computer printers produce accurate and reliable duplicate originals. Documents covered by the original writings rule include all written or electronic documents, recordings, and photographs. Neither the modern rule nor the traditional rule applies to oral testimony.

The modern rule specifically provides that duplicates are admissible to the same extent as an original unless there is a question about the authenticity of the original, or some other unfairness. The modern rule also provides that if neither the original nor a duplicate exist, if the original and copies have been inadvertently lost or destroyed, or if the documents cannot be obtained by any available judicial process or subpoena, other evidence of the contents of the writing is admissible.

Example:

Examining Attorney:

Q: Is there a lease for the rental property in Jurassic Park?

A: Yes. There is a printed, signed lease.

Q: Describe the terms of the lease regarding giant frilled lizards.

Objecting Lawyer:

Objection. The best evidence of the terms of that lease requires that the written lease be introduced instead of oral testimony about the lease.

Judge:

Sustained.

Some evidence that is contained in a document may be admissible through oral testimony without the need to introduce the document. There are three specific situations where oral testimony provides reliable evidence without the need for the available document to be admitted.

a.   Short Descriptions

A witness may testify to a few or several words inscribed on a sign, label, tag, subject matter line, poster, display, and similar documents. Because there may be only a few prominent words on these items, the testimony is reliable. If an item contained a lengthy statement, then the original writing rule would apply. For example, a witness can testify that a sign read "no trespassing," but cannot testify regarding a sign containing several detailed sentences of information.

b.   Independent Facts

Facts that exist independently of a document and that are known to a witness may be established without requiring that the document be produced. For example, a witness may testify that a payment was made and not have to produce a credit card paid receipt or a reproduction of a paid bill. For another example, a tenant may testify to the amount and due date of the rent paid without having to produce the original lease. In these examples, the facts are independently known without reliance on the document because the witness paid or received the money. On the other hand, a written document is required to establish facts that are not independent of the document, such as detailed terms or provisions.

c.   Collateral Matter

If the writing, recording, or photograph is collaterally (indirectly) related to the issue to be proved, and the need for producing the original is minimal, secondary evidence by way of oral testimony will be permitted. For example, if a witness testifies to a date that appears in a diary or electronic calendar, the original of the diary or calendar need not be introduced unless the actual date is very significant in the case.

2.   Lack of Authentication (Fed.R.Evid. 901 and 902)

Writings, both paper and electronic, must be authenticated to be admissible, that is, they must be shown to be what they purport to be. Authentication is a foundation requirement for writings. Section 8.6 explains authentication requirements for various documents. A lack of authentication objection is identical to a lack of foundation objection.

Example:

Evidence:

In a copyright case, Shakespeare introduces a letter that he claims was written and signed by Roger Bacon.

Objection:

The letter is not authentic because there is no testimony that the signature of Mr. Bacon is genuine and he denies writing it.

Ruling:

Sustained

If evidence of the authenticity is introduced, the exhibit is admissible.

3. Parol Evidence Rule

The parol evidence rule provides that a written agreement cannot be contradicted or modified by oral or written evidence of a prior or contemporaneous agreement. Exceptions to this rule include: when the contract is ambiguous, when the writing is not intended to be a complete expression of the agreement, or when fraud or mistake was committed in the formation of the contract.

Example:

Evidence:

Phineas Fogg agreed to buy a hot air balloon from Jules Verne for $65,000. Verne said he would supply propane gas for one year without charge. Fogg and Verne signed a contract that stated Fogg purchased the balloon for $65,000, but did not mention anything about the gas. When Fogg later attempted to obtain the propane gas, Verne told him he would have to pay for it. Fogg sued Verne, and Fogg attempts to testify about the free fuel term.

Objection:

The parol evidence rule prohibits testimony contradicting or modifying a writing.

Ruling:

Sustained.

If the agreement regarding the gas was indeed part of this contract, it should have been in writing.

E. CONSTITUTIONAL LIMITATIONS IN CRIMINAL CASES

Evidence that may be reliable under the rules of evidence may be excluded in a criminal case because it was not obtained by the government in a fair way. The Bill of Rights and the Fourteenth Amendment establish limitations on the government. Criminal constitutional exclusionary rules were developed by the federal and state courts to exclude evidence obtained in a way that violated the defendant's constitutional rights. For example, if evidence or statements were obtained from a defendant through an unconstitutional search or improper interrogation of the defendant by the police, they will not be admissible even though they would be admissible under the general rules of evidence.

F. HEARSAY (FED.R.EVID. 801 AND 802)

Hearsay is an out-of-court statement offered to prove the truth of the matter asserted. See Fed.R.Evid. 801. Hearsay occurs when a witness repeats an out-of-court statement. The declarant of the statement can be either the testifying witness or another person. Hearsay is excluded because it involves defects making it unreliable:

- The fact finder has no opportunity to observe the credibility of the declarant when the statement was made, to gauge the sincerity, perception, or memory of the declarant, or to resolve ambiguities in the declarant's statement.

- The out-of-court statement may not be restated accurately because the witness may have misheard or misunderstood the statement.

- When the statement was made the declarant was not under oath.

- It may not be possible to cross-examine the declarant.

Most hearsay statements are admissible either because the statements do not meet the legal definition of hearsay or because an exception provides for their admissibility. Most out of court statements may be repeated in a trial or hearing because they are sufficiently trustworthy for the fact finder to rely on them. Cross-examination is available to reduce their reliability.

This section provides a method of analyzing out-of-court statements to assess whether they are or are not hearsay and to determine whether exceptions exist to admit the hearsay statements. This section defines hearsay, explains why many out-of-court statements are not hearsay, and describes the more common exceptions to the rule against hearsay.

1. Definition (Fed.R.Evid. 801)

There are three essential factors to a hearsay statement. If any one factor is absent, the statement is not hearsay.

The first factor is that the "statement" must be an oral or written assertion or nonverbal conduct intended to be an assertion. Hearsay statements may be oral, written, or asserted conduct. Oral testimony and written documents are hearsay statements, but not all conduct is a statement within the meaning of hearsay. Only assertive conduct constitutes hearsay. Assertive conduct is conduct that is intended by the actor to be an assertion. For example, during a line-up, the victim points her finger at the defendant. This is assertive nonverbal conduct. The statement implied in that conduct is "the defendant did it."

The second factor is that the statement must be an "out-of-court" statement. A hearsay statement is a prior statement made by a declarant outside the courtroom that is repeated by the witness in court. Three examples illustrate this factor:

- If the witness, Ichabod Crane, on the stand states, "Brom Bones said the horseman is headless," that statement is an out-of-court statement.

- If witness Ichabod Crane on the stand states, "I said the horseman is headless," that statement is also an out-of-court statement.

- If witness Ichabod Crane on the stand states, "The horseman is headless, and I saw it," that testimony is not hearsay.

The first two examples are out-of-court statements because they were made outside of the courtroom and were repeated in the courtroom. The third example is not a restatement of a prior statement, but a description of an event.

The third factor is that the out-of-court statement is offered to prove the truth of what the statement says. If the statement is offered for any other purpose, it is not hearsay. One way of determining whether the third factor has been met is to compare "what the statement proves" with "what the proponent is trying to prove." If there is a match, the statement is hearsay. If there is not a match, the statement is not hearsay. For example, a witness testifies that Mr. Black Elk said it was snowing on Mt. Rushmore on May 1. If the statement is offered to prove that it was actually snowing on Mt. Rushmore on May 1, the statement is hearsay. If the statement is offered to prove that the witness could identify the voice of Mr. Black Elk, the statement is not hearsay.

2. Out-of-Court Statements That Are Not Hearsay (Fed.R.Evid. 802)

Out-of-court statements that are admissible include:

- Statements not offered for the truth of the matter asserted.

- Nonassertive conduct.

- Non-propositions.

- Verbal acts.

- "Statements" by a declarant that is not a person.

a. *Statements Not Offered for the Truth of the Matter Asserted*

An out-of-court statement offered to prove the truth of the matter asserted is inadmissible hearsay. A statement offered to prove a fact other than the truth of the matter asserted may be admissible. For example, a witness overheard the groom say "I do. I do." If offered for the truth of the matter asserted—that the groom said "I do. I do."—it is inadmissible hearsay. If offered for some other purpose, it is not hearsay.

For example, if offered to prove the groom could talk, it is not hearsay. When offered for another purpose, the contents of the statement need not be believed for the evidence to be relevant. The mere fact that the statement was made independent of its truth is what is reliable.

A statement may appear to be offered for its truth but is primarily offered for another purpose. Common examples of such statements include statements offered to prove that an individual had notice or knowledge of something. For example, if a service station attendant tells a driver that his engine needs oil, that statement may be introduced to determine a breach of warranty claim brought by the driver. The statement is introduced primarily to show that the driver had notice that his engine needed oil and not for the truth of the matter asserted.

b. *Nonassertive Conduct*

Nonassertive conduct—conduct not intended by the actor to stand for the matter to be proved—is not hearsay. For example, an issue at trial is whether it was cold and windy at an intersection, and Sherlock Holmes testifies that, "I observed from my window people standing at the intersection all facing in one direction, wearing heavy coats, with their collars upturned, and their hands in their pockets." The nonverbal conduct by the pedestrians is nonassertive conduct because they did not intend their acts to stand for the proposition sought to be proved—that it was cold and windy. Nonassertive conduct is admissible because it is reliable.

c. Non-Propositions

Statements are hearsay only if they contain a "proposition," that is, a statement that is offered for the truth of its contents. A common non-proposition statement is a question. Questions are usually not hearsay because they often do not contain any proposition. For example, a statement "I said, 'What did you say?' " is usually not hearsay, but the statement "I said, 'Elaine, who is with you at the toy store on Michigan Avenue?' " is hearsay because it contains a proposition that Elaine is at the Michigan Avenue toy store.

d. Verbal Acts

Statements known as "verbal acts" or "operative words" are not considered hearsay because they are offered for their legal or logical significance and not for the truth of the matter asserted. The making of the statements creates legal duties or obligations irrespective of the matter asserted. The most common examples are statements that constitute the words of an offer or acceptance creating a contract, or defamatory words spoken to establish slander. For example, in a real estate contract case, the witness can testify: "I heard Lord Grantham say 'I will sell you Blackacre if you sell me Downton Abbey.' " Further, in a defamation case, a witness can testify: "Chambers said Hiss was a communist."

A verbal act may also logically permit a statement to prove the declarant spoke. For example, in a personal injury case, if the defendant claims the accident rendered the plaintiff unconscious, the plaintiff could introduce a statement from a witness bystander who heard the plaintiff crying out after the accident. Whether the plaintiff was crying out "That hurts" or "Call for help," the statement proves plaintiff was conscious.

e. Declarant Not a Person

A statement is hearsay only if made by a person. A "statement" not made or produced by a person is not hearsay. A result produced by an inanimate object such as a machine or the conduct of an animal is not hearsay. As examples, the following are not hearsay statements: the number produced by a radar device which displays the speed of an automobile; the pointing to a package by a dog that was trained to smell narcotics; a witness who testifies that her watch said "two-thirty." These situations may raise foundation issues regarding their admissibility.

3. Statements Not Defined as Hearsay

Some out-of-court statements that are offered for the truth of the matter asserted are defined by both federal and state rules of evidence as non-hearsay. These include:

- Party admissions,
- Prior statements by witnesses, and
- Prior identifications.

a.   Party Admissions (Fed.R.Evid. 801(d)(2))

Any statement made by an opposing party or the party's agent, employee, or representative is not hearsay and is admissible when offered against that party. An admission is defined as a statement made or an act done by a party to a lawsuit. A working definition of party admissions is: anything an opposing party ever said or did or wrote that has anything to do with the case will be admissible. A plaintiff can testify to what a defendant said, and a defendant can testify to what the plaintiff said. A witness can testify to what any party said if offered by the opposing party against the declarant party.

Statements by an opposing party are admissible because the party should assume responsibility for statements made and because the party has a full opportunity to explain why the statement was made. Admissions extend to statements made by agents, authorized persons, co-conspirators, and to adopted or approved statements made by other representatives of the party. Statements made by employees of a party are admissions if made within the scope of employment. For example, Thomas, an engineer of defendant's train, tells an investigator, "The Tank engine broke down at the station." The investigator can be called by the plaintiff to repeat Thomas' statements.

Some state jurisdictions treat party admissions as an exception to the hearsay rule, rather than as non-hearsay statements. This treatment yields the same results as the federal rule.

b.   Prior Statements by Witnesses (Fed.R.Evid. 801(d)(1))

Prior inconsistent statements made by witnesses under oath at a trial, hearing, deposition, or other proceeding are admissible as substantive evidence of the statements made. Prior consistent statements are admissible to rebut an indirect or express charge against the witness of recent fabrication, improper influence or motive. The declarant must testify and be subject to cross-examination. The federal rules and similar state rules admit prior inconsistent statements in evidence as substantive proof. Some states only permit prior statements to be introduced for impeachment purposes and not as substantive proof.

For example, during a deposition, Paul Revere states "There was one lamp in the belfry arch." After the deposition, Paul Revere makes changes in his deposition testimony and now states "There were two lanterns in the belfry." During direct examination at trial, Paul Revere says "There were two lanterns in the belfry." On cross-examination, Paul Revere can be asked: "Prior to this trial, you stated that there was one lamp in the belfry arch." This statement is offered to prove the truth of the matter asserted—that there was only one lamp—and also offered to impeach the witness.

During redirect examination, Paul Revere can testify that he said after the deposition that there were two lanterns. This statement is offered to corroborate the direct testimony and to rebut the impeachment by the prior inconsistent statement. In states that do not follow the federal rules, the prior statements are only admissible to impeach and to rebut impeachment and not to prove there was one lamp.

c.   *Prior Identification (Fed.R.Evid. 801(d)(1))*

Prior identification of a person made by a witness after observing the person is admissible if the declarant testifies at trial and is subject to cross-examination. This rule allows a witness to testify to a prior identification statement made during or shortly after viewing the person or after identifying a photo of the person.

For example, a witness, Cole Porter, who saw an assailant, tells the police that the assailant was "Five foot two with eyes of blue." At trial, Mr. Porter can say: "I told the police that the person who attacked me was five foot two with eyes of blue." Also at that trial, the officer can state: "Mr. Porter told me that the suspect was five foot two with eyes of blue."

G.   HEARSAY MYTHS

A number of myths exist regarding hearsay that arise from a misunderstanding of the application of the hearsay rules. An explanation of these myths may clear up some hearsay misperceptions.

- *Myth: All out-of-court statements are inadmissible hearsay.* Most out-of-court statements are admissible because they are reliable.

- *Myth: A witness on the stand can testify to whatever the witness has said in the past.* A witness on the stand who repeats what he or she has said in the past is testifying to an out-of-court statement that may or may not be admissible under the hearsay rules. The declarant's mere presence on the stand does not automatically permit the witness to repeat what he or she said in the past.

- *Myth: If a witness can be cross-examined, all prior statements of that witness are admissible.* Merely because a witness has testified or is available to be cross-examined does not make all prior statements by that witness admissible. The hearsay rules determine whether out-of-court statements by that declarant are admissible.

- *Myth: If the proper foundation is laid to authenticate a relevant document, the document is admissible.* Authentic and relevant documents are admissible only if they contain admissible out-of-court statements. The contents of the document must comply with the hearsay rules to be admissible.

- *Myth: Affidavit statements made under oath are admissible.* An affidavit is a hearsay statement, and must satisfy a hearsay exception, such as past recollection recorded, to be admissible.

- *Myth: Affidavits are admissible if the witness is unavailable.* An affidavit made by a person who is unavailable to testify is not a substitute for the live testimony of that person and constitutes inadmissible hearsay. Deposition testimony may be admissible.

- *Myth: Res gestae makes much of hearsay admissible.* The phrase "res gestae" (which means "the things done") has been replaced by modern rules of evidence. The phrase means different things to different advocates, and is only recognized in a few jurisdictions.

- *Myth: Judges flip a coin when ruling on hearsay objections.* Most judges base their ruling on the applicable hearsay rules. Some judges are inclined to overrule hearsay objections because of the unlikelihood that an appellate court would reverse their evidentiary ruling and grant a new trial. Some judges misunderstand or misapply the rules of hearsay and improperly overrule hearsay objections. Hearsay objections should, however, be made in an attempt to exclude unreliable evidence and to make a record for appeal.

- *Myth: After a hearsay statement has been admitted, little can be done about its impact.* Even if questionable hearsay is allowed in, much can be done to reduce its effect. Cross-examination questions can demonstrate its unreliability, and the defects of the evidence can be pointed out during summation.

- *Myth: No one understands hearsay, so who cares?* Ninety percent of the hearsay situations and rules are relatively easy to understand and apply. It is the remaining ten percent that require more analysis.

- *Myth: Hearsay is fun to learn and not at all frustrating.* The most frustrating aspect of hearsay is that different judges and lawyers have different understandings of the hearsay rules. Hearsay can become less frustrating if the advocate flexibly adapts to the judge's view on hearsay and offers evidence consistent with those views.

- *Myth: There is always a hearsay exception that makes the hearsay statement admissible.* A hearsay statement must meet the requirements of a hearsay exception to be admissible.

There are a reasonable—but nonetheless limited—number of hearsay exceptions.

H. HEARSAY EXCEPTIONS (FED.R.EVID. 803 AND 804)

Many hearsay statements are admissible because one or more exceptions to the hearsay rule make them admissible. Federal and state jurisdictions have developed numerous exceptions. The federal rules of evidence have codified twenty-nine separate exceptions, and many states recognize more.

There are a number of rationales as to why these exceptions have been developed. A common rationale is that the hearsay exceptions recognize that many hearsay statements are reliable and trustworthy. If the traditional defects of unreliability and untrustworthiness do not exist, the statement ought to be admissible.

A second rationale supports those hearsay statements where the declarant can be cross-examined. If there is an opportunity to cross-examine the person who made the hearsay statement, it may be appropriate to allow that statement to be admitted.

A third rationale is there is no efficient or economical way of proving the fact except through the hearsay statement. Some exceptions to the rule against hearsay have been created in part to respond to the pragmatic needs of introducing evidence. If there are no other practical means of proving something critical to the case, hearsay may be admissible.

The following sections explain the most commonly recognized hearsay exceptions. Most jurisdictions, including the federal system, divide hearsay exceptions into two general groups that depend upon the availability of the declarant to testify at trial.

Hearsay statements that are exceptions to the hearsay rule *regardless of whether the declarant is available to testify* at the trial include:

- Sense impressions,

- "State of mind" assertions,

- Records, and

- Reputation evidence.

Additional hearsay statements that are exceptions to the hearsay rule *only when the declarant is unavailable to testify* include:

- Former testimony,

- Statements against interest,

- Statements of personal or family history, and

- Dying declarations.

In addition to these exceptions, some hearsay statements will be admissible if certain specific requirements of reliability are met. The federal rules and many state jurisdictions designate this exception as the "residual" exception.

1.   General Hearsay Exceptions

a.   *Sense Impressions*

This exception includes two types of statements: present sense impressions and excited utterances.

i.   *Present Sense Impressions (Fed.R.Evid. 803(1))*

Statements describing or explaining an event or condition made while the declarant was perceiving the event or condition, or immediately thereafter, are admissible as present sense impressions. This is a broad exception and covers many statements made by persons involved in or who observe an event. This exception has two specific requirements:

- The statement describes or explains an event or condition, and

- The statement is made immediately or shortly after the declarant perceives the event or condition.

These spontaneous statements are deemed reliable because of the lack of time for reflective thought that can result in a changed perception of the event, and because the witness is likely to have a fresh memory of the event at the time the statement was made.

Example:

Bo Jangles is injured falling on a dance floor. Mr. Jangles' attorney calls Eleanor Powell, a witness, to testify about Bo's accident.

Examining Attorney:

Q: Where were you standing?

A: I was standing next to Ms. Caruthers, and both of us were standing near Bo when he fell.

Q: What did Ms. Caruthers say when Mr. Jangles fell?

Objecting Lawyer:

Objection. Hearsay.

Judge:

Overruled.

A: Ms. Caruthers said to me "This dance floor is very slippery, I almost fell myself a moment ago."

Q: What did you do next?

A: I walked over, slowly, to help Bo.

Q: What did Mr. Jangles say?

Objecting Lawyer:

Objection. Hearsay.

Judge:

Overruled.

A: He said "This floor has some slippery stuff on it."

Both objections are overruled because both declarants, Ms. Caruthers and Mr. Jangles, made statements about a condition immediately after perceiving the event. The statement by Mr. Jangles is not a party admission because it is not being offered against him, but rather is being offered on his behalf.

ii.   *Excited Utterances (Fed.R.Evid. 803(2))*

Statements made by the declarant while under stress or excitement caused by a startling situation, and which relate to that situation, are admissible as excited utterances. This exception only applies if:

- The statement is made by the declarant while under stress,

- The declarant has personal knowledge of the event by participating in or observing the event,

- The statement is prompted by the startling event, and

- The statement relates to the event.

The rationale for this exception is that spontaneous statements made under stress or during a startling event are reliable because a person does not have time to fabricate such statements.

Example:

In a personal injury case, Jill witnesses a startling event and testifies that she said, "Oh no, the handle of the pail cracked and Jack fell down and broke his crown!" The opposing lawyer, representing the landowner, anticipating Jill's response, would object to the statement as hearsay. The judge would overrule the objection because the statement is an excited utterance, and is also a present sense impression.

Many statements are both excited utterances and present sense impressions. An excited utterance statement differs from a present sense impression in two aspects:

- While an excited utterance usually occurs during or immediately after an event, it need not occur at those times. As long as the declarant is still upset by the event when the statement is made, it is an excited utterance. The present sense impression must be made at the time of the event or immediately thereafter.

- The excited utterance need only "relate" to the startling event, while a present sense impression must "describe or explain" an event or condition.

b.   *State of Mind or Body Exceptions*

There are two related exceptions that involve statements regarding the declarant's state of mind or body: Existing mental, emotional, or physical conditions, and medical treatment statements.

i.   *Existing Mental, Emotional, Physical Condition (Fed.R.Evid. 803(3))*

Statements by a declarant involving the declarant's existing state of mind, emotion, sensation, or physical condition (such as intent, plan, motive, design, feeling, pain, and bodily harm) are admissible. These statements are reliable because of their spontaneous nature. They are made at the time the declarant experiences the condition.

Example:

In a products liability case, a witness called by the plaintiff testifies that he heard the plaintiff, Knievel, state right after the jumping accident: "My head is throbbing. I feel depressed. I hate the guy who sold me this motorcycle. I am going to go back to the cycle store and complain." All these statements are admissible as statements of existing physical, emotional, and mental conditions.

This exception does not include statements of past conditions. For example, if Knievel also said: "Last week, my back hurt," the statement is inadmissible hearsay because it refers to a past condition. If Knievel said: "My back hurts," the statement is admissible because it refers to a present, existing condition.

ii. *Medical Treatment Statements (Fed.R.Evid. 803(4))*

Statements made by a person who describes medical history, past or present pains, or symptoms to a medical professional for purposes of medical diagnosis or treatment are admissible. These statements are deemed reliable because the declarant who seeks medical treatment has little or no incentive to lie.

Example:

In a personal injury accident, the plaintiff's treating physician is called to testify at trial on behalf of the plaintiff.

Examining Attorney:

Q: When did you examine Whiplash Willie?

A: About two weeks after the accident.

Q: What did Mr. Willie tell you about his injuries at that time?

Objecting Lawyer:

Objection. Hearsay.

Judge:

Overruled.

A: He said that right after the accident his neck hurt a lot and that up until the day before he saw me he could not turn his head to the right or left.

Q: What else did he say about his injury?

Objecting Lawyer:

Objection. Hearsay.

Judge:

Overruled.

A: He said he had a lot of pain in his lower back when he tried
     to bend over or sit down, and blamed his bad fortune.

Q: What did he say about the cause of the injuries?

Objecting Lawyer:

Objection. Hearsay.

Judge:

Sustained.

The first objection is properly overruled because the testimony consists of a medical diagnosis. The second objection is also properly overruled because the cause of the injury is a relevant part of the information the doctor needs to properly diagnose and treat the injury. The third objection is properly sustained because any further statement, such as "It was defendant's reckless driving that caused my neck injury," is not a part of the patient's medical history.

c.   Records

Several hearsay exceptions permit the admissibility of specific categories of records. These records are deemed reliable because the information they contain is usually entered and maintained in an accurate, trustworthy manner including:

- Business records,
- Public records,
- Specific records,
- Absent records, and
- Past recollection recorded.

i.   Business Records (Fed.R.Evid. 803(6))

Records kept in the ordinary, regular course of a business or other organization are admissible. Records include memoranda, reports, emails, data compilation, documents, or any other type of written or electronically stored information. Recorded information includes facts, opinions, and other information. The term "business" includes any business, institution, association, profession, occupation, and organization, whether profit or nonprofit. The records are admissible hearsay written statements if:

- The entries are made at or near the time of the event or act,

- A person with knowledge records the information or transmits the information to someone who records it,

- The records are kept in the course of a regularly conducted business activity or duty,

- The recording of the specific information is a regular practice of that business,

- The custodian or the qualified witness testifies to these facts, and

- The records are reliable and trustworthy.

Example:

In a commercial arbitration case, Ms. Zloty testifies that she is the manager of a bank currency exchange office, that it is the business of the bank to make and maintain records of exchanges, that Exhibit No. 3 contains documents made contemporaneously with the information recorded on the documents, and that the documents were made in the regular course of the business of the bank. Exhibit No. 3 is admissible.

The witness must testify to the specific requirements of the business exception rule, which commonly requires the examining attorney to ask leading questions to establish these factors. In most civil cases and many criminal cases business records are introduced through a stipulation or in response to a request for an admission. There is usually no need to take the time to subpoena a witness to lay the foundation for the hearsay exception, unless the records are controversial. Many of these records will also be self-authenticating under the rules of evidence and may be introduced through a witness who can testify to their relevance.

ii.　Public Records (Fed.R.Evid. 803(8))

Public records are generally reliable because government officials record the information pursuant to a public duty or the law and have no interest in recording information that favors one side or the other. Several types of public records are admissible:

- Records that describe or explain the activities of an office or agency, such as published reports by the government summarizing what the office or agency does. An example is a document published by a state department of transportation that explains how it conducts drivers' licensing exams.

- Records of matters observed and recorded pursuant to a duty imposed by law. Documents maintained by government officers concerning their official activities are examples of such records. Another example is public housing records listing the names of tenants and their addresses.

- Factual findings resulting from investigations made pursuant to authority granted by law, such as reports prepared by government investigators. Only those parts of an investigation report that are factual findings, factual conclusions, and historical facts will be admissible. Conclusions or opinions are not admissible. For example, a fire investigative report that includes a description of the accident is admissible, but a portion of the report that concludes the Triangle Shirtwaist Factory fire was caused by arson because the defendants were in desperate financial situations is inadmissible. In some cases, determining what is an admissible "factual finding" and what is an inadmissible "conclusion" is difficult. Courts have held that "factual conclusions" are admissible under the public records exception. The resolution in each case depends on the exact words used in the report.

- Land records and property documents maintained in a public office, including deeds, certificates, entries in ledgers, and computer data relating to property interests. These documents are reliable.

- Public reports are generally more likely to be admissible in civil cases. In criminal cases, a defendant has a right to confront witnesses and cannot cross-examine a report. For example, public reports containing observations of law enforcement personnel are not usually permitted in criminal cases under this exception.

iii. Other Specific Records

The rules of evidence in most jurisdictions render admissible the following specific types of documents:

- Market reports and commercial data. Hearsay statements are contained in market reports, financial summaries, commercial documents, and business transaction data. These statements include facts, opinions, and evaluative or interpretive information. Examples are market quotations, stock prices, financial information, business directories, and other compilations. The rationale for their admissibility is that since the financial and business world relies upon them, so should the law. (Fed.R.Evid. 803(17)).

- Records of vital statistics, including birth, death, and marriage information. (Fed.R.Evid. 803(9)).

- Records of religious organizations, including birth, marriage, divorce, death, and other personal or family records kept in the ordinary course of an organization's activities. (Fed.R.Evid. 803(11)).

- Marriage, baptismal, and other certificates. (Fed.R.Evid. 803(12)).

- Family records, including personal or family history or facts listed in sources such as holy books and inscriptions. (Fed.R.Evid. 803(13)).

- Ancient documents and statements contained in authentic documents in existence for 20 years or more. (Fed.R.Evid. 803(16)).

- Judgments of previous convictions and judgments involving personal, family or property data. (Fed.R.Evid. 803(22) and (23)).

Many records are admissible under more than one hearsay exception. A record may qualify as a business record, public record, and a specific record. Some records may appear to be admissible under a rule but have been held to be inadmissible by the courts. For example, police reports are not admissible in criminal cases, even though such reports may technically qualify as business records or public records, because the defendant has a constitutional right to cross-examine witnesses, and a record cannot be cross-examined. Case decisions or statutes may expand or narrow the rules of evidence governing the introduction of various types of records.

iv. Absence of Business or Public Records (Fed.R.Evid. 803(7) and (10))

The lack of an entry in a business or public record is admissible to prove an event did not occur. Before the lack of a record or entry is admissible, the attorney must establish that the information was the type of information that would have been recorded and that a search has been made of the records. Most jurisdictions allow two ways to prove the absent record search. A witness with personal knowledge may testify to the diligent search that was undertaken, or the proponent may offer a self-authenticating certificate that describes the unsuccessful search.

v. Past Recollection Recorded (Fed.R.Evid. 803(5))

Records concerning a matter that a witness no longer remembers, but that the witness once knew and accurately recorded when the matter was fresh, will be admissible evidence. Written or electronic records of prior events are admissible if:

- The testifying witness does not presently fully or accurately recall the event,

- The witness has personal knowledge of the record,

- The witness made the record or adopted it as correct at a time when the memory of the witness was fresh, usually close in time to the occurrence of the event, and

- The witness testifies that the report is accurate or that the record would not have been signed or adopted if it were inaccurate.

Section 8.6(M) explains past recollection recorded evidence.

Example:

In an antitrust case involving computer records, the witness maintained a database of Bell Labs email conversations made three years before the trial describing inventions and discoveries. At trial, the witness is unlikely to remember the details of three-year-old conversations. The relevant database may be admitted as past recollection recorded by having the witness establish the existence of the foundation factors for past recollection recorded.

---

vi. Learned Treatises (Fed.R.Evid. 803(18))

A learned treatise is a book, periodical, article, website information, pamphlet, or magazine established as reliable authority on a matter, ordinarily the subject of expert opinion, which is relied upon by an expert in direct examination or called to the attention of an expert witness during cross-examination. Sections 10.5(G) and 10.7(B)(14) describe the introduction and use of learned treatises.

d. Reputation Evidence (Fed.R.Evid. 802(19), (20), & (21))

Reputation evidence is a collection of hearsay statements in which specific hearsay exceptions render certain types of reputation evidence admissible. Reputation evidence concerning personal or family history, such as marriages, births, deaths or other events of family significance are admissible. Fed.R.Evid. 803(19). Reputation evidence regarding general history or land boundaries or customs is also admissible.

Fed.R.Evid. 803(20). Reputation evidence of a person's character among associates or in the community is likewise admissible as a hearsay exception. Fed.R.Evid. 803(21). Section 7.10(D) explains when reputation evidence is relevant.

2. Declarant Unavailable Exceptions (Fed.R.Evid. 804)

Some hearsay statements are only admissible if the declarant is unavailable to testify at trial. Fed.R.Evid. 804(a).

The "unavailability" of a witness includes situations where the declarant:

- Is absent from the hearing or trial and the proponent of the statement is unable to secure attendance by a subpoena or other process.

- Is unable to be present because of an existing physical or mental illness or death.

- Testifies to a lack of memory of the subject matter of the statement.

- Is exempted from testifying by a ruling on the ground of privilege.

- Persists in refusing to testify despite a court order.

Hearsay statements admissible if the declarant is unavailable include:

- Former testimony,

- Statements against interest,

- Statements of personal or family history, and

- Dying declarations.

a. Former Testimony (Fed.R.Evid. 804(b)(1))

In a civil trial, the testimony given by a witness at a deposition or another hearing may be admitted if the party against whom the testimony is offered had an opportunity to previously examine the witness. The most common use of former testimony in a civil trial involves the introduction of deposition testimony because the lay or expert witness is unavailable. In criminal cases, this hearsay exception is less often applicable because of the defendant's constitutional right to cross-examine witnesses. Section 7.10(A) explains the introduction of prior testimony.

b. Statements Against Interest (Fed.R.Evid. 802(b)(3))

A statement made by a person contrary to that person's interests is admissible. The contrary interests include statements adversely affecting a person's pecuniary or proprietary interests or which tend to subject the person to civil or criminal liability. The rationale for this rule is that reasonable individuals do not make statements against their own interests unless those statements are accurate. This exception need only be used where the declarant is not a party. If a party makes such a statement, the statement is admissible as a party admission. See Section 4.8(F)(3).

Example:

In a civil case, the user of an addictive product has sued the manufacturer of the product. An employee of the manufacturer made a statement to an agent of the Food and Drug Administration. The plaintiff calls the FDA agent to testify.

Examining Attorney:

Q: What did Ms. Marlboro tell you during your investigation?

Objecting Lawyer:

Objection. Hearsay.

Judge:

Overruled.

A: Ms. Marlboro told me that she and others routinely added candy to the tobacco in violation of company policy.

---

c. Statements of Personal or Family History (Fed.R.Evid. 803(b)(4))

Statements regarding the personal or family history of the declarant are admissible. These statements are generally allowed as long as the declarant was related to a person or intimately involved in a family and likely to have accurate information even though the declarant had no means of personally knowing the matter.

Example:

In a probate case, a daughter is called to testify to what her father had told her.

Examining Attorney:

Q: What did your father, Gluskap, tell you about his family?

Objecting Lawyer:

Objection. Hearsay.

Judge:

Overruled.

A: He said he had one brother whose name was Malsumus.

---

d.   Dying Declaration (Fed.R.Evid. 803(b)(2))

A statement concerning the cause or circumstance of the declarant's impending death that is made by the declarant who believes death is imminent is admissible. The rationale is that the declarant, who faces death, is telling the truth.

Example:

In a murder case, the victim's husband is called to testify by the prosecution.

Examining Attorney:

Q: After your wife was shot, what did you do?

A: I ran over and knelt next to her.

Q: What did she say?

Objecting Lawyer:

Objection. Hearsay.

Judge:

Overruled.

A: She said, "Darling, I'm dying. Jeeves did it."

---

3.   Residual Hearsay Exception (Fed.R.Evid. 807)

Hearsay statements that are not covered by a specific hearsay exception may be admissible if:

- The statement is offered as evidence of a material fact,

- No other evidence exists which is more probative,

- Its admission will serve the interests of justice, and

- The offering party provides opposing counsel with prior notice of the introduction of such a statement.

This "residual" or "catch-all" exception to the hearsay rule may render other reliable, trustworthy hearsay admissible. This exception is useful in limited situations where no other rule or exception permits hearsay to be admissible. This exception is not intended to and has not been interpreted by courts to make inadmissible hearsay admissible. The exception is reserved for unusual circumstances in which a reliable and trustworthy hearsay statement should be admissible in the interests of justice because no other exception covers the situation. For example, hearsay statements made by consumers who report their experiences with a product in a reliable consumer survey may be admissible under this exception.

4.   Multiple Hearsay (Fed.R.Evid. 805)

A statement may contain more than one hearsay statement. This multiple form of hearsay is called "hearsay within hearsay." Each statement must be analyzed to determine whether there is multiple hearsay and whether each part of the statement falls within an exception or is defined as non-hearsay.

Example:

Curley sues Moe for civil assault. At trial, Curley testifies that "Moe said to me, 'I meant to poke you in the eyes because Larry said he was in a lot of pain because you had just slapped him.'" *The attorney for Moe objects to this multiple hearsay. There are two statements within this testimony: the statement by Moe to Curley and the statement by Larry to Moe. The first statement— that of Moe to Curley—is a party admission and is admissible. See Section 4.8(F)(3)(a). The second statement—that of Larry to Moe—is admissible as a hearsay exception, either as a present sense impression or as a statement of an existing physical condition. See Section 4.8(H)(1)(b). The entire statement is admissible.*

A common situation of multiple hearsay occurs with documents. Documents introduced during trial commonly contain hearsay information. The document may contain admissible statements and inadmissible hearsay. Each document must be analyzed to determine which sentences, phrases, and words are admissible and which are not. See Sections 8.6(B)–(D).

Example:

A plaintiff lays a foundation through a medical record custodian that a hospital record falls within a business record exception to the hearsay rule. See Section 4.8(H)(1)(c).

The witness is a medical record custodian, Patch Adams. The exhibit is the medical record of plaintiff Worf offered by the plaintiff. The witness testifies that he is the Director of the Emergency Room, that it is the business of the hospital to make such medical records, that this exhibit was made contemporaneously with the events recorded, and that the record was made in the regular course of the hospital's business. The record falls within the business record exception to the hearsay rule. Parts of the record may or may not be admissible depending upon the applicable hearsay exceptions. The record contains the following statements:

- A statement by Dr. Beverly Crusher: *"Administered alien steroids to patient."* Admissible. Business record exception.

- A statement by Dr. Kathleen Pulaski: *"Set patient's broken antenna in a cast."* Admissible. Business record exception.

- A statement by the plaintiff Worf: *"My third eye hurts."* Admissible. Statement by person made for diagnosis.

- A statement by the defendant Picard: *"I was warping around 3000 light years when I hit the rear end of his tractor beam."* Admissible. Party admission offered against that party.

- A statement by a bystander in the Twilight Zone: *"Wow, its (referring to the plaintiff) head was all covered with green blood right after the accident."* Admissible by most judges and arbitrators. Present sense impression.

- A statement by a Romulan who observed the accident: *"Picard sure looked euphoric when I saw him much later after the accident."* Inadmissible, by most. No exception applies.

§ 4.9   QUESTIONABLE OBJECTIONS

Certain objections—some of which are commonly made—are improper, inappropriate, or not recognized in a jurisdiction. These improper objections vary among jurisdictions, and include the following:

Irrelevant, Immaterial, Incompetent. This broad objection may be inappropriate because it is too general. Irrelevancy is a proper ground for an objection. "Immaterial" is no longer a term recognized by the Federal Rules of Evidence. "Incompetent" refers to the ability of a witness to testify and not to specific questions or answers.

Improper and Unfair. This objection is too general and does not specify the ground of an objection. A reference to a more specific reason must be made, or this objection will commonly be overruled.

Self-Serving. This objection is usually groundless. In a general sense, evidence the opposing side attempts to introduce is self-serving, that is, it will serve that side's interests and harm the other side's case.

Prejudicial. This objection is also improper, for reasons similar to the inappropriateness of the self-serving objection. It is not sufficient that evidence is prejudicial for it to be excluded, the evidence has to be "unfairly prejudicial." See Fed.R.Evid. 403.

Invades the Province of the Fact Finder. This objection may be too ambiguous to be useful. An expert witness can testify to an ultimate opinion; lay witnesses are able to testify to many common opinions. These admissible responses can be said to invade the province of the fact finder.

§ 4.10 OBJECTION ANALYSIS

The following lists provide a summary of objections and a work form to prepare for evidentiary objections.

FORM 4.1
OBJECTION PLANNING WORKSHEET

Case _____   File _____

Anticipated Objections to be Made by Adversary

Witness/ Exhibit	Evidence	Objection	Grounds for Objection (Rule/Statute Case Law)	Response to Objection	Other Sources of Evidence	Offer of Proof	Limited Admission

Anticipated Objections to Adversary's Evidence

Witness/ Exhibit	Evidence	Objection	Grounds for Objection (Rule/Statute Case Law)	Limited Admission	Curative Instruction

Pretrial Evidentiary Motions

Motions in Limine	Anticipated Ruling	Alternative Way to Introduce Evidence

Common Objections
IMPROPER FORM OF QUESTION

Leading
   FRE 611
      Lawyer Testifying

Multiple Questions
   FRE 611
      Compound Questions

Narrative
   FRE 611
      No Question Before
      Witness

Assuming Facts Not in Evidence
   FRE 611 & 701-704
      Inaccurate
      Hypothetical

Non-Responsive
   FRE 611
      Volunteered

Misstatement of Testimony
   FRE 611
      Mischaracterization of
      Evidence

Cumulative/Repetitious
   FRE 403 & 611
      Asked and Answered

Argumentative
   FRE 611
      Badgering

Vague
   FRE 401-403
      Ambiguous
      Confusing
      Misleading
      Unintelligible

Improper Impeachment
   FRE 613
      Collateral Issue

Beyond Scope
   FRE 611

Common Objections
EXCLUSIONARY RULES OF EVIDENCE

Relevancy
    FRE 401-411
        Irrelevant
        No Probative Value
        Unfairly Prejudicial
            Improper Character
            Improper Habit
            Subsequent Reme-
                dial Measures
            Offers of Compro-
                mise
            Payment of Medi-
                cal Expenses
            Plea Bargains
            Liability Insurance
            Religious Beliefs/
                Opinions

Privileges
    FRE 501
        Attorney/Client
        Doctor/Patient
        Spousal Testimony
        Marital Communica-
            tions
        Clergy/Penitent
        Trade/Business
            Secrets
        Informer Identity
        Governmental Informa-
            tion
        News Sources
        Other

Competence
    FRE 601-602
        Incompetent
        Lack of Personal
            Knowledge
        Lack of Memory

Foundation
    FRE 601-602
        Lack of Foundation

Lay Opinion
    FRE 701
        Impermissible Opinion
        Impermissible Conclu-
            sion
        Speculation

Expert Opinion
    FRE 702-705
        Unqualified Witness
        Impermissible Opinion

Authentication
    FRE 901-902
        Lack of Authenticity

Original Writings
    FRE 1001-1007
        Signs
        Independent Facts
        Collateral Matter
        Unauthentic Copy
        Non-genuine Original

Parole Evidence
        Statutory or Case Law

Criminal Constitutional Issues

Common Objections
SUMMARY HEARSAY ANALYSIS

Hearsay
    Declarant
        Not Under Oath
        Not Subject to Cross
        Credibility Not Observ-
          able

Definition FRE 801
    Offered to Prove Truth of
        Statement
    Out-of-Court Statement
    Assertive or Nonassertive
    Non-propositions
    Verbal Acts
    Declarant Not Person

Non-hearsay 801(d)
    Party Admissions
    Prior Statements

Hearsay Exceptions
    Sense Impressions
        Present Sense Impres-
          sion 803(1)
        Excited Utterance
          803(2)
    State of Mind
        Existing Mental/Emo-
          tional/Physical
          Condition 803(3)
        Treatment Medical
          Statements 803(4)

Records/Documents/
    Writings
    Business Records 803(6)
    Public Records 803(8)
    Past Recollection
        Recorded 803(5)
    Vital Statistics 803(9)
    Absent Entries 803(7)
        &(10)
    Commercial Data
        803(17)
    Property Records
        803(14) & (15)
    Official Certificates
        803(11) & (12)
    Family Records
        803(13)
    Ancient Documents
        803(16)
    Learned Treatises
        803(18)
    Previous Convictions
        803(22)
    Other Judgments
        803(23)

Reputation
    Character 803(21)
    Family 803(19)
    General History 803(19)

Declarant Not Available
    Former Testimony 804(b)(1)
    Statement Against Interest
        804(b)(3)
    Personal History 804(b)(4)
    Dying Declaration 804(b)(2)
    Reliable Hearsay 807

CHAPTER 5

JURY SELECTION

■ ■ ■

5.1   Introduction
    A.   Role of the Attorneys
    B.   Client Participation in Jury Selection
    C.   Role of the Judge
    D.   Familiarity with Procedures
5.2   Objectives of Jury Selection
    A.   Support a Challenge for Cause Motion
    B.   Exercise Peremptory Challenges
    C.   Educate the Jury
    D.   Develop Rapport with the Jurors
    E.   Neutralize Negative and Enhance Positive Attitudes and Beliefs
    F.   Obtain Commitments
5.3   Procedure
    A.   Jury Pool
    B.   Juror Summons
    C.   Jury Orientation
    D.   Jury Panel
    E.   Number of Prospective Jurors
    F.   Seating Prospective Jurors
    G.   Preliminary Information About Panel
    H.   Jurors' Oath
    I.   Preliminary Remarks
5.4   Questioning the Panel
    A.   Mechanics
    B.   Questioning Exclusively by the Judge
    C.   Questioning by Judge and Attorneys
    D.   Introductory Remarks by Attorneys
5.5   Jury Selection Questions
    A.   Types of Questions
    B.   Selecting Types of Questions
    C.   Concluding Questions
5.6   Theories of Jury Selection Questioning
    A.   Impressionistic Evaluations
    B.   Generalizations and Stereotypes
    C.   Character and Personality Traits
    D.   Nonverbal Behavior
    E.   Jury Profile
    F.   Social Science Research

————————

Trial Advocacy Supplement
Jury Selection

An example of a jury selection process in a civil jury trial appears in the *Supplement to Trial Advocacy Before Judges, Jurors, and Arbitrators*. The transcript of the *Rita Riley v. Garfield House Apartments* jury trial presents the strategies and skills that are explained in this chapter. Commentary accompanies the transcript that explains jury trial procedures and the tactics and techniques used by the lawyers.

REFLECTING ON ADVOCACY

A jury consists of twelve persons chosen to decide who has the better lawyer.

—ROBERT FROST

The audience is the most revered member of the theater . . . Without an audience there is no theater . . . They are our guests, our evaluators . . . They make the performance meaningful.

—VIOLA SPOLIN

§ 5.1   INTRODUCTION

Jury selection is the first stage of the jury trial. Before the trial begins, people from the jurisdiction where the trial is to be held are summoned to serve as jurors. Court administrators and judges select prospective jurors from whom the lawyers choose those they prefer and de-select those they do not want, leaving the panel that decides the case.

The primary purpose of jury selection is to identify and select jurors who can fairly determine a party's case. Voir dire, another name for jury selection, means to "speak the truth." The jurors answer questions asked by the judge, and in many jurisdictions, by the attorneys, to reveal their impartiality and fairness and their biases and prejudices.

The jury selection process is the first opportunity the attorneys have to establish professional contact with prospective jurors and the only opportunity counsel have to enter into a dialogue with the jurors. This process, within limits, may be used to achieve other objectives, such as: educating the jurors, developing rapport with them, neutralizing negative and enhancing positive juror attitudes and beliefs, obtaining commitments from the jurors, and introducing case themes and theories. See Sections 5.2 and 5.7. During the rest of the trial, the attorneys either speak to the jurors or present evidence through witnesses to the jurors.

The process of selecting jurors is actually a means of de-selecting jurors. Attorneys use peremptory challenges and, occasionally, motions to strike for cause to remove a limited number of prospective jurors. Attorneys may remove jurors who appear unfavorable to their side or favorable to their opponent. The process has some additional limitations. Factors such as race, gender, and religion cannot be a reason for removal.

This process of de-selection is a difficult task because of the relatively short amount of time available for jury selection. Attorneys can only obtain a limited amount of information from jurors during the selection process. It would take an extensive amount of questioning and a lengthy period of time for attorneys to obtain enough information to make thoroughly informed judgments. Within the time available, the best an attorney can accomplish is to make a reasonable judgment based on the information provided.

This chapter explains jury selection procedures, how to prepare for and conduct jury selection, effective selection approaches, various types of jury questions, procedures for the removal of jurors, and strategies and tactics involved in this selection process.

A.   ROLE OF THE ATTORNEYS

The role of the attorney in jury selection varies among jurisdictions. In all jurisdictions, attorneys may bring motions to strike jurors for cause and may exercise a limited number of peremptory challenges to remove jurors. In those jurisdictions where the judge asks all questions of the prospective jurors, the role of the attorney is limited to submitting proposed questions to be asked by the judge and to making the final decision to remove jurors from the panel. In jurisdictions where the attorneys may question the prospective jurors, the role of the attorney becomes more substantial.

The process of asking questions of the jury panel involves a number of intricate skills. Attorneys can ask questions of the prospective jurors and engage them in a dialogue about matters that often relate to their lives. While the questions must be planned in advance, the lawyers must make ongoing judgments regarding the scope of the questions, what issues should be probed, and when to end the questioning. The attorneys also hope to gain the trust and respect of the jurors during this dialogue.

Jury selection is not as predictable or structured as other parts of the trial. The attorneys usually do not know the answers they will receive and must assess biases and prejudices jurors may have based on the answers to their questions. And the lawyers must continually assess the effect questions and answers have upon individual jurors and the group dynamics of the panel.

B. CLIENT PARTICIPATION IN JURY SELECTION

The extent to which clients are involved in jury selection is a matter of professional and personal preference. Many trial attorneys believe their client's input is extremely valuable, while others limit their client consultations. In deciding to what degree the client should be involved and relied on as a resource the attorney should consider:

- The client's understanding of the case and the jury selection objectives,

- The ability of the client to make informed decisions about the jurors,

- The mutually agreed approaches that have been chosen for jury selection,

- The professional relationship with the client,

- The impression made on the jurors when an attorney/client "team" selection effort is demonstrated,

- The ramifications of a disagreement by counsel with the decision the client has made about a juror, and

- The lawyer's belief in the appropriate role of a client in the case and the corresponding ethical obligations involved.

C. ROLE OF THE JUDGE

The role of the judge varies among jurisdictions and the preferences of individual judges. In jurisdictions where the judges ask all the questions, some judges ask only a limited number of questions they select, while other judges ask most of the questions submitted by the attorneys. In jurisdictions where the attorneys also ask questions, some judges may be actively involved in asking questions while others may be passive.

Active judges may limit their questioning to standard questions, allowing the attorneys to ask specific questions about the case. Passive judges may ask few, if any, questions, and permit the attorneys to conduct whatever questioning the attorneys believe appropriate. Counsel can ask the judge to take a more active or passive role or request permission for the lawyers to ask specific questions.

D. FAMILIARITY WITH PROCEDURES

The advocate must become completely familiar with the jury selection procedures used by the judge. Prior to trial, the attorney may learn how a judge conducts jury selection by watching the judge conduct jury selection in other cases. Colleagues and court personnel are also sources of information about a judge's jury selection preferences.

During the pretrial conference or immediately before jury selection begins, specific procedures for jury selection should be discussed thoroughly with the judge and opposing counsel. If the judge or counsel suggests that jury selection be conducted in the "usual" way, the attorney should ask what are the "usual" procedures. There is a tendency by novice attorneys to pretend they know how judges conduct jury selection in order to avoid revealing their inexperience. There is no one standard way to conduct jury selection. Even the most experienced trial lawyers ask the judge to explain what procedures the judge prefers to follow, suggest alternative procedures, and request permission to conduct the jury selection process in a way that helps their client's case.

§ 5.2   OBJECTIVES OF JURY SELECTION

There are six goals trial lawyers try to achieve during jury selection:

- Obtain information to make challenges for cause;

- Obtain information to exercise peremptory challenges;

- Educate the jury about the case, facts, issues, clients, parties, witnesses, and law;

- Develop rapport with the jurors;

- Neutralize negative and build on positive juror attitudes and opinions; and

- Obtain commitments from the jurors.

The first two objectives are uniformly accepted. The remaining four are not described in jury selection rules but are objectives that may be achieved while asking questions to obtain information and to exercise appropriate challenges to jurors. The extent to which all the objectives can be achieved depends upon the rules of a jurisdiction, the practice of the judge, and the attorney's ability to question jurors.

A. SUPPORT A CHALLENGE FOR CAUSE MOTION

Questions concerning factors that establish obvious or apparent bias or prejudice on the part of a juror determine whether grounds exist to support a motion to challenge a juror for cause. Areas of such questioning include: prior knowledge of the case, familiarity with the parties or attorneys, existing attitudes regarding issues in the case, and related matters. Questions asked by the judges usually include these types of questions, examples of which appear in Section 5.7(A).

B. EXERCISE PEREMPTORY CHALLENGES

Questions that reveal information about the jurors concerning opinions, feelings, beliefs or attitudes that may reveal biases or prejudices that fall short of providing a challenge for cause may assist the attorney in making peremptory challenge decisions. These questions may include all aspects about jurors including: their hobbies, leisure time, literature they read, television they watch, websites they view, family background, and other information. Examples of questions appear in Section 5.7(A).

C. EDUCATE THE JURY

Attorneys may also use jury selection to educate the jury about the parties, facts, witnesses, issues, and strengths and weaknesses of the case. Jury selection is the first opportunity the attorneys have to describe the case to the jurors. The first impression jurors have about a case can influence their verdict.

Lawyers attempt to inform the jurors about aspects of the case through the questions they ask them. See Section 5.7(B). Some jurors will be fairly knowledgeable about the legal system and familiar with legal terms and procedures. Potential jurors may have access to information about a case and the parties because of social network sources, websites and blogs, and media reporting. Advocates can use the jury selection process to discover what potential jurors generally understand about our legal process and what they may specifically know about a case.

Attorneys may explore and explain weaknesses or problems that include concerns applicable to all cases as well as those that are specific to the case. Case weaknesses may include: the type of client (for example, a large corporation against a sole proprietor), the type of remedy (a substantial amount of money), the sensitive nature of the case (sexual harassment or criminal sexual abuse), the type of defense (consent or self-defense), the type of witness (a felon), and the facts involved (drugs). The attitudes and feelings of the jurors regarding these problems and weaknesses must be explored for several reasons. These topics are important areas to probe for prejudices that may significantly affect a juror's ability to be fair and impartial. An open discussion of these topics may reduce the chances that the jurors will use these weaknesses to adversely decide the case. Affirmatively revealing problems reduces the impact of the weaknesses and prevents the jurors from first hearing about a case weakness from the opposing party. The questioning attorney may be able to obtain a commitment from the jurors to base their decision on all the evidence presented and not just on controversial facts.

Jury selection questions can be designed to anticipate and counter efforts by opposing counsel to educate the jury to their advantage. Questions can be asked that explore juror reactions to the other side's positions. These questions may reveal biases jurors have in favor of the opposing side that cannot be remedied, requiring the removal of these jurors. The attorney who questions jurors second may be able to change jury attitudes about the other side's case from favorable to a neutral or negative perception.

D. DEVELOP RAPPORT WITH THE JURORS

Trial attorneys want the jurors to trust, respect, and even like them, and to have a favorable impression of their client. These goals can be achieved through questions and answers, which develop a professional rapport between the jurors and the attorneys. A lawyer hopes to engage in an effective conversation with jurors to significantly increase the likelihood that the jurors perceive the advocate to be caring, sincere, and honest. See Section 5.7(C).

E. NEUTRALIZE NEGATIVE AND ENHANCE POSITIVE ATTITUDES AND BELIEFS

The questioning process may be used to overcome negative opinions, attitudes, and beliefs jurors may have. Questions can also build on positive feelings and reactions the jurors may already have toward the case and a client. See Section 5.7(D).

F. OBTAIN COMMITMENTS

An effective method of gaining support from jurors is to obtain their commitment regarding issues in the case. Trial attorneys may seek to have jurors promise that they will not hold unfavorable matters against the client, that they will be impartial and put aside biases and prejudices, or that they will follow the law as explained by the judge. These commitments may guide the jurors during deliberations. Not all courts permit questions seeking commitments. See Section 5.7(E).

§ 5.3   PROCEDURE

Jury selection procedures are controlled by statutes, rules of procedure, local court practice, and the preferences of individual judges. This section summarizes procedures generally followed in federal and state jurisdictions, which processes subsequent sections of this Chapter describe in more detail.

A. JURY POOL

Jurors are obtained from the community where the case is heard. The area of this community is usually the same as the venue boundaries of the court, such as the district or county boundaries where the court is located. The names of prospective jurors are obtained from public records including voter registration cards, driver's licenses, utility records, property documents, telephone directories, city directories, tax records, and other sources that identify possible jurors. The process used to identify potential jurors must meet constitutional standards, which require that the jury pool include individuals from all segments of the community and not exclude any class of people.

B. JUROR SUMMONS

The clerk of court (known as the court administrator in many jurisdictions) sends a summons to individuals living in the community selected to serve as jurors. The summons tells the prospective jurors to appear at the courthouse on a certain day and time and usually includes an explanation of how an individual may be excused from jury duty. A statute or court rule will typically list the legitimate reasons for which a juror may be excused: for example, severe physical illness, personal or family emergencies, or disqualifying employment status (such as judges). Most jurisdictions reject common excuses (e.g., inconvenience, work) and require representative members of the community, including lawyers, to serve jury duty. Prospective jurors may also be asked to complete a printed informational form and return it or complete an online form. Jurors are ordinarily scheduled for jury duty for a set period of time, such as a few weeks. Jurors complete their jury service after this time period has elapsed or after they reach a verdict in a case for which they sat as a juror. A number of individuals called for jury duty never actually serve as jurors because they are removed or because they are not needed.

C. JURY ORIENTATION

Prospective jurors arrive at the courthouse on the scheduled day and time and may complete an information form if they have not already done so. The clerk may review this information to determine whether any of the jurors should be excused because of personal circumstances or special employment situations. Many jurisdictions make these information forms available to the attorneys who will be selecting from among the prospective jurors. The clerk usually conducts an orientation program for the jury pool, including a lecture regarding jury duty, the distribution of a pamphlet explaining jury service, or the showing of a video describing the roles of jurors.

After orientation, the jurors may stay at the courthouse and wait to be called for a case or may leave for home or work. If they stay at the courthouse, they usually wait in a room where they may read, talk, use the internet, play games or watch selected television programs. If they leave, the clerk may contact them by phone, text, or email or tell them to return on a specific day or contact them in the future if they are needed. Federal courts use an Integrated Voice Response (IVR) electronic system to notify jurors of dates, times, and changes in their jury duty.

D. JURY PANEL

The clerk selects a panel of prospective jurors for a specific case from the pool of individuals summoned for jury duty. This process may be done randomly or in the order they were initially notified. A bailiff or other court official escorts this panel to the trial courtroom and typically seats the prospective jurors in the back or side of the courtroom.

E. NUMBER OF PROSPECTIVE JURORS

The total number of prospective jurors in a panel usually includes the following: the number of jurors who will deliberate, plus one or more alternate jurors, plus the number of individuals equal to the peremptory challenges the attorneys may exercise, plus additional individuals to replace any juror who may be removed for cause. For example, a panel of prospective jurors in a civil case may include: the 6 jurors who will make up the six-member jury; 1 or 2 alternate jurors; more alternate jurors if the trial is expected to last longer than several days; 4 additional persons who will be struck when the two parties each exercise their two peremptory challenges; and a few additional individuals who can replace any jurors removed for cause.

In other cases, the panel will consist of more jurors. If a case requires twelve jurors to deliberate, additional alternative jurors will sit and more peremptory challenges are provided each party. For example, in a criminal case, there may be 12 jurors, a minimum of 2 alternates, 8 more for possible peremptory challenges, and additional alternatives for long trials and individual replacements for those removed by cause challenges.

F.   SEATING PROSPECTIVE JURORS

The court clerk randomly selects prospective jurors from the panel seated in the courtroom who take a seat in the jury box. In some jurisdictions only those members of the panel selected to be prospective jurors are seated in the jury box to be questioned; the remainder return to the waiting room. In other jurisdictions, the remaining members of the jury panel remain seated in the courtroom until they are needed. If they are not selected, they return to the jury waiting room. If more jurors are needed, they are obtained from the pool of jurors in the waiting room.

G.   PRELIMINARY INFORMATION ABOUT PANEL

A list of the prospective jurors may be available and provided to counsel, along with information about each of the individuals. This data may include their name, address, employment status, family status, and information obtained from the form completed during orientation. If the names of the prospective jurors are not provided, the attorneys or an assistant can record the names as the clerk calls their names. Most lawyers write down the phonetic pronunciation so they will be able to pronounce the names properly. If no preliminary information about the jurors is provided to counsel, questions should be asked by the judge or attorneys to obtain this preliminary information.

Internet search engines and other sources are available to obtain public information about potential jurors. While further, detailed information can be obtained, the process can be time consuming and expensive. The importance of the case, its cost, and the time available are factors that determine the efforts that should be made.

H.   JURORS' OATH

The prospective jurors take an oath or affirmation, usually given by the clerk, to answer all questions truthfully and completely.

I.   PRELIMINARY REMARKS

The judge ordinarily makes introductory remarks to the prospective jurors. These remarks typically include an explanation of the purpose and procedures of the jury selection process; an introduction of the parties, attorneys, and the court officials; a brief description of the case; and instructions regarding the role of jurors in the case. The content of these introductory remarks varies among jurisdictions and judges. The comments usually cover information needed by the prospective jurors to understand what is happening. The judge then typically asks questions to gain information from the prospective jurors about their familiarity with the parties and the attorneys, their knowledge of the case, their previous jury trial experience, and other relevant matters.

Example (Judge):

Members of the Jury, this is a medical malpractice case. The plaintiff, Laura Fischer, is seated at the counsel table to your left, next to her attorney, Frank Galvin. The defendant, Wesley Brophy, is seated at the other table, next to his attorney, Ed Concannon, from the law firm of Concannon and Kaplan.

The plaintiff claims the defendant negligently diagnosed and failed to properly treat her condition when she sought medical treatment from him for her severe headaches. The defendant denies he was negligent and asserts the plaintiff did not tell him about the severity of her headaches. The plaintiff seeks to recover damages for her injuries and pain she claims to have suffered as result of the alleged negligence. Defendant denies he is responsible for those damages.

Q: Are any of you familiar with, or have any of you heard about, the incident that I described to you? Please raise your hand if you have.

A: (No affirmative responses).

Q: Are any of you familiar with, or do any of you know, any of the parties or attorneys that I have introduced to you?

A: (No affirmative responses).

As you know, I am Judge Harold T. Stone. Two other court officials who will be assisting me with this trial are Lana Wagner, who is the clerk of court, and MacIntosh Robinson, who is the court reporter.

This part of the trial is the jury selection process. We need an impartial jury that can decide this case fairly. To determine which of you can be fair and impartial, the attorneys and I will be asking you some questions. We ask these questions to obtain information about your ability to sit as a juror in this case. You must answer the questions honestly and completely. We do not ask the questions to pry into your private lives but only to seek helpful information so that the parties in this case can select jurors you would want in this case if you were a party: a jury made up of fair and impartial individuals.

In some jurisdictions, the judge may decide not to make some or all of these comments, instead allowing the attorneys to address the jury and make the preliminary remarks. An attorney who is first to make such remarks may gain an advantage by initially establishing some rapport with the jurors. The attorney who is second may then add whatever preparatory remarks the first lawyer did not cover or add other remarks about the case that were omitted.

§ 5.4   QUESTIONING THE PANEL

The panel of prospective jurors is questioned either by the judge and the attorneys or by the judge alone. This process varies among jurisdictions. See Section 5.4(B). The applicable federal rules and state rules provide judges with discretion in conducting jury selection. These rules give the court authority to conduct the entire examination or to permit the parties or their attorneys to conduct the examination of prospective jurors. See Fed.R.Civ.Proc. 47(a) and Fed.R.Crim.Proc. 24(a).

A.   MECHANICS

1.   Presence of Judge and Reporter

While most judges are present during the jury selection process, some may leave the bench while the jury is being questioned. In many jurisdictions a court reporter may not record the jury selection, and the judge may not be present to monitor the process. When there is no record of the questions being asked or when the judge is not in the courtroom, it is more difficult to control the questioning by opposing counsel. An attorney should usually request that the judge remain in the courtroom and/or that a court reporter make a record of the questions and responses.

2.   Attorney Movement

The lawyers may be permitted to walk around while questioning jurors or may be required to remain at a lectern or at counsel table. Some advocates prefer to sit in front of the jury box. The physical arrangement or the acoustics of the courtroom may prevent movement or require the lawyers to move to a particular location so they can be heard.

3.   Order of Questioning

In many jurisdictions, defense counsel is the first attorney to ask questions, followed by the plaintiff/prosecutor while other jurisdictions have the plaintiff/prosecutor go first. If uncertain, the advocate can ask the judge the preferred order at the pretrial conference. An attorney who plans to ask many preliminary questions and then realizes that the other side gets to ask those questions first may be left without much to ask, appear to be unprepared or be unable to accomplish specific objectives.

4. Discussion of Law

Generally, a discussion of the law by the attorneys is not permitted, although what is allowed varies among judges. An inappropriate discussion of the law may result in a reprimand from the judge. Counsel can ask the judge to explain the relevant law.

5. Amount of Time Available

Some judges strictly limit the amount of time the lawyers are permitted to question the jury; others permit the time preferred or requested by the lawyers. There is a common sense, reasonable duration that naturally restricts the time spent on questioning. The time varies, depending on the seriousness of the case, its complexity and length, any pretrial publicity, the lawyer's ability, the patience and schedule of the judge, and the court docket.

6. Open Courtroom

The public is permitted in the courtroom during the jury selection process, as well as during all other stages of the trial. Judges rarely set limits on who may be in the courtroom. Limits will be set only in those exceptional cases where there is an overriding interest that requires privacy, security protection or juror anonymity. The constitutional right of a defendant in a criminal case and the substantial interest of the public and media make the presumption of openness extremely difficult to overcome. Prospective witnesses who will be sequestered during the trial may be prohibited from attending jury selection.

7. Jury Selection Materials

Effective advocates organize and have readily available the materials they need for jury selection. These materials include the questions to be asked, a summary of the case issues, a list of witnesses and exhibits about which the jurors may be questioned regarding their knowledge, information about the jurors gathered from juror questionnaires or other sources, the law regarding challenges for cause and peremptory challenges, and objections that can be made during jury selection.

8. Recording Information During Jury Selection

The lawyer, co-counsel, an assistant or the client usually take notes and record information obtained during the questioning process on a laptop, tablet or notepad. This information may include observations of the juror's behavior and dress, juror responses to questions, and other factors that may help to rate prospective jurors as favorable or unfavorable. The extent of the note taking depends upon the lawyer's approach and the desired objectives.

Note taking can also create some problems during jury selection. It may unnecessarily interfere with and delay asking questions. Some jurors may be suspicious, bothered or offended by note taking. Jurors may wonder why their responses are being taken down in such detail and what will happen with that data. Extensive note taking can distract the lawyer from observing and listening to the jurors.

Notes should be taken in an organized manner. A large number of notes containing excessive information may be difficult to organize and apply. A system should be designed so that there is sufficient space for all relevant information and so the notes can be easily reviewed. Some lawyers develop a shorthand method that is neither distracting nor offensive, while others do not take notes at all, preferring instead to pay close attention to what the jurors say and how they say it. When colleagues record information, the trial attorney is free to ask questions without having to be concerned about note taking.

A jury chart is indispensable as a means to record information about the jurors. See Form 5.1. A chart used to record information may be constructed as the clerk reads the names of the prospective jurors, or the information to create the chart may be provided by the court clerk in advance. Information obtained during jury selection can be recorded by using abbreviations, symbols, or initials.

B. QUESTIONING EXCLUSIVELY BY THE JUDGE

Judges ask all jury selection questions in about one-fifth of the state courts and approximately two-thirds of the federal courts. The attorneys may—and usually do—submit questions for the judge to ask. The rules in most jurisdictions require that the court allow the attorneys to submit proposed questions in writing or orally.

An advantage of the judge asking all the questions is efficiency. The jury selection process is shortened, often taking less than thirty minutes or an hour. The disadvantages are that the judge does not know the case as well as the attorneys and may not ask necessary questions; the jurors may be hesitant to answer some questions in a forthright manner because the judge is an authority figure; and the lawyers have little opportunity to follow-up on answers, educate the jurors, neutralize their attitudes, develop rapport with them, or obtain commitments from them.

After a judge asks the questions, the attorneys may request that the judge ask clarifying or additional questions, with the record containing the questions proposed by the attorneys the judge did not ask. After the questioning has been completed, the lawyers may bring motions to strike jurors for cause, which the judge may grant or deny, and then the lawyers are able to exercise their peremptory challenges. See Section 5.8.

C. QUESTIONING BY JUDGE AND ATTORNEYS

In most state courts and in some federal judicial districts, the judge and attorneys share the questioning. In these jurisdictions, the judge typically asks initial questions to determine grounds for challenges for cause, followed by questions from the attorneys. The extent to which a judge is involved in the questioning of potential jurors depends primarily on the philosophy and preferences of the judge.

State court rules and procedures vary widely with regard to the way jury selection is conducted. In major civil and criminal cases, the lawyers commonly conduct intensive and extensive examinations. In most civil cases, the judges limit the scope and extent of questions asked by the attorneys and set a time limit for jury selection.

The advantage of the shared questioning system is that the attorneys are able to obtain more relevant information from the jurors in order to properly exercise their challenges and to establish rapport. The disadvantage is that the process is time consuming and attorneys may misuse the system by attempting to argue their case instead of obtaining information. The attorneys make their challenges for cause during or after all the questioning has been completed and exercise their peremptory challenges after all the questions have been asked of individual jurors or the entire panel.

1. Questions Directed to the Panel

Ordinarily, jurors are questioned as a panel. The lawyers first ask general questions of the entire panel and follow up with questions to individual jurors. It is important to determine just how those questions are phrased, which questions are directed to the entire panel, and which are asked of individual jurors. When jurors are questioned as a panel, the attorneys usually make their challenges for cause and exercise their peremptory challenges after all the questioning has been completed.

2. Questions Directed to Individual Jurors

In some courts, the attorneys question each prospective juror on the panel individually. The attorneys ask all questions of one prospective juror before questioning another member of the panel. After questioning an individual prospective juror, the attorneys may exercise a challenge for cause, exercise a peremptory challenge, or accept the juror. The attorney then questions the next prospective juror on the panel. The process continues until the required number of jurors has been selected.

3. Questions to an Individual Juror Outside the Presence of the Panel

This process is used only in major criminal cases and some significant civil cases that involve sensitive matters and is quite time consuming. Prospective jury members are individually questioned by attorneys outside the presence of other jurors. In these cases one juror at a time is brought in the courtroom and questioned individually to prevent a response from prejudicing or influencing other members of the panel. The attorneys then make a challenge for cause, exercise a peremptory challenge, or accept the juror. Jury selection is completed when the required number of jurors has been reached.

D. INTRODUCTORY REMARKS BY ATTORNEYS

In jurisdictions that permit the attorneys to ask questions, the lawyers are usually able to make introductory remarks about the case before beginning questioning. The scope of these remarks depends upon what the judge and opposing attorney have said to the jurors. The remarks can include identifying the client, the purpose of jury selection, and a concise explanation of the factual story and legal issues.

Example (Plaintiff's Attorney):

Members of the Jury, I represent Jacob Marley, the plaintiff in this case, who sits next to me. Mr. Marley, a business partner of the defendant Scrooge, is here to obtain money from the defendant for the breach of a partnership agreement involving a financial institution they owned and operated.

As Judge Jarndyce has explained, I will be asking you some questions to obtain information regarding the issues in this case. Both sides need to know your attitudes and feelings regarding these issues in order to determine that you will be fair and impartial. My questions are not intended to make you uncomfortable or nervous, although it's normal and natural for you to feel anxious because being in court can be an unsettling experience. If you don't understand a question, please tell me and I'll rephrase the question to make it understandable. I'll be asking some questions directed to all of you, and some questions directed to individuals. If you have any information, regarding any question that I ask another juror, please raise your hand and I will call on you.

It is improper for an attorney to make closing arguments during the introductory remarks to jury selection. Those should be reserved for summation.

Example (Improper Comments):

This civil case is about an extremely hardworking and trustworthy employee, Bob Cratchit, who is the poor plaintiff who had to sue Scrooge to obtain his meager salary. Bob signed a valid employment contract with this miserly defendant, who illegally refused to pay Mr. Cratchit the salary he deserves. At the end of this case, we're certain you'll right this terrible wrong.

---

§ 5.5　JURY SELECTION QUESTIONS

A.　TYPES OF QUESTIONS

The scope of jury selection questions depends on what counsel wishes to accomplish. The extent of questioning also depends on what the judge has asked the jurors, the limits placed on the questioning, what information is already available to the lawyers, and what the attorney believes is needed to achieve the objectives of jury selection.

There are several types of questions counsel may ask:

- Open-ended questions,
- Close-ended questions,
- General questions to the entire panel,
- Specific questions directed to the entire panel,
- General questions to an individual juror, and
- Specific questions directed to an individual juror.

1.　Open-Ended Questions

Open-ended questions allow jurors to explain answers and express their opinions.

Examples:

Q: Sloan Sabbith, what do you do on a typical evening in the newsroom?

Q: What do you like to do at home after reading WSJ?

FORM 5.1
JUROR INFORMATION

Name   _____

Address   _____

Approximate age/
    demeanor/dress   _____

Knowledge about case   _____

Knowledge about attorneys/ parties/witness   _____

Occupation   _____

Employer   _____

Education   _____

Marital status   _____

Spouse's occupation/employer   _____

Children   _____

Past claims/lawsuits   _____

Similar case experience   _____

Past/present jury duty   _____

    Civil   _____

    Criminal   _____

Opinion about case   _____

Attitude toward client/case   _____

Hardships   _____

Other   _____

2.   Closed Ended Questions

Closed ended questions gather a relatively small amount of information from a juror and they are phrased to obtain a "yes" or "no" response. They are generally used to obtain specific factual information, to obtain commitments, and to educate the juror.

Example:

Q: Ms. Segal, have you met Mr. Capone?

Q: Have you been at his store in Mercer?

Q: Can you be fair to Mr. Capone as you listen to his testimony?

---

3.   General Questions to the Entire Panel That Require an Explanatory Response

---

Examples:

I am going to ask some general questions about the Hockey Hall of Fame and follow up with some more specific questions.

Q: How any of you visited the Hockey Hall of Fame in Virginia, Minnesota?

Q: Tell us about your experience at the Hall of Fame.

---

4.   Specific Questions Directed to the Entire Panel Requiring "Yes" or "No" Answers and That May Require Follow-up Questions

---

Examples:

Q: Have any of you attended a Tommy Tutone auction?

Q: Have any of you bought anything at his auction?

---

5.   General Questions to Individual Jurors Requiring Narrative Responses

---

Examples:

Q: Ms. Benz, you said that you were involved in an automobile accident. Please tell us about that experience.

Q: Mr. Du Bois, you raised your hand when I asked if any of you knew any members of the union. How do you know someone with the union?

---

6. Specific Questions Directed to Individual Jurors Requiring "Yes" or "No" or Short Explanatory Responses

---

Examples:

Q: Ms. Kachina, you said you attended ceremonial dances on the reservation, did you participate in the dances?

Q: About how many ceremonial dances did you attend?

B. SELECTING TYPES OF QUESTIONS

The type of questions that should be asked depends upon the limits the judge has placed on the questioning, the preference of the lawyers, the responses of the jurors, the nature of the case, the time available for juror interviews, and the purpose for asking the questions. General questions directed to the panel as a whole are usually appropriate if "yes" or "no" answers or short explanations are expected. Specific questions directed to individual jurors may be asked as follow up inquiries or to probe new areas.

The jurors also need to know how they are expected to respond to questions. The lawyer should make clear, especially in asking questions of the entire panel, whether the jurors should respond verbally or by raising their hand. If there are many prospective jurors, asking them to raise their hands makes it easier to identify individuals.

Some types of questions should be directed to the panel as a whole, while other types should be asked of jurors individually. The nature of the questions and the anticipated answers often determine when and what types of questions should be asked of jurors. Attorneys often ask questions of the entire panel during the beginning of the jury selection process, postponing individual questions until they establish some rapport with the jurors. Questions seeking grounds for challenges for cause are commonly asked of all panel members because the questions are less threatening when all jurors are asked. Questions involving sensitive or personal matters may also be more effectively directed to the entire panel because the impact initially will be less intrusive on individual jurors.

Questions should be asked in a manner that involves all jurors. A mix of general and specific questions usually maintains the attention of the entire panel. Jurors should be treated equally. However, if a lawyer knows for certain that a juror will be struck, that juror need not be questioned in the same way other jurors are questioned.

C. CONCLUDING QUESTIONS

The concluding questions of jury selection should elicit a positive and affirmative response that supports a verdict for the client.

Example (Civil Plaintiff):

Members of the Jury, after we present evidence that proves Ms. Kramer's case, will each of you be able to return a verdict in favor of the plaintiff?

Example (Civil Defendant):

Will each of you agree that you will not decide this case until you have heard all the evidence, and that you will keep an open mind and wait until after we have presented our case on behalf of Mr. Kramer, the defendant, before reaching any decision?

---

§ 5.6   THEORIES OF JURY SELECTION QUESTIONING

Successful trial lawyers have developed their own jury selection theories to determine whether a juror will be favorable or unfavorable. Theories used to determine which jurors will be biased or prejudiced are varied and diverse. Whatever theory is used, it is important to remember that jury selection theories are more art than science.

Attorneys develop and employ approaches based largely on their experience, judgment, intuition, and feelings. These different jury selection theories produce approaches not necessarily based on objective, discernible factors. Specific approaches should not be used without a great deal of consideration given to their predictive accuracy.

The following paragraphs present several theories used by trial lawyers in determining which jurors should be removed from the panel.

A. IMPRESSIONISTIC EVALUATIONS

This approach relies largely on the intuition of the attorney and frequently on the intuition of the client as well. The attorney, or the attorney and the client, determine which jurors the attorney and client like or do not like, and which jurors seem to like the client, the case, and the attorney. These judgments are based upon the attorney's subjective assessment of each juror. It may be based on the simple analysis of "I like this juror" and "This juror appears to like me."

B. GENERALIZATIONS AND STEREOTYPES

Many attorneys select jurors based upon generalizations regarding people. The attorney relies upon characterizations to predict how a juror will react and vote. Some of these generalized stereotypes may have merit (loan officers at small banks are often fiscally conservative); other stereotypes may be speculation (rural inhabitants dislike corporations); still other stereotypes are nonsensical (obese individuals whose grandparents came from Crete favor defendants). The stereotyping of an individual based on generalizations applicable to a class of people can be detrimental or helpful, depending on the validity of the underlying data.

C. CHARACTER AND PERSONALITY TRAITS

Some attorneys identify favorable jurors based upon the apparent character and personality traits of the juror. The attorney obtains information and observes the jurors to determine these traits. The attorney then decides which of these jurors may be most favorable to a client. Examples of character and personality traits include: how authoritative or assertive the juror appears, how good a communicator or listener the juror is, and how honest and open the juror will be.

D. NONVERBAL BEHAVIOR

Attorneys may rely on the nonverbal behavior revealed by jurors in addition to their verbal responses to assess their real attitudes and feelings. They observe the jurors closely for positive and negative body language and attempt to interpret this behavior in assessing the jurors' biases and prejudices.

E. JURY PROFILE

Advocates can attempt to develop a profile of an effective juror involving social, family, economic, political, educational, and psychological attitudes and views. The goal is to identify potential jurors who may be favorably inclined toward the position of one party or unfavorably predisposed toward an opponent's position. This approach is based upon a jury profile developed in advance of trial to indicate in general terms how a particular juror will make a decision in a case based on specific backgrounds or upon generalizations derived from a larger group in society. A jury profile attempts to describe the characteristics of the ideal, mythical juror. This juror is hopefully someone who is prone to return a winning verdict.

Some attorneys believe this process is very worthwhile and would not proceed to trial without this effort. Other lawyers do not find this procedure as useful because it is too speculative, and they feel that the chances of finding an ideal juror on the panel are remote. However, many lawyers believe it is worthwhile to create a profile that can be used as a reference to evaluate the prospective panel of jurors. A jury profile should not be a mechanical replacement for the judgment of counsel and the client who have the ultimate responsibility to select jurors.

A jury consultant or a psychologist or sociologist with expertise or experience with jury selection may help design a juror profile. If sufficient economic resources are available, this approach might be useful in supplementing the attorney's and the client's assessment of prospective jurors. This information may also be obtained less expensively from books, articles, treatises, or websites. A jury profile may be created by reviewing the factual and legal issues, considering how jurors might identify with the client, witnesses, and the attorney, and by predicting how jurors might vote in jury deliberations. Jurors are then selected from the panel who most closely match the characteristics of people who identify with the case theory, the participants, and the issues.

A jury profile of unfavorable jurors may also be designed. This anti-juror profile corresponds to the opponent's favorable, mythical juror. Characteristics and traits of individuals who are least likely to identify with the client, case theory, participants, and the issues are identified. During jury selection, prospective jurors who have these characteristics and traits may be challenged or struck from the panel.

F. SOCIAL SCIENCE RESEARCH

Attorneys can rely on social science data to select jurors in cases where clients have the resources to pay for the development of this information. This approach identifies characteristics that favorably correlate with the significant issues in a case. Reputable jury consultants can research appropriate demographic factors and sample the community to determine which jurors may have these characteristics. Information about a juror's financial situation, job, marital status, neighborhood, and hobbies reveal information that may match favorable factors. This approach relies upon the expertise of social scientists or experts in other behavioral disciplines, and many lawyers are reluctant to rely extensively upon these non-lawyers in selecting jurors.

G. IMPROPER THEORIES

There are some juror selection theories that are improper. It is unconstitutional to use race, gender or religion as the sole or primary reason in choosing jurors; and trial lawyers must avoid using these factors in jury selection. If a prohibited factor appears to be the reason why a juror is being struck, the attorney has the burden to establish the legitimate reasons why a juror is being removed. See Section 5.9(H).

§ 5.7   QUESTIONS AND APPROACHES TO ACHIEVE OBJECTIVES

The judge has discretion to allow or disallow questions depending upon the purpose and nature of the question. In all jurisdictions where the attorneys may ask questions, the attorneys have a right to ask questions to obtain information to support grounds for a challenge for cause. The attorneys may also ask questions to obtain information needed to exercise peremptory challenges.

Judges have broad discretion to permit questions that serve the other jury selection objectives. Many judges allow the attorneys to ask a wide range of questions that educate, develop rapport with, and obtain commitments from jurors. Other judges restrict the scope of these questions or prohibit them altogether. The attorney should obtain information about limitations the judge places on the questioning process. See Section 5.4.

Many jurisdictions limit jury selection questions to areas that establish bias or prejudice and prohibit or limit questions designed to educate or indoctrinate prospective jurors. However, many jurisdictions do permit attorneys to question jurors to achieve broader objectives. Categorizing jury selection questions into those that are designed to show bias or prejudice and those that are designed to educate or indoctrinate the jury is often difficult. Many questions serve multiple purposes, and legitimate questions in all jurisdictions designed to elicit bias and prejudice may also achieve broader objectives.

Counsel should follow common sense communication guidelines questioning jurors:

- Engage the jurors in conversation.
- Be receptive and responsive.
- Encourage the jurors to give complete and honest answers.
- Listen carefully to answers.
- Observe nonverbal demeanor.
- Reward helpful answers with verbal and nonverbal responses.

A. OBTAINING INFORMATION

1. Information About Jurors

In order to identify favorable jurors, the lawyer should collect and review as much information that is readily available about prospective jurors. In most cases, the attorneys do not know who the jurors will be until the jurors arrive in the courtroom, limiting the opportunity to obtain preliminary information. In some jurisdictions, information about the prospective panel of jurors may be obtained before trial. Addresses of the panel provide generalized information concerning the neighborhood, home, and socioeconomic status of the prospective jurors. Information about size of family, occupation, prior jury duty, and other background information may also be useful.

In jurisdictions that provide advance information and with a client that has substantial resources available, an investigation may be conducted of the prospective jury members. Investigators may contact neighbors and friends to gather information about panel members, but no personal contact may be made directly with prospective jurors. In some jurisdictions, records are maintained about jurors' prior jury service. Prosecutors, criminal defense counsel, plaintiff's personal injury trial lawyers, or defendant's insurance attorneys may also maintain information about jurors, particularly in smaller communities. Internet search tools are available that can provide helpful information concerning prospective jurors. The approach that is taken must not violate the privacy rights of prospective jurors or their family and friends. Lawyers and retained investigators must comply with any federal or state laws or regulations that restrict inquiries and investigations.

2. Information About Jury Duty

Trial attorneys need to review the jury orientation program to discover what information prospective jurors receive before they appear in the courtroom. This may be done by obtaining a copy of the information, by watching the recorded presentation, or by talking with court personnel. The location of the jury waiting room and juror activities while waiting may also influence jurors' perceptions about the legal system. Counsel should become familiar with the jury room, whether wireless or internet access is available, what kind of magazines or books the jurors have access to, what kind of games or other activities the jurors participate in, and where jurors are likely to have lunch. The more the attorney learns about what happens to the jurors prior to jury selection, the better able the attorney is to ask effective questions.

3. Information from Observations of Jury Activity in the Courtroom

a. *Prospective Jurors in the Courtroom*

The trial attorney should begin observing the jurors as they enter the courtroom. The lawyer should observe the appearance of the jurors, including their conduct, any apparent physical discomforts, with whom they talk, and whether individuals appear talkative, quiet, nervous, or alone. This first impression may be helpful in deciding questions to ask and in making a final selection.

b. *Prospective Juror Associations*

Some of the prospective jurors may have spent time together or may have formed friendly or unfriendly relationships. Particular attention should be paid to these relationships, as they will affect the cohesiveness of the jury. Attention should also be paid to those jurors who appear to emerge as leaders, as they may influence other jurors.

c. *Juror Body Language and Appearances*

Nonverbal cues prior to jury selection and during the selection process may help determine if a juror is more or less favorable. Did the juror make more eye contact with the attorney or client? Did the juror appear to be interested or alert during questioning? Did the juror seem more at ease in answering one side's questions? Jurors who appear to be comfortable or calm in the courtroom may be willing to follow instructions more readily than someone who is uncomfortable being in court.

d. *Observations by Team Member*

Another trial team member may sit in the courtroom to observe the jurors during jury selection and advise trial counsel regarding those observations. This individual, not occupied with questioning, will have a better opportunity to observe juror behavior.

4. Factual Information

If a question seeks particular information, the question should be phrased to generate a specific response. There are several areas of questions that should be considered with every juror. The following examples provide sample questions:

Examples:

Employment Status

Q: What kind of work do you do, Mr. Krebs?

Q: What are your responsibilities as a supervisor?

Q: How do you feel about being a supervisor?

Family Status

Q: You said you have one child, Ms. Gillia. A girl or a boy?

Q: What school does he attend?

Q: Do you ever get the chance to help out at school?

Educational Level

Q: After high school, did you go to any other school, Ms. Menniger?

Q: Have any of you taken courses where the law has been taught or discussed?

Q: What kinds of courses were they?

Life Experiences

Q: Mr. Armitage, what do you do on a typical Saturday? Sunday?

Q: What are your hobbies?

Q: What do you do with your vacation time?

Previous Jury Experience

Q: Have you ever sat as a juror before?

Q: What kind of a case was it, Ms. Gilroy?

Q: Do you have any positive or negative feelings about our system of justice based on your experience?

Experience with the Court System

Q: Have any of you ever been involved as a plaintiff or defendant in a case?

Q: Please tell us about that experience, Professor Pomfritt?

Q: Does that experience affect how you may consider this case?

Experience in Fields Relating to the Case

Q: Do you have any relatives or friends who are teachers, Ms. Byron?

Q: Mr. Osborne, do you know anyone who's been the victim of a crime?

Knowledge of Case

Q: Because you have heard of the defendant S. Peter Pryor Junior College, do you have any feelings, one way or the other, that may affect your judgment about this College that educates students here in our community?

5.   Relationships with Parties, Lawyers, and Witnesses

These questions are often asked by the court at the start of jury selection. Counsel may inquire further to clarify a juror's answers.

Examples:

Q: Minny Jackson, you raised your hand when the judge asked you if you knew the plaintiff this case. How do know Hilly Holbrook?

Q: A few of you indicated you have heard about the defendant Madea Simmons. I'll start with juror Ms. Breaux, how do you know about Ms. Simmons?

---

6.   Opinions and Attitudes

These questions seek opinions and attitudes of the jurors, and may be phrased either as open-ended or leading questions.

Examples:

Q: Have you heard about the concept of a living will, Luis Kutner?

Q: Have you heard about the concept that people, before they die, can choose to have extraordinary life support ended if they have a terminal illness and there is no hope at all for continued life?

Q: Will the fact that this case involves Transylvania Transplant Hospital which employs people in this community influence you one way or the other in reaching a verdict based on the facts ?

---

7.   Demonstrating a Bias

Sensitive and difficult issues of possible bias and prejudice should be addressed.

Example:

Q: Mr. Wallace, you have told us that it would be very difficult for you if your child were to marry someone of a different race and that your feelings about race are very important values in your life. You know that this is a race discrimination case. Because your feelings are so strong and, perhaps, even controlling, would you agree that it would be impossible for you to be fair and neutral as you evaluate the evidence in this case?

8. Pretrial Publicity

Websites, blogs, news media, and television and radio may have an influence on the ability of the jurors to listen to the case.

Examples:

Q: What do you recall reading on the internet about this case, Mr. Turing?

Q: How do you feel about the defendant in this case based on what you have seen on any websites, Mr. Babbage?

The words people use to describe the publicity may reveal their attitudes and provide a basis for asking more questions about their views.

B. EDUCATING THE JURY

Questions may be asked that provide information to the jurors.

Appropriate questions can be designed to tell the jurors about the evidence, the law, and other facets of the case.

1. About the Case and Facts

Examples:

Q: Are you all aware, from what Judge Wapner told you, that this is not a criminal case involving Ms. Simpson, but is a civil case?

Q: In this case the plaintiff is saying that the defendant unlawfully caused the death of a person, her husband, Homer. Do you understand that this is unlike a criminal case, and in this case no one will go to jail if you find that the defendant is responsible for Mr. Simpson's death?

2. About the Clients or Parties

Example:

Q: Judge Erskine-Brown asked you if you knew Horace W. Rumpole, who is the plaintiff in this case. He is a widower. His wife, Hilda Rumpole, died last fall. She was very active in community affairs in our city. Did any of you know her?

Example:

Q: The plaintiff in this case emigrated from Somalia five years ago. Because of that move, he lost everything and had to start anew in this country. The plaintiff was a doctor in Somalia but because of our medical regulations he cannot practice medicine. He has taken laboring jobs to provide for his family. Do you know anyone who has moved from another country and has had those or similar experiences?

Example:

Q: Coco Chanel is a fashion designer and consultant and she will testify in this case as an expert witness. Have any of you bought her haute couture?

---

3. About the Witnesses

a. Lay Witness

Example:

Q: Cass Gilbert is the only eyewitness who will testify in this case. He will tell you that after work he had two bottles of beer and chicken wings and left to go home. Then he saw the building collapse. Do any of you doubt that someone like Mr. Gilbert who earlier ate and drank at a bar can later observe an event clearly and remember it?

---

b. Expert Witness

Example:

Q: Dr. Rose Mayo will be testifying and will be telling you that she is a graduate from New York Medical College and a California Board Certified orthopedic surgeon. She currently serves with Doctors Without Borders. Will you be able to weigh her expert testimony based on her qualifications, training, and experience, and not be influenced because Dr. Mayo has been recently practicing only in foreign countries?

4. About the Law

a. Burdens of Proof

The common standards of proof—"beyond a reasonable doubt" in a criminal case and "preponderance of evidence" in a civil case—may be unfamiliar to jurors. To avoid jurors confusing the different types and degrees of proof, it is important they understand the differences from the beginning so they do not apply the wrong standard.

Example Criminal Case:

Q: In a criminal case the defendant does not have to take the stand and testify. It may be that some people might consider the defendant guilty if she does not testify. Will you be able to set aside any such thought and follow the law that allows the defendant not to testify?

Q: Do you understand that as Tyler White sits here in this courtroom, she is presumed innocent?

Example Civil Case:

Q: Do you understand that the burden of proof in a civil case is by a preponderance of the evidence that is much lower than the burden of proof beyond a reasonable doubt that you might have heard about in a criminal case?

Q: Will you be able to apply this burden of proof in this civil case involving an alleged civil assault by my client, George Pickett?

b. Liability

Questions can also help the jurors understand liability issues.

Examples:

Q: One of the issues in this case is whether the defendant Ghostbusters Proton Pack Company is strictly liable for what happened. Has anyone heard of strict liability?

Q: Do you think it is reasonable to say that the company that made the product is responsible for the deaths of others caused by the defect, even if it didn't intend to cause any injuries or was unaware of a problem?

c. Damages

And questions can help the jurors understand damages.

Examples:

Q: If you find the defendant Professor Prosser liable for the personal injuries suffered by the plaintiff, the law holds him responsible to pay money damages to compensate plaintiff for her loss. Do you understand that?

Q: Plaintiff may be able to recover for her pain and suffering in this case. Have you heard of that legal term—pain and suffering—before?

d. Defenses

If a juror may be unwilling to accept a particular defense, the juror could be removed for cause. Questions can inform jurors about the correct legal standard.

Examples:

Q: In this case the defendant Mandrake the Magician is going to tell you that he was somewhere else with his friends and couldn't have committed the crime. That is called an alibi. Are all of you familiar with that term?

Q: Do you think it's possible that a person can be accused of something and actually be the wrong person?

e. Elements

Jury selection also provides the opportunity for the lawyer to teach the jurors about elements of a case.

Examples:

Q: Do you understand that in this case where Goliath was killed by a staff and sling, there may be a number of different possible offenses that describe what might have happened?

Q: Do you understand that the term "manslaughter" is a lesser offense than first-degree murder?

5. About Weaknesses and Strengths in the Case

The attorney may acknowledge weaknesses during jury selection. If dealt with in a straightforward manner, the effect of the weaknesses may well be diminished.

Example:

Q: Frances Stevens has a criminal record. Five years ago she was convicted of burglary. She will take the stand and tell you that her days of being a "cat burglar" with John Robie have long been over. Will you be able to decide the case on the evidence presented in court about what happened in this case and not what happened five years ago?

C. DEVELOPING RAPPORT WITH THE JURY

Jury selection questions must be asked in a way that develops a positive rapport with the jury. The trial lawyer who makes a favorable impression during jury selection benefits from the lasting effect of this impression throughout the trial.

Rapport can be created and developed in several ways. The attorney must project a sincere and honest attitude in the case. A respectful approach, a caring outlook, appropriate eye contact, attentive listening, appropriate body language, and a genuine interest help reduce juror anxiety and build rapport.

The lawyer must also be well prepared. Poorly phrased questions, inappropriate inquiries, and aimless questioning portray the attorney as ill prepared and unprofessional. The more comfortable and at ease the jurors become with the attorney and client, the more attention and focus they can devote to the case.

1. Developing Rapport Begins Early

The jurors often will notice the attorneys and parties upon entering the courtroom. Counsel and clients should be prepared at counsel table to receive the jurors. The jurors may observe the lawyer, the client, and witnesses in the courtroom or elsewhere in the courthouse and as they converse with clerks, bailiffs, and other court personnel. The attorney must appear professional and confident at all times in front of the jurors.

2. Properly Addressing the Panel

Jurors should be addressed respectfully by their surnames. While some jurors may be more sensitive to this issue than others, every effort should be made to make sure of the juror's preference, such as Mr. Figaro, Ms. Carmen, Mrs. Electra, or Madame Butterfly. A military person may expect to be addressed by a title such as "Captain" or "Sergeant." A scientist or medical doctor may prefer to be addressed by the title "Doctor." Attorneys should review the juror questionnaires, or ask the jurors their preference, or request that the judge or clerk obtain that information before the lawyers question them.

3. Using Appearances to Develop Rapport

Attorneys and clients must consider how they wish to appear and whether they appear that way in the eyes of the jurors. Section 1.8 discussed considerations of physical appearance, clothing style, gestures, body language, and related considerations. These factors should be used to effectively enhance rapport with the jurors.

4. Using Questions to Develop Rapport

a. *Manner of Asking Questions*

An effective approach is to use a conversational style with the jurors. Questions should be delivered with a calm voice using appropriate pauses and interesting modulation. This helps the attorney appear interested in the question as well as the juror's answer. Careful listening and paying attention enhance interest. Questions that are read or delivered in a monotone voice appear to be routine questions and, while they may get some information, they do little for developing positive rapport.

b. *Recognizing Jurors' Discomfort/Anxiety*

If the attorney recognizes that a juror is uncomfortable or anxious about being questioned, counsel should sincerely acknowledge the discomfort and attempt to help the juror relax. Lawyers should not be overly solicitous to avoid appearing insincere.

Example:

Q: You are Elle Woods, right? It appears to me that you are troubled with the question I just asked you. I'll rephrase it so it makes better sense.

---

c.   *Questions That Permit the Juror to Clarify Previous Statements*

The attorney can demonstrate sensitivity and interest by allowing the juror to correct a misstatement or expand on an answer.

Example:

Q: Earlier I asked you questions about damages and you indicated that you would award damages to someone who has proven severe emotional distress. However, later you said you felt it would be hard to judge the level of distress suffered because people experience it differently. Dr. Freud, will you be able to make a fair judgment about the emotional distress the plaintiff suffered after you hear and see all that tragically happened to her?

---

d.   *Style and Tone of the Questions*

A juror may be bothered by an awkward or rambling question or by the tone in which a question is asked. The lawyer must accept the blame for asking that kind of question and rephrase it, rather than implying that the juror is at fault.

Example:

Q: What I am really trying to ask is prior to the last question that I asked you, before I was speaking to you about the following information ... I'm sorry, that just didn't make sense. Let me try it again, Ms. Malaprop.

---

5.   Dealing with Hostile Jurors

Questioning a juror who is obviously hostile or appears angry or upset is difficult. One approach is simply not to ask a hostile person any questions, with the idea that the person will be removed later on a peremptory challenge. In so doing, the attorney may avoid the risk of an angry juror influencing other jurors through negative answers to questions. However, an open, direct approach to resentment or antagonism may go a long way toward developing rapport with the other jurors, or may work towards diffusing the hostility so that the juror becomes an asset rather than one who has to be removed. If this approach fails, a basis for a challenge for cause may be established by showing the hostile juror to be prejudiced against the case, client, or attorney.

Example:

Q: Ms. Nightingale, you appeared upset when I asked you about lawsuits against surgeons. You told us you thought these doctors were a bunch of "overpaid prima donnas."

A: You bet I did.

Q: Do you ever go to a doctor yourself for any kind of treatment?

A: I've been to some doctors, but never a surgeon.

Q: Have you ever been treated in a hospital?

A: Fortunately not.

Q: Now, you have told us that you have children. Have they ever gone to a doctor?

A: I've never taken them. My husband does.

Q: You haven't taken them to have shots or any kind of preventive treatment or health care?

A: I don't like dealing with doctors.

Q: Would you agree that it would be very difficult for you to be fair to a defendant doctor and listen to all the evidence before making up your mind?

A: I can't trust what they say. I don't believe them.

6. Avoiding Embarrassing Situations

Frequently attorneys must ask questions that are personal and potentially embarrassing to the jurors. Counsel must be aware of possible adverse reactions to such inquiries. Questions should be worded carefully to avoid or minimize negative jury reactions.

Example:

Q: Mr. Marx, if you were out on the street one day and an interviewer stopped you and asked you whether you saw yourself as a liberal or conservative, how would you describe yourself and why?

Q: Sue Sylvester, if you could go back and see your favorite high school cheerleading teacher and that teacher asked you how things were going for you, what would you say?

Comedic attempts may also cause embarrassments. Jokes are dangerous because it is possible that the attorney will appear flip and uncaring. Natural humor, suitable in a situation or as a natural response to a juror's humor, may create an appropriate light-hearted moment.

7. Giving the Jurors a Chance to Talk

When asking open-ended questions, the attorney should listen to the relevant answer and not interrupt. Encouraging narrative juror responses generates more information about them. If a juror appears to hesitate, the attorney can be supportive by using a silent pause, an affirmative head nod, or phrases like, "Go on" or "Please continue." If a juror rambles on, counsel may politely interrupt and ask another question.

8. Thanking Jurors

The attorneys may recognize the willingness of prospective jurors to be jurors. It is appropriate to sincerely thank them for being candid and open with their responses.

Example:

Thank you all very much for being so direct with me and for answering my questions honestly. We all appreciate the fact that you have been thoughtful in answering these questions, even the difficult ones concerning personal matters.

D. NEUTRALIZING NEGATIVE AND BUILDING ON POSITIVE ATTITUDES AND BELIEFS

Obviously, jurors bring their opinions and life experiences with them to the courtroom. All jurors have some biases and prejudices and hold misperceptions about trials, jury duty, what trial lawyers do, and what clients deserve. People have difficulty publicly admitting their biases and prejudices, especially in a courtroom in front of strangers. Sometimes their answers are incomplete half-truths, misleading, or even false. Questions can be crafted to encourage complete, honest answers.

Example:

Q: Except for what Judge Soong has told you about this case, you don't know anything about the case, do you?

A: That's right.

Q: As you sit here now, you have no strong feelings one way or the other about this case, do you Mr. Data?

A: I don't.

Q: You don't have any biases or prejudices that unduly influence you one way or another toward either the plaintiff or the defendant in this case?

A: That's right.

Q: And the only evidence you are going to rely on to decide this case is the evidence presented during this trial?

A: Yes.

Of course, those answers are not quite accurate. Nobody is completely neutral. Jurors' experiences and beliefs influence their decision-making, and a major objective of the jury selection process is to learn about these attitudes. Questions that are designed to discover bias and prejudice should be used to neutralize negative opinions and build upon positive feelings that jurors may have toward the case, client, or counsel.

Example:

Q: Real trials are not like television programs such as "Law and Order" and reruns of "The Practice." And, you know, of course, lawyers don't behave in real courtrooms like they are so often portrayed in the movies, don't you?

As importantly, attorneys must deal with inappropriate stereotypes regarding client or witnesses.

Example:

Q: You are going to learn that Tom Joad, the plaintiff in this case, is unemployed. He has not been able to find a job for over a year and has had to receive financial assistance to support himself, which he is entitled to receive from the government in order to live. The fact that Mr. Joad has not worked does not affect in any way what happened to him in this case. Will all of you be able to set aside feelings you might have about unemployed people receiving public aid in making the decisions in this case?

The jurors may have preconceived notions about issues in a case such as soft tissue injuries, psychiatric issues, high monetary verdicts, or questionable lawsuits similar to the case on trial. These attitudes likely need to be explored.

Example:

Q: This case involves a corporate acquisition. While the deal may appear to be complex and confusing, the events are simple and straightforward. Do you have any personal or professional experiences that are negative or positive about any Quaker executives involved in the Snapple takeover?

E.　OBTAINING COMMITMENTS

The lawyer may attempt to obtain a promise from the jurors to not hold some fact or weakness against a client or a witness. Such a request should be phrased as a question seeking a "yes" or "no" response.

Example:

Q: In this case Mata Hari is going to tell you that she was sexually assaulted by the defendant. She will also tell you that although she is a prostitute, she told the defendant that she didn't want to have sexual relations with him. He then brutally forced her to have sex with him by punching and beating her. Do you believe that everyone, no matter who they are, has the right to make a voluntary decision about their own sexual partners?

While seeking to obtain commitments can be difficult and troublesome, questions may be designed to properly obtain appropriate responses. Most jurors will hold themselves and other jurors to these commitments. Studies of video recorded jury deliberations confirm that some jurors speak up and remind the others about a commitment if that subject arises as an improper factor in reaching a verdict. Commitments made during jury selection can be used during summation to remind the jurors that they must approach deliberations with the understanding that they need to honor their promises.

§ 5.8　CHALLENGES

Attorneys may remove a juror based on two primary types of challenges: challenges for cause and peremptory challenges. A third type of challenge, rarely available, is a challenge to the array. This third challenge claims that the process used to select the pool of jurors was unlawful or unconstitutional because the selection system excluded or restricted certain classes of people from the jury pool. In the past, prospective jurors in some jurisdictions were selected only from voter registration records that excluded some citizens. Lawful and constitutional procedures were developed to identify and obtain jurors from all parts of the community. Challenges to the array are historical events, although it is possible that impermissible selection procedures exist somewhere.

A. CHALLENGES FOR CAUSE

A motion to challenge for cause seeks to remove a prospective juror from the panel. Trial lawyers may request a judge to exclude a juror for one or more of three reasons:

- Lack of juror qualifications (e.g., a person has a major disability making it impossible to be in a lengthy case),

- Actual bias or prejudice (e.g., a juror has expressed overt bias or prejudice), or

- Implied bias (e.g., a juror has a significant relationship with a party or witness).

Statutes, rules, or case law ordinarily establish the grounds supporting a challenge for cause. Certain types of persons are legally disqualified for jury duty. These persons include judges and relatives of parties and attorneys. The judge or a clerk often screens the jurors and disqualifies those individuals who are excluded by law.

A challenge for cause may be based on either actual or implied bias. Actual bias is present when the juror has a state of mind regarding a particular case, the parties, or witnesses that prevents the juror from acting with impartiality and without prejudice to the substantial rights of either party. For example, a juror may admit that she strongly dislikes the defendant car dealer because of previous bad experiences in having her car serviced by an affiliated auto dealer. Implied bias may be based on existing relationships between a prospective juror and a party or major witness even without a showing of actual bias. For example, a juror who is a good friend of a party will be excluded.

1. Establishing Bias or Prejudice

In order to be granted a challenge for cause it must be shown that the juror is so obviously sympathetic or prejudiced that it would be impossible for the juror to be fair. In establishing a cause challenge, having jurors simply admit that they are biased or prejudiced is usually insufficient. Their answers must reveal reasons why they are unable to be fair and impartial followed by responses confirming bias or prejudice.

Example:

Q: Would all those reasons make it very difficult, or impossible, for you to be fair and impartial in this case, Mr. Hamlet?

Q: You would agree that it would be better for you if you served as a juror in some other case that does not involve the fratricide issues involved in this case, is that correct?

Example:

Q: Ms. Paige, you understand that the plaintiff is claiming that the defendant got very angry and struck her on the back with a baseball bat. Is there anything about this case, before having heard the evidence, that may lead you to believe you could not be fair and impartial to both sides?

A: Yes.

Q: Could you tell us, please, what that might be?

A: I've been at Little League games and watched how parents get out of control. I'm terribly bothered by anyone assaulting another person. I heard about what happened in this case from my Dad, and such anger is crazy.

Q: As you sit here, I understand that it would be difficult or impossible for you to sit as a fair juror in this case.

A: That's true. My mind is pretty well made up.

2. Procedure

An attorney challenges a juror by moving the court to strike the juror for cause. An attorney may indicate acceptance of a juror by advising the court that the attorney finds the juror acceptable or by using a phrase such as "I accept this juror," "I pass this juror" or "I waive the right to challenge this juror." Some judges ask the attorneys whether they wish to challenge any juror, while other judges expect the attorney to affirmatively bring a motion to challenge. If there are no challenges, counsel can state to the court: "Both my client and I accept these jurors and find them to be fair and impartial." An attorney who challenges a juror for cause must state the motion and specific grounds.

Example:

Your Honor, it is clear from Ms. Pomfrey's answers that her past experiences with the staff at Hogswart School of Witchcraft and Wizadry make it impossible for her to be fair and impartial toward my client. She agreed she wouldn't be able to put aside her negative attitudes and bad feelings about the School in reaching a verdict. For these reasons, we request she be excused.

In some jurisdictions, this challenge is made at a bench conference or in chambers. In other jurisdictions, this challenge is made in front of the jurors. Preferably, challenges for cause should be made outside the hearing of the jury. If an attorney announces in front of the jury "We challenge Mr. Macbeth for cause because it is clear that he could not be fair and impartial in this case," problems may arise. The making of the challenge may diminish rapport with jurors who have befriended Mr. Macbeth, or may create a bad impression on other jurors. If the court denies the challenge, the attorney will have to exercise a peremptory challenge to remove him because of the natural, adverse reaction he would have toward the challenging attorney. It may be a better practice if the challenging attorney explains reasons for a challenge outside the hearing of the panel.

It may be effective, however, to move to strike a juror in front of the panel if a particularly prejudiced juror can be challenged in a way that provides useful information to the rest of the jurors. A challenge for cause stated in front of the panel must be stated in a way that does not embarrass a juror or diminish rapport with other jurors. The challenging attorney may say: "We ask the Court to excuse Mr. Macbeth so that he may be a juror in another case, and thank him for his time today."

3.   Numbers of Challenges

There are no limits to the number of challenges for cause that may be made. However, courts are conservative in granting these challenges because removing a juror extends the jury selection process and delays the trial, and may encourage other jurors to try to get out of jury duty. Judges realize that most jurors have some adverse attitudes and consequently require a showing of substantial bias or prejudice which significantly affects the juror's ability to be fair and impartial before granting a challenge for cause.

Judges realize that some jurors may not want to sit as a juror and may admit to a bias or prejudice to avoid jury duty. Judges do not want to encourage jurors to exclude themselves and try to discourage this effort by not allowing other prospective jurors to be easily removed. Judges who make it difficult to exercise a cause challenge decrease the chances attorneys will make unnecessary challenges and superfluous motions.

4. Strategies for Exercising Challenges

In most jurisdictions, attorneys must bring challenges for cause before exercising peremptory challenges. The timing for cause challenges depends upon the trial procedures. In some courts, the cause challenge must be made as soon as the reason for the challenge surfaces during the questioning. In other jurisdictions, the challenges for cause cannot be made until the questioning of the challenged juror is completed. In some other courts, the challenges for cause cannot be made until all the jurors have been questioned.

An attorney must consider several factors in determining whether to exercise a challenge for cause:

- Sufficiently objective reasons must be established before a cause motion can be made. If objective reasons have not been established, the attorney should either ask further questions or pass the juror.

- An attorney must assess whether the judge freely or grudgingly grants motions to remove for cause. The judge's practice influences whether an attorney brings or declines to bring a cause challenge.

- The type of case may also determine whether a challenge for cause is more likely to be granted. Challenges for cause are more often granted in criminal cases, especially if requested by defense counsel. A challenge for cause is more likely to be granted in a civil case when the case involves significant issues.

- If peremptory challenges may not be available to remove all unfavorable jurors, a motion for cause is more likely to be made. If there are a sufficient number of peremptory challenges, there may be no need to make a cause challenge.

- Attorneys can compare the replacement jurors from the panel with prospective jurors in the jury box to determine whether replacement jurors may be better or worse.

5. Options for the Challenging Attorney

An attorney has four options regarding the removal of a juror for cause. First, the attorney can convince the prospective juror to explicitly admit to being biased or prejudiced and unable to be fair and impartial. This option might not be available before judges who do not want jurors to remove themselves and do not want lawyers trying to convince them they are unfit jurors.

Second, the attorney can hope the judge will decide to excuse the juror without a request from the attorneys. This may occur in situations where a juror has obvious bias or prejudices, or objective factors have been revealed that make it unlikely that the juror will be fair. This option is available before those judges who take an active role in the jury process, but may not be available before judges who take a passive role.

Third, the attorney can hope opposing counsel will challenge a juror for cause. This likely occurs when a juror is unfavorable to all parties.

Fourth, the attorney can challenge the juror for cause.

6. Options for the Opposing Attorney

An attorney who faces a challenge for cause brought by the opposing counsel has a number of options. The attorney can oppose the challenge for cause and argue the juror is qualified. The attorney can request that the judge ask rehabilitative questions. The attorney can ask permission of the judge to ask questions that rehabilitate the juror and remove the bases for the opposing party's challenge for cause. Or, the attorney may also join in the challenge for cause and ask that the juror be excused.

This latter option may be appropriate and effective in cases where it is clear to everyone that the juror would not be impartial. In these trials, the attorney who agrees that an obviously prejudiced juror be excused and replaced with an unbiased juror may be perceived by the judge and jurors as being fair and trustworthy. There may be a tendency to oppose the cause challenge or ask rehabilitative questions, based on the adversarial notion that an attorney should oppose whatever the opposing lawyer seeks.

7. Rehabilitation Procedures

After an attorney has asked questions to establish grounds for a challenge for cause or after the challenge for cause has been made, an opposing attorney or the judge may ask questions of the prospective juror for "rehabilitation" purposes. These questions are an effort to establish that the juror can be fair and impartial.

Example:

Q: You have just told us that you have a particular bias against vloggers. In this case there will be vloggers from Video Game High School who will be called as witnesses. If the judge tells you that you must set aside your opinions and decide the case solely on the facts presented to you, will you be able to follow the instruction that the Judge gives you?

A: Yes.

> Q: If Judge Blaylock tells you that it's your duty not to let your feelings or attitudes about the case adversely affect you, can you follow the Judge's instructions and be fair to both sides?
>
> A: Yes, I will be able to do that.

Rehabilitation questions permit new information to be developed to rebut any facts or inferences supporting a challenge for cause or to help establish the degree of bias or prejudice the juror may have. The judge may also wish to rehabilitate in order to avoid having to call a replacement juror, which would extend the length of the jury selection process. In permitting or asking rehabilitative questions, the judge must determine if the juror can be fair and if it is appropriate to require opposing counsel to exercise a peremptory challenge instead of granting a challenge for cause.

> **Example (By the Judge):**
>
> Q: You have just told us that you had a particular attitude against vloggers. If I were to tell you that you must set aside your attitude and decide the case solely on the facts presented to you, and if I tell you that it is the law, I take it that you will be able to set aside that attitude and decide the case solely on the evidence given to you in this case.
>
> A: Of course.

Rehabilitation may force the opponent to use a peremptory challenge if the challenge for cause is unsuccessful. If rehabilitation establishes that the juror can be fair and impartial, the challenging attorney will need to exercise a peremptory challenge to remove that juror, reducing the number of peremptory challenges available.

8.   Reversing Apparent Bias or Prejudice

An attorney may not be able to bring a motion for cause or have a sufficient number of peremptory challenges available to remove all questionable jurors. Some jurors have an appearance of prejudice against a party that further questioning may be able to neutralize. In these situations, the attorney may need to ask questions of a juror to either reduce the apparent prejudice so the juror may be kept, or to reveal a prejudice by that juror against the other side, causing opposing counsel to consider exercising a challenge. The goal of the examining attorney opposing a challenge for cause is to establish reasons why the juror can be impartial and to obtain a commitment from the juror to be fair.

Example:

Q: Would it be difficult for you, Ms. Pocahontas, to be fair and impartial in this case because the defendant has a captain job similar to yours?

A: Well . . . I don't think so.

Q: Would you be able to set aside your attitudes and feelings about your job and decide this case upon the evidence presented to you in this case?

A: I would do my best to try.

Q: You would be able to determine whether the conduct of the defendant in this case was legal or illegal based upon what you hear as evidence and not based upon what may happen in your company?

A: Yes.

Q: Would you hold the defendant in this case to the standards of a reasonable employer as established by the applicable law and not to some higher standard you may have experienced in your professional life?

A: Of course.

Q: If the facts establish to your satisfaction that the defendant illegally fired the plaintiff in this case, you would be able to find in favor of the plaintiff?

A: Sure.

Q: As an executive, have you had to fire an employee if there was good cause to fire that employee?

A: Unfortunately, yes.

Q: But you yourself have never been fired?

A: Not yet (laughter). Seriously, no.

Q: You believe you can be fair and impartial in determining the credibility of the plaintiff in this case?

A: Yes.

Q: And you promise us to be fair and impartial as a juror in this case?

A: I do.

This line of questioning, if successful, can establish the importance of setting aside biases and prejudices all the jurors have in deciding a case. It may also result in jurors bending over backward during deliberations to appear to be fair and impartial.

If this line of questioning works, opposing counsel may even become concerned with the juror developing a bias in favor of the opposing party and with the possibility of the examining attorney establishing overly effective rapport with the juror. If this approach does not work, however, the examining attorney may still be able to exercise a peremptory challenge and remove the juror.

9. Replacement Jurors

When a juror has been removed for cause, a replacement juror takes that juror's place. The replacement juror may be called from the panel that is seated in the courtroom or may be called from the jury waiting room. If the replacement juror has been in the courtroom during the selection process, many of the preliminary statements may have already been made. However, if the replacement juror has not been in the courtroom, preliminary matters must be repeated. If the replacement jurors are in the courtroom during the interviews of the prospective jurors, attention should be paid to the replacements because it is possible that an unknown replacement juror is less favorable than the juror who was removed from the panel for cause.

B. PEREMPTORY CHALLENGES

Peremptory challenges permit the attorney to remove a limited number of prospective jurors from the panel without any reason or explanation to the court, with some limitations. An illegal basis, such as race, religion or gender, cannot support a peremptory challenge. A statute or court rule determines the number of peremptory challenges available to each party. The number of available peremptory challenges varies among jurisdictions and depends upon the type of case.

In civil cases, each party may have two or more peremptory challenges. In criminal cases, each party usually has more than two peremptory challenges. In federal criminal trials, if the offense is punishable by imprisonment for more than a year, the government is entitled to six peremptory challenges and the defendant is entitled to ten peremptory challenges. If the offense is punishable by imprisonment for no more than a year, each side is entitled to only three peremptory challenges. See Fed.R.Crim.Proc. 24(b).

An attorney has two options when exercising a peremptory challenge: the attorney can use a challenge and remove a juror, or the attorney can hope opposing counsel removes the juror by using a peremptory challenge. The actual process of making peremptory challenges varies widely and it is important that the attorney know which process will be used. Three common ways include:

- At the conclusion of the questioning, both sides approach the bench where plaintiff strikes the permitted number of jurors. The defense then strikes a similar number leaving a final panel.

- When questioning is completed, a chart containing the names of jurors not removed for cause is passed between the attorneys. The defense first strikes one juror, followed by the plaintiff, with remaining strikes made alternately until the appropriate number of jurors are removed.

- Following completion of questioning and motions for cause, each side independently lists the names of the jurors to be removed. The judge compares the lists and seats the first six or required number of jurors not removed.

The limited number of peremptory challenges makes it difficult for attorneys to remove as many undesirable jurors as possible. For example, the plaintiff may want to get rid of five jurors but has only four strikes. If the plaintiff thinks that one of those jurors is bad but is as undesirable for the defense as for the plaintiff, the plaintiff's attorney can make an educated guess that the defense will strike the juror. This gives the plaintiff the chance to strike the other four jurors.

If the jurors are struck alternately, each side can watch the progress and an extremely bad juror can be struck last if the other side has not removed the juror. However, if each side strikes four jurors independently and the judge seats the first six unchallenged jurors, neither side can rely on the other to remove the undesirable juror. If both sides strike a juror, the strikes overlap and fewer unacceptable jurors are removed.

C. ALTERNATE JURORS

Alternate jurors are often included in trials, and always in lengthy or complex trials. An alternate juror is selected to sit as an extra juror throughout the trial and will be called to replace a juror who becomes ill during the trial, is unable to attend the trial, or is unable to deliberate. The selection of alternate jurors occurs at the same time and is identical to the procedure used for selecting regular jurors.

The court usually permits an additional peremptory challenge when alternate jurors are selected. Typically, at least one alternate juror will be selected for a six-person jury and two to three alternates for a twelve-person jury, depending on the potential length of the trial. Alternate jurors may be excused from duty when the jury begins deliberations. Many judges allow alternate jurors to remain on the jury and deliberate.

D. REMOVING JURORS FROM THE PANEL

The last decision the attorneys make in the jury selection process is to exercise peremptory challenges and to strike individuals from the panel. What the striking process presumes is that the attorneys have obtained enough information about the prospective jurors to make an accurate determination about the people they want to have sit on the jury, and those they want to remove. As Section 5.8(B) explained, the number of peremptory challenges and choices are limited. A successful determination about whom to strike depends on the lawyer's ability to obtain useful information about each juror, to analyze this information, and to make accurate judgments about people.

Making an accurate final decision is difficult. The following example demonstrates two approaches and two attorneys who interpret the information obtained from the jurors in completely different ways.

Example:

Judge:

Counsel, are you prepared to exercise your first peremptory challenge?

Counsel O:

Your Honor, may co-counsel and I have a few minutes to confer?

Judge:

Yes, you may.

(Counsel O and Z conferring)

Counsel O:

I think that we should strike juror No. 5 first. He does not fit my profile.

Counsel Z:

What do you mean?

Counsel O:

We have an emotional, sympathetic case and I don't believe that the juror will react favorably to our client or our case. He is middle aged, owns his own business, lives in a wealthy suburb, watches news programs that are not fair and balanced, and reads unreliable blogs. My profile shows that he would be a very bad juror for our side.

Counsel Z:

Wait a second. That juror grew up in poverty. His parents died when he was young and he was raised by his grandparents. He made his own way and worked his way through college washing dishes in the college cafeteria. He told us that he volunteers for the Scouts and is very involved in developing educational programs for underprivileged children and has donated a lot of laptops to schools. I think he's terrific.

Counsel O:

But he is of Hittite descent, likes the color purple, and sits up too straight, and all that is a sure sign that he will not vote our way.

Counsel Z:

You've got to be kidding. Where in the world did you get that stuff?

Counsel O:

I was surfing the net.

Counsel Z:

Let's strike juror No. 2. She doesn't look at us at all. When I questioned her, she sat with her arms folded and a scowl on her face. I don't think I related to her. She made me feel uncomfortable.

Counsel O:

I think that we should keep her. Her experience fits my profile.

Counsel Z:

I also think that we should strike juror No. 8. He just doesn't seem to think the way anybody else thinks. I can't understand what he is talking about, and he regularly watches professional wrestling, and doesn't have a computer.

Counsel O:

But he's perfect for our case. He is a head nodder, appears upbeat, and looks like a lot of fun. He will react with empathy, and that's what we want.

Counsel Z:

Well, he may fit your profile. Let's ask our clients who they prefer to decide their case.

§ 5.9   MISCONDUCT AND OBJECTIONS

State and local rules of procedure, the Model Rules of Professional Responsibility, rules of decorum, and common sense establish standards for proper conduct by attorneys and jurors during jury selection.

A. INADMISSIBLE EVIDENCE

Any questions or behavior by counsel designed for the sole purpose of prejudicing the jury are improper. For example, questions that inform the jury that a defendant is wealthy or an atheist, if not relevant, are not permitted, are objectionable, and probably constitute grounds for a mistrial. The general rule is that evidence may be referred to in jury selection as long as it bears upon an issue at trial, will be introduced at trial, and is relevant to the jury selection process. In addition, questions must be designed to provide a basis for exercising challenges for cause or peremptory challenges.

B. IMPROPER QUESTIONS

Questions asked to meet improper objectives may not be asked during jury selection. Whether a question is legitimate or inappropriate depends upon the law of the jurisdiction and the discretion of the judge. For example, questions seeking solely to educate or indoctrinate jurors may be proper in one court but improper in another.

C. IMPROPER OR QUESTIONABLE TOPICS

Questions must be asked in good faith. Inquiries that touch on questionable areas must be phrased carefully. For example, in a personal injury case it is improper to mention insurance coverage. If a question is asked for the purpose of informing the jury that either the defendant or the plaintiff is insured, the question is improper and may be grounds for a new trial. However, an attorney may inquire whether any of the jurors work for an insurance company to legitimately determine their bias or prejudice. When a specific insurance company is a party to a lawsuit, jurors may be asked if they have an interest in, or a relationship with, that insurance company. In cases involving questionable or potentially prejudicial topics, the attorney may request permission to ask a specific question or may ask the judge to inquire to avoid errors made by counsel.

D. CURRYING FAVOR

Communication with jurors by counsel before and during trial is forbidden except in the course of official proceedings. "Currying favor," or trying to seek or gain favors through flattery of the jurors or exaggerated interests with their concerns or comfort, is improper. Issues regarding jury matters should be brought to the attention of the judge who will then assist the juror. Similarly, social and business arrangements with jurors must be avoided. The judge will, or should, advise the jurors that the lawyers are prohibited from talking to the jury during the trial, and that if the attorneys appear to ignore the jurors during recesses, it's because they are not allowed to communicate with jurors.

E. JUROR MISCONDUCT

Jurors commit misconduct if they answer jury selection questions falsely, violate rules of court or fail to follow the directions of the judge. Some jurors will wrongfully tweet, text or blog during a trial about their experiences, or may improperly view websites and search for information about parties or witnesses. Counsel have a duty to inform the court of jury misconduct immediately upon learning it. Acts of jury misconduct cannot be kept secret and used later as grounds for a new trial.

F. IMPROPER CONDUCT BY ATTORNEYS

Attorneys must maintain a fair and impartial relationship with prospective and actual jurors during the trial. It is improper and unethical for attorneys to:

- Talk with jurors individually or in a group,
- Contact any friends or relatives of jurors, or
- Indirectly have a colleague contact a juror.

G. OBJECTIONS

Counsel may object to the jury selection questions and conduct of opposing counsel. In determining whether to object, an attorney should consider strategic factors such as:

- The prejudicial impact of the questioning;
- The extent that opposing counsel is actually using jury selection for purposes other than to determine challenges for cause and peremptory challenges; and
- Whether the judge has a reputation for taking control of jury selection after becoming frustrated with prolonged questioning that strays from challenges.

1. Arguing the Case, the Law, or the Facts

Questions may be asked concerning the case, the law, and the facts to obtain information to support a cause or peremptory challenge. However, in most jurisdictions, it is improper to present arguments in these areas during jury selection.

Example:

Objection. Counsel is making a final argument and not asking questions.

Response to Objection:

- Rephrase the question to seek information from the jurors rather than making a statement to the jurors.

- Alter tone of voice making the question sound appropriate.

- Advise the judge prior to the beginning of questioning that some questions may appear to be objectionable but are not and clarify why not.

- Explain to the judge that you need to question the jury about the case to properly exercise your challenges.

2. Improperly Indoctrinating the Jury

In many jurisdictions, questions that attempt to indoctrinate the jurors are improper. What are appropriate questions that seek to "educate" jurors varies among judges and attorneys. Section 5.7 explained the use of jury selection to provide appropriate information to the jurors through the use of proper questions.

Example:

Objection. Counsel is improperly indoctrinating the jury.

Response to Objection:

- Rephrase the question to avoid objectionable phrasing.

- Explain to the judge the need to obtain answers regarding juror positions and reactions to questions.

- Clarify that a promise from the jurors to vote in favor of the client is not being sought, but that the jurors are being asked whether they can keep an open mind after hearing certain evidence.

3. Referring to Inadmissible Evidence or Topics

Inadmissible evidence and prejudicial topics may not be referred to during jury selection. Section 5.9(C) explained inappropriate areas of inquiry during jury selection.

Example:

Objection. Counsel has mentioned inadmissible evidence and improper topics during jury selection. We request the court to admonish counsel and to instruct the jurors to disregard what counsel mentioned.

Response to Objection:

- Explain why the evidence is admissible or why the topic is not improper.

- Explain that while the area is a sensitive topic, the subject must be explored because of specific legitimate reasons.

4. Repeating Questions

Areas of jury selection already explored by the judge or opposing counsel may not be repeated. Counsel may, however, clarify or ask more detailed questions in areas already explored. Whether or not the questions are repetitive is a matter of judicial discretion.

Example:

Objection. Counsel is improperly repeating questions and asking questions in areas already covered during prior jury selection.

Response to Objection:

- Prior to jury selection, advise the court and opposing attorney that certain areas will be explored and that the court and opposing counsel may also wish to explore the same areas.

- Explain that additional information must be gathered from areas previously covered in order to obtain more complete information from the jurors.

5. Asking the Jurors to Prejudge the Case

Questions that ask the jurors to prejudge the case are improper. Questions that seek commitments regarding an issue or evidence in the case may be improper because the scope of the commitment may exceed what the jurors may properly promise.

For example, a party who has a felony conviction may be impeached with the introduction of that felony conviction. The attorney for this felon may properly inform the jurors of the conviction during jury selection to obtain a commitment from them that they will base their verdict on the evidence in the case and not automatically discredit the story of the party based on the felony conviction. In most jurisdictions the attorney may not ask jurors to promise that the felony conviction will not influence them because the conviction is a credibility factor the jurors may consider.

Example:

Objection. Counsel is asking the jurors to prejudge the evidence.

Response to Objection:

- Rephrase the question to avoid seeking a commitment or promise from the jurors.

- Rephrase the scope of the commitment or promise sought from the jurors.

6. Irrelevant Questions

An attorney may not ask irrelevant questions or questions designed to improperly influence the jurors.

Example:

Objection. Counsel is asking questions that are irrelevant regarding the qualifications of the jurors and is improperly attempting to unfairly influence them.

Response to Objection:

- Explain to the judge how the information sought relates to a challenge for cause or peremptory challenge.

- Rephrase the question to avoid the appearance of it being to influence the jurors.

7. Questions That Improperly or Incorrectly Explain the Law

Questions that ask jurors if they understand or will apply the law as explained by the judge are appropriate. Questions that incorrectly state the law are objectionable.

Example:

Objection. Counsel is incorrectly explaining the law.

Response to Objection:

- Explain why the attorney needs the response of the jurors to the legal issues stated in the question.

- Rephrase the question by advising the jurors that the judge will explain the law.

- Restate the law correctly.

8. Questions That Are Unfair, Embarrassing, or Pry Improperly into the Personal and Private Life of a Juror

Questions that seek legitimate information about jurors are appropriate. Overly sensitive, embarrassing, or unfair questions that seek inappropriate personal information about jurors are improper.

Example:

Objection. Counsel is asking unfair and embarrassing questions.

Response to Objection:

- Apologize to the jurors and to the court.

- Stop being insensitive or unfair.

H. IMPROPER REASONS TO REMOVE A JUROR

Discriminatory reasons that are used to support a peremptory challenge or a motion to remove for cause may be illegal. A prospective juror cannot be removed for racial, religious or gender reasons. Some jurisdictions prohibit removal for other reasons. The attorney must know the reasons a juror cannot be removed and provide a proper basis for removal. An attorney may object to a removal based on improper grounds. It if appears to the judge illegitimate factors are being used, the advocate will need to explain why legitimate reasons support removal.

CHAPTER 6

OPENING STATEMENT

■ ■ ■

6.1 Introduction
    A.   Purposes
    B.   What Can Be Presented
6.2 Preparation
    A.   Pretrial/Prehearing Evidentiary Rulings
    B.   Opening Based on Jury Trial Events
    C.   Opening Based on Final Argument
    D.   Anticipating Opponent's Positions
    E.   Selecting Visual Aids and Exhibits
    F.   Meeting Expectations
    G.   Order of Opening Statement
    H.   Length of Opening Statement
    I.   Waiving or Reserving the Opening
    J.   Prepared Outline or Detailed Script
    K.   Rehearsal
    L.   Specific Requirements
6.3 Organization
    A.   Structure
    B.   Parts of the Opening
    C.   Opening Statement Critique
6.4 Content
    A.   Prefatory Phrases
    B.   An Effective Story
    C.   Details
    D.   Parties/Witnesses
    E.   The Event
    F.   Circumstances
    G.   Visual Aids and Exhibits
    H.   What Happened
    I.   How it Happened
    J.   Why it Happened
    K.   Disputed Issues
    L.   Claims and Defenses
    M.   The Law
    N.   Burden of Proof
    O.   Damages in a Civil Case
    P.   Amount of Damages
    Q.   Request for Relief

6.5   Techniques
    A.   Offensive/Defensive Approaches
    B.   Anticipating Defenses
    C.   Asserting Promises
    D.   Making a Compact with the Jury
    E.   Employing Understatement
    F.   Avoiding Overstatement
    G.   Asserting Challenging Positions
    H.   Describing Case Weaknesses
    I.   Explaining the Absence of Evidence
    J.   Qualifying Remarks to the Jury

6.6   Presentation and Delivery
    A.   Location of the Presentation
    B.   Movement
    C.   Appropriate Distance
    D.   Gestures
    E.   Eye Contact
    F.   Transitions
    G.   Observing the Fact Finder
    H.   Notes and Outlines
    I.   Visual Aids and Exhibits

6.7   Objections and Motions
    A.   Improper Comments
    B.   Objections
    C.   Curative Instructions
    D.   Opening Statement Motions

Trial Advocacy Supplement
Opening Statements

Examples of complete opening statements appear in the *Supplement to Trial Advocacy Before Judges, Jurors, and Arbitrators* in three cases. A jury trial, an arbitration, and an administrative law hearing demonstrate and explain opening statement strategies, tactics, and techniques discussed in this Chapter.

REFLECTING ON ADVOCACY

The best way to win an argument is to begin by being right. . . .

—JILL RUCKELSHAUS

Speeches cannot be made long enough for the speakers, nor short enough for the hearers.

—JAMES PERRY

§ 6.1   INTRODUCTION

A.   PURPOSES

The opening statement provides the advocate with the opportunity to explain the evidence to the fact finder and to describe the issues to be presented during the trial or hearing. A compelling, convincing opening statement has a significant impact on the decision maker's initial understanding and impression of the case. Judges have reported that they often form an early impression of a case during a trial based on the opening statement. Jury surveys have established that during final deliberations jurors often vote consistently with early positions formed during the opening. This result, of course, will be affected by other events such as the introduction of persuasive evidence, credible witnesses, or a compelling closing argument. Nonetheless, the more effective an opening statement is, the more likely a favorable decision will be forthcoming.

The purposes of an opening statement are to:

- Tell an interesting and compelling story.

- Describe the relevant evidence to the fact finder.

- Portray events using effective verbal communication skills and exhibits.

- Summarize what the case is about including theories, issues, claims, defenses, and positions.

- Persuade the fact finder of the merits of the case.

- Motivate the fact finder to want to render a favorable decision.

- Assist the judge or arbitrator in determining the legal issues that need to be decided.

- Establish an appropriate atmosphere in the court or hearing room.

Opening statements should always be made in jury trials, and unless there is a good reason not to do so, they should also be made in bench trials, arbitrations, and administrative hearings. In bench trials and arbitrations, if the advocates have been able to previously explain the case to a judge or arbitrator, then it may be unnecessary to present an entire opening statement. It may be sufficient to conduct a short opening providing the judge or arbitrator with the essential information that has not been communicated. In administrative hearings, this approach also works unless opening statements are not permitted. Often, an effective opening to a judge or arbitrator lists and identifies the issues that need to be resolved and explain how they should be decided.

Some judges and arbitrators may suggest or tell the lawyers not to conduct openings because they believe they already know enough or to save time. It may be inappropriate to deliver an opening to a decision maker who does not want to hear it. But, the advocate should insist on making an opening statement if the advocate believes it will increase the knowledge of the judge or arbitrator, help win the case, not waste time, and not irritate the judge or arbitrator. See Section 3.11(A). A well-presented, concise opening may actually shorten case presentation as the decision maker better understands the story, the theory of the case, the evidence, and the issues.

B. WHAT CAN BE PRESENTED

This chapter describes the presentation of opening statements for all trials and hearings, including jury trials. Most of the strategies and techniques described in this chapter also apply to bench trials, arbitrations, and administrative cases, but there are important differences as explained in Section 3.11.

1. Facts and Opinions

An opening statement presents in a story format facts and opinions that will be introduced as evidence. The facts that can be described include direct and circumstantial evidence and reasonable inferences drawn from this evidence. The opinions that can be described include admissible lay and expert opinions. In a jury trial, an opening statement consists primarily of a presentation based on the evidence.

The goal of the advocate is to tell a story about the evidence. Any admissible evidence, even if in dispute, can be presented. An attorney can refer to facts and opinions from any source, including information to be introduced by opposing counsel. Not all evidence will be referred to during the opening. A skilled advocate selects significant evidence that meets the purposes of an effective opening without including unnecessary details or insignificant information.

2. Theories and Issues

Section 2.5 described the importance of selecting a case theory to support a favorable verdict. During the opening, the advocate should use theme words and phrases to introduce the case theories and issues.

3. Argument

The general rule is that it is improper to present arguments during an opening. An attorney cannot provide explanations, propose conclusions, comment on the evidence, or otherwise advance arguments. The attorney should, however, present the most persuasive opening possible, and a skilled advocate will present an opening statement that may touch the line of argument but does not cross over that line.

There is often a fine line between what argument is and what may or should not be stated during an opening statement in jury trials. And there can be a fine line between what is a fact supported by the evidence and what is a conclusion advanced by the advocate. Judges and lawyers may disagree where the lines are to be drawn. Advocates must know the limits of openings statements and the restrictions that may be placed on openings and not be overly cautious in straddling the line.

Advocates presenting openings before judges and arbitrators have greater latitude in the scope and content of their opening. Opening statements presented before professional decision makers may include both factual and legal statements. While summation is the more appropriate opportunity to argue the case, opening statements before judges and arbitrators can effectively raise the issues and state how they should be decided.

4. Issues

Before jurors, the best opening provides a realistic story of what occurred within the context of the issues they need to resolve. In the story portion of the opening statement, the advocate can recreate what happened through the "story" of the case. Unlike a fictional story, the opening statement provides a real picture of the facts as the advocate wants them portrayed. These statements need not identify all specific issues that need to be resolved but can generally state the decisions the jurors need to make. For example, in a criminal case, references may be made by defense to the jury finding the defendant not guilty.

Before professional decision makers, advocates may specifically advise the judge or arbitrator about the issues they need to decide. If there are several issues, they could be numbered and provided on a chart or exhibit. Issue statements make clear what needs to be decided and provides helpful guidance to the judge or arbitrator.

5. The Law

In a bench trial, arbitration, and administrative hearing, the advocate can ordinarily discuss the law and explain legal issues. In a jury trial, the judge has the responsibility of explaining the law and may do so through preliminary jury instructions about the applicable law. The jury trial attorney may make accurate short references about the law during the opening in almost all jurisdictions. The lawyer can concisely refer to the legal issues in the case, the elements that comprise a claim or defense, and the burden of proof. The advocate can also show how the facts establish the issues, prove the elements, and meet the burden of proof. And, a lawyer may briefly mention how the law applies to the facts or how the facts support the law. To be sure not to breach the opening statement rules and the expectations of the judge or arbitrator, the attorney can inquire regarding what is inappropriate if in doubt.

6. Visual Aids and Exhibits

Visual aids and real and demonstrative exhibits are often used in openings. The information contained and portrayed with these sources can help the fact finder better understand and remember more about the case. The use of power point presentations and computer generated lists and charts provide a helpful way to present an opening and to have the fact finder follow along and pay attention.

The use of real and demonstrative exhibits that will be introduced during the trial or hearing also help the fact finder see and understand the evidence. Many cases involve electronically stored information, social network communications, and digital evidence that can be effectively presented as exhibits. During the opening, critical evidence can be presented using computer aided and generated exhibits. Jurors, judges, and arbitrators may expect the advocates to use visual displays and printed words in addition to the spoken word. Because of these expectations, it is effective to use available trial exhibits or create visual aids for use in the opening, which may also be used in summation.

7. A Test

One effective "test" to determine whether an attorney can include information during opening to a jury is to determine whether a witness, a document, or some other form of evidence will provide such information. If the answer is yes, the statement may be made during the opening; if no, then that statement is probably inappropriate and objectionable.

Adherence to this conservative test minimizes objections to an opening statement. Strict adherence, however, may deprive an opening statement of the persuasive explanation needed to be most effective, including an appropriate explanation of the case theory and issues. Most judges and opposing lawyers allow more latitude in an opening statement than described in this narrow test.

Ideally, an effectively presented opening statement would result in the decision maker jumping up, hugging the advocate, and telling the client that the remainder of the case is a mere formality and the client will win. This fantasy may not happen. There is no recorded instance of this ever occurring in the annals of trial practice, but it's an aspiration.

§ 6.2   PREPARATION

This section discusses planning considerations including: the efficient preparation of an opening statement; the selection of the evidence to be explained, the theories and issues to be described, and the law to be explained; and choosing the most effective way to present this information.

A.   PRETRIAL/PREHEARING EVIDENTIARY RULINGS

When determining which evidence to present during the opening statement, the attorney must ascertain whether an in limine ruling is necessary before presenting that evidence. An opening statement may not refer to evidence that is inadmissible. Pretrial and prehearing evidentiary rulings permit the attorney to plan an opening statement knowing what evidence will be admitted.

Section 4.5(A) described the procedure of bringing a motion in limine to obtain a pretrial or prehearing evidentiary ruling. An attorney may want to obtain an advance ruling to avoid an objection by the opposing lawyer to questionable evidence. An opposing attorney may want to obtain a pretrial ruling to prevent jurors from hearing information that will not be admissible evidence during a jury trial.

Not all evidentiary problems will be resolved in a pretrial or prehearing motion. The judge may defer ruling on admissibility until that point in the case when the evidence is actually introduced. An attorney may decide not to seek an advance ruling for tactical reasons. An attorney may prefer to assume the evidence will be admissible, or may not want to suggest to the opposing counsel or to the judge or arbitrator that some evidence might be objectionable. In these and other situations the advocate may need to plan the opening without the benefit of an advance ruling, and without knowing if some evidence will be excluded.

B.   OPENING BASED ON JURY TRIAL EVENTS

An opening statement should be based in part on what has happened during the judge's initial explanations and jury selection. Remarks made during jury selection and during preliminary instructions by the judge to the jury may affect what should be said and how it should be said during opening. In jurisdictions where jury selection questioning has been extensive, it may not be as necessary for the attorney to spend time establishing a rapport with the jurors. But, where jury selection is limited, the attorney may need to provide the jurors with more information and to establish a favorable impression of the case during the opening. In a similar fashion, where the judge provides an objective explanation of the issues in a case, it may not be necessary for the attorneys to detail the claims and defenses. But, where the judge gives few preliminary instructions, a detailed explanation of the issues, claims, and defenses may be necessary.

C. OPENING BASED ON FINAL ARGUMENT

The final argument constitutes the foundation for the opening statement. Summation must be planned before the trial starts. See Sections 2.4(A) and 11.3(A). If a fact, opinion, theory, issue, or position is not going to be a part of the closing statement, it should not be part of the opening statement or the rest of the case. The opening must be consistent with and based on what will be included in the final argument.

D. ANTICIPATING OPPONENT'S POSITIONS

When preparing an opening statement, an attorney needs to review the case from the perspective of the opposition. The advocate must anticipate and attempt to diffuse the other side's opening statement, theories, evidence, and case. The more accurately an attorney anticipates the other side's positions, the more effective the attorney can present an opening that rebuts what the other side has said or will say.

E. SELECTING VISUAL AIDS AND EXHIBITS

An attorney must decide the best use that may be made of visual aids and exhibits during the opening statement. Consideration should be given to the persuasive impact these devices may have on the decision maker and how they will make the opening statement more understandable and interesting. The fact finder is more likely to recall important parts of the opening when those parts are presented using visual aids and exhibits. The opening can focus on critical pieces of real evidence by displaying their contents and can highlight important demonstrative evidence. Openings in cases that involve electronically stored information can use computer technology to enhance this evidence. The use of these aids and exhibits is described in Section 6.4(G) and Chapter 8.

F. MEETING EXPECTATIONS

Planning and preparation decisions need to be made in the context of what the fact finders/decision makers expect. Judges and arbitrators who routinely hear and observe openings have both general and specific expectations. They know the procedural rules and anticipate the advocates will follow those mandates and guidelines. They each will also have their own individual preferences for what happens in an opening. Advocates can discuss their preferences with the decision maker before the opening.

Jurors and even some professional decision makers will be influenced by what they believe may happen and what they know about other similar presentation situations. Years ago, people were used to hearing long speeches, reading lengthy newspaper articles, and viewing detailed news programs. Today many are used to seeing short, concise presentations via the media and online or live presentations. The proliferation of TED like talks, controversial chat shows, specialized blogs, and website displays has created an expectation about how openings could be presented.

Advocates need to choose the most effective means and the most persuasive content in preparing an opening. They also need to reflect what the expectations might be of their particular audience. It makes little sense to craft an opening that appeals to the advocate but does not to the judge, jurors, or arbitrator.

G. ORDER OF OPENING STATEMENT

In bench trials, arbitrations, and administrative hearings, opening statements occur at the beginning of the case. In jury trials, opening statements usually occur immediately after jury selection. In some administrative cases, opening statements are not common or permitted.

The general rule is that the party with the burden of proof gives the first opening statement. A plaintiff/claimant/prosecutor has the burden of proof in a case and makes the first opening. The defendant/respondent then has an opportunity to present an opening immediately or may delay the opening until after the plaintiff/claimant/prosecutor has presented evidence and rested, as explained in Section 6.2(I). In cases with multiple parties, the order of the opening statements is determined by the judge or arbitrator, usually based on one or more of the following factors: which party has the greater burden of proof, the chronology of the factual events, and which party has the more substantial claim or defense.

H. LENGTH OF OPENING STATEMENT

The opening statement should be long enough to explain what needs to be stated and short enough to maintain the attention of the fact finders. Some opening statements may only last five minutes, others will extend for an hour or more. Most openings do not exceed twenty to thirty minutes.

There is no optimum length for an opening statement because each opening depends upon the evidence and circumstances of the case and the speaking ability of the attorney. The use of visual aids and exhibits may permit a longer and more in depth opening that keeps the attention of the fact finder focused on important events.

Some judges and arbitrators set limits on the length of an opening. Restrictions can be discussed with the judge or arbitrator before the presentation begins. An attorney who anticipates that the opposing lawyer may exceed a reasonable time may ask for an appropriate restriction.

I.   WAIVING OR RESERVING THE OPENING

An opening statement may be waived. In a jury trial, however, an opening statement should never be waived because of the advantages an effective opening provides. In a case before a judge or arbitrator, an opening may be waived if an advocate has had an opportunity to fully explain the case to the judge or arbitrator prior to the trial or hearing.

Federal and state court jurisdictions permit the defendant to present an opening statement immediately after the plaintiff/prosecutor or to reserve the opening statement until the plaintiff/prosecutor rests and the defense case begins. Local rules or practice may prohibit or restrict the defense option of delaying an opening statement. In the vast majority of civil cases and in most criminal cases, the defendant should give the opening statement immediately following the opening by the plaintiff/prosecutor. This approach provides the jury with an explanation of both sides of the case, places the plaintiff/prosecutor's case in perspective, and counters an effective opening statement. When the defense opening is delayed, the jury may attach undue weight to the initial opening statement and not fully consider available defenses.

In civil cases, because of liberal discovery rules, pretrial conferences, and settlement efforts, the defense knows what issues the plaintiff will attempt to prove and what evidence will be offered. In these cases, the advantages in immediately giving the opening far outweigh any advantage gained from delaying it. The defendant's own story can be explained at the outset, and the jurors provided with additional facts and perspectives to be considered while the plaintiff presents evidence.

In criminal cases, there may be an advantage to the defendant in reserving an opening statement, especially if discovery has been limited and some evidence may or may not be available or introduced. Reserving the opening statement in such situations prevents the prosecution from modifying the presentation of its case to reduce the impact of the defense described in the defense opening. In a case where alternative defenses exist and a defense attorney is unsure what defense may be best, it may be more effective to make that decision after the prosecution has presented its evidence. In some cases where the defense attorney is not certain whether the defendant will testify, delaying the opening may also be a useful tactic. Not giving a prompt opening, however, may create an impression that the prosecution's case is stronger than it really is. If delayed, defense counsel should advise the jury the opening will be forthcoming.

J.   PREPARED OUTLINE OR DETAILED SCRIPT

The material for an opening statement should be organized into an outline format, including an introduction, body with segments, and conclusion. The use of an outline helps organize the facts and issues of the case into a readily accessible format. As the attorney prepares other facets of the case, the outline may be modified and should remain flexible. Form 6.1 is an example of an outline of elements to be considered.

Some attorneys find it helpful to prepare a complete opening statement. This draft may then be reviewed and improved. The drawback of using a script during an opening statement is the temptation to read it. A better approach is to prepare a key word outline and practice the presentation until the advocate has learned rather than memorized a script. The advocate should be able to present the opening using only the key word outline. When notes are used, they should be used in a forthright fashion.

Outlines and notes can be prepared on a laptop and displayed as a visual aid on the monitor during the opening statement. The outline can be written on a paper pad, or can be printed on a poster or white board, and displayed as the contents are discussed. The advocate can create visual aids that contain an outline of all or part of the opening and use it as a guide while speaking. How the notes should be used or displayed depends upon how best they augment the content of the opening.

K. REHEARSAL

After the attorney has prepared the outline or script, practice is necessary to be adequately prepared for the presentation. Opening statements should not be read aloud from a set script, nor should they be rigidly memorized. The attorney should not necessarily try to remember exact words used during the practice sessions, but rather express the ideas that have been rehearsed in these sessions.

The attorney may want to think through the opening statement silently and then practice verbally, concentrating on content. Practice should include rehearsing the use of any visual aids and exhibits. As the content of the opening is mastered, the advocate can work on stylistic improvements to enhance the delivery. After this preparation the attorney should continue rehearsing the opening statement until it is as good as it can be. The attorney may use an audience of colleagues, family, a mirror, or video for review and critique.

The attorney should rehearse until the story can be told in a persuasive, compelling manner. The key to an effective presentation of an opening is that the attorney knows the ideas and important phrases that need to be conveyed, is comfortable with and confident about this story, and can make a sincere, believable, and understandable presentation. Novice advocates will need to practice until they are well prepared. Skilled advocates can rely on prior experiences in presenting an opening.

FORM 6.1
OPENING STATEMENT PLANNING WORKSHEET

Case _____ **File** _____

Case theory

Theme words of case

Significant issues

Structure

Introduction

Significant story facts

Event/circumstances

What/how/why it happened

Parties/witnesses

References to the law

Visual aids/exhibits

Case weaknesses

Request for verdict/decision

Conclusion

Other tactics/approaches/techniques

Possible objections adversary may make

L. SPECIFIC REQUIREMENTS

The attorney should determine before the trial or hearing whether the judge or arbitrator has any special requirements or limitations or whether applicable rules set limits on the content or presentation of the opening statement. This determination avoids having the opening interrupted and reduces the chances of opposing counsel making objections.

§ 6.3　ORGANIZATION

A. STRUCTURE

Opening statements must be presented in a structured fashion, allowing the entire case to be framed in the opening and helping the fact finder easily understand the facts and issues. The following are examples of various structures that can be used effectively:

1. Chronological

A chronological description of events is relatively easy to remember, makes sense, and is easy to understand. The attorney describes the events in the order in which they occurred. For example, in an employment arbitration, the opening can begin when the plaintiff was hired and end with events occurring on the date the plaintiff was fired.

2. Flashback

The beginning of the opening can explain the end of the story, and the remaining story can be told by flashing back to earlier events. For example, in a murder trial, the murder can be described first, followed by the events leading up to the murder, including the planning of the crime.

3. Parallel Actions

The actions of the plaintiff and the defendant or victim and criminal defendant can be told separately with the conclusion being the final event at which they came together. For example, in an automobile accident case, the routes of the plaintiff and defendant can be separately described with the conclusion being the collision.

4. Claims, Defenses, Topics

The opening can be structured around the claims, defenses or related topics that will be proved during the trial. For example, in a breach of contract arbitration, the opening can describe the elements: creation of a contract, its breach, and the resulting damages.

5.   Order of Evidence

The opening can be structured to reflect the order in which the evidence is presented, the witnesses testify, and the documents are introduced. For example, in a real estate administrative hearing involving lay and expert witnesses and numerous documents, the opening statement can follow the order in which the witnesses will testify and documents will be introduced. Available exhibits consisting of real and demonstrative evidence may also be a guide for part of the opening structure.

6.   Liability and Damages

In civil cases, the opening can first discuss liability and then damages. For example, in a personal injury case, the story can describe how the accident happened and then what injuries the plaintiff suffered.

7.   Mixture of Substructures

A number of these approaches can be used for parts of the opening, as substructures. For example, a civil case could begin with the flashback technique, use chronology to present the liability facts, and explain the damages in the order in which the witnesses will describe the damages.

B. PARTS OF THE OPENING

An opening statement has at least three major parts: the introduction, the body, and the conclusion.

1.   Introduction

An opening should begin with an introduction that draws the fact finder into the case when they are alert and interested in learning about what happened and why. The principles of advocacy and persuasion explained in Sections 1.5 and 1.6 apply with special force to the introduction of the opening statement.

Starting the statement in an interesting and dramatic way may be the most effective way to begin an opening. Beginning remarks in an opening statement need to take into account what has occurred previously. In a case before a judge or arbitrator, if the decision maker is very familiar with the case, the opening may be limited to outlining the major issues to be decided. In a jury trial, the beginning depends in part upon what introductory remarks and instructions the judge may have given and what information the jury has learned about the case during the jury selection process. An illustration of a judge's explanation follows.

Example (Judge):

Members of the Jury, at this beginning stage of the Jorge Mario Bergoglio vs. Sons of Anarchy trial the attorneys will now make what is called an opening statement. Each of them will tell you the evidence that will be introduced in this case. After these opening remarks, each of the parties will present their case. The plaintiff will proceed first, and present witnesses and introduce documents that support his case. Defense counsel will then have an opportunity to cross-examine the plaintiff's witnesses. After the plaintiff introduces all his evidence, the defendant will then present witnesses and exhibits in support of their case, and the plaintiff will have a chance to question the defense witnesses. After both parties have completed presenting their evidence, the attorneys will have an opportunity to summarize and explain the case to you in final argument. I will then instruct you on the law by explaining the law that applies to this case. You will go to the jury room, deliberate, and reach a verdict concluding this trial.

Counsel for plaintiff will now make an opening statement.

Ordinarily, a judge provides a similar, or more concise or lengthy, explanation to the jury describing how the trial will be conducted. If the attorney is uncertain what instructions may be given, the attorney can request that the judge provide particular instructions and preliminary remarks concerning the purpose of the opening, the identity of the parties and attorneys, and the trial procedures. If a judge does not explain to the jury the trial process, the attorney may provide that information at some point during the opening statement.

a. Explanation of Purposes

An opening statement may begin with an explanation of who the attorneys are, whom they represent, and the purposes of an opening statement. The following examples of introductory comments demonstrate how some lawyers begin their opening. These remarks are not the most persuasive way to begin an opening. However, they provide a comfortable way to begin and may help reduce initial anxiety.

Example (Purpose):

Members of the Jury, this opening statement allows me to explain to you the evidence that you will hear and see in this case. The evidence will be presented on behalf of Will Shortz in bits and pieces and not in the order in which the events happened. This opening will provide you with an overview of the case and help you understand what happened.

Example (Explanation):

My name is Atticus Finch. I represent Tom Robinson, who is sitting here. I now have the privilege of speaking to you about the evidence that will be introduced during this trial. This case will be presented to you like a jigsaw puzzle. Each witness who testifies and each document that is admitted will be a piece of that puzzle. At the end you will be able to put that picture together by yourselves. In the beginning, this opening statement allows me an opportunity to describe to you each of the pieces so that you will better understand the complete picture.

Example (Personal Injury):

Daisy Werthan, the plaintiff, has suffered severe and permanent injuries caused by the negligent driving of the defendant, Hoke Colburn. As you know, I am Vincent Gambini, the attorney representing Ms. Werthan. As the judge explained, this opening statement permits me to talk with you about what happened to cause that accident and those disabling injuries that have cost Ms. Werthan a long and well deserved retirement. I will tell you the story of what happened and a summary of the evidence.

Example (Employment Contract Case):

You have already met the plaintiff, Begum Hussain. She is in court today to be paid the salary the defendant promised her. I am here to present the facts through witnesses and documents which show that she has a right to that money. You are here to listen to the evidence and award the money owed her.

The advantage of these or similar preliminary remarks is that the jurors may better understand the purpose of the opening statement and the identity of the attorneys and parties. The disadvantage of such remarks is that they may not be the most persuasive way to begin the presentation of the case. The jurors can initially be told the theory of the case, and later about identities of participants and opening statement procedures.

b.   *Explanation of Theme*

An opening statement may begin with an explanation of the case theory described in a compelling and dramatic way to develop interest and capture the attention of the fact finder. The advantage of this approach is that the fact finder gains a favorable impression of the case and is more likely to recall the theme words used to describe the important facts and issues. The disadvantage is that issues may be overstated, or the opening made too melodramatic. However, this approach can be quite effective in any type of case before any decision maker if done well.

Example (Personal Injury):

This case is about the life and death of a man, a husband, a father, and a productive member of this community. His name was Walter White. He was killed when the all-terrain vehicle he was carefully driving rolled over unexpectedly, throwing him dangerously out of the defective three wheeler and over the cliff where he fell to his tragic death. He was thirty-nine years old with a loving family, wife, and two children He was a much admired high school chemistry teacher leading a fascinating life.

Example (Product Liability Plaintiff):

You are going to hear a case of corporate deception and greed by one of the largest pharmaceutical corporations in the world. The case is about the marketing of the Precon Shield, an untested and unsafe product. The case is about the selling of this product to thousands of women without caring about the serious injuries they suffered because of this dangerous and defective product.

Example (Criminal Prosecution):

Members of the Jury, on a clear summer evening on June 19, Liz Lemon got off the commuter train in Elmhurst. She was coming from work in Rockefeller Center where she works as a television director. The train pulled away from the station. She began walking to her car parked a block from the station. As she walked into the entrance of the parking ramp, she heard a noise. She turned to her right and confronted that man (looking at the defendant). On behalf of the people of this state, I am here today to tell you the facts of what happened when she met that man (referring to the defendant). After hearing those facts, it will be clear beyond a reasonable doubt that that man (turning to the defendant) brutally assaulted Ms. Lemon and stole her purse, her money, and her sense of security and peace of mind.

Example (Criminal Defense):

This is a case of mistaken identity. Mr. Abdulyadej did not commit any crime on the evening of July 15. He is innocent of what the prosecutor has claimed he did. Under our system of justice, the prosecution has the burden to prove to you beyond a reasonable doubt that my client is guilty. Under our system of justice, he is presumed to be innocent. Indeed he is innocent as he sits here in this courtroom. The facts that you will hear in this case will convince you that Mr. Abdulyadej was not anywhere near the scene of the crime. The case for the prosecution consists of one eyewitness who attempts to identify my client. That identification, members of the jury, was made under circumstances that make it totally unreliable.

---

2.   The Body

The content of the opening depends upon what the fact finder knows. A judge or arbitrator may know some aspects of the case, and the content should cover matters not known. Jurors may only know a bit about the case depending upon the extent of jury selection and preliminary statements made by the judge. The advocate should design a presentation to explain the unknown facts and issues of the case.

An opening statement may answer six questions: who, what, how, where, when, and why? Who is involved, what happened, how did it happen, where, when and why did it happen? The most effective way this information can be presented is usually by the attorney telling a compelling and complete factual story. This description of events should parallel the substance of the evidence, and the summary that will be given in the closing argument. The attorney, particularly a defense counsel, may need to explain what the evidence will not show as well as what it will show. Section 6.4 provides examples of the components of the body of an opening.

3.   Conclusion

An opening statement should have a strong conclusion. This may be achieved with a concise summary of the vital facts, with a compelling statement justifying a decision, or with a dramatic summary of the major theme of the case. A strong conclusion will have an impact because the fact finders often remember what they hear last. A strong presentation can be hindered by an apologetic or weak conclusion. The final words should be well thought out, so the conclusion will be effective both in content and delivery.

Example (Civil Plaintiff):

Members of the jury, at the end of this trial, after you have heard all the evidence, we'll ask that you find the defendant responsible for the damages suffered by Anita Lizana and that you find that he must compensate her for her medical expenses, for the wages and income she has lost, for her inability to play professional tennis, and for the pain and suffering she has endured and continues to endure to this day as a result of the defendant's negligence. We're confident you will hold the defendant accountable for his carelessness and indifference.

Example (Civil Defendant):

Those facts will clearly establish the defendant was not negligent and has no responsibility to the plaintiff in this case. At the end of this case the evidence will demonstrate the defendant did no wrong and bears no legal responsibility. The facts, the testimony and the evidence will demonstrate that the plaintiff cannot prove her case and a verdict should be returned in favor of Phil Wenneck against the plaintiff.

Example (Criminal Prosecution):

At the conclusion of this trial, I'll have an opportunity to talk with you again and discuss some of the things I've said today and the evidence you will hear in the trial. I'll ask you at that time to return a just and fair verdict and find the defendants Bonnie and Clyde guilty of robbery.

Example (Criminal Defendant):

At the end of this case, I'll discuss what you have heard and seen during the trial. By that time, you will have more than reasonable doubt that Mr. Baggins was not involved in the incident. By that time, you will be convinced that Bilbo Baggins did not steal the ring and is not guilty. By that time, you'll know he's innocent, and you will want to return a verdict on his behalf.

C. OPENING STATEMENT CRITIQUE

Questions that may assist in determining whether an opening statement has been properly constructed include the following:

- Does the opening statement tell what happened?
- Does the opening tell why to find for the client?
- Does the opening statement tell how to find for the client?
- Are visual aids and exhibits available to be used?
- Does the opening statement have a helpful structure?
- Is the opening consistent with what will be proved in the case and with what will be argued in summation?
- Does the opening statement make the decision maker want to find for the client?

§ 6.4   CONTENT

The content of an opening depends upon the facts and circumstances of the case and the strategic and tactical decisions of the advocate. The following factors may be considered when preparing the opening.

A.   PREFATORY PHRASES

Advocates may use a variety of prefatory phrases during opening statements. Some common prefaces include "I will prove" and "the evidence will show." Whether prefatory phrases should be used is a matter of debate among advocates. Some lawyers suggest that none of these phrases should be used but that the attorney should simply tell a story without any qualifying prefaces. Some advocates believe the attorney must use phrases like "I will prove to you" or "We will present evidence" to establish the attorney's position in a case and to have as powerful an influence as possible on the fact finders. Other advocates believe that more objective phrases such as "the evidence will show" or "you will learn" are the more appropriate phrases. Some judges and arbitrators expect or require advocates to preface their remarks with these phrases. The use of some phrases during an opening may prevent a presentation from sounding like an argument. A neutral qualifying introduction such as "you will learn" or "the evidence will show" may be an effective way of preventing an objection. If this tactic is overused, however, and it becomes apparent it is being used to argue or to introduce otherwise inappropriate information, an objection will be sustained.

Example (Criminal Case):

I will prove the defendant, Lucas McCain, did not intend to shoot the rifle. I'll present evidence to you that will establish this incident was all a tragic accident.

Example (Civil Case):

You'll learn from the evidence that the defendant, Mr. Wong, was negligent. Because he was negligent he is responsible for what happened. The facts will prove that, because Mr. Wong is responsible, he must be held accountable and must compensate the plaintiff, Ms. Wight, for what he did to her.

B.   AN EFFECTIVE STORY

The opening statement story should be told with simple language, in as dramatic a fashion as is appropriate, and in an interesting way. Statements and approaches that make a story believable and persuasive appear in great works of literature, art, and theatre, and they are the same factors that make an opening very effective. See Section 1.5.

Example (Commercial Case):

This is a case of a lost business opportunity, a lost invention, a lost dream—unfairly taken from a creative individual by a large irresponsible corporation. On February 14, Dr. Joan Clarke, while working hard and long hours, by herself for herself, in her home workshop, invented a new and innovative enigma computer device. Sometime later she visited the offices of the defendant—a huge corporation. She offered the defendant an opportunity to buy this invention. The lawyers for that conglomerate drafted a 12-page document. The executives of that corporation told the plaintiff that if she wanted to market her invention she would need to sign this contract. She willingly signed it. They signed it. She lived up to her end of the bargain. They have not lived up to their end of the contract. They breached the terms of that binding document. They didn't do what they told her they would do. They haven't paid her what they said they would pay her. We are here today to hold them to their promise, to their word, to their contract.

Example (Negligence):

On the evening of July 20, Mary Stands With A Fist was just finishing the last half mile of her three-mile run down Badlands Highway here in Fort Sedgwick. Mr. Dunbar had just finished drinking his fifth martini at the No Name bar. As Mary was running about four miles an hour on the marked jogging path along Badlands, Defendant Dunbar was weaving his car from side to side about 60 miles per hour traveling in the same direction on southbound Badlands Highway. Mary never saw the car that ran her down. Mary never saw the driver that killed her. She is gone. Her life is over. But we see him, he is with us. He sits in that chair there. This trial is to hold him responsible for the reckless killing and negligent homicide of Mary Stands With A Fist—a tragedy that never should have happened.

C. DETAILS

The facts presented during an opening statement should be as detailed as necessary to provide a clear and complete story. The advantage of providing a detailed story is that the story is usually perceived by the decision maker as more credible and more persuasive. Details that provide necessary information for a full understanding of events and explain sources of corroboration and credibility bolster the essential aspects of a case. The disadvantage of detailing specific facts is that the subsequent presentation of that evidence may not be as specific as the opening suggested. Additionally, too much detail can be confusing and boring.

Example (Personal Injury):

Defendant administrators violated school district safety rules regarding fitness activities. These rules require gym mats to contain three inches of thick foam. The defendants were using pads with only two inches of foam. The school district rules also require one supervisor for every ten kids using the gym mats. The defendants at the Charming school had only one supervisor for twenty kids. The mats had much less foam and there were fewer supervisors than required. The district administrators knew it, and they were irresponsibly negligent.

Example (Technical Data):

We will hear a lot of technical data about this Fornistan machine. We will see instruction manuals, diagrams, graphic designs, and other documents. And although these engineering details may appear very complicated and technical, the basic issue in this case is simple and straightforward. We will be focusing on only one part of the machine that was properly designed, was safely used, and did not cause the accident.

D. PARTIES/WITNESSES

Information about the parties and witnesses can be explained during opening. The advocate can explain who will testify and what each person will say. Witnesses should be described in a way that will make their story understandable and their testimony credible.

The fact finder needs to understand or be reminded that a case involves people and not merely abstract legal problems. The more a party and key witnesses are personalized and described as individuals who will testify to what happened, the more likely they will be perceived as believable. Statements should be made which help the fact finder identify, relate to, and empathize with the witnesses.

Whether every witness needs to be identified during opening statement depends on the facts of the case and the importance of the witness. The more critical the individual is to the case, the more essential it may be to identify that individual. If the testimony of the witness should be highlighted, identifying the witness in the opening will help do so. If a distinguished expert will testify, identifying that expert will help.

Fact finders may have a difficult time identifying with witnesses who are not described during an opening. They have no useful way of forming a picture in their mind of the witness. A party or witness who is present can be identified. Key witnesses may be present during the opening so the attorney can introduce them. The names and identities of the witnesses can be written on a visual aid or contained in an exhibit.

Fact finders can find it difficult to remember details and the names of witnesses. The struggle to remember and identify witnesses may distract them from remembering more important details of the opening. Highlighting the source of the evidence by generally describing the witness (an eyewitness to the accident, a bank vice president, a police officer) may be sufficient. This identification helps the fact finders understand what happened without burdening them with names.

Statements about the background of a witness may also be included. This information can be effective if the fact finders have things in common with the background of the witness or if the description portrays the witness as a responsible, believable individual. The backgrounds of minor or problem witnesses need not be detailed in the opening.

Describing a witness during the opening commits the attorney to calling that witness to testify. Only witnesses who are sure to be called ought to be described. If there is uncertainty about whether a witness will testify, no specific reference ought to be made to that witness. A defense attorney may decide not to call a witness to testify based on the way the plaintiff/claimant/prosecutor presented a case and should not specifically refer to these optional witnesses in the opening.

Whatever is said about a witness and testimony should be proved during the trial or hearing. An advocate should not offer incomplete information or exaggerate the background or testimony of the witness. Exaggeration may create unfulfilled expectations with the fact finder. Misstatements provide an opportunity for opposing counsel to correct the inaccurate or incomplete description during opening or comment during final argument on the failure to prove such statements.

Example (Corporation):

Marvel Comics is a group of people, of individuals who work at their trade providing consumers with fun adventures. The people of this company include workers, managers, and shareholders. Anya Sofia Corazon who sits here, represents all those individuals involved in the business. She'll stay throughout the entire trial, and she will also take the stand and testify.

Example (Witnesses):

Please consider the testimony of the witnesses carefully. Consider what they say and assess their believability. See which one has a reason to be less than truthful. See which one was in the best position to observe what happened. We know what Jack Bauer will say in this case because we had an opportunity to interrogate him and ask him questions under oath before trial. He'll tell you the same things he told us.

Example (Experts):

Rachel Carson will testify that in her opinion this product is harmful to the environment. We'll hear all about her environmental expertise, her extensive professional experiences, the many articles she has written, the teaching positions that she holds, and her excellent reputation in her field of expertise. We'll also hear her expert opinion, the facts that support that opinion, and the reasons why this product is so very harmful.

E. THE EVENT

The description of important incidents, occurrences, and events is a typical part of an opening statement. The portrayal should be accurate and complete and should enable the fact finders to compose a clear picture in their minds. Verbal descriptions of scenes can become complicated if too much detail is given, or if complex explanations are made. Only those details that portray the scene accurately should be provided. It can be difficult for fact finders to follow directions or visualize matters in the abstract. References to compass directions (north, south), degrees (a 90 degree turn), angles (a sharp right turn), and similar references are difficult to visualize. Visual aids and exhibits may be used to describe scenes in order to ensure a better understanding.

Example (Use of Computer Generated Diagram):

The streetcar was headed east, in this direction, left to right, on the diagram, along Elysian Fields. The bus stopped at this intersection here at the southwest corner of Desire Street. Elysian Fields runs east and west, and Desire runs north and south along this line. The plaintiff, Stella Kowalski, got off the streetcar at this intersection on this corner. She waited for the lights to change and waited for the walk sign to be lit up and then began walking in the crosswalk across Elysian Fields to the northwest side of the intersection to this spot marked SK.

F. CIRCUMSTANCES

Information about the circumstances surrounding the incident or event may be important and may need to be explained during the opening. Explanations of the time, date, weather, vehicles, equipment, and other information should be provided to the extent necessary. The more important the circumstance is to the story, the more detail should be provided. If the time of the day is critical to the case, the precise time should be mentioned. If the exact weather conditions are important, atmospheric details should be provided.

The extent to which details need to be described depends upon how precise the witnesses will be and how necessary it is that the fact finder visualizes an accurate picture. It may be enough to describe a car simply as a "car" if a further description is not necessary. If it is important that the fact finder accurately visualize the bumper of a car, then a digital photo of the bumper or an actual bumper should be introduced.

Example (Criminal Case):

As Georgia O'Keefe walked down the first block towards her studio, she saw a number of apartment buildings on her left, and to her right she saw a gas station, a grocery store, and a few homes. As she walked down the second block, she could see more apartments and more homes on both sides of the street. It was twilight. The street lamps were on. There were three street lamps on the short second block: one the middle and one at each end. The apartment buildings all had exterior lights that were turned on. The evening sky was clear.

G. VISUAL AIDS AND EXHIBITS

The use of visual aids and exhibits significantly increase the effectiveness of an opening statement. These devices help fact finders understand the facts and details of cases and help advocates accurately and persuasively present openings.

Visual aids may be created exclusively for use during opening statement. Exhibits that will be real or demonstrative evidence during the trial or hearing can also be used. Exhibits vary from simple diagrams to video presentations to computer generated reconstructions of events. The content of some visual aids will be obvious (a printed poster), while others may need to be previewed (a software demonstration) by the judge or arbitrator. The nature of the visual aid will determine whether it needs to be reviewed by an opposing lawyer and the judge before it is used.

Some jurisdictions have specific restrictions about the use of visual aids and exhibits. Permission for their use will need to be sought from the judge or arbitrator before the opening to avoid an interruption or objection from opposing counsel. While most judges and arbitrators routinely permit the use of visual aids and exhibits, some may be reluctant to permit them because they are not familiar with their use.

Example (Injuries):

You will see some horrific images of the plaintiff's injuries and computer generated graphic scenes of the terrible accident during this trial. Some of them will be difficult to look at. But you need to see them so that you can understand the full extent of the plaintiff's injuries. They are not shown to you for their shock effect. If they do trouble you, remember that they are only a pale imitation of what the actual injuries were and they are much less dreadful than if you saw the real injuries in the flesh. I'm going to show you a few now. This first shows how the plaintiff, Constance Langdon, looked one day after the accident.

Example (Product Liability):

Please look at the monitors in front of you. Here is a chart listing the design and manufacturing defects. We need to review each of these items with you. This first column in blue lists the defects. This second column in green lists the dates when the defendant Transformers Incorporated, and its managers, first knew about the defects, and this third column in red lists what injuries the defects caused. This chart will help you understand what went wrong, when it went wrong, and why it went wrong.

H. WHAT HAPPENED

The fact finder obviously needs to know what happened. The facts and circumstances of a case dictate the parameters of the story. A description of what happened includes references to the parties, the scene, and circumstances. An effective description includes statements that are objectively accurate, complete, and believable. A description that is too abstract, too subjectively biased or incomplete is not persuasive.

Example (Criminal Case):

Zatanna Zatara was holding the straps of her magic bag in her right hand as she walked toward the Justice League. The defendant came up to her and grabbed one strap of the bag and attempted to steal it from her. She immediately looked right at the defendant, and instinctively gripped the handle of the bag tightly. As he tried to pull it from her, she again stared at the defendant and pulled the bag towards herself. He held onto that bag, and was pulled closer towards her until the defendant's face was only about a foot away from Ms. Zatara's face.

I.   HOW IT HAPPENED

Usually an issue in a case revolves around the question of how something happened, and an explanation will be part of the opening. A clear description of the "how" of what happened is essential.

Example (Civil Case):

Trung Trac suffered a ruptured disc in the accident. We will learn from the doctors who will testify that the spinal column is made up of a number of bones or vertebrae, one on top of the other. Between each of these bones is a disc called an intervertebral disc. It is shaped like a donut and acts like a shock absorber. The center of the donut is filled with something called nucleosis pulpesis, a gelatin or jelly-like substance. If the vertebrae are jammed together pressure can be put on these "donuts" and the "jelly" squirts out the side (descriptive gesture). This is a rupture and the injury is called a ruptured disc. This model shows the vertebrae and discs, and will help us understand how the severe and painful injuries suffered by Ms. Trac happened.

Example (Civil Case/Third Party Defendant):

The evidence will show that it was the Minions who were at fault. They didn't oil the machine; they didn't check the machine's temperature; and they didn't replace the worn parts. The defendant did not cause the machine to explode and did not cause the plaintiff's injuries. The Minions did it all. The evidence will show that the defendant is not accountable for what happened, but rather the Minions are the irresponsible parties.

J.   WHY IT HAPPENED

Explaining the what and the how of a story may not be sufficient if the why has not been explained. The why may not be of critical importance in a legal sense, but the fact finders will be curious about why something happened. If a good reason exists to explain the "why," then a concise explanation should be included in an opening. If no good reason exists to explain an event, then an explanation should be avoided.

Explanations of why something happened usually are limited in an opening because a detailed or lengthy explanation may go beyond the evidence of a case and become improper argument. If an explanation cannot be based on direct or circumstantial evidence, then an explanation should be reserved for final argument.

Example (General):

Why were the defendants in a hurry? Because they were late for the start of the Minecraft adventure game.

Example (Medical Negligence):

This is a case about medical negligence. Doctor Meredith Grey was careless when she performed surgery on the plaintiff. She is not a bad doctor. She is not unfit to practice medicine. She made a serious mistake and must be held responsible the same way any professional must be held responsible for a serious mistake that causes pain, suffering, and damages. She made the serious mistake, in part, because she was exhausted. She had been up all night working at the hospital and hadn't slept. She acted irresponsibly and must be held accountable for her negligence.

K. DISPUTED ISSUES

The fact finder needs to focus on the disputed issues between the parties. A reference to the conflict in the evidence or testimony helps define what needs to be decided.

Example (Tort Case):

There will be a dispute in the evidence presented to you—a disagreement about who saw what. Ren Suzugamori will say the light was red, while Lyserg Diethel will say the light was green. The lawyers and the witnesses know about this dispute because we have had the opportunity to learn about the facts of this case before coming to trial so we know who will say what. After hearing everything, we believe you will agree that Ms. Suzugamori is wrong and Mr. Diethel is right and find that the light was green.

Example (Contract Arbitration Case):

The dispute between the parties in this case resolves around who is to blame for the breach of the contract. Each side blames the other side. We contend the plaintiff Wyldstyle is legally to blame for the breach and here are three reasons why. The first is. . . .

L.   CLAIMS AND DEFENSES

In most cases references to the claims or defenses should be made. These descriptions focus attention on what must be decided.

Example (Civil Claimant):

The evidence will show that Aklar Shah signed this contract and failed to deliver the precious gems that she promised to deliver to Daria-i-Noor according to the terms of this contract. The issue you will need to resolve is whether the diamonds that respondent sent were the diamonds the claimant ordered under their agreement. The evidence will show that Aklar Shah sent the wrong precious gems and breached their contract.

Example (Civil Respondent):

The primary question you will need to answer in this arbitration is whether this piece of paper is a legally enforceable contract. The evidence will show that this paper is not a contract and that Daria-i-Noor is not responsible to Aklar Shah. Counsel for claimant has told you about the diamonds the claimant expected to receive from the respondent. That is not the main issue. The real issue is whether Exhibit No. 1 is a binding contract. It's not.

M.   THE LAW

The advocate may refer to the law and may blend an appropriate discussion of the law with the facts. Trial counsel may not explain the law in detail to a jury.

Example (Negligence by Defendant):

You will learn that there was a stop sign at the intersection of Boardwalk and Park Place and that a person driving through that intersection must come to a complete stop and look in both directions before proceeding. The evidence will show that the defendant failed to come to a full, complete stop at the stop sign at this intersection as she was required by law to do.

Example (Lack of Negligence):

Judge Edward Coke will instruct you that negligence is the failure to exercise ordinary care or the failure to do something that a reasonable prudent person would have done under the same or similar circumstances. You will apply this legal standard to the facts of this case. When you do, it will be clear that the defendant Rachel Lapp did exercise ordinary care when she drove her buggy and is not responsible for the accident.

N. BURDEN OF PROOF

If the judge in preliminary instructions does not explain to the jury the burden of proof in the case, it may be appropriate to briefly mention the burden in the opening statement. A reference regarding the burden should be brief because references to matters of law must be limited. A reference to the burden should be made if doing so is tactically advantageous. Section 2.12 discussed burden of proof strategies in detail.

Example (Civil Case):

This is a civil case. The burden of proof in a civil case is called "preponderance of the evidence." That means that the plaintiff wins if it is more probable than not that her story is true. We will prove that it is more likely than not that what the plaintiff said happened, actually happened. The burden of proof is not beyond a reasonable doubt, which is a much heavier burden. That applies in criminal cases, not in civil cases like this one. Judge Trudy-Kessler will explain this lesser burden of proof later during the trial, and we will apply it to the facts to show you why the plaintiff Mitch Brockden is entitled to your verdict.

O. DAMAGES IN A CIVIL CASE

In a civil case, the plaintiff needs to explain the types of injuries, expenses, and other damages. All damages that are recoverable under the claim brought by the plaintiff should be mentioned. In a contract case, the damages may be computed by referring to the terms of the contract or by establishing the lost income or profits. In a tort case, personal injury damages should include an explanation of the injury, diagnosis, treatment, and prognosis of temporary or permanent injuries.

Example (Personal Injury):

This case is about what happened to Clark Kent. He was one person before the accident and a different person after. Your task is to put a value on the differences between what Clark was and what he has become and will remain for the rest of his life.

Example (Pain and Suffering):

Almásy will tell you the horrors he went through during four months of intensive burn treatments. He will describe how his twice daily bath was so excruciatingly painful he screamed and cried. He will tell you that he has never experienced any pain like the agonizing pain caused by his burns. He will explain that he couldn't use enough drugs to stop the pain because the drugs made him sicker. He'll describe the terrible pain with which he has to live, despite the great care he was provided by Hana.

P. AMOUNT OF DAMAGES

Lawyers who prefer a detailed description of damages want the fact finder to know from the outset the extent of the damages sought. Mentioning a dollar amount creates a frame of reference, provides some guidance during the case, establishes the extent of the damages, suggests that the attorney knows what the case is worth, and preconditions the fact finder to a request in summation for an appropriate damage award. Lawyers who prefer a minimal description of damages want the fact finder to first hear the details during the presentation of the evidence. Not mentioning the dollar amount during the opening delays the disclosure of damages to the introduction of damage evidence, creates suspense, avoids locking the attorney and witnesses into set positions, and gives the fact finder an opportunity to hear the witnesses describe the injuries before a request for specific damages is made.

If the injuries that caused the damages are slight, less emphasis should be placed on them. If the injuries that caused the damages are great, more prominence should be placed on them during the opening. In jury trials, references to damage amounts may also be made during jury selection that may influence what should be said during the opening.

Example (Damages Described):

This case involves the irresponsibility that Matrix Solutions bears as a result of its computer hacking scheme. The law measures the amount of responsibility in dollars. You will hear evidence about the substantial damages Mr. Neo has suffered as a result of the personal extortion attempts and the breach of his privacy. These damages amount to $10,199,900, which is a substantial amount of money—but an amount which is very fair and reasonable because the responsibility the defendant owes to the plaintiff is equally substantial.

Example (Damages Reserved):

At the conclusion of the case, we will discuss the evidence that you have heard. We will ask then that you return a verdict that fairly and adequately compensates the Bar-ba-loots for what they have endured. We will also ask you to return a verdict that will include punitive damages—damages that punish Once-Ler Factory for gross and willful misconduct. Punitive damages are available under the law in cases like this when a company destroys food-producing truffula trees causing famine and rampant disease. Punitive damages tell the defendant it wantonly ravaged the environment and should never do it again. The defendant corporation has a net worth in excess of $500 million, that is over one half a billion dollars. At the end of the case, I will come back and ask you to award the plaintiffs a substantial amount of money that will compensate them for what happened and award them additional monies to punish the defendant for its reckless and irresponsible actions.

Q. REQUEST FOR RELIEF

An opening statement should contain an explanation of the decision or verdict that the facts will support. This explanation should be clear so the fact finders understand the precise conclusion they must reach to find for a party. Some attorneys will say that the facts and law require that a specific award or verdict must be returned because the client is entitled to or has a right to such a result. Other attorneys explain that the fact finders have an opportunity, and even a duty, to decide in favor of a client based upon the law and facts of the case.

Example (Civil Arbitration):

That concludes my opening. You will hear from the witnesses just what happened, and you will have documents that will support that testimony. At the close of this arbitration, I am going to ask you to issue an award in favor of Forthright.

Example (Criminal Case):

The facts will prove that the Defendant is guilty of murder in the first degree beyond a reasonable doubt. The testimony and exhibits prove that the Defendant shot and killed J.R. Ewing. The evidence will prove that the Defendant intended to kill Mr. Ewing, decided to shoot him, and planned to murder him three days before he killed him. These facts prove beyond a reasonable doubt that the defendant is guilty of first degree murder.

§ 6.5   TECHNIQUES

The following sections involve techniques for the effective presentation of an opening statement. These approaches need to be reviewed to determine their applicability to openings in particular cases.

A.   OFFENSIVE/DEFENSIVE APPROACHES

An opening statement should lead the fact finder to a conclusion that the client is entitled to win. The plaintiff/claimant/prosecutor will naturally take the "offensive" and explain the story in a positive way. Some defense counsel may think it appropriate for the opening statement to be explained in a "defensive" way because the other side has the burden of proof. A more effective tactic may well be for the defense to take the offensive and explain what the defendant's evidence will prove and then defend the case by stating what the plaintiff's evidence won't prove.

Counsel for the defendant who presents an opening after the opening by the plaintiff/claimant/prosecutor must decide whether and how to respond to the opening by the opposing attorney. Defense counsel should be careful not to appear weak by responding in a completely defensive way. The opening should describe the case of the defendant/respondent and, after that has been explained, respond to the extent necessary to statements by the other side in the initial opening statement. Even in a criminal case where the defendant will not testify, the opening statement for the defense should be as positive as possible. The defense will present evidence through cross-examination of the prosecution's witnesses, and this information can be used to support reasonable doubt.

At the end of an opening by a plaintiff/claimant/prosecutor, counsel may raise some questions or make some remarks that suggest the defense lawyer should answer or address during the opening for the defendant. The lawyer for the defendant should present the prepared opening statement and avoid directly responding to this ploy, unless a response is necessary or would be more effective than not responding.

Example (Civil Case):

At the end of her opening statement, counsel for the plaintiff suggested to you that I should tell you what facts we had which differed from the facts she explained to you. You may have wondered why I didn't respond to the questions Alicia Florrick raised until now. The facts that I just explained to you, that you will hear from the witnesses who take that stand and which you will read in these documents, will answer those questions. There is no need for me to do what plaintiff's counsel asked. You will do that later during your deliberations; and our facts will lead to you to the right conclusion: verdict for the defense.

B. ANTICIPATING DEFENSES

After making an opening statement, the plaintiff/claimant/prosecutor has no opportunity for rebuttal after the defense opening. Defenses need to be anticipated and dealt with in the opening. In civil cases, the plaintiff will usually know and can explain away the defenses.

Example (Accident Case):

The defendant cannot avoid responsibility in this case by telling you the accident was Alice's own fault—that she wasn't watching where she was walking. But after hearing all the evidence, you will learn this was an area where people walked all the time and no one, including Alice, expected there to be a hole in the ground.

Example (Automobile Case):

Now I must tell you that the defendant will try to put some of the blame for this accident on T.E. Lawrence. The defendant will claim that Mr. Lawrence should have slowed his motorcycle or swerved to avoid the accident. But you will learn the defendant came over the crest of that hill so fast there was no way Mr. Lawrence could have avoided the collision. He just could not have seen defendant's bicycle in time to avoid this tragic accident.

In criminal cases, the constitutional rights of the defendant limit comments that can be made by the prosecution. The prosecutor may not directly comment on evidence the defense may produce. A prosecutor can explain evidence that will be introduced during the prosecutor's case and state indirectly that such evidence overcomes potential defenses, but the prosecution cannot comment on possible testimony by the defendant because the defendant need not and may not testify or present evidence.

C. ASSERTING PROMISES

A "promise" that specific evidence will prove a certain fact can be effective as long as the attorney can fulfill that pledge. A promise that is not kept causes the fact finder to lose confidence in the attorney and in other facts as well. Assurances must be employed carefully. If a lawyer does make promises during an opening or otherwise asserts that certain evidence will be proved, the opposing lawyer should note all these statements and mention during summation all promises not kept.

Example (General):

I promise you that I will present evidence showing the defendant lied to the plaintiff about the value of her land. After hearing this evidence, you will conclude that the defendant misrepresented the facts and defrauded Ms. Gaza. At the end of this case, I'll ask you to put us to the decisive test: Did we prove to you what we said we would prove? If we have, we will ask you then for a verdict in favor of the plaintiff against the defendant.

D. MAKING A COMPACT WITH THE JURY

The attorney may make a compact with the jury during the opening. The attorney may promise the jurors that the attorney will never mislead or misdirect them or intentionally misstate any evidence or exaggerate the facts. The attorney may ask the jurors to hold the attorney to this statement and to hold the opposing lawyer to the same standard. This approach impresses the jury with the sincerity of the lawyer and reduces the chances the opposing lawyer will engage in misdirection or exaggerations. This tactic can be used in situations where there is a concern the opposing lawyer will present an unfair and improper opening.

Example (General):

Everything I've told you in this opening about the evidence is what you will hear from this witness stand and see and read in these dispatches. I will prove that the events in this historic case happened the way I just described. I ask you to hold the other parties, Czar Nicholas and Alexandra, to this same standard.

E. EMPLOYING UNDERSTATEMENT

Understatement can be a useful credibility-building device for an opening statement presentation. Understating a case sets the expectation of the fact finder at a level that will be exceeded during the trial or hearing. The presentation of the evidence will then surpass the fact finder's expectations, enhancing the credibility of the case and the attorney. Understatement may also arouse curiosity. If the attorney does not describe all the details of an event or a conversation during the opening, the fact finders may pay special attention because they have been eagerly waiting to hear or see the evidence. The use of understatement does have disadvantages. It may reduce the attorney's ability to explain facts in a persuasive way, and a fact finder may initially perceive an understated case to be weaker than the attorney intended.

Example (Civil Case):

Judy and Doralee talked that day about Violet and her future with the group. They will take the witness stand and tell you what they said. When you hear what they said, you will understand the plans they had for Violet from 9 to 5.

F. AVOIDING OVERSTATEMENT

Advocates should avoid the use of overstatement during an opening statement. The fact finder may be initially impressed, but this impression will not last long once it is realized that the evidence does not match what the attorney proffered. Further, opposing counsel may comment during summation about the absence of the exaggerated evidence.

G. ASSERTING CHALLENGING POSITIONS

The facts and issues in some cases will be more challenging for advocates to promote and more difficult for fact finders to accept than in other cases. Usually, it is easier to prove that a person was negligent, failed to do something, or made a mistake rather than having to prove that a person intentionally did something, acted very unreasonably, or lied. For example, in a negligence case where contradictory statements were made by the plaintiff and defendant regarding the color of a traffic light, the plaintiff can win by proving that the defendant could not accurately see the color of the light or was confused about the color of the light without proving the defendant is a liar. In some cases the more challenging position is necessary as part of the proof and problematic facts must be addressed in the opening. For example, a discrimination case may require the plaintiff to prove the defendant committed an intentional discriminatory act that the defendant denies. In the opening, the attorney needs to assert the defendant lied and acted reprehensibly. These assertions are more challenging to substantiate than claims with easier to prove facts.

Example (Civil Plaintiff):

We will prove to you that the defendant stated that he didn't want "them" working for him, and if it is not now appropriate for me to call the defendant D.W. Griffith a racist, by the end of the case it will be clear to you that he is a racist.

Example (Criminal Defendant):

I will prove to you that the witness for the prosecution is a liar. Fletcher Reede, whom the prosecutor has described as the key witness in this case, has lied a number of times in the past regarding what he did on the night of February 14th. He lied to the police when they questioned him. And he took an oath—the same oath he took today—to tell the truth and lied to a judge at a previous court hearing.

H. DESCRIBING CASE WEAKNESSES

An attorney must consider whether to describe weaknesses in a case. Weaknesses that will be brought out in testimony must be presented in a forthright manner. Weaknesses in a case that have not been explained and most likely will be mentioned during the opponent's opening or later in the case should be addressed during opening statement. A candid disclosure usually enhances the appearance of sincerity and credibility of the attorney while reducing the impact of the opposition's strong points.

Example (Negligence):

A moment ago, I told you that I would describe everything that happened. You will learn that the plaintiff Amanda Bonner had stopped at a local bar on her way home from her law office. Ms. Bonner will tell you herself that she had dinner and two glasses of wine with her dinner a couple of hours before the accident. The evidence will show, however, that those events had nothing to do with the accident, which happened only because the defendant ran a red light smashing his car into the back of plaintiff's car. The defendant is the irresponsible party in this case, and Ms. Bonner deserves your verdict.

Example (Contract):

We told you that we would put everything before you, the good and the bad. You will learn in this case that Beanie Baby has a criminal record—she was convicted of income tax evasion five years ago. But that has nothing to do with the fact that she had an employment contract with the defendant and that she has a legal right to her commissions.

Example (Personal Injury):

In the interest of fairness, and holding nothing back, you will hear evidence from Dexter Morgan that he was a trespasser—he did not have permission to be on the property when he got hurt. But you will learn that the owner, the defendant, must take care not to injure people who are on her property whether they have permission to be there or not.

I. EXPLAINING THE ABSENCE OF EVIDENCE

During the opening the attorney can describe what facts will not be proved, what documents will not be introduced, and what evidence will not be presented, and briefly explain why such information will not be offered. Usually this explanation is appropriate where evidence does not exist or was not preserved. Fact finders may wonder why some evidence is not introduced, and this tells them what they will not hear or see.

Example (Missing Witness):

The plane was behind schedule when Amelia Earhart boarded it. She will tell you it was over a day late. The pilot of the van will not be able to tell you how late it was because he moved away from our city over a year ago and cannot be located despite our very best efforts to find him.

Example (Absent Evidence):

The evidence will be that Kinner Airster did insufficient testing on this biplane model. Our expert, Dr. Sheldon Cooper, will testify that in his opinion proper testing would have shown the biplane to be unreasonably dangerous and defective.

J. QUALIFYING REMARKS TO THE JURY

Some attorneys emphasize to jurors that what an attorney says during opening does not constitute evidence. Other attorneys may explain that the jurors' function is to determine the facts after hearing the evidence during the trial. Comments like this reduce the impact of an opening statement presentation and are often unnecessary because the same statement may be contained in the judge's preliminary instructions to the jury. Defense counsel may want to make such comments in an attempt to reduce the effectiveness of a particularly persuasive plaintiff's opening statement and to remind the jurors that they must wait to determine the evidence as it is introduced during the trial.

Example (General):

You will hear a lot of lawyer talk in this case. You have just listened to the opening statement for the plaintiff by his lawyer, Patty Hewes. What we lawyers say is not evidence. The judge will tell you that you are not to decide this case based upon what we as lawyers have said but rather on what the evidence will prove. You are not to rely on lawyer talk in reaching the verdict in this case. You are to rely on the testimony of the witnesses who will come before you and testify and the documents that will be introduced. Now let me describe what the evidence will show.

---

§ 6.6   PRESENTATION AND DELIVERY

The manner in which the attorney delivers the opening statement affects the fact finders' understanding of the evidence, significantly influences their initial impression of the attorney and the strengths and weaknesses of the party's story, and shapes their perspective of the entire case. The following factors are matters that will affect the quality of the opening presentation. These factors supplement the considerations relating to presentation and delivery explained in Section 1.7.

A.   LOCATION OF THE PRESENTATION

Advocates typically conduct opening statements in trials standing behind or by a lectern or table in front of the fact finder. In arbitrations and administrative hearings, the opening may be delivered sitting down. Trial lawyers may be able to conduct an opening while standing close to the jury, and if preferred, may ask the judge for permission to do so. Wherever located, the advocate should be in the direct view of the jury, judge, or arbitrator.

In some courts, local rules require that the attorney stand behind a lectern without moving when presenting the opening. In these situations, the attorney can ask permission of the court to stand away from the lectern in order to make a more effective presentation. If the attorney must remain at a lectern, visual aids or exhibits may be used to emphasize points and to provide an opportunity for movement away from the lectern.

B.   MOVEMENT

Some movement is useful, particularly if the opening is long. Movement and stance should be orchestrated so as not to be distracting. An attorney may use movement as a transition or to provide emphasis. Movement that appears purposeless is disconcerting and is to be avoided.

C.   APPROPRIATE DISTANCE

The attorney must maintain an appropriate distance from the fact finder. This distance should neither be so far away that personal contact is lost nor so close that the fact finders feel uncomfortable. A distance of between five and ten feet can be used as an appropriate guide, but the optimum distance varies depending on circumstances. An advocate can observe the fact finders' reaction and move close when appropriate and stand further away when necessary. For example, when the attorney approaches the jury box, the attorney may stand in front of jurors in the first row, speak with a quieter voice, and make primary eye contact with jurors in the second row.

D. GESTURES

The attorney should use gestures that are appropriate to the content of the opening statement and that appear natural. Gestures should be made even if the attorney stands behind the lectern. Fact finders will become bored with a talking head, which is all that they might see if the attorney stands behind a lectern without using any gestures, movement, or visual aids. Wild gestures, flailing hands, random pacing, and fiddling with pens are distracting and are to be avoided.

E. EYE CONTACT

An effective way to establish credibility and sincerity is to look directly at the fact finder during the opening. Good eye contact also helps hold attention and allows the attorney to observe reactions. Advocates should vary their eye contact and not stare. It should be sufficiently long to establish contact but not so long it becomes uncomfortable.

F. TRANSITIONS

The opening statement is more effective if the attorney employs transitions. Prefatory remarks, silence, a louder voice, a softer voice, visual aids, movement, and gestures can signal a transition.

G. OBSERVING THE FACT FINDER

The attorney must observe a fact finder's reaction during the opening statement and adjust the presentation when necessary. The initial impressions displayed during the opening will be useful in determining how the evidence is later presented and what might be an effective closing argument position. However, it is difficult to determine accurately what people are thinking just by watching them during a presentation. Care must be taken not to overreact and not to change an approach completely because of a perceived reaction.

H. NOTES AND OUTLINES

When notes are used, the attorney should avoid pretending they are not being used. An obvious use of notes done openly is appropriate. Fact finders understand the need to use notes.

A prepared outline can be effectively employed in an opening as a visual aid. A diagram, whiteboard, easel paper, or computer monitor may contain an outline of the opening that highlights important matters and assists the attorney in explaining the facts.

I.   VISUAL AIDS AND EXHIBITS

As mentioned previously, the use of visual aids and exhibits can enhance the manner of the presentation and affect the above factors discussed in this section. Important parts of real and demonstrative evidence exhibits may be shown to the fact finder to help them understand the case and remember key facts and issues. Visual aids can be crafted for use during the opening to make the evidence and issues clear and memorable.

§ 6.7   OBJECTIONS AND MOTIONS

A.   IMPROPER COMMENTS

Certain statements and comments made during an opening are objectionable. References to the following evidence and comments are improper:

1.   Referring to Inadmissible or Unprovable Evidence

Counsel must not refer to inadmissible evidence or unprovable facts during opening statement. This prohibition extends to evidence excluded by pretrial or prehearing rulings, or likely to be excluded by the rules of evidence, as well as facts, opinions, or inferences that are not supported by evidence. The standard for determining whether an attorney may refer to specific evidence is whether the attorney has reasonable, good faith grounds to believe the evidence is admissible. The standard to determine whether a matter can be proved is whether there is a source of admissible evidence to prove the matter. The opening statement is not to be used as a subterfuge to present inadmissible or nonexistent evidence or to circumvent the rules of evidence and professional responsibility.

Objection:

Counsel has referred to evidence that is neither admissible nor provable in this case. We request those statements be stricken and counsel admonished for making such references.

Response to Objection:

- Explain the evidence law that supports the admissibility of the questioned evidence.
- Describe the source of evidence that supports the statement.
- Advise the judge/arbitrator and opposing counsel before the opening that there will be a reference to potentially objectionable evidence, and seek a preliminary ruling as to its admissibility.

2.   Explaining Details of the Law or Jury Instructions

The attorney should not explain details of the law or give instructions to the jury. While making brief references regarding the law in the case is proper, lengthy descriptions or detailed explanations of the law are not proper. These comments are only appropriate in summation.

The precise extent to which an attorney may refer to the law during an opening varies among jurisdictions and among judges. Some courts strictly limit an attorney's explanation of the law during opening statement, while other courts permit reasonable latitude to the attorneys to explain the law applicable to the facts. See Section 6.1(B).

Objection:

Counsel is improperly explaining the law or jury instructions during opening statement.

Response to Objection:

- Avoid lengthy or detailed references to the law or jury instructions.

- Briefly mention the law or jury instructions several times during the opening, rather than describing it in one lengthy explanation.

- Combine a description of the facts with an explanation of the law to make these statements sound more factual.

- Use prefatory remarks such as "The evidence will show" before explaining the law.

- Remind the jurors that it is the judge and not the attorneys who will explain the law to them.

3.   Making Argumentative Statements

Counsel should not make argumentative statements during the opening. The opening statement is an opportunity to present the evidence that will be offered and not to argue issues in the case. See Section 6.1(B).

Objection:

Counsel is making argumentative statements.

Response to Objection:

- Explain that the reference to the facts, law, or case is proper for the opening and is not an argument.

- Avoid speaking with an argumentative tone of voice, or with over-emphatic gestures, or in a loud, aggressive manner.

- In a jury trial, request a bench conference to avoid being admonished by the court in front of the jury.

4.   Stating Personal Beliefs and Opinions

The attorney should not give a personal opinion or belief concerning the evidence or the case. The fact finder is to determine the case based upon the facts and the law and not upon the personal statements of counsel. Phrases such as "I personally believe" or "It is my opinion" are objectionable. The lawyer may state "I will prove" or "I submit" because the lawyer is not asserting a personal position and there is supporting evidence.

Objection:

Counsel is stating a personal belief or opinion.

Response to Objection:

- Rephrase the remarks and avoid interjecting personal ideas and opinions.

- Use phrases such as "We will present evidence to you that will show" and "You will learn that" rather than phrases that suggest personal beliefs.

5.   Putting Fact Finders in the Place of the Party

Counsel may not ask judges, jurors, or arbitrators to put themselves in the place of a party or witness in determining an issue. They are to base their decision on the evidence and not substitute their personal experiences or reactions for that of the evidence presented in the case.

Objection:

Counsel is improperly referring to personal experiences of the fact finder.

Response to Objection:

- Avoid suggesting fact finders rely on their own experiences;

- Save references to common life experiences until final argument.

- Use general references to real life or common sense. For example, "Mr. Burns did what most people would do" and

"Ms. Allen used common sense when she turned on the television to watch the comedy hour."

6. Speculating About the Other Side's Case

In a criminal case, a prosecutor cannot suggest what the defense will prove because the defense has no obligation to prove anything. In a civil case, speculation about the other side's case may be argumentative, may not represent what the evidence will show, and would be improper.

Objection:

Counsel is improperly speculating regarding what we will prove.

Response to Objection:

* Explain the statements relate to evidence the other side will introduce and are proper.

* Explain it is necessary to describe facts the other side will prove in order to understand all the facts of the case.

7. Making Disparaging Remarks

Counsel may not make remarks during opening statement that disparage opposing counsel, the opposing case, the opposing party, or witnesses. Such conduct is improper, unfairly prejudicial, and unethical. The decision maker should reprimand the offending attorney. Severely disparaging remarks may be a ground for a mistrial.

Objection:

Counsel is making improper remarks. Counsel has said I was mendacious and I ask your Honor to admonish counsel and insist she apologize to me.

Response to Objection:

* Try to explain that the remarks are not improper.

* Admit a mistake and apologize.

* Accept an admonition from the court without argument.

8. Additional Prohibitions

The issues involved in specific cases may further restrict certain references made during opening statements. In a personal injury case, references to insurance are inappropriate. In a criminal case, a prosecutor cannot comment on the refusal of the defendant to testify. In all cases, counsel may not refer to matters that may overly influence the passion or prejudice of the jury, such as appeals to the family circumstances of a party or references to the wealth or poverty of a party.

B. OBJECTIONS

If an objection is made during opening, the judge will rule on the propriety of the objection. If the objection is sustained, the attorney should correct the mistake and continue with the opening. If the objection is to the content of the opening statement, then the subject ought to be avoided. If the objection is to the form of the statement, the statement can be rephrased. If the objection is overruled, the attorney should continue with the opening and may repeat or emphasize the statement, and may preface it with "As I was saying" or "Before the interruption."

Tactically, an attorney may decide not to object but rather write down what was said and use this against the opposing attorney in closing argument. Many attorneys extend a professional courtesy to one another and do not object during opening statement unless the opponent is saying or doing something that is clearly improper and quite damaging to the case. Most attorneys want the openings to be presented zealously and without interruptions. However, an objection and a request for a curative instruction may be necessary to preserve an issue for appeal.

C. CURATIVE INSTRUCTIONS

In jury trials, after an objection has been sustained, the attorney making the objection should consider asking the judge to instruct the jurors to disregard the improper comment. This curative instruction may reduce the negative impact of the improper comment. Some jurisdictions require the curative instruction be requested to preserve an issue for appeal. A request for a curative instruction may call more attention to the improper statement, however, and ought not to be made if the disadvantage caused by highlighting the improper comment outweighs the effectiveness of the curative instruction. See Section 4.5(D).

D. OPENING STATEMENT MOTIONS

An opposing party may bring a motion to dismiss or for a judgment as a matter of law or a directed verdict on an issue in the case based on admissions made by counsel during opening statement. Admissions made during the opening can have a binding legal effect on the party. Because the opening is part of the record of the case, facts conceded by counsel may be binding admissions. This motion is seldom available because rarely will the opposing counsel make such adverse admissions.

A motion to dismiss or for a judgment as a matter of law may also be brought on the ground that the opposing party has failed to establish a prima facie case during the opening. Generally, the failure to mention specific evidence in the opening does not preclude subsequent introduction of the evidence. As long as the pleadings and previous proceedings placed matters in issue, the rules of evidence and not the scope of the opening statement determine what evidence will be permitted.

In a civil case, a trial court has the discretion to grant a summary disposition based upon the opening statement of counsel. If an opening statement contains admissions or fails to refer to sufficient supporting evidence, there may be grounds for a motion to dismiss or a directed verdict. In criminal cases, a decision maker may direct a verdict for the defendant on the basis of the prosecutor's opening statement if no reasonable juror could convict the defendant based upon the facts stated in the opening statement.

The purpose for a summary disposition based upon the opening statement is judicial economy. A trial is unnecessary if, based on the opening statement, it is obvious that no claim, defense, or case exists. Summary dispositions are rarely granted. Opening statements usually contain more than enough information to support a claim or defense. If a case is so weak that no facts exist to support a claim or defense, the weakness will be apparent at the pretrial or prehearing stage and the case should be dismissed or resolved at that time. If counsel fails to refer to facts sufficient to support a claim or defense, the judge or arbitrator may allow the case to proceed. If a summary disposition motion is granted, and evidence exists which was not described, the losing side can move to reopen the case and supplement the opening statement.

Other possible motions include:

- A motion to have the court set restraints on the opponent's opening regarding time, scope, detail, and demeanor. If an attorney exceeds the reasonable standards for an opening, this motion may be granted.

- A motion by plaintiff to present additional facts in response to defendant's opening. This unusual motion may be appropriate in a situation in which the defendant raises unanticipated issues.

CHAPTER 7

DIRECT EXAMINATION

■ ■ ■

Trial Advocacy Supplement
Direct Examinations

Examples of direct examinations appear in the *Supplement to Trial Advocacy Before Judges, Jurors, and Arbitrators*. Three cases demonstrate direct examinations of witnesses in a jury trial, an arbitration, and an administrative law hearing. These examples present the strategies, tactics, and techniques explained in this chapter.

REFLECTING ON ADVOCACY

Any fact is better established by two or three good testimonies than by a thousand arguments.

—NATHANIEL ERAMENS

If you can't be direct, why be?

—LILY TOMLIN

§ 7.1   INTRODUCTION

A.   PURPOSE

Testimony from witnesses is the primary source of evidence in our dispute resolution system. An advocate asks questions, and the answers of the witness provide the facts, describe what happened, and tell the story. The focus of attention—the spotlight—is on the witness and the story that is being told.

Direct examination requires an advocate to present evidence that:

- Is legally sufficient to survive a motion for a directed verdict, a judgment as a matter of law, or a motion to dismiss.

- Meets or exceeds evidentiary admissibility requirements.

- Convinces the fact finder of the truth of the story being told.

- Is easily understood and remembered by the fact finder.

- Stands up to the test of cross-examination.

- Anticipates, counters or contradicts opposition evidence.

The direct examiner asks questions that permit the witness to recreate an event so the fact finder will see, feel, hear, sense, and perceive the event as experienced by the witness. The story told by the witness must be clear, interesting, credible, and persuasive. It is the primary responsibility of the direct examiner to ask questions to develop this story and enable the witness to communicate effectively.

A good direct examination sounds and looks easy. The witness describes the events in an understandable and persuasive way while sounding and looking believable. The fact finder is engrossed in the story. There are no interruptions while the examination flows. The opposing attorney can make no objections that would be sustained. All the evidence needed to prove the case is introduced. All that is the goal of successful direct examinations.

It may appear that a good direct examination depends on an effective witness, an easy case, or just plain luck. But, the success of a direct examination depends significantly upon the abilities of the direct examiner. The advocate provides the structure and orchestrates the telling of an interesting and persuasive story through a credible and convincing witness who has been properly prepared to testify.

B. TAKING OF TESTIMONY

The taking of the testimony of witnesses in trials is primarily done orally. The process begins with the judge asking counsel to call a witness, or counsel saying: "The plaintiff calls Agatha Christie as our first (or next) witness." The judge or clerk may ask the witness, who is seated at the counsel table or in the courtroom, to come forward and stand in front of or enter the witness box. Witnesses are asked to raise their right hand, and in some jurisdictions, may place their left hand on a Bible or other holy book such as the Torah or Quran. The clerk or judge then administers an oath or affirmation. A witness may affirm to tell the truth under penalty of perjury rather than swear to an oath that includes the word "God." Then, the witness sits in the witness box.

The clerk or judge may then ask the witness: "Please state your full name and spell your last name for the record." In a few jurisdictions, witnesses may also be asked to give their address. The judge may then state to counsel, "Counsel, you may proceed," or the attorney may automatically begin asking questions. The direct examiner need not have witnesses repeat their name and address and can begin the direct examination with a relevant or welcoming question.

In arbitrations and administrative hearings, the process is similar to court trials with the arbitrator or administrative hearing officer administering the oath or affirmation. In lieu of testifying in person, witnesses may testify over the phone, by internet video or satellite transmission, or through other electronic means, including a previously recorded video that includes both direct and cross-examination.

§ 7.2   EVIDENCE CONSIDERATIONS

Four primary evidentiary considerations apply to direct examination:

1. The witness must be *competent* to testify.
2. The testimony must be *relevant*.
3. *Foundation* questions must establish the *reliability* of the testimony.
4. The form of the question must be *proper*.

A. COMPETENCY

There are four competency requirements. A witness must:

- Give an *oath* or an affirmation,
- *Perceive* something,
- *Remember* what was perceived, and
- *Communicate* this information.

The judge or arbitrator decides whether a witness meets these requirements. A witness who fails to satisfy these four factors is obviously not going to be helpful and will not or should not be called to testify.

1. Oath or Affirmation

A witness must agree to tell the truth either in response to an oath ("I do") or an affirmation ("I affirm that what I say will be the truth."). The witness must understand the meaning of an oath or affirmation. This ability of a witness is obvious and typically goes unchallenged.

Witnesses may be challenged if they may not understand what it means to tell the truth. Such witnesses include young children or people with mental, learning, memory, or communication disabilities. It may be necessary for the direct examiner to ask a series of questions that demonstrate the witness' ability to understand and tell the truth.

Example:

Lawyer Examining Young Child:

Q: Malcolm, how old are you?

A: Seven.

Q: What does it mean to you when someone asks you to tell the truth?

A: It means I shouldn't lie.

Q: What is a lie?

A: It's when I don't tell the truth about something.

Q: What happens to you when you don't tell the truth?

A: Ah ... I can't play with my PlayStation, or I can't do something that I really want to do.

Q: Has that happened to you?

A: Yea.

Q: What will you tell us today?

A: What happened to me.

Q: Will it be the truth?

A: Yes.

In jury trials, it may be necessary to conduct a hearing outside the presence of the jury for the judge to determine whether a witness is competent. An attorney who plans to conduct a direct examination of a questionable witness may ask the court to rule on the competency of the witness before that witness takes the stand to avoid the opposing party from objecting to a witness in front of the jurors. The direct examiner may ask questions of the witness to lay a foundation to establish competency. A judge may prefer to meet the witness in chambers and talk with the witness to determine competency.

2. Perception

The degree to which a witness must perceive something to be competent depends upon the nature of the testimony. A witness is competent if the witness has personal knowledge of the matters about which the witness is to testify. The rules of evidence exclude testimony about matters the witness did not observe or had no opportunity to observe. See Fed.R.Evid. 602. Witnesses acquire personal knowledge through any of their senses. For example, witnesses who hear or see something can testify to what they heard or saw. See Section 4.8(C).

Witnesses can testify to opinions within the realm of common experience that help the fact finder understand an issue. Common lay witness opinions include speed, time, distance, emotions, feelings, age, health, and sobriety. A lay witness can testify to an opinion if it is rationally based on the perception of the witness and if it is helpful to an understanding of the testimony or the determination of a factual issue. See Section 4.8(C)(3)(b).

A witness may be qualified to testify as an expert witness if the testimony is not generally within the knowledge of the fact finder and the testimony will assist the fact finder in understanding the case or will help establish a fact issue. Expert testimony includes scientific, technical, or other specialized knowledge outside the scope of the common experiences of the fact finder. A witness is qualified as an expert when the witness has sufficient knowledge, skill, experience, training, or education to render a helpful opinion. Chapter 10 explains the use of expert witnesses.

3. Recollection

A witness must recall what they perceived. A witness whose memory may have been affected between the time of observing an event and the trial may be challenged as incompetent. For example, witnesses who suffered an injury adversely affecting their memory may be challenged.

4. Communication

A witness must be able to communicate. Witnesses must testify to what they perceived through their own words or those of an interpreter. A witness with communication difficulties may be assisted by the direct examiner who can ask leading questions to help the witness testify. See Section 7.7(B). This tactic must be limited in use to avoid highlighting the inability of the client to testify independently of the attorney.

B. RELEVANCE

Testimony must be relevant before it may be considered by the fact finder. Relevant testimony has a tendency to make more or less probable any facts of consequence to the case. Fed.R.Evid. 401 and 402. See Section 4.8(A). If the testimony is relevant, it is admissible. If the testimony has no logical relationship to events, it is not relevant and not admissible.

While almost all relevant testimony is admissible, there are some exceptions. If the prejudicial value of the evidence unfairly outweighs its probative value, or if the testimony confuses the issues, misleads the fact finder, causes undue delay, or is a needless presentation of cumulative evidence, the evidence will not be permitted even though relevant. Fed.R.Evid. 403. In addition, there are other types of unfairly prejudicial evidence described in Section 4.8(A)(4) that will not be permitted for important policy reasons even if relevant: improper character evidence (Fed.R.Evid. 404 and 405) , improper habit evidence (Fed.R.Evid. 406), subsequent remedial measures (Fed.R.Evid. 407), offers of compromise (Fed.R.Evid. 408), payment of medical expenses (Fed.R.Evid. 409), plea bargains (Fed.R.Evid. 410), and liability insurance (Fed.R.Evid. 411).

C. FOUNDATION

Evidence based on unknown or unreliable sources is not admissible. Foundation consists of the facts that establish the reliable basis of the evidence. Before evidence of "Y" can be introduced, evidence of "X" must be established—which is the factual foundation. See Section 4.8(C)(4).

Example:

Examining Attorney:

Q: What happened when you arrived home?

A: Someone was in the kitchen with Dinah.

Q: Who was it?

Objecting lawyer:

Objection: Lack of foundation.

Judge:

Sustained.

Examining Attorney:

Q: What did you do when you got to the house?

A: I walked into the kitchen.

Q: What did you see?

A: I saw someone in the kitchen with Dinah.

Q: What did you see this person doing?

A: Strummin' on the ol' banjo.

Q: What else was this person doing?

A: He was singing "Fee Fi Fiddley I Oh."

Q: Did you recognize this person?

A: Yes.

Q: How?

A: I had seen and heard him strum his banjo and sing this song at the Grand Ol' Opry.

Q: Who was he?

A: J.H. Cave

Q: Who?

D. RELIABLE EVIDENCE

Direct examination evidence must be reliable. The following questions assess sufficient evidentiary reliability:

- Does the witness have personal knowledge of the matter? Fed.R.Evid. 602.

- Has a sufficient foundation been laid to establish the source of the information? Fed.R.Evid. 901.

- Is the opinion testimony rationally based on the perception of the witness? Fed.R.Evid. 701.

- Is the out-of-court statement not hearsay? Fed.R.Evid. 801.

- Is the testimony admissible based on an exception to the hearsay rule? Fed.R.Evid. 803 and 804.

If these questions are answered in the affirmative, the evidence is admissible. The following examples illustrate questions establishing reliable testimony:

Example: (Personal Knowledge of an Event):

Q: What happened with the harpoon?

A: The harpoon was launched, striking the whale.

Q: What did the whale do?

A: The stricken whale flew forward and dove beneath the sea.

Q: What happened with the harpoon line?

A: With igniting velocity the line ran through the groove until it ran afoul.

Q: What happened after the line ran afoul?

A: Captain Ahab stopped to clear it, but the flying line caught him around the neck.

Q: Then what happened to Captain Ahab?

A: He was shot out of the boat, voicelessly as warriors bowstring their victim.

Q: What did you see?

A: He was gone. He disappeared into the depths of the sea.

Q: What did you see next?

A: After a while, the whale breached. It shot out of the water.

Q: Did you see Captain Ahab?

A: Yes.

Q: Where was he?

A: He was strapped to the whale, bound by the harpoon lines.

Q: How did he look?

A: Peaceful. His arm was waving at us, beckoning us to follow him.

Example (Description of Sensations):

Q: Shortly before you saw the fire, did you smell anything, Ms. Nero?

A: Yes.

Q: What did you smell?

A: I smelled smoke.

Q: Did you hear anything shortly before you saw the fire?

A: Yes.

Q: What did you hear?

A: A violin.

Example (Identification of a Voice):

Q: Do you know Jan Dean?

A: Yes, I do.

Q: How?

A: I was his friend for years.

Q: Have you spoken to him in person?

A: Yes.

Q: How often?

A: Weekly.

Q: Did you speak to him on the telephone?

A: Yes.

Q: Did you recognize his voice?

A: Yes.

Q: How?

A: He had a distinctive way of speaking that I would recognize anywhere.

Q: Did he talk to you on the telephone about the accident?

A: Yes, he did.

Q: What did he say?

A: He said, "Gosh, I sure wish that I hadn't gone so fast around Dead Man's Curve."

Example (Opinions Based on Observation):

Q: What did Norma Rae do?

A: I saw her run over to the foreman and shake her fist at him.

Q: How far away from them were you?

A: About ten feet.

Q: Did you see how Ms. Rae looked?

A: Yes.

Q: How did she look?

A: She was quite flushed and very excited.

Q: What did she do next?

A: She yelled loudly at the foreman.

Q: Then what did you see?

A: She grabbed a sheet of paper, wrote on it, and held it up.

Q: How long did you see Ms. Rae do all this?

A: For over a minute.

Q: How would you describe her actions?

A: She was very angry and very determined.

Example (Explanation of an Incident):

Q: What did you see, Mr. Frost?

A: Two roads diverged in a yellow wood.

Q: What were you thinking?

A: Sorry I could not travel both and be one traveler.

Q: What happened next?

A: Long I stood.

Q: What did you see as you were standing there?

A: I looked down one as far as I could see.

Q: What did you do?

A: I took the one less traveled by.

Q: Why?

A: Because it made all the difference.

---

§ 7.3   PREPARATION

A. OVERALL PREPARATION

The preparation of direct examination begins with a review of the evidence needed to establish the theories, facts, and issues of the case.

1. Legal Theories

The elements of each claim or defense must be reviewed to ascertain what direct examination testimony is needed to prove these legal elements. A review of the jury instructions in a jury trial and the proposed findings of facts in a bench trial provide this information.

2. Factual Story

A direct examination must introduce those facts and opinions the witness knows or holds that are part of the factual story of the case, including the foundation for the admissibility of exhibits. The direct examiner must anticipate the cross-examination of the witness and introduce facts that reduce the effectiveness of the anticipated cross-examination questions. The advocate must also review the theories, facts, and issues of the opposing party's case and determine what evidence should be introduced that contradicts or rebuts these matters.

3. Significant Issues

The direct examiner must review the significant issues in a case to determine which witnesses should be asked questions regarding those issues. A witness who has information about important facts, buttresses the credibility of another witness, provides additional information from which the fact finder may draw favorable inferences, or has any other helpful information, should testify to this evidence.

B. EVIDENCE/WITNESS CHART

Form 7.1 provides an analytical framework to prepare an effective direct examination.

C. WRITTEN PREPARATION

The presentation of a successful direct examination requires the preparation of written or printed materials. These materials may be an outline of topics, a list of questions, or a combination of topics and questions. A written outline provides an organized and structured approach to the examination and includes the major topics about which the witness will testify. A printed list of questions acts as a script for the direct examination and contains the sequence of questions to be asked. The materials should be composed in large, easy to read font, with important words, phrases, and questions highlighted.

A combination outline/script provides the advantages of both while reducing the disadvantages of each. An outline may be effective for easy questions and simple topics, but may be inadequate for complex or difficult matters. A detailed script lists the questions to be asked, but may not permit sufficient flexibility and may encourage the attorney to read questions instead of asking questions in a conversational manner. A well-prepared outline/script contains a comprehensive list of topics to be covered and specific questions to be asked in certain areas. This preparation ensures that the direct is complete and comprehensive and provides an easy-to-follow format.

In preparing direct examination materials:

- List all the topics that need to be covered.

- Organize related topics together.

- Compose questions for topics that need prepared questions.

- Review the lists and sequence topics appropriately.

- Edit and supplement the materials during trial preparation.

FORM 7.1
DIRECT EXAMINATION WORKSHEET

Case_____ File_____

Elements of Claim/ Defense	Fact/Opinion	Witness	Exhibit	Possible Objections	Response to Objection	Other Proof

Witness Preparation Example for Personal Injury Auto Accident:

Background

Name

Address

Family

    Spouse

    Children

Education

    High school

    College

    Degrees

Hobbies

Job

    Present

        Duties

        Duration

        Responsibilities

    Prior Work

        Duties

Duration

Responsibilities

Day of Accident

Date—March 15, 2015

Location—294 Wild Flower Lane, Green Acres

Before accident

Where

When

From—to

At accident

Where standing

Lighting

Weather conditions

Other cars

Intersection

Other witnesses

Arrival of police

Scene

Intro diagram: fair and accurate representation

NE corner—corner where standing—gas station

SE corner—opposite corner—straight ahead corn field

NW corner—corner to left—grocery store

SW corner—diagonal opposite—ball diamond

Action

Blue Chevy going west—right to left on Wild Flower Lane

Red Ford going east—left to right on Wild Flower Lane

Foundation for speed of Chevy

How long in view

From what distance

From where to where

Drove car for 20 years

Estimated speed of own car and other cars

Opinion: 30 m.p.h.

Collision

> Standing on corner
>
> Waiting to cross street
>
> Watching traffic
>
> Saw collision
>
> Describe collision
>
> Front end of Chevy hit driver's door of Ford

After collision

> Ran over to Chevy
>
> Passenger opened car door and got out
>
> How did the passenger appear to you?
>
> Did the passenger say anything to you?
>
> What did the passenger say?

Leave scene

> Went home

D. PRACTICE/REHEARSAL

An effective way to prepare a direct examination is to practice asking the questions out loud, following the prepared outline/script. There is no need initially to have a witness provide the answers. Verbalizing the questions familiarizes the advocate with the direct examination, makes the lawyer more comfortable with the questions, and increases the attorney's level of confidence. Changes can be made after this rehearsal.

The direct examination can be structured in segments. The advocate can practice the segments rather than rehearsing the entire examination or can easily move the segments around to increase their effectiveness. For example, in an accident case, the direct examiner can:

- Start the examination with an overview of the accident,
- Describe the sequence of the accident,
- Move to the events before the accident,
- Cover information about the witnesses,
- Discuss the accident in detail, and
- Conclude with a detailed discussion of the injuries.

Successive rehearsals allow the attorney to experiment with timing, pacing, voice modulation, gestures, and movement. Practice should continue until the attorney knows the material and is comfortable and confident with the direct questions and anticipated answers.

§ 7.4   WITNESS PREPARATION

An attorney must develop a system to ensure that all witnesses who will testify on direct examination have been contacted and subpoenaed. All witnesses, even friendly witnesses, should be subpoenaed a reasonable time before testifying to assure attendance as well as generate neutrality. Form 7.2 provides a checklist for witness selection and preparation.

Witnesses should be prepared and familiar with the testimony they will give. Factors that should be considered include:

- Who conducts the preparation? Does the witness feel comfortable with the attorney who is to conduct the preparation?

- When does preparation occur? Will the witness be more comfortable if the preparation occurs at a convenient time?

- Where does the preparation occur? The location and physical layout may affect the comfort of the witness.

- Why does the preparation take place? Do the witnesses understand the importance and significance of their testimony in the case?

A.   OBTAINING INFORMATION

The gathering of information from witnesses occurs before the initiation of the lawsuit and continues through pretrial proceedings. The attorney must determine how the information is to be gathered. Every contact with the witness is an opportunity to obtain information about:

- What facts the witness knows,
- What opinions the witness has,
- What exhibits the witness can identify,
- Prior statements the witness has made,
- Weaknesses that may be covered by the cross-examiner, and
- Prior experience as a witness.

FORM 7.2
WITNESS INFORMATION WORKSHEET

Case _____   **File** _____

Name of Witness   _____

Address   _____

Phone: Home_____   Cell   _____

Email   _____

Employer   _____

Statement taken _____   Deposition completed _____

Subpoena/Duces tecum served   _____

Witness given copy of statement/
   Deposition to review   _____

     Deposition transcript summarized   _____

Former testimony to be used   _____

Purpose(s) of witness   _____

_____

Exhibits to be introduced through witness   _____

_____

Witness prepared   _____

Appearance date _____   Time   _____

After the advocate learns what a witness knows and the evidence about which the witness can testify, the attorney can structure the direct examination and should consider:

- What does the witness contribute to the case?
- How important is this witness to the case?
- What are the strengths and weaknesses of this witness?
- What are the abilities of the witness to observe, perceive, remember, and communicate?
- How vulnerable is this witness to cross-examination?

B. METHODS OF PREPARATION

The advocate must meet with the witness in order to fully and properly prepare that witness for direct examination. The type and extent of preparation varies from case to case, from attorney to attorney, and from witness to witness. Areas to be covered with the witness include the legal theories, the factual summary, and significant issues. The more crucial the witness is, the more thorough this explanation must be.

There are a variety of ways advocates prepare witnesses. Many prefer to conduct a direct examination as a "dress rehearsal," complete with questions and answers, and the probable cross-examination, conducted by the attorney or a colleague. Some attorneys video record witnesses so the witnesses can view their answers and their demeanor. Other attorneys prefer to prepare a witness by outlining the structure of the examination without rehearsing specific answers to specific questions. Advocates need to decide the best way to prepare each individual witness to make them as confident and comfortable as possible.

Attorneys can take the witness to the courtroom or hearing room where the case will be tried. When the court is in session, the witness can see where everybody sits and watch the proceedings. When the court is out of session, the witness can sit in the witness chair and walk around the courtroom and become more comfortable with the surroundings.

The appropriate method depends upon the type of case, the ability of the witnesses, the evidence, the time available, and the skill of the advocate. Witnesses may be prepared individually, in groups, during one interview or several interviews. Some witnesses may have problems that require special consideration before trial. Children, people with communication disabilities, and extremely nervous people are among witnesses who may need special care during preparation. Doctors, linguists, therapists, or interpreters may assist attorneys with these witnesses. Some witnesses may be rambling, defensive, arrogant, or sarcastic, and the advocate must discuss these problems with the witness to reduce or eliminate their negative impact.

The goal of witness preparation is to prepare the witness to testify truthfully and believably. When attorneys prepare a witness by "sandpapering" and "sanitizing" their testimony, the witness looks rehearsed and is not believable. All witnesses have some weaknesses and problems that need to be dealt with in a forthright manner. An attorney can adjust the preparation, depending upon the experience the witness has in testifying, the importance of the testimony, the witness' ability to testify, and the witness' effectiveness in communicating.

In addition to personally meeting with a witness, the attorney may communicate with the witness through email, by sending a letter, or providing a booklet or a video recording. These communications can provide general information about the trial process, the role of a witness, what the witness may expect to occur during trial, and specific information about the case. If the witness is a client, this information will be protected by the attorney/client privilege and not be discoverable by the opposing lawyer, except to the extent the information refreshes the recollection of a witness. If the witness is not a client, the communications can be discovered by the opposing lawyer.

Before the trial, the attorney should instruct the witnesses to keep the attorney informed of their whereabouts and of any new information concerning the case, and to bring their individual subpoena to court.

C. PREPARATION FOR DIRECT EXAMINATION

Witnesses must know what is expected and what will happen at the trial or hearing. Several areas need to be covered including explanations about procedures, truthfully answering questions, and witness demeanor.

Procedural matters that need to be explained are:

- The stages of the trial or hearing.

- The role of the judge, jury, arbitrator, witnesses, attorneys, and court personnel.

- Objection procedures, including the meaning of the words "overruled" and "sustained."

- Practical matters such as transportation to the trial or hearing, complying with a subpoena, the location of the trial or hearing, when to appear, the place to meet the attorney, the place to wait, and what to do after testifying.

- Preparation and use of diagrams or demonstrative evidence.

- What the attorney may do if the witness forgets something, such as using leading questions and refreshing recollection.

Instructions about testifying truthfully include:

- Walk confidently to the witness stand or witness chair and remain standing if possible while taking the oath. Say "I do."

- Speak clearly and loudly. Do not mumble or cover your mouth.

- Tell the truth.

- Testify only to what you saw, did, said, or heard.

- Avoid speculation, guesses, and assumptions.

- Avoid memorizing answers.

- Think about the event and the details. Picture the scene, the persons present, what happened, and what was said.

- Answer with positive, definite answers. Avoid saying "I think," "I believe," "I'm not real sure," or "In my opinion" when you actually know the facts. But if you are uncertain about an answer, say so.

- Listen carefully to the questions and understand them before answering. If for some reason you do not understand, ask for the question to be repeated or rephrased until you understand it.

- If your answer was incorrect or unclear, you may correct it then or wait until re-direct examination when you may be asked more questions. It may be appropriate to say: "I want to clarify something."

- Use your own words and language, not the language of the attorney or someone else's words.

- When testifying, talk as you normally do in a conversation.

- Be aware of and address the fact finder when testifying.

- Answer the question asked; do not second-guess why the question was asked or add additional information.

- Immediately stop when an attorney objects or when the judge or arbitrator interrupts. Don't try to slip in an answer.

- If there is an objection to the question, listen to the objection and what the attorneys and judge say. You may learn something about the question and how it should be answered from these statements.

Descriptions of proper demeanor include:

- Be aware of body posture, sit comfortably, and don't slouch.

- Dress neatly and appropriately for a serious event.

- Do not bring any written notes or material unless told to.

- Be courteous, don't disagree with the lawyers or make jokes.

- Do not ask the judge or arbitrator for help answering. I'll assist you.

- Do not make distracting gestures or facial expressions.

- Anticipate being nervous; it is normal and expected.

- If you feel ill or overly fatigued, ask for water or a break.

An attorney may need or wish to provide witnesses with additional information. If the witness is a client, obviously that person will need to be involved in all aspects of the case and know everything about it.

D. PREPARATION FOR CROSS-EXAMINATION

Directions for cross-examination answers and responses include:

Instructions about witness answers:

- Answer leading questions directly and simply, with a "Yes" or "No," if appropriate.

- Do not volunteer information or attempt to explain an answer. I may have you explain something on redirect examination if it is necessary.

- Take your time, if you need to, in answering a question.

- If you don't understand a question, say so. Never answer a question you do not fully understand or before you have thought your answer through.

- If your answer is complete and truthful, stop talking. Do not continue talking even if the cross-examiner looks at you expecting you to say more. If the examiner asks you if that is all you recall, say "Yes" if that is the truth.

- Testify to only what you have personally seen, done, said, or heard. Do not speculate, guess, or assume anything. If you do not "know" something because you have not seen, done, said, or heard it, your answer should be, "I don't know."

- Testify only to your best recollection. If you do not recall something, do not hesitate to say so, even if you fear this may make you appear to look foolish.

- Do not exaggerate, and avoid unnecessary superlatives such as "never" or "always."

Directions regarding how to respond:

- Do not allow the cross-examiner to put words in your mouth. Do not necessarily accept the cross-examiner's characterization of events. If a question is inaccurate, state "I can't answer that question" even if the attorney tries to force you into agreeing or disagreeing with the question or saying yes or no.

- If information is contained in a document and you are uncertain of an answer, state you do not recall the contents or say you would need to see the document.

- If you are asked a question which was asked during a deposition or a prior statement, answer the question if you recall the answer. Otherwise, say you do not recall.

- If you say something that is inconsistent with your prior testimony, do not panic. Mistakes happen. If you make a misstatement, correct it. If you make a mistake, admit it.

- Expect the cross-examiner to obtain some information that may weaken your story. Every lawsuit has two sides, and the opposing lawyer is trying to tell the other side's story.

- If the cross-examiner seems confused, don't attempt to help.

- Answer trick questions properly:

  "Your lawyer told you to say that, right?

  > Say "My lawyer told me to tell the truth."

  "Who else besides your lawyer told you what to say?"

  > Say "I'm telling what I saw and heard."

  "Have you talked to anyone about this case?"

  > If I do not object, mention individuals you have talked with about the case, including me or other witnesses. It's normal and expected to have talked to lawyers and others.

  "Are you being paid to testify in this case?"

  > Say "No." You are not being paid to testify. You may be receiving some compensation for your travel and expenses.

E. CLIENT GUIDELINES

A client who sits throughout the case at the counsel table may need to be advised about certain procedures. Clients should be told that:

- They will be periodically watched by the decision maker and should always be conscious of being observed.

- They should periodically maintain eye contact with the decision maker. This helps personalize the client.

- They should not interrupt the attorney unless necessary or when the attorney seeks advice. It is usually preferable for the client to write a note to the attorney.

- They must pay attention throughout the case, focus on the evidence and arguments, and watch the decision maker, the other lawyer, and other witnesses. The client may be able to observe something the attorney missed.

F. SEQUENCE OF WITNESSES

The sequence in which witnesses testify in a case can be a critical aspect of case presentation. Factors such as the best order, type, and timing of witnesses must be determined by the advocate.

Order of Witnesses

- *Chronology*. Witnesses can testify the way the story unfolds.

- *Topical Order*. Witnesses may testify following the order of the topics.

- *First and Last Impression*. The witness providing the best first or last impression about the case should be called first or last.

- *Overview*. A witness who provides a general overview of important events should be called first or early on.

Type of Witness

- *Party Witness*. This critical party should be called when her or his testimony will have the most impact.

- *Foundation Witness*. A witness who has information needed to establish the foundation for the introduction of other evidence should be called before that evidence is offered.

- *Critical Exhibit Witness*. In a case involving important exhibits, it may be necessary to introduce the exhibit at the outset of the case and to call the witnesses necessary to lay the foundation for the introduction of the critical exhibits.

- *Corroborating Witnesses.* A witness who has information corroborating the testimony of another should follow that witness.

- *Adverse Witness.* If a party calls the opposite party as an adverse witness, and if the adverse witness must testify to damaging admissions, this evidence should be presented at a compelling time.

- *Weak Witness.* An unimportant witness or an important witness who has credibility problems or who may be boring should be called when the negative impact is at a minimum.

- *Concluding Witness.* The last witness in a case should serve one or more purposes, such as: highlighting the case theory, emphasizing important facts, and providing compelling evidence. The concluding witness should not be especially vulnerable on cross-examination. In a case involving expert witnesses, strong expert witnesses typically make effective final witnesses.

- *Rebuttal Witnesses.* An important witness should not be saved for rebuttal. If the opponent chooses not to present the anticipated information needed for the witness to rebut, the witness may not be allowed to testify. See Section 3.6(F).

Timing of Witness

- *"Sandwich" Sequence.* Strong witnesses should be called in the beginning and at the end, with weak witnesses called in between.

- *Lay Before Expert Witnesses.* Lay witnesses who establish facts that support expert opinions should be called first.

- *Availability of Expert Witnesses.* Experts may only be available at predetermined times, limiting when they can be scheduled. Often they will appear in recorded videos.

- *Deposition Testimony.* In civil cases, when witnesses are unavailable to testify in person, their deposition transcript may be read or their deposition video shown to the fact finder. The advantage is that the testimony can be edited to provide concise and relevant evidence. The disadvantage is that this means of providing testimony is often not as interesting or persuasive as live testimony.

- *Time of Day/Place in Case.* The time of the day when witnesses testify and the place they testify in a multi-day trial or hearing may affect the impression they make on the fact finder. Important or complex evidence may be better received when the fact finder is more alert or interested in paying attention. The period before or after a lunch or recess may be less productive because the fact finder may be thinking about lunch, the need for a break, or home.

Whatever order of witnesses is selected, the advocate must be prepared to change that sequence. Flexibility may be needed because witnesses may be late or become unavailable on a scheduled day. The prediction the lawyer made regarding the time needed to introduce evidence may be wrong, and the planned sequence of witnesses may need to be adjusted. The attorney may request that the judge or arbitrator allow for a recess or a break in the case, but it is unlikely this request may be granted because of other scheduling priorities.

§ 7.5   ATTORNEY PRESENTATION

A. LOCATION AND MOVEMENT

Many courts have established rules that restrict the attorney's location and movement in the courtroom during direct examination. Some courts require the attorney to stand at or near a lectern while questioning, and some require the attorney to stand behind the lectern, permitting the attorney to move only a short distance on either side of the lectern, unless an exhibit is being introduced. Other jurisdictions, including arbitration forums and administrative tribunals, require the attorney remain seated at counsel table during questioning. Still other jurisdictions provide the attorney with some freedom, and the attorney can decide whether it is best to stand, sit, or move about.

An attorney who is in a jurisdiction that restricts location and movement may ask permission to ask questions from a different location. Permission should be sought if there is a tactical advantage in conducting the examination the way the attorney wants. Such requests may be summarily denied or readily granted. If the judge or arbitrator asks for a reason, the attorney should explain why the witness will be better able to testify or how the fact finder will be better able to see the evidence.

The examiner should consider selecting a location that works best for the witness, fact finder, and reporter. The place from which the attorney conducts the direct examination should be a place that permits the fact finder to easily hear the witness and see exhibits and allows the reporter to hear and see what is said to ensure a complete and accurate record.

In jury trials, some direct examiners prefer to place the jury between the witness and the direct examiner. This placement encourages both the witness and the attorney to speak loud enough so that the jurors can hear easily, focuses the jurors' attention on the witness because the attorney is out of their line of sight when they look at the witness, and encourages the jurors to move their heads periodically back and forth between the witness and the attorney, keeping the jurors more alert.

B. APPROACHING THE WITNESS

Judges permit attorneys to approach the witness when the attorney needs to show the witness an exhibit. Some judges, especially those who are conservative in permitting movement, require the attorney to ask for permission before approaching a witness. See Section 3.5(D).

Example:

Examining Attorney:

Q: What did you do with the gold medal, Ms. Didrikson-Zaharias, when you picked it up?

A: I etched my initials on the back of it.

To the Court:

Your Honor, may I approach the witness with the exhibit that has been marked for identification as Exhibit No. 1932?

Judge:

Yes, you may.

Many judges do not require the attorney to ask for permission to approach the witness. They assume that if the attorney approaches the witness, it is for a good reason. Those judges that do require attorneys to ask for permission may only expect the request to be made the first time an attorney approaches the witness. See, again, Section 3.5(D).

C. PROCEDURES

Local and informal rules and idiosyncratic preferences by individual judges and arbitrators may affect how a direct examination proceeds. If unsure, the advocate can ask about these expected procedures.

§ 7.6   STRUCTURE OF DIRECT EXAMINATION

Direct examinations must be organized in a manner that most effectively presents an interesting, persuasive, and credible story.

A. BEGINNING OF DIRECT EXAMINATION

A common and effective way to begin a direct examination is to establish the background of the witness. Another way used by many direct examiners is to begin an examination with a few preliminary questions and promptly proceed to the relevant event and weave background information into the questioning as this information applies to the evidence. Background questions accomplish a number of direct examination goals. They:

- Relieve some of the initial anxiety and nervousness of the witness and put the witness at ease. Questions regarding family, employment, and hobbies are easy to answer.

- Build confidence in the witness to provide longer and more detailed answers as the examination proceeds.

- Help establish personality and credibility and humanize witnesses by reflecting the way they naturally talk.

- Identify similarities between the witness and the fact finder, especially jurors. Similarities can strengthen witness credibility because the fact finder unconsciously or consciously identifies with the witness, reinforcing the integrity and sincerity of the witness.

- Establish a foundation to support a witness' statement or opinion in the case. Statements should be sought about the background of the witness that strengthen the witness' ability to testify. For example, if a witness testifies to detailed facts, there may be some prior work or other experiences the witness had which favorably affect the ability of the witness to observe or remember detailed facts.

The extent to which an attorney can develop the background of a witness depends on the type of case, the relevance of the testimony to a legal issue in the case, the kind of decision maker, the predisposition of the judge or arbitrator to allow a reasonable number of background questions, and the tactical decision by the opposing attorney to object to unnecessary background questions. Administrative law cases may focus on specific, limited issues to which the background of the witness is irrelevant. Many background questions are not legally relevant to a case. For example, whether an eyewitness to an accident has a family or has lived in the community for a long period of time is legally irrelevant to the issues in the case.

Most judges allow a reasonable number of background questions, even though the questions are technically irrelevant, as long as they establish the background of the witness or help establish credibility. The more important a witness is in a case, the more likely judges permit extensive background questions. The more crucial issues are in a case, the more leeway may be given background questions. For example, felony cases may permit more witness background inquiries than misdemeanors cases. Opposing attorneys may object to background questions that are too numerous or go beyond reasonable information. Judges will overrule these objections if the direct examiner can establish a link between the background question and an issue in the case including credibility.

Preliminary background questions typically begin a direct examination, unless the case is an administrative hearing where these questions are not necessary. Background questions with many witnesses may be more effectively asked at a later stage of the direct examination. For example, the hobbies of a car crash victim may have more impact on damages when explained by the witness after the witness has related the injuries suffered which prevent the witness from pursuing the hobbies. Background questions that relate to a specific issue the witness will address should be delayed until the witness testifies regarding the issue.

Example:

In the following example, the background of the witness is directly applicable to the witness' ability to identify a defendant in a robbery case.

Examining Lawyer:

Q: Then what happened?

A: He came right up to me and demanded all my money.

Q: What do you do for a living, Ms. Pritchett?

A: I am a life coach beauty consultant.

Q: How long have you been doing this?

A: Fifteen years.

Q: What are some of the things that you do on your job?

A: One of the most important things I do is pay attention to the detail of people's faces.

Q: Why?

A: In order to make the correct decisions about what is best for the beauty of my clients.

Q: What have you done to help you with your job?

A: Actually, I study people's faces. Sometimes I am embarrassed because I get caught staring at people.

Q: When you were robbed, Gloria, what did you do?

A: I stared at the man so I'd be able to remember his face.

Q: Describe his facial features.

A: He had brown hair, brown eyes, a bent nose, thin lips, a small triangular shaped chin, a black mole on his left cheek, a scar on his right cheek, and an eagle tattoo on his neck.

B. STRUCTURE

The following are ways to construct a direct examination:

1. Chronology

The witness can describe the events in the order in which they occurred.

2. Elements of Claim or Defense

Witnesses can testify in the order in which the elements of a claim or defense need to be proved. For example, in civil cases, a witness can first discuss the facts that establish liability and then explain the facts that support damages. In a criminal case, the witness can establish facts that show a conspiracy and then describe events that prove the criminal act.

3. Flashback

The witness can summarize an event and then describe it in detail. The direct examiner can ask the witness short narrative questions that provide an overview of the entire event and then ask the witness detailed questions that explain the event step by step. Subsequent specific questions present the details of the incident and are not repetitious.

Example:

Examining Lawyer:

Q: Ms. Daae, please tell us what you did at 8:00 p.m. on November 2.

A: I attended a play.

Q: What play?

A: Phantom of the Opera.

Q: What happened after the play?

A: A man came into the box where I was seated.

Q: What did you notice about the man?

A: He was wearing a mask.

Q: Then what happened?

A: He grabbed me and carried me away through a trap door in the stage.

Q: Where did he take you?

A: To the pit.

At this point the direct examiner can have the witness describe the incident in detail.

Q: I want to take you back and have you tell us the details of what happened that night step by step. What time did the play end?

A: Around 10:00 p.m.

Q: What is the very first thing you saw immediately after the play ended?

A: I saw. . . .

---

§ 7.7 PROPER QUESTION FORM

A witness may answer direct examination questions that are phrased properly but not those that violate the rules of evidence. The following analysis helps determine whether questions are proper as to their form.

- Does the question suggest and contain the answer? If so, it is a leading question. Fed.R.Evid. 611(c).

- Does the question call for a narrative response? If so, it may be overly broad and improper. Fed.R.Evid. 611.

- Is the question a multiple question? If so, it may result in an improper compound answer. Fed.R.Evid. 611.

- Is the question vague or ambiguous? If so, it may be confusing or unintelligible. Fed.R.Evid. 403.

- Is the question repetitious? If so, it may produce cumulative, unnecessary evidence. Fed.R.Evid. 403 and 611.

A. LEADING QUESTIONS

A leading question is a question that *suggests* and *contains* the answer. Every question is leading to some extent in that it suggests a topic or a result. Pure non-leading questions are: Where? Who? Why? When? How? Direct examiners would not get very far if forced to ask these neutral, broad questions, such as "What?" instead of "What is your job?" A direct examination question *may suggest* something happened, may refer to a topic, may ask whether someone spoke, and may propose a result, as long as it *does not contain* the answer.

Example:		Explanation:
Q:	Did you go anywhere?	This question does not give information and lets the witness tell the story. It is not leading.
A:	Yes.	
Q:	Where?	
A:	Downtown.	

Example:		Explanation:
Q:	Where did you go?	This question suggests that the witness went somewhere, but does not tell where and is proper.
A:	Downtown.	

Example:		Explanation:
Q:	Did you go downtown?	This question suggests that the witness went somewhere and suggests the place. Although it does not actually suggest the answer, it is more leading than the previous example, yet it is probably not improper.
A:	Yes.	

Example:		Explanation:
Q:	You went downtown, Ms. Petula Clark, didn't you?	This question is leading and contains the answer, and may be permitted only under an exception.
A:	Yes.	

Leading questions are prohibited on direct examination because the witness is to testify and not the attorney. These questions do not allow the witness the opportunity to tell the story and may draw objections that interrupt the flow of testimony. The witness should be the focus of attention, but may fade into the background if the attorney "testifies" through leading questions. A fact finder cannot accurately judge the credibility of a witness on critical matters and may react negatively if the attorney in effect takes over. Even if the opposing advocate does not object to leading questions, they should be avoided to permit the witness to tell the story, unless there is a good reason to ask them.

B. PERMISSIBLE LEADING QUESTIONS

The general rule that "leading questions are not permitted on direct examination" is a rule of limitation and not an absolute prohibition. Proper leading questions can:

- Help a witness testify by suggesting familiar topics.

- Speed up the presentation of information.

- Provide an opportunity to introduce variety into the examination.

- Demonstrate honesty by bringing out negative information.

- Reveal the attorney's knowledge of the facts.

- Make the testimony more interesting and compelling.

Federal Rule of Evidence 611(c) and similar state rules permit leading questions when they are necessary to develop testimony. Rule 611(c) has been interpreted to mean leading questions are permitted to:

- Bring out preliminary matters;

- Reduce anxiety and help the witness become comfortable;

- Elicit non-controversial or undisputed facts;

- Establish inconsequential facts;

- Suggest new topics;

- Act as a transition;

- Bring out negative facts;

- Examine an adverse witness;

- Question a hostile witness;

- Lay the foundation for certain exhibits;

- Establish complex foundations;

- Examine a witness who has difficulty communicating because of age, disability, or unfamiliarity with language;

- Refresh a witness' recollection; or establish past recollection recorded (see Section 7.10(B)); and

- Ask a witness to disagree with statement made by another.

Not all judges recognize these exceptions. Many judges will not permit the use of leading questions in all of these situations. Judges in bench trials and administrative hearings and arbitrators may be more inclined to permit leading questions because they believe it is a faster way to introduce evidence. Some of them will encourage advocates to lead witnesses, to save time. The advocate should resist this suggestion if the witness and not the attorney is the better source of the evidence.

The following examples illustrate permissible leading questions recognized by most judges and arbitrators:

1.   Preliminary Matters

Example:

Examining Lawyer:

Q: Madame Solis, you served as Secretary of Labor?

A: I did.

Q: Were you the first to have served in that position?

A: Yes. I was the first Latina to serve in a presidential cabinet.

2.   Witness Comfort

Example:

Examining Lawyer:

Q: On the fifth day of August, at noon, you were at Millennium Park?

A: Yes.

Q: Where had you been?

A: At work.

Q: Now, you work for the city, don't you?

A: Yes.

Q: What do you do, Mr. Emanuel?

A: I am the mayor of the greatest city in the world.

Q: Why were you at the Park?

A: I was there to give a talk at the grand opening of the new lake front wind turbine.

3. Eliciting Non-controversial or Undisputed Facts

Assume the example below involves a motorcycle accident in which the issue is fault, not the identity of the rider.

Example:

Examining Lawyer:

Q: Mr. Lawson, you were driving Mr. Robert's motorcycle, right?

A: Yes.

Q: It was a VMAX, wasn't it?

A: Yes, it was.

---

4. Establishing Inconsequential Facts

Example:

Examining Lawyer:

Q: You were planning to visit the Great Wall of China, weren't you, Ms. Buck?

A: Yes.

Q: So, much of your conversation was about the trip?

A: Yes.

---

5. Suggesting a New Topic

Example:

Examining Lawyer:

Q: Dr. Ezekiel, what was your occupation?

A: I was the medical examiner for the county of Galilee.

Q: How long were you medical examiner?

A: Fifteen years.

Q: What do you do now?

A: I am retired.

Q: Before you retired you performed an autopsy on the body of Lazarus, didn't you?

A: Yes, I did.

6. As a Transition

Example:

Examining Lawyer:

Q: Mr. Enron, what did you do on Monday?

A: I happily destroyed documents in my office using my portable shredder.

Q: Now, on Tuesday you stayed home with your kids?

A: Yes.

Q: What did you do on Wednesday?

A: I was at the office cheerfully deleting electronic documents.

7. Bringing Out Negative Information

Example:

Examining Lawyer:

Q: What did you see?

A: I saw a munchkin run right down the middle of the road.

Q: You don't know who the munchkin was?

A: No, I don't.

Q: Did you see where the munchkin went?

A: Yes.

Q: Where?

A: Straight down the yellow brick road.

Q: Out of sight?

A: Yes.

Q: And you have seen the munchkin since that day?

A: Never.

8. Examining an Adverse Witness

Occasionally, a witness who has information necessary to prove a critical element in a case is the opposing party or a person closely identified with the opposing party, such as an employee or agent. The theory behind direct examination is that witnesses called by one side cooperate with the direct examiner and give information candidly and truthfully, but this is not necessarily true with opposing witnesses. An adverse party is not usually willing to cooperate, and an adverse witness likely favors the other party. Both may attempt to provide answers that damage the direct examiner's case. The advocate may examine an adverse party or witness using leading questions as if the witness were being cross-examined.

Example:

Examining Lawyer (To the Court):

Your Honor, may I call the defendant, Mr. Earnhardt, as an adverse witness?

Judge:

You may.

Examining Lawyer:

Q: You are a successful racecar driver, aren't you?

A: Yes I am.

Q: On April 17, you were driving your car, correct?

A: Yes.

Q: Your car is a 1935 Pierce-Arrow?

A: Yes. It's a beauty.

Q: You drove your car into the back end of the plaintiff's car?

A: Yes.

Q: Immediately before the collision, your foot slipped on your gas pedal?

A: Yes.

Q: It was embarrassing for you to have your foot slip?

A: Of course.

Q: So, that's why you told the police the plaintiff had backed her car into yours at a speed of 25 miles per hour?

A: I'm afraid so.

---

9. Questioning a Hostile Witness

An independent witness who demonstrates a reluctance to testify or hostility toward a party becomes a hostile witness, and at that time it is within the discretion of the judge or arbitrator to permit the direct examiner to examine the witness using leading questions. A showing of actual hostility in the courtroom and surprise answers by the witness is often a predicate, but surprise is not always a necessary element. If it is clear in advance of the case that the witness will be hostile, the attorney should make a preliminary showing of anticipated hostility. Some witnesses may become hostile during an examination, and the lawyer can then ask for the witness to be treated as a hostile witness.

Example:

Examining Lawyer (To the Court):

Your Honor, this witness is a hostile witness. She is angry with the police and my office for prosecuting her friend. While she initially said she would not talk about how much the defendant had to drink, she is now willing to do so but with much reluctance. I am uncertain what she will say. I request the opportunity to use leading questions during the direct examination under the provisions of Rule 611(c).

Judge:

You may do so.

Examining Lawyer:

Q: Ms. Mondavi, you are a friend of the defendant?

A: Yes.

Q: It's fair to say you are a good friend?

A: I believe so.

Q: You're angry with the police for arresting him for drunk driving?

A: Yeah. He was just being his usual self.

Q: You want to help the defendant?

A: If I can.

Q: You don't want to be here to testify for the prosecution, do you?

A: Nope.

Q: You told the police you wouldn't tell anybody about how much you saw him drink?

A: Maybe . . . yeah.

Q: It's true that you saw the defendant drink an entire bottle of wine and then drive away in his Tesla?

A: Yes, that's all true, but it was an exquisite 1991 California Meritage with extraordinary clarity and a wonderful bouquet with just a hint of jasmine infused berries.

10. Foundation for Exhibits

Example:

Examining Lawyer:

Q: Mr. Noah, I have just handed you a photo that has been marked for identification as Exhibit 2. Do you recognize it?

A: Yes, I do.

Q: What is it?

A: It is a lovely picture of our Ark.

Q: How do you know?

A: Well, it looks just like we left it when we joyfully beached it on Mount Ararat.

Q: Is Exhibit 2, marked for identification, a fair and accurate representation of how your Ark looked after the flood?

A: Indeed it is.

11. Establishing Complex Foundation

Example:

Examining Lawyer:

Q: As a laboratory analyst, Dr. Curie, based on your education, training, experience, and the testing of this substance, do you have an opinion to a reasonable degree of scientific certainty what this stuff is?

A: Yes.

Q: What is your opinion?

A: It is law school vending machine "food."

12. Examining a Witness Who Has a Difficult Time Communicating Because of Age or Disability

Example:

Examining Lawyer:

Q: How old are you, Gretel?

A: Four.

Q: Do you remember what happened to your brother, Hansel?

A: Yes.

Q: He's not here anymore, is he?

A: No.

Q: Do you know what happened to him?

A: Yes.

Q: What happened?

A: We were playing in the woods.

Q: Did you see a house in the woods?

A: Yes.

Q: Did you go into the house?

A: Yeah.

Q: What happened?

A: I saw an old lady trying to put Hansel in the microwave.

13. Refreshing a Witness' Recollection

A witness may have a memory lapse on the stand. A previous statement or a leading question may help the witness recall the answer. It is not unusual for a witness under the stress of an examination to forget something and need help to remember something specific.

The examining lawyer may show a document or anything to the witness to refresh the witness' memory. The examining attorney must first establish that the witness now has no memory of the answer about which the witness is being questioned. The witness may review the statement or item and then must set it aside before answering, since the answer must not be from the document itself, but must be from actual refreshed memory.

The witness should not read from the document for two reasons. First, it is improper and objectionable. If the witness reads a prior statement, that statement is actually being introduced as past recollection recorded and not a present memory. Federal Rule of Evidence 803(5) requires a specific foundation for the introduction of a document as a previously recorded recollection. See Section 4.8(H)(1)(c).

In practice, the difference between refreshing recollection and past recollection recorded is often ignored and witnesses are frequently permitted to review their notes while testifying. Second, if the witness reads from a document, the witness becomes vulnerable to cross-examination questions that highlight that the witness has no independent recollection of what occurred and may not be believable.

Documents used to refresh recollection do not need to be marked, because they are not offered as evidence, unless the judge or arbitrator requires them to be marked. The cross-examining lawyer has a right to see the written statement or document or item used to refresh, and can use it during cross-examination. See Fed.R.Evid. 612. The opposing attorney may have the document marked and introduce it into evidence for impeachment or as an admission.

In some situations witnesses may bring notes with them to help refresh recollection. Police officers, administrators, and some experts often bring a file with them to the witness stand and use it to refresh their memory during testimony. The opposing lawyer may insist that the notes be used properly. That is, the lawyer may either ask the judge or arbitrator that the witness put the notes away and testify independently without reference to the notes or have the examining attorney lay the proper foundation for the reliability of the notes.

Example:

Use of Leading Question:

Q: Mr. Chase, when you loaded up the car for your cross country vacation, what did you pack?

A: Picnic gear, clothes, suitcases, Wally World map, Aunt Edna . . . oh, let's see, I think that's it.

Q: Do you remember putting anything else in the trunk?

A: That's all I can remember.

Q: Did you pack five sets of scuba gear and five pairs of snow skis?

A: How silly of me, of course.

Alternative Example:

Use of Document:

Q: Mr. Chase, do you remember putting anything else in the trunk?

A: That's all I can remember. There may have been more.

Q: Is there anything that would help refresh your recollection as to what else you might have put in the trunk?

A: Yes, my email to the insurance company. I listed everything that was stolen.

Q: I have just given you Exhibit 2. Do you recognize it?

A: Yes, it's my email to the insurance company.

Q: Read it to yourself please.

A: All right.

Q: Does reading your email refresh your recollection as to what else you put in your trunk?

A: Yes.

Q: May I have it back, please?

A: Yes, here's the email.

Q: Do you now remember what else you put in the trunk?

A: Yes.

Q: What?

A: Five sets of scuba equipment and five pairs of snow skis.

---

14. Asking a Witness to Disagree with a Statement Made by Another

---

Example:

Examining Lawyer:

Q: Ms. Duran, you heard your son testify that the noisy argument took place out on the patio deck, didn't you?

A: Yes, I heard that.

Q: Is that what you recall about the argument?

A: No, it isn't.

Q: Do you agree with your son where the argument occurred?

A: No, I don't.

Q: Where did the argument take place?

A: The argument occurred in the ring with de la Hoya.

C. NARRATIVE QUESTIONS

A narrative question may be proper or improper, depending upon the scope of the question, the timing of the question, the ability of the witness to answer, and the ability of the attorney to control the witness. A narrative question is improper if:

- The witness responds with a long, uncontrolled story, or

- The narrative response denies the opposing attorney the opportunity to anticipate objectionable evidence and the ability to make a timely objection, or

- The narrative question reduces the ability of the examining attorney to control the direction or the scope of the examination.

Judges and arbitrators have broad discretion in permitting or limiting the use of narrative questions. In determining whether to allow their use, the judge or arbitrator:

- Assesses the capabilities of the witness to properly testify and the capabilities of the direct examiner to control the examination,

- Is unlikely to allow a witness to answer a narrative question if the witness may be unable to provide a concise response or has a tendency to introduce objectionable testimony,

- Will not permit a narrative response if the witness is unprepared or the attorney is insufficiently experienced to interrupt and control the witness who begins to ramble,

- Is likely to permit narrative questions asked by an effective examining attorney or by a witness who has properly answered narrative questions without rambling,

- Will allow narrative responses to establish background or foundation, or to complete the description of an event.

Specific forms of narrative questions are commonly asked during direct examinations. Narrative questions that are limited in scope or that act as transition questions are usually appropriate, such as "What happened next?" or "Then what happened?" A proper narrative question avoids allowing the witness to tell the entire story, but acts as a directed question allowing the witness to continue telling part of the story.

Example:

Examining Lawyer:

Q: Mr. President, what happened in the voting booth on the second Tuesday in November?

A: I voted for Alfred E. Neuman.

Q: Then what happened?

A: I lost the election.

Q: Please explain how that changed your life.

D.　IMPROPER QUESTION FORMS

1.　Vague or Ambiguous Questions

All questions must be reasonably clear and specific so that the witness knows what is being asked, the other side knows whether to object, and the fact finder can understand the testimony. It may happen that the attorney's mind is racing ahead and what is asked makes little sense, or that the lawyer uses the wrong words. Vague, ambiguous, confusing, unintelligible, and misleading questions must be avoided.

Example:

Examining Lawyer:

Q: Did you, subsequent to your verbal conversation with the professional investigator, affix or otherwise impress your distinctive signature to a testimonial document satisfying the statute of frauds?

A: Well . . . Huh?

Q: Let me rephrase the question. Did you sign the piece of paper that Guy Noir gave you?

A: Oh! Yes, I signed it.

2.　Repetitious Questions

A witness is generally permitted to describe what happened only once, and an advocate is not permitted to gain unfair advantage by repeating favorable testimony. The form of the question need not be identical to be repetitious. Questions may be asked during direct examination to clarify prior responses, add descriptive details to a story, and emphasize testimony. The key is to avoid asking questions that sound repetitive or produce answers that are repetitious.

Example:

Examining Lawyer:

Q: Then what happened to you and your purse, Ms. Prada?

A: I held on to the strap of the purse, and he had hold of the other end pulling it away from me. I tried to pull it back from him, and he yanked hard pulling it out of my grasp.

Q: How did you try to pull it away from him?

A: I held my smart phone in my left hand, and my right hand gripped the purse strap. I tried to pull my arm towards my body, but he was trying to yank the purse off my arm.

Q: How did he yank the purse from your arm?

A: He was pulling it real hard, as I tried holding onto it.

Q: How did he pull it away from you?

A: He pushed me away with one of his hands, and then grabbed the bottom of the purse with both hands, and I fell back.

When more than one witness provides the same information, it becomes cumulative. While it is certainly permissible for witnesses to corroborate each other, it is within the discretion of the judge or arbitrator to place limits on the extent of the cumulative testimony.

3.   Multiple Questions

Multiple or compound questions are impossible to understand and create a jumbled record. It is often unclear what part of the multiple question the witness answered. Compound questions should be withdrawn and rephrased.

Example:

Examining Lawyer:

Q: When did you wake up, and what did you see when you awoke? Excuse me. I'll withdraw the question and rephrase it. What day did you wake up, Mr. Van Winkle?

---

§ 7.8   QUESTION AND ANSWER TECHNIQUES

This section presents a variety of questioning techniques that can be employed to produce effective testimony.

A.   ESTABLISHING THE CHARACTERS

Storytelling involves the description and depiction of the characters who bring the story to life. Witnesses are those characters in trials and hearings. Questions can establish who they are and how and why they are involved.

1.   Putting a Witness at Ease

Easy to answer questions can be asked to help put the witness at ease as well as establish that the witness is competent.

Example:

Examining Lawyer:

Q: What is your name?

A: Luke.

Q: How old are you, Luke?

A: I am going to be eight.

Q: When are you going to be eight?

A: When my birthday comes.

Q: Who are your Mom and Dad?

A: They're over there.

Q: What is your Dad's name?

A: Phil.

Q: And Mom's name?

A: Claire.

Q: Do you have any brothers or sisters?

A: Haley and Alex.

Q: What do you like to do most of all?

A: Play with my laptop.

Q: What is your favorite computer game?

A: I love Lawyer Hunt.

---

2.   Establish a Witness' Background

Information about witnesses helps explain their background.

Example:

Examining Lawyer:

Q: Tell us your name please.

A: Vanna Gray.

Q: Ms. Gray, what is your occupation?

A: I am a hostess for a television game show.

Q: What does that involve?

A: I dress fashionably and turn letters on a big board as contestants guess them.

Q: Is that it?

A: Yes, it is.

Q: Do you have to do much talking on the show?

A: No.

Q: How did you get into that business?

A: When I finished college, I moved to California and for the fun of it, I auditioned for the job and got it.

Q: When did you move to California?

A: About thirty years ago.

Q: Where did you go to college?

A: The University of Linguistics.

Q: What did you get your degree in?

A: I received a degree in etymology.

---

3.   Demonstrate Credibility

The experiences of a witness help establish the credibility of that witness. Information that establishes a connection between the experiences of a witness and the evidence should be established.

Example:

Examining Lawyer:

Q: Mr. Chan, were you requested to investigate an automobile accident in which April Woo was involved?

A: Yes, I was.

Q: What did you do to investigate this accident?

A: I immediately went out to the accident site and inspected Ms. Woo's black sports utility vehicle and the other car. I also photographed and video recorded the scene from many different vantage points.

Q: What else?

A: I noticed the skid marks on the street, used a laser to measure their length, and made a video recording of that scene. I also took close-up photos of both damaged vehicles.

Q: Anything else?

A: I used Google Earth to map the area and the accident site.

Q: Then what?

A: I composed a report on all of my observations including all the photos and videos, all of which I provided the client.

Q: Describe the training that you have had in accident reconstruction and particularly in analyzing accident scenes.

A: I worked as a member of a highway patrol accident scene team for over 20 years until my retirement 3 years ago. Since then I've had my own business, Fu Manchu Investigative Services. I'm board certified as an accident reconstructionist with the American Society of Accident Investigators.

Q: Can you estimate how many accident scenes you have investigated over the last twenty-four years?

A: Yes.

Q: How are you able to do that?

A: When I started my business, I knew it would be important to be able to provide that information in order to show my experience in the field. I went back to the highway patrol office and went over all of my reports through the use of the computer and storage files and was able to determine how many accidents I had investigated. Since I started my own business, I have kept careful electronic records.

Q: How many accident scenes have you investigated over the course of your professional career?

A: Very close to 2,852.

---

4.   Display the Sincerity of the Witness

When witnesses are given the opportunity to talk about their lives, jobs, friends, and acquaintances, in their own words, they can demonstrate they are honest and sincere persons.

Example:

Examining Lawyer:

Q: Mr. Cassidy, as a bank robber, what kinds of things do you have to do?

A: I have to plan every robbery, buy the bullets, feed the horses, keep track of the money, and be able to shoot accurately.

Q: What details do you plan?

A: We must plan each robbery with great care. We must know how many persons are working in each bank and how many guards are on duty. We must determine how long we can be in each bank before the sheriff shows up; and, of course, we have to know when the payroll arrives at the bank.

Q: How often do you rob banks?

A: Quite regularly. In the winter we head south. In the summer we head north.

Q: Do you take any breaks between bank robberies?

A: Yes.

Q: How do you take these breaks?

A: Well, every robbery is a little bit different, and so are the breaks. We usually take a week break between banks, sometimes longer, if we get chased.

Q: Where do you usually go?

A: To Hole-in-the-Wall.

Q: Are these breaks important?

A: Yes.

Q: Why?

A: Well, there is some strain in robbing banks and to relieve tension, Sundance, the boys, and I take regular breaks to relax and to help us keep our skills sharp.

---

5. Identify Similarities Between the Witness and the Fact Finder

It can be helpful to identify similarities between the witness and fact finder. In this example, jurors have indicated similar interests.

Example:

Examining Lawyer:

Q: Tell us your name?

A: Mr. Spock.

Q: Where do you live?

A: Live?

Q: Yes, where are you from?

A: I see. I am from the Planet Vulcan and that is where I make my home when I am not working.

Q: Where do you work?

A: I am assigned to the Star Ship Enterprise.

Q: And where is the Enterprise now?

A: In the Milky Way—coordinates star point 4896.12.

Q: What is your assignment on the Enterprise?

A: I am the first officer.

Q: Do you have any time for hobbies?

A: Yes, I do.

Q: Tell us please what your hobbies are.

A: Well, I do like to travel. I enjoy camping. One of my favorite places is Yosemite. I like sports, particularly bowling. I enjoy reading, especially twenty-first century history.

B. ESTABLISHING FOUNDATION TO SUPPORT FACTS

1. Establish Perception

Facts must be established to show that the witnesses saw or heard what they say they saw or heard.

Example:

Examining Lawyer:

Q: What happened next?

A: I saw this man walk up to the movie ticket window where I was working and stand right in front of me.

Q: What were the lighting conditions like at that time?

A: There were bright lights on both sides of the ticket window, and there was a light on in the ticket window.

Q: Describe the ticket window you were looking through when you saw the man standing in front of you.

A: It's a clear plate glass window, about 2 feet wide and 3 feet high with a 6-inch opening to pass money and tickets.

Q: What condition was it in on that day?

A: It was clean, and there was nothing blocking my view.

Q: Describe the man you saw, Ms. Grauman.

---

2. Enhance Foundation

Foundation questions should be asked that enhance the reliability and accuracy of the story told by the witness.

Example:

Examining Lawyer:

Q: Mr. Fife, where were you at 3:00 p.m. last April 23?

A: I was at the northeast corner of the intersection of Lexington and Grand Avenues in our city.

Q: What were you doing?

A: I was working as a crossing guard, watching traffic.

Q: What is the most important part of your job?

A: Keeping a careful watch for cars and children.

Q: What did you see?

A: I saw a collision between a tan VW and a blue Bentley.

Additional foundation questions further enhance the reliability and accuracy of the witness' story.

Example:

Examining Lawyer:

Q: Where did you graduate from high school, Mr. Fife?

A: I have a degree from Mayberry High School.

Q: How long ago?

A: Thirty-three years.

Q: Since you graduated from high school, what further education have you had?

A: Police courses like driving school, traffic control, weapons training, not with real bullets, of course, and other courses to sharpen my keen law enforcement skills.

Q: Since graduation what has been your police experience?

A: Well, I haven't worked a lot in the field, but I have been a Deputy here in town for 25 years with Sheriff Andy Taylor.

Q: Have you had any special titles?

A: Yes, I am the Guard in Charge of the Mayberry Elementary School crossing.

Q: What are your responsibilities?

A: It is my duty to make sure that all the children get across the street safely, and that means that I have to watch the cars and the children very carefully.

Q: Have you had any special training for this assignment?

A: Yes.

Q: What?

A: Well, Sheriff Taylor sent me to traffic training where I learned the most modern methods of school crossing techniques. And when the kids are in school, I go to the crossing to practice making cars stop and go.

Q: Describe what you saw at the intersection of Lexington and Grand Avenues at 3:00 p.m. on April 23 last year.

3.   Establish Foundation to Support an Opinion

Before a witness can render an opinion, questions need to be asked to show the witness perceived events that support the opinion or conclusion.

Example:

Examining Lawyer:

Q: Were you in the room when John Greystoke signed the will?

A: I most certainly was.

Q: Did you see what he was doing before he signed the will?

A: Yes, I did.

Q: What was he doing?

A: He was chattering like a baboon, swinging from the chandelier, and yelling for Jane.

Q: How long had you know Mr. Greystoke?

A: Twenty years.

Q: How often had you seen him?

A: Weekly over that time.

Q: Why so often?

A: I brought him fresh fruit every week.

Q: Had you ever seen him swing from the chandelier before?

A: Too many times.

Q: How did he sign the will?

A: He first tried to squash his banana on it.

Q: Then what?

A: His butler gave him a pen and he made a "T" on the will.

Q: Do you have an opinion if Mr. Greystoke knew what he was doing when he signed the will?

A: Yes.

Q: What is that opinion?

A: He had no idea what he was doing.

---

4.   Develop Facts to Bolster Conclusion

It is critical to provide fact finders with facts to support positions. The key is to establish facts that lead them to the correct conclusion.

Example:

Examining Lawyer:

Q: Ms. Payne, where were you when your laptop case was taken from you?

A: It was noon, and I stopped in front of the restaurant entrance to wait for my friend.

Q: As you stood there, how far could you see?

A: I could see down the block.

Q: How far down the block could you see?

A: Well past the intersection.

Q: Describe how your laptop case was taken.

A: I heard someone running up to me, and I turned and saw the defendant who tried to wrestle the case from my shoulder. I immediately grabbed the laptop and pulled the case toward my body, and he sort of came along with it.

Q: Then what did you see, Doris?

A: I saw his face. He was right there in front of me.

Q: How far away from you was his face?

A: About a foot and a half, maybe less.

These questions allow the fact finder to conclude that the victim got a very good look at the robber. If she could see a block ahead, she could very clearly see 18 inches away. These questions are in contrast to asking the witness: "Did you get a real good look at him?" That question requires the fact finder to focus on the credibility of the witness. The former questions lead the fact finders to conclude on their own that the witness got a good look. They reach their conclusion based on the facts and not on the opinion of the witness.

C. SETTING THE SCENE

Most stories, plays, motion pictures or re-creations of actual events must be placed in a setting that the audience can visualize. The same is true with a direct examination. The scene must be established before the action can make any sense. Once that scene has been established by primary witnesses, later witnesses may be placed at the scene to confirm the accuracy of what has been established and then to describe the action from their perspective. As the action shifts to a new location, the scene must be described again by witnesses. The extent to which a witness must establish the scene depends on the order of witnesses, the importance of the witness to the case, and the witness' relationship to other witnesses. The direct examiner must determine what can be left to the imagination of the fact finder and what must be carefully described verbally or by exhibits.

1. View of the Witness

The direct examiner should select the view from which the examiner wants the fact finder to see the scene. The scene may be described from two perspectives: through the eyes of the witness or from an overview. The first has the witness act as a storyteller and use phrases "I saw" and "I could see," and is generally more effective. The second has the witness act like a historian and describe a scene and can be more difficult to picture. The ideal goal is for the fact finder to see the actual scene from the same perspective as the witness.

Example:

Examining Lawyer:

Q: Were you were going?

A: I was on my way home, to Tara

Q: As you were walking up the cobblestone driveway, what did you see directly in front of you?

A: I saw large, old oak trees and magnolia trees lining both sides of the path.

Q: As you were looking around, tell us what was to your right?

A: I could see a large home with white columns and ivy growing on the brick walls.

Q: And what was to your left?

A: I saw the burned-out shell of the house that was destroyed by the explosion and fire.

Q: As you continued walking toward your house, please describe what you saw, Ms. O'Hara.

This technique draws the fact finder into the scene. It is as if the fact finder is walking along with the witness and is there at the scene when the event unfolds. Further questions can enhance this notion that the fact finder is not being told what happened but is experiencing what occurred.

---

2. Detail

The determination of what to describe and what to leave to the imagination of the fact finders should not be left to chance. The fact finders should be told the details necessary to accurately understand the scene as the attorney wants them to understand it and to satisfy their reasonable curiosity.

Example:

Examining Lawyer:

Q: What kind of neighborhood was it, Ms. Valdez?

A: It was mostly a residential neighborhood.

Q: Describe the buildings at the intersection.

A: There were large old wooden homes on two corners, an empty lot on one, and a modern brick building on the other corner. There was a coffee shop, the Coffee Cantata, in the lower floor of that building and three floors of condominiums above the store. Aria Liesgen lived on the top floor.

Fact finders may interpret this response differently. What does "residential neighborhood" mean to a twenty-year-old college student juror, a sixty-five-year-old judge, or an arbitrator who was an architect? What do "large old wooden homes" mean to an arbitrator who lives in a rural area, an inner city juror who grew up in a two-room flat, or a judge who grew up in a suburban house? Is the "coffee shop" one of a chain of stores or an independently owned store located in the condo building? The details necessary for the fact finder to get an accurate picture should be included in the examination when relevant.

D. DESCRIBING THE ACTION

A witness can describe events as they happened. The direct examiner should ask questions in a structured way so that it's easy for the witness to explain events enabling the fact finders to clearly visualize what occurred. A chronological order is easy to follow. Most people describe an event the way it happened and expect a story to be told the same way.

1.   Detailed Description of a Person

Example:

Examining Lawyer:

Q: After you came downstairs and went into the living room, what did you see?

A: I saw a man standing by the fireplace.

Q: How were you able to see him?

A: The table light and all the Christmas tree lights were on.

Q: What was he wearing?

A: A red outfit.

Q: Please be more specific.

A: He was dressed in fur, from his head to his foot.

Q: Were his clothes clean or dirty?

A: They were all tarnished with ashes and soot.

Q: Describe his general build for us.

A: He was chubby and plump.

Q: What did his face look like?

A: His eyes twinkled. He had dimples and appeared merry.

Q: Go on.

A: His cheeks were like roses, his nose like a cherry.

Q: What was his mouth like?

A: He had a droll little mouth drawn up like a bow, and he had a beard on his chin that was as white as the snow.

Q: Did he have anything in his mouth?

A: Yes.

Q: What?

A: Well, he had a stump of a pipe held tight in his teeth.

Q: Was he carrying anything?

A: Yes.

Q: What?

A: He had a bundle of toys that he had flung on his back.

Q: What did he look like?

A: He looked like a peddler just opening his pack.

Q: What else can you remember about this man?

A: He had a broad face and a round little belly that shook when he laughed, like a bowl full of jelly.

Q: Is there anything else that he did besides laugh?

A: Yes, he winked at me and twisted his head.

Q: What did you feel when he did that?

A: I felt that I had nothing to dread.

---

2.   Detailed Description of an Event (Criminal Case)

A detailed examination is important to provide sufficient information so the fact finder has a clear understanding. An effective story can be told through a short question/answer format.

Example:

Examining Lawyer:

Q: What is your name please?

A: Officer Lenny Briscoe.

Q: Where do you work?

A: For the City of New York.

Q: What do you do for the City?

A: I am a police officer.

Q: How long have you been a police officer?

A: Ten years.

Q: Were you working on May 1st this year?

A: Yes.

Q: At 11:00 p.m. on May 1st this year were you on duty?

A: Yes, I was.

Q: Where were you at 11:00 p.m.?

A: At the corner of Stone Canyon Way and Mockingbird Lane.

Q: Were you on foot or in a car?

A: In a police car.

Q: What did you see?

A: I saw a bright red Chrysler Roadster.

Q: Which way was it traveling?

A: North to south on Mockingbird Lane.

Q: What did you see about the car?

A: It was traveling on the wrong side of the road and appeared to be traveling very fast.

Q: What did you do?

A: I began to follow the car.

Q: What was the car doing?

A: It was weaving wildly from side to side. Twice it jumped up the curbs and bounced back down on the road.

Q: Were you able to determine how fast the car was traveling?

A: Yes.

Q: How?

A: I sped up and got behind the car, and I was able to match my speed with the car for about a block. I stayed about four car lengths feet behind because of its weaving from side to side. My speedometer indicated 45 miles per hour.

Q: Do you know what the posted speed limit is on Mockingbird Lane where you were?

A: Yes, I do.

Q: What is it?

A: Thirty miles per hour.

Q: What did you do?

A: I followed the red Chrysler for about two blocks and then I turned on my overhead lights and siren.

Q: What happened?

A: The car kept going on the wrong side of the street for a block, and it finally stopped on the wrong side of the street.

Q: What did you do?

A: I turned on the video camera and walked up to the driver.

Q: What did you see when you approached the car?

A: I saw a man in his early sixties sitting behind the wheel. He was wearing a white suit, no tie.

Q: What else did you notice?

A: When the man rolled down the window of his car, I could smell a strong odor of alcohol coming from inside the car.

Q: What did you do next?

A: I asked him to get out of the car and he did. I asked if he had a driver's license.

Q: Did he give you a license?

A: No.

Q: Did he say anything to you?

A: Yes, he did.

Q: What?

A: He said that he didn't have a license, had never had one, and didn't need one.

Q: How did he speak?

A: His speech was very slurred. It was hard to understand.

Q: Could you see his face clearly?

A: Yes.

Q: How?

A: I had my flashlight shining near his face and we were standing directly under a street light.

Q: Describe his face for us.

A: His face was flushed and reddish. He appeared to be sweating, and his eyes were bloodshot, glassy, and watery.

Q: Could you smell his breath at that time?

A: Yes.

Q: How close were you when you could smell his breath?

A: About two feet.

Q: What could you smell?

A: I could smell the strong odor of an alcoholic beverage.

Q: What did you do next?

A: I asked him to take what are called "field sobriety tests."

Q: Why do you ask a person to take field sobriety tests?

A: To determine a person's ability to coordinate movements, follow simple directions, and perform balance tasks.

Q: What is the first test that you asked him to perform?

A: I asked him to stand erect with his feet together and arms outstretched. I told him to close his eyes and touch the tip of his nose with his right index finger and then with his left.

Q: How did he do when he tried to touch his nose?

A: First he started to fall over and I caught him and stood him up. However, he didn't open his eyes. He then touched the middle of his forehead with his index finger and slid it down along his nose to the tip.

Q: How did he perform with his left hand?

A: He touched the side of his lip and slipped his finger up.

Q: Did you ask him to perform another test?

A: Yes, I did.

Q: What?

A: I asked him to say the alphabet.

Q: How did he do?

A: He did fine until he got to the letter "K" and he then said "K" eight or nine times and finally said, "That's all, eh."

Q: Did you ask him to take any more tests?

A: Yes.

Q: What test?

A: To walk a straight line, one foot in front of the other.

Q: Did he take that test?

A: No.

Q: Did he tell you why?

A: Yes.

Q: What did he say?

A: He said, "I ain't takin' any more tests. I'm as drunk as an old skunk. You've got me now and you know it."

Q: Did you record these tests?

A: Yes, a video camera in our vehicle recorded his taking, and failing, the tests.

Q: What did you do then?

A: I placed him under arrest for driving while under the influence of an alcoholic beverage. I then drove him to the county jail and offered him a breath test.

Q: What happened when you offered him a breath test?

A: He refused to take a breath test. I then offered him a chance to provide a urine or blood sample.

Q: Did he give you any samples?

A: No.

Q: What did you do then?

A: I left him at the jail with the county sheriff and went back on patrol.

Q: Did he ever tell you his name?

A: Yes, he said his name was Bacchus.

Q: Just Bacchus?

A: That's right. He said that was the only name he had.

Q: In the years on the police force have you arrested people for driving under the influence of alcohol?

A: Yes, hundreds of times.

Q: Do you ever drink alcoholic beverages?

A: Yes, I do, on occasion.

Q: Have you seen other people drink?

A: Yes.

Q: Have you seen some of these people come under the influence of alcohol?

A: Yes, I have.

Q: Based upon your own experience, your observations of others, and your observations of Mr. Bacchus, do you have an opinion whether he was under the influence of alcohol the night that you arrested him?

A: Yes, I do.

Q: And what is that opinion?

A: He was very much under the influence of alcohol.

Q: Officer, did you bring the video recording to show the jury?

A: I did.

3. Detailed Description of an Event (Civil Case)

Example:

Examining Lawyer:

Q: What did you do on that Thanksgiving holiday?

A: My daughter, Molly, and I were going to be alone that day, and we were invited to go into the country for dinner at the home of some people with whom I work.

Q: What is their name?

A: Mr. and Mrs. Baskerville.

Q: How old was Molly at the time?

A: She was six.

Q: What time did you arrive?

A: We were invited for dinner at two p.m., and we arrived a few minutes after that as we got lost on the way.

Q: Had you ever been to the Baskervilles' home before?

A: No, I had not.

Q: What did you do when you got there?

A: Their farm is a long ways off the county road. We drove up the driveway by the barn and parked in front of the house.

Q: Where is the barn located in relation to the house?

A: It is across the driveway.

Q: How far is the barn from the house?

A: About 100 feet.

Q: How far from the house did you park?

A: About 30 feet. There is a fence around the front yard, and we parked right by the gate.

Q: What did you do?

A: I got out of the car and waited for Molly.

Q: What happened?

A: As Molly was walking in front of the car, I saw something out of the corner of my eye from the direction of the barn.

Q: What did you do?

A: I turned my head to see what it was.

Q: What did you see?

A: An enormous shaggy brown dog sprinting towards Molly.

Q: Did it make any noise?

A: No, it was running real fast and was making no noise at all.

Q: How big was this animal?

A: It was massive. Its head was higher than my waist. It had a huge mouth, and I could see its large, sharp teeth.

Q: What did you do?

A: I screamed and ran to Molly.

Q: What happened?

A: I grabbed her and started to pick her up. The beast leaped at Molly biting her on the back of her neck,

Q: Go on.

A: We fell to the ground. I couldn't get my hands loose, and the dog was biting and snarling and tearing at us. We were both screaming and crying for help. Molly was bleeding.

Q: What was the next thing that happened?

A: I heard a woman yelling.

Q: What did she say?

A: I heard something like, "Down Hound! Stop that! You bad dog! You should be ashamed!"

Q: What did the dog do?

A: It let go and sat down, snarling and growling at us.

Q: Did you see who the woman was?

A: Yes, Mrs. Baskerville.

Q: What did the dog look like?

A: It was a huge filthy hound. It had long, shaggy, matted brown hair covered with dirt. It smelled just awful. It had an enormous head with yellow eyes. It had huge teeth and was growling, drooling, and quivering as it sat there.

Q: What happened next?

A: Mrs. Baskerville took us inside the house and tried to stop Molly's bleeding while her husband called an ambulance.

Q: Did she say anything to you?

A: She said that the darn dog was always jumping on people and that they should have locked the dog in the barn.

Q: Had she ever said anything to you about a dog before you came to the house that day.

A: Never! I didn't even know that they had a hound.

E. DETAILING CONVERSATIONS

The foundation needed to admit a relevant conversation is fairly easy when the conversation occurs face-to-face and the witness can identify the person making the statement. However, foundation is more difficult with phone conversations, as the witness has to be able to identify the voice in order to show that the conversation relates to the case.

Example (Prior Familiarity with Voice):

Examining Lawyer:

Q: Did you conduct an investigation of the collapse of the ski lift gondola?

A: Yes, I did.

Q: What did you do?

A: I called up Stein Eriksson, the owner of the resort, on the telephone.

Q: Had you ever spoken to Stein Eriksson before?

A: Yes, many times.

Q: Did you recognize his voice when you called him?

A: Yes.

Q: How?

A: I recognized the sound of his voice and his accent.

Q: Did he identify himself to you in any other way?

A: Yes.

Q: How?

A: When he answered the phone he said, "Allo, dis is Stein Eriksson speking."

Q: Then what did he say?

A: He said, "I sure vish we had fixed da dern cable car."

Example (Subsequent Identification of a Voice):

Examining Lawyer:

Q: What did you do on the fifth of January?

A: I called on my cell phone to talk about the variety show.

Q: Did you talk to someone?

A: Yes, a man.

Q: Did you know who it was?

A: No.

Q: Did you recognize his voice?

A: Not at first.

Q: Have you heard his voice since that conversation?

A: Yes.

Q: Where?

A: In the courtroom today when he testified for the plaintiff.

Q: How can you recognize his voice?

A: It is very distinctive and high-pitched—and he has a silly laugh.

Q: What is the name of the man whose voice you heard today?

A: Peewee Herman.

Q: What did he tell you about the show when you phoned him?

A: He said that he wanted a prime time show.

Example (Extrinsic Sources of Identification):

Examining Lawyer:

Q: Had you ever spoken to Lilly Tomlin before March 3 of last year?

A: No.

Q: Have you spoken to her since?

A: No.

Q: On March 3, what did you do?

A: First, I went online and looked up the phone number of the Rowan Martin Comedy Club

Q: Then what?

A: I called the number and a man answered "Comedy Club."

Q: What did you do?

A: I asked to speak to Ms. Tomlin.

Q: What happened?

A: First, music played, then the phone rang and a woman answered saying, "What character do you want to talk to?"

Q: What did you say?

A: Lilly Tomlin.

Q: What did she say?

A: She's talking to you.

Q: Then what happened?

A: I asked her whatever happened to Ernestine?

Q: What did she say?

A: Telephone operators are extinct.

Q: How did she sound?

A: Just like on television, with a noisy raspberry lilt.

F. ASKING PERSUASIVE QUESTIONS

The direct examiner should ask understandable questions that develop an interesting story using the following techniques.

1. Simple Words

Words that reflect the language of fact finders should be used. Simple, everyday, easy to understand conversational words are generally more effective for jurors. Complex, multi-syllable words or legalese sound snobbish and can be confusing. The ordinary language used in the community is most effective, excluding vulgar or crude language, unless such language is relevant to the case. More sophisticated language can be used with professional decision makers such as a judge or arbitrator.

Example:

Examining Lawyer:

Simple:

Q: Before the accident, where were you?

Complex:

Q: Prior to the accident, where were you situated in relation to this event?

Simple:

Q: Did you see something?

Complex:

Q: Did you have occasion to observe anything material at all?

Simple:

Q: What happened on December 14?

Complex:

Q: Calling your attention to the date of December 14, what, if anything, occurred on that date?

Simple:

Q: Then what happened.

Complex:

Q: Did anything unusual happen that you can recall?

---

2. Impact Words

A careful choice of impact words can have an effect on testimony. Impact words are graphic words that vividly describe something in support of a perception the witness attempts to depict. See Section 1.5(G).

Example:

Examining Lawyer:

Neutral Words:

Q: What was the *speed* of the two cars?

Impact Words:

Q: How *slowly* were you driving?

Q: How *fast* was the other car going?

Neutral Words:

Q: What was the *distance* between you and the other woman?

Impact Words:

Q: How *close* were you to the other woman?

Q: How *far* away were you?

Neutral Words:

Q: How *much* water was in the glass?

Impact Words:

Q: How *full* was the glass?

Q: How *empty* was the glass?

---

3.   Explaining Terms

The attorney should make sure the witness explains terms that have specialized or multiple meanings.

Example:

Examining Lawyer:

Q: What was the man like?

A: He was a big and scary.

Q: Describe what you mean by big.

A: He wore a full metal suit, that looked like armor.

Q: And describe what you mean by scary.

A: His face was covered with only masked slits showing his eyes, and he had a light arc reactor on his chest.

Q: Did you recognize him?

A: Oh, yeah.

Q: Who was he?

A: Iron Man.

---

4.   Clarifying Answers

The lawyer needs to ask follow-up questions that clarify unclear or ambiguous answers. This can be difficult because the advocate knows the case better than the fact finder and often makes assumptions that a fact is obvious and need not be presented. The testimony must be understood, assumptions should not be made, and the necessary details must be presented. The advocate must hear the answers from the perspective of the fact finders who are hearing the evidence for the first time.

Example:

Examining Lawyer:

Q: Captain Raydor, where were you driving to?

A: To the Los Angeles Major Crime Division.

Q: What happened on the way there?

A: I saw a man run out of a store carrying a shotgun. I slammed on my brakes, stopped the car, jumped out, and yelled at him to stop and drop the shotgun.

Q: Were you armed?

A: Yes, I carry my police firearm at all times.

Q: How close was he to you?

A: Well beyond the range of his shotgun.

5. Listening Carefully

The attorney must listen carefully to every response. Witnesses may misunderstand a question, make mistakes, or assume that the attorney wants an answer not called for by the question. And the attorney may be preoccupied with other thoughts, such as the next question or problems that may arise. Or the attorney may expect certain answers and not pay attention when the witness says something different.

When a witness makes a mistake or does not answer the question precisely, the attorney needs to intervene. There will be occasions when the witness has made a factual error, or is rambling, or has added information that is improper and the lawyer must interrupt. Occasionally, the answer may be okay, but the lack of demonstrated control may cause a problem. Controlling the witness demonstrates that the attorney seeks only proper, responsive answers, bolstering the credibility of the attorney and the witness.

Example:

Examining Lawyer:

Q: What did you see, Ms. Rodman?

A: *(At a very rapid pace.)* There was this strange looking creature with a head of rainbow colored hair and who was wearing a boa. He was jumping up and down and dribbling a basketball towards me and he must have really been excited and I thought that he was going to dunk the ball in the basket I was carrying and then he started yelling at me. . . .

Q: I have to stop you right here for a moment. We are going to have to take it one step at a time. I'm going to ask you short questions, and you give responsive answers. Okay?

A: Oh, yes.

Q: You can't tell us what this gentleman said to you because
     that's hearsay and not allowed in this case. Now when he
     did speak to you, were you looking at his face?

A: Yes.

Q: Did you see what if anything he was wearing in his nose?

A: Oh yes, I did.

Q: What was it?

A: Several nose rings that were quite elegant.

---

6. Exhibits

Exhibits should be used in a way that enhance the testimony of a
witness and are introduced at an appropriate time during an
examination. Exhibits can be important to a case and helpful to a witness
and the fact finder. A separate chapter focuses on the proper and effective
use of exhibits. See Chapter 8.

G.   DEVELOPING FACTUAL DETAILS

Effective storytelling for trials and hearings involves the
development of sufficient facts to support a case. The following techniques
provide alternative ways to establish such detailed facts.

1.   Asking Short Questions

Short questions make it easier for the lawyer to control testimony
and to direct a witness to provide detail. Long, drawn out questions can
be confusing, delay the flow of testimony, and waste time.

Example:

Examining Lawyer:

Q: What were you doing?

A: I was the scorekeeper at the quidditch match.

Q: Where were you?

A: I was sitting at mid-field at the scorer's table, about four
     meters back from the sideline.

Q: Who was playing?

A: Gryffindor and Slytherin.

Q: What did you see shortly before the end of the first half?

A: I saw a man wearing a Gryffindor scarf jump out of the bleachers and run right up and punch the captain of the Slytherin team right on the jaw.

2. Using Narrative and Specific Questions

The following examples demonstrate three comparative approaches to the development of a story: a story elicited with a narrative question, with specific questions, and with a combination of the two.

a. *Narrative Example*

Example:

Examining Lawyer:

Q: Tell us what you remember about that afternoon.

A: When the kids got home from school and had their snack, I sent them out to play. They had on light jackets and boots. The golf course across the street has a pond. The kids had skated there all winter. Some time later, Maggie returns screaming they fell through the ice. I ran to the pond to pull them out. I first got Bart on the shore and then I waded back into the water to find Lisa. She was below the ice and I couldn't see her. I went under the ice as fast as I could and felt with my hands until I felt her arm. I grabbed her and pulled her out, and she was blue.

b. *Specific Question Example*

Example:

Examining Lawyer:

Q: What is the first thing that happened when your kids came home from school on March 15?

A: They had a snack—crackers and milk.

Q: After the snack, what did they do?

A: They put on their play clothes and jackets to go outside.

Q: What kind of jackets?

A: Light, spring jackets.

Q: Why didn't they wear winter jackets?

A: Because it was a mild day. The snow was melting.

Q: Where do the children like to play?

A: They like to play on the golf course in the winter because there are hills for sliding and a pond they skate on.

Q: Where is the golf course?

A: Right across the road.

Q: On that day, did you say anything about the pond ice?

A: Yes.

Q: What?

A: I told them to stay off the ice because it was unsafe.

Q: After the children got dressed, what did they do?

A: They went outside.

Q: What happened next?

A: I heard Maggie rush into the house screaming that Bart and Lisa fell through the ice.

Q: What did you do?

A: I ran as fast as I could to the pond.

Q: What did you see when you got there?

A: I saw that the ice had broken through.

Q: What did you do?

A: I jumped into the water to find my kids.

---

c. *Combination Narrative and Specific Example*

An effective direct examination employs a mix of questions that call for short, narrative responses combined with short, controlled questions that elicit appropriate details. This mix of questions guides the witness in telling the story, permits the attorney to control the direction of the story, provides clarifying details, and holds the interest of the fact finder.

Example:

Examining Lawyer:

Q: After the children got dressed, what did they do?

A: They went outside, and I saw them run to the golf course.

Q: What did you do after you saw the children run towards the golf course?

A: I thought they might go to the pond, so I got dressed and ran after them. I was scared they would fall through the ice.

Q: Then what happened?

A: The ice had already given way, and both Bart and Lisa were in the pond. I ran out to pull them from the water. I took my sweater off and held one its arms and swung it out to Bart so that he could grab the other arm. He did, and I got him on the shore. And then I waded back into the water to Lisa.

Q: Where was she?

A: She was below the ice, and I couldn't see her.

Q: What did you do?

A: I went under the ice as fast as I could and felt with my hands and after a bit I felt her arm. I was so frightened.

Q: After you felt her arm, what did you do?

A: I grabbed her and pulled her out. I saw she was blue, and I cried out for help.

---

3. Developing a Detailed Sequence

A story may be told in various stages. The witness may first provide a short summary of what happened and subsequently explain the details of the events. This format allows the witness to highlight and emphasize the critical facts. The advocate can structure the questions from the general to the specific and follow up with further relevant questions.

Example:

Examining Lawyer:

Q: What did you do after touring the house, Ms. Lloyd Wright?

A: I decided to buy it! I loved the architectural style, and was excited but also anxious. I drove to the real estate agent's office where he gave me some papers to sign. He answered my questions, and then I reviewed and signed several papers.

Q: How long a time where you in his office?

A: About half an hour.

Q: What was the first thing that happened in his office?

A: He said I would really enjoy living in that neighborhood, and he handed me some papers he had prepared.

Q: What did he say when he handed you the papers?

A: He asked me if I had any questions.

Q: I want you to answer my next questions as carefully as you can. What was the first question you asked?

A: I asked about the nearest elementary school to the house.

Q: What did he answer?

A: He said it was four blocks away.

Q: What was the next question you asked him?

A: I recall asking him about nearby parks. . . .

4.   Using Double Direct

"Double direct" is a technique in which part of a previous answer is used as a preface to the next question. This tactic emphasizes critical information so the fact finder hears the information more than once and should be reserved for important evidence.

Example:

Examining Lawyer:

Q: When you finished studying Mr. Bolt, what did you do?

A: I went out to jog around the stadium.

Q: Which way did you go to get to the stadium?

A: I came off Arapahoe and headed toward the track.

Q: What time was that?

A: 3:00 p.m.

Q: How was the weather at that time?

A: It was clear and sunny and warm out.

Q: What happened next?

A: I jogged towards the track. When I got about 150 feet off Arapahoe, I passed a large hedge on my right. I heard branches scraping and twigs snapping.

Q: When you heard those noises, what did you do?

A: I ran faster, and I felt someone running up behind me.

Q: How do you know?

A: I heard the running steps and then my arm was grabbed from behind and was twisted hard behind my back.

Q: As your arm was being twisted, what happened to you?

A: I lost my balance and fell into the hedge.

Q: What happened when you fell into the hedge?

A: The man put a knife to my throat.

Q: As the man put a knife to your throat, what did you see?

A: I saw a rose and violet tattoo on his neck.

Q: The tattoo on his neck, please describe it.

A: It was the size of two small flowers. The rose petals were red, and the violet part was blue.

5. Completing a Sequence

Sometime during an examination, the direct examiner realizes that something has been left out of an earlier part of the examination. Important information may need to be added timely to the event.

Example:

Examining Lawyer:

Q: What happened to you then Ms. Dewey?

A: Well, the man attacked me. He was hitting and kicking me. I was yelling for help and trying to get away.

Q: And were you able to get away?

A: Yea, I ran back to the library as fast as I could.

Q: I didn't ask earlier what time you got off work after you finished cataloging the online decimal system. When did you leave the library?

A: About 4:30 p.m.

Q: What time did you get back to the library?

6. Volunteering Weaknesses

Weaknesses in the witness' background or testimony may need to be presented during the direct examination to minimize its impact and to enhance the credibility of the witness and the attorney. Negative information about the witness or testimony that is not revealed on the direct and is first exposed on the cross-examination can be harmful. Weaknesses revealed on direct examination demonstrate that neither the attorney nor the witness has anything to hide, reducing the adverse effect of the weakness. In addition, the witness has the opportunity to explain the weakness in the witness' terms, not in the opposing counsel's words. If addressed, weaknesses should be explained in a matter-of-fact way with as little embarrassment or concern as possible.

The decision to admit weaknesses can be difficult. If a weakness cannot be excluded by the rules of evidence, and the cross-examiner is expected to expose that weakness, then perhaps it's wise to bring the weakness out on direct. It's possible to deal with a weakness on redirect in the hope that the cross-examiner will not bring up the matter or that the explanation will be so good that the cross will appear foolish. This, however, is a defensive and difficult position to assume and can backfire.

Another option regarding a weakness is to avoid it altogether on direct or re-direct. The advocacy notion is that devoting any time to it only highlights the weakness more, and it's better tactically to ignore it. This tactic prevents more time being unnecessarily spent on the matter.

Example:

Examining Lawyer:

Q: What color was the light?

A: Green.

Q: Did you talk with Lt. Columbo the day of the accident?

A: Yes.

Q: Did he write up a statement?

A: Yes, on a scrap of paper.

Q: Did that statement say the light was fuchsia?

A: Yes.

Q: Did you sign the statement?

A: Yes.

Q: Can you explain why you did that?

A: Yes, I can.

Q: Tell us please.

A: When Lt. Columbo was taking the statement, I was in the hospital in a lot of pain. I didn't read the statement. I just signed it to get rid of him. He was always hanging around asking me lots of questions.

§ 7.9　REDIRECT EXAMINATION

The direct examiner may conduct a redirect examination after the completion of the cross-examination. Redirect examination provides the direct examiner with the opportunity to have the witness clarify or explain points raised on cross-examination and to cover new material raised by the cross that was not dealt with on the direct examination.

With proper preparation, the direct examiner can predict the areas of cross-examination and may cover those areas on direct examination and limit the effectiveness of a cross. In addition, a redirect examination can be planned in advance so that the anticipated areas of weakness or vulnerability can be clarified or explained. Important testimony and significant issues need to be addressed on direct, and a direct examiner should not usually reserve vital evidence to be introduced during redirect.

A.　LIMITED SCOPE

The general rule is that redirect examination may only cover new material raised by the cross-examination. Redirect should not be used to go over the same information covered by the direct examination or raise new areas not covered by either the direct or cross-examinations. If this occurs, most judges and arbitrators will sustain an objection that the redirect examination is repetitious or beyond the scope of the cross. The application of these restrictions is uneven with a broad scope allowed by some judges and arbitrators, while others are more restrictive.

Example:

Cross-Examination of an Eyewitness:

Q:　Is it fair to say, Ms. Sybil, that you have seen someone on the street you thought you recognized and waved at that person only to realize the person was a complete stranger?

A:　Yes, that has happened to me.

Q:　It was embarrassing to have that happen, wasn't it?

A:　Well, yes it was.

Q:　I have no further questions.

Redirect Examination of the Same Witness:

Q:　Ms. Sybil, when you thought you recognized a stranger, did that person stand two feet in front of you, face-to-face and demand all your money as the defendant did in this case?

A:　Never. The only time I've been robbed is by that defendant.

B. FOREGOING REDIRECT EXAMINATION

A well-prepared case and a good direct examination may make a redirect examination unnecessary. In making the decision whether to conduct a redirect examination, the following factors should be considered:

- The witness may not have been prepared for certain redirect questions and should not be asked surprise questions.

- The witness may not understand the point the attorney wants to make and misspeak.

- Having the last word is not that important. The same information need not be repeated just to get the last word.

- Continuing with redirect examination may bore or bother the fact finder and add nothing new to the evidence.

- Closing argument may be a better time to emphasize the important parts of the case, and not redirect examination.

- A case may be damaged by asking too many questions. A witness who repeats answers may look rehearsed, and mistakes can be made going over the same testimony.

- Redirect examination gives the opponent the opportunity for a recross-examination.

C. QUESTION FORM

The same rules of evidence apply to redirect and direct examination, with the same restrictions applying to the use of leading questions. There may be a greater latitude allowed by some judges and arbitrators who permit a broader range of leading questions during redirect examination in order to permit the attorney to focus on matters within the scope of the cross-examination and to speed the redirect to completion. Since the witness has testified on both direct and cross-examination, the redirect examiner may refer to previous answers and lead the witness to a specific topic through the use of this prior testimony. The opposing attorney might not object because the cross-examination consisted of leading questions, and the attorney may be so used to leading questions that leading questions on the redirect examination may not sound improper.

D. CORRECTING MISTAKES/REFRESHING RECOLLECTION

Redirect examination may be used to refresh the witness' recollection if the witness has misstated or forgotten information during the cross-examination. See Fed.R.Evid. 612.

Example (Redirect Examination):

Examining Lawyer:

Q: During the cross-examination you told us that the man held you by the throat with his left hand while he had a knife in his right. Are you sure that he had the knife in his right hand, Mr. Bowie?

A: Oh my, did I say right hand? I didn't mean that. He had the knife in his left hand and was choking me with his right.

Q: How do you know that?

A: Because I had grabbed his left hand so I wouldn't be knifed.

E. RESERVING THE INTRODUCTION OF EVIDENCE

Direct examination evidence should not be withheld for later presentation during a redirect examination. An attorney who reserves important evidence runs the risk of not being able to present it because the opposing attorney may not cross-examine at all or may not cover that particular area, rendering some areas beyond the scope of the cross. It can be dangerous to run the risk of delaying the introduction of evidence during redirect for the tactical purpose of having the last word or outwitting the opponent.

There are some occasions where the delaying of the introduction of information is worth this risk. If the direct examination is structured in such a way so that the cross-examiner is quite likely to cross-examine on the topic and damage will not be done to the case if the evidence is not dealt with, evidence may be reserved for redirect.

Example:

During the direct examination, the main eyewitness to a robbery has identified the defendant as the robber and has said that she looked carefully at the defendant for about a minute during the course of the robbery. The robbery took place in a well-lit store. The witness has testified that when she was seen staring at the defendant, he told to knock it off, but she kept looking at him. He then struck her, knocked her to the floor, and kicked her.

On both the direct and cross-examination she testified that she was scared, that the robbery happened quite fast, and that she was concerned for her young child and for the other people in the store. She testified that she had a great deal of money in her possession and was angry that it was being stolen. She also testified that she had never seen the robber before the day of the robbery and the only other time that she had seen him was in court during the trial where the defendant was seated next to his attorney. She has testified further that she has not seen any photos of the defendant before the trial and never participated in any line-up identification.

Redirect Examination:

Q: Ms. Van Brittan-Brown, we have asked you a number of things about the robbery, but one of the things that neither I nor the other attorney has asked you is this: Why did you keep staring at the robber even after you were told to stop?

A: I never wanted to forget the face of the man who stole from us. I hoped that I could help catch him someday.

Q: I have no further questions.

If a topic was not covered either on the direct or the cross-examination, some courts will permit the direct examiner to reopen the direct examination to permit the witness to be recalled to cover the new topic. The decision to permit the reopening of a direct examination of a witness falls within the discretion of the judge or arbitrator.

§ 7.10 DIRECT EXAMINATION SITUATIONS

This section presents several direct examinations of specific types of witnesses involving special considerations.

A. FORMER TESTIMONY

In civil trials, testimony of a witness may be introduced through former testimony given at a deposition or another hearing. This testimony is either read to or by the fact finder, or if video recorded, shown during the case. Former testimony is admissible in lieu of live testimony if the previous testimony was given under oath, the witness is unavailable to testify, and the party against whom the testimony is offered had the opportunity to previously examine the witness, or if another party with substantially the same interest or similar motive had that opportunity.

The most common use of former testimony in a civil case involves the introduction of deposition testimony because the witness is unavailable. Many civil cases include this type of evidence. Depositions are often taken to preserve testimony when the offering attorney anticipates that witnesses will be unavailable at the trial, arbitration, or hearing. The deposition of these witnesses is taken and their testimony is commonly video recorded or stenographically preserved. It is very common that the testimony of expert witnesses, who are unavailable because of their professional schedules, is presented in this way.

The procedure to introduce the former testimony is similar to the introduction of live testimony. The video recorded testimony can be shown to the fact finder. If there is only a transcript available, a judge or arbitrator can read the testimony. In jury trials, the transcript can be read to the jury, usually with the attorney reading the questions and another person sitting in the witness stand supplying the answers. The offering attorney should select a person to read the answers who looks credible, is interesting to listen to, and sounds persuasive to gain as much impact as possible from the reading of the deposition.

Prior to the showing of the video or reading of the transcript, the opposing attorney may object to questions or answers contained in the former testimony. The judge or arbitrator rules on each of the objections and, if sustained, the inadmissible question or answer is deleted. If a deposition transcript is read, the portions of the transcript ruled inadmissible are not read. If the video recording is used, the portions ruled to be inadmissible are not shown to the fact finder.

There are a number of technical ways this can be done. If evidentiary rulings are made a reasonable time before the recording is shown, an edited copy of the original recording can be made and that revised version shown. Otherwise, the recording can be advanced to eliminate the inadmissible portions, or the monitor turned off, or the sound muted while the recording continues to play. In jury cases, neither the written deposition transcript nor a recording of the deposition goes with the jury to the jury room for deliberations. This is to avoid the jurors giving recorded evidence more weight than oral evidence from live witnesses.

Example (Deposition Transcript):

Examining Attorney:

Your Honor, Leslie Knope, an eyewitness, is unavailable to testify. Ms. Knope testified at a deposition. Both opposing counsel and I were present and examined her. We now request permission to read her deposition transcript to the jury.

Opposing Counsel:

We have reviewed those parts of her former testimony that the plaintiff plans to introduce, and we have no objection to the introduction of that evidence. After counsel for plaintiff completes the direct examination of Ms. Knope, we will introduce our cross-examination questions and answers.

Judge:

Members of the Jury, counsel for plaintiff will now present the testimony of a witness who is unavailable to be here today. You are to consider the testimony of this witness with the same degree of attention and consideration that you give the testimony of any other witness. Counsel, you may proceed.

Counsel:

I will read the questions, your Honor, and a colleague from my firm, Amy Poehler, will read the answers.

Court:

Ms. Poehler, you may come forward and sit in the witness stand. Counsel, you may begin.

Example (Video Deposition):

Examining Attorney:

Your Honor, Dr. Temperance Brennan, an expert witness, is unavailable to testify. We previously recorded a video deposition of her testimony, and counsel was present. Your Honor has reviewed this recording and has ruled on defendant's objections. Those questions and answers you ruled inadmissible have been edited from this recording. We now request permission to show the recorded testimony of the Doctor, also known as Bones.

Judge:

You may proceed.

In criminal cases, former testimony is usually inadmissible because the defendant has a constitutional right to be confronted by live witnesses and to cross-examine them. Former testimony in a criminal case may be admissible when there is a retrial of the same defendant, or if the defendant stipulates to its admissibility.

B. PAST RECOLLECTION RECORDED

When a witness has no present recollection and efforts to refresh recollection have failed or would fail, the introduction of past recollection recorded may be used to present evidence on direct examination. Federal Rule of Evidence 803(5) provides an exception to the requirement that a witness testify verbally to a present memory in court.

The examining attorney will have prepared a witness for the use of past recollection recorded. It should not come as a surprise when a witness has no current recollection of an event. Statements introduced as past recollection recorded need to be marked and offered into evidence because they constitute the substantive evidence substituted for the verbal testimony of the witness. The foundation for the introduction of the recorded item includes:

- The witness has no present, independent recollection,
- The witness at one time personally knew the relevant information,
- The information was written, composed, or recorded by the witness or at the witness' direction,
- The writing, digital version, or recording was created or adopted when the information was fresh in the witness' memory,
- The writing, composition, or recording accurately contains the information, and
- The witness authenticates the exhibit.

Some witnesses (police, investigators, doctors, experts) may have to rely upon prior statements and reports to assist them during testimony. In many routine cases involving such testimony, the judge or arbitrator do not expect and do not require the laying of a full foundation for these documents as past recollection recorded because they have heard the foundation laid before in similar cases, and they want to save time and move the case along. The opposing attorney may not be satisfied with this approach and can object to the lack of proper foundation.

Example:

Examining Attorney:

Q: What do you do for a living?

A: I'm a state highway trooper.

Q: How long have you been a state highway trooper?

A: Fifteen years.

Q: What are your primary duties?

A: To enforce highway traffic laws and to assist with highway accident scenes.

Q: Do you know how many tickets you give out each year?

A: Approximately.

Q: How many?

A: Between 750 and 1000 a year.

Q: Do you remember the details of all the accident scenes you have investigated?

A: Not all.

Q: Do you remember the details of all the traffic tickets that you have written?

A: No.

Q: What is your procedure when you give a ticket?

A: After I give a ticket, I immediately compose a report while sitting in my police car on the electronic ticket form describing all the important details of the incident.

Q: Do you recall giving a ticket to the defendant in this case on June 1, last year?

A: Yes, I remember giving him a ticket.

Q: Do you remember the details of the incident?

A: Not completely.

Q: What do you remember?

A: I remember it was a careless driving violation.

Q: Do you remember any other details?

A: Not for sure.

Q: How come?

A: Because I see so many reckless driving and speeding cases I can't accurately and completely remember all the details.

To the Court:

Your Honor, may I approach the witness?

Judge:

Yes you may.

Examining Attorney:

Q: Trooper Estrada, I hand you Exhibit No. 1. What is it?

A: It is an electronically printed copy of the ticket and report I was speaking about.

Q: Do you recognize it?

A: Yes I do.

Q: How?

A: I recognize the form, my notations, my trooper number, and the name of the defendant with the date and time.

Q: Does reading this document, Exhibit No. 1, help refresh your recollection as to the details of the incident?

A: No, not really.

Q: Do you have any recollection of the details of that incident as you sit here today?

A: Some but not all.

Q: At the time that you composed this report, did you remember the details of the incident?

A: Yes.

Q: When you composed it, did you include the true and correct version of what you had observed?

A: Yes.

Q: Would you have signed it if it had not been a true and complete version of what you observed?

A: No, I would not have.

To the Court:

Your Honor, I offer Exhibit No. 1 as past recollection recorded.

Judge:

Any objections Counsel?

Opposing Counsel:

No objections.

Judge:

It is received.

Examining Attorney:

At this time, Trooper Estrada, please read what you wrote:

A: "I was proceeding on routine patrol on my CHP motorcycle when I observed the subject vehicle, a stunning twin turbo sapphire blue Porsche cabriolet sporting the requisite spoiler, go zooming by me on the left-hand shoulder at an extraordinarily high rate of vvvvrrrroooommmm."

Q: Very interesting. Go on.

A: "At that time. . . ."

C. WITNESSES WITH COMMUNICATION ISSUES

A child or a mentally challenged or disabled witness may require special consideration as a direct examination witness. The decision maker must determine if the witness is competent to testify. Often a questionably competent witness is the only person who can testify in a case, such as a child abuse, sexual assault, incest, neglect and dependency case. Federal Rule of Evidence 611(c) permits leading questions to assist this witness in communicating. However, the more the attorney asks leading questions, the less competent the witness will appear to be and the less persuasive the testimony becomes.

A witness who has communication problems must be made to feel at ease in the court or hearing room. The preparation may require that the witness be brought to the room, rehearse testifying, and allowed to spend sufficient time in the room to become comfortable with an unfamiliar and potentially frightening place. A mix of leading and non-leading questions assists the witness in testifying, and helps the attorney develop critical testimony which should be given without the over-use of leading questions.

D. CHARACTER EVIDENCE

Character evidence is evidence of a trait or characteristic of a person offered to prove that the person acted in conformity with such character. The evidence rules of almost all jurisdictions are consistent with the common law doctrine that character evidence is not admissible to prove that an individual acted in conformity with the individual's character on a specific occasion. Evidence of wrongs, bad acts, or crimes is generally inadmissible to prove that a party is a bad person or possesses a bad character. For example, evidence that a party has a trait for speeding while driving a car to prove that party was speeding is inadmissible.

Conversely, evidence of good character, good deeds, or an exemplary life is inadmissible to prove that a party is a good person or possesses a good character. For example, proof that a defendant is a careful driver is inadmissible to prove that the defendant was not negligent. Character evidence may be relevant, but the unfair prejudice and confusion of the issues resulting from the character evidence outweighs the probative value of such evidence. See Section 4.8(A)(4)(a).

1. Civil Cases

In a civil case, character evidence is usually inadmissible to prove that the person acted in conformity on a particular occasion, but may be admissible in the following instances:

- Evidence of the character of a person or a pertinent trait may be admissible to prove motive, opportunity, intent, preparation, plan, knowledge, identity, or absence of mistake or accident.

- Evidence relating to the character for untruthfulness may be offered against the person testifying.

- Evidence of the truthful character of a witness is admissible after the character of the witness for untruthfulness has been attacked.

- If character is an issue or an element of liability or damages, evidence is admissible on that issue. Civil cases in which character is an issue include defamation cases (reputation).

2. Criminal Cases

In criminal cases, character evidence is admissible when relevant:

- An accused may offer evidence of a pertinent personal trait. The defendant who claims self-defense in an assault case may offer evidence regarding the defendant's reputation for peacefulness.

- The prosecution may offer character evidence to rebut the pertinent trait suggested by the accused. In a self-defense case, the prosecutor can offer evidence of the defendant's reputation for violence.

- The accused may offer evidence of a pertinent trait of the character of a victim and the prosecution may offer evidence in rebuttal.

- The prosecution may offer evidence of a character trait of peacefulness of the victim in a homicide case to rebut evidence that the victim was the first aggressor.

- Evidence relating to the character for untruthfulness may be offered against the person testifying.

- Evidence of the truthful character of a witness is admissible after the character of the witness for untruthfulness has been attacked.

- Character evidence may be admissible to prove motive, opportunity, intent, preparation, plan, knowledge, identity or absence of mistake or accident.

- Character evidence that may otherwise be proper may be deemed inadmissible as unfairly prejudicial. See Section 4.8(A)(4).

3. Introduction of Character Evidence

There are three ways in which character evidence may be introduced during direct examination of a witness:

A. Opinion testimony: A witness may testify to a personal opinion about the character of a person if a foundation is established regarding what the witness knows or has observed about the person over time.

> "I have personally known the defendant for 30 years, and I consider him to have an excellent reputation for honesty."

B. Reputation testimony: A witness can testify to the general reputation of a person through a foundation establishing what the witness has heard expressed about that person in the defined community. Reputation is the general community consensus about an individual.

> "I have lived in this community for 30 years, and I have heard that the defendant's reputation for honesty is excellent."

C. Specific instances of conduct: A witness may testify to firsthand knowledge about a person.

> "The defendant has been a marriage encounter counselor, a Red Cross volunteer for 10 years, and is currently a member of the Honest-To-Goodness Club."

In all cases, character evidence is admissible by reputation testimony and opinion testimony. Federal Rule of Evidence 803(21) and similar state rules make such testimony admissible hearsay. Testimony of specific instances of conduct is not admissible to prove character on direct examination. Specific instances of conduct may be more convincing, but such specific evidence also has the potential to create undue prejudice, confuse the issues, and consume unnecessary time. Reputation and opinion testimony are less convincing, less prejudicial, and take less time.

Where character evidence has been admitted on direct examination, specific instances of misconduct may be explored during cross-examination. A witness who testifies on direct that a party has good character may be cross-examined regarding knowledge about specific instances of bad character about that person. This line of inquiry may show that the witness may not have known about these specific instances, or ought not to be believed.

In cases in which a character trait of a person is an essential element of the case, proof of the trait may be made by specific instances of conduct. If a character trait is a direct issue in a case, then specific instances of good conduct may be introduced on direct examination to prove such an issue. Specific instances of bad conduct may be raised on cross-examination to disprove the issue, and specific instances of bad conduct may be introduced on direct examination through a witness testifying on behalf of the adverse party to further disprove the character established. All questions regarding specific instances of good conduct or bad conduct must be asked in good faith and must be based on facts. Advocates cannot suggest such instances exist through innuendo or ask unsubstantiated questions.

Example (Direct Examination):

Examining Attorney:

Q: How long have you lived in Washington?

A: 10 years.

Q: What do you do now?

A: I'm a consultant.

Q: Before you were a consultant, what did you do?

A: I was a senator.

Q: How long were you a senator?

A: Six years.

Q: Why did you quit being a senator?

A: I was defeated in an election.

Q: Do you know Congressman Russo?

A: Yes.

Q: How long have you known him?

A: Ten years.

Q: Have you ever socialized with him?

A: Yes.

Q: How often?

A: Several times a year over the last decade.

Q: Do you know other people in the Washington area who have socialized with Congressman Russo?

A: Yes.

Q: How many?

A: Hundreds.

Q: Tell us some of the people you know who have socialized with the Congressman.

A: Other senators, representatives, employees of the House and Senate, and other consultants like myself.

Q: Have you ever talked to these people about Congressman Russo's drinking habits?

A: Yes.

Q: How often?

A: Many times.

Q: Have you ever seen the Congressman drinking?

A: Yes.

Q: How many times?

A: Multiple, frequent times.

Q: Do you know him to be known by any nickname?

A: Oh, yeah.

Q: What was he called?

A: Congressman Boozemeister.

Q: Based on your own observations and your discussions with others, do you know Congressman Russo's reputation for sobriety in the community of Washington?

A: Yes, I do.

Q: What is that opinion?

A: His reputation is that he is a very sober person when he is not drinking.

E. HABIT EVIDENCE

Evidence of a particular habit of a person or the routine practice of an organization is admissible to prove that a person or organization acted in conformity with that habit on a particular occasion. If the evidence of an otherwise relevant habit is unfairly prejudicial, an objection is proper and will be sustained. See Section 4.8(A)(4)(b).

Federal Rule of Evidence 406 does not define habit. Habit is generally defined as a regular response to a repeated specific situation. Definitions may be found in treatises, statutes, case law and rules. It is within the discretion of the judge or arbitrator to determine if the specific situation has been repeated enough to establish a true habit.

§ 7.11 IMPROPER DIRECT EXAMINATION

This section describes improper uses of direct examination that are unethical and grounds for an objection, mistrial, new trial or hearing.

A. FACILITATING THE PRESENTATION OF PERJURED TESTIMONY

The knowing use of fraudulent, false or perjured testimony is prohibited. Attorneys have a duty to prevent the misrepresentation of testimony. If the client in a civil case insists on testifying falsely, the attorney must inform the tribunal of the fraud in some manner. Disclosure may occur by making a record of the fact that the client is taking the stand against the advice of counsel or by actually telling the decision maker about the perjury. If a client in a criminal case insists on presenting false testimony, the attorney has the same duty but may be limited by constitutional considerations in determining how or if the perjury may be revealed. A criminal defense lawyer may have to allow the defendant to testify but may not ask the witness any questions or use the false testimony as a part of the final argument. If an attorney knows that a witness, who is not a client, will offer perjured testimony, the lawyer may not call that witness to testify.

In both civil and criminal cases, an attorney may request to withdraw from the case, but the request may be denied. Denial of the request to withdraw usually occurs when the trial is well underway and the withdrawal will cause unfair delay that may cause prejudice to the opponent or to the administration of justice.

B. SOLICITING INADMISSIBLE RESPONSES

It is improper for an attorney to solicit inadmissible responses. For example, it is highly improper in an automobile accident case for a plaintiff's counsel to ask, "Did you ever take photos of that car before the repairs were made?" anticipating the witness will respond with, "No, but the insurance company did." A direct examiner must comply with the exclusionary rules of evidence and cannot attempt to prompt an inadmissible response from a witness, even with a question that is not objectionable. A direct examiner who attempts to contravene the rules of evidence commits misconduct which may result in a mistrial or a reversal. Further, the integrity of the attorney will be severely damaged, and the decision maker may conclude the attorney is untrustworthy. Ultimately, the attorney may be reported to the governing professional responsibility or lawyer licensing board.

C. INADVERTENT WITNESS MISCONDUCT

The inadvertent blurting out of inadmissible evidence by a witness can result in an admonition or even a mistrial or reversal. The examining lawyer needs to control the witness. This can be achieved by a preparation session before trial in which the witness is advised of the dangers of volunteering information and in not responding to the questions. Some witnesses disregard such advice and want the decision maker to know certain information, which is excluded by the rules of evidence. For example, a witness may want to tell about some rumors and gossip the witness heard about a party, which is inadmissible hearsay. The direct examiner must explain to the witness what information is inadmissible and the impropriety of attempting to disclose it.

D. ALLOWING THE CLIENT OR WITNESS TO DISRUPT THE TRIAL OR HEARING

Allowing a client or witness to disrupt a case may bring disciplinary action against the lawyer. Lawyers should not stand mute as their clients misbehave. Not only may the lawyer be sanctioned, but a client or witness can be cited for contempt as well.

E. USING TRICKS TO CONFUSE IDENTIFICATION

The deliberate substitution of someone other than a party at the trial or hearing is improper. An attorney must disclose to the tribunal the name of the client that the attorney represents. In a case in which identification is an issue, it may be unethical for a lawyer to seat someone other than the client at counsel table for the purpose of eliciting an erroneous identification or to test an eyewitness' identification. However, full disclosure of the tactic to the judge or arbitrator and opposing counsel beforehand may permit the use of this technique.

CHAPTER 8

EXHIBITS

■ ■ ■

8.1 Introduction
    A.   Real Evidence
    B.   Demonstrative Evidence
    C.   Visual Aids
8.2 Preparation of Exhibits
    A.   Identifying Potential Exhibits
    B.   Assessing Use
    C.   Planning the Presentation
    D.   Disclosing Exhibits
    E.   Managing Exhibits
8.3 Modern Technology
    A.   Introduction
    B.   Technology Systems
    C.   Use of Technology
    D.   Communication Technology
8.4 Evidentiary Considerations
    A.   Relevancy and Unfair Prejudice
    B.   Levels of Foundation
    C.   Chain of Custody
    D.   Demonstrative/Illustrative Evidence
    E.   Limited Purposes
    F.   Redacting an Exhibit
    G.   Judicial Discretion
8.5 Introduction of Exhibits
    A.   Legal Terminology
    B.   Steps for the Admissibility of Exhibits
    C.   Other Ways Admitting Exhibits
8.6 Elements of Evidentiary Foundation
    A.   Physical Objects and Properties (Products, Clothing, Appliances, Weapons)
    B.   Documents (Electronic Documents, Contracts, Digital Data, Leases, Signed or Printed Documents)
    C.   Personal and Business Correspondence (Letters, Memos, Notes, Files, Bills, Mail)
    D.   Electronic Business and Personal Correspondence (Emails, Text Messages, Blog Entries, Chat Room Comments, Web Communications)
    E.   Internet Communications and Information (Websites, Social Networks, Search Engine Data, Internet Archives, Cloud Server Data)

  * Dianna Case, Connect Litigation, and Litigation Insights assisted with the content and design of demonstrative exhibits.

Trial Advocacy Supplement
Federal Rules of Evidence

The Federal Rules of Evidence appear in the *Supplement to Trial Advocacy Before Judges, Jurors, and Arbitrators.* References to evidentiary rules in this Chapter refer to the Federal Rules of Evidence.

The explanations, descriptions, and examples in this Chapter reflect both federal rules and state rules modeled on the federal rules widely adopted in the majority of states. The reasons and rationales underlying these evidentiary rules are applicable to federal and state courts, arbitrations, and administrative hearings.

These evidence rules determine the admissibility of exhibits in judicial forums and influence or control the admissibility of relevant and reliable exhibits in arbitrations and administrative hearings. The foundation examples in this Chapter establish the proper foundation for the admissibility of exhibits in these forums.

REFLECTING ON ADVOCACY

Few things are harder to put up with than the annoyance of a good example.

—MARK TWAIN

A pleasant illusion is better than a harsh reality.

—CHRISTIAN NESTELL BOVEE

§ 8.1   INTRODUCTION

Judges, jurors, and arbitrators expect to see visual evidence as well as hear oral testimony. Exhibits meet these expectations. Well-prepared and well-presented exhibits help witnesses and attorneys communicate and present an interesting and persuasive case.

Outside the court and hearing rooms, learning is often accomplished through images and graphics. People view astonishing websites, flashy magazines, amazing television programs, dazzling movies, and the graphic world of the internet. They expect to learn and to be entertained.

It usually takes more than the spoken word to keep people interested and focused. It takes illustrative aids to help people learn and remember. This is just as true in the courtroom and in the hearing room as it is anywhere else.

An exhibit is anything other than oral testimony that can be perceived by the senses and presented as evidence. A presentation that combines verbal and visual evidence is more likely to be understood and remembered. There are three major types of exhibits: real evidence, demonstrative/illustrative evidence, and visual aids.

A.   REAL EVIDENCE

Real evidence consists of exhibits that are objects, writings, or data containing facts relevant to a case. Real evidence includes such things as physical objects, written documents, electronically stored information, printed papers, and digital evidence. Examples include the knife used in a homicide, DNA material found on a victim, the blender involved in a product liability case, a written agreement in a contract case, an email in a fraud case, an Instagram in a property dispute, and a video in a tort case. These relevant items of real evidence are probative by themselves. Proper foundation establishes their relevancy and admissibility.

Example:

Examining Lawyer:

Q: I have just handed you an exhibit that has been marked for identification as Exhibit No. 1. Do you recognize this Exhibit?

A: Yes.

Q: How do you recognize Exhibit No. 1?

A: I own this book. I recognize it by its title, my initials on the title page, and my handwritten notes. I picked it off the floor after the defendant threw it.

Q: What is Exhibit No. 1?

A: It's the book entitled *Ghandi* that I saw the defendant use to hit plaintiff.

Q: Is Exhibit No. 1 in the same condition as it was when you saw the defendant hit the plaintiff with it?

A: Yes.

To the Court:

I offer what has been marked for identification as Exhibit No. 1 into evidence.

Real evidence adds another dimension of proof in a case. A physical object or document provides the fact finder with a lasting impression of the facts. For example, the claw hammer murder weapon can be seen; the defective medical implant can be touched; the emailed libelous statement can be read; the terms on the small print contract can be highlighted; the controversial DNA results can be explained; the video taken by a wearable or mountable camera can show the horrors of the accident.

B. DEMONSTRATIVE EVIDENCE

Demonstrative/illustrative evidence refers to those exhibits that are not part of the "real" event or transaction but are a representation of an object, writing, or data. They are based on the evidence and are usually created after the fact. Demonstrative or illustrative evidence includes photos, graphics, diagrams, computer generated data, drawings, maps, diagrams, videos, animation, simulation, models, power point presentations, and anything that augments verbal testimony. These exhibits are admissible if they:

- Assist a witness in testifying, or
- Help the fact finder understand the evidence.

Example:

Examining Lawyer:

Q: I show you Exhibit F marked for identification. Do you recognize it?

A: Yes.

Q: What is Exhibit F, Ms. Michelangelo?

A: It is a three-dimensional model of the sculpture.

Q: Is the diagram a fair and accurate depiction of the sculpture that was created five hundred and ten years ago?

A: Yes.

Q: Would this model assist you in explaining the birth of the Renaissance?

A: Yes, it would.

To the Court:

Your Honor, at this time I offer Exhibit F as illustrative evidence, and ask that the witness be allowed to use it during her testimony.

Demonstrative/illustrative evidence adds a powerful visual dimension to the case. A diagram can provide an overview of an event; a digital photo can bring to life the details of a scene; a video recording can show the lengthy, deliberate path the defendant took to the murder scene to establish premeditation; a working model with movable parts can simulate a product; a diagram of an intersection with magnetic cars can assist a witness in describing an accident; a computer generated recreation of an airline accident can bring to life the final fatal moments. See Sections 8.7 and 8.8.

C. VISUAL AIDS

Visual aids are created and used to effectively communicate information to the fact finder and to help the fact finder understand the presentation. Visual aids are neither real nor demonstrative exhibits and are not considered evidence. Visual aids may be used during final argument, opening statement, and direct and cross-examination. Examples of visual aids include: a power point outline of an opening statement, final argument, or expert testimony; a part of opening or argument prepared on a poster board; summary charts of witness testimony; a whiteboard or easel paper listing words and dates; summary information presented with a document camera; graphs depicting product information; photos of places; a computer generated flowchart of events and amounts; and an enlarged verdict form for use during summation. Although there is no specific foundation that ordinarily must be established to use visual aids, it is necessary to either describe what will be used or obtain permission from the judge or arbitrator.

Example:

To the Arbitrator:

We have prepared a list of each transaction between Wookie and Hans Solo involved in this case. We can display this summary evidence on the monitor screen. It will help us present our summation and assist you in understanding the multi-galactic transactions. We ask permission to use it.

Arbitrator:

You may do so.

Visual aids can persuasively emphasize evidence in opening statements and summation. For examples, a line or bar graph can favorably portray evidence. Summaries of testimony can highlight and compare evidence. A software program can recreate and dramatize a story. Printed words displayed on a chart can create a summation outline. Power point slides can present reasons to support a verdict.

§ 8.2   PREPARATION OF EXHIBITS

Planning the use of exhibits includes several considerations:

- Identifying potential exhibits.
- Assessing the use of exhibits.
- Choosing the witness(es) through whom the exhibit will be offered and used.
- Planning a professional presentation.
- Managing exhibits.

A. IDENTIFYING POTENTIAL EXHIBITS

The identification of exhibits occurs during investigation, discovery, and preliminary stages and continues throughout the case. Real evidence is located, gathered, and preserved. Demonstrative evidence is created before and during the trial or hearing. Visual aids are developed at a reasonable time before they are needed.

B. ASSESSING USE

Advocates select exhibits that effectively communicate the case theory, tell a story, present substantive information, emphasize important areas of evidence, and refute the opponent's evidence. The following questions help evaluate the use of exhibits:

- Will the exhibit improve the ability of the witness to testify more effectively? Will it enhance the ability of the advocate to present evidence?

- Will the fact finder better understand and remember the evidence portrayed by the exhibit? If it may be distracting or confusing, it should not be introduced.

- Will the fact finder expect the exhibit to be introduced? The failure to introduce it may have the fact finder draw an adverse conclusion from its absence in the case.

- Can the exhibit foundation be established through the testifying witness? Some exhibits involve a chain of custody foundation, and require more than one testifying witness before an exhibit is introduced or used. See Section 8.4(C).

- Will the exhibit be admitted into evidence or used for demonstrative purposes?

- Will the exhibit take too long to introduce or use? The examining attorney should efficiently refer to the exhibit.

- Will the relevant, probative value of the exhibit outweigh any unfair prejudicial impact? If the exhibit shocks the fact finder, is vulgar or in bad taste, or is unnecessarily cumulative or repetitive, it should not be offered.

- What is the cost and amount of time needed to make or obtain the exhibit? The expense, in dollars and time, should not exceed the exhibit's overall usefulness.

- Will electronically stored, digital, or computer-based evidence be easily presented and understood? Technology can either enhance or weaken evidence presentation.

- Will the exhibit be perceived by the fact finder as unfair? Expensive, elaborate, or numerous exhibits used by one side may create the perception that the party with significant resources is overwhelming the party with lesser resources.

- What are the rules for disclosing exhibits to opposing counsel, the judge, or arbitrator prior to the trial or hearing?

- What technical problems might there be with the exhibit? Does the court or hearing room have facilities and equipment to present the exhibit? Have adequate steps been taken to ensure any problems can be overcome?

Advocates need to decide what type of exhibit is or may be available and whether it should be used. Client resources, available preparation time, the length of the trial or hearing, and available technology, are other factors that affect the use of exhibits. Technology can be compelling and fascinating, but it can divert attention from the evidence and be a distraction. Simple presentations may be just as persuasive.

C. PLANNING THE PRESENTATION

Advance preparation is needed for exhibits. Advocates need to prepare and rehearse the use of exhibits ahead of time to effectively present them. A qualified witness or witnesses must identify and lay a foundation for the admission of the evidence. Exhibits may also be admitted as evidence through a stipulated agreement.

D. DISCLOSING EXHIBITS

The timing and requirements to disclose exhibits to opposing counsel, judges, and arbitrators depends on the type of exhibit and the applicable rules. The existence of real evidence is usually known to all the parties. Demonstrative/illustrative evidence is typically generated after the relevant events and a reasonable time before its use. Visual aids may be produced during case preparation or shortly before their use.

The rules and fairness will determine when an advocate must advise opposing counsel and the decision maker of the availability and use of exhibits. Pretrial and pre-hearing rules commonly require the advocates to identify and list the exhibits they plan to introduce or use, including all types of exhibits. This prevents an opposing party from being unfairly surprised. The rules or case order usually include a deadline for the notification and disclosure of exhibits. If a lawyer decides to use an exhibit after a deadline, permission from the judge or arbitrator or opposing counsel will be needed.

The decision to use an exhibit must be made far enough in advance so the exhibit can be prepared or created and disclosed to avoid objections to its use. This notice permits an opponent to make timely objections, informs the proffering attorney that the exhibits are not objectionable, and allows the judge or arbitrator an opportunity to rule on the admissibility of exhibits before the trial or hearing. Subsequent sections in this Chapter explain these procedures.

Demonstrative/illustrative evidence and visual aids may not be known about or anticipated to be used in a case by opposing parties. To avoid problems with their use, the advocate may seek timely permission of the judge or arbitrator to use them. Decision makers have discretion in admitting or rejecting these types of exhibits. See Section 8.9. Judges and arbitrators may have their own views on how these types of exhibits are to be handled. Typically, demonstrative exhibits are marked and introduced, and visual aids need not be marked or introduced as they are not considered "evidence." Some decision makers expect all exhibits to be marked and introduced.

In jury trials, real evidence is usually made available for a jury to view during deliberations in the jury room. Demonstrative/illustrative evidence may be made available if it would assist the jurors in their deliberation. Visual aids are usually not available for jury deliberations. Judges have discretion in deciding what goes to the jury room.

E. MANAGING EXHIBITS

Organization is of particular importance in introducing and using exhibits. So much is going on during a case that foundation questions can be forgotten, and exhibits too easily misplaced. Advocates can prepare specific electronic or paper lists and files itemizing and containing the exhibits to be used, the necessary foundation for those exhibits, and the witnesses who will provide that foundation. All exhibits should be labeled with an exhibit number or reference name, whether or not they are admitted into evidence.

An organized format helps assure the exhibit is introduced and received in evidence. Forms 8.1 and 8.2 illustrate an effective system. Exhibits can be included in an exhibit case notebook or electronic file with copies provided to the fact finder, opposing lawyer, and witnesses. Technology provides efficient ways to label and manage exhibits using electronic tags and bar codes.

FORM 8.1
EXHIBIT FOUNDATION WORKSHEET

Case_____ File_____

Exhibit

Elements of Admissibility	Which witness will provide	What witness will say
(1)		
(2)		
(3)		
(4)		
(5)		
(6)		
(7)		
(8)		
(9)		
(10)		

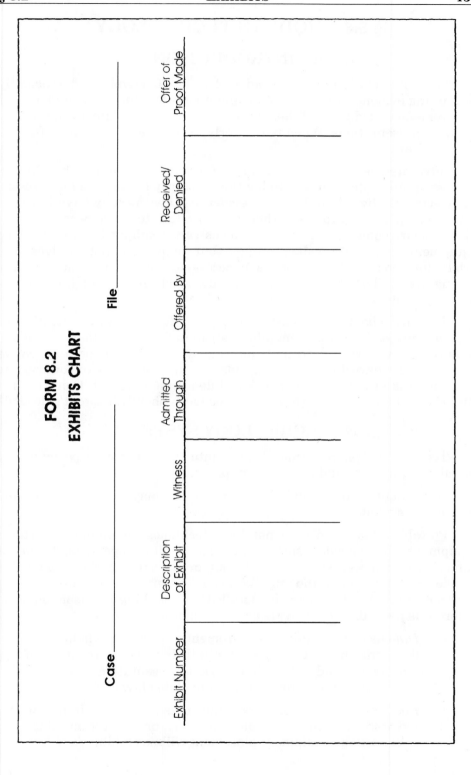

§ 8.3 MODERN TECHNOLOGY

A. INTRODUCTION

Modern technology assists advocates in effectively and efficiently presenting evidence and arguments and allows fact finders to understand and remember evidence. When used well, it can explain evidence and enhance presentations. When used poorly, technology can inhibit effective communication.

Advocates need to understand the technology available, when its use is most appropriate, and how to lay the necessary foundation and present the electronic, digital, and camera evidence. Lawyers may have law firm technology personnel to assist them or can retain technology consultants. Many courtrooms and hearing rooms are equipped with modern equipment and multimedia systems, but many are not. Judges and arbitrators commonly use or have access to computers and monitors during cases. Clerks and reporters may use electronic and digital systems to track exhibits.

To learn about available technologies before a trial, arbitration or hearing, advocates can contact administrators for information or visit the courtroom or hearing room. Judicial, arbitral, and administrative websites may have technology information. It's also wise to confirm the equipment is in working order or schedule a time to test it. Confirmation that the system is still operational can be made shortly before it's needed.

B. TECHNOLOGY SYSTEMS

Technology systems generally fall into two categories: permanently installed equipment and portable equipment.

Permanent. Court and hearing rooms may have an existing technology system.

Portable. If a room does not have technology equipment, portable equipment will be needed, such as: laptops, monitors, speakers, document cameras, and power supplies. A layout or drawing of the room helps decide what equipment and supplies are necessary and the best setup. It is crucial that the equipment is installed and working a reasonable time before it is needed. The following are the major things to look for:

- *Dimensions*. Obtain measurements. This will help with decisions on what equipment will fit in the courtroom, easel placement, and selection for what presentation system to utilize (monitors, projector, flat panel displays).

- *Line of sight issues*. Check line of sight views from the judge's bench, counsel tables, jury box, or arbitration tables to ensure the equipment placement will not inhibit viewing.

- *Power and connectivity*. Confirm location of all power outlets, internet connections, and cabling for the systems.

- *Approval*. Obtain permission. Authorization is usually required from an administrator for delivery and installation.

- *Equipment security*. Confirm how secure the room will be when empty. Determine if the equipment and materials can remain in the room to avoid daily setup.

C. USE OF TECHNOLOGY

The use of proper exhibit technology equipment relies on the judgments of the advocates and the discretion of the judge or arbitrator. Exhibit and room limitations also determine the appropriate apparatus.

- *Monitors/screens*. Many court and hearing rooms have screens, and some rooms are outfitted with flat panel displays or computer monitors allowing the participants to view the evidence. Judges have ultimate control over jury viewing, through override switches controlled from the bench. For a bench trial or arbitration, four or fewer monitors are sufficient (one for the judge/arbitrator, witness, and each advocate). For a jury trial, five or more monitors may be necessary. In some cases, one large monitor screen may be used if it can be seen by all. An amplifier may also be necessary to broadcast the signal.

- *Document cameras/projectors*. If using monitors, a projector is not necessary. With a screen, a projector is needed.

- *Smart boards*. The court and hearing rooms may be equipped with a smart board (electronic whiteboard) that is connected to computers and can display large images. The board can be written on with special markers producing an image that can be preserved in the computer. Printed copies can be made to display and for the record.

- *Sound systems*. Audio equipment may be needed depending upon the size of the room and the number of participants. Many rooms have some sound projection equipment and may have battery powered "lapel" microphones. Speakers are required when a video deposition is shown.

- *Power lecterns*. Many courtrooms have adjustable lecterns for the comfort of advocates. Tall or short advocates can adjust the height of the lectern.

- *Computer assisted transcription (CAT)*. Reporters in some court and hearing rooms enter evidence into viewable, real-time files, which can be searched, reviewed by lawyers and witnesses, and referenced during the proceeding. Arrangements for real-time reporting may need to be made in advance of the case.

- *Bar code technology.* In a case with numerous exhibits, bar code technology permits an advocate to select a labeled document and quickly reference a particular page and paragraph appearing on a screen for all to see instantly.

Supplies augment both technological and traditional equipment, including easels with flip charts and white boards with marking pens. Advocates may need to bring extension cords, scissors, tape, white out, correction tape, post notes, marking pens, and highlighters.

D. COMMUNICATION TECHNOLOGY

Exhibits may be presented digitally or electronically or in combination.

1. Document Camera Presentations with Prepared Documents

Document cameras, also referred to as visual presenters, are devices that combine a video camera with projection equipment. As the witness examines a document during testimony, the exhibited document is placed on the document camera and is shown to the fact finder. The advocate may also display exhibits during opening or summation. Typically, the document camera is either hooked up to a projector that reflects the image onto a screen, or is connected to monitors in the room.

There is no need to scan documents and photos ahead of time. Printed or reproduced documents, as well as tangible exhibits, can be placed on the document camera surface. Documents can be marked highlighting the witness' testimony.

There are limitations. Document cameras are often formatted with landscape (11″ x 8.5″) orientation, making it difficult to see detailed portrait (8.5″ x 11″) documents without zooming in on particular data. And, it is difficult to compare documents.

2. Digital Exhibit Presentations Using Computers

Electronic evidence presentations most commonly include a computer with files to display case information through the use of a projector or monitor. Original exhibits, such as documents and photographs, are scanned and made into digital files, loaded into a computer, and viewed with a software application. Effective systems allow retrieval of documents in any order (not just sequentially) and permit multiple document comparisons and zooming, highlighting, and marking the documents during the presentation.

Once documents and other evidence are digitized, files can be stored in multiple directories and searchable formats. When presenting evidence using a computer, there is no paper shuffling or document rummaging. Exhibits may be maintained on a laptop in separate lists or files and readily opened when needed. This method is useful in cases with a modest number of exhibits.

In cases with numerous exhibits, presentation software allows lawyers to type in a code or use a bar code reader to retrieve documents, making their use smooth and efficient during evidence presentation. Features allow the advocate to bring up more than one document at a time, zoom in when needed, or focus on several areas at once. Presentations can be prepared which display facts, one at a time.

Streaming and recorded video can present evidence. Live witnesses who are not present may appear on a video monitor by using a telecommunications software application. Recorded evidence can be presented through electronic media. Prior deposition, trial or hearing testimony can be presented as previously recorded.

Video evidence can be copied onto a CD-ROM and synchronized with a prepared transcript so the two can be shown at the same time. Attorneys can present computer-generated simulations and animations to supplement the testimony of expert and fact witnesses. These presentations help fact finders understand complex events.

Software programs that produce these various uses of exhibits are available on line at no cost or from proprietary vendors. It takes practice, time, and experience to develop the knowledge and skills to produce these exhibits. It is not rocket science, and technologically challenged advocates can readily become proficient in their use.

§ 8.4   EVIDENTIARY CONSIDERATIONS

Real and demonstrative exhibits are subject to the rules of evidence. Some exhibits, like physical objects, may be easy to introduce. Other exhibits, such as documentary evidence, have to satisfy rules regarding the admissibility of hearsay and original writings before being received into evidence. Chapter 4 on Evidence and Objections described the applicable evidentiary procedures and rules for all forums including jury and bench trials. Exhibits in administrative hearings and arbitrations may be subject to less formal and less rigid admissibility requirements.

The following sections discuss additional exhibit issues:

- Relevancy and unfair prejudice.

- Levels of foundation.

- Chain of custody.

- Demonstrative evidence.

- Exhibits used for limited purposes.

- Redaction of an exhibit.

- Exercise of discretion by the judge or arbitrator.

A. RELEVANCY AND UNFAIR PREJUDICE

An exhibit must be relevant to be admissible. An exhibit is relevant if it has any tendency to make more or less probable the existence of any fact that is of consequence to the case determination. See Section 4.8(A).

Example:

Examining Attorney:

Q: I am showing you what has been marked for identification as Exhibit No. 10. Do you recognize it, Mr. Dumbo?

A: Yes.

Q: How?

A: I brought it with me.

Q: What is it?

A: It's a peanut shell. I ate the peanut part before I took the stand.

Q: Why did you eat the peanut?

A: To help my memory so I can testify better.

To the Court:

Your Honor, I offer Exhibit No. 10.

Opposing Counsel:

Your Honor, I object. This has nothing to do with this case and is irrelevant.

Judge:

Objection sustained.

Even when an exhibit is relevant, it may be excluded from evidence if it tends to confuse the issues or mislead the fact finder, causes undue delay, wastes time, is cumulative, or if the probative value of the exhibit is substantially outweighed by its unfairly prejudicial impact. A motion in limine can obtain a ruling regarding inadmissible or unfairly prejudicial exhibits. See Section 4.5(A).

Some exhibits may be susceptible to a claim of undue prejudice because of their visual impact. This impact may indeed be prejudicial to the opponent, but the harm is not necessarily unfair. For example, a photo or video showing injuries that a plaintiff has suffered demonstrates the extent of the injury and communicates the pain and suffering the plaintiff endured. The impact of this image is undoubtedly more harmful to the defendant's case than if the plaintiff verbally described the injuries. This harm does not rise to the level of unfair prejudice unless the exhibit is unnecessarily gruesome. Some exhibits may be excluded because of the unnecessary impact they have in a case or the way they distort the evidence.

Example:

In a criminal trial, presume the prosecution is introducing a series of photos of the deceased victim through a police officer.

Examining Attorney:

Q: Detective Chief Leigh Johnson, I am showing you what has been marked for identification as State's Exhibit No. 83. It is a digital photo. Do you recognize it?

A: Yes, I do.

Q: What is it?

A: It's another photo in the series you have just shown me of the body of the victim.

Q: Is Exhibit 83 like the other photos—Exhibits 79 through 82—we have introduced, a fair and accurate representation of the victim's body as you saw it on the day of the murder?

A: Yes, it is.

To the Court:

Your Honor, I offer State's Exhibit No. 83.

Opposing Counsel:

Your Honor, I object to Exhibit No. 83 on the grounds that a fifth photo of the same body is unduly prejudicial, a waste of time, and cumulative.

Judge:

Your objection is sustained.

Example:

In a civil trial, presume the witness is an eyewitness to an auto accident that occurred at 9:00 p.m. on a summer night.

Examining Attorney:

Q: Officer Shibuya, I show you what is marked for identification as Exhibit C. Do you recognize this photo?

A: Yes.

Q: What does it show?

A: It shows the pedestrian scramble intersection at Rodeo Drive where the accident happened.

Q: Is Exhibit C a fair and accurate representation of the scene of the intersection that you saw?

A: Yes, for the most part, except it's brighter.

To the Court:

Your Honor, I offer Defendant's Exhibit C into evidence.

Opposing Counsel:

I object, your Honor, to the introduction of Exhibit C. This photo was apparently taken during the day and doesn't show the intersection the witness saw at dusk, as the sun was setting. It distorts the facts and is confusing.

Judge:

Sustained.

B. LEVELS OF FOUNDATION

There are two levels of foundation for exhibits that must be met during a case. The first is the legal foundation that must be established before the exhibit can be admitted as evidence, and the second is the persuasive foundation. The judge or arbitrator always determines whether the minimum legal foundation has been met and whether the exhibit is admitted in evidence. The fact finder, including the jury in a jury trial, determines the persuasive weight and decides whether the exhibit is really what it claims to be. See Section 4.2(B).

The threshold legal foundation is the minimum requirement for the admissibility of an exhibit. While this admissibility foundation can be minimal, the advocate must expand or clarify the foundation to increase the weight the fact finder will give to that exhibit. This is the persuasive foundation. Detailed facts must be established so that sufficient evidence exists to satisfy both levels of foundation.

1. Legally Sufficient Foundation

The judge or arbitrator determines whether there is sufficient evidence to support a finding that the exhibit is what it purports to be. The foundation for real evidence is established by a witness testifying that the tangible object or document is what it is claimed to be. Fed.R.Evid. 901(b)(1). There are two primary types of real evidence:

- Evidence that is *readily identifiable* because it is unique or singular, and

- Evidence that is *fungible* and which lacks unique or identifiable characteristics.

The minimum evidentiary foundation is established for real evidence when a witness can identify the object by its distinctive characteristics and can state that the object is in the same or substantially the same condition as it was at a relevant time. Federal Rule of Evidence 901(b)(4) permits identification by "distinctive characteristics" such as "appearance, contents, substance, internal patterns, or other ... characteristics."

Example:

Examining Attorney:

Q: I show you what is marked for identification as Exhibit No. 101. What is it?

A: It's my rubber duckie.

Q: How do you recognize it?

A: It looks identical to my rubber duckie. It's the same shape and color. It feels the same. It has the same exact watermarks on it from the last time I used it, and I recognize the missing paint from its beak.

Q: Ms. Kwakk Wakk, is Exhibit No. 101 in the same, or substantially the same, condition now as it was when you last saw it in your bathtub?

A: Yes.

To the Court:

Your Honor, we offer Exhibit No. 101 into evidence.

Evidence law does not require that a witness be completely sure or state with absolute certainty that an exhibit is the identical object. An exhibit will be admitted as long as there is reasonable evidence to support a finding that the exhibit is what it is claimed to be. A qualified identification of an exhibit may affect the weight (persuasive value) the fact finder gives to the exhibit but may not affect admissibility.

2. Persuasive Foundation

After a judge or arbitrator has ruled that sufficient evidence has been established to admit an exhibit, additional testimony may be needed to convince a fact finder that the exhibit is real, accurate, complete, or true, depending on the type of exhibit. The more detailed the facts are to support the authenticity or accuracy of an exhibit, the more likely the fact finder will conclude the exhibit is what it is claimed to be.

The following example illustrates the levels of evidentiary foundation and persuasive foundation with respect to the opinion testimony of an expert regarding an exhibit.

Example:

Presume J.E. Hoover has been qualified as an expert crime laboratory analyst and has analyzed two separate bullets: one from the body of the deceased and the other from the test gun.

Examining Attorney:

Q: You have told us that you examined what has been marked for identification as State's Exhibit A—a bullet from the body of the deceased?

A: Yes.

Q: Did you examine State's Exhibit B, which is the bullet you told us was fired from the test gun?

A: Yes.

Q: Did you compare the bullets?

A: Yes.

Q: How did you do that?

A: With a comparison electronic microscope.

Q: What is that type of microscope?

A: A comparison electronic microscope is an instrument that allows me to place two bullets under separate eyepieces so they can be rotated, and I can look for similarities in both the vertical and horizontal bullet markings.

Q: Based on your examination with the comparison microscope, do you have an opinion whether the bullet from the body of the deceased matches the bullet fired from the test gun?

A: Yes, I do.

Q: What is it?

A: They match identically.

Q: Describe how you made this comparison.

A: The markings on both bullets, which are known as striations, matched.

Q: What caused the striations?

A: Striations are caused by scratches and imperfections in the barrel of the pistol that in turn causes marks or striations on the bullet.

Q: How do these striations help you make bullet comparisons?

A: These striation markings will be the same on every bullet fired from the same gun.

Q: Do you have an opinion whether the bullets, Exhibits A and B, were fired from the same gun?

A: Yes.

Q: What is the opinion?

A: They were definitely fired from the same gun.

Q: How do you know?

A: I rotated the bullets so I could see that the scratches or striations on the two bullets were identical.

C. CHAIN OF CUSTODY

The foundation for most exhibits can be established through a witness who testifies that an exhibit looks or feels like the real thing. Some exhibits may not be readily identifiable. Objects that are not unique, that do not have distinctive characteristics or that have not been marked in any identifiable way may require a chain of custody foundation to make the exhibit admissible.

A chain of custody accounts for the whereabouts of the exhibit during all relevant times of the case. Examples include: in a drug case, the bag containing the drug needs to be accounted for from the time the bag was seized from the defendant until its transport to the courtroom; in a criminal case, a bloody glove found at the scene must be carefully marked and preserved; in a contaminated beverage case, the bottle needs to be accounted for from the time of consumption until the time of trial.

There are two ways of establishing an unbroken chain of custody:

- The exhibit has been *at all times in the continuing,* safe, and sole possession of one or more individuals; or

- The exhibit itself was *distinctively identified,* or was sealed and placed in a safe, tamper-proof container or preserved in a secure, virus proof device.

Testimony from one or more witnesses must show there have been no significant breaks in the links of the chain of custody. Typically, evidence need not establish a perfect unbroken chain or the whereabouts of an exhibit over the entire period of relevant time. Judges and arbitrators recognize that a chain of custody is flexible and that a reasonable amount of relevant evidence is sufficient to meet the admissibility foundation. Additional evidence may be necessary to meet the persuasive foundation and convince the fact finder that the exhibit is the actual real evidence and there has been no loss, misplacement, mix-up, unexplained changes, or tampering.

Example:

This example shows how the chain of custody is established when the exhibit was in the continual, sole possession of individuals.

Examining Attorney (First Witness Establishing Foundation):

Q: On July 4, at 12:00 noon, where were you?

A: I was at the Mudville Ball Park.

Q: What were you doing there?

A: I was there with my husband and my daughter, and we were having a picnic before the team began batting practice for the big game.

Q: What happened?

A: One of the baseball players was walking out toward home plate before anyone else even arrived.

Q: Did you know who it was?

A: Yes.

Q: Who?

A: Casey.

Q: How do you know it was him?

A:　I recognized him. I had seen him many times before at games and in town.

Q:　What was he doing?

A:　Limbering up and signing autographs.

Q:　Then what happened?

A:　I heard the sound of a crack of a big bat.

Q:　Then what?

A:　Well, I was quite surprised.

Q:　Why?

A:　Because it was long before any batting practice or the game.

Q:　What happened next?

A:　I was suddenly hit on the head by a ball.

Q:　What happened to you?

A:　I ended up with a big, ugly cut and a very painful bruise on my head.

Q:　What did you do?

A:　I picked up the ball.

Q:　Then what did you do with it?

A:　I handed it to my daughter.

Q:　Did you look at it carefully?

A:　No, I was bleeding a lot.

Q:　Can you identify the baseball that hit you on the head?

A:　Not specifically. It looked like any baseball.

Examining Attorney (Second Witness Establishing Chain):

Q:　You are the daughter of the plaintiff who was hit in the head with the baseball, correct?

A:　Yes.

Q:　Describe for us what happened?

A:　I was standing next to my Mom when she cried out, and I turned and she handed me a baseball.

Q:　Did you see your mom get hit with the ball?

A:　Not really.

Q:　What did you do with the ball?

A: I've kept it in my possession since that time.

Q: Why did you do that?

A: Well, I watch Court T.V. and thought Mom might have a good lawsuit.

Q: How did you keep it?

A: Well, I carried it home with me.

Q: Then what did you do with it?

A: I locked it in my desk drawer and put the key on a chain that I carry around my neck.

Q: Does anyone else have a key to your desk drawer?

A: No.

Q: When did you remove the baseball?

A: I took the key from around my neck today, unlocked the desk drawer, removed the baseball, and brought it with me to court today.

Q: Do you have that baseball with you right now?

A: Yes, I do.

Q: Will you hand it to me, please?

A: Yes.

Q: I am showing you what has been marked for identification as Exhibit No. 1. What is it?

A: It's the baseball with that red stain that I kept in my possession since my mom gave it to me and that I just took out of my pocket and gave to you.

Q: By the way, how did Casey do that day?

A: He struck out.

Example:

This example deals with an exhibit that cannot be specifically identified but which has not been tampered with because it has been kept in a sealed container.

Examining Attorney:

Q: What were you doing on November 5?

A: I was in my dorm room with a professor.

Q: What was his name?

A: Professor Kingsfield.

Q: What were you doing?

A: We were smoking marijuana.

Q: What did you do after you smoked the marijuana?

A: I picked up this partially smoked marijuana cigarette that had been smoked by the professor.

Q: What did you do with it?

A: I placed it in an envelope, sealed the flap, wrote my name over the seal, and the date and the time.

Q: Why did you do that?

A: Well, I thought that someday Professor Kingsfield might be up for an appointment to the World Court, and maybe I'd be asked if he smoked pot.

Q: I am showing you what has been marked for identification as Exhibit No. 1. Do you recognize it?

A: I do.

Q: What is it?

A: It is the envelope on which I wrote my name and the date after putting in the marijuana cigarette.

Q: What did you do with this envelope, Exhibit No. 1?

A: I placed it in a box in my house in the attic.

Q: Where has Exhibit No. 1 been for the past year?

A: In that box in my house in the attic.

Q: Has the envelope been opened?

A: No, it has not.

Q: How do you know?

A: It is still sealed and has my name over the flap. The envelope is intact.

D. DEMONSTRATIVE/ILLUSTRATIVE EVIDENCE

Demonstrative/illustrative exhibits are not real evidence. However, they may involve issues relating to authenticity depending on the nature of the particular exhibit. Witnesses must be able to testify that they are familiar with or know that the information portrayed or contained in or on the exhibit is accurate. Illustrative aids that are plainly visible, including prepared diagrams and models, can be described by the witness. Exhibits such as a video recording, DVD, and computer generated demonstrative aids require a witness to establish that the image or information has been reviewed and is accurate. See Sections 8.7 and 8.8 for examples.

E. LIMITED PURPOSES

An exhibit, like any other form of evidence, may be admitted for a limited purpose. Federal Rule of Evidence 105 and similar state rules authorize evidence to be offered for a limited purpose. See Section 4.5(E). The contents of some exhibits may be admissible for one purpose but inadmissible for other purposes. In these situations, the offering lawyer should indicate the limited purpose the exhibit serves.

Example:

Presume the plaintiff artist has testified the injuries she sustained in an accident due to the defendant's negligence caused her to lose physical control over her arm and hand and she is now unable to draw freehand. A defense witness has testified he saw the plaintiff draw a sketch now being introduced as real evidence.

Defendant's Counsel:

Your Honor, I offer Exhibit No. 1.

The Court to Plaintiff's Counsel:

Do you have any objections?

Plaintiff's Attorney:

Not to the introduction of the creation of the drawing, Your Honor, but we do to its depiction of Your Honor that is quite . . . well Judge . . . very unflattering. May we have an instruction that Exhibit No. 1 is being offered for a limited purpose?

Judge:

Yes, you may. (To the jury): Members of the Jury, I am instructing you that Exhibit No. 1 is being offered for the limited purpose to show that Ms. Catherine of Bologna could draw freehand. The content of the sketch itself is not evidence in this case and should not be considered by you as such.

Example:

Presume the defendant consumer testified that she paid for repairs done to her Hard Candy Purple Sportster and she has identified a $497 repair bill, Exhibit No. 2, as the copy of the bill that she received marked "Paid."

Defendant's Counsel:

I offer Exhibit No. 2 into evidence for the limited purpose of proving that the defendant paid this bill.

Plaintiff's Attorney:

Objection, your Honor. This bill contains hearsay information that certain repairs were done on the defendant's motorcycle and is inadmissible.

Defendant's Counsel:

Your Honor, we don't offer the bill to prove the repairs were performed, but only to prove that the defendant paid money and received a receipt.

Judge:

Overruled. Exhibit No. 2 is received for that limited purpose.

F. REDACTING AN EXHIBIT

Some exhibit documents contain both admissible and inadmissible evidence. The examining attorney should offer only those parts of the documents that are clearly admissible. In jury trials, when the judge sustains an objection to part of a document, the ruling will require that the inadmissible portions of the document be redacted (removed) before the jurors see the document. The examining attorney may anticipate such objections and prepare an alternate exhibit, which does not contain the inadmissible statements. The alternate exhibit can be shown to the jury in lieu of the original document.

Example:

Examining Attorney:

Your Honor, we offer Exhibit No. 12 into evidence, which is a copy of the manuscript, *Paradise Lost in Law Studies: An Empirical Survey* written by John Milton XII. My client, the plaintiff, wrote comments in the margins that contain statements that are irrelevant to this case. Counsel for defendant has seen those comments and agrees with us they are inadmissible. We eliminated those comments from this exhibit.

Opposing Counsel:

Your Honor, we have no objection to the admissibility of Exhibit No. 12 with those comments removed.

Judge:

Exhibit No. 12 is received.

There are a number of ways that inadmissible portions of a document may be eliminated. If only a few words or phrases need to be redacted, they may be easily obliterated by using whiteout tape or a marking pen. If substantial portions of a document need to be deleted, those parts can be covered up with a piece of paper and a copy made of the document, or the document can be scanned, word processed, and edited. Emails, tweets, and social network communications may be edited to remove inadmissible contents. If the form of the document is unimportant, the admissible portion of the contents may be recreated on a blank page and that new document admitted into evidence. Whatever method is employed, jurors should only be allowed to see the admissible portions of the document. Taping a piece of paper over the inadmissible parts of a document is not wise because the jurors may be tempted in the jury room to peek under the taped portion.

Example:

Examining Attorney:

Your Honor, we offer Exhibit No. 7, a dental report prepared by the plaintiff's dentist, Doc Holliday, into evidence.

Opposing Counsel (At the Bench):

Your Honor, we object to the second and third sentence of the first paragraph of the report. Those sentences contain inadmissible hearsay because those statements were not made to the good Doctor for purposes of diagnosis or treatment.

Judge:

Sentences two and three of the first paragraph of Exhibit No. 7 are ruled inadmissible. The remainder of the exhibit is received into evidence. Counsel, before you may show this exhibit to the jurors, you must remove those two sentences.

Examining Attorney (At the Bench):

Yes, your Honor. We have redacted them on this copy.

Opposing Counsel (At the Bench):

Your Honor, we ask that the court instruct the jurors to disregard the removed portion of the dental record and that they not guess about what it contained.

Judge:

Members of the Jury, you will have the dental record of the plaintiff, but you are not to consider statements that were deleted. You are not to draw any inference or guess about what was deleted or why it was removed.

G. JUDICIAL DISCRETION

The judge or arbitrator has discretion in ruling on the admissibility and use of exhibits. This discretion is limited with real evidence. Since the admissibility of real evidence is determined as a matter of law, it is admissible if the proper foundation is made.

Discretion is broader in regard to demonstrative/illustrative evidence and visual aids. The determination is more one of fact than law regarding the admissibility of these types of exhibits. They will be permitted if the judge or arbitrator decides that the demonstrative evidence or visual aid assists the witness or helps the fact finder.

§ 8.5 INTRODUCTION OF EXHIBITS

A. LEGAL TERMINOLOGY

Many exhibits require the examiner to use precise legal terminology for their introduction and use. Specific questions, which are often technical and formalistic, must be asked to establish the proper foundation. Most witnesses would never be able to come up with these words by themselves, and so the attorney is allowed—and required in many situations—to state the foundation words in the form of leading questions. This "litany" of questions elicits the precise elements of foundation necessary for the introduction and use of exhibits and reduces the time a witness would need to testify to such matters if leading questions were not used. Other reasons may also justify the use of leading questions in laying the foundation for exhibits. See Section 7.7(B).

Examples:

Q: Is this photo a fair and accurate representation of the scene as you saw it on February 14, Ms. Valentine?

Q: Are these records made in the ordinary and regular course of your travel business, Mr. Gulliver?

Q: Is this musket in substantially the same condition as it was the day you first saw it at the scene of the shooting, Ms. Crockett?

B. STEPS FOR THE ADMISSIBILITY OF EXHIBITS

The introduction of exhibits requires several steps that must be mastered and committed to memory. The witness must provide testimony that establishes the necessary foundation for the particular exhibit. Specific illustrations of the foundation required for various types of exhibits appear in Section 8.6. While the precise steps vary among decision makers and differ among types of exhibits, the following directions provide a general format:

- Qualify the witness by laying the *foundation* to identify the exhibit.

- Make certain the exhibit has been pre-marked before the trial or hearing or before the witness testifies, or have the item *marked* as an exhibit during the examination.

- Ask permission from the judge or arbitrator to *approach the witness*. Many do not require this.

- *Show* the exhibit to opposing counsel (this step is not required because counsel has already seen the exhibit, but may be done as a matter of courtesy).

- Request that the witness *examine* and *recognize* the exhibit.

- Have the witness *identify* the exhibit.

- *Offer* the exhibit into evidence by referring to its exhibit number or letter.

- Provide *opposing counsel* the opportunity to *review* the exhibit if not done previously (counsel may want to make an objection and review the exhibit).

- *Respond to* any *objections* made by opposing counsel if necessary.

- Obtain a *ruling* from the judge or arbitrator on the record.

- If admitted, *show* the exhibit *to* the *fact finder* in an appropriate way.

ILLUSTRATION OF ADMISSIBILITY STEPS

Plaintiff's Examining Attorney:

Q: What is your name?

A: Ms. Little.

Q: Where were you last June 1 at 3 o'clock in the afternoon?

A: Out in the chicken yard.

Q: What happened?

1. *FOUNDATION*

A: A brick fell into my yard and nearly hit me.

Q: What did you do?

A: I picked it up.

Q: Why?

A: I thought the sky was falling.

Q: What did you do with the brick you had picked up?

A: I scratched my name on it with my claw.

2. *MARKED*

To the Court Reporter:

May I have this marked for identification as Exhibit No. 1?

Court Reporter:

Your exhibit has been marked for identification as Exhibit No. 1.

3. *APPROACH*

To the Court:

Your Honor, may I approach the witness?

Judge:

Yes, you may.

4. *SHOW TO OPPOSING COUNSEL*

Would you care to look at Exhibit No. 1?

Opposing Counsel:

No. I have already seen it.

5. *EXAMINE AND RECOGNIZE*

Q: I have just handed you an object marked for identification as Exhibit No. 1. Do you recognize it?

A: Yes.

Q: How?

A: I recognize the size and the shape and I recognize my name that I scratched on it with my claw.

6. *IDENTIFY*

Q: What is Exhibit No. 1?

A: The brick that fell in my yard last June 1.

Q: Is Exhibit No. 1 in the same condition as it was on June 1?

A: Yes.

7. & 8. OFFER AND REVIEW

To the Court:

Your Honor, at this time I offer Exhibit No. 1, and I am handing it to opposing counsel.

9.   RESPONSE

Opposing Counsel:

No objection, your Honor.

10.   RULING

Judge:

Exhibit No. 1 is admitted.

11. SHOW TO FACT FINDER

Plaintiff's Attorney:

May the brick be shown to the jurors?

Judge:

Yes. You may pass it to them.

Plaintiff's Attorney:

Your Honor, may I wait just a minute before I ask any further questions of this witness so the jurors can look at the exhibit?

Judge:

You may have just a short time, counsel, and then proceed.

The following paragraphs explain each of these steps in detail.

1.   Qualifying the Witness (Foundation)

Questions need to be asked of the witness to lay the foundation for the witness to identify the exhibit. The witness must testify that the witness saw the exhibit and is able to recognize it. Naming the exhibit or briefly describing it is usually sufficient.

Example:

Q: What happened after the conference?

A: I signed the pact, and I saw Prime Minister Chamberlain sign the pact.

Example:

Q: What did you see?

A: I saw the defendant, Ma Barker, holding the machine gun.

In these two examples, after the witness testifies to the existence of the evidence, the attorney can begin asking questions to introduce the exhibit.

---

2. Marking the Exhibit

Most exhibits will be pre-marked before the trial or hearing or before the witness testifies. Many judges require the attorneys to have all the exhibits marked by the court reporter or clerk before the start of the trial, and administrative judges and arbitrators typically ask the attorneys what exhibits they plan to introduce before the hearing and mark them at that time. In a situation where an exhibit is not pre-marked, the attorney can have the exhibit marked during the trial or hearing.

Exhibits will be marked either by a number or a letter. The practice among tribunals varies. In most forums, the exhibits are marked with consecutive numbers. In other forums, all of the plaintiff's exhibits are marked with numbers and the defendant's exhibits with letters. The person marking will know the proper system, and the attorney need not suggest whether a number or letter should be used. The judge or arbitrator or reporter will also usually maintain a list and keep track of the sequence of exhibits, and will know the next letter or number that should be used.

3. Approaching the Witness

Some judges and arbitrators require the attorney to request permission before approaching the witness with an exhibit. Some expect the attorney to seek such permission only with the first exhibit, or the first witness. Most do not require or expect the attorney to ask for such permission, because they recognize the attorney must approach the witness in order to show the exhibit to the witness. The attorney can ask the judge or arbitrator about the preferred practice if the attorney is uncertain whether a request should or need be made. See Section 3.5(D).

4. Showing to Opposing Counsel

There is no formal rule requiring that the exhibit be shown to opposing counsel at this point, and many advocates do not. However, as a matter of courtesy, some advocates will show the exhibit to counsel at this time. This assures what the exhibit is and avoids an interruption by opposing counsel who may want to be sure what exhibit is being used.

5.　Examination and Recognition of Exhibit by the Witness

The attorney needs to describe on the record (if there is one) the handing of the exhibit to the witness. The attorney should always refer to the number or letter marked on the exhibit to identify the exhibit for the record. There are a number of alternative phrases that may be used:

Examples:

I hand you what has been marked as Exhibit No. 6 for identification, Valentina Tereshkova.

I am handing you . . . Or, You have in your hands . . . Or, I've just handed you . . . I show you . . . Or, I am showing you . . .

Or, Here is . . . Or, oops, I dropped it.

The witness must recognize the exhibit and explain how the witness is able to do so.

Example:

Q:　Do you recognize Exhibit No. 6 for identification?

A:　Yes.

Q:　How?

A:　I wore these night vision goggles while on surveillance. They are the same size and shape. And my initials are on the strap.

Q:　Anything else?

A:　Oh, yes. They remind me of my years of service in the military.

Q:　You have our most profound and deepest gratitude.

Some judges require references to an exhibit not yet received in evidence include the phrase "marked for identification." Most judges consider this an unnecessary technicality and do not require the use of this phrase.

The attorney should not describe the exhibit that is being shown and should refer to it by its exhibit number or letter to avoid improperly leading the witness. Some exhibits may be generically described by counsel when handed to the witness: if it is obvious to everyone what the exhibit is, or if the identification of the exhibit is not in issue, or if leading questions are permissible.

Examples:

Q: I hand you what has been marked as Exhibit No. 6. Do you recognize this telescope, Mr. Galileo?

Q: Here is Exhibit No. 3. It is an iPad, Ms. Gates.

---

6. Identification of Exhibit by the Witness

The witness identifies the exhibit with a brief, accurate description.

Example:

Q: Please look at Exhibit C, Mr. Daguerre, and tell us what it is.

A: It is a photo I took of the cathedral of Notre Dame de Paris.

Example:

Q: Mr. Fitzgerald, what is Exhibit No. 3?

A: It is a letter I received from Zelda.

It is improper for the attorney to describe an exhibit that is not identifiable by sight or is an issue in controversy.

Example:

Examining Attorney:

Q: I show you Exhibit No. 1, which is a Bar Exam Interactive Fun Video game.

Opposing Counsel:

Objection, Counsel's testifying. There is no basis for that identification.

Arbitrator:

Objection sustained.

---

7. Offering the Exhibit into Evidence

The attorney must offer the exhibit into evidence. The attorney must refer to the exhibit by the assigned number or letter and direct the offer to the judge or arbitrator.

Examples:

Your Honor, I offer Exhibit No. 1 into evidence.

Respondent offers the computer disk marked as Exhibit E, Ms. Arbitrator.

The attorney should avoid using unnecessary words in making the offer, such as "I would like to offer into evidence" because it does not matter what the attorney "would like" to do. A short, simple declarative statement is sufficient: "I offer . . ." is enough.

8.   Examination of the Exhibit by Opposing Counsel

After the exhibit is offered by the proponent, the opposing attorney may object to its admission. The opposing attorney must usually wait until the proponent has offered the evidence before an objection regarding admissibility can be made, unless there is a reason for making an earlier objection. Early objections to an exhibit may be made through a motion in limine, or before the witness testifies, or before the exhibit is shown to the witness. The opposing attorney may also need to object to an exhibit if displaying it is unfairly prejudicial or otherwise objectionable, or if the examining attorney asks improper questions trying to lay a foundation for the introduction of a questionable exhibit.

Some attorneys show the exhibit to opposing counsel at the same time they offer the exhibit into evidence. The attorney may hand it to counsel if the examining attorney wants the opposing counsel to look at the exhibit, or if the opposing counsel wants to review the exhibit. The offering attorney may remark that counsel has been provided with an opportunity to previously see the exhibit. The attorneys will have seen the exhibits, and it may be unnecessary to physically show the exhibit to opposing counsel because of counsel's familiarity with the exhibit.

In some jurisdictions the exhibit may be shown to opposing counsel at an earlier stage of the offer. In some tribunals, the exhibit is shown to opposing counsel before it is shown to the witness. In these jurisdictions, it may be necessary for the examining attorney to show the exhibit to the opposing counsel before showing it to the witness. In other forums, the exhibit is shown to opposing counsel after it is shown to the witness but before it is offered in evidence. Whatever the requirements are in a jurisdiction, the examining attorney should follow them.

The nature and type of exhibit determine how and when opposing counsel can see the exhibit. Electronically stored information and digital evidence may not be readily observable before it is displayed during a case, and the lawyers will have had to review it ahead of time to make sure the evidence is admissible and to ascertain whether the computer or device that contains the information will properly and timely display it. All counsel will have had to review it before it is introduced to make certain it is the evidence that is to be introduced. This process requires trust by all parties that the proffering attorney will not attempt to introduce something that opposing counsel does not know about or has made objections to that the judge sustained.

9. Responding to Objections

The examining lawyer may need to respond to objections interposed by the opposing attorney to the introduction of the exhibit. The judge or arbitrator often rules immediately and overrules the objection without expecting any response from the offering lawyer. If a response is expected or if the examining lawyer believes the objection may be sustained, the advocate should ask to be heard and explain why the exhibit is admissible. If an objection is sustained, the examining lawyer should ask additional questions to remedy the evidentiary deficiency or make an offer of proof if the exhibit is excluded. See Section 4.5(B).

10. Ruling

The judge or arbitrator will make a ruling. Occasionally a decision maker will fail to rule on the admissibility of an exhibit. Advocates can and should insist on a ruling. If the exhibit is not received in evidence, it is not a part of the case, not a part of the record, and may not be used in final argument or as part of an appeal.

11. Showing the Exhibit to the Fact Finder

How an exhibit is shown to the fact finder depends upon the forum, the type of exhibit, the exhibit's importance to the case, how the attorney prefers to present the exhibit, and how the judge or arbitrator wants the exhibit presented. In bench trials, administrative hearings, and arbitrations, the judge or arbitrator may be able to easily and readily review the exhibit. In jury trials, a number of options may be available.

a. Tangible Objects

Objects that are large, easily seen or dangerous need not be handed directly to the jury. The jurors can see these tangible objects while the witness is on the witness stand. For example, it is sufficient for the jurors to see a gun from a distance, and it may be unnecessary or inappropriate for them to handle the gun.

Some tangible objects may need to be handled and individually seen by the jurors. Objects that are small or difficult to see from a distance may need to be shown to the jurors up close. If the actual weight of an object is in issue, or if the use or function of an object is in dispute, the jurors may need to handle the object.

i. *Documents*

There are a variety of ways a document may be shown to the jury. It may be:

- Read to the jury by the attorney or clerk (a neutral person),
- Passed among the jurors,
- Copied, with one copy distributed to each juror,
- Enlarged, placed on an easel, and explained by the witness,
- Displayed on a monitor screen, or
- Shown with relevant portions highlighted.

The attorney should decide which method will be the most effective and efficient and make arrangements for that distribution or display.

ii. *Photos and Videos*

Photos may be used for a variety of purposes. In automobile accident cases, photos of the scene, the automobiles, and injuries to the parties are common. A video recording of the day in the life of a severely disabled plaintiff may be shown. Photos of the scene of the crime are typical in criminal cases. Aerial photos may be used in condemnation proceedings. Drones may capture relevant scenes. Computer generated videos may display recreations of events with three dimensional, rotating views.

Photos and videos are usually demonstrative evidence, while some constitute real evidence. A recording of a bank robbery taken with a surveillance camera is actual evidence of facts in a case. A video taken by a helicopter camera depicts an event. A wearable or mountable camera captures videos of real life accidents and crimes.

The foundation for real or demonstrative photos and videos is usually the same. The witness' testimony that the photo or video accurately depicts what appears is sufficient to establish foundation. In some cases, a witness may have to testify as to how the video recording or presentation was made, if the making affects authenticity or accuracy.

iii. *Diagrams, Drawings, and Computer Displays*

A witness may use a prepared diagram or may create a freehand drawing on a whiteboard, on an easel paper using marking pens or on a computer or tablet screen using a mouse or light pen. While freehand drawings may be used because of time or financial constraints, prepared diagrams are more effective because few witnesses draw well.

iv. Visual Aids

During opening statement and summation, a lawyer may use a prepared chart of key facts, a list of damages, or a summary of evidence. This information may be presented on a board or a monitor screen.

In a jury trial, during final argument, an attorney may refer to an enlarged copy of the jury instructions or the verdict form, which are placed on an easel in front of the jury or shown on a monitor. During witness examination, the advocate may write key words of a witness' testimony or have an expert summarize opinions on a pad or monitor.

b. Displaying Exhibits

How long an exhibit is displayed depends upon the type of exhibit. Items of real evidence are usually left on counsel table or on the clerk's table during a case, unless their presence is unfairly prejudicial or otherwise objectionable or because of space limitations. Demonstrative evidence is displayed during the testimony of a witness who uses the exhibit. If an opposing counsel does not want the evidence or visual aid to be continually displayed, counsel may either physically move the exhibit, ask the examining lawyer to put the exhibit away, or ask permission to have the exhibit removed.

c. Attention of Fact Finders

The examining attorneys should provide the fact finders with sufficient time to understand, view or touch evidence before continuing with the examination of a witness or the introduction of other evidence. If an exhibit is being read by a judge or arbitrator or if jurors are reviewing exhibits, the attorney should delay continuing until the fact finders can devote their full attention to the additional evidence. Some judges may limit or not permit a delay in testimony for jurors to examine an exhibit.

C. OTHER WAYS ADMITTING EXHIBITS

1. Stipulations

Advocates may stipulate to the foundation of an exhibit to avoid the need to ask detailed questions during the case and may agree on the procedures to be used in presenting exhibits. Stipulations can significantly reduce trial and hearing time and should be voluntarily entered into between counsel if there is no real dispute concerning the authenticity or accuracy of the exhibits. Counsel will usually prefer to stipulate to the admissibility of exhibits, particularly those with difficult foundation requirements, in cases where both lawyers have similar exhibits to introduce, including, for example, social network or computer data evidence.

Judges in bench trials and arbitrators encourage or expect certain types of evidence to be admitted by stipulation. For example, hospital records will often be entered into evidence by stipulation because these records are usually reliable. A prepared stipulation should be introduced during the trial or hearing, or an oral agreement summarized on the record. In jury trials, the offering attorney must request permission to introduce the stipulation by reading it or have someone read the stipulation. Stipulations are more common and expected in civil cases, and less so in criminal cases when the defense insists that the prosecution prove all elements for the introduction of an exhibit.

Example:

Claimant's Attorney:

Ms. Arbitrator, at this time I offer Exhibit No. 13. It is a print duplicate of a GiveMeHope email lyric sent between the parties on May 30, the admissibility of which both Respondent's counsel and I have agreed to through stipulation.

Arbitrator (To Counsel for Respondent):

Is that correct, counsel?

Respondent's Counsel:

Yes, your Honor.

Arbitrator:

Exhibit No. 13 is received.

Even when opposing counsel are likely to be cooperative and agree to stipulate to the admission of exhibits, there are occasions when laying the foundation is advantageous and may be important for persuasive foundation. In these situations, counsel should ask questions that establish a complete foundation for the exhibits. Counsel may need to reject a proffered stipulation from the other side or resist the urgings of the judge or arbitrator to accept such a stipulation. In rejecting a stipulation, the examiner must decide that laying the foundation is strategically necessary for its persuasive value.

2. Pleadings, Admissions, and Discovery Responses

Pleadings and discovery documents are a part of the case but are not considered as evidence by the fact finder unless or until an attorney affirmatively offers such information as evidence during the case. The evidence may be offered during the direct or cross-examination of the witness who originally provided the information, or may be read directly during the offering party's case in chief or on cross-examination.

Example:

Plaintiff's Attorney:

Your Honor, we offer Exhibit No. 1, the letter containing the libelous statement made by the defendant about Oscar Wilde. The authenticity of the letter was admitted in Defendant's Answer, paragraph three, making it admissible.

Example:

Defendant's Counsel:

Your Honor, I offer Exhibit No. 25. It's an electronic copy of the home page of the Beatles vs. Rolling Stones Website relevant to this case. Plaintiff admitted to its authenticity in a discovery admission that appears in Plaintiff's Response to Defendant's Request for Admissions No. 4.

3. Abbreviating the Foundation

When there is a series of exhibits for which the foundations are similar, the attorney may abbreviate the process of laying foundation after the first few exhibits have been introduced. The attorney can ask the witness whether the response given to the foundation questions for the previous exhibits would be essentially the same for subsequent exhibits. Once the judge or arbitrator and opposing attorney know the attorney is prepared to present an extensive foundation, the evidence may not be necessary or may prompt a stipulation regarding admissibility.

Example:

Presume the witness has testified that she seized ten items from the defendant's airplane hangar and that she used a marker to identify each item.

Examining Attorney:

Q: I am showing you what we have already marked for identification as Exhibit No. 1. Do you recognize it?

A: Yes.

Q: How do you recognize it?

A: I recognize it because I marked my initials and the date on the fuselage.

Q: What is Exhibit No. 1 for identification?

A: It's the drone I found in the defendant's Kitty Hawk hangar.

Q: Where did you first see Exhibit No. 1?

A: I saw this staggering discovery in the defendant's hanger.

Q: When did you put the markings on it?

A: At the time I seized it from the defendant, Mr. Wright.

To the Court:

Your Honor, we offer Exhibit No. 1.

Judge:

With no objection, it is received.

Examining Attorney:

Q: I show you Exhibit No. 2. What is it?

A: It's a photo of the first drone I also found in the hanger.

Q: What did you do next?

A: I was flabbergasted, of course. I placed my initials and date on the back.

Q: Are those your initials on Exhibit No. 2 with the date you discovered it?

A: Yes.

To the Court:

Your Honor, we offer Exhibit No. 2.

Judge:

Received.

Examining Attorney:

Q: I hand you Exhibit No. 3. What is it?

A: It's an unopened bottle of champagne.

Q: Is that also an exhibit you found in the defendant's hangar and marked in the same way as Exhibits No. 1 and 2?

A: Yes.

And so on with the following seven exhibits.

---

4. Self-Authenticating Documents

Some exhibits are self-authenticating. Federal Rule of Evidence 902 and similar state rules make it unnecessary to introduce evidence authenticating these exhibits:

- Domestic public documents under seal.

- Domestic public documents not under seal.

- Foreign public documents.

- Certified paper or electronic duplicates of public documents.

- Official publications issued by public authorities.

- Newspapers and periodicals.

- Trade inscriptions.

- Acknowledged and notary public documents.

- Commercial paper and related documents.

After the attorney establishes that an exhibit falls into one of these categories, the attorney need not introduce any other evidence to establish its authenticity. The exhibit may be offered, unless some other evidence rule has not been met.

Example:

Examining Attorney:

I offer Exhibit No. 5 for identification into evidence. It is a computer disk officially distributed by the government. The disk has the trade name "X-Files" inscribed with "The Truth is out there." This exhibit is self-authenticating.

Arbitrator:

It is received, Ms. Scully.

---

§ 8.6   ELEMENTS OF EVIDENTIARY FOUNDATION

The necessary evidentiary foundation questions vary from exhibit to exhibit but, typically, responses are sought that establish the exhibit's existence, identity, authenticity, and completeness or accuracy. The following checklists of foundation elements and examples demonstrate the legal grounds for introducing various exhibits.

A. PHYSICAL OBJECTS AND PROPERTIES (PRODUCTS, CLOTHING, APPLIANCES, WEAPONS)

To admit a tangible object into evidence, the following elements must be proved:

- The exhibit is relevant to the case.

- The witness recognizes and can identify the exhibit.

- The witness can recall what the exhibit looked like at the previous relevant time.

- The exhibit is now in the same or substantially the same condition as when the witness saw it at the previous relevant time.

Example:

Examining Attorney:

Q: When you entered the Borden house, where did you go?

A: The bedroom.

Q: What did you see?

A: I saw an axe.

Q: Where was it?

A: On the floor.

Q: What did you do?

A: I picked it up carefully.

Q: Why?

A: Because it was covered with blood.

Q: Was there anything else you noticed about the axe?

A: Yes, it had a chip on the handle.

Q: What did you do with it?

A: I bagged it and marked the bag with my police ID. Then I took it with me to the police department and put it in my evidence locker.

Q: How long was it there?

A: Until today.

Q: What did you do with it today?

A: I took it out of the evidence locker and brought it to court.

Q: Officer, I have just removed from the bag and placed on the table in front of you what I have had marked as State's Exhibit No. 1. Do you recognize it?

A: Yes. It's the axe.

Q: How do you recognize it?

A: I recognize the chip on the handle, the size, and the red stain.

Q: What is it?

A: It is the same axe I found in the living room of the Borden house.

Q: Does it appear to be in the same condition as it was when you picked it up?

A: Yes, except the red stain is now dry.

To the Court:

Your Honor, I offer State's Exhibit No. 1 into evidence.

B. DOCUMENTS (ELECTRONIC DOCUMENTS, CONTRACTS, DIGITAL DATA, LEASES, SIGNED OR PRINTED DOCUMENTS)

To admit documents into evidence the following elements must be proved:

- The document is relevant to the case.

- The document was composed on a computer accessible by password, contains a signature and was handwritten, printed, or bears other identifying characteristics.

- The electronic or handwritten signature, handwriting, composition, or characteristic belongs to or identifies a person.

  — The witness saw the person sign, write, or compose the document; or

  — The witness knows, is familiar with, or can recognize the characteristic; or

  — The witness recognizes and can identify the content; or

  — The witness is a party and admits signing, writing, or composing it; or

  — A handwriting expert states that the signature or writing is by a certain person or that the document can be identified by its characteristics; or

  — A computer expert states that the document was created on a computer accessible to or used by the relevant person; or

  — A qualified witness can testify to the process and system that was used to create, store, and produce the information; or

— The document contains unique characteristics or distinctive information.

- The document is authentic.

- The document is an original or an admissible duplicate or other reliable copy.

- The document is now in exactly the same or substantially the same condition (if exactness is not required) as when it was made and has not been altered.

Example (Signed Document):

Examining Attorney:

Q: Tell us your name please.

A: John Hancock.

Q: Where were you on July 4, 1776?

A: I was in Constitution Hall in Philadelphia.

Q: Why were you there?

A: To attend a meeting of the signing of the Declaration of Independence.

Q: Did you see the document being signed?

A: Yes.

Q: Whom did you see sign the Declaration?

A: Some other founding fathers and myself.

Q: Would you recognize the Declaration if you saw it again?

A: Yes.

Q: How?

A: By my signature on it, and I remember the words of the document.

Q: I have just given you what has been marked for identification as Exhibit No. 4. Do you recognize it?

A: Yes.

Q: How?

A: I recognize the words and I recognize my signature.

Q: Your signature is rather large, isn't it?

A: Yes.

Q: How come?

A: I was feeling particularly revolutionary that day.

Q: Tell us please, what is Exhibit No. 4?

A: It is the same Declaration of Independence that I signed on July 4, 1776.

Q: Has it been changed or altered in any way?

A: No.

To the Court:

Your Honor, I offer Exhibit No. 4.

Example (Contract):

Examining Attorney:

Q: You said you entered into a contract for employment as a first year associate?

A: Yes, I did.

Q: How was that contract created?

A: Brachman, the senior partner of the firm, sent me an email that detailed the terms of the contract, including the starting salary.

Q: How much was the starting salary?

A: $199,999.99 a year.

Q: Did you accept the contract terms?

A: Oh, yes. Quite happily.

Q: I have just handed you what I have marked for identification as Exhibit No. 5. It is a printed document. Do you recognize it?

A: Yes, I do.

Q: How do you recognize it?

A: It's the email I received from Brachman, the senior partner, which contained the contract terms and salary.

Q: How do you know it's from Brachman?

A: It has his email address; it refers to terms he and I had previously discussed in person; it has the law firm's information; and it's in the same format as other emails I received from him.

Q: What is his email address?

A: Brachman@lalaw.com

Q: What did you do after you received this email?

A: I immediately replied that I accepted the terms and position as a first year associate, and then I went to celebrate.

Q: Did you later determine that your reply was sent to Brachman?

A: Yes.

Q: How did you do that?

A: I reviewed the "sent" folder in my system and saw it had been sent to him.

Q: Did you also learn whether the email you sent was opened?

A: Yes, I received a "read receipt" reply that same day when the email was sent.

Q: Have there been any changes to this email since you accepted it?

A: No.

Q: What is Exhibit No. 5?

A: It's the contract that I agreed to last year on April 18.

To the Arbitrator:

I offer Exhibit No. 5.

C. PERSONAL AND BUSINESS CORRESPONDENCE (LETTERS, MEMOS, NOTES, FILES, BILLS, MAIL)

Personal or business correspondence has similar foundation requirements as legal documents. A witness may recognize the writing, signature, or content of the document. Some business correspondence may require additional foundation evidence to prove it was sent or received. In these instances, the additional elements include:

- The correspondence was addressed or routed to a person.

- The witness saw or signed the original, duplicate original, or an authentic copy.

- The witness placed the correspondence in an accurately addressed delivery envelope; or sent the message through an email account to a current email address; or the witness supervised a person who in the normal course of business mailed or otherwise sent it.

- The envelope was placed in a mailbox or given to a private delivery carrier; or the message was sent through the regular email network; or the witness supervised a person who in the normal course of business sends such correspondence.

- The copy of the original is an accurate duplicate.

- The original correspondence was received by the addressee or never returned to the sender.

Example (Correspondence):

Examining Attorney:

Q: Ms. Heloise, do you know a man by the name Abelard?

A: Yes.

Q: How do you know him?

A: We have been quite good friends.

Q: How long?

A: We met twenty years ago. Then I went into a convent and he went into a monastery.

Q: How was your relationship continued?

A: Through correspondence over twenty years.

Q: How often did you correspond?

A: Frequently. Often on a weekly basis.

Q: Did you write to him?

A: Yes.

Q: Did he write to you?

A: Yes.

Q: Can you recognize his signature?

A: Of course.

Q: How?

A: Well, I had seen him sign his name before I went into the convent, and I received hundreds and hundreds of his handwritten notes over the past twenty years.

Q: I have just given you a piece of paper with handwriting on it which I have had marked for identification as Exhibit No. 1. Do you recognize it?

A: Yes.

Q: How do you recognize it?

A: By the signature, Abelard, handwriting, and by the date. And I recall the poetry.

Q: What is it?

A: The last love note I received from Abelard.

To the Court:

Your Honor, I offer Exhibit No. 6.

Example (Business Documents):

Examining Attorney:

Q: Tell us your name.

A: Colonel Tom Parker.

Q: For whom did you work?

A: Elvis Presley.

Q: What did you do?

A: I was his business manager.

Q: You are holding a paper that has been marked for identification as Exhibit No. 3. Do you recognize it?

A: Yes, I do.

Q: How do you recognize it?

A: I typed it, and I remember the words. These are my initials on the bottom, and I recognize Mr. Presley's signature.

Q: How?

A: I have seen him sign his name hundreds of times.

Q: What is Exhibit No. 3?

A: It is the letter suggesting a personal interview that I prepared for Elvis Presley which he signed and I mailed.

Q: Do you remember what you did with that letter that you prepared after it had been signed by Elvis?

A: Yes. I mailed it.

Q: How did you mail the letter?

A: I placed it in an envelope and sealed the envelope.

Q: Did the envelope have any writing on it?

A: Yes.

Q: What was the writing?

A: It was addressed to: Publisher, National Enquirer, Eden, MN 55347.

Q: Do you know how the address got on there?

A: Yes.

Q: How?

A: I wrote it on myself before I placed the letter in it.

Q: What did you do next?

A: I licked the stamp and put it in the upper right-hand corner.

Q: Then what did you do?

A: I walked outside to a U.S. postal service mailbox.

Q: Then what?

A: I dropped it in the mailbox and went back to work.

Q: Did you ever get the envelope and letter returned to you?

A: No. Never.

To the Court:

Your Honor, I offer Exhibit No. 3.

Example (Oral Contract Reduced to Print):

Examining Attorney:

Q: On March 19, Sir, did you receive a phone call around 16:00 hours?

A: Yes.

Q: Did the caller give any form of identification?

A: Yes. She identified herself.

Q: What did the caller say?

A: The caller said she was calling from D.C. where she worked for the husband of the President. She said that the First Gentleman had a hobby workshop in the basement of the White House and he wanted to start whittling carbon fiber replicas of the Presidents.

Q: Did she say anything else?

A: Yes. She said she wanted to order a digital force power titanium implanter.

Q: What do you do for a living, sir?

A: I manufacture hammers.

Q: What did you do next?

A: I told her I needed an order, preferably done on our website, from the person ordering the goods from my company.

Q: Did you ever receive such an order?

A: Yes. Our company received a website order for a hammer with an email name and address bearing information from the White House.

Q: Showing what is marked for identification as Claimant's Exhibit No. 1, do you recognize it?

A: Yes, I do.

Q: How do you recognize it?

A: Well, it has a White House logo, and it reads that it's from the office of the First Gentleman and contains an electronic signature with the name of the First Gentleman.

Q: Anything else?

A: Yes. It is an order for a digital force power titanium implanter for $997.

Q: How did you obtain this document, marked for identification as Claimant's Exhibit 1?

A: I made a printed copy of the email order.

Q: After you received the email order, what did you do?

A: I sent an email reply confirming the order.

Q: Handing you what is marked for identification as Claimant's Exhibit No. 2, do you recognize that?

A: It's a printed email reply that confirmed the hammer order.

Q: How do you recognize it?

A: It's exactly what I emailed in reply to the order, and it has the confirmation number: 1600.

To the Arbitrator:

We offer Claimant's Exhibits No. 1 and 2.

Arbitrator:

Received.

Examining Attorney:

Q: What did you do after that?

A: Well, our company staff worked creatively for a couple weeks and came up with a modified hammer model. We packaged this hammer in a designer container and included a bill for $997.

Q: How was the package delivered?

A: I addressed the package to the First Gentleman at the White House and completed the Express Delivery form. Then I put it in the "Delivery" box on my desk.

Q: What is the pick up and delivery procedure in your office?

A: Our company procedure is that all packages are picked up periodically by our messenger. She goes through all the offices, picks up everything from the "Delivery" boxes and sends them.

Q: Did you ever notice in your "Delivery" basket that the package was no longer there?

A: Yes, I did. Later that same day, the basket was empty.

Q: I am showing you what has been marked for identification as Claimant's Exhibit No. 3. Do you recognize this?

A: Yes, I do.

Q: How?

A: By its contents.

Q: What is it?

A: This Exhibit is a duplicate of the bill that I sent to the First Gentleman along with the hammer.

Q: Who made the duplicate?

A: I did. I had prepared this bill on our computer database system, and in preparation for this trial, I printed a duplicate of the bill from our computer database.

Q: How else do you recognize this bill?

A: The $997 amount and terms are the same as the bill I had prepared and placed in the package that was sent to the First Gentleman.

To the Arbitrator:

Claimant offers Exhibit No. 3.

D. ELECTRONIC BUSINESS AND PERSONAL CORRESPONDENCE (EMAILS, TEXT MESSAGES, BLOG ENTRIES, CHAT ROOM COMMENTS, WEB COMMUNICATIONS)

Courts have developed foundation requirements for electronically stored information including emails and other digital documents. These foundation elements include:

- The message was addressed to a certain person.

- The message was sent electronically to that person.

- The message was received by that person, or the system used to send the message operated properly, or the system receiving the email verified the message was received.

- The duplicate of the message introduced is an accurate copy.

Other foundation elements may include:

- The receiver acknowledged receiving the email.

- The receiver sent back a reply.

- The receiver forwarded a copy of the email.

- The sender and receiver communicated about the contents.

- Meta-data of the email establishes that it was received.

Example (List Serve Messages):

Examining Attorney:

Q: Are you a member of a club?

A: Yes.

Q: What club?

A: The Long Distance Ironbutt MC Riders.

Q: Does the group have a list serve?

A: It does.

Q: What is the list serve?

A: It's a way that members can communicate with each other about topics of mutual interest regarding endurance riding.

Q: Are you an Ironbutt list serve member?

A: Indeed, I am.

Q: How does it operate?

A: We basically send emails to other members, and all members who are registered for the service receive those emails, and can read them and reply.

Q: How long have you been a list serve participant?

A: Over 3 years.

Q: How often do you read list serve messages?

A: Very frequently.

Q: Did you receive a list serve email relating to a party in this case last July?

A: I did. I got an email from TooFast. He's an Ironbutt member and a regular contributor to the list serve.

Q: How do you know?

A: I am a friend of TooFast, and know him personally. And I see his messages routinely on the list serve.

Q: How do you know the messages are from him?

A: They have his trademark electronic signature, and over the years, I've talked to him about some of his messages.

Q: Please view the monitor for what has been marked as Exhibit No. 11, and tell us what it is.

A: I see the message TooFast sent to me and other Ironbutt members.

Q: How do you know?

A: It has my email address on the "To" line, and the subject line reads "Coast to Coast Nonstop." I remember it really well because I was shocked.

Q: Why was that?

A: I didn't think that TooFast could do that ride in less than 50 hours, as the message boasted.

To the Arbitrator:

I offer Exhibit No. 11.

E. INTERNET COMMUNICATIONS AND INFORMATION (WEBSITES, SOCIAL NETWORKS, SEARCH ENGINE DATA, INTERNET ARCHIVES, CLOUD SERVER DATA)

Foundation requirements for electronically stored, created, and produced information on the Internet include:

- The party or witness is the owner of the website or is otherwise responsible for its contents.

- The witness entered the website URL in a reputable search engine and the website was accessed.

- The witness logged on and reviewed the relevant information on the website.

- The exhibit accurately reflects the contents of what the witness reviewed (the exhibit could be a print out, a hard copy, or displayed on a monitor screen or other display).

The possibility exists that the website information had been manipulated and is not authentic or accurate. The opposing party can offer evidence challenging the contents or claiming a hacker created or tampered with the information. In determining these challenges, decision makers consider whether:

- The information is still on the website.

- Other sources prove or disprove the website contents.

- Others saw or relied on the website contents.

- The information is consistent with the website purposes.

- The information is otherwise published or republished.

- Meta-data proves the information was on the website.

Example (Website):

Examining Attorney:

Q: How did you first learn about the defendant's business?

A: From her website.

Q: How did you locate her website?

A: I used a search engine, Google, to find businesses that sold cakes and confectioneries on line. I came across her Razzle Dazzle site.

Q: What do you recall about her website?

A: I especially remember that it listed a testimonial from me.

Q: On the laptop in front of you, please search for the Razzle Dazzle website.

A: Ok . . . here it is.

Q: Please describe what is displayed on the large monitor.

A: That is the Razzle Dazzle website.

Q: How do you know that?

A: It obviously says Razzle Dazzle, and I recognize it because it's the same website I first saw.

Q: How did you locate the testimonial you mentioned earlier?

A: I clicked the "Reviews" window and saw it.

Q: Please do what you had previously done.

A: Alright . . . there it is. That's what I had read last year.

Q: Is that statement exactly the same as you first read it last year?

A: It's identical.

To the Arbitrator:

We submit an exact printed duplicate of the display shown on the website screen as Respondent's Exhibit A.

Arbitrator: Received.

To the Arbitrator:

Respondent requests that the witness read the testimonial review as it appears on the website screen.

Arbitrator: He may do so.

A: It reads: "At best, the so-called 'squishy substance' snack was tastier than the Wall-E Twinkie might have tasted."

F. BUSINESS RECORDS (MEMORANDA, REPORTS, WRITINGS, ELECTRONIC FILES, DATA COMPILATIONS)

Records maintained in the ordinary course of business may be introduced through a witness who does not have personal knowledge of the recorded information but does have personal knowledge concerning the business recording process. The introduction of this type of relevant information is allowed through the foundation elements detailed in Fed.R.Evid. 803(6) and similar state rules. The term "business" includes any business, hospital, institution, organization, association, profession, occupation, and nonprofit. The content of "records" includes facts, events, conditions, opinions, or conclusions. The elements to be proved include:

- The report must have been "made at or near the time" of the occurrence which gave rise to the report.

- The record was made by "a person with knowledge" of the information or was made "from information transmitted by" a person with knowledge.

- The record was made "in the regular practice of that business activity."

- The record was kept "in the course of a regularly conducted business activity."

- The witness is the "custodian" of the documents or a "qualified witness."

Example (Medical Records):

Examining Attorney:

Q: What is your name, sir?

A: Carla Espinosa.

Q: Where do you work?

A: Scrubs Hospital Clinics.

Q: What is your current job?

A: I am the medical records librarian.

Q: As a medical records librarian, what do you do?

A: I am the custodian in charge of all the records at Scrubs.

Q: Do you have a staff working for you?

A: Yes. They all work at my direction and control.

Q: Do you have a policy in your hospital concerning the making of records?

A: Yes, we do.

Q: What is that policy?

A: All medical records must have been made at or near the time of the occurrence of the information contained in them. The record must be made by a person with knowledge of the information or from information given to that person by someone with knowledge.

Q: I am showing you what has been already marked for identification as Exhibit No. 23. Tell us what it is.

A: Yes, these are medical records obtained from our medical records library of a patient with the patient number 2345, which corresponds with the name Denise Mahoney.

Q: Are these records kept under your control?

A: Yes.

Q: You reviewed these records?

A: Yes.

Q: Reviewing these records, did you determine whether these records were made at or near the time of the occurrence of the listed information.

A: Yes, they were.

Q: How do you know that?

A: The different occurrences are dated and timed and the time the information was recorded is also dated. My examination of both the records and the notes shows that they were made at or near the time of the occurrences.

Q: Looking at these records, can you determine whether the records were made by a person who had knowledge of the record information?

A: Yes, I can.

Q: How?

A: In each of these cases the person making the record was a doctor, and the doctor was assigned to the case by patient name and number.

Q: Are these records kept in the course of the regularly conducted business of your hospital?

A: Yes, they are.

Q: Was this record made in the course of a regularly conducted hospital and clinical activity?

A: Yes, it was.

To the Court:

I offer Exhibit No. 23.

Computer data may readily qualify as business records. When computer records will not initially qualify as business records, additional foundational questions relating to the input, storage, and retrieval methods of the computer system and its reliability will be necessary. Decision makers generally permit these exhibits to be admitted unless there exists a genuine issue regarding their authenticity or unfairness regarding their admission or unless there are issues regarding accuracy, hacking, tampering, or unreliability.

Example (Computer Data):

Examining Attorney:

Q: Ms. Mandarin, at Guangzhou Fidelity Company has it been the regular practice that a person with knowledge of the data enters that information in your computer database?

A: Yes.

Q: As custodian of your Fidelity's computer records are you familiar with the method of entry, storage, and retrieval of data in the system?

A: Yes, I am.

Q: Is that system reliable?

A: Yes.

Q: How do you know it is reliable?

A: We have established reliability protocols that meet or exceed the standards established by the ITU—the International Transmission UN Agency—and the ATM Forum—the asynchronous transfer mode industry consortium.

Q: Are there safeguards that detect and correct systemic errors

A: There are.

Q: Does the computer produce reliable retrieved data?

A: Yes.

Q: Is the information necessary for notices of delinquent accounts programmed into the computer at or near the time invoices are emailed?

A: Yes, on the first working day of each month.

Q: Do you know Fidelity's procedure for keeping records of the delinquent accounts and its notifying customers in default in March, 2015?

A: Yes.

Q: Please explain those default and notification procedures.

A: The data reflecting all activity on the account are verified by a staff person. Then the verified data is keyed into the terminal and copied on a hard drive. Every working day the processor merges the new data with the information already on the accounts record for the month. The computer, by the 15th of the month, finds all accounts not currently paid. To find these accounts, the computer uses instructions from a program to search and identify delinquent accounts. As instructed, the computer produces these accounts. This data is held five days. If the account is paid up within that time, no additional interest is assessed; but additional interest is assessed if the account remains unpaid. As programmed, all the accounts, delinquent or otherwise, are put into monthly statements. Using the program, the computer produces the statement for each Fidelity account, confirms the next payment's due date, and forwards this data to our email system where it is transferred electronically to individual accounts and then sent to individual account holders. Millions of accounts are handled monthly.

Q: What steps does Fidelity take to ensure the computer finds and identifies delinquent accounts so accurate notices of default notify customers?

A: Special control procedures are built into the system. Transcriptions of data are verified by two different terminal operators. Accounts identified as unpaid by the 15th are rechecked. If these accounts remain unpaid during the next five days, notices are produced and included with the proper email statement. Our data system re-verifies the accuracy of this information.

Q: Here is Exhibit No. 8. It's labeled a delinquency notice and it's attached to a Fidelity statement. What is this document?

A: It's Charles Ponzi's delinquency notice.

Q: How do you recognize it?

A: This is a duplicate of the statement on our computer system.

Q: Was this duplicate made in the regular course of business?

A: Yes.

Q: Was this notice and statement prepared by the computer system you have described for us this afternoon?

A: Yes.

Q: Is the information on Exhibit No. 8 correct?

A: It is correct for the date stated.

To the Arbitrator:

I offer Respondent's Exhibit No. 8.

Opposing Counsel:

Your Honor, may I examine the witness for the purpose of laying a foundation for an objection?

Arbitrator:

Yes, you may.

Opposing Counsel:

Q: Ms. Mandarin, Exhibit No. 8 was completed on March 20, 2015, correct?

A: Yes.

Q: You did not yourself make any data entry on this statement from which Exhibit No. 8 was made, did you?

A: No. The accounts receivable operators and the computer system read the data, and the computer program carries out the accounting procedure.

Q: Does the computer itself read documents like the statement, Exhibit No. 8?

A: Only if the computer is equipped with an optical scanner.

Q: But your computer does not have such a scanner, does it?

A: It does not for this purpose.

Q: So your computer cannot read this statement, can it?

A: No, only the data stored on the disk.

Q: How often does the computer store account information?

A: Daily, but only on accounts that have had activity. The transcription of daily activity is run through the system to merge with the last cumulative drive. The computer, by program, performs the necessary accounting on active accounts and updates the database.

To the Arbitrator:

We object. Exhibit No. 8 is unreliable hearsay. The witness admits no personal knowledge of input or retrieval.

Arbitrator:

Overruled. This is a business record produced in the regular course of Claimant's financial business. Exhibit No. 8 is received.

G. COPIES/DUPLICATES

Modern copying, reproduction, and computer equipment creates accurate copies of original documents and records. These "duplicate" originals are admissible. However, the original may be the most persuasive and, if available, should be offered to prove its content. See Fed.R.Evid. 1002. A duplicate original may be routinely admitted unless it is of questionable authenticity or it would be unfair to admit a copy. See Fed.R.Evid. 1003. A copy may also be admissible if the original has been lost or destroyed, or is in the possession of the opponent, or is otherwise not obtainable. See Fed.R.Evid. 1004.

Example:

The witness has testified that he saw and read the original agreement.

Examining Attorney:

Q: Brother Timothy, I am showing you Exhibit No. VII. Do you recognize it?

A: Yes.

Q: What is it?

A: It's a duplicate of the rental agreement for the abbey.

Q: How do you know?

A: I recognize the names and terms. It has my signature on it as well.

Q: How was this duplicate made?

A: Immediately after we both signed the lease, I saw the land baron scan and produce this duplicate that he handed me. I brought this lease home and put it in the abbey vault.

Q: Has it changed in any way?

A: No.

Q: Is this the lease, Exhibit No. VII, that you removed from your vault?

A: Yes.

To the Court:

Your Honor, I offer Exhibit No. VII.

H. ELECTRONIC RECORDINGS (AUDIO, VIDEO, DIGITAL, COMPUTER RECORDINGS)

The elements to establish a foundation for the introduction of recordings are:

- The electronic recording is relevant to the case.

- The operator was qualified to run the equipment.

- The recording equipment was checked before its use and operated normally.

- The witness heard or saw the event being recorded.

- After the event had been recorded, the witness reviewed the device and determined that it had accurately and completely recorded the event.

- The witness can recognize and identify the sounds or images on the recording.

- The recording is in the exact same condition at the time of trial or hearing as it was at the time of the recording.

Example (Video Event):

Examining Attorney:

Q: Sheriff, where were you on the 24th day of November, 1963?

A: I was in the Dallas jail.

Q: Where in the Dallas jail?

A: I was in the basement garage by the exit ramp.

Q: What did you see?

A: I saw a man I later learned was Jack Ruby point a gun in the direction of Lee Harvey Oswald and shoot at him.

Q: Sheriff, I have given you a video recording that has been marked for identification as Defense Exhibit No. 155. Do you recognize it?

A: Yes, I do.

Q: How do you recognize it?

A: Well, I wrote my initials on the label of the recording that I saw before coming into this courtroom today. After I saw it, I also wrote my initials on a card that indicates that I have seen the recording.

Q: What is on the recording?

A: It's a recording of what I just described . . . of the shooting I saw on the 24th day of November in 1963.

Q: Is this video a complete and accurate representation of what you saw?

A: Yes, it is.

To the Court:

I offer Defense Exhibit No. 155.

Example (Sound Recording):

Examining Attorney:

Q: Mr. Jagger, what do you do for a living?

A: I install electronic digital sound recording devices with my partner, Mr. Richards, all over the world.

Q: Have you ever installed sound recording devices in corporate offices?

A: Yes, I have, as well as for royalty.

Q: Where have you installed recording devices?

A: In the First National Bank in New York.

Q: Why did you do so?

A: At the direction of the head of security, a Ms. Marshall.

Q: Where did you do the installation?

A: In the office of an employee, Teresa Doolittle.

Q: What did that consist of?

A: I set up a secret electronic digital recording device in her desk. I put the receiving device in another room.

Q: Did you ever test the device?

A: Yes, I did.

Q: How did you do that?

A: I started the recording equipment in her office when she was conducting a meeting. After one hour, I stopped the recording to verify it was operating properly.

Q: How did you do that?

A: I listened to the one-hour conversation that I had just digitally recorded.

Q: Whose voice did you recognize on the recording?

A: I recognized the distinctive voice of Ms. Doolittle.

Q: Did you later record another event in her office?

A: Yes.

Q: What did you do with that recording?

A: I created an electronic file for it, marked with my name and date, and secured it in password-protected server, where it has been until I downloaded a duplicate on a USB drive that I brought with me to court today.

Q: Did you listen to the recording before you came in here?

A: Yes.

Q: Whose voices are there?

A: There is only one voice.

Q: Whose voice is it?

A: The USB drive just contains the voice of Ms. Doolittle, as she was talking to others on her cell phone, and then singing to herself.

Q: Have you made any additions or subtractions or changes to that recording, or tampered with it in any way?

A: No I haven't.

Q: You have in your hand State's Exhibit No. 23. Do you recognize it?

A: Yes, that's the recorded jump drive.

Q: How do you recognize it?

A: I marked it with the identifying character "Jack" and placed it in a secure USB case I carried with me to court.

Q: What did you do with it?

A: I unlocked the case in chambers before trial started today, then gave the flash drive to you.

To the Court:

I offer Exhibit No. 23. Counsel, this is the recording that we gave to you in discovery before this trial started.

Judge:

Exhibit 23 is received.

Examining Attorney:

Q: May I play relevant parts of the recording at this time, your Honor?

A: Yes, you may.

I.   TEST RESULTS (DNA, MRI EXAMS, CT SCANS, MEDICAL IMAGES, X-RAYS, LABORATORY WORK, COMPUTER ANALYSES)

Exhibits containing results from tests, exams, scans, and other procedures require special foundation information to be introduced. These are the elements to be proven:

- The exhibit is relevant to the case.

- The witness is qualified to operate the equipment.

- There exists a procedure that regulates the testing or analysis process.

- The witness personally conducted or supervised an operator who conducted the testing, produced the results, or completed the analysis.

- The equipment was in normal operating condition.

- The witness can identify the results or conclusions.

- The results or analysis are in the same condition as when they were completed.

Example (MRI):

Examining Attorney:

Q: Mary Shelley, what is your position?

A: I am a MRI Radiologist employed by Arkham Asylum Health Services.

Q: Were you working Friday, July 3, at the Igor Medical Clinic?

A: I was.

Q: Ms. Shelley, I'm handing you what's been marked for identification as Exhibit No. 2. Do you recognize it?

A: Yes, I do.

Q: What is it?

A: It's a magnetic resonance image I generated on July 3.

Q: How do you know?

A: My name, the date and location, and the patient's identifying number are affixed to the MRI. That number is on the medical record at the Igor Clinic.

Q: Ms. Shelley, I'm handing you Exhibit No. 1, already stipulated as Mr. Frankenstein's medical chart and received into evidence. What is the medical record number?

A: (Reading) 01133026.

Q: Now I'm handing you what's been marked as Exhibit No. 2, the MRI. What number indicates the patient's chart?

A: It's next to the date.

Q: What is that number?

A: (Reading) 01133026.

Q: Are you a certified radiologist and MRI operator?

A: Yes.

Q: How was the image prepared?

A: An MRI machine created a detailed internal image of the patient's body including the brain.

Q: Was the machine functioning properly?

A: Yes, it had been periodically tested to ensure its accuracy and reliability, and there was no problem in its operation.

Q: After the image was made, what did you do?

A: I retained the original image, put my ID, the date, location, and patient's ID on it. Then I began to read and review it.

To the Court:

I offer Exhibit No. 2.

J. DIGITAL IMAGES, PHOTOS, SOCIAL NETWORK PICTURES, AND ELECTRONICALLY PRODUCED IMAGES (VIDEO, DVDS, FILM, MOVIES, DIGITAL RECORDINGS)

The elements to be proven to admit digital and electronic images into evidence are:

- The image or images are relevant to the case.

- The witness is familiar with the scene displayed in the image at the relevant time of the event.

- The image fairly and accurately depicts the scene at the time of the event.

There is no need to establish the sources of the image, or the video or photo sharing site, or the type of equipment used, or other imaging details, or even when the image was created, unless these facts are an issue in a case. Images from a variety of sources may be used including cameras, websites, and image sharing sites. Section 8.8 describes and displays these exhibits.

Example (Facebook Page):

Examining Attorney:

Q: How did you and the defendant become friends?

A: It all started on Facebook.

Q: How did it happen?

A: Both of us were users. He asked me to befriend him. I did.

Q: What happened after that?

A: Well, one day I went to my home page and saw that he had updated his photo on his profile . . . and that's when I noticed the tuffet and the web . . .

Q: Ms. Muffet, I'm going to stop you there. Take a moment and compose yourself . . . Now, please use the laptop in front of you to locate your Facebook page.

A: Alright . . . I have it here.

Q: Is that photo of the defendant, that you just mentioned, on your page, in his profile?

A: Oh my . . . yes it is.

Q: Is that the same photo you first saw of him?

A: It's the same.

To the Court:

Your Honor, we have a digital photo that is exactly the same as the one Ms. Muffet just identified, which we previously provided counsel. We now offer Exhibit 6, which is that photo.

Court:

Hearing no objection, it's received.

Example (Instagram App):

Examining Attorney:

Q: How did you and the plaintiff first meet?

A: We met online, sort of. I had an Instagram account and shared pictures on Tumbler and Flickr and the Plaintiff apparently was a user as well. I was especially attracted to the hashtag. We shared photos and messages and began following each other online.

Q: What were the shared photos?

A: We did mostly goofy things that we captured with our smart phone camera and posted the photos.

Q: Did you exchange photos on April 1 last year?

A: Of course. That is a special day.

Q: You have your smart tablet that is connected to the monitors here. Please go to your Instagram app and account.

A: It only takes a moment . . . here it is opening and there. . . .

Q: Please identify the April 1 photo the plaintiff posted that day.

A: Here it is.

Q: Before you describe it, can you identify it as the photo the plaintiff posted that day?

A: Yes.

Q: How?

A: I recognize her on the beach at Malibu with her trademark surfboard and wave.

To the Arbitrator:

This photo has been previously disclosed and marked as Exhibit 10. It appears in the Exhibit Files we provided you and counsel.

Q: Mr. Koohona, is the photo marked as Exhibit 10 the April 1 photo you just described?

A: Yes.

To the Arbitrator:

We offer Exhibit 10.

Arbitrator:

Received.

Examining Attorney:

Q: Tell us, sir, what wave is the plaintiff Gidget trying to catch in this photo?

K. SUMMARY EXHIBITS

Summaries of evidence may be introduced as an efficient and effective means to explain evidence to the fact finder. Summary exhibits may include a chart detailing the testimony of one or more witnesses or a summary description of documents. Federal Rule of Evidence 1006 and similar state rules permit summaries of writings to be introduced as evidence. The elements for introduction of summaries include:

- The information summarized must be relevant.

- The witness has knowledge concerning the information contained in the summary.

- The witness has reviewed the exhibit and verified that it is an accurate summary.

Example:

Examining Attorney:

Q: You've told us you're an Informational Technology Expert, Ms. Cleopatra?

A: Yes.

Q: What have you done in preparing this case for arbitration?

A: I have prepared a CD-ROM photo exhibit of the 457 exhibits containing a photo of each of the items that have been admitted in this case as having come from King Tut's tomb.

Q: I am showing you what has been marked for identification as Exhibit No. 458 which is a CD-ROM disk. Are you familiar with this disk?

A: Yes.

Q: How are you familiar with it?

A: I personally prepared the entire database on this disk.

Q: What does it contain?

A: Photos of the 457 exhibits indexed with a bar code system.

Q: Is it a fair and accurate portrayal of each of the exhibits?

A: Yes.

To the Court:

Ms. Arbitrator, at this time we offer Exhibit No. 458, the exhibit summary of all Plaintiff's exhibits introduced into evidence.

L. JUDICIAL/ARBITRAL/ADMINISTRATIVE NOTICE

A judge or arbitrator may take notice of facts, at any time during a proceeding, that are accurate, verifiable by reliable sources, and undisputable. See Fed.R.Evid. 201 and Section 3.6(K). These facts may appear in an exhibit.

Example:

Plaintiff's Attorney:

Your Honor, it is crucial to this case that we prove what day September 11, 2001 fell on, as well as the days of the week upon which other dates fell in 2001. I have marked a 2001 calendar as Exhibit A. At this time, I ask the court take judicial notice of the accuracy of this calendar and admit Exhibit A in evidence.

Judge:

I will take judicial notice of Exhibit A and admit it into evidence.

M. PAST RECOLLECTION RECORDED

A witness who, at the time of trial, does not have an independent recollection of an event may have previously made a record of the event and that record may be introduced as an exhibit of real evidence. The elements to establish the foundation of past recollection recorded exhibits appear in Section 4.8(H)(1)(c) and include:

- The witness has no present recollection of the event.

- The witness once had knowledge of the event.

- The witness made a record of the event when the matter was still remembered.

- The recorded recollection accurately reflects the knowledge of the witness.

- The exhibit is in the same condition now as when made.

Example (Lack of Memory):

Examining Attorney:

Q: Ms. Lovelle Wentworth Howell, do you remember what happened to you after you boarded the S.S. Minnow?

A: I was injured in a boating accident when the tiny ship was tossed, if not for the courage of the fearless crew the Minnow would have been lost.

Q: Do you remember any other details of that accident?

A: No. I haven't been able to recall the details since the day after my accident.

Q: The day of the accident, did you give a statement to anyone?

A: Yes, I did.

Q: To whom did you give a statement?

A: I gave a statement to a Coast Guard officer.

Q: At the time you gave the statement, did you remember what details occurred to you at the accident?

A: Yes, I did.

Q: Do you have a memory of those details now?

A: I do not.

Q: At the time you gave the statement to the Coast Guard officer, what did you do?

A: I read it, and I signed it.

Q: Showing you what has been marked by the court reporter as Exhibit No. 50—it's a three-page handwritten, water-stained statement with your signature on each page and the date—do you recognize this document?

A: Yes, I do.

Q: What is it?

A: It is a statement I wrote and signed the day of the accident.

Q: Would you please read the statement silently to yourself.

A: Yes.

Q: Having read the statement, does it refresh your recollection as to the details of what happened in the accident?

A: Not really. I still can't recall the details.

Q: Would you have signed this statement if it had not been complete?

A: No, I would not have.

Q: Would you have signed this statement if it had not been accurate?

A: No.

To the Court:

Your Honor, at this time I offer Exhibit No. 50 as past recollection recorded.

Judge:

Received.

Example (Detailed Facts):

Examining Attorney:

Q: Ms. Stephen, do you recall going to Bloomsbury Warehouse on November 27 last year?

A: Yes, I do.

Q: You accompanied Minny Thackeray, the defendant, who was inventorying books shipped from her mother's Hyde Park, Kensington home?

A: Yes.

Q: How did you assist Ms. Thackeray?

A: As she opened each box and told me the contents and condition of each book, I used a digital dictator recorder to record the information.

Q: Each box was inventoried?

A: Yes.

Q: What did you do after you completed the inventory?

A: We returned to the office, and I downloaded the recording to my computer system.

Q: Does the data include all the information from the recorder?

A: Yes, and it includes the value for each title based on its condition.

Q: When did you obtain the value?

A: Thursday, after I entered the information. Ms. Thackeray told me what value to put by each book, and I did so.

Q: Do you remember the valuation of the volumes written by Virginia Woolf?

A: Not really.

Q: Would it help you to look at the data for those valuations?

A: Yes, it would.

Q: Ms. Stephen, here is Exhibit 59. Do you recognize it?

A: Yes, this is the list I printed from the book database and these are the values I inserted next to each title after Ms. Thackeray's appraisal.

Q: Is the list in the same condition as when you prepared it?

A: Yes, it looks the same.

To the Arbitrator:

I offer Exhibit 59 into evidence.

Arbitrator:

Received.

Examining Attorney:

Q: Ms. Stephen, please read the Virginia Woolf titles and their value as set out on page four of Exhibit 59.

N. REAL EVIDENCE HIGHLIGHTED

Real evidence exhibits can be selectively used and highlighted to emphasize relevant evidence. During the examination of a witness, after a real evidence exhibit has been introduced, offered, and received into evidence, the witness can be asked questions about the most relevant portions of the exhibit. This can be done by combining some of the techniques used with demonstrative evidence, discussed in the next section, with questions relating to portions of real evidence exhibits.

Common uses of this approach include highlighting portions of exhibit documents by using marking pens or software specifically designed to highlight in color or create larger font portions of an electronic document. The witness can point to, further explain, and emphasize the highlighted portions of the document. The examining lawyer can operate the software and highlight the portion the witness describes. These highlights can also be used during opening and summation to remind the fact finder of the evidence.

Additional techniques allow documents or charts listing events and times to be compared and contrasted on a screen or monitor. This approach can be used to buttress or rebut other evidence. These images can have a positive effect on how evidence is understood by the fact finders, especially regarding conflicting testimonies. Operational software programs are available to produce these images. Otherwise, there are always highlight marking pens and paper charts to use.

The ubiquitous use of cameras on smart phones, selfie sticks, wearable and mountable devices, and other apparatus make many sources of photos and videos available of actual events. These displays can show what really happened augmented by testimony of witnesses. Images can be paused, enlarged or highlighted, allowing witnesses to describe what is happening.

§ 8.7 DEMONSTRATIVE EVIDENCE AND VISUAL AIDS*

A. DESIGN

Various types of demonstrative evidence may be useful during the presentation of a case. Witnesses may testify more accurately, comfortably, and effectively with illustrative aids described in Section 8.1B. Exhibits should be designed in such a way that they are user friendly and visually attractive. Advocates can learn to prepare and use these types of exhibits by exploring web sites that explain their use, by obtaining software programs that create these exhibits, and by retaining professional trial and hearing support consultants or employees.

There are three pertinent questions to ask when designing demonstrative evidence:

- What does the fact finder need to know from the exhibit?

- What is the minimal amount of information needed to provide this information?

- Which type of exhibit is the most effective and affordable?

Photo and Digital Recordings.

These exhibits should be sufficiently large and clear to be seen by the fact finders. A digital photo may be enlarged so that it can be easily seen. Photos may be displayed on a monitor screen. A digital recording or computer file may be created to show a procedure or to recreate an event.

Diagrams, Drawings, and Computer Displays. Enlargements of simple diagrams can be made inexpensively and quickly. Displays of lists or transactions may be presented with a computer program and monitor.

Charts/Graphs. There are several types of charts and graphs:

- Line—This graph is helpful to display timelines, trends, and prices. Avoid placing information too close together or including too much information.

- Pie—This chart is best used for a division of one number or percentages. Avoid pie charts with more than seven slices and charting numbers that are so small they disappear when compared to other pie pieces.

---

* Dianna Case, Connect Litigation, and Litigation Insights assisted with the content and design of demonstrative exhibits.

- Bar—This graph has a wide variety of uses, including comparisons for multiple numbers, events, or groupings of data. Make sure the labels and colors are distinct.

Exhibit Boards. Minimum size for a board is 30″ x 40″, and recommended sizes are 36″ x 48″ for an average-sized room and 45″ x 60″ for a large room. The greatest benefit of using boards is that unlike computer and document camera exhibits, boards can remain displayed during other evidence presentations. The disadvantage of using boards is the difficulty of placing them where they can be seen by everyone.

Computer Slide/Video Projectors. Portable projectors are available that can be connected directly to the laptop, and also to camera equipment or video or digital players, to display various sizes of exhibits. Projectors can display accurate renditions, while old style slide projectors may distort part of an exhibit and require the room to be darkened.

Notebooks for Written/Printed Exhibits. Some exhibits can be duplicated and placed in individual notebooks with tabs for use by the fact finders, lawyers, and witnesses or available as electronic files displayed on computer monitors.

B. COMPOSITION

Factors to consider in composing demonstrative/illustrative exhibits are:

Format. Proper formatting creates the right size, not too small or large.

Font. Big is often better.

Lines. Too many lines clutter the exhibit. 5 lines with 5 words is reasonable.

Spacing. The use of white space and margins is important to keeping the viewer focused on the display contents.

Color. Color tends to hold a viewer's attention longer than black-and-white and has more retention value. Whether the presentation is on a board or the computer, contrast is the key to good visibility. Certain colors signify different things to different people; however, some colors have natural messages, such as green and red—go and stop, good and bad, fast and slow. Too many colors on an exhibit distract from the key message and should be avoided.

Contrast. Viewers need to be able to distinguish the contents. Light or white backgrounds with dark text or dark or black backgrounds with light text increase readability.

Orientation. Either a landscape (11″ x 8.5″) or a portrait orientation (8.5″ x 11″) can be used.

Visual Output. When designing an exhibit, the visual output determines the best format—computer screen, large format exhibit board, or projector screen. Certain items that are too small for an exhibit board may look fine on a large projection screen. In the alternative, some images may be best viewed on multiple exhibits if the writing is too small for a single exhibit.

Size. Exhibit size may depend on the limitations or advantages of the room size for easels, boards, monitors, and other displays.

Computer Displays. Additional displays for computer exhibits include: (1) split screens e.g., (side-by-side presentations of conflicting testimony/documents), (2) call-outs (highlighted text segments "brought out" from their location on a displayed document page in larger font), or (3) builds (sequential additions to a graphic exhibit) showing evidence along with testimony.

C. ADMISSIBILITY

The introduction and use of demonstrative evidence is subject to a variety of approaches depending upon the practice in a jurisdiction and the preferences of the judge or arbitrator. See Section 8.2(C).

In some forums, the examining attorney need not formally offer a demonstrative exhibit into evidence but need only ask permission for the witness to use the demonstrative exhibit. In these jurisdictions this permission makes the exhibit part of the file or record. In other tribunals, a demonstrative exhibit is not offered into evidence until after the witness has used it during testimony or has marked on it. The record should indicate what the demonstrative evidence is and how it is being used.

In cases where more than one witness uses or marks a demonstrative exhibit, the procedures for its introduction may also vary. If a second witness uses or marks the exhibit, the demonstrative evidence may have to be re-offered because new information now appears on the exhibit. The markings may be distinguished by the use of a different color marker or by the placement of clear plastic cover over the drawing or chart that the witness draws on to distinguish those markings from the markings of the first witness.

The following examples demonstrate the admissibility and use of major demonstrative exhibits.

Digital Photos/Digital Recordings

The elements to be proven to admit photos/digital recordings into evidence are:

- The exhibit is relevant to the case.

- The witness is familiar with the scene displayed in the photo/digital recording at the relevant time of the event.

- The photo/video fairly and accurately depicts the scene at the time of the event.

- The photo/video will assist the witness in describing/explaining what happened.

There is no need to establish the source of the image or the photo or video sharing site, the type of camera used, film speed, focal lens, shutter speed, lens opening, other photography details, or even when the picture was taken, unless these facts are in issue.

Example—Digital Photograph

Examining Attorney:

Q: Ms. Jetson, on July 1, 2988, at approximately 2:00 sundial time, were you at the SkyPad and Orbit Lanes intersection?

A: Yes, I was.

Q: What were you doing there?

A: I was waiting for the space shuttle.

Q: While you were waiting for the shuttle, what did you observe?

A: I saw two electric, driverless vehicles, a Masarocket and a Lambomissle, enter the intersection and collide.

Q: I show you what has been marked as Plaintiff's Exhibit No. 1 for identification and ask you to examine it. Do you recognize it?

A: Yes, I do.

Q: What is it?

A: It's a photo of the intersection where the accident occurred.

Q: Is the scene on the photo in any way different from the scene that you observed on July 1, 2988?

A: No.

Q: Is the photo a fair and accurate depiction of the scene of the accident that you observed on July 1?

A: Yes, it is.

Diagrams, Charts, Drawings

The foundation elements for the introduction of a diagram, chart, or drawing are:

- The witness is familiar with the scene or event.

- The witness recognizes the facts depicted in the diagram or chart or is familiar with the exhibit.

- The exhibit will assist the witness in explaining testimony or will aid the fact finder in understanding the testimony.

- The exhibit is reasonably accurate (or is drawn to scale) and is not misleading.

A copy of the diagram may be introduced as part of the record. A photo may be made of a freehand drawing and included in the record.

Example—Prepared Diagram

Examining Attorney:

Q: Ms. Monroe, are you familiar with the intersection of Hollywood and Vine?

A: Yes, I am.

Q: Do you recall what the intersection looked like on April 20?

A: Yes, I do.

Q: How do you remember?

A: That was the day that, as I was leaving the drugstore, I saw an accident.

To the Court:

Your Honor, may I approach the witness?

Judge:

Yes, you may.

Examining Attorney:

Q: Ms. Monroe, I show you a diagram marked as Exhibit No. 6 that has already been prepared. Have you seen it before?

A: Yes, I have.

Q: Is this diagram a fair and accurate representation of the location of the streets and the buildings at the intersection of Hollywood and Vine on April 20, 2 years ago?

A: Yes, it is.

Q: Would this diagram assist you in describing what you saw that day?

A: Yes, it would.

To the Court:

Your Honor, I offer Exhibit No. 6 for demonstrative purposes.

Judge:

It is received.

Examining Attorney:

Your Honor, may I place it on the easel and have the witness approach?

Judge:

Yes, you may.

Examining Attorney:

Q: Ms. Monroe, there is an arrow on the diagram indicating north is to the top of the diagram. Is that correct?

A: Yes.

Q: Which way does Hollywood run?

A: It runs from north to south.

Q: And that is from top to bottom on the diagram?

A: Yes.

Q: Would you take the red marker and mark an "M" to indicate where you were at that intersection when you saw the accident?

A: I was right here.

Q: You have placed an "M" on the northeast corner of the intersection. Is that right?

A: Yes.

Q: Now, what did you see?

A: I saw one car coming from the east and one car coming from the west, and they met head-on in the middle of the intersection.

Q: Did you learn who was driving the car from the east?

A: Yes, he told me his name was Arthur.

Q: What about the car from the west?

A: The driver said his name was Joe.

Q: Will you label the car coming from the east and one from the west with the initials A and J placed in the center of the cars?

A: Yes.

Q: Will you draw a line from the cars from the east and west showing where they collided in the intersection?

A: Yes, I will.

Q: Will you mark with a "C" the spot of the crash?

A: All right.

To the Court:

Your Honor, at this time I re-offer the exhibit as marked.

Judge:

It is once again received.

Example—Model

Examining Attorney:

Q: Dr. Pierce, did you have the opportunity to examine the knee of my client, Ms. Houlihan?

A: Yes, I did.

Q: Did you do any surgery on Ms. Houlihan's knee?

A: Yes, I did.

Q: Would a model of a knee assist you in explaining what you saw during the visual and surgical examination of my client's knee?

A: Yes, it would.

Q: You have in your hand Exhibit No. 1. What is it?

A: It is an anatomical model of a person's knee.

Q: Is that an accurate model of a person's knee?

A: Yes, it is.

Example—Freehand Drawing

Examining Attorney:

Q: Now you said earlier that had an idea for some kind of cartoon character?

A: Yes, I did.

Q: What kind of character?

A: A rodent.

Q: Would it assist you in explaining your idea to us if drew your idea on this whiteboard using the black marking pen?

A: Yes, it would.

Q: Now sir, I see you have drawn some sort of animal.

A: It's a rodent.

Q: Are you sure that's a rodent, it looks like a rat?

A: It is a rodent.

Q: What are you drawing on the rodent?

A: Pants and shoes.

Q: And now what are you drawing?

A: Three-fingered gloves.

Q: Do you have a name for this character?

A: Yes, I do.

Q: And what is that name?

A: I have been thinking about Ralph.

Examining Attorney:

Your Honor, may I take a photo of the drawing to preserve it for the record and have the photo marked as an exhibit?

Judge:

You may.

D. DEMONSTRATIONS

Live demonstrations or experiments in court are difficult and dangerous. They may work well at rehearsal before trial, but can fail too easily. An effective alternative is to prepare a video recording of the experiment or demonstration or a computer generated recreation, and if it works and is persuasive, show it during the case.

A simple demonstration that can be easily performed may be conducted if appropriate. A witness who displays an injury or shows how an object was held can assist the fact finder in understanding what happened. Anything more complex should be recorded or recreated before the trial or hearing, or, if resources do not permit, not done at all.

Problem Example (Demonstration):

Examining Attorney:

Q: Ms. Chiquita, where were you on January 6, two years ago?

A: I was in the produce department of the Foods Unlimited supermarket.

Q: Did anything happen to you there?

A: Yes.

Q: What?

A: I was walking down the aisle when I slipped on a banana peel that was lying on the floor.

Q: Did you see the banana peel before you slipped?

A: Yes.

Q: When?

A: Just as I stepped on it, I looked down and saw it under my left foot.

Q: What happened?

A: Both feet went out from under me. My feet went up in the air and I came down hard on my right elbow.

Q: What happened to you?

A: I felt terrible pain in my elbow and saw a bone sticking out of my arm and lots of blood.

Q: Would you be able to demonstrate how you fell in the store?

A: Yes.

Q: Would that assist you in explaining to us what happened?

A: Yes.

To the Court:

May the witness please demonstrate what happened?

Opposing Counsel:

I have absolutely no objections.

Judge:

Are we insured for this kind of thing?

§ 8.8   DISPLAYING EVIDENCE AND DEMONSTRATIVE EXHIBITS

A.   COURTROOM/HEARING ROOM TECHNOLOGY

The layout and available technology in the courtroom or hearing room is important to the planning, organization, and presentation of exhibits. Advocates need to know the room layout and prepare a diagram including location of electrical outlets; available equipment; movability of furniture; sight lines; and acoustics, including possible dead spots. Wiring and cabling installation may be needed for technology equipment.

DIAGRAM 8–1

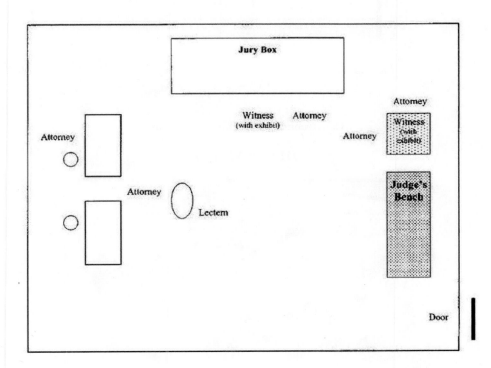

Courtroom Without Technology

DIAGRAM 8–2

Courtroom with Technology Option

DIAGRAM 8–3

Courtroom with Technology Option

DIAGRAM 8–4

Courtroom Technology Installation

DIAGRAM 8–5

Technology Network Scheme

DIAGRAM 8–6

Courtroom with Screen

DIAGRAM 8–7

Courtroom with Monitors

B. VISUAL PRESENTATION AND EXHIBIT DISPLAYS

Advocates need to thoroughly prepare for the use of exhibits:

- Plan well enough ahead to select real exhibits and create demonstrative exhibits.
- Review the resources available for exhibit development.
- Select the best medium for your presentation.
- Prepare exhibits that are simple, clear, and understandable.
- Be familiar with the court or hearing room and preferences of the decision maker.
- Use professional, persuasive exhibits.
- Practice and rehearse using the equipment and exhibits.
- Test run the technology to display exhibits.
- Double check viewing distance, readability, and comprehension.
- Present the information confidently and as a seamless evidence introduction.

The Exhibit Displays:

1. Photographs

PHOTOGRAPH 8–8

Viking Stadium under construction January 2015, Minneapolis, Minnesota
(photograph with permission of Minnesota Vikings)

PHOTOGRAPH 8–9

Viking Stadium before demolition for new stadium

2. Models

MODEL 8–10

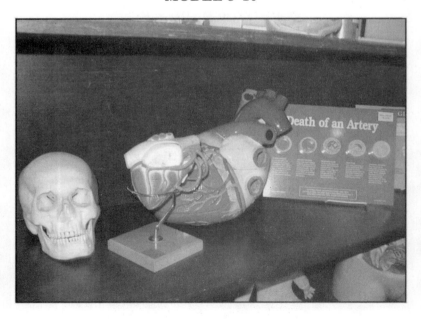

Model with Display Board

MODEL 8–11

Camera

3. Computer Models

ILLUSTRATION 8–12

3D Model Display

4. Display Board

ILLUSTRATION 8–13

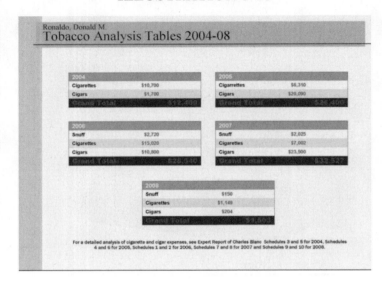

Financial Loss Due to Smoking

5. Diagrams

MAP 8–14

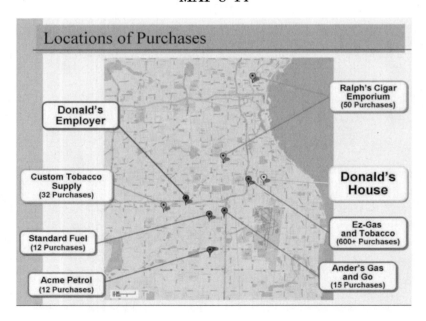

Tobacco Purchase Locations

DIAGRAM 8–15

Evidence that Smoking Cigarettes Causes Cancer

	YES	NO
Is there a plausible biological mechanism?		
Is there medical literature supporting causation?		
Is there a temporal relationship between exposure and presence of the disorder? (Challenge – Dechallenge)		
Is there evidence of causation in defendants' internal documents?		

Final Argument Checklist

DIAGRAM 8–16

Construction Diagram

6. Illustrations

MECHANICAL ILLUSTRATION 8–17

Precipitator

MEDICAL ILLUSTRATION 8–18

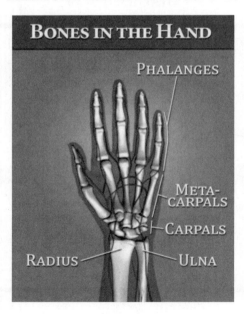

Medical Hand

MEDICAL ILLUSTRATION 8–19

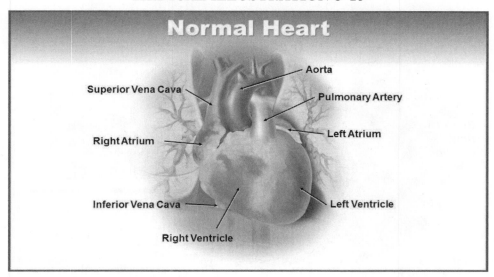

Normal Heart

MEDICAL ILLUSTRATION 8–20

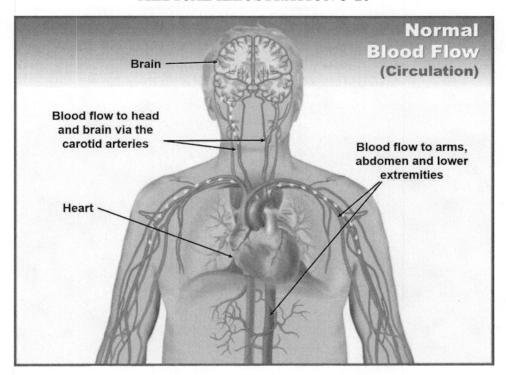

Normal Blood Flow (Circulation)

MEDICAL ILLUSTRATION 8–21

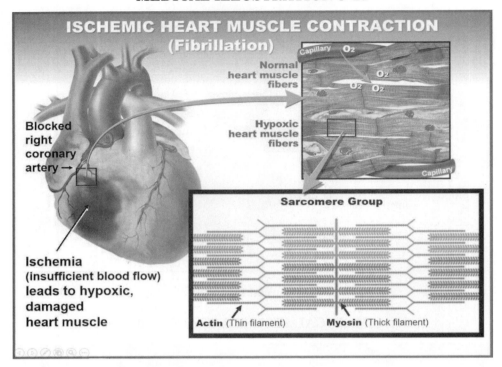

Ischemic Heart Muscle Contraction (Fibrillation)

ARCHITECTURAL ILLUSTRATION 8–22

New Viking Stadium illustration aerial view *(with permission of Minnesota Vikings)*

ARCHITECTURAL ILLUSTRATION 8–23

New Viking Stadium illustration (with permission of Minnesota Vikings)

7. Maps

MAP 8–24

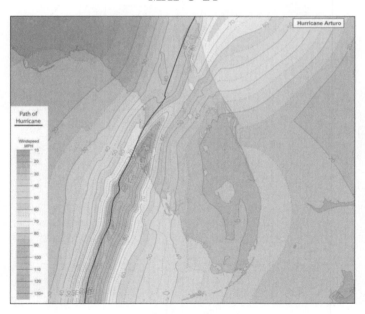

Path of Hurricane

MAP 8–25

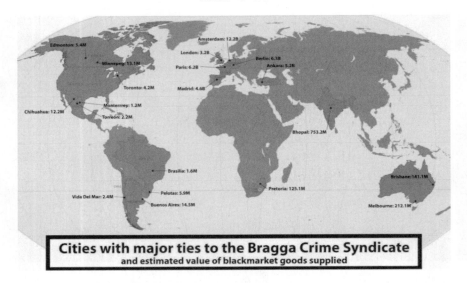

World Drug Locations

MAP 8–26

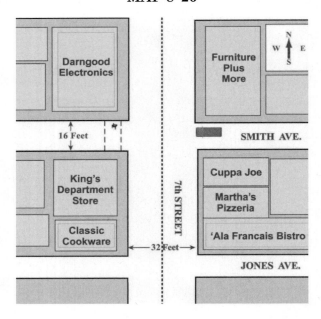

Street Map

8. Timelines

TIMELINE 8–27

Financial Loss

TIMELINE 8–28

Event Timeline

9. Charts and Graphs

CHART 8–29

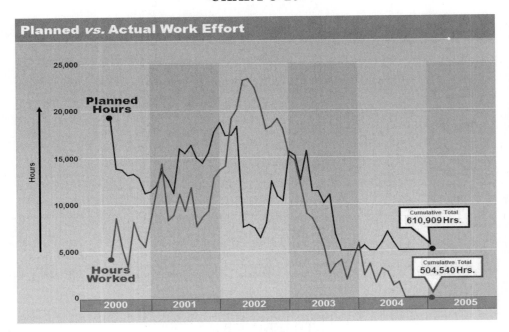

Line Chart

CHART 8–30

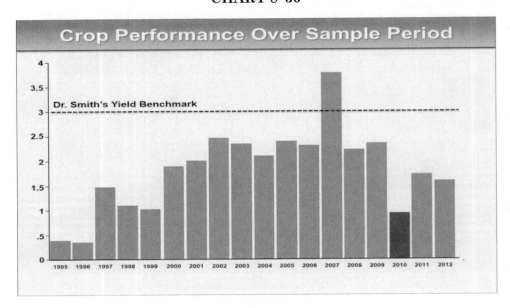

Bar Chart

CHART 8–31

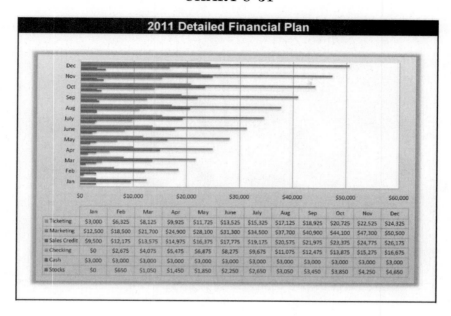

Bar Chart with Detail

CHART 8–32

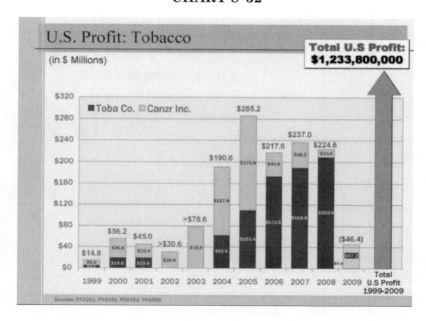

Bar Chart Comparison Timeline

CHART 8–33

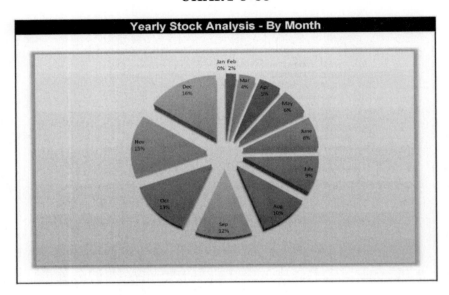

Pie Chart

CHART 8–34

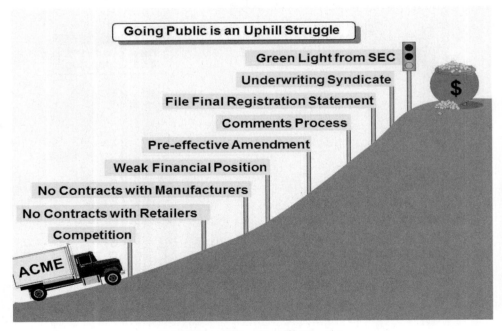

Event/Chart Timeline Illustration

10. Callouts

DOCUMENT CALLOUT 8–35

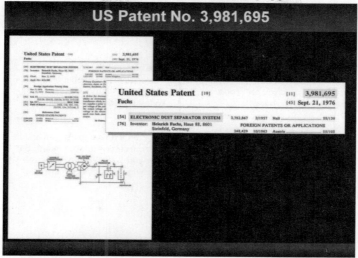

Emphasis on Callout

ILLUSTRATION 8–36

Precipitator with Callout

11. Comparisons

COMPARISON 8–37

Mr. Anderson's	*Mr. Smith's*
"The spoon is the best utensil. Period. You can cut with it if it has a nice sharp tip and you can scoop. What more do you need?"	"The best utensil? I'd say a knife. There's so many varieties of knives. Sharp knives, butter knives, serrated knifes. I could go on forever. "
"Why use anything other than a spoon? Can you scoop with a fork? I don't think so. The only other utensil I would ever consider would be a spork. But even that is pushing it."	"Granted, it is hard to eat with a knife with out cutting up your mouth, but have you ever tried cutting a steak with anything else? Its worth the pain."

Side-by-Side Testimony

COMPARISON 8–38

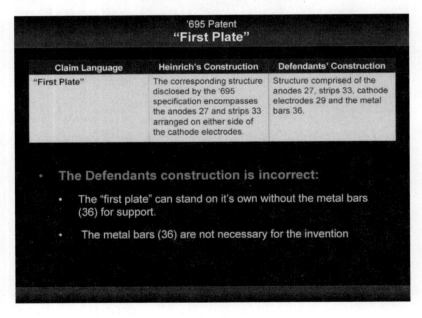

Patent Claim Construction Comparison

12. Computer Animation

ANIMATION 8–39

Hard Drive Animation

ANIMATION 8–40

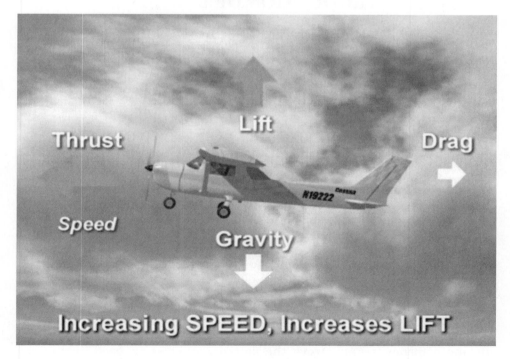

Flight Animation

ANIMATION 8–41

Hard Drive Animation

§ 8.9   OBJECTIONS TO THE INTRODUCTION OF EXHIBITS

A. PREPARING FOR OBJECTIONS

Advocates need to anticipate and prepare for any possible objections to the introduction of an exhibit. An objection, whether sustained or overruled, slows the presentation of the case. And protracted legal arguments interrupt the flow of the presentation.

B. RESPONDING TO OBJECTIONS

If an objection to the introduction of real evidence is sustained, advocates may:

- Make an offer of proof explaining the exhibit and the grounds for its admissibility. See Section 4.5(B).

- Offer the exhibit for a limited purpose. See Section 4.5(E).

- Offer the exhibit as demonstrative evidence, and not as real evidence.

The foundation for illustrative evidence is less than that required for the introduction of real evidence and may permit the exhibit to be received for illustrative purposes. For example, in an assault case, if the offering attorney cannot prove the actual hockey stick used during the assault is the stick offered as real evidence, the attorney could offer the hockey stick as illustrative evidence to assist the witness in testifying and to help the fact finder understand what happened.

C. QUESTIONING THE WITNESS

Opposing counsel may question the witness after an exhibit has been offered to determine if there is a basis for an objection or to lay a foundation for an objection. Counsel may ask questions (witness voir dire) to determine whether the foundation is lacking.

Example:

Q: Your Honor, may I ask some questions of this witness for the purpose of laying a foundation for an objection to the introduction of this *Toys* exhibit?

Section 4.3(J) explains this questioning procedure. The scope of this voir dire examination is very limited. The questions should not be about the weight to be given the exhibit but only about the foundation. Voir dire examination should not be used unless the exhibit is likely to be excluded. Cross-examination is a more effective tool to reduce the evidentiary effect of an exhibit. The proponent of the exhibit has the right to object if the witness voir dire questioning goes beyond permissible questioning.

D. COMMON OBJECTIONS

Exhibits are subject to appropriate evidentiary objections, including:

- Irrelevant. Fed.R.Evid. 401 and 402.

- Unfairly prejudicial or gruesome. Fed.R.Evid. 403.

- Misleading or inaccurate. Fed.R.Evid. 403.

- Waste of time or undue delay. Fed.R.Evid. 403.

- Exhibit does not assist the witness or aid the fact finder. Fed.R.Evid. 401.

- Cumulative or repetitious. Fed.R.Evid. 403.

- Lack of foundation, authentication, and identification. Fed.R.Evid. 901 and 903.

- Inadmissible hearsay. Fed.R.Evid. 801 and 803.

- Violation of original writing rule. Fed.R.Evid. 1002.

- Constitutional objections in criminal actions (i.e., denial of right to cross-examine).

This section provides examples of objections to improper or questionable exhibits.

1. Unfairly Prejudicial Exhibits

Example:

The prosecutor wishes to introduce a two foot by three foot color photograph displaying the victim's dead body found at the scene of the crime.

Prosecutor:

Your Honor, the state offers State's Exhibit No. 3, a photo of the victim's body, showing there were two shotgun blasts: one to the head, and one to the knees.

Defense Counsel:

Objection, your Honor, may I be heard at the bench?

Judge:

Please approach the bench.

Defense Counsel:

Under Federal Rule of Evidence 403, this exhibit is not admissible. Any probative value is substantially outweighed by the unfairly prejudicial nature of the exhibit. It is revolting, unnecessary, gruesome, and unfairly prejudicial. It has minimal probative value because the state's medical expert already testified to the cause of death. There is no reason for the jury to be shocked by this photo.

Prosecutor:

Your Honor, may I be heard?

Judge:

Yes, Mr. Murdoch.

Prosecutor:

This photo establishes there were two separate shots, supporting the state's claim of premeditation. It's essential for the jurors to see this exhibit.

Judge:

The objection will be sustained as to State's Exhibit No. 3. It is unnecessarily large and unfairly prejudicial.

Prosecutor:

Your Honor, we have a smaller 16-inch by 20-inch color photo of the same scene which we now offer as State's Exhibit No. 4.

Defense Counsel:

We continue to object, your Honor. There is no need for this photo to be introduced and no need for it to be in color.

Judge:

Objection overruled. State's Exhibit No. 4 is received.

Defense Counsel:

Your Honor, we request that the photo be briefly shown to the jurors and that it not be used by the State again during the trial.

Judge:

I will allow each individual juror to view the photo and permit the State to refer it during final argument. Proceed Counsel.

Problems can be anticipated and resolved in advance. The offering attorney can:

- Prepare alternative pieces of demonstrative evidence if the initial exhibit is held not to be admissible. Some attorneys will also have prepared a large black and white photo as an alternative, if the judge refused to admit a color photo.

- Explain to the judge the exhibit provides the jury with relevant and realistic facts that are essential to an understanding of the case.

- Bring a motion in limine to obtain a preliminary ruling as to its admissibility.

2. Emotionally Laden Exhibits

Example:

The plaintiff lost both legs in an accident. The defendant provided plaintiff with prosthetic devices as artificial legs. The plaintiff claims the devices are defective.

Examining Attorney:

Your Honor, we offer as demonstrative evidence Plaintiff's Exhibit No. 12, a video recording that shows the difficulty the plaintiff has in putting on and wearing the prosthesis and the operational defects with the design.

Objecting Lawyer:

Objection, your Honor. This video recording is unfairly prejudicial as it plays to the passion and prejudice of the jury, which substantially outweighs its minimal probative value. Further, your Honor, this evidence is repetitive because the plaintiff has already testified to the difficulty she has had with the prosthesis. However, we are willing to stipulate to the introduction of a still photograph of her wearing the prosthesis.

Judge:

Overruled. The plaintiff, Ms. Cairo-Thebes, is entitled to show the jury how the prosthesis works.

In preparing the exhibit, the attorney may:

- Prepare a realistic video and not an exaggerated staged effort

- Introduce the demonstrative evidence before substantial evidence has been introduced which may trigger an objection on the grounds of repetition.

- Have the witness perform a live demonstration instead of the video demonstration. This is problematic because live demonstrations can fail, and the demonstration may not establish what is sought to be proved.

3.   Misleading or Time Consuming Exhibits

Demonstrative evidence may mislead or confuse the fact finder or distort the facts. Drawings not drawn to scale, photos taken at a time far removed from the incident, and models not similar to the real evidence are examples of misleading evidence.

Example:

In a wrongful death action in which the plaintiff died from injuries sustained in an automobile collision, the plaintiff's accident reconstruction expert witness re-created the accident with a computer program.

Examining Attorney:

Your Honor, Plaintiff offers Exhibit No. 10, a computer disk containing a recreation of the scene prepared by our expert witness reconstructing the accident

Opposing Counsel:

Objection, Your Honor. This recreation is misleading and distorts the facts. The expert who recreated this event has no personal knowledge of the accident; this re-creation is not drawn to precise scale; and the re-creation does not include all of the evidence in this case concerning the accident.

Examining Attorney:

Your Honor, in response to the objection, this computer re-creation will help our expert testify and help the jurors' understand the facts.

Court:

Overruled. Exhibit No. 10 received.

Examining Attorney:

May we have the expert witness, James Byron Dean, explain what is depicted on the monitor as it's being shown?

Court:

Yes, you may.

Sometimes a presentation of demonstrative evidence may be time consuming or require extensive preparation. In these instances, the value of the demonstrative evidence must be weighed against the cost of time and delay. Demonstrative evidence that does not significantly add to the case will frequently be rejected. Illustrative evidence that does not assist the fact finder in understanding testimony or interpreting facts is objectionable and ought not to be allowed or used.

4. Unconstitutional Exhibits

In criminal cases, the introduction of demonstrative evidence may be objectionable as a violation of the defendant's constitutional right to cross-examine the witnesses. The defendant may not be able to cross-examine the person who created the exhibit. This objection is best used in conjunction with another ground supporting an objection.

Example:

Prosecutor:

Your Honor, I offer State's Exhibit N—the police report.

Defense Counsel:

Objection, your Honor. This is not within the public record hearsay exception. The report is conclusory, and my client has a right to cross-examine Officer Cagney who prepared this report.

Prosecutor:

Your Honor, we wish to use the diagram prepared by Detective Lacey on the lower third of the report as demonstrative evidence of the burglary scene and offer that portion of Exhibit N.

Judge:

The diagram part of State's Exhibit N is admitted as illustrative evidence. The remarks and conclusions surrounding the diagram by Detective Lacey must be redacted.

Prosecutor:

Your Honor, we have scanned the diagram into a computer that can be displayed on the monitor without showing the redactions.

Judge:

You may proceed.

---

5. Objections to Computer Exhibits

Objections regarding computer created or digital exhibits may involve issues regarding authenticity and the original writing/best evidence rule (Fed.R.Evid. 1001–1106):

- Computer generated originals presented in a digitized alternative format (e.g. on a CD in a standard file format) are admissible if it can be shown that the conversion of the original was accurately reproduced from the original.

- Scanned documents of computer documents and images are admissible if they can be authenticated and do not distort the original evidence.

- Charts summarizing data not itself introduced into evidence are admissible if the underlying voluminous data was made available to the opposing parties for review and a witness has laid the proper foundation.

- The rule of completeness for writings or recorded statements may require that the entire exhibit be introduced if the computer software only displays part of the relevant evidence in a document or recording.

- The rule of completeness may also apply to digital photos that have been cropped or partially enlarged and require the contemporaneous introduction of other scenes.

CHAPTER 9

CROSS-EXAMINATION

■ ■ ■

———————

Trial Advocacy Supplement
Cross-Examination

Examples of cross-examinations appear in the *Supplement to Trial Advocacy Before Judges, Jurors, and Arbitrators*. Three cases demonstrate cross-examinations of witnesses in a jury trial, an arbitration, and an administrative law hearing. These examples present the strategies, tactics, and techniques explained in this Chapter involving both supportive and destructive cross-examination.

REFLECTING ON ADVOCACY

Bromidic though it may sound, some questions don't have answers, which is a terribly difficult lesson to learn.

—KATHARINE GRAHAM

A lie may live and even wiggle after it has been spiked, but not beyond the sundown.

—HEYWOOD CAMPBELL BROUN

§ 9.1   INTRODUCTION

Cross-examination is the method of examining an opposing party or adverse witness. An effective cross-examination reveals information that supports the cross-examiner's case and that damages the opposing party's case. A primary purpose of cross-examination is to obtain evidence necessary to prove a case and to support statements made in summation.

There are two types of cross-examination:

- *Supportive cross.* Supportive cross-examination develops evidence supporting the cross-examiner's case. These questions can elicit new favorable information or bolster positive and constructive evidence.

- *Discrediting cross.* Discrediting cross-examination discredits the testifying witness, or another witness, or the opponent's case. This may be accomplished by attacking the credibility of the witness or testimony and by reducing the evidentiary and persuasive value of the opposition's evidence.

A.   SUPPORTIVE CROSS-EXAMINATION

The following questions assist in formulating supportive, helpful cross-examination responses from a witness:

- What statements in summation rely upon the testimony of this witness? If a witness is the only source of helpful information, that evidence must be elicited during cross-examination. For example, if a witness is the only person who can identify a signature on a document, then that witness needs to authenticate that document.

- What helpful information does the witness know? This information ought to be elicited through cross-examination. For example, if a witness has personal knowledge of the identity of individuals present during a conversation, the witness can identify those individuals.

- What admissions has the witness made? If a witness has made written, electronic, or oral statements, these admissions must be reviewed to determine which of them might be helpful to the cross-examiner's case. For example, in a breach of contract case, discovery may produce a statement that the opposing party failed to make contract payments on time. One way to introduce this admission is to ask leading questions of the opposing party on cross.

- What information does the witness have to corroborate favorable evidence? An opposing witness may have information to support a favorable fact established by another witness. For example, an opposing expert witness may support the scientific methods used by another expert who reached a contrary opinion.

- Can the witness bolster or rehabilitate the credibility of favorable witnesses? In addition to introducing proof of a fact through an adverse witness, testimony of that witness corroborating the testimony of a favorable witness may increase the credibility of the favorable witness. For example, if the testimony of a husband testifying in support of his wife can be corroborated by the opposing party, the credibility of the husband is enhanced.

- What portions of the direct examination were helpful? Helpful testimony from direct examination may be highlighted and expanded on cross-examination. For example, an eyewitness called by a plaintiff who observed a traffic accident that occurred during a rainstorm can be asked questions by the defense on cross-examination to establish poor visibility and slick roads.

There are factors common to typical disputes that may be established to enhance supportive cross-examination. In civil cases, a common theme involves *accountability*—which party is held legally accountable for causing the dispute. Tort cases involving negligent acts and contract cases involving breach of conduct are often decided by determining which party is more accountable for the misfeasance or misconduct. Questions can be designed to develop and highlight these favorable factors.

B. DISCREDITING CROSS-EXAMINATION

The purpose of discrediting cross-examination is to discredit evidence or impeach a witness by demonstrating that the testimony developed on direct examination and the evidence introduced by the opposing party is unreasonable, inaccurate, incomplete, inconsistent, implausible, improbable, impossible, or unbelievable. Discrediting cross-examination undermines the other side's case and reduces the credibility of the other side's witnesses. It is unlikely that the other side's case or the credibility of a witness will be totally discredited on cross-examination. It is more likely that bits and pieces of damaging information will be revealed which collectively hurt the opponent. See Section 9.4.

A common discrediting theme for cross-examination focuses on the *irresponsibility* of the opposing party or adverse witness. In criminal cases, the police may have acted unreasonably during the investigative stages of the case. In civil cases, the defendant very likely acted irresponsibly. Questions that establish the nature of the unreasonable and irresponsible conduct or statements will highlight the damaging effect of this evidence. See Section 9.4(A).

C. CHALLENGES OF CROSS

Challenges arise on cross-examination because the witnesses are adverse, hostile or uncooperative. The advocate seeks to elicit helpful information from an opposing witness who wants to or tries to harm the case of the advocate. Cross-examination questions are designed to make witnesses agree with facts or conclusions they want to deny, disagree with or ignore. The goal is to get witnesses to admit facts or opinions that hurt their case and help the case of the opposing party.

Witnesses on cross-examination are usually well aware of these efforts by advocates. The opposing lawyer has prepared the witnesses for direct and has also prepared them regarding the likely or exact cross-examination topics and questions that will be asked. Unprepared witnesses may be surprised at some cross-examination questions, but well prepared witnesses will understand what is being asked and why.

This is the major challenge of cross: how to obtain helpful answers from a witness who does not want to provide such evidence and how to do so effectively, reasonably, and compassionately without badgering the witness into submission and losing the effect of the favorable answers?

A fundamental question underlying this challenge is: why would witnesses agree with questions they don't want to agree with? The answer can be found in basic human nature responses: witnesses agree when they have to or when they want to. While they do not want to *have to* answer the questions as asked, they must. Several reasons exist to compel them to do so.

First, the answer may well be the truth. Witness agree because it is the truth and they have taken an oath to tell the truth, however unpleasant. Secondly, they are compelled to agree because of their previous statements or actions. They said or did so in the past and they have to admit consistency. Thirdly, they want to agree because it makes them look or sound good. Questions that flatter them or make them appear to have done something well will cause them to agree. Fourthly, they prefer to agree to avoid looking unreasonable or acting irresponsibly. They cannot reasonably or fairly deny, disagree with or ignore the questions. Fifthly, well-composed leading questions containing the answers compel them to have to respond agreeably or even reluctantly. These and other factors described in this Chapter explain effective ways to meet the challenges of cross-examination.

D. RISKS OF CROSS

Cross-examination needs to be conducted with realistic expectations and an assessment of the inherent risks. Cross-examination will not necessarily "win" a case or produce a miracle. Risky questions that have little hope of obtaining helpful information are typically asked out of desperation because the cross-examination is not well conceived. These risks can be reduced or eliminated by using leading questions that contain and suggest the answer, that require the witness to agree, and that control the witness' answer. Risks increase by asking bad questions that are ineffective or objectionable, such as:

- Non-leading questions, such as: "What do you mean by that?"

- Open ended questions that permit a witness to explain, such as: "How do you possibly explain your answer?"

- Narrative questions, such as: "Come on, tell us what really happened."

- Why questions, such as: "Why do you say that?"

- Disbelieving and desperate questions, such as: "You don't expect us to believe that, do you?"

- Curiosity questions with little or no hope for a helpful answer, such as: "Are you sure, I was rather hoping you would say the opposite."

- Repetitive questions, such as: "Now, on direct examination you said . . . is that what you actually meant to say?"

- Lengthy questions, which consist of subordinate clauses and passive voice, and confuse the witness and decision maker.

Thoroughly preparing proper questions and resisting the urge to ask these terrible questions prevent cross-examiners from making these egregious mistakes. Should you think about asking such awful questions or hear yourself starting to ask one . . . stop, stop, stop.

E. GOOD FAITH BASIS

An advocate must have a good faith basis for cross-examination questions. An attorney cannot ask a question on cross-examination unless the attorney has proof of the underlying facts. The attorney must have a source of reliable information, such as a witness or document that supports the statement made on cross. For example, a cross-examiner cannot ask a witness, "You drank ten beers that evening, right?" unless the attorney has available evidence to prove that fact. The rationale for this requirement is to prevent the cross-examiner from suggesting false or misleading facts through leading questions. While a cross-examiner must not fabricate and must have proof of the facts underlying the questions, the proof need not be admitted as evidence.

F. MYTHS ABOUT CROSS-EXAMINATION

There are myths about cross-examination that arise from a misunderstanding of cross-examination strategies and tactics.

- *Myth: Only an experienced lawyer can be an effective cross-examiner.* Any advocate who thoroughly prepares and asks proper questions can be effective. All advocates, regardless of experience, have the abilities to conduct an effective cross.

- *Myth: The cross-examiner must not be caring or sensitive.* Decision makers may identify with the witness. The witness may be perceived as a nice, decent person or may have a background similar to the background of the decision makers. They expect ordinary witnesses to be treated courteously and respectfully, and not to be treated in an uncaring or insensitive manner.

- *Myth: Cross-examination should be conducted very aggressively.* An attorney who conducts an overly aggressive cross-examination may be perceived as manipulating the witness and the evidence. An attorney must be perceived as fair and should be politely insistent and professionally assertive rather than excessively aggressive.

- *Myth: The witness must be destroyed on cross-examination.* The purpose of cross-examination is not necessarily to make the witness look or feel bad, but to obtain evidence to win a case. After a good cross, a witness may leave the stand without feeling "destroyed."

- *Myth: The witness should always be shown to be a liar.* Attacking the credibility of witnesses by suggesting or inferring that they are lying is ill advised unless there is direct evidence of a lie. Many witnesses make honest and good faith efforts to describe an event and will not look like or sound like they are making things up. However, it is not uncommon for witnesses who see or hear only a portion of an incident to add details they assume occurred. These witnesses may then blend their recollection of what actually occurred with the presumed details. This mistaken recollection and misbelief forms the basis for their testimony. The witness is mistaken, but not lying. A direct attack on the veracity of such a witness may be ineffective.

- *Myth: The cross-examiner must know all the details of expected answers before asking the question.* The reality is that often the lawyer will know the witness' prior statements and know what the witness will repeat at trial. But, there may be no complete, verbatim transcript or prior statement for some witnesses. The cross-examiner will still need to ask leading questions, and can effectively do so by accurately predicting what the witness will say. The more accurate the prediction, the more effective the leading question will be.

- *Myth: Cross-examinations must produce dramatic results.* A cross-examination that does not leave the fact finder gasping, the witness crying, or the attorney exalting does not indicate that the cross has been ineffective. Some cases involve dramatic moments, many do not.

- *Myth: Cross-examination is an opportunity to debate with the witness.* Argumentative questions are improper and likely to draw an objection. The cross-examiner wants to obtain "yes" or "no" responses from a witness and to avoid debating with the witness.

- *Myth: Cross-examination often escalates into a shouting match between the witness and the attorney.* There is seldom a need to ask questions in a loud or harsh manner. Few witnesses deserve or require this treatment.

- *Myth: Cross-examination should result in the witness "confessing."* Witnesses seldom "confess" their guilt or liability on the stand. Some witnesses, including informers and criminals, can be made to admit to their lies and crimes. Civil cases seldom involve such witnesses.

- *Myth: Cross-examinations that appear on television or in the movies are realistic and appropriate.* More often than not, cross-examination questions asked in a television program or motion picture or theater play are unrealistic and inappropriate. A witness does not deserve to be treated in the way commonly depicted in television and the movies, nor will they as readily change their testimony.

- *Myth: Cross-examinations should always be short.* A cross-examination should be as long as necessary to obtain the required information from the witness. With some witnesses, cross-examination will be short, and with others, long. There is no set time limit for effective cross-examinations. The facts, witnesses, and circumstances determine the content and length.

- *Myth: Cross-examination should cover one point.* Some advocates suggest that cross-examination should only cover one or a few points. This is appropriate advice if that's all the information a cross-examiner needs to develop. Many cross-examinations require the development of more points. What one experienced advocate considers to be one point with six sub-points, another lawyer may consider to be seven points. Regardless of the semantics or the counting system used, a cross should fully cover what is necessary.

- *Myth: Cross-examination is the most difficult advocacy skill.* A well-prepared cross-examination, seeking answers already known or reasonably predicted by the cross-examiner, need not be any more difficult than other parts of the case.

§ 9.2 PREPARATION

A. PLANNING

Cross-examination can be very difficult, awkward, embarrassing and damaging if questions are phrased improperly, inappropriate areas are explored, or the attorney loses control over the witness. Thorough planning, preparation, and understanding of successful cross-examination techniques are necessary to plan an effective cross-examination.

You undoubtedly have been involved in numerous cross-examination experiences in your life. You have been both a cross-examinee (remember being a teenager) and a cross-examiner (recall a relationship, perhaps). And you have vicariously experienced cross-examinations through literature and the arts. You may also have had professional or other experiences that influence your perspective.

These events have shaped your approach and can affect how you prepare and believe a witness should be cross-examined. It's best, for now, to suspend your views on what you believe effective cross-examination techniques entail until you complete this Chapter. Then you can revisit your views and approaches and modify them to be an effective professional cross-examiner at a trial or hearing.

Preparation for a cross-examination begins during the preliminary stages of a case. Witnesses are interviewed, witnesses' statements are taken, documents are preserved, and depositions are completed. The responses obtained from these discovery sources provide information useful for cross-examination.

Before trial or hearing, the different areas of cross-examination are reconsidered and specific questions are planned. Preparation continues until the moment cross-examination begins. The cross-examiner listens carefully to the answers the witness gives on direct examination and adds, deletes or modifies questions to be asked during cross.

After the witness has testified on direct, the cross-examiner is usually able to ask a high percentage of prepared questions. The well-prepared cross-examiner recognizes or can predict what the witness will testify to on direct, what the witness knows and does not know, and what the witness previously has said, written, or composed.

Adjustments may be necessary during the cross-examination itself. The witness may not respond as anticipated, or may give unresponsive or rambling answers. The attorney must listen thoughtfully during the cross and flexibly adapt to the responses by asking insistent follow-up questions that produce the desired responses.

B. SHOULD THERE BE A CROSS-EXAMINATION?

The decision to cross-examine must be made during trial preparation and again during the trial or hearing. Whether cross-examination should be conducted as planned, or whether any cross-examination should be conducted at all must be finally resolved after the witness has completed direct examination. The vast majority of witnesses merit some cross-examination. The following factors provide guidance in determining whether a witness should be cross-examined or asked certain questions:

- Has the witness damaged the case? If the witness has not provided damaging evidence, the cross may be unnecessary. A witness who did not appear credible, or whose story is not credible, or who has not been sufficiently contradicted may need to be selectively cross-examined.

- Is the witness unimportant to the other side? The less significant a witness, the more likely a cross is unnecessary.

- Will the decision maker expect cross-examination? Witnesses who have provided damaging information or who are important to the other side need to be examined to meet expectations of the decision maker and to prevent opposing counsel from commenting on the failure during summation.

- Did the witness omit important adverse information on direct examination? Cross-examination regarding that information may be unwise. Occasionally, an opposing attorney may intentionally withhold evidence during the direct examination of a witness anticipating the evidence will be disclosed on cross or redirect. If there is no cross-examination regarding this evidence, this information may never be disclosed. Some experienced lawyers set this trap for the inexperienced cross-examiner.

- Will cross unavoidably bring out information that is harmful to the case? If cross-examination will yield more harmful than helpful information, it may be best not to cross.

- Are questions being asked only for the sake of asking questions? If the cross will serve no better purpose, it should not be conducted.

- Does this witness present any difficulties that may cause substantial problems? If a witness is a very difficult witness, the decision to cross-examine should be reconsidered.

- Are there questions that need not be asked in light of the direct examination answers? While the witness should be asked some prepared cross questions, other questions may be deleted.

FORM 9.1
CROSS-EXAMINATION WORKSHEET

Case _____ Witness _____ File_____

Supportive Cross-Examination Information:

Discrediting Cross-Examination:

    Implausible/Improbable/Impossible:

    Inconsistencies:

    Impeachment: Facts/Opinions/
                                                Modifiers/Synonyms

        Interest/Bias/Prejudice

        Competency Deficiencies

        Inadequate Observation/
           Lack of Perception

        Poor Recollection

        Inconsistent Conduct

        Criminal Record

        Specific Instances of Untruthfulness

        Prior Inconsistent Statements
           Written/Oral/Omissions

        Other Areas:

C. FULL AND FAIR OPPORTUNITY TO CROSS

A party has a right to fully and fairly cross-examine a witness. Unusual situations may arise when a witness who has testified on direct examination cannot be cross-examined. These situations include: (1) the assertion of a privilege by the witness permitting the witness to refuse to answer questions, (2) a witness becoming ill or otherwise incapacitated before or during cross-examination, and (3) the refusal of a witness to answer a question which the judge or arbitrator orders the witness to answer. In these situations, the cross-examiner may request that the direct examination testimony of the witness relating to the cross-examination topics be stricken because no opportunity exists to cross-examine the witness regarding those matters.

D. SCOPE OF CROSS-EXAMINATION

The scope of cross-examination is usually limited to the following two areas: the subject matter of direct examination and matters affecting credibility issues. The law in most jurisdictions, including the federal system, limits cross to the scope of the direct and to matters that discredit the witness or the case. See Fed.R.Evid. 611(b). Judges and arbitrators, however, have broad discretion to permit inquiries into additional matters. Cross-examiners will typically have a lot of latitude to explore relevant areas affecting the case or the credibility of a witness.

While the rules of a given jurisdiction may appear to restrict the scope of cross-examination, practice often permits broader inquiries. However, some judges and arbitrators enforce the rules strictly and sustain an objection that the cross exceeds the scope of the direct. When this occurs the cross-examiner should advise the judge or arbitrator that the questions apply to credibility permitting a broader cross-examination.

If an area of inquiry on cross exceeds the scope of the direct examination and does not involve credibility issues, the cross-examiner has several options. First, the questions may be asked and the opponent may not object. Second, the question may be asked, the opponent may object, and the objection may be overruled, permitting the answer. Third, the cross-examiner can seek permission to allow a broader cross-examination. In this case, the attorney may advise the judge or arbitrator that the witness could be called back later to testify, and it would be more efficient if the examination was completed at one time. Fourth, if the questions are disallowed, the attorney can call the witness to testify at the next opportunity in the case and introduce the affirmative evidence.

E. PREPARING TOPICS AND QUESTIONS IN ADVANCE

Cross-examination is most effective when topics and questions are prepared in advance. Experienced lawyers may be able to effectively cross-examine by relying solely on a list of topics. Many lawyers, however, especially novice advocates, need to write out questions to be effective. The extent of question preparation depends upon the significance of the question or topic, the type of witness, and abilities of the advocate.

Effective cross-examination often demands that the attorney ask precise questions containing specific words. In these situations the attorney, particularly the novice cross-examiner, is well advised to compose the questions. Most prepared questions need not be altered significantly during the case, but an attorney must adapt the questions to changing circumstances. The attorney should avoid simply reading prepared questions and must pay attention to the witness' verbal and nonverbal responses to ask follow-up, clarifying, and leading questions.

F. STRUCTURE

Cross-examination questions should be asked in an order that makes the cross-examination most effective, interesting, persuasive, and memorable. An effective way to organize cross-examination points is to:

- List all the points expected to be made.

- Divide the points into the two broad categories of cross-examination: supportive cross and discrediting cross.

- Rank each point from most to least important in the two categories.

- Select the most effective order of the more important points.

- Organize the sub-points in a sequence that works best.

- Review all the listed points and determine whether the initial assessment of their rank, order, and sequence appears effective.

G. ORDER

If both supportive and discrediting questions are to be asked, the supportive cross-examination questions ought to be asked first for a number of reasons: (1) These questions elicit helpful information and will be emphasized by being asked at the beginning of the cross-examination. (2) The questions follow the pattern of questions asked on direct examination that was just completed. (3) The witness may be more cooperative at the beginning of a cross-examination. And, (4) the credibility of the witness has not yet been attacked and the decision maker may perceive the witness to be more believable.

The order of the supportive cross-examination questions should follow a prepared structure, with important questions beginning and ending the line of questioning, and with the other points asked in the middle. The final point of supportive cross-examination may serve as a transition into the discrediting category of cross-examination.

The shift from supportive to discrediting cross-examination may cause a problem. The cross-examiner wants the fact finder to believe the admissions elicited during the supportive cross-examination and to find the witness not credible as a result of the discrediting cross-examination. The transition questions that begin the discrediting cross-examination should be selected to reduce this problem. The discrediting cross may render testimony so unbelievable that the fact finders will not believe the supportive cross-examination answers. In these situations, it may be better to avoid asking supportive cross-examination questions altogether, unless there is no other source for this information.

The order of the discrediting cross-examination questions should also follow a prepared structure. Important points should be made at the beginning and at the end of this category of questions, with other points interspersed in the middle.

An occasionally used alternative to a logical sequence of planned questions is to probe areas in a random fashion. This "jumping around" or "hop and skip" approach has the advantage of causing problems for a witness who may be fabricating responses. Such a witness, if asked questions in a logical or chronological order, may maintain the fabrication, but if asked questions in a random order, may testify inconsistently. This approach has disadvantages. The cross-examiner may have difficulty remembering what has been asked, and the fact finder may find it difficult to follow an unstructured cross-examination. This alternative requires practice and experience to be effective.

H. CONCLUDING QUESTIONS

The concluding questions of a cross-examination should:

- End the examination on a high note with an effective point.

- Not be objectionable to avoid disrupting the conclusion.

- Be the type the witness will readily agree with.

I. RECROSS EXAMINATION

The scope of recross examination is limited to the subject matter of the redirect examination. A primary purpose of conducting a recross is the same as conducting a cross-examination: Is there any information this witness has that is needed for summation? Recross examination questions can refer to the redirect answers: "During the redirect examination by your attorney, you stated that. . . . However, it is true that. . . ."

If no recross is necessary, the cross-examiner can say: "Your Honor, there is no reason for any further questions." There often is no need to conduct a recross, and a recross should not be conducted merely because redirect questions were asked. Recross questions should not be asked if the redirect was ineffective, or if the examination of the witness has been overly lengthy and the fact finder cannot absorb more from this witness.

J. LOCATION AND MOVEMENT

The cross-examiner must be visible to the fact finders. The cross-examiner asks the questions containing the evidence the fact finders need to hear and see. Unlike direct examination where the testimony comes from the witness during cross-examination, it is the advocate, in effect, who provides the evidence through leading questions.

The cross-examiner may have the option to sit or stand. Many jurisdictions require the cross-examiner to stand behind a lectern and not move about. Cross-examiners may approach the witness when showing the witness an exhibit or using a visual aid. Many jurisdictions require the attorney to remain seated behind counsel table, especially in administrative hearings and arbitrations. In some small hearing rooms, the cross-examiner may sit only a few feet away from the witness.

In jurisdictions where counsel has an option to stand and move, the cross-examiner should determine what location is best. This will depend upon the type of questions asked and the demeanor and responses of the witnesses. If the cross-examiner wants the fact finder to observe the witness displaying guilt or uncertainty, the cross-examiner should stand in a location that requires the witness to look in the direction of the fact finder and that permits the fact finder to see the attorney.

If the cross-examiner can move during cross-examination, movement should be purposeful. It may be effective to move closer to the witness during impeachment or when significant questions are asked to control the response of the witness. Further, the closer the cross-examiner is to the witness, the more the witness may become uncomfortable and not credible. The cross-examiner, however, cannot stand too close or "crowd" a witness. Opposing counsel will object, and/or the judge or arbitrator will ask the cross-examiner to move away a suitable distance or to sit down.

K. DEMEANOR

Compassion and confidence are two critically important cross-examination traits. The vast majority of witnesses deserve to be treated decently because of the facts or just because they are persons. And, the decision maker may expect witnesses to be treated fairly. Further, if the witness perceives that the cross-examiner is confident, the witness is more likely to be agreeable and less evasive.

The most effective demeanor for a cross-examiner is to be firm, yet sensitive. This is especially true during the beginning of a cross-examination attempting to elicit supportive evidence. An empathetic or sympathetic cross-examiner is more likely to elicit favorable information. Some witnesses deserve special treatment, including witnesses such as young children, a victim of a crime, or a bereaved spouse.

Other situations may require more assertiveness on the part of the attorney, particularly during impeachment or when controlling an evasive or rambling witness. The cross-examiner should avoid becoming overly aggressive or combative with the witness and avoid displays of anger. Such behavior is usually inappropriate or ineffective and will draw an objection that typically will be sustained.

§ 9.3   TACTICS AND TECHNIQUES

The goal on cross is to ask leading, short, fact-based questions.

Effective cross-examination requires the use of proper tactics and techniques. Many of these approaches are principles or "commandments" which should seldom be violated.

They include:

- Ask proper leading questions,

- Select the precise right content, usually fact based,

- Compose short, concise, simple questions,

- Seek agreement from the witness,

- Control the witness' responses,

- Emphasize helpful points,

- Utilize safe questions, and

- Design appropriate questions for special witnesses.

The tactics and techniques described in this section should be reviewed before every cross-examination to determine which should be employed. Not all of the techniques ought to be used in every cross, but many will be applicable. If a problem does occur during cross, it is usually because one of these tactics was not properly employed.

Cross-examination questions must be carefully crafted and precisely asked. The difference between an effective cross-examination question and an ineffective one is often very subtle. One wrong word, the slight mistiming of a question, too long a question, or a momentary loss of control may cause problems. A witness may properly refuse to respond, may claim a question is unclear, and may try to explain an answer, because the cross-examiner failed to ask a precise and concise question.

A. FORM OF QUESTIONS

1. Leading the Witness

Only leading questions that suggest or contain the answer should be asked on cross. Questions that require a "yes," "no," or short, anticipated answers should be asked. Non-leading questions that permit a witness to explain or expand an answer should be avoided because they are open-ended, may result in damaging testimony, and cannot be controlled.

Example:

Q: You are Chicago, correct?

A: Yes.

Q: You are hog butcher for the world?

A: Yes.

Q: Toolmaker, correct?

A: Yes.

Q: Stacker of wheat?

A: Yes.

Q: You're a player of railroads and the nation's freight handler?

A: Yes.

Q: It is fair to say you are stormy?

A: Yes.

Q: Husky?

A: Yes.

Q: Brawling?

A: Yes.

Q: You are the city of the big shoulders?

A: Sure.

Q: And your poem was written by Carl Sandberg?

A: Of course.

---

2. Form of Leading Question

Leading questions should be formulated to prompt responsive answers. A properly phrased leading question requires the witness to agree with the question. There are a variety of ways effective leading questions can be asked.

Example:

Ask: You saw Olivia Pope on the Capitol steps?

Not: Did you see the defendant on the Capitol Steps?

Phrases may be added to leading questions to obtain an answer. These prefaces or clauses may be useful in prompting a response. The repetitive use of these phrases ought to be avoided, however, because they may detract from the substance of the question. Examples include:

Example:

You saw the defendant on the African Queen, isn't that correct?

Or,

It is true that you saw the defendant on the African Queen?

Or,

You saw the defendant on the African Queen, right?

Leading "questions" may also be asked in the form of statements that sound like questions because of the cross-examiner's voice inflection.

Example:

Q: You met Buddy Holly at the **airport** (emphasis)?

A: Yes.

Q: At about **11:00 p.m.** (emphasis)?

A: Yes.

Q: That was the **first time** (emphasis) you met Mr. Holly?

A: Yes.

Q: And the **last** (emphasis)?

A: Yes.

Different types of leading questions should be used for variety and to prevent a cross from sounding monotonous.

3. Simple, Short Questions

Short, straightforward questions in simple, understandable language are most effective. Lengthy or complex questions likely will be confusing.

Example:

Ask:

Q: The fight began?

A: Yes.

Q: The referee stood in the middle of the ring?

A: Yes.

Q: Ali stood in one corner?

A: Yes.

Q: Frazier stood in the opposite corner?

A: Yes.

Q: Ali began to move toward the center of the ring?

A: Yes.

Q: Frazier also began to move towards the middle of the ring, right?

A: Yes.

Not:

Q: As the fight began both Ali and Frazier stood in their respective corners at the opposite sides of the boxing ring and then each of them began to move towards the center of the ring, isn't that what happened?

---

4. Avoid Multiple Negative Questions

Questions that contain double or multiple negatives are bewildering.

Example:

Do Not Ask:

Q: It is correct is it not you don't know who was on Galactica?

Q: It is not true, is it, that you are not from Battle Star?

B. CONTENT OF QUESTIONS

1. Fact Based Questions

Questions that include the relevant facts prompt responsive answers. The factual words included in the cross-examination question must be based on accurate facts to compel a witness to admit the accuracy of the question. Questions that seek an unsupported conclusion, or employ words with multiple meanings or are not fact based permit the witness to be non-responsive or to explain an answer.

Example:

Avoid Asking:

Q: When you visited Michael Cory, you wanted to sell him as much insurance as you could? (conclusion not fact)

A: He came to my office. I told him I could provide him with an insurance policy that met his needs.

Ask Instead:

Q: You asked Mr. Cory to come to your office?

A: Yes.

Q: When he was in your office, he said he needed insurance?

A: Yes.

Q: You told him you could provide him with insurance?

A: Yes.

Q: You wanted to sell him insurance?

A: Yes.

Q: Your job was to sell him insurance?

A: It was, and I did.

Some words appear to be "facts" but are conclusory words. Each cross-examination question should be reviewed to determine whether the precise words used are specific and concise facts.

Avoid Asking:

Q: Mr. Churchill read the lease agreement, correct?

A: He may have skimmed the lease.

Q: He understood the terms of the lease, didn't he?

A: I don't know.

Ask Instead:

Q: You handed Mr. Churchill the lease agreement?

A: Yes.

Q: You saw him look at the lease agreement?

A: Yes.

Q: He sat there for some time looking at the lease?

A: Yes.

Q: The two of you discussed the lease for over an hour?

A: Yes.

Q: He asked you some questions about the lease?

A: Yes.

Q: You answered his questions?

A: Yes.

Q: You asked him if he had other questions about the lease?

A: Yes.

Q: You believed he understood the lease?

A: I thought so.

Q: You asked him whether that lease met his country's needs?

A: Yes.

Q: And he said, "Victory is at hand."?

A: Correct.

Q: He signed that lease?

A: Yes.

---

2. Effectively Asking for Opinions

An effective way to induce a witness to provide an opinion is to first establish the factual basis for the opinion. For example, if you want eyewitnesses to admit they were tired at the time they made an identification, you first need to establish the factual basis for their being tired before you ask questions about their being tired.

Example:

Q: Mr. Chavez, your pickup truck was stolen at approximately 8:30 p.m., correct?

A: Yes.

Q: You got up that morning about 6 a.m.?

A: Approximately 6 o'clock.

Q: You worked from 7 a.m. until 6 p.m.?

A: Yes.

Q: You worked hard all day?

A: Sure.

Q: You rushed to get the job done by 6?

A: We always work hard to get things done on time.

Q: You had someplace to go right after work?

A: Yes.

Q: You drove to a union meeting with your fellow workers?

A: I did.

Q: That lasted from 6:30 to 8:30 pm?

A: It did.

Q: You are the union president and led the meeting?

A: I did.

Q: Working 11 hours is a tiring experience.

A: It can be.

Q: And you were very busy over 13 hours that day?

A: Yes.

Q: You were naturally tired at the end of that day?

A: Somewhat.

Q: It was quite a long day.

A: A typical day for me.

Q: You were going home and looking forward to resting?

A: Sure.

Q: Because you had quite a tiring day, right?

A: I did.

Q: And that's when you first saw the stranger by your truck?

A: Yes.

If the witness was asked the opinion question before the factual questions, the witness could have tried to bring up reasons for not being tired. Factual questions establish the conclusion that the witness was tired and prevent the witness from reasonably explaining away an answer. Even if the witness refused to admit to being tired at the end of the day, the fact finder would believe the witness was tired and would not believe the witness' denial.

3. Using Modifiers

The use of adjectives and adverbs as modifiers may help in obtaining favorable responses from a witness. Different impressions may be created on cross if appropriate modifying words or phrases are used. For example, a witness may be willing to admit to different degrees of being tired depending on the sequence of questions and the modifying words used.

Example:

Q: You were somewhat tired after working a *full* day, correct?

A: Yes.

Q: Working *all* those hours made you feel *tired*?

A: Yes.

Q: Working those *additional* overtime hours made you *more* tired than usual?

A: Perhaps.

Q: The *hard* day you had made you feel *very* tired at the end of the day?

A: Some, yes.

Q: Your work that *long* day caused you stress?

A: Well, some.

Q: It's fair to say that you felt a *lot* of stress by the end of the day, correct?

A: At the end, sure.

Further questioning with some witnesses may have them agreeing to being "extremely tired" at the end of the day. Using various modifiers—a little, somewhat, quite, very—is an effective way to have the witness gradually agree to a position.

4.   Using Synonyms

If a specific word is being sought on cross-examination, a synonym may be useful instead of trying to force the witness to admit to one specific word. A thesaurus provides alternative words that more effectively describe a situation. In the eyewitness example, having the witness agree to being "exhausted" at the end of the day rather than just being "tired" is much more effective. Synonyms can more accurately portray the event you prefer the jurors perceive. In addition to the word "tired," other words such as fatigued, worn out, weary, sleepy, drowsy, rundown, bushed, drained, or tuckered out could be used. If a witness denied feeling some of these effects at the end of a tiring day, the fact finder would disbelieve the witness about not being tired or would conclude the witness is not a credible witness.

C. SEEK AGREEMENT WITH THE WITNESS

1.   Be Considerate

Witnesses ordinarily deserve courteous treatment. Some witnesses may deserve righteous indignation and some may be questioned with an aggressive approach, but no one deserves to be questioned in an obnoxious manner. The cross-examiner can usually be more effective by being insistent, politely assertive, and persistent and by showing appropriate consideration rather than overt aggression.

Example:

Q: Ms. Lindberg, I understand this is a difficult time for you. We all know the kidnapping and death of your son was a terrible tragedy. You realize I need to ask you some questions so we all can understand what happened.

---

2.   Flatter the Witness

An effective way to obtain a responsive answer to a leading question is to ask a question that makes the witness look good. Witnesses are much more likely to agree with a position that serves their self-interest or flatters them in some way. For example, if the purpose is to get the witness to admit to being tired, then questions should be asked which show the witness had legitimate reasons to be tired.

Example:

Q: Tom Sawyer, you consider yourself a good worker?

A: Yeah.

Q: You work hard when your job requires it?

A: You bet.

Q: Sure. And your work is demanding?

A: I'll say.

Q: You want to succeed at your job, don't you?

A: I'd like to, yes.

Q: You try to do the best possible job you can?

A: I try.

Q: And you are a very dedicated, committed worker?

A: I try to be. Yes.

Q: You worked a long day?

A: I did.

Q: And it's fair to say you were tired at the end of your long, hard day of work?

A: I was.

These and additional questions lead to the inevitable conclusion that a hardworking and dedicated employee who worked a full day would naturally be tired at the end of that day. Positive, supportive, and flattering questions usually result in an agreeable witness.

3. Establish Concepts

One of the purposes of cross-examination is to provide the fact finder with a different perspective and explanation of a situation. These views can be established by asking questions that develop these "concepts." The cross-examiner wants the witness to show agreement with a "concept" by agreeing with the question. However, a witness may disagree with certain words used to establish the concept. The cross-examiner should then focus on establishing the concept and not necessarily force the witness to agree to specific terms or descriptions. The use of various words can lead the witness to agree with the overall concept. The technique of using synonyms described in section 9.3(B)(4) helps establish concepts.

Example:

Q: The game was vigorous?

A: Yes.

Q: You played hard?

A: Yes.

Q: You were hot?

A: Yes.

Q: Sweaty?

A: Yes.

Q: You were tired at the end of the game, Ms. Hopscotch?

A: Yes.

Q: You were not totally exhausted?

A: That's right.

Q: But you were very tired?

A: Yes.

Q: All that hopping and bending did wear you out?

A: Yes.

Attempting to have the witness agree with a conclusory word before asking a sufficient number of appropriate fact questions is likely to backfire. It is much wiser to ask the preliminary questions establishing the facts so the witness has to agree. The summation can then be used to explain that the ability of the eyewitness to make an identification was diminished because the witness was tired or distracted.

4. Use Indirection

Cross-examiners sometimes use indirection in asking questions. Indirect questions may not alert the witness about why a question is being asked or the purpose of a line of questioning until the point is made. During witness preparation, the direct examiner will advise the witness of the anticipated areas of cross-examination, and the witness will understand the purpose behind some questions. This advance information may not be sufficient to alert witnesses to all areas of cross, and their unfamiliarity with the legal process may reduce their ability to think clearly and anticipate questions, making indirection an effective tactic.

Example (Cross-Examining the Employee):

Presume the cross-examiner represents an employer who fired an employee who then sues the employer for breach of the employment contract. The employer in defense claims the employee was an "at will" employee and could be fired at any time without cause, and cross-examines the employee.

Q: You could quit your job at any time, Ms. White, is that correct?

A: Yes.

Q: The dwarfs could not force you to stay?

A: Not if I wanted to leave.

Q: Yes. If you no longer wanted to work there, you could leave?

A: That's true.

D. CONTROL RESPONSES AND THE WITNESS

Effective cross-examiners are insistent and persistent. They expect a responsive answer and they will ask follow up questions if an answer is non-responsive. There are a variety of methods that can produce prompt, favorable responses and that reasonably control the witness.

1. Know the Answers

A cardinal rule of cross-examination is to ask only a question to which the answer is already known by the cross-examiner. Many answers will be known because they appear in a witness statement, a deposition, a document, or are within the knowledge of another person. If the witness refuses to answer properly, the source of the information can be used to remind or impeach the witness. See Section 9.4(E). Further, because the witness knows a source of information exists, the witness will give the expected answer, effectively controlling the response and witness.

Example (Controlling a Response Using a Witness Statement):

Q: You were driving your broomstick approximately 5 light-years an hour, isn't that correct Mr. Potter?

A: I'm not sure how fast I was going.

Q: You were going approximately 5 light-years an hour?

A: I don't know.

Q: You recall that you gave a written statement in this case to an investigator, correct?

A: Yes, I did.

Q: In that statement you said you were going approximately 5 light-years an hour?

A: Oh, that's right.

2.   Predict the Answers

There are situations in which the precise answer is not known but may be reasonably deduced. There may not be a complete statement of a witness; there may be questions that were not asked during a deposition; there may be an administrative hearing or arbitration without prior statements from the witness. These situations are common and frequent.

A successful cross-examination approach is to reasonably predict what the answers will be. An effective cross may be based upon a reasonable deduction of what the witness is likely, or very likely, to say. This determination can be based on what a reasonable person would have said or done or what is quite likely to have occurred.

Example:

Presume a witness views an accident while walking home on Valentine's Day. Presume also that the cross-examiner does not know the precise answers to the following questions but can reasonably deduce the answers and demonstrate that the ability of the witness to observe was diminished.

Q: Ms. Knightley, the day of the accident was Valentine's Day?

A: Oh, yes.

Q: You had some plans that evening?

A: Yes.

Q: While you were standing on the corner, were you thinking about your plans?

A: Yeah. About going to a movie.

Q: And you were looking forward to going to the movies?

A: Yes. I was.

Q: It was a film you wanted to go see.

A: Yes, a movie I love actually.

Q: And those thoughts were pleasant thoughts?

A: Yes, you could say that.

Q: The accident occurred while you were thinking about your plans for the evening?

A: Well, yes.

This approach can be successful in one of two ways. The witness may agree with the questions, as illustrated above. Or, if the witness disagrees, the fact finder will conclude the witness is being evasive or does not want to admit the obvious that is harmful. Either way, the cross has established a favorable point.

3.   Avoid the Dangerous Unknown

A cross-examiner might be tempted to ask important questions to which the answers are unknown, not predictable, and cannot be reasonably deduced. This temptation may arise because the cross-examiner has not properly prepared the case or because the attorney is playing a hunch or thinks any possible response can be handled. These temptations need to be avoided. If a witness on direct examination adds some new details that are unfamiliar to the cross-examiner, impeachment by prior inconsistent statements or omission may be available. See Section 9.4(E). The cross-examiner should prepare questions and techniques for dealing with surprise testimony during direct examination.

4.   Pursue the Reasonably Anticipated

Some cases do not involve extensive discovery and the advocate may not know a lot about what the witness will say on direct, as described previously. An effective cross can still be conducted by reasonably predicting and thoroughly preparing for the anticipated answers. A party or another witness can be an excellent source of information about what an adverse witness knows. The previous examples illustrate effective ways to cross when not everything is sufficiently known.

5.   Listen and Observe

The cross-examiner needs to listen carefully to the answers and observe how the witness responds. The advocate must concentrate and listen to and observe the subtleties and nuances of the exact answers. The attorney may need to follow up on nonresponsive or ambiguous answers, to repeat or rephrase questions if a witness is perplexed, and to comment on the appearance and credibility of witnesses during summation.

Example:

Q: You were not at the Pollock studio, were you, Ms. Krasner?

A: No.

[Does the answer "No" mean "No, I wasn't there," or "No, I was there"? The inflection the witness uses in responding may make the response clear. If not, the cross-examiner should follow up:]

Q: That means you were not there?

A: That's right.

Example:

Q: It is true that you don't remember exactly what Mr. Hale said, right?

A: Yes.

[This question is awkwardly phrased because it contains the words "true," "right," and the negative: "don't." The attorney needs to clarify the response:]

Q: Your answer is that you don't remember?

A: Yes.

Example:

Q: Ms. Thayer, you were the waitress that refused to take the chicken salad sandwich order from Mr. Nicholson, correct?

A: I . . . think so.

Q: Excuse me, your facial expression indicated that you may not have understood that question.

---

6.   Techniques to Control the Witness

The most effective way to control witnesses is to ask short, precise questions to which they must agree. Fact questions that are accurate will require the witness to agree. Questions that contain an answer that the witness has previously provided will prompt the correct response. Examples in the previous sections that rephrased inappropriate questions illustrate this type of control. Imprecise questions or questions that contain non-factual conclusions will give the witness the opportunity to respond incorrectly or give a narrative, non-factual answer or explanation. Lengthy or complex questions need to be avoided.

Example:

Avoid Asking:

Q: At the time the fight started you were standing behind the bar at the cash register giving change to a customer, isn't that correct, Mr. Gleason?

A: Not really. I was watching to see who started the fight, and I saw your client hit the plaintiff.

Rather Ask:

Q: A fight broke out, didn't it Mr. Gleason?

A: Yes.

Q: You were behind the bar?

A: Yes.

Q: You were standing at the cash register?

A: Yes.

Q: You were giving change to a customer?

A: Yes.

Additional ways to maintain control include:

a. Repeat the Question

Example:

Q: You were standing behind the bar?

A: Well, yes, but I was looking up.

Q: You were standing behind the bar?

A: Yes.

b. Insist on an Answer

Example:

Q: You were giving change to a customer?

A: Well, let me think about that. You see, there was this noise. . . .

Q: But that was not my question. You were giving change to a customer, correct?

A: Yes.

---

c. Rephrase the Question

Example:

Q: You were giving change to a customer?

A: I heard this noise.

Q: Perhaps my question wasn't clear enough. Let me ask it this way. When you heard a noise, you were handing change to a customer?

A: Yes.

---

d. Advise the Witness to Answer

Example:

Q: You closed the cash register drawer?

A: As I was looking over in the corner.

Q: You walked away from the cash register?

A: A customer called me over.

Q: Mr. Gleason, please limit your answer to the question I asked in order to help us understand what happened.

A: All right.

Q: You closed the drawer?

A: Yes.

Q: You did walk away from the cash register?

A: Yes I did.

---

e. Further Advise the Witness

Example:

Q: The customer asked you for a drink?

A: She was thirsty.

Q: She asked you for a bottled beer?

A: We don't sell beer on tap.

Q: Mr. Gleason, in the interests of time, please answer the specific question asked. If you don't understand the question, tell me and I'll rephrase it so it's clear. If you can't answer it yes or no, tell me and I'll rephrase it.

f. Seek Cooperation from the Witness

Example:

Q: Mr. Gleason, during your direct examination you answered questions your attorney asked you. You will be able to give me that same degree of cooperation you gave your attorney, won't you?

A: I'll try.

g. Request a Curative Instruction

If a witness gives a nonresponsive answer, the judge can be asked in jury trials to instruct the jury to disregard the answer that was not responsive to the question asked.

Example:

Q: You walked down to the far end of the bar?

A: But I'm sure your client started that fight.

Cross-Examiner:

Your Honor, we ask that you instruct the jury to disregard that last answer as being nonresponsive and improper.

h. Ask the Judge or Arbitrator for Further Assistance (If Nothing Else Works)

Advocates can ask the judge or arbitrator to instruct the witness to answer the questions asked. Some judges and arbitrators may do this on their own to prevent a witness from being unresponsive. However, some may refuse to assist the attorney and tell the attorney to conduct the examination. It is ordinarily more effective to ask for assistance after a witness has failed or refused to answer a number of questions and after the advocate has used techniques to obtain responsive answers. Many judges and arbitrators expect an attorney to control the witness and to ask for assistance only if those attempts fail. Others, however, will control a non-responsive witness without being asked.

Example:

Q: The bottled beer was in a fridge below the bar, wasn't it?

A: I could clearly hear your client yelling.

Q: Again, Mr. Gleason, answer the question asked.

A: I'm trying.

Q: You bent down to get beer from the fridge below the bar?

A: Just for a brief moment.

Q: You opened a refrigerator?

A: How else could I get the bottles out? It only makes sense. . . .

Cross-Examiner:

Your Honor, I object on the grounds of nonresponsiveness and ask you to instruct this witness to answer the question asked.

---

6.   Close Loopholes

To increase the chances a witness will agree with a question, ask a witness a series of preliminary foundation questions as a predicate to obtain responsive answers.

Example:

Q: Mr. Pinkman, you gave *the police a description* of the person you saw sell the methamphetamine?

A: Yes.

Q: The events were *fresh* in your memory?

A: Yes.

Q: The description you gave was *accurate*?

A: Yes.

Q: You wanted to *assist* the police in finding this person?

A: You bet.

Q: You did *not withhold* any information from the police about the description of this person?

A: I did not.

Q: You gave the *best possible* description you could?

A: I did.

Q: And the description you gave was. . . .

These preliminary questions lay a foundation requiring the witness to respond favorably because no reasonable person would disagree with the resulting conclusion. Predicate questions take away any excuse a witness may give for not saying or doing something. In the above example, the witness may attempt to explain the prior description given to the police was not accurate in an effort to change the description of the drug dealer at trial. The preliminary questions compel the witness to agree to what they said and did previously and to what is reasonable.

7. Avoid Asking One Question Too Many

Questions should be designed to produce necessary information. When that information is obtained, the attorney should stop asking questions. Asking too many questions may hurt the case because the witness is given another opportunity to explain an answer. The explanation can be saved for summation.

Example:

Q: After the robbery, you gave a description of the person who started the fight to the police?

A: Yes, I did.

Q: You told the police that person was about 5′10″ tall?

A: Yes.

Q: Weight around 200 pounds?

A: About that.

Q: Had brown eyes?

A: Yes.

Q: Black hair?

A: Yes.

Q: And wearing a tee shirt and jeans?

A: That's right.

Q: Now that description fits many people who live in this community, doesn't it, Mr. Schrader?

A: I will never forget the guy who took my money. That's him sitting right there.

The last question is one question too many. The attorney can explain that point in closing argument without trying to get the witness to agree.

8.   Avoid Explanations

As explained previously, questions that permit a narrative response, or that ask "how" or "why," invite disaster in a cross-examination. A witness should not be given an opportunity to explain something that diminishes the point made on cross-examination. The opposing attorney may ask questions on redirect examination, but the cross-examiner should not ask questions that prompt explanatory responses.

Example:

Do Not Ask:

Q: So, tell us *why* you're so sure my client, Lex Luther, did it?

A: I've never seen anybody commit such a brutal act. I'll never forget that man as long as I live. I see him in my mind and I see him sitting there next to you. He did it.

---

9.   Anticipate the Unexpected

Witnesses usually agree with leading questions, but advocates need to be prepared in case they do not. A prior statement can be used to refresh their recollection or impeach them. See Section 9.4. The cross-examiner must know all the details of prior statements.

If there are no prior statements or ready sources to hold the witness accountable, there are some things that can be done to prepare for these situations. First, prepare alternative questions, so questions need not be asked spontaneously if there is an unexpected answer. If the expected answer is yes, presume the witness will say no and prepare for a "no" response. Also, have additional questions on related topics prepared in case the witness says, "I don't remember." This preparation can be a time-consuming process, but necessary. Second, focus on asking questions about concepts and not words. If witnesses will not agree with the choice of words, change the words and get them to agree with the concepts. See Section 9.3(C). Lastly, avoid arguing with witnesses if they disagree with proposed answers. When a witness gives an unexpected response, don't argue with the witness or ask objectionable or ineffective questions listed in Section 9.1(D). Thorough preparation for unanticipated responses will provide the next question.

E. EMPHASIZE POINTS

1. Expand a Point

It is an effective technique during cross-examination to ask a series of short, precise questions rather than one broad, general question. Concise questions highlight the point and are easier to understand.

Example:

Avoid Asking:

Q: You had 3 drinks at the bar that night waiting for Shrek?

Rather Ask:

Q: You arrived at the bar at approximately 6 p.m.?

A: Yes.

Q: You ordered one martini?

A: Yes.

Q: And you drank that martini?

A: Yes.

Q: You ordered a second martini?

A: Yes.

Q: You drank the second martini?

A: Yes.

Q: Then you had a glass of wine?

A: Yes.

Q: You say you left the bar at approximately 7 p.m.?

A: Approximately.

Q: Princess Fiona, you had two martinis and one glass of wine during that hour you were at the bar?

A: Yes.

---

2. Save Point for Summation

An effective cross-examination helps the fact finder remember and understand the point made during cross-examination. Therefore, questions should be crafted so that at the end of a series of questions the fact finder understands the point being made. Sometimes, the purpose of a series of questions may be unclear. There is always a temptation to ask a final summary question to make a point obvious. A final question may give the witness an opportunity to clarify or explain, and it may be best to avoid the summary question and explain the reasons in summation.

Example:

Q: Officer Krupke, you consider yourself a good police officer?

A: Yes.

Q: You take pride in your work?

A: Yes.

Q: You have been a police officer for ten years?

A: Yes.

Q: You graduated from the Police Academy?

A: Yes.

Q: You regularly attend police training programs?

A: Yes.

Q: You hope someday to become a captain?

A: That would be my hope.

Q: You were the detective in charge of this case investigation?

A: Yes.

Q: You spent many hours conducting that investigation?

A: Yes.

Q: You spent several weeks involved in that investigation?

A: Yes.

Q: You developed a profile of the person who you believe committed this crime?

A: Yes.

Q: It is fair to say that you had an instinct about the person who committed this crime?

A: Yes.

Q: After further investigation, you selected two individuals who you thought may have committed this crime?

A: We initially narrowed our investigation to two.

Q: But you were not sure?

A: That's true.

Q: And you conducted a thorough investigation of the first person on your list of suspects?

A: Yes.

Q: You later decided this first person didn't commit the crime?

A: That's right.

Q: You then investigated the second person on your list?

A: We continued our investigation of the second person.

Q: And after still further investigation, you decided the second person could not have committed the crime?

A: Yes, that's correct.

Q: And you still were not sure?

A: Yes.

Q: You started all over again?

A: Yes.

Q: And then you decided to begin an investigation of Mr. Riff, the defendant in this case?

A: Yes.

Do Not Ask the Final Summary Question:

Q: So you really were not sure of anybody, and Mr. Riff was not on the top of your guilty list?

That question will likely produce an answer that explains that Riff committed the crime. Instead, during summation argue: how uncertain the police were regarding their suspicions about the defendant; how long it took to conduct their unsuccessful investigations; how reluctant the police were to have arrested the defendant in the first place; and there were other possible suspects who more likely committed the crime.

F.　ASK SAFE QUESTIONS

1.　Repeat Supportive Direct Examination

The general rule is that direct examination testimony should not be repeated on discrediting cross-examination because the repetition of the direct will only emphasize the opponent's case. However, repetition of direct examination testimony will be effective if that part of the direct is supportive of the cross-examiner's case. Leading questions are the effective way of presenting supportive evidence on cross-examination.

Non-leading questions already asked on direct may be effective on cross only if the answer is very favorable and witness control is not a problem.

Example:

Q: Humpty Dumpty, as you told us on direct examination, you approached the wall on your own?

A: Yes.

Q: You then decided to sit on top of the wall?

A: Yes.

Q: You were able to climb the wall on your own?

A: Yes.

Q: You sat on the top of the wall, correct?

A: Yes.

Q: Then you fell off the wall?

A: Yes.

Q: There was no one around when you fell off the wall?

A: That's right.

Q: No one pushed you?

A: No one.

Q: And that was a great fall?

A: Sure.

Q: Some people came immediately to help you?

A: Yes.

Q: All the King's men came?

A: There were a lot of them.

Q: And all their horses?

A: Apparently.

---

2.   Ask "Neutral" Cross-Examination Questions

Safe, neutral questions are helpful to control the witness and prompt responsive answers. On cross-examination, problems with a witness may arise, and precise questions help get the witness back on track.

Example (*Volunteer Witness*):

Q: Ms. Bjorg, you were asked to be a witness in this case by the attorney for the plaintiff, correct?

A: Yes.

Q: You were not served with a subpoena ordering you to come to court to testify, were you?

A: I was not served.

Q: You came here today because the attorney asked you to come?

A: Yes.

Example (*Familiarity with Evidence*):

Q: Mr. Olijuwon, you have talked with the attorney for the plaintiff about this case?

A: Yes.

Q: You discussed the testimony that you were going to give in this case?

A: Yes.

Q: You also previously talked to the plaintiff?

A: Yes.

Q: And you discussed with the plaintiff what happened in this incident?

A: Yes.

Q: And you talked with other witnesses in this case about this incident?

A: I did.

Q: Before coming into court to testify today, you had some idea of what the plaintiff was going to say, didn't you?

A: Yes.

Q: Because he told you?

A: Yes.

Q: And you also had some idea of what some of the other witnesses were going to say?

A: Yes.

Q: Because they told you as well?

A: Yes.

Example (*Reviewed Documents*):

Q: You were not present in court when the plaintiff testified, were you, Mr. Ali-Baba?

A: No.

Q: You had a chance to read the deposition of the plaintiff that was taken before this trial, didn't you?

A: I did.

Q: And you had a chance to read statements the attorney for the plaintiff showed you?

A: I did.

Q: And those statements contained the stories of some of the witnesses in this case?

A: I believe so.

Example (*Favorable Testimony*):

Q: Ms. Aguilera, you pretty much understood why the plaintiff had brought this lawsuit?

A: Yes.

Q: You knew that your testimony would help the plaintiff's case?

A: I believe it will.

Q: In fact, you understood that the plaintiff expected you to testify favorably?

A: Well, I assume that's why they asked me to come and sing my testimony.

These questions and answers may not establish information useful for cross-examination purposes, compared to the other approaches and techniques explained in this Chapter. However, they may be useful in situations where safe, neutral or indirect questions need to be asked. Arguments may be made based on answers to the questions that the witness appears biased, over-prepared by the other attorney, or has no actual knowledge of the facts.

G. DESIGN QUESTIONS FOR SPECIFIC WITNESSES

1. Witnesses with Communication Issues

Certain witnesses require special consideration in conducting cross-examination. These include children, vulnerable witnesses, and individuals who have communication difficulties. With these types of witnesses, careful crafting of questions is especially important. The use of easy to understand words and a softer tone can be effective.

2.   The Evasive Witness

Some witnesses may give evasive answers to cross-examination questions even though the questions are effectively phrased. They may display selective memory, forgetting information that hurts them and only remembering information that helps them. Rambling witnesses provide nonresponsive answers, defeating even the best efforts to control their responses. Occasionally, witnesses may take on an adversarial demeanor or hostile attitude, even though the cross-examiner is tactful and polite. Still other witnesses may repeatedly answer by saying "I'm not sure," "I can't remember," "I don't recall," "Maybe," or "I don't know," even though the question is simple and direct.

Evasive witnesses, if allowed to continue, usually destroy their own credibility. Fact finders perceive these witnesses to be unreasonably evasive and do not believe their story. One way to cross-examine them is to continue to ask them questions and permit them to continue to be evasive. The more a witness testifies in an unreasonable manner, the more likely it is that their testimony will be ignored. The negative impact created by evasive witnesses may extend beyond their story and adversely affect other parts of the opponent's case.

During summation, the cross-examiner can compare the selective memory or evasive answers of these witnesses given during cross-examination with the good memory and cooperation of favorable witnesses on direct examination.

3.   The Reputation Witnesses

Because the character of a party or witness is usually not an issue, few cases involve the examination of reputation witnesses. The credibility of each witness who testifies can be attacked by the testimony of another who states that the witness' reputation for telling the truth is poor. As a practical matter, this occurs infrequently because most people have decent reputations for telling the truth. Also, it is difficult to locate a person who can convincingly testify to a witness' propensity for being untruthful. Consequently, the opportunities to cross-examine reputation witnesses do not arise often.

When such opportunities occur, reputation witnesses can be cross-examined like any other witness. They may also be cross-examined as to specific instances of misconduct that contradict the character trait in issue. Cross-examination questions can establish bad acts, prior misconduct, convictions, and other instances that contradict the reputation established on direct examination. Some cross-examination techniques are:

- If the reputation witness testifies that the person has a good reputation in the community, the question, *"Have you heard . . . "* of specific instances of misconduct can be asked.

- If the reputation witness testifies that in the witness' opinion the reputation of the person is good, the question, *"Do you know . . . "* of specific instances of misconduct can be asked.

- Reputation witnesses can also be effectively cross-examined by questions that establish their lack of personal knowledge about the events of the lawsuit:

"You were not online when Mr. Assange's computer was hacked?"

"You did not see the defendant with Ms. Liwynske?"

Another line of questioning may establish the limited knowledge of the reputation witness and the narrow basis of the testimony:

"Thousands of people live in Hakuna Matata's community? You have only talked to a few of them about the defendant's reputation for truth?"

Or

"You only spend a limited amount of time with the defendant in politics? You are unaware of how the defendant treats his family at home?"

Some jurisdictions restrict the type of cross-examination questions that may be asked of a reputation witness. All jurisdictions require that the cross-examiner have a good faith basis and available proof to establish the prior misconduct.

§ 9.4   DISCREDITING CROSS-EXAMINATION

As explained in the introduction to this Chapter, a primary function of cross-examination is to discredit the opponent's case. Questions are designed to discredit the testimony of witnesses and their credibility and other evidence offered by the opponent. These questions attack the legitimacy, integrity, and persuasiveness of the opponent's positions.

As with supportive cross-examination approaches, there are factors common to typical disputes that may be established to enhance destructive cross-examination. In civil cases, a common theme involves notions of responsibility. The party who has acted responsibly should prevail over the party that acted irresponsibly. This is often a balancing determination because both parties to the dispute likely have been irresponsible, with the victor being that party who has been less irresponsible. The goal of discrediting cross, in part, becomes an effort to show the opposing party to be solely or more irresponsible and, accordingly, deserving of losing the case.

This section describes and provides a variety of cross-examination techniques and tactics that discredit evidence and impeach witnesses. Section A explains how to attack a story that is implausible, improbable, or impossible. Section B describes how to establish inconsistencies between witnesses. Section C explains impeachment strategies. Section D describes common areas of impeachment.

A. IMPLAUSIBILITY, IMPROBABILITY, IMPOSSIBILITY

When preparing the case, the evidence may reveal that the testimony of a witness is too farfetched to be believed. Cross-examination can establish that the story told by a witness ought not to be believed because it is implausible, improbable, or impossible.

1. Implausible

The story may be implausible because it does not make sense or reflect common life experiences. For example, a witness may testify that four years before the trial, while repairing floor tile in the hallway outside the office of the CEO of M & M Company, he recalled overhearing the CEO say these exact words: "I just placed an order for 750 units at a price of $138,000, delivery to Los Alamos, and they agreed to send a letter of credit before emailing the bill of lading and to pay for transit loss insurance." The complexity of the words and details demonstrate the story told by the witness is implausible. The attorney may argue in summation that such recollections are too implausible to be believed.

2. Improbable

A witness' version of a story, or part of a story, may be improbable. It may be very unlikely the story could have occurred the way the witness describes. The more unlikely the story, the more easily a showing of improbability may be made. For example, a witness may testify that she was no more than 100 feet away from a building while peddling her bicycle at a speed of 15 miles per hour toward the building when she heard the explosion and saw the defendant running away. During cross-examination, the attorney may place a mark on a diagram showing her position in the alley at the time of the explosion. During summation, the attorney can use a mathematical formula for the number of feet per second a bicycle travels at 15 miles per hour to show that either she was at least 300 feet away or that she was peddling over 35 miles per hour, which, while possible, is improbable.

3. Impossible

Some witnesses may sincerely tell an impossible story. While they may honestly believe what they perceived and remember, they are still wrong. For example, a witness may testify that, while parked behind the crosswalk at the intersection of Oak and Elm, he saw the defendant's motorcycle traveling at a high rate of speed. The cross-examination may ascertain the exact position of the witness when he said he saw the accident. During the defendant's case, the cross-examiner may call an investigator to introduce photographs or a video taken through the car window from the spot where the witness said he was stopped showing a brick building blocking the witness' view.

B. ESTABLISHING INCONSISTENCIES BETWEEN WITNESSES

A witness' story may be inherently correct and complete, but may contradict the story told by another witness. Cross-examination can establish these inconsistencies. For example, Police Officer Hernandez testifies that Sergeant Schultz was holding the shotgun in her right hand with the barrel pointed toward the ground. The defense cross-examiner may have Officer Hernandez repeat part of this testimony to highlight it for the fact finder. Officer Garibaldi subsequently testifies for the defense that Sergeant Schultz held the shotgun in both hands with the barrel pointed at the deceased. The defense can then argue these material inconsistencies during summation and point out why a particular witness (Officer Garibaldi) ought to be believed.

It is improper to ask one witness to comment on the credibility of another witness or to ask whether a witness believes another. It is permissible to ask a witness if that witness agrees or disagrees with a story told by another witness. For example, it is improper to ask: "Do you believe Officer Hernandez is telling the truth?" However, in most jurisdictions, one may properly ask Officer Garibaldi: "Officer Hernandez testified that Sergeant Schultz held the shotgun in her right hand. Do you agree or disagree with Officer Hernandez's statement?"

C. IMPEACHMENT STRATEGIES

Impeachment is a tactic designed to reduce the credibility of the testifying witness, the credibility of a story, or the credibility of another witness. Any witness may be impeached. A declarant of a hearsay statement who does not appear as a witness in person may also be impeached. Federal Rule of Evidence 806 and similar state rules permit the impeachment of a hearsay declarant to the same extent that a live witness can be impeached.

1. Using Material and Significant Evidence to Impeach

Effective impeachment covers material evidence and important issues. If an issue is collateral—immaterial or insignificant—the impeachment is usually ineffective or disallowed. Whether impeachment evidence is collateral depends upon its impact on the issues in the case and on the credibility of the witness. Impeachment evidence may be introduced if the evidence relates to a significant issue, reduces the credibility of a witness or is otherwise important.

Impeachment is most effective when it relates to significant facts or opinions adversely affecting the credibility of the witness or story. A "reasonableness" test is the standard that is commonly used to determine the value of impeachment material. If it is reasonable that the testimony of a witness might be adversely affected, or if the witness' testimony is unreasonable because the witness has testified differently on separate occasions, the impeachment is sensible and should be conducted.

The following examples illustrate the reasonableness factor:

- If a witness is a good friend of a party, it is reasonable to demonstrate that the witness may be biased in favor of that party. If a witness is merely an acquaintance of a party, that remote fact may not sensibly establish bias.

- In an attempt to establish bias on the part of the witness in favor of a party, it is reasonable to show that the witness is a current, loyal employee of the party for whom the witness is testifying. On the other hand, it would be ineffective for the cross-examiner to establish bias if the witness had worked for the employer for one month ten years ago and had no contact with the employer since that time.

- It is reasonable to demonstrate that the witness has made a significant change in testimony concerning details of an event. For example, if a witness testifies at a deposition she was "pretty sure" it was the defendant who was driving the car, and then testifies at trial she "is certain" the defendant was driving the car, such a significant change in her opinion will make impeachment worthwhile.

- It is not reasonable to impeach a witness on minor details. A witness to a crime may testify that she was standing at a store "laptop" display when she saw the defendant. Investigation reveals she stood by a smart tablet display and not a laptop display. An attempt to impeach the witness by showing the display was for tablets and not laptops may be so insignificant that it's unproductive.

Impeachment efforts regarding minor discrepancies usually backfire because the fact finder may conclude that if the trivial issue is the best the cross-examiner has, the case must be very weak. Witnesses may have made prior statements that contain slight inaccuracies when compared with the actual evidence. These inaccuracies may be so insignificant they are not worth impeachment of the witness.

Minor inaccuracies may be worth the impeachment effort if there are a significant number and cumulatively they add up to substantial mistakes. A witness who makes many small errors may be disbelieved on a major issue. The advocate can argue in summation how these discrepancies reduce the credibility of the witness.

2. Impeaching a Witness Using Extrinsic Evidence

A witness may occasionally deny the impeaching evidence. For example, a witness may testify that she is not an employee of defendant corporation or a witness may deny having a felony criminal record. The cross-examiner is usually able to introduce extrinsic (meaning from a source other than the witness) evidence to establish the impeaching fact. For example, the cross-examiner may call the personnel director of defendant corporation to testify that the witness is an employee, or the cross-examiner may introduce a certified copy of the criminal conviction or ask the court to take judicial notice of that fact.

Extrinsic evidence may not be admissible if the impeaching issue is collateral. An issue is collateral if there is no direct connection between the impeaching fact and a relevant issue in the case. For example, a witness may testify on direct examination that she saw a restaurant glass window crack as she was drinking her vanilla shake. The cross-examiner asks her whether, in fact, the shake was chocolate, not vanilla, and she denies that it was chocolate. The cross-examiner will not be able to call the waiter to testify as to the flavor of the shake because the type of shake is only collateral and not related to any material issue.

However, if the same witness testifies on direct examination that she saw the glass window crack when she was sitting in a window booth, the cross-examiner may ask her whether she was in fact sitting at a wall table. If the witness denies sitting along the wall at a table, the cross-examiner may call the waiter as a witness to testify that the witness was sitting by the wall with her chair facing away from the glass window, preventing her from seeing out. This issue is non-collateral because it directly relates to the ability of the witness to see and perceive.

3. Responding to Impeachment Evidence by the Direct Examiner

The cross-examiner must consider the tactics available to the direct examiner who must deal with impeachment. The direct examiner has a number of options when facing impeachment evidence.

First, the direct examiner can object to the impeachment effort. The accusation may be collateral or insignificant and improper impeachment.

Second, the direct examiner may request the judge or arbitrator to allow related statements explaining the impeachment to be introduced immediately to reduce the impact of the impeachment. Jurisdictions commonly have a rule permitting the introduction of statements related to the area of impeachment contemporaneously with the impeaching statement. See, e.g., Fed.R.Evid. 106. The rationale for this rule is to permit statements to be placed in proper and complete context.

For example, a witness may testify during a deposition: "The car was traveling around 30 miles per hour. But it may have been going slower." On direct examination, the witness testifies that the car was traveling "around 20 miles an hour." On cross-examination, the cross-examiner introduces the prior statement that the car was traveling "around 30 miles per hour" to impeach the witness. The direct examiner can ask that the prior statement—"But it may have been going slower"—be introduced at the same time during cross-examination to present the complete context of the statement. This request should be allowed, and the statement can be read from the prior statement.

Third, the direct examiner can offer the impeaching evidence during the direct examination. It is less harmful if the witness voluntarily explains a mistake or problem on direct. For example, it is a preferred practice for a witness who made a significant prior inconsistent statement to admit making the mistake during direct examination and explain why.

Fourth, the direct examiner during redirect examination can have the witness explain significant impeaching evidence. This may be necessary, even if the witness first explains it on direct examination, depending upon how damaging the information is and how it was elicited during cross-examination. For example, if a witness during direct testified on a critical issue that there were three firefighters at the scene, and during cross admits there were only two, a redirect examination question would be: "Why did you say there were two and not three firefighters at the scene during cross-examination?"

Fifth, the direct examiner may rehabilitate an impeached witness with a prior consistent statement, if it rebuts a charge of fabrication or improper motive. See, e.g., Fed.R.Evid. 801(d)(1)(B). If there is an available prior consistent statement, the statement can be introduced as an exhibit. If the prior consistent statement was made orally to another person, that person may be called to testify to the prior statement.

Sixth, in a jury trial the direct examiner may request that the judge give the jury an instruction limiting the jury's consideration of the impeaching evidence to its effect only on the credibility of the witness and not as substantive proof of the evidence. See Section 4.5(E).

D. COMMON AREAS OF IMPEACHMENT

There are eight established areas of impeachment:

- Interest, Bias or Prejudice,
- Competency Deficiencies,
- Inadequate Observation/Lack of Perception,
- Poor Recollection/Lack of Memory,
- Inconsistent Conduct,
- Criminal Records,
- Specific Instances of Untruthfulness, and
- Prior Inconsistent Statements/Omissions.

1.   Impeachment Based on Interest, Bias or Prejudice

Witnesses may have an interest in a case that motivates them to testify in a certain way. This interest might be financial gain or an emotional reason, such as revenge. Establishing these factors on cross can demonstrate the underlying motivation behind a witness' testimony and may significantly reduce the credibility of that witness' testimony.

Bias and prejudice are factors that prevent a witness from being impartial. A witness may have a bias in favor of, or a prejudice against, a party or a case. Bias or prejudice can result from a variety of causes. The basis for the bias or prejudice is usually a relationship the witness has with a party or an interest the witness has in the case. The most common sources are family, personal relationships, employment situations, and life experiences. Establishing these factors during cross demonstrate the underlying influences which make impartiality difficult or impossible.

If a witness denies the existence of an interest or a relationship, extrinsic evidence of that fact can be established. The cross-examiner can introduce such a fact through a witness or an authenticated document.

Example (Prejudice):

Q: Mr. Bluto, you do not consider Popeye a friend, do you?

A: He's not a friend.

Q: You have argued with him over the years?

A: Yes.

Q: You've had many fights with him?

A: We have.

Q: Popeye has taken Olive Oyl, the woman you love, from you?

A: He's trying.

Q: That makes you angry?

A: Well, yea.

Q: It is fair to say, Mr. Bluto, that you hate Popeye?

A: Without a doubt.

Example (Bias and Interest):

In a personal injury case, the father of the plaintiff was a passenger in the car that the son was driving at the time of the accident. The father was not injured.

Q: You were the passenger in your son's car at the time of the accident, correct Mr. Stiller?

A: Yes.

Q: You have a close relationship with your son?

A: Sure.

Q: You talk to him about many things?

A: We do.

Q: And you talked to him about this accident?

A: A few times.

Q: Your son has told you he hopes to get money for this case?

A: Yes.

Q: You and he were driving back to the comedy theater?

A: We were.

Q: He was going there for training to be a comic?

A: Yes.

Q: It costs a lot of money for that training?

A: It's not cheap.

Q: Your son pays for all that training?

A: Yes.

Q: And you pay for his living expenses?

A: Yes.

Q: And those expenses are quite high?

A: Yea, it's pricey.

---

2.   Impeachment Based on Competency Deficiencies

Section 7.2(A) described the four competency requirements for a witness: oath, perception, recollection, and communication. Cross-examination may establish that a competent witness has deficiencies that reduce credibility. The competency requirements of perception and recollection are two areas most frequently attacked on cross-examination.

The two other requirements of an oath and the ability to communicate are not usually areas for cross-examination inquiry. If a witness is unable or has difficulty taking an oath or affirmation, the opposing attorney will argue that the witness is incompetent. After the judge or arbitrator makes a determination that a witness has properly taken an oath or affirmation, that requirement will usually not be an effective area to be probed on cross. Further, Federal Rule Evidence 610 prohibits evidence of a witness' religious beliefs or opinion to be used for the purpose of reducing or enhancing the witnesses' credibility.

Occasionally, a child witness or another witness who has difficulty discerning the truth may be cross-examined to establish an inadequate or inappropriate understanding of the oath or affirmation. Because of the delicate nature of the issue and the vulnerable status of the witness, cross-examination on the matter of oath or affirmation may cause the fact finder to empathize with the witness and to perceive the cross-examiner negatively. Effectively cross-examining a witness on the abstract notions of truth is difficult. Cross-examination in regard to the oath or affirmation is usually conducted without the jury being present. Cross-examination can be effective when a record exists showing the witness has lied under oath or affirmation previously, or has told a story different from that told on direct examination. See Section 9.4(D)(7).

Communication problems that witnesses have will ordinarily not be effective areas for cross-examination. If a witness cannot communicate, an interpreter will be made available by the examining attorney or court to translate the testimony in an understandable fashion. See Section 3.6(E). If a witness has difficulty communicating because of a disability, cross-examination inquiries may make the fact finder more sympathetic toward this vulnerable witness rendering the cross ineffective. If a witness has difficulty because of nervousness or some other reason, that factor may be self-evident and not require any cross questions. Cross-examination concerning the ability of a witness to communicate is usually conducted outside the presence of a jury. The judge then makes a ruling.

3. Impeachment Based on Inadequate Observation/Lack of Perception

To reduce their credibility, the ability of witnesses to observe an event or to perceive a situation may be challenged on cross-examination. Most witnesses do not observe or perceive everything, and the inadequacies of observations and the lack of perception may be established on cross-examination. Common causes for inadequate observation and lack of perception are:

- Witness was not expecting the event,

- Witness was distracted,

- Event happened quickly,

- Circumstances were unusual,

- Event frightened the witness,

- Situation surprised the witness,

- Witness was doing something else during the event,

- Witness' perception based on sight, taste, hearing, smell, or touch was adversely influenced by other factors, and

- Details of the event were not previously described by the witness.

Example (Car Driver):

Q: Professor Knapp, you were driving east on Summit?

A: Yes.

Q: You were on your way to the law school?

A: Yes.

Q: You approached the intersection of Summit and Victoria around noon?

A: Yes.

Q: Your class begins at noon?

A: Yes. When I get there.

Q: You were going to be late for that class?

A: Sadly, yes.

Q: You were anxious to get to school?

A: Yes.

Q: You were in a hurry?

A: A bit. But I wasn't speeding.

Q: You spend a fair amount of time planning your classes?

A: Yes.

Q: Sometimes you think about your classes at home?

A: Yes.

Q: And sometimes when you are driving your car?

A: Yes. But I pay attention.

Q: Your class was on your mind as you drove east this day on Summit Street?

A: Yes, I suppose.

Q: As you approached the intersection of Summit and Victoria, the stop and go traffic light turned red?

A: Yes.

Q: You noticed there was a crossing guard standing on the sidewalk to your right?

A: Yes, she was on the southwest corner.

Q: While you were waiting at the intersection, you would from time to time glance up at the light to see if had changed?

A: Yes.

Q: And you looked around to see if there were any kids in the intersection crossing the street?

A: Yes.

Q: I believe you said on direct examination you saw two students to your right talking to the crossing guard?

A: Yes.

Q: Your radio was on in your car at this time?

A: I listen to public radio.

Q: It was noon time and the news was on the radio?

A: Yes.

Q: Cars were driving north and south through the intersection?

A: Yes, I saw some cars drive by and Dean Gordon's limo.

Q: You were not expecting to see an accident at that time, were you?

A: No.

Q: That surprised you?

A: Yes.

Q: When you first heard the collision it startled you?

A: I was startled.

Q: You had a passenger in your car on the way to law school?

A: Yes.

Q: You were driving that day with Professor Juergens?

A: Yes.

Example (Car Passenger):

Q: You were in the car with Professor Knapp, correct?

A: Yes.

Q: You both were on your way to school?

A: Yes.

Q: During the drive you talked with Professor Knapp?

A: Yes.

Q: He told you he was in a hurry because he was late for class?

A: He mentioned he was late.

Q: The car you were both in was stopped at an intersection by a crossing guard?

A: Yes.

Q: While the car was stopped, Professor Knapp made some remark about the crossing guard?

A: Yes.

Q: He said he wished he were a crossing guard instead of a law professor?

A: Yes.

Q: And you said, "There is not much difference."?

A: As a joke, obviously.

Q: After the accident, both of you drove on to the school?

A: Yes.

Q: You don't recall Professor Knapp saying anything to you about the accident during that drive, do you?

A: No, I don't recall.

Q: You do recall that he said after the accident he was going to be late for class?

A: He said that, and he was sad.

---

4.   Impeachment Based on Poor Recollection/Lack of Memory

Most witnesses will not remember everything they observed or perceived. Other witnesses may have had their recollection influenced by what they learned after an event. Cross-examination can reveal reasons why the witness' memory is lacking or unduly influenced. If the witness denies the underlying fact showing poor or absent memory, the cross-examiner can introduce that fact through extrinsic evidence. Common factors that diminish the recollection of a witness include:

- The passage of time,
- The absence of any record,
- Discussing the matter with others,
- Being involved in similar situations,
- Inability to distinguish this event from others, and
- Matters that adversely affect the memory of the witness.

Example: (Car Driver Inability to Remember Details):

Q: After the accident, you immediately drove on to the law school, correct Professor Knapp?

A: Yes.

Q: You did not wait at the accident scene?

A: No.

Q: You didn't give your name or address to anyone?

A: I did not.

Q: You did not tell anyone at that time what you saw?

A: No.

Q: Back at the law school, you discussed the accident with Professor Juergens, the passenger in your car?

A: Yes.

Q: You discussed what you saw?

A: We talked about it.

Q: You taught four hours of classes that day?

A: Yes.

Q: You stayed in your law school office and sent some emails?

A: Yes.

Q: You bought some—I won't mention what—from eBay on the Internet?

A: For my collection.

Q: You did not talk about this accident with anyone else while you were at the law school?

A: No.

Q: After school, you went home for dinner?

A: Yes.

Q: You recall you told your wife, Ms. Jesson, and your children—Chris, Nathan, and John—that you saw an accident that day?

A: I mentioned it at dinner.

Q: You don't recall the details of what you told them, do you?

A: No, not really.

Q: About a week later you talked to an investigator about this accident?

A: Yes.

Q: During that week after the accident you don't recall whether you talked to anyone else about the accident, do you?

A: No.

Q: Some time later you talked with an investigator, a Brad Cousins, and received an accident report form, didn't you?

A: Yes.

Q: That was a blank form with instructions to be completed?

A: I believe so.

Q: You never filled out that form, did you?

A: No.

Q: You never made any notes about the accident, did you?

A: No, they're not a part of my memoirs.

Example: (Experienced Police Officer/Lack of Details):

Q: Detective McConaughey, you mentioned on direct that you thought the street lights were working at the corner where the drug sale took place, correct?

A: Yes.

Q: This event took place approximately two years ago?

A: Almost two years ago.

Q: You arrived at the scene shortly after the event took place?

A: Yes.

Q: You immediately began an investigation, correct?

A: I did.

Q: You talked with witnesses at the scene?

A: Yes.

Q: During an average week would you say you talked to over a hundred different potential witnesses?

A: It's difficult to say, but that's likely.

Q: You may talk to more than a hundred different people during your week?

A: Some weeks more, some weeks less.

Q: How long have you served as a police officer?

A: Six years.

Q: It's fair to say you can't remember all the details of all the cases you have worked on?

A: I can't recall them all, no.

Q: When you conduct an investigation and talk with a witness you complete a report, correct?

A: Yes.

Q: You can't possibly remember all the details these witnesses tell you?

A: That's correct.

Q: You have investigated many cases over the past two years since this event?

A: Yes that's true.

Q: It's impossible to remember all the details of those cases?

A: That's true.

Q: That's why you need reports?

A: Yes.

Q: These reports need to be accurate?

A: Yes.

Q: And complete?

A: Yes.

Q: The reports need detailed information?

A: Yes.

Q: If the reports don't have the details, an incident can be confused with another?

A: Yes, that can happen.

Q: You complete a report to make a record of the investigation?

A: Yes.

Q: That written report can help refresh your memory about the details of an investigation?

A: Yes.

Q: The investigation report you completed in this case included the important information the witnesses told you?

A: Yes.

Q: It also had all the important details that you saw?

A: Yes.

Q: There is no mention anywhere in your report that the streetlights were working, correct?

A: There is no mention.

Example (Salesperson/Lack of knowledge/memory):

Plaintiff has sued defendant for breach of an express warranty made during a car sale. The salesperson has testified under direct examination that he does not recall stating that the car had no major mechanical problems and denies that the plaintiff consumer asked whether the car had major mechanical problems.

Q: You have been a salesperson with Courtesy Car Company for three years, Mr. Loman?

A: Yes.

Q: Would you say that you have sold three or four cars a week on the average over the three years?

A: That would be a fair average.

Q: You, of course, talked with each of these customers?

A: Of course.

Q: Some of these customers leave and come back to the car dealer a number of times before deciding to buy a car?

A: Yes.

Q: In addition to all these customers, you also talk with other potential customers who decide not to buy a car?

A: Yes.

Q: Would you say that you talk to another 20 or 30 potential customers during an average week?

A: That is more difficult to estimate. Some weeks more, some weeks fewer.

Q: With each of these customers and potential customers you talk about the features of the cars they are interested in?

A: Yes.

Q: You talk about the exterior of cars?

A: Yes.

Q: You talk about the interior of cars?

A: Often.

Q: You talk about the engines?

A: Sure.

Q: You talk about gas mileage?

A: Frequently.

Q: You talk about many features of the various cars the customers look at?

A: Yes.

Q: The plaintiff, Betty Buckley, bought a used car from you two years ago?

A: Yes.

Q: When you first met her on the sales lot she was like any other customer, correct?

A: Yes.

Q: And when she returned to buy the car, she was also like any other customer?

A: Yes.

Q: Most customers ask you questions about the cars they are interested in?

A: Yes.

Q: And Ms. Buckley asked you some questions about the car she purchased?

A: I assume so.

Q: You cannot remember the specific questions she asked you, can you?

A: Not really.

Q: Customers often have questions based on what they want in a particular car?

A: Yes.

Q: You don't recall whether Ms. Buckley asked about a satellite radio that gets Broadway musicals, do you?

A: I don't recall.

Q: You can't remember what she asked you about the engine?

A: Not specifically.

Q: Nor what she asked about the transmission?

A: I can't say I do.

Q: As a salesperson it's important for you to meet the needs of your customers?

A: Well, yes.

Q: And you try your best to satisfy your customers?

A: You bet.

---

5.   Impeachment Based on Inconsistent Conduct

Testimony of a witness may be discredited because the conduct of the witness may be inconsistent with the witness' direct examination. Cross-examination can disclose that the actions of the witness are inconsistent with the witness' testimony. If the witness denies the inconsistent behavior, the cross-examiner can introduce extrinsic evidence of the inconsistent conduct.

Example:

In a personal injury case, the plaintiff Joyce Simmons has testified regarding the extent of injuries to her lower back, including pain and suffering.

Q: Ms. Simmons, immediately after the accident you got out of your car?

A: Yes.

Q: You walked over to the defendant's car?

A: Yes.

Q: You talked to Mr. Candy, the defendant?

A: I did.

Q: He called the police.

A: He told me he did.

Q: Neither of you called for an ambulance?

A: Not that I know of.

Q: You then walked over to a gas station?

A: Yes.

Q: That was about a hundred yards from the accident scene?

A: I would guess so.

Q: You used the restroom there?

A: Briefly.

Q: You talked to the gas station attendant?

A: I told her what had happened.

Q: You did not ask for an ambulance or for a doctor?

A: I did not.

Q: You then walked back to the accident scene?

A: Yes.

Q: You stood around and waited for the police?

A: Yes.

Q: The police arrived about fifteen minutes later?

A: About that.

Q: You talked with the police?

A: Yes.

Q: You didn't ask for an ambulance or a doctor then, did you?

A: No.

Q: A tow truck arrived?

A: Yes.

Q: You stood around and watched the truck tow your car away?

A: Yes.

Q: About an hour after the accident, the police drove you home?

A: Yes.

Q: You didn't ask to go to a hospital?

A: No.

Q: When got home, you told your family about the accident?

A: Yes.

Q: You then ate dinner?

A: Yes.

Q: After dinner you and your husband went to a movie?

A: To relax.

Q: After the movie you went home and went to bed?

A: Yes.

Q: The next morning you got up?

A: Yes.

Q: You ate breakfast?

A: Sure.

Q: You went to work at the grocery store?

A: Yes.

Q: You didn't go see a doctor then?

A: No.

Q: You talked with your friends at work about the accident?

A: A few.

Q: You worked a full day that day?

A: Yes.

Q: Later that day you decided to telephone a medical clinic?

A:　I did.

Q:　You then made an appointment to see a doctor three days later?

A:　Yes.

Inconsistent conduct that reduces the credibility of witnesses and their action or inaction may also be established through a showing of what a reasonable witness should have or could have done. A witness may fail to do what a *responsible person should have done* or what *a reasonable person could have done.* These failures give rise to impeachment inquiries that show the witness to have acted irresponsibly or unreasonably under the circumstances. The witness is held to this common sense standard: how a responsible person would have acted and what a reasonable person could have done.

Example:

In a real estate leasing dispute, the plaintiff book store lessee sues the defendant lessor for breach of the lease term that required the lessor to maintain the commercial property in reasonable repair. A roof water leak damaged the book inventory of the lessee. Ms. Randolph, the lessor, claims Mr. Hearst, the book store lessee, failed to timely notify her when he initially noticed the leak before it got worse and damaged his book inventory.

Q:　Mr. Hearst, you first noticed the water leak in the ceiling on April 17, correct?

A:　I did.

Q:　You placed a pail under the leak, correct?

A:　Yes.

Q:　You didn't notify Ms. Randolph of the leak at that time, did you?

A:　I didn't. It didn't seem like much of a problem then.

Q:　The pail filled up daily with water from the leak?

A:　Yes.

Q:　And you emptied the pail every day?

A:　Yeah.

Q:　The pail held about two gallons of water when filled?

A:　About that.

Q:　By the week's end, you emptied over 12 gallons of water?

A: About that much.

Q: And you still had not notified my client, Ms. Randolph?

A: I had not.

Q: You decided not to notify her?

A: I was busy.

Q: You could have phoned her?

A: Perhaps.

Q: You could have texted her?

A: I'm not sure I had her cell phone number.

Q: You could have emailed her?

A: Yeah.

Q: You chose, instead, not to notify her, right?

A: Well, it was a busy time.

Q: The next week, water was still leaking from the ceiling?

A: It wasn't getter any better.

Q: And you had to empty the pail several times that week?

A: I recall doing that.

Q: And you still failed to notify Ms. Randolph?

A: I wouldn't say it was a failure.

Q: You decided not to contact her?

A: I did not contact her then.

Q: That was your choice: not to tell her about the leak?

A: I guess I didn't tell her then.

Q: You know you did not notify her then?

A: That's right.

---

6. Impeachment by Criminal Record

A witness may be impeached by introducing a prior criminal conviction of that witness. Federal Rule of Evidence 609 and similar state rules determine the type of criminal convictions that may be used to impeach and establish the foundation for the judge or arbitrator to admit evidence of a criminal record. In general, convictions for a crime of fraud, dishonesty, false statements, or felony convictions (convictions of crime punishable by a term in excess of one year) may be used if the conviction or the release from confinement occurred within ten years from the date of the present trial. Convictions may be inadmissible if their unfairly prejudicial impact substantially outweighs their probative value. The fact that a witness has been arrested or convicted of misdemeanors or juvenile offenses is usually inadmissible as a basis for impeachment.

Most jurisdictions allow all witnesses to be impeached through cross-examination questions revealing criminal convictions, but some jurisdictions permit only party witnesses to be impeached by prior convictions. Questions may be asked of the witness that reveal the crime involved, type of conviction, date and location of the conviction, and the sentence imposed. Some jurisdictions do not allow witnesses to be cross-examined in regard to their prior convictions and only permit impeachment to be proven through a certified record of the conviction.

Cross-examination questions cannot usually delve into the facts or details of the crime to avoid unfair prejudice. Ordinarily, direct or redirect examination questions may be asked of the witness to explain the circumstances of the conviction or crime to reduce the impact of the conviction and the negative impact on the credibility of the witness. If the witness denies the conviction, the cross-examiner can introduce extrinsic evidence, commonly a certified copy of the judgment of conviction.

7.   Impeachment by Specific Instances of Untruthfulness

Evidence relating to the untruthfulness of a witness may be introduced against that witness during the cross-examination of that witness. Federal Rule 608(b) and similar state rules provide a judge or arbitrator with discretion to permit a witness to be cross-examined regarding specific instances of misconduct that relate to the untruthfulness of the witness. The cross-examiner may ask leading questions which show the witness has committed relevant and material acts establishing an untruthful character.

Example:

Q: Mr. Gandalf, you have lied when you applied for jobs, haven't you?

A: I'm not sure what you mean.

Q: Three years ago, you applied for a job with Equilaw, correct?

A: Yes.

Q: You filled out an application form for a job with Equilaw?

A: Yes, I did.

Q: On that application form, you wrote that you had five years experience in human relations, right?

A: So.

Q: You didn't have any experience in human relations, did you?

A: Not necessarily in that type of job.

Q: What you wrote on the Equilaw application was untrue?

A: I didn't have that experience.

Q: That statement was a lie, was it not?

A: It was incorrect.

Q: Two years ago you applied for a job with the Fellowship of the Rings?

A: Yes.

Q: You interviewed with the personnel director there.

A: I believe so.

Q: You told the director you previously worked for Equilaw?

A: I may have said that.

Q: Equilaw never hired you?

A: I never worked there.

Q: That statement you made to the Fellowship of the Rings personnel director was untrue?

A: Yes.

Q: That statement was a lie?

A: Yes.

Evidence of the untruthful character of the witness may be introduced through opinion and reputation by witnesses called to testify on direct examination, as explained in sections 9.3(G)(3) and 7.10(D). These witnesses may be cross-examined like any other witness, and they may also be asked questions about specific acts of truthfulness by the witness who is being impeached. Further, to contradict the testimony of these impeaching witnesses, other witnesses may testify on direct to the reputation for truthfulness of the witness who is being impeached. These witnesses may also be cross-examined like other witness, and may be asked questions about specific instances of untruthfulness by the witness.

These situations infrequently occur. The information needed to establish the untruthful character of a witness is seldom available. Even if the information is available, it may be inadmissible because it is unfairly prejudicial or collateral to the issues of the case. Further, the tactic may backfire, because the fact finder may perceive the attack to be unfair and unrelated to the issues of the case.

Example:

A witness testifies on direct examination that a party has a reputation for truthfulness.

Q: Did you know the witness lied in the past to employers?

A: No, I didn't know that.

Q: Did you know he had lied to Equilaw when he falsely told them he had five years of experience in human relations?

A: No.

Q: Did you know he lied to the Fellowship of the Rings when he told them he had worked for Equilaw?

A: No.

---

8. Refreshing Recollection Instead of Impeaching a Mistaken Witness

There are situations when the cross-examiner wants to prove a fact and will prefer to refresh the witness' recollection rather than impeach the witness. This may occur when the witness is not fabricating information but has made a mistake or cannot remember an event.

Refreshing recollection can be accomplished by showing the prior statement to the witness. If a witness on cross-examination forgets a fact the cross-examiner wants to establish affirmatively, it will be more effective for the cross-examiner to refresh the recollection of the witness through a prior statement. The cross-examiner may use a leading question to introduce the answer, but displaying to the fact finder and witness the source of the prior statement may be more effective.

Example:

Q: On direct examination, you testified that the Forum arbitration clause was signed on November 17?

A: I believe so.

Q: Do you now recall that you signed the arbitration clause on October 17?

A: No, it was November.

Q: I show you the original of the Forum clause. Please look at the bottom of the page.

A: I see it.

Q: You did sign the arbitration agreement on October 17?

A: Apparently.

Q: October was the month you signed?

A: Yes.

E. IMPEACHMENT WITH PRIOR INCONSISTENT STATEMENTS

The credibility of a witness may be diminished on cross-examination by the use of prior inconsistent statements. To be used on cross-examination, prior statements must be inconsistent or contradictory. The obvious point to be made is that the witness provided testimony on a previous occasion that was significantly different from the direct examination testimony. Effective cross-examination establishes and emphasizes the difference between a prior inconsistent statement and the testimony at the trial or hearing.

Testifying witnesses may be impeached *only* with prior statements *they* made. A witness cannot be impeached with prior statements made by others. Witnesses can only be held accountable for inconsistencies in their conflicting stories. The loss of credibility arises from the fact that the witness has given different responses at different times about the same event. Contrary statements by other witnesses can reduce the credibility of a witness, but these statements cannot be used to impeach with a prior inconsistent statement.

1. Impeachment Preparation

The cross-examiner has to be intimately familiar with the witness' prior statements so that the prior statements can be easily located during cross-examination. The statements need to be readily available so the cross-examiner can refer to and use them during cross.

2. Stages of Impeachment

The use of prior inconsistent statements usually includes four stages.

a. *Reaffirm the Direct Examination Testimony*

The cross-examiner commits the witness to the direct examination testimony by having the witness repeat the testimony to reaffirm the evidence. This ought to be done in a way that does not unnecessarily alert the witness to the cross-examiner's intentions. Direct examination testimony that differs from a prior inconsistent statement should be selected. Precise questions should be asked which restate as exactly as possible the direct examination testimony. The cross-examiner should avoid asking questions that paraphrase or improperly summarize the testimony to avoid disagreement from the witness. Repetition of the direct testimony prevents the argument that there was no inconsistency, reduces the witness' ability to explain away some ambiguity in their own testimony, and highlights the contrasting answers.

b. Describe the Circumstances of the Prior Inconsistent Statement

The cross-examiner can then lead the witness through a series of questions describing the circumstances and type of prior inconsistent statement. These questions establish the date, time, place, and circumstances of the previous statement. If the fact finders are to believe that the prior inconsistent statement is accurate, questions that establish the reliability of the prior statement need to be asked.

Some prior inconsistent statements are admissible as substantive proof. Federal Rule of Evidence 801(d)(1)(A) provides that a prior inconsistent statement made under oath at a legal proceeding is not inadmissible hearsay, but is substantive evidence. Some states provide that other prior inconsistent statements may also be considered substantive evidence. If the cross-examiner does not want the fact finders to believe that either statement is true, then questions that establish the reliability of the prior statement need not be asked.

The Federal Rules of Evidence and similar state rules no longer require an attorney to call the witness' attention to the circumstances of the prior inconsistent statement. However, strategic considerations usually mandate such an explanation. These questions explain the circumstances of the prior statement, increasing the fact finders' understanding of what happened and the impact of the inconsistent statements. These background questions also reduce the witness' opportunity to explain away the prior statement, further increase the anxiety of the witness, and highlight the importance of the witness' mistake. There is no required number of questions that should be asked to establish the circumstances. The case, the witness, the prior inconsistent statement, and the purpose of cross-examination determine how many and which questions will be asked.

c. Introduce the Prior Inconsistent Statement

The cross-examiner then introduces the prior inconsistent statement. Usually, the most effective way is to read the inconsistent statement to the witness, while the witness reads a duplicate copy silently along, and have the witness admit making it. Another way to introduce the statement is to have the witness read it aloud. The problem with having a witness read a prior statement is that the witness may not read it with the same degree of emphasis as the cross-examiner. Opposing counsel ought to be told of the source of the statement and either the page number or line number of the source. The prior inconsistent statement need not be marked (unless the judge or arbitrator insists) if the document itself is not being offered as evidence. The reading of the prior statement and the witness' verbal affirmation of the answer is typically the evidence offered. See Fed.R.Evid. 615(a). If the advocate prefers to have the document marked and introduced, an offer may be made.

d. Obtain the Witness' Response to the Inconsistent Statement

Ordinarily a witness will admit to making the inconsistent statement. The direct examiner will most likely have instructed the witness to admit making the statement. The direct examiner may even have covered it on direct, or plans to have the witness explain it on redirect. Impeachment questions should not be asked on cross which allow the witness an opportunity to explain away the inconsistency.

If the witness admits making the statement, the impeachment process is concluded. If the witness does not admit the prior inconsistent statement, the cross-examiner must prove that the statement was made. If the witness denies making the statement, or cannot recall making it, the cross-examiner will need to establish the witness made the statement. Usually, extrinsic evidence is introduced to establish the statement. The type of extrinsic evidence depends upon the type of statement made. The following sections describe the various types of prior inconsistent statements and the necessary extrinsic evidence.

It is highly unlikely that witnesses will deny they made a statement appearing in an email or text message, or in a video or on a transcript, or that their signature does not appear on a written statement. A witness may attempt to be evasive and say the transcript may be inaccurate or the written statement incomplete, but further questioning will usually be successful in having the witness admit the prior statement is authentic.

Example:

Q: You have told us you saw both cars just before the crash?

A: Yes that's true.

Q: Are you sure you saw both cars before the crash?

A: Absolutely!

Q: Do you remember when Investigator Lestrade visited with you the day after the accident?

A: Yes.

Q: That was at your home, wasn't it?

A: Yes.

Q: He asked you some questions, didn't he?

A: Yes.

Q: And he wrote your responses down in a statement?

A: Yes.

Q: Investigator Lestrade gave you a chance to read that statement, didn't he?

A: Yes he did.

Q: And you did read it?

A: Yes.

Q: You signed that statement, didn't you?

A: Yes.

Q: You signed it because it was true and correct?

A: Yes.

Q: You wouldn't have signed it if it wasn't true and correct, would you?

A: No.

Q: Now, in about the middle of that statement you told Investigator Lestrade: "I only saw the BMW before the crash, and not the other car." Do you see that?

A: That's what it says.

Q: Have you now read that statement?

A: Yes.

Q: And that is what you said?

A: Yes.

This method of impeachment repeats the direct examination. An alternative method accomplishes the same thing but does not require that the direct examination be repeated. Repeating the direct examination may over emphasize that information. The following alternative technique avoids highlighting the direct examination.

Example:

Q: You only saw one car just before the accident, didn't you?

A: No.

Q: Are you sure you saw more than one car?

A: Yes I'm sure.

Q: Didn't you tell Investigator Lestrade you only saw one car?

A: I may have.

Q: Well, you do recall the day after the accident you told Investigator Lestrade you saw only one car?

A: I talked to an investigator after the accident.

Q: And you gave him a statement?

A: Yes.

Q: He wrote it down?

A: Yes.

Q: You read it?

A: Yes.

Q: It was true?

A: Yes.

Q: You signed it?

A: Yes.

Q: I hand you a written statement and ask you to look at it. That is your signature on the statement, correct?

A: Yes.

Q: Read silently along with me. In that statement it's written: "I only saw the BMW before the crash, and no other cars."

A: Yes, I see that.

Q: That is what you said?

A: Apparently. Yes.

---

3. Significant Prior Inconsistent Statements

The nature of the impeaching material varies from significant to minor. Section 9.4(C) explained why impeachment efforts should be made only with significant, material evidence. If a witness testifies at a deposition that a car was a "light green" color and at the trial or hearing states the car was "green," it may be ineffective to impeach the witness on this minor discrepancy, unless the precise color of the car was significant. Minor inaccuracies will not adversely affect the credibility of the witness unless there is a pattern or a significant number of these inaccuracies. Fact finders understand that witnesses do not have perfect recall.

4. Introducing Contemporaneous Prior Statements

The direct examiner can request that additional portions of the prior statement be introduced contemporaneously with the impeaching part of the statement to prevent a cross-examiner from introducing selective facts out of context. Federal Rule of Evidence 106 and similar state rules permit an opposing attorney to request that the judge or arbitrator require the contemporaneous reading of other relevant portions of the statement. See Section 9.4(C).

5. Types of Prior Inconsistent Statements

There are five major types of prior inconsistent statements:

- Prior statements under oath,
- Discovery responses and verified pleadings,
- Written or composed statements,
- Oral statements, and
- Omissions.

The following sections demonstrate examples of each of these types of prior inconsistent statements and the extrinsic evidence that is necessary to prove impeachment if the witness denies the prior statement.

a. *Prior Statements Under Oath*

Prior statements under oath include testimony provided at depositions, previous trials, motion hearings, preliminary hearings, grand jury hearings, inquests, and hearings before various boards.

Example:

Q: Ms. Kostrzewa, you testified on direct examination that you were traveling in your car at 25 miles per hour just before you entered the intersection?

A: Yes.

Q: You further testified that you knew the speed to be 25 miles per hour because you had just looked at your speedometer immediately before driving through the intersection?

A: Yes.

Q: That is your testimony under oath today before this jury?

A: Yes, that is what I said.

Q: Do you recall that you previously testified under oath regarding the facts of this case?

A:　Yes, I remember.

Q:　You remember we call that procedure a deposition?

A:　Yes.

Q:　There was a court reporter there taking down your statements just like there is a court reporter here today?

A:　Yes.

Q:　You took an oath and promised to give truthful answers?

A:　Yes.

Q:　You recall that your attorney was there with you?

A:　Yes.

Q:　And you recall that I was there?

A:　Yes.

Q:　Before that deposition, you had an opportunity to talk with your attorney about the deposition?

A:　Yes.

Q:　You had an opportunity to prepare for the deposition and think about what happened at the intersection?

A:　Yes.

Q:　That deposition occurred just a few months after the accident?

A:　Yes.

Q:　The events of the accident were still fresh in your mind at the time of your deposition?

A:　Yes.

Q:　During your deposition, questions were asked of you and answers were given by you just like today in court?

A:　Yes.

Q:　At the beginning of the deposition you were told if you didn't understand a question to say so and it would be rephrased?

A:　Yes.

Q:　The questions and answers at the deposition related to what happened at the intersection of May Lane and Ridgeway?

A:　Yes.

Q:　You answered those questions at the deposition as best you could, correct?

A: Yes.

Q: You gave complete and honest answers?

A: I tried.

Q: You did not withhold any information, did you?

A: No.

Q: Ms. Kostrzewa, I'm handing you a document. Please look at it. Is this a transcript of your deposition?

A: It appears to be.

Q: Please turn to page 69 and look at line 10. You were asked this question then: "How fast were you driving when you first entered the intersection?" Do you see that?

A: Yes.

Q: And your answer to that question was: "At least 30 miles an hour. I'm not real sure." Do you see that?

A: Yes.

Q: The next question you were asked was "Did you look at your speedometer any time before you entered the intersection?" And your answer was "I don't believe so." Do you also see that response?

A: Yes.

Q: Those were your answers a year ago, under oath?

A: That's what is written here.

Q: And those are your answers?

A: Yes.

Q: Do you recall after the deposition going to your attorney's office to read your deposition transcript?

A: Yes, I recall that.

Q: And you read over the answers that you gave to make sure they were correct?

A: Yes.

Q: After reading your deposition you signed the deposition?

A: Yes.

Q: Your signature appears on the last page of that transcript, correct?

A: Yes, that's my signature.

The redirect examination can include the direct examiner's introduction of any segment of the deposition that helps bolster the accuracy of the direct testimony, reduces the impact of the prior statement, explains what the witness meant to say during the deposition, or shows that cross-examining counsel used a response out of context.

Example (Continued):

Judge:

Redirect, counsel?

Direct Examiner:

Q: Yes, your Honor. Ms. Kostrzewa, please turn to page 115 of that same deposition, and look at line 8. That question was asked of you later in the deposition and it reads "Do you have any other basis for determining how fast you were going just before you entered the intersection?" Do you recall that question being asked of you that day?

A: Yes.

Q: Would you please read from your deposition the answer that you gave that day?

A: I said, "My long years of driving experience. And it's very likely, come to think of it, that I looked at my speedometer, which I often do."

Q: That was your testimony a year ago, under oath?

A: Yes.

Proof of Prior Testimony

If a witness denies giving a deposition answer, a statement appearing in a deposition may be proved by offering that portion of the original deposition transcript into evidence. In most jurisdictions, the original deposition is not part of the file or record. Usually, the attorney who took the deposition has possession of the original transcript. The certification page prepared by the reporter is attached to the original transcript certifying it to be the original.

There are three ways to place a deposition transcript into evidence.

1. The judge or arbitrator may take notice of the original transcript and receive it in evidence.

2. In some jurisdictions, the attorney must authenticate the document, overcome any hearsay problems, and establish the transcript as an original writing. The original transcript of the

deposition, which contains an attestation by a notary public, is self-authenticating under the rules of evidence, and a duplicate copy is also self-authenticating. See Fed.R.Evid. 902(1) and 902(4). The transcript can be established to be an original writing or an admissible duplicate by the certification signed by the notary at the end of the transcript stating it is the original. See Fed.R.Evid. 1001(3) and 1001(4).

Hearsay problems may be overcome in one of two ways. If the deponent is an adverse party, the transcript can be offered as a party admission. See Fed.R.Evid. 801. If the deponent is a non-party, the transcript may be offered solely for the limited purpose of impeaching the witness (not for the truth of the matter asserted) rendering the transcript non-hearsay. See Fed.R.Evid. 801(c). If the witness is a non-party and the filed transcript is offered as substantive proof in addition to its impeachment value, the transcript can be offered in evidence as a public court record exception to the hearsay rule. See Fed.R.Evid. 803(8).

3.   In a few jurisdictions, the reporter may have to be called as a witness to establish that the reporter is a qualified reporter, that the reporter was present at the proceeding and swore in the witness, and that the reporter prepared a verbatim record of the testimony.

Prior testimony that appears in a judicial or other proceeding may be proved by introducing a certified copy of the transcript of that portion of the proceeding containing the witness' testimony. The clerk of court or other administrator can provide a certified copy of the transcript prepared by the reporter. The judge or arbitrator may take notice of a certified transcript. In a few jurisdictions, the reporter who transcribed the judicial testimony may need to be called as a witness and a foundation similar to that of a deposition reporter may have to be established.

The transcript should usually be marked as an exhibit and introduced in evidence. The portion of the transcript that contains the prior inconsistent statement ought to be read to or by the fact finder.

b.   *Discovery Responses and Verified Pleadings*

Prior inconsistent statements may appear in answers to interrogatories, responses to requests for admissions, a verified complaint, or other legal documents signed by the witness under oath.

Example:

On direct examination, a party testifies that he cannot remember whether he received a video. An answer to an interrogatory states he did receive the video.

Q: Mr. Kreskin, you testified on direct examination that you did not see the Copperfield YouTube video, is that correct?

A: Yes.

Q: You do recall that as part of this lawsuit, you received some written questions from us?

A: I think so.

Q: Those questions are called interrogatories?

A: Yes, I remember them.

Q: You, with the assistance of your attorney, provided written answers to those questions?

A: Yes.

Q: You swore under oath that your answers were true?

A: Yes.

Q: Do you recall question No. 5 which asked, "Identify all videos you watched related to the Copperfield performance."?

A: That sounds familiar.

Q: Your sworn answer to that question was, "I recall watching parts of the Copperfield YouTube extravaganza."

A: If that's what it says.

Q: That is what you stated in writing under oath at that time?

A: Yes.

Q: You discussed your answers with your attorney?

A: Yes.

Q: You understood that you had to provide complete and accurate answers?

A: Yes.

Q: And, that's what you did back then?

A: Yes.

Proof of Discovery Responses and Verified Pleadings

Discovery responses and verified pleadings that appear in the file can be proved by introducing those documents. Discovery responses that are not in the file may be proved by introducing the originals of those documents, which are usually in the possession of the attorney receiving the response. The opposing attorney will usually agree that the originals are accurate and authentic, and the court will receive them in evidence. The opposing attorney will usually also agree that the original is accurate and authentic and that stipulation will be sufficient for the court to receive the transcript into evidence.

c.   *Written or Composed Statements*

Written and composed statements include documents that have been created, signed, agreed to, or approved by a party. Writings include: written statements given to a police officer or investigator; notes handwritten by the witness; printed statements signed by a witness; affidavits from judicial, administrative, or arbitration proceedings; memoranda prepared by the witness; and letters and other documents. Composed statements include electronically created or stored documents, including emails, text messages, tweets, and other social network communications. These documents may be personal or business records.

Example:

The witness has testified during direct examination that the defendant was not present at a meeting on December 6. In a memorandum the witness prepared and signed, the witness stated the defendant was present at the meeting.

Q: Ms. King, you have told us that the defendant, Dr. King, was not present during that December 6 meeting, correct?

A: That's right.

Q: You remember the other two people who were there but not the defendant?

A: He was not there.

Q: After that meeting on December 6, you prepared a summary memo?

A: I may have.

Q: It was your normal business practice to prepare a memo after a meeting that summarized the meeting?

A: Yes, it was.

Q: And after the December 6 meeting, you prepared such a memo?

A: That is likely.

Q: I hand you Exhibit No. 6. Your name appears as the author of this memo, right?

A: Yes.

Q: It's dated December 6?

A: Yes.

Q: The subject line refers to the meeting on that day?

A: That's what it reads.

Q: The memo summarizes a meeting that occurred at 3:00 p.m. that day?

A: That's the date and time.

Q: Exhibit No. 6 is the memo you prepared after the meeting?

A: Yes.

Q: In the first paragraph of that memo, you identified the individuals who were present at the meeting?

A: Yes.

Q: You state in Exhibit No. 6: "Present were Ralph Abernathy, Rosa Parks, and Martin Luther King."

A: Yes.

Q: In that memo you identified Dr. King as being present at that meeting?

A: It appears so.

Proof of Written, Signed, Composed, or Sent Statements

If a witness denies making a prior statement, the prior statement can be proved by calling any witness who can identify the writing, signature, composition or creation of the document. The questions are the same as those needed to authenticate a document. See Section 8.6(B).

d. Oral Statements

Any oral statement a witness has made to anyone may be used as a source for impeachment. This includes oral statements made to investigators, police officers, business personnel, family, friends at a social gathering, or to any person at any time at any place. The oral statement can be proved by extrinsic evidence.

Example:

A witness to a robbery was interviewed by a police officer and told the officer that she did not see the person who robbed the bar. The prosecution called this witness and on direct examination she identified the defendant as the robber.

Q: On direct examination, you testified the defendant was in the saloon?

A: Yes.

Q: You identified the defendant as the robber in the saloon?

A: Yes.

Q: You believe it was the defendant who was in the saloon the day it was robbed?

A: Yes.

Q: Ms. Kitty, you do recall talking to Marshal Dillon shortly after the robbery?

A: Yes.

Q: Marshal Dillon asked you what you saw?

A: I think so.

Q: You wanted to help the Marshal find the robber?

A: Yes.

Q: You wanted to tell Marshal Dillon everything you knew?

A: Yes.

Q: Marshal Dillon was taking notes when he talked to you?

A: I'm not sure.

Q: Ms. Kitty, at that time you told Marshal Dillon that you did not see the person that robbed the saloon?

A: I don't recall saying that.

Q: Ms. Kitty, you told Marshal Dillon that you did not know who robbed the saloon?

A: I don't believe I said that.

Proof of Oral Statements

If the witness denies making the prior oral statement, the previous oral statement can be proved by calling any witness who can testify that the witness made the prior statement.

Example (Continued):

Q: Marshal Dillon, did you speak to Ms. Kitty shortly after the robbery?

A: Yes.

Q: Did she say anything about the robbery?

A: Yes.

Q: What did she say?

A: She said she didn't see the person who robbed the saloon.

Q: Anything else?

A: She also said she didn't know who the robber was.

---

e. Omissions

A common method of impeachment involves the cross-examination of a witness regarding a matter testified to on direct examination that does not appear in a prior statement. Witnesses frequently fail to include all important details in prior statements. The omission is significant because there is no record of this material statement in any report, statement or testimony. The absence of this important information can be revealed on cross-examination and be used to reduce the credibility of the witness.

The impeachment process by omission is similar to impeaching with a prior inconsistent statement except the omission does not appear in the prior statement. A witness who testifies to an important matter that does not appear in a prior statement can be impeached by establishing the absence of this material matter from the previous statement. Common prior statements that may omit significant facts include emails, social network communications, reports by police officers, memoranda by investigators, deposition testimony, and other documents or sources of information. The impeachment process can establish that the prior statement was made at a time when the events were fresh in the witness' mind and can suggest that the witness may be adding facts or making things up because the current statement was not included in the prior statement. This process is a subtle form of impeachment because the cross-examiner is establishing the nonexistence of a fact or opinion.

Example:

In an automobile accident case, the plaintiff, Mr. Hardy, has testified on direct examination that the defendant said, "I'm

sorry. It was my fault." In his previous deposition the plaintiff
never testified the defendant said those words.

Q: On direct examination, you stated the defendant, Mr. Laurel, said to you after the accident, "I'm sorry. It was my fault."?

A: Yes, that's what he said.

Q: Your testimony is the defendant made that statement to you immediately after the accident?

A: Yes.

Q: Now, Mr. Hardy, you recall your deposition was taken in this case?

A: Yes.

Q: At that deposition you testified under oath just like you were testifying under oath today?

A: Yes.

Q: Your attorney was present at that deposition?

A: Yes.

Q: And I was there asking you questions about the accident?

A: Yes.

Q: You remember I told you if you did not understand a question I would rephrase it so you could understand it?

A: I believe so.

Q: That deposition was taken three months after the accident?

A: Yes.

Q: And the accident happened over two years ago?

A: That's about right.

Q: Before that deposition you talked with your attorney about the accident?

A: Yes.

Q: And after that deposition you had an opportunity to read the transcript of your testimony?

A: Yes, I believe so.

Q: And you did read and sign it?

A: Yes.

Q: You recall that during the deposition I asked you this question—on page 35, line 16: "What did Mr. Laurel say to you immediately after the accident?"

A: I believe so.

Q: Your answer was: "He said 'I'm sorry this all happened.' "?

A: If that's what it says.

Q: I show you your deposition transcript and ask you to read the next question that was asked you on line 18.

A: "Did the defendant say anything else?"

Q: Please read line 19 with me as I read it out loud. It says "No, I don't believe so." Right?

A: Yes.

Q: Nowhere in these answers did you say the defendant said, "It was my fault."

A: That's correct.

Example:

On direct examination, a police officer testified he found a cell phone on the defendant with the victim's information on the contact list. That statement does not appear in his police report.

Q: Detective McNulty, after you arrested the defendant, you searched his pockets?

A: Yes.

Q: On direct examination, you said you found a throw away cell phone in one of his pockets?

A: Yes.

Q: You also told us the victim's name and phone number were on the contact list of that phone?

A: Yes.

Q: You are sure about that?

A: Yes.

Q: After you arrest someone you prepare a report?

A: Yes.

Q: You have been trained on how to prepare such a report?

A: Yes.

Q: You were trained to include all important facts?

A: Yes.

Q: You were trained to prepare a complete and accurate report?

A: Yes.

Q: After you arrested the defendant, you prepared a report?

A: Yes.

Q: You wanted the report to include all important matters?

A: Yes.

Q: And you wanted it to be complete and accurate?

A: Yes.

Q: Let me show you your report. This is your report, correct?

A: Yes.

Q: After you completed the report, you read it over?

A: Yes.

Q: And after reading it, you signed it?

A: Yes.

Q: One of the purposes of this report is that the prosecutor relies on it to determine what happened, true?

A: Yes.

Q: Another purpose is to help you refresh your memory before testifying at trial?

A: Yes.

Q: You read this report before testifying here today?

A: I looked it over.

Q: You did so to help you recall what you did that evening?

A: In part, yes.

Q: Detective McNulty, nowhere in this report did you state that you found a cell phone in the defendant's pocket?

A: That's not in the report.

Q: Nowhere in this report did you state that you found a throw away cell phone anywhere on the defendant?

A: That's not in there.

Q: Nowhere in the report did you state that you found a cell phone with a name and phone number on the contact list?

A: That's not in the report either.

Proof of Omissions

Once the witness admits the information is missing, the impeachment is completed and the omission has been proved. If the witness denies the omission, the relevant portion of the transcript or the written statement must be introduced and shown to the fact finder to prove the absence of the significant fact or opinion. Omissions can be proved by introducing the prior documented statement using the same methods to introduce deposition transcripts and documents described in the previous subsections.

F.   COMPLETION OF CROSS-EXAMINATION

A well prepared cross will produce responses that both support the case of the cross-examiner and reduce the favorable impact of the direct examination. During redirect examination, counsel may have an opportunity to reflect on the cross and determine whether any questions or areas were overlooked that may be covered on re-cross examination. All these points will be highlighted and their significance explained during summation.

CHAPTER 10

EXPERTS

■ ■ ■

Trial Advocacy Supplement
Experts

Examples of the direct and cross-examinations of expert witnesses appear in the civil jury trial in the *Supplement to Trial Advocacy Before Judges, Jurors, and Arbitrators*. The transcript of the *Rita Riley v. Garfield House Apartments* trial demonstrates the strategies and skills that are explained in this Chapter regarding experts. Commentary accompanies the transcript that explain effective tactics and techniques.

REFLECTING ON ADVOCACY

Even when experts agree, they may well be mistaken.

—BERTRAND RUSSELL

Expert opinion . . . is only an ordinary guess in evening clothes.

—HON. CURTIS BOK IN

KERSTETTER V.
COMMONWEALTH

§ 10.1 INTRODUCTION

Expert witnesses are used when the scientific, technical, or other specialized knowledge of the expert will assist the non-expert fact finder understand the evidence or determine a fact in issue. In both simple and complex cases, expert testimony may be needed to explain, interpret, or apply the facts so a correct verdict, decision, or award can be rendered. One or both parties may need experts in order to prove their case.

This Chapter covers experts who testify in trials, arbitrations, and hearings. Many of the strategies, tactics, and techniques explained in Chapter 7 on direct examination and Chapter 9 on cross-examination regarding lay witnesses also apply to expert witnesses. The following sections explain additional approaches particularly applicable to experts. There are other types of litigation experts (e.g., retained or consulting experts) that assist with pretrial discovery who do not testify at trial that are not covered in this Chapter.

In civil cases, parties know what the testifying experts will say. Discovery has produced prepared expert reports and the experts have usually been deposed. This process allows the lawyers to evaluate the expert opinions and may prompt a settlement before trial or hearing.

It is common for expert testimony in civil cases to be presented through a video recording or through an audio or stenographically recorded transcript. Recorded testimony assures that the fact finders will hear or read the expert testimony, avoids problems with scheduling experts who have conflicting schedules, and reduces overall expert costs.

Experts in civil cases commonly undergo two discovery or deposition stages. The first consists of a combination of disclosure and discovery methods including interrogatories, document production requests, and discovery depositions. These methods provide the opposing party with information about the expert, the expert's opinions, and bases of those opinions. The second is a deposition taken to preserve testimony with the proffering party conducting direct examination of the expert followed with the opposing lawyer conducting cross-examination. Objections are made on the deposition record; and the judge or arbitrator will later rule on the objections, with the recorded testimony edited to reflect the rulings.

In criminal cases, both the prosecution and defense exchange information about expert opinions and testimony as required by applicable law. The timing for this exchange of information often depends on which side has the burden of proof on an issue. These experts usually testify in person in court during the trial as required by constitutional and case law provisions.

§ 10.2 EXPERT WITNESSES

A. PURPOSES OF EXPERT TESTIMONY

Expert testimony serves several purposes. An expert may:

- Provide factual information. For example, a treating physician can testify to the injuries suffered by a civil plaintiff.

- Apply expert knowledge to the facts of a case and render an opinion. For example, a design engineer can explain information about product design and render an opinion regarding its defects.

- Explain scientific principles and theories. For example, in a homicide case, a forensic pathologist can explain the medical principles involved in determining the cause of death.

- Introduce relevant, compelling evidence. For example, in a civil case, an expert can explain the DNA results that prove a party's relationship with a person relevant to the case.

- Describe test procedures and results. For example, a chemist can explain the testing procedures to identify cocaine and describe the test results, which prove the substance to be cocaine.

- Explain real evidence introduced in the case. For example, a radiologist can explain the operations of an MRI.

- Review the facts and render an opinion regarding the likelihood of an event or occurrence. For example, an accident reconstruction expert may testify to likely causation.

- Calculate the amount of recoverable damages in a civil case. For example, an economist can testify to the present value of projected lost earnings of an injured plaintiff.

- Render an opinion that contradicts the conclusions of an expert who testified for the opposing party. For example, a prosecution psychiatrist can testify that a defendant was not mentally ill at the time the crime was committed, which contradicts the expert opinion of a defense psychiatrist.

B.   WHO IS AN EXPERT

A person who has scientific, technical or other specialized knowledge gained by education, training, experience or skill may be qualified as an expert. Professionals, such as doctors, engineers, and economists, who have had extensive formal education and training, may be easily qualified. Other individuals whose expertise has been derived primarily from experience or skill, such as mechanics and technicians, may also be qualified if they have the requisite background. The laws of a jurisdiction determine who may be an expert, as explained below and in Section 10.3.

C.   AREAS OF EXPERTISE

An area of knowledge that contains scientific, technical or other specialized knowledge may constitute an area of expertise requiring expert testimony. A general test that most jurisdictions apply is: whether the area of expertise has gained general acceptance within the relevant scientific, technical or other specialized expert community. A scientific theory which has gained general acceptance within the relevant scientific community or which has been verified by reliable experiments is ordinarily recognized as a proper expert topic. These fields of expertise include medicine, engineering, economics, psychiatry, accounting, computer science, and law. Additional fields of generally recognized expertise include firearm analysis, ballistics, mechanical repairs, property assessments, laboratory analysis, electronic data recovery, and computer systems.

Other areas may not ordinarily be recognized by a judge or arbitrator unless experts in the subject and related areas recognize and accept the subject as one reflecting specialized knowledge. Developing subjects that are accepted areas of expertise include expert testimony regarding child abuse syndrome and posttraumatic stress disorders. Some fields of expertise are not widely accepted and many require proof of reliability. These fields include hypnosis and voice spectrograms. Other areas that are not traditionally considered areas of expertise or that are unusual may not be recognized by the decision maker as an area of expertise. For example, individuals proficient in operating lie detector machines are not usually considered experts because their opinions and lie detectors have not been recognized as accurate or reliable.

Judges and arbitrators commonly recognize or take judicial or arbitral notice of the recognized area of expertise. An expert may need to be asked questions to establish reliability of the field: "How well recognized is this area of expertise? Do experts like you recognize this area as reliable and accurate?" The law of a jurisdiction determines the scope of acceptable expertise, as further explained in the next section.

§ 10.3   THE LAW OF EXPERT TESTIMONY

Every jurisdiction has specific laws regarding the qualifications of experts and the recognized areas of expertise. The primary sources of the law for each jurisdiction are evidence rules and judicial decisions applying and interpreting the rules. In federal cases, Fed.R.Evid. 702 and related rules and federal case law regulate expert testimony, including Daubert v. Merrell Dow Pharmaceuticals, 509 U.S. 579 (1993).

Different approaches to the admissibility of expert testimony are defined by Federal Rule 702 and the *Daubert* case and by an earlier case, Frye v. United States, 293 F. 1010 (D.C.C.C. 1923). The federal rules and the *Daubert* case, presently used in federal court cases, establish non-exclusive factors to assess the admissibility of expert testimony.

Federal Rule 702 codifies the *Daubert* standards and states:

A witness who is qualified as an expert by knowledge, skill, experience, training, or education may testify in the form of an opinion or otherwise if:

(a) The expert's scientific, technical, or other specialized knowledge will help the trier of fact to understand the evidence or to determine a fact in issue;

(b) The testimony is based on sufficient facts or data;

(c) The testimony is the product of reliable principles and methods; and

(d) The expert has reliably applied the principles and methods to the facts of the case.

This rule and the *Daubert* standards provide that judges or arbitrators are the gatekeepers to determine the admissibility of expert opinions. They must find it more likely than not that the expert's methods are reliable and reliably applied to the facts in the case. The following factors help decision makers determine the propriety of expert testimony.

An opinion by a qualified expert may be admissible if the underlying theory, method or technique:

- Is generally accepted by a relevant expert community;

- Has been subject to peer review or publication;

- Has been or can be tested or determined to be falsifiable or refutable;

- Has an acceptable potential error rate; or

- Is controlled by legitimate, recognized governing standards.

Additional factors that influence whether an opinion by a qualified expert is admissible include:

- If the expert's inferences and opinions are adequately supported by the evidence;

- If the expert considered alternate explanations regarding outcomes or results and can explain why other explanations were rejected;

- If the expert applied a sufficient level of intellectual rigor in forming the opinion;

- If the field of expertise to which the expert belongs is known for reliable conclusions; and

- If the opinion was developed independently of the case or for the purpose of providing expert testimony.

A majority of states have adopted the federal approach. Other states have modified it by adding other factors, such as: the extent to which the theory/method/technique relies on the subjective interpretation of the expert and the degree to which non-judicial uses have been made of the theory/method/technique.

About one quarter of the state courts use the *Frye* test, also known as the "general acceptance test." These jurisdictions broadly permit expert testimony if the opinion to be offered is based on a principle that has gained general acceptance in the particular expert field in issue. The expert can testify whether a principle has gained this general acceptance.

The remaining jurisdictions use a combination of the *Daubert* and *Frye* factors. State appellate court decisions and evidence rules will explain the specific approach used. Arbitrators and administrative law judges commonly follow the expert evidence law applicable to the case.

§ 10.4 DIRECT EXAMINATION OF EXPERT WITNESSES

A. ATTORNEY PREPARATION

The attorney should know the subject that the expert will testify about as well or better than the expert. Without this specialized information, the attorney may fail to recognize critical information or be unable to identify errors or discrepancies with the expert testimony. This failure will result in ineffective direct and cross-examinations.

There are a variety of ways advocates can become well informed. They can become "experts" through studies, schooling, training, and learning. They can research topics through books, websites, treatises, articles, and other sources. They can also seek advice from colleagues and other advocates who are knowledgeable with the area of expertise.

The advocate may hire a consulting expert in the field to assist in this educational process. These individuals will not be called to testify but serve to educate the attorney and offer suggestions for direct examination of testifying experts and for the cross-examination of opposing experts. An expert may also serve as both a consulting expert and a testifying expert in appropriate situations to reduce costs. Some areas of expertise may have a limited number of potential experts or only a few experts may be available to testify, requiring one expert to serve more than one role.

In addition to these preparation efforts, the advocate can study videos and transcripts of previous cases in which an expert testified. This approach can help prepare an informed direct examination and can reveal areas of vulnerability for cross-examination. The attorney can also review recorded testimony from other individuals who are experts in the same or related areas and cases.

B. WITNESS PREPARATION

Expert witnesses need to be prepared properly for their testimony. The approaches and guidelines explained in Section 7.4 for lay witness examinations are also applicable to experts. There are additional considerations specifically related to experts that are covered in the subsequent sections of this Chapter.

Expert preparation can differ from lay witness preparation in several ways. It can be easier. The expert witness may have substantial experience testifying in cases, and understands how to be an effective witness and how to avoid being ineffectual. The expert knows the subject matter area very well and does not require much substantive preparation. And the expert is a professional who has been selected in part because of her or his ability to communicate clearly and credibly.

There are likely to be some preparation challenges. The expert may believe he or she knows it all, and may come across as arrogant or haughty. The professional witness may not take kindly to directions from an advocate who seemingly knows less than the witness does if a different approach is preferred. And the busy expert may not have the time or be willing to take enough time to prepare with the lawyer.

Whether it's easy or challenging, it is crucial for the attorney to thoroughly prepare an expert. Rehearsing direct and cross-examination are just as important for an expert as they are for a lay witness. Video recorded experts need to see and hear what they look and sound like on video. All experts need to be prepped on how they may win or lose a case.

FORM 10.1
EXPERT TESTIMONY PLANNING WORKSHEET

Case _____ File _____

Name _____ Fees _____

Qualifications _____

Opinions _____

Sources of Information _____

Personal Knowledge _____

Other Sources _____

Bases of Opinions _____

Exhibits _____

Technical Terms to be Explained _____

Treatises _____

Probable Cross-examination Areas _____

Redirect Examination _____

C. QUALIFYING THE EXPERT

The rules of evidence require that the expert must be qualified in the area about which the expert will testify. See Fed.R.Evid. 702. The judge or arbitrator rules on whether an individual is "competent" and qualified to be an expert witness. This means that:

- The expert has education, training, experience or skill in a field beyond the knowledge of the fact finder;

- The scientific, technical, or other specialized knowledge of the expert will assist triers of fact to understand the evidence or to determine a fact in issue they cannot decide based on common knowledge; and

- The expert's opinion is based on education, training, knowledge, experience or skill and not on unfounded speculation or conjecture.

The foundation necessary to qualify an expert is relatively straightforward and generally not difficult to prove if the expert has sufficient qualifications. Examples demonstrating the legal foundation for almost every area of expertise may be found in articles, books, treatises, and websites on the subject of expert examinations. After sufficient foundation has been laid to establish the qualifications of an expert, the advocate may continue with the questioning to elicit expert testimony.

PREPARATION OUTLINE OF EXPERT TESTIMONY

Name

Title, degree

Personal Background

Address (work, home)

Family

Length of residence

Hobbies

Clubs

Social organizations

Charitable organizations

How, When Expert Becomes Involved

Treating physician

Consultant

Examination for trial or hearing (plaintiff or defense)

Neutral expert

Retained by plaintiff or defense

Fees

Occupation

Employer

Position/description/responsibilities—how long

Prior employers/positions/responsibilities

Education

Undergraduate degrees

Institution

Graduation date

Advanced degrees

Institution

Graduation date

Training

What

Where

When

By whom

Certificates/licenses

Professional Organizations

Name

Purpose

Length of membership

Authority in organizations

Professional Achievements

Books

Articles

Websites

Blogs

Teaching

Presentations

Consultations with other professionals

Awards/honors

Legal Experience

As Witness

Plaintiff or defense

Frequency of testifying

Consultant

Organization or parties

Frequency

Specialized Experience

Type of experience

Tests

Examinations

Study

Consulting with others

Personal interview

Specific Examination or Tests Involved in Case

Number of tests

Why

When

Where

How

Results

Reports

Date

Summary

Supplement

Opinions

Basis of Opinions

Sources of Opinions

Report

Exhibits

Other Information

Exhibits

Exhibits already prepared

Exhibits to be prepared

Weaknesses/Cross-Examination Areas

Weakness of profession

Weakness of expertise

Weakness of opinion

Bias/Prejudice

Favorable or adverse interests

Lack of objective information

Lack of reasonable testing

D. ESTABLISHING QUALIFICATIONS

Federal Rules of Evidence 704 permits experts to testify to an opinion and provide reasons for that opinion without first testifying to the underlying facts or data for that opinion. This Rule also provides the judge or arbitrator with the discretion to require the disclosure of underlying facts or data before the introduction of the opinion. The expert may likely be cross-examined regarding some of the underlying facts or data.

Because of the flexibility of Fed.R.Evid.704 and similar state court rules, there are optional ways to establish qualifications of an expert. Qualifications may be presented in sequence at the beginning of the examination, or may be mixed throughout the examination and presented as they apply directly to a particular point. Whatever method is used to establish qualifications, an effort should be made to "personalize" the expert and demonstrate that the expert is very knowledgeable and believable. The expert's education, work history, and personal background help humanize the expert. Some experts may sound arrogant when describing their background because in effect they are telling the fact finder how brilliant they are. Questions need to be designed to establish how smart the expert is without resulting in boastful answers.

The following examples demonstrate two different ways of presenting an expert's qualifications.

1. Qualifications at Beginning of Examination

It is traditional and easier to present the expert's qualification in sequence at the beginning of the examination. Many courts and arbitrators are familiar with an expert examination presented in this way and are comfortable with the sequence. However, this approach may not be the most persuasive way of presenting the expert. Lengthy qualifications presented at the beginning of the direct may bore the fact finder as the tedious qualifications may not appear to relate to the case.

Example:

Lawyer: The plaintiff calls Dr. Rebecca Lee Crumpler.

Q: Dr. Crumpler, what kind of medical doctor are you?

Q: Do you live in our city?

Q: How long have you lived in our community?

Q: Do you have family?

Q: Where did you go to college?

Q: In what fields did you get your degree?

Q: Where did you go to medical school?

Q: When did you graduate from medical school?

Q: Where did you serve your internship?

Q: Where did you complete your residency?

Q: Did you specialize?

Q: Explain what that means?

Q: Are you board certified?

Q: What does that mean?

Q: What experience do you have in your specialty?

Q: Have you done any lecturing or teaching in your specialty or related areas?

Q: Have you written any books or articles or created any blogs or websites in the area of your expertise or in related areas?

Q: Do you belong to any professional organizations?

Q: Have you ever testified in court before?

Q: How often?

Q: Have you testified for both the plaintiff and the defense?

---

2. Qualifications During the Examination

When qualifications are woven into the direct examination, the qualifications, analysis, and opinion relate to the case and focus on issues.

Example:

Lawyer: Defendant calls Dr. Doug Ross as his expert witness.

Q: Where did you go to medical school?

Q: When did you graduate from medical school?

Q: What medical post-graduate training have you had?

Q: Did you train in a specialty?

Q: Explain your specialty?

Q: How long have you been practicing your specialty?

Q: Now Doctor, at my request, did you examine the knee of Mr. Baryshnikov?

Q: When was that?

Q: Where did the examination take place?

Q: How long did the examination last?

Q: Did you have sufficient time for the examination?

Q: Tell us what you did to perform the examination.

Q: While you were at medical school, what training did you have in conducting this kind of examination?

Q: Have you had any specific training or education to treat injuries of the type that Mr. Baryshnikov has?

Q: Please explain.

Q: Was that training and experience helpful to you in diagnosing his injury?

Q: How?

Q: Have you ever lectured on the type of injury that Mr. Baryshnikov has suffered?

Q: What have you presented?

Q: Does your lecturing help you in diagnosing and treating injuries of this nature?

Q: Have you written any books or articles or composed blogs or websites regarding that type of injury?

Q: What have you authored?

Q: Do your publications assist you in your diagnosis and treatment of injuries of this kind?

Q: How so?

3.   Early Introduction of Opinion and Qualifications

It may preferable to introduce opinions very early during an expert's testimony, followed by a presentation of the specific qualifications for each opinion. Fed.R.Evid. 705 permits an expert to give an opinion without first testifying to the underlying facts or data. The federal rules and state rules allow the early introduction of expert opinions. The early introduction places the expert's education, experience, and work into context making the expert testimony more relevant and interesting.

Example:

Q: Dr. Konrad Zuse, what doctorate degree do you have?

Q: What does this degree prepare you to do?

Q: Did you examine and analyze the HAL 9000 computer at issue in this case?

Q: Describe your examination and analysis.

Q: How long did your examination take?

Q: Describe the computer chip you examined.

Q: Do you have an opinion whether the Eniac chip you examined violates the 3,120,666 patent at issue?

Q: What is that opinion?

Q: Where did you learn to analyze computer chips?

Q: At BIT, what courses did you take that helped you learn how to analyze computer chips?

Q: What research did you conduct that assisted you in being able to analyze computer chips?

Q: What publications or websites did you author explaining the computer chip analysis method you used in this case?

E.   RESUMES AND STIPULATIONS

An expert may also be qualified to testify by submission of the expert's resume as an exhibit or through stipulations to the qualifications of the expert by opposing counsel. Judges and arbitrators may allow the curriculum vitae of the expert to be introduced as an exhibit in addition to their oral testimony or in lieu of such testimony. If the case involves many experts, the attorneys may prefer, or the judge or arbitrator may require, the attorneys to submit complete or summary resumes instead of questioning the experts about their qualifications. This procedure shortens examinations, allowing the focus to be on the expert opinions.

An attorney may stipulate to the qualifications of an opponent's expert, making it unnecessary for that expert to be qualified. An attorney may decide a stipulation is preferable to having oral testimony of the other side's expert qualifications. This will be particularly true if the opponent's expert has better qualifications. Some judges or arbitrators may urge the attorneys to stipulate to each other's experts to save time.

An advocate must consider whether the submission of resumes or an offer of stipulation is tactically wise. It may be more effective for the fact finder to hear the expert testify to qualifications, especially if the qualifications are impressive. An attorney can refuse the offer of the opposing attorney to stipulate to qualifications and establish them through testimony. In non-jury cases, discussions with the judge or arbitrator about the preferred ways to proceed with expert qualifications can be done before the trial or hearing. In jury trials, discussions with the judge about the use of resumes and offers of stipulations should be conducted outside the hearing of the jury to avoid adversely influencing the jurors with comments by the attorneys or rulings by the judge.

F. TENDERING THE EXPERT

Some jurisdictions require that the examining attorney request the judge or arbitrator to accept the witness as an expert or "tender" the witness as an expert before continuing with the testimony: "Your Honor, we tender Dr. Watson as an expert forensic scientist." The judge then decides that the witness is not qualified or permits the witness to proceed to testify as an expert. An opposing lawyer could "pass/accept" the witness and not oppose the witness testifying as an expert. In jury trials, unless the attorney is completely certain the judge will accept the expert, this motion should be made outside the hearing of the jury, in case the judge may decide the expert is not qualified. Neither the federal rules nor most state rules require a proffering lawyer to make this formal request (tender). The process of tendering an expert needs to be followed in those state jurisdictions that require tendering.

§ 10.5 EXPERT OPINIONS

A. OPINIONS

After a judge or arbitrator is convinced that a witness is qualified to give an expert opinion, the direct examiner must convince the fact finder that the expert is worth believing. Establishing this persuasive foundation requires the direct examiner to present the information in a way that is accurate, reliable, convincing, authoritative, and understandable. The examiner must establish that the opinion of this expert is reliable and the opinion of the opponent's expert is unreliable.

An expert will usually testify to a number of opinions. A case may involve a major and several subordinate or minor opinions. Some judges may require the attorney to use specific traditional words (legal jargon) as a predicate to the introduction of an opinion.

Example:

Q:　Do you have an opinion based upon a reasonable degree of medical (or psychiatric, accounting, or other) certainty?

A:　Yes.

Q:　What is that opinion, Dr. Hfuhrvhurr?

Example:

Q:　Doctor, based on your experience, training, and education in the area of fingerprint analysis and, in addition, based on your examination of the fingerprints that you found on the dashboard of the car and your comparison of those fingerprints with the known fingerprints of the defendant, do you have an opinion to a reasonable degree of certainty whether the fingerprints found on the dashboard are the defendant's fingerprints?

A:　Yes, I do.

Q:　What is your opinion, Dr. Jan Evangelista Purkinje?

A:　The fingerprints that were found on the dashboard of the car identically match the defendant's left thumb and forefinger.

B.　OUTLINE OF EXPERT OPINION

A summary outline of the direct examination of an expert ordinarily includes the following topics:

- The subject matter of the opinion,
- Principles that support the area of expertise and opinion,
- Sources of information relied upon by the expert,
- Any standard tests or routine procedures used in the area,
- Specific tests or procedures used in the case,
- Other bases of the opinion of the expert,
- The opinion or conclusion, and
- An explanation of the opinion and conclusion.

C. SOURCES OF INFORMATION

An expert witness must explain the sources of information or facts that support the expert's opinion. This information is critical to comply with the evidence rules and to convince the fact finder. Federal Rule of Evidence 705 and similar state rules permit an expert to give an opinion without first having to provide the sources of the information or facts underlying the opinion. This rule permits flexibility regarding the order of the expert testimony. The expert may explain the sources either before or after rendering the opinion, as previously explained in Section 10.4(C).

There are a variety of sources of information an expert may rely on:

- Personal, firsthand information perceived prior to the case.

- Information obtained from experts, documents, records, files, witnesses, and other sources, before or during the case.

- Evidence including testimony heard by or told to the expert.

- Hypothetical questions.

Whatever information the expert relies upon must be of a type "reasonably relied upon" by experts in the same area of expertise in forming an opinion. See Fed.R.Evid. 703. This broad standard permits an expert to testify to any source of information, whether admissible or inadmissible, as long as experts reasonably rely upon the information.

1. Personal, Firsthand Information

An expert may have personal firsthand knowledge of information learned or perceived prior to the trial or hearing. The witness may testify to these sources after a proper foundation has been laid that includes the testing, analysis, observations or perceptions made, when and where these observations occurred, how the expert made these observations, who was present, and a description of the work performed.

Example:

Q: Fire Chief Molly Williams, were you at the scene of the fire?

A: Yes.

Q: When did you arrive at the scene?

A: We received the first alarm about ten minutes after the fire started, and I arrived at the casino about five minutes after we received the alarm.

Q: What did you see when you arrived at the casino building?

A: Flames were shooting out of all the windows on the west side of the building, and the walls on the east side had partially collapsed.

Q: What did you notice about the flames?

A: They were a very bright orange color and were spreading rapidly from north to south through the building.

Q: Who was at the scene of the fire when you arrived?

A: The owner of the casino, Samantha Jane Marquez.

Q: Did you talk with her?

A: Yes.

Q: What did she say?

A: She said, "It's all good. The World Poker Tour cancelled." Then she tented her fingers whispering " Well done."

An expert who has firsthand knowledge about physical evidence may need to testify to establish the appropriate chain of custody of the exhibit. Section 8.4(C) describes establishing the chain of custody. For example, an expert who examined and tested strands of hair seized at the scene of a crime will testify to opening the sealed container containing the hair and resealing the container after the tests have been completed to demonstrate the hair that was tested is the same hair offered as evidence.

Experts who examine or test an item of physical evidence may not be able to recall the specific exhibit. An expert who routinely handles and examines many physical objects may have no independent recollection of a specific exhibit. Notes made by the expert may be used to refresh the recollection of the expert. Questions may be asked which first establish the regular, standard or correct procedure used by the expert followed by questions that establish that those recognized procedures were followed with the specific exhibit.

2. Information Obtained from Other Sources Prior to the Trial or Hearing

An expert may rely upon sources other than personal observations and experiences, as long as the type of information is relied upon by other experts in the same area to reach conclusions. This type of information may include evidence that is inadmissible at trial. The most common form of inadmissible evidence is hearsay. For example, in practice an expert may rely upon a hearsay statement, which the rules of evidence would exclude as unreliable. If, however, experts ordinarily rely upon hearsay information, this expert may rely upon hearsay in forming an opinion.

An expert may explain these sources of information if they helped form the basis of an opinion even if they are not admissible. It is unclear to what extent an expert may describe or explain the details of the inadmissible sources of information. Federal Rule of Evidence 703 permits an expert to describe the source of the information and to testify that the information was relied upon as the basis of the opinion; however, judges and arbitrators disagree as to the admissibility of the information. Many decision makers permit the expert to testify that the expert relied upon information from another person, but don't permit the expert to testify to what that person said or composed if it is inadmissible evidence.

Example:

Examining Lawyer:

Q: Have you had an opportunity to examine the plaintiff?

A: No. There was no need to.

Q: Dr. Who, what have you done to learn about the plaintiff's medical condition?

A: I followed expert protocols.

Q: What have you done?

A: I have studied the entire medical record of the plaintiff. I have spoken with Dr. Harleen Frances Quinzel, and I have read her medical reports. In addition, I've read the accident reports prepared by the police department and I've read the statements given to the police by the two accident witnesses.

Q: Is this the type of information that experts in the field of orthopedic surgery, like you, normally rely on to reach a conclusion or to form an opinion about a person's injuries?

A: Yes, it certainly is.

Q: Based upon this information, and your experience, training, and education, do you have an opinion about the nature or type of injuries suffered by the plaintiff?

A: Yes, I do.

Q: What is that opinion?

A: I cannot find any evidence the plaintiff has suffered any injury whatsoever.

---

3. Information Perceived or Made Known During the Case

An expert may base an opinion upon evidence introduced during the trial or hearing. The expert may obtain this evidence by sitting through the case, watching a video of the testimony, reading a transcript of the evidence, or by obtaining a summary of this information. The substance of this evidence must also be the type of information that an expert in the same area relies upon to form an opinion.

Example:

Q: Dr. Jung, have you been here in court during the testimony of the defense psychiatrist, Dr. Jennifer Melfi?

A: Yes, the entire time.

Q: Have you been here during any other part of the trial?

A: No.

Q: Have you read any files or records concerning this trial?

A: Yes.

Q: What have you read?

A: I have read the court file in this case and the transcripts provided me by the court reporter of each day's testimony.

Q: Is the type of information you received from listening to the defendant's psychiatrist and from reading the daily transcripts of the testimony of all the other witnesses, the kind of information a forensic psychiatrist generally uses to form an opinion as to whether the defendant knew what she was doing or whether she knew what she did was wrong at the time she shot the security guard?

A: Yes, it is.

Q: Based upon this information and your education, training, and experience, do you have an opinion whether the defendant knew what she was doing or if she knew it was wrong at the time she shot the victim?

A: Yes, I do.

Q: What is that opinion?

A: My opinion is that the defendant knew exactly what she was doing when she shot the security guard and she knew it was wrong when she did it.

D. HYPOTHETICAL QUESTIONS

An expert may base an opinion upon a hypothetical question. The direct examiner asks the witness the hypothetical question that contains facts that have been or will be introduced during the trial or hearing. The expert, not having personal knowledge of these facts and not having heard these facts during the case, is asked to assume facts set out in the hypothetical question in forming an opinion. The Federal Rules of Evidence and similar state rules no longer require hypothetical questions to be used to introduce an opinion. Hypothetical questions are usually cumbersome and less effective than relying on one of the previously explained sources of information upon which experts can rely.

If used, hypothetical questions should be prepared in advance with the help of the expert. They should be written out in order to avoid mistakes and should be accurate, complete, and as short as possible. The attorney should practice reading the question so that the question can be presented in an interesting way. Long, complicated hypothetical questions can be cumbersome and sound monotonous.

Example:

Q: Dr. Necessiter, I ask you for your opinion based on the following hypothetical facts: Assume that on June 21, 2015, a thirty-nine year old man was employed as a groundskeeper in the Chicago school system. He was riding a lawnmower on the grounds at Quigley High School, which were hilly and wooded. This man was mowing at about a speed of two miles per hour. His hands were on the controls and he occasionally had to look back over his shoulder. The mower hit a stump that stuck out of the ground about eight inches high and twenty inches wide. The force of the impact knocked the man off the seat of the mower and he fell to the ground. He hit his head on the turf and became unconscious. A passerby saw the accident and came to his aid. When the man became conscious, after about five minutes, the passerby took him to Rush Hospital where he was examined. The examination included an MRI of his head. The test results revealed a fracture line on his skull which extends from the anterior side of the external auditory meatus through the middle of the right parietal bone about four inches. The man complains of severe headaches.

Dr. Williams, assuming all these facts, do you have an opinion based on a reasonable degree of medical certainty whether the injury suffered by Groundskeeper Willie to his head was caused by the fall from the mower?

A: Yes I do.

Q: Please tell us that opinion.

There is a tendency to oversell a case with a hypothetical question and ask the expert to give an opinion far beyond the expert's capability. The hypothetical question should not be used to argue the case. The more that is put in the question, the more there is a chance for exaggeration and error, and the more opportunities there are for the cross-examiner to challenge the basis of the expert's opinion.

E.   QUESTIONS CALLING FOR NARRATIVE RESPONSES

Direct examination tactics of expert witnesses parallel many of the approaches and techniques applicable to a lay witness. There are some differences in questioning. A direct examiner usually wants an expert to answer broad questions with detailed narrative responses. Judges and arbitrators typically allow expert witnesses significant leeway. Many experts testify as if they were a teacher explaining information.

Experts generally are permitted to testify with narrative responses. The attorney needs to retain control over the direction of the testimony and ask questions that develop the opinions of the expert. Some experts with courtroom experience can provide useful suggestions regarding how their opinion ought to be introduced and what questions should be asked. The advocate should monitor and interrupt answers if words or concepts need to be explained or if the expert is rambling or becomes boring.

F.   EXPLAINING SPECIALIZED TERMS

The direct examiner must understand and know how to pronounce all of the expert's specialized terms. The testimony of an expert often includes technical words and concepts because they are required to lay a foundation for an opinion or because they buttress the credibility of the expert. It is crucial to an understanding of the expert testimony that definitions of terms be fully explained. The expert should define technical terms after using them, or the direct examiner should interrupt and ask the expert to explain the terms in plain, understandable language.

Examples:

Q: How does a stethoscope work?

Q: What is a CAT scan?

Q: You used the term "metacarpals." What are they?

Q: Chief Sitting Bull, how does a surveyor do a triangulation?

Example:

Q: Mr. Branson did your former business partner Reginald Denny fly a drone over the White House?

A: Yes. It was inadvertent.

Q: Can the drone be programmed to avoid this occurring again?

A: Oh, yes. We are able to prevent it from happening again.

Q: How is that?

A: We can re-design the directional system, which we are in the process of doing.

Q: Explain the system that can be installed on a drone aircraft to keep this from happening in the future.

A: A firmware system can be installed on a drone that uses a GPS to prevent it from flying over restricted areas such as the White House.

Q: Explain what you mean by the term firmware?

A: Firmware is the combination of persistent memory data and computer program code in a directional control system.

Q: Explain the term "GPS"?

A: The Global Positioning System—GPS—is a space-based satellite navigation system that provides guidance to the firmware.

Q: Tell us in layperson's language what they are and how they work.

Technical terms need to be correctly spelled for the record. The advocate should provide the reporter with a list of terms the expert uses.

Demonstrative exhibits and visual aids may be effectively used to help experts explain information. Charts, diagrams, models, power point presentations, and computer-generated graphics may be prepared which illustrate what an expert describes. For example: A drawing of a gas chromatograph (a device that measures blood alcohol levels) helps explain the testing. A model of a human body allows a doctor to explain the relevant parts of a body. A video recording which shows a testing process demonstrates visually what is difficult to describe orally. A visual aid may be created by the attorney while the expert testifies by writing key words of the witness on an easel pad or computer screen.

G. TREATISES

Treatises include books, periodicals, articles, and website compositions. A treatise may be used on direct or cross-examination. The authenticity of a treatise may be established by a reliable authority, through the admission of a witness, through another verifying expert or through judicial notice. A treatise may be introduced as evidence for any purpose. Treatises do not become exhibits, but the portions of a treatise offered in evidence are introduced in the record.

When a treatise is in general use and is relied on in a particular field, most experts will admit that it is an authority. An expert cannot prevent being cross-examined by a recognized treatise by saying the particular treatise is unreliable. If one witness is able to testify that the treatise is authoritative, it may be used to cross-examine another expert, even though that expert refuses to recognize the authority of the treatise. The authoritative parts of the treatise may be read by the attorney or by the expert. This evidence may be offered for any purpose. Whether used for impeachment purposes or as substantive proof of its contents, a treatise may substitute for a live expert and may corroborate an expert's opinion.

Example:

Examining Lawyer:

Q: Doctor, are you familiar with a website article in the National Journal of Medical Research, entitled "The Diagnosis of Migraine Headaches Suffered by Law Students," by Dr. Langdell?

A: Yes, I am.

Q: Have you read that article?

A: Yes, I have.

Q: Have you used the information in that article in your work?

A: Yes, I have.

Q: Do you consider it authoritative?

A: It is a very reliable authority.

By the Attorney:

Your Honor, if I may, I would like to read one sentence on page 4 of that article entitled, "The Diagnosis of Migraine Headaches Suffered by Law Students."

Judge:

You may do so.

Examining Lawyer:

"The severity of a migraine headache of an average law student bears a direct relationship to the number of law school classes attended by the student."

---

§ 10.6 EXPERT CROSS-EXAMINATION

A. PREPARING CROSS-EXAMINATION

Thorough preparation for cross-examination of an expert begins during discovery and case preparation. Information must be obtained regarding the expert's identity, qualifications, opinions, basis for opinions, supporting facts, information relied on in forming opinions, publications, websites, and fees. To effectively cross-examine an expert, the attorney must become knowledgeable about the area of expertise involved in the case. The same efforts the advocate employs in preparing expert direct examination applies to cross preparation. See Section 10.4(A).

B. CROSS-EXAMINATION AREAS

The cross-examination approaches and techniques explained in Chapter 9 that apply to lay witnesses also apply to expert witnesses. Further, this section explains additional tactics that may be used to cross-examine experts, including both supportive and discrediting cross.

Supportive Cross-Examination

- Obtain concessions.
- Criticize the other side's positions.

Discrediting Cross-Examination

- Disclose expert fees and financial interests.

- Establish bias or prejudice based on experiences.

- Expose unreliability of the purported area of expertise.

- Dispute the facts relied on by the expert.

- Challenge sources of information buttressing the opinions.

- Establish unreliability or insufficiency of bases of opinions.

- Highlight the expert's lack of knowledge about the case.

- Illustrate insufficient testing.

- Establish existence of other causes.

- Show inappropriate or insufficient expertise.

- Establish differences of opinions among experts.

- Challenge subjective opinions.

- Introduce inconsistent prior statements.

- Discredit hypothetical questions.

- Use treatises to impeach.

- Expose other deficiencies.

The attorney must review these techniques and determine which of them are applicable. Experts do not often change their opinion or admit making a major mistake on cross-examination. Directly attacking an expert opinion may not be productive. Indirect challenges can reduce the reliability of the opinions and the credibility of the expert.

The attorney must control the responses of the expert and not allow the witness to reply with damaging answers. Experienced expert witnesses who have testified in previous cases may be able to evade answering questions or attempt to explain answers. The advocate may have difficulty controlling the responses from these experts if the attorney attempts to accomplish too much. The last part of this Chapter presents questions that may be asked to reduce the risk of losing control of an expert while discrediting the testimony. See Section 10.7.

C.   DEVELOPING A PLAN

It is important to develop an effective cross-examination plan, implement it, and revise it as necessary during the case. Following a plan prevents ill-conceived attempts by the advocate to ask unprepared questions. A well-designed plan incorporates alternative lines of cross-examination that may be asked depending on the expert's answers.

A case may require experts to investigate a site, conduct tests, or review research to support their opinion. For example, an expert in a products liability case may be asked if the expert conducted a certain test. If the expert says "no," the cross-examiner can proceed to demonstrate what this test would have revealed. If the expert answers: "It wasn't necessary," the cross-examination can to establish the poor choices the expert made and what information was not obtained.

§ 10.7   SUPPORTIVE AND DISCREDITING CROSS-EXAMINATION

A.   SUPPORTIVE CROSS-EXAMINATION

The advocate ought to be able to identify some areas of agreement the cross-examined expert has with the advocate's experts. It is likely that opposing experts will agree on some issues, such as:

- Factual matters, including some of the important underlying facts.

- The sequence of events and the way things happened.

- Opinions generally recognized in the expert community.

- Reasonable differences of opinions that exist among experts.

The cross-examiner can seek concessions from the expert and highlight problems with the opponent's case.

1. Obtaining Concessions

An opposing expert may be used to establish, agree with or corroborate positions and opinions propounded by supporting experts. Questions can be asked which obtain admissions regarding generally accepted theories, principles, and opinions among experts and which show that the opposing expert agrees with the cross-examiner's experts.

Example (Cross-Examination by Defendant):

Q: Do you agree with Dr. Jekyll that schizophrenia can be effectively treated with certain drugs?

A: Yes.

Q: One of those drugs is Schizophryn?

A: Yes.

Q: Another one of those drugs is Psychophryn?

A: In many situations.

Q: You heard Dr. Jekyll state that the conduct of the defendant on the day of the crime was a classic reaction of a person with a schizophrenic personality.

A: Yes, I recall that statement.

Q: You do agree with that conclusion?

A: I do.

This concession can be effectively used during summation: "The prosecution's expert agreed with our expert. Mr. Hyde, who testified for the defense, in support of our position. He said. . . ."

2. Criticizing the Other Side's Position

The opposing expert may be used to criticize a part of the opposing party's position, statements or conduct. Questions can establish that what the opposing party said or did was inappropriate or otherwise deficient.

Example:

Q: After the machine's butterfly valve failed to close, the defendant didn't replace the valve, Mr. Papillion?

A: That is my understanding.

Q: Had the defendant replaced Exhibit No. 2, the butterfly valve, at that time, this accident may not have happened?

A: That's true.

Q: After the accident, the defendant removed the butterfly valve from the machine and left it outside?

A: Yes.

Q: Exhibit No. 2 was exposed to the sun and the wind and other elements of the weather?

A: Yes.

Q: The elements affected the condition of the valve as it sat outside for approximately a month?

A: To some degree, yes.

Q: If the defendant had placed the butterfly valve in a safe protected environment, say inside a building, the condition of the valve would have been protected?

A: Yes.

Q: You conducted tests on the valve after it had been outside?

A: Oh, yes.

Q: These tests were conducted after the Exhibit No. 2 had been kept outside for about a month?

A: Yes.

B. DISCREDITING CROSS-EXAMINATION

The most effective way to reduce the impact that an opposing expert has in a case is by discrediting the expert testimony. There are a variety of sources that can provide the bases for discrediting cross-examination.

1. Expert Fees and Financial Interests

An expert usually receives money for time spent in preparing for and testifying at the trial or hearing. The amount of money paid may be introduced or emphasized on cross-examination. It may be reasonably inferred that the testimony of the expert is being influenced by the fee. Sometimes the fee is or appears to be excessive. Financial interests in a case can be also be demonstrated if the expert has testified in similar cases for the opposing attorney or expects to testify in similar cases for the opposing attorney in the future. These fees and ongoing relationships infer that the expert has been influenced to testify favorably.

Example:

Q: Dr. Scrivello, you received a fee from the plaintiff's attorney for the hours you spent in preparing for this case, correct?

A: Yes.

Q: And you received a fee for the hours you are spending in court during this case?

A: Yes.

Q: You will be sending your bill for these fees to the attorney for the plaintiff?

A: Yes.

Q: The amount of those fees that you receive will be more than $19,000?

A: Yes.

Q: You have been asked to testify in previous cases by the plaintiff's attorney, correct?

A: Yes.

Q: And you testified in several similar previous cases?

A: Yes.

Q: And you expect to testify again in the future?

A: I may.

The direct examiner will often bring out the existence of the fee, the amount of the fee, and involvement in previous cases during direct examination to reduce the impact of this area on cross. The direct examiner may also ask redirect questions allowing the expert to explain that the opinion has not been influenced by fees or financial interest. Fees and financial interest may not be an effective area for cross-examination if the cross-examiner expects to call an expert to testify on direct examination and that expert has similar fees and financial interests.

These fee and financial questions need to be carefully crafted to avoid explanatory responses. The cross-examiner should not ask the question, "You are being paid a lot for your testimony today, aren't you?" An experienced expert witness will reply that the payment is not for the testimony but is compensation for time, and that the charges are the same fee for time spent by the expert working elsewhere or testifying.

2. Bias or Prejudice

A professional expert witness who testifies frequently may have developed an apparent bias or prejudice because of involvements in previous cases. There are a number of experts who only testify for one side because of circumstances (e.g., treating physicians who testify for injured plaintiffs), and there are experts who testify because of choice (e.g., insurance defense experts). Other experts may not testify exclusively for one type of party, but still may testify more often for either plaintiffs or defendants or prosecutors or criminal defendants.

The extent of the bias or prejudice is influenced by whether the expert has somehow been involved with the facts before liability arose or whether the expert was hired as an advisor to support the case. If an expert was a treating expert or was retained before the trial or hearing, the expert can be shown to have been a major participant in the case. If an expert was retained late in the case, the expert may have been influenced by the fact that the expert knew what opinion the attorney wanted the expert to form and assert.

Example:

Q: Doctor Mendoza, you have testified approximately 20 times in court before?

A: Yes.

Q: Of those 20 times, 18 have been on behalf of the defense?

A: I believe so.

Q: Approximately 90% of the times you have previously been in court have been in support of the defense regarding the recovery of meta data from a computer?

A: Yes.

Example:

Q: Dr. Childs, the information you used to form your opinion was sent to you by the plaintiff's attorney?

A: Yes.

Q: The attorney told you that she represented the plaintiff?

A: Yes.

Q: The plaintiff's attorney also told you she thought plaintiff's injury was caused by the faulty Julia cooking oven?

A: She told me that.

The direct examiner may anticipate this line of questioning and portray the expert as an independent professional who has high ethical standards. The direct examiner may also conduct redirect examination to highlight the integrity of the expert.

3. Inadequate Sources of Information

Questions may reveal that an expert relied upon incomplete or inadequate sources of information in forming an opinion. The adverse inference is that the expert did not have all the available information necessary to form a proper opinion, or did not know of a source of information essential to forming an objective opinion. The expert may have received information primarily from the attorney who hired the expert; the expert may not have had information accessible to other experts; or the expert may not have reviewed information essential to forming a proper opinion.

Example:

Q: Doctor Hellion, you based your opinion in this case on information that the plaintiff provided you, correct?

A: Yes.

Q: You were not present at the scene of the fire?

A: No.

Q: You never went to the scene of the fire, did you?

A: No.

Q: You never conducted your own investigation of the remains of the building?

A: I did not.

Q: You don't have personal knowledge about how the fire started?

A: No.

Q: You relied exclusively on the information the plaintiff who hired you provided you?

A: Yes.

Q: That information was contained in electronic file documents?

A: Yes.

Q: You never talked to the owner of the building, who is the defendant in this case, did you?

A: No.

Q: You never talked to the fire marshal in this case?

A: No.

Q: You never talked to anyone except the plaintiff and members of the law firm representing the plaintiff, did you?

A: Correct.

Q: You never asked for any other information?

A: That's correct.

Q: You used what they provided you?

A: Yes.

Q: And nothing more?

A: That's true. It wasn't necessary.

Q: And because you concluded it wasn't necessary, you chose not to ask for more information?

A: Yes.

---

4. Unreliable or Insufficient Information

Some experts may base an opinion on subjective facts obtained from a party. This is particularly true of treating or examining physicians, psychiatrists, or psychologists who derive their information from a patient. The expert's reliance on this information suggests their opinion is unreliable because of the partisan source of questionable facts.

Example:

Q: Doctor, you examined Marion Barbara Carstairs' lower back, correct?

A: Yes.

Q: She told you she had some pain in her lower back, right?

A: Yes.

Q: She told you she thought the injury she suffered in the boat accident caused that pain?

A: Yes.

Q: You relied on her regarding her claim of lower back pain?

A: Yes.

Q: You examined her lower back that day?

A: Yes.

Q: There was no bruising in the area of her lower back?

A: No.

Q: There was no apparent muscle spasm present, was there?

A: No.

Q: You performed no tests on her back?

A: There was no need to.

Q: Yes, and that's why you choose not to conduct any further examination, correct?

A: I did nothing further.

---

5. Disputed Facts

During direct examination the expert reveals facts that form the basis for the expert opinion. Some of these facts will be in dispute. On cross-examination the attorney can ask the expert if the opinion would change if the expert relied on other facts. If the expert agrees with this conclusion, the attorney can argue in summation that the opposing expert agrees with this favorable conclusion. If the expert disagrees, the attorney can argue that the opinion of the expert is suspect because the expert stays with the same opinion regardless of differences in facts.

Example:

Q: Doctor Lavoisier, you based your opinion on the fact that the glucose content was five percent, correct?

A: Yes.

Q: If the glucose content were only four percent, would that fact affect your opinion?

A: It might.

Q: Would the fact that the glucose was less than three percent change your opinion?

A: Yes.

6.　Lack of Thoroughness

Experts have limited amounts of time to spend in preparing and forming opinions. They may not prepare carefully or thoroughly. Questions can be asked to establish how little an expert has done and how much more an expert could have done.

Example:

Q: Marie Laveau, you are not a medical doctor, are you?

A: No.

Q: It's fair to say you are a practitioner of the scientific voodoo folkways.

A: I am.

Q: You conducted a psychological examination of the defendant?

A: Oh, yes.

Q: You met with the defendant for an hour and a half?

A: Yes, I spent that time with her.

Q: Those 90 minutes were the only time you spent with her?

A: Yes.

Q: If you had spent more time with the defendant you may have acquired more information?

A: Sure.

Q: That additional information may have affected the opinion that you formed about the defendant?

A: It's possible.

Q: You may have learned some things about the defendant you didn't learn during your only interview with the defendant?

A: True.

Q: You don't know what else you may have learned, do you?

A: I guess I don't know.

Q: Well, we are not here to guess, Ms. Laveau. It's fair to say you don't know what else you may have learned, correct.

A: Yes.

---

7. Insufficient Testing

An expert may not have conducted sufficient tests or procedures to support an opinion. The cross-examiner's own expert can tell the examiner what tests an expert should have or could have conducted before being able to render an opinion. Questions on cross-examination can establish that the expert failed to conduct ordinarily necessary tests, did not obtain information that experts typically rely on before forming an opinion, and may not have obtained crucial test results that would have changed the expert's opinion.

Example:

Q: Dr. McCoy, you removed the cast two weeks after the break?

A: Yes.

Q: At that time, you did not test to determine any loss of weakness in the muscle, did you?

A: Not at that time.

Q: You didn't believe it worthwhile?

A: It wasn't.

Q: You chose not to conduct a test because you didn't want to?

A: That's right.

Q: You could have given other tests rather easily?

A: I could have.

Q: And you did not conduct any test to determine any weakness with the nerve, did you?

A: No.

Q: You didn't think that was worthwhile either?

A: No.

Q: And you decided not to do any type of further tests?

A: That's correct.

Q: You placed a new cast on?

A: Yes.

Q: You removed this cast four weeks later?

A: Yes.

Q: Some fractures require much more time in a cast, correct?

A: Yes.

Q: Serious fractures?

A: Usually.

Q: When you removed this final cast, you didn't perform an electromyography, did you?

A: No.

Q: Isn't it true an electromyography, if performed early enough, would make it possible to demonstrate a weakness in a muscle or nerve before a permanent loss of strength developed?

A: In some cases.

Q: And this is a case in which that would be true, correct?

A: Yes.

---

8. Existence of Other Causes

Often there are alternative explanations for expert opinions. Cross-examination can reveal those alternatives by establishing other causes in addition to the cause the expert advances. The cross-examiner's expert can provide these other possible causes of an event.

Example:

Q: Doctor Zhivago, there can be other causes for back pain, yes?

A: Yes.

Q: A degenerative condition can cause back pain?

A: Yes.

Q: Or stress?

A: Do you mean physical stress or mental stress?

Q: Physical stress.

A: Yes.

Q: And mental stress?

A: I suppose, yes.

Q: And infectious conditions?

A: Yes.

Q: Heredity?

A: Yes.

Q: Congenital conditions?

A: Yes.

Q: Even a preexisting injury?

A: Yes.

---

9.   Inappropriate or Insufficient Expertise

The expertise of an expert may be in areas different from those directly involved in the case. An expert may have experience in a broad area, and the case may involve a very narrow area. Or an expert may have expertise on a very narrow subject, and the case may involve a broader subject. An expert may be vulnerable to challenges based on the lack of education, training or experience with a crucial issue in the case.

The emphasis attached to this area of cross-examination depends on how the opposing expert contrasts with the cross-examiner's own expert. If a broad area of expertise is applicable to the case, the cross-examiner should attempt to narrow the expertise of the opponent's expert. If a narrow area of expertise is appropriate to the case, the expert should attempt to broaden the expertise of the opponent's expert.

Example:

Q: Ms. Veranzano, your Master's degree is in structural engineering?

A: Yes.

Q: You did not major in electrical engineering, did you?

A: I did not major in it, but I had some courses in it.

Q: Your experience has primarily been in the field of structural engineering?

A: Primarily.

Q: More of your professional life has involved structural engineering as contrasted with electrical engineering?

A: Yes.

Q: You have published numerous professional articles?

A: Yes, many.

Q: Those articles have dealt with structural engineering?

A: Yes.

Q: You have written articles on bridge construction?

A: Yes.

Q: And you have written articles that have appeared in structural engineering magazines and on related websites?

A: Yes.

Q: None of those articles deal with the electrical engineering issues in this case, do they?

A: They do not.

Q: You have not relied on any of those articles as a basis for your opinion in this case, have you?

A: I didn't need to.

Q: Because those articles didn't deal with the issues at stake in this case?

A: They do not.

---

10. Differences of Opinion Among Experts

Opinions in some areas of expertise are subject to significant and legitimate differences among qualified experts. This is especially true in fields of expertise involving subjective or interpretive fields, such as psychiatry or economics. Questions can be asked that establish different experts have legitimate differences of opinion and the testifying expert has been wrong sometimes and right sometimes in the past.

Example:

Q: Doctor Yellen, it's difficult to predict with accuracy the rate of inflation for future years?

A: Yes.

Q: Prominent economists differ among themselves regarding the future rate of inflation?

A: Yes.

Q: This area of predicting the rate of inflation is subject to significant differences of opinion among experts?

A: Yes.

Q: You have been an expert economist for over thirty years?

A: Yes.

Q: During that span of time, you have had occasion to predict the rate of inflation?

A: Yes.

Q: Sometimes your predictions have been accurate?

A: Yes.

Q: And sometimes your predictions have been inaccurate?

A: Yes.

Q: You have disagreed with the predictions of experts whom you consider to be renowned in the field of economics?

A: Yes.

Q: And these experts who are authorities in their field and whom you recognize as authorities have disagreed with your predictions regarding the rate of inflation in the past?

A: I suppose.

Q: And sometimes their predictions—and not yours—have been accurate?

A: Yes.

---

11. Subjective Opinions

An expert may admit that the opinion the expert reached is a matter of informed judgment and not based on some immutable principles. This technique is useful for areas of expertise that are subjective in nature rather than scientific or technical. For example, opinions based on interpretations and beliefs can be effectively challenged.

Example:

Q: The assessment of the value of real property is not a science, is it Ms. Monopoly?

A: No, it is not a science.

Q: There are many variables that affect the value of a piece of property, correct?

A: Yes.

Q: Some of these variables are based on subjective evaluations and not objective data?

A: That is true.

Q: Some of these factors require an appraiser individually to interpret property values, correct?

A: Yes.

Q: And appraisers may reach different conclusions about the value of the same piece of real estate?

A: Yes, they may.

12. Inconsistent Prior Statements

An expert witness can be cross-examined using any oral or written statement made by that expert that contradicts or is inconsistent with a position taken on direct examination, as with a lay witness.

Example:

Q: Dr. Keynes, you testified on direct examination that the defendant properly used the FIFO method in this transaction because it is the "preferred method" employed by accountants, is that right?

A: Yes.

Q: Doctor, you prepared a written report summarizing your opinions in this case, didn't you?

A: Yes.

Q: The attorney for the plaintiff retained you and paid you for your time in preparing that report?

A: Yes.

Q: Before preparing the report you thoroughly reviewed all the facts, correct?

A: Yes.

Q: You consider yourself an expert with regard to accounting procedures, don't you?

A: Yes.

Q: The report that you prepared was accurate, wasn't it?

A: Yes.

Q: Doctor, I would like to show you your printed report. You do recognize this report as the one you prepared, correct?

A: Yes.

Q: Your signature appears at the end of the report on page 5?

A: Yes.

Q: Please turn to page 3, second paragraph, 4th line.

A: Okay.

Q: You wrote what's contained on that line in that paragraph in that report, didn't you?

A: Yes.

Q: You wrote on line 4 that: "Neither the FIFO nor the LIFO method is preferred in a case such as this."

A: Yes I did.

---

13. Hypothetical Questions

If a hypothetical question is used on direct examination, an effective way to cross-examine the expert is to ask the expert concise hypothetical questions that contain facts different from the direct examination hypothetical. This approach is similar to the technique discussed in Section 10.5(D) and can be used with similar success.

14. Treatises

Treatises can be used during the cross-examination of an expert to impeach that expert as well as for other purposes. Federal Rule of Evidence 803(18) and similar state rules provide:

- Treatises may be used on cross-examination of an opposing expert, or on the direct examination of an expert.

- Treatises include books, periodicals, articles, professional magazines, and websites.

- Treatises must be established as "reliable authority" by admission of a witness or by another expert or by notice.

- Treatises may be introduced as evidence for any purpose.

- Treatises are read on the record and do not become exhibits.

Some experts who have written extensively may have published a position contrary to their position taken at the trial or hearing. Other experts may be impeached with treatises another person authored. This impeachment process requires a thorough review of all the publications in the area and a detailed index of these publications for use during trial.

An expert on cross-examination need only admit that a treatise is a reliable authority generally recognized in an area. The expert does not have to have relied upon the treatise or professionally agree to its position. Leading questions that establish that the treatise has successive editions, is used extensively in professional schools, or appears in the offices or smart tablets of many experts, may establish this foundation.

If an expert on cross-examination denies the general reliability of the treatise, the treatise may still be used but will need to be established as authoritative by another expert, the book editor, a librarian, or a website publisher. Some jurisdictions still require the witness on cross-examination concede that the treatise is authoritative and that the witness relies on it before it can be used for impeachment.

The attorney proffering the treatise may read it to the fact finder or introduce it as evidence and it becomes part of the record. The treatise is admitted for all purposes: for impeachment, as substantive proof of its contents, to substitute for the views of another expert, or to corroborate another expert's opinion. The opinion of an author of a treatise or other learned publication can be introduced through the treatise even though the author does not testify. See Section 10.5(G).

Example:

Examining Attorney:

Q: Dean Wyeth, are you familiar with a text entitled, The Economics of Advocacy Practice?

A: Yes.

Q: This book has been a reliable authority in the field of law and economics for many years, correct?

A: Yes.

Q: Do you consider this text to be authoritative?

A: It's one authority.

Q: Dean, do you agree with the following statement that appears on page 150: "The median salary for advocates is in inverse proportion to their LSAT scores and their law school class rank at graduation."?

A: I would hope not. But, yes I agree.

To the Arbitrator:

I now would like to read a short paragraph from page 666.

Arbitrator:

You may do so.

Examining Attorney:

"The major factor bolstering the success of advocates in practice is their abiding affection for their law school advocacy text."

I have no further questions.

---

15. Safely Exposing Deficiencies

Additional areas that can be established on cross are topics that do not depend upon circumstances relating to the specific area of expertise. These areas include "safe" questions that can be asked if questions suggested in the previous subsections are not appropriate or are too risky.

- The late entry of the expert into the case. The opposing attorney may not secure an expert until immediately before the case is heard.

- The very limited amount of time the expert spent reviewing the information and data.

- The information the expert relied upon has been provided primarily by the party who retained the expert.

- The facts relied on by the expert are not the facts upon which other testifying experts relied.

16. Lack of Reliability of the Field of Expertise

This subject may be available if the advocate does not call an expert to testify in opposition to the other side's expert or if an opposing expert claims an expertise that is questionable. The judge or arbitrator may permit the expert to render an opinion, but the opposing lawyer can still challenge the so-called expert. The advocate may ask cross-examination questions establishing the unreliability of the field of expertise or the failure of experts in related areas to accept and recognize the area as a reliable field of expertise. And, the cross-examiner may show the expert opinion to be unreliable and not credible. Topics that may be successfully covered using these approaches include:

- Lack of sufficient education, training, or experience of the expert;

- Differences between related areas of expertise that have been generally unrecognized;

- Unreliability of the procedures or tests used; and

- The observation that the field of expertise is merely the application of common sense that fact finders may apply on their own.

CHAPTER 11

SUMMATION/FINAL ARGUMENT

■ ■ ■

Trial Advocacy Supplement
Summation

Examples of complete closing arguments appear in the *Supplement to Trial Advocacy Before Judges, Jurors, and Arbitrators* in three cases. A jury trial, an arbitration, and an administrative law hearing demonstrate and explain summation strategies, tactics, and techniques discussed in this Chapter. Commentary accompanies the transcript that helps explain the approaches used by the lawyers.

REFLECTING ON ADVOCACY

Facts, as such, never settle anything. They are working tools only. It is the implications that can be drawn from facts that count.

—CLARENCE BELDEN RANDALL

A good speech is a good thing, but the verdict is the thing.

—DANIEL O'CONNELL

§ 11.1 INTRODUCTION

A. SCOPE

Summation is the last opportunity the lawyer has to make an oral presentation to the fact finder. During summation, the advocate can explain the evidence, describe the law applicable to the facts, and present reasons why the judge, jurors, or arbitrator should render a decision in favor of the advocate's client. It is the final culmination that hopefully leads to a well-deserved victory and justice.

Summation occurs after the close of all the evidence. It is also known as final argument or closing argument, although the term "argument" may misstate the primary purpose of summation. It is not enough to merely "argue" the rightness or wrongness of positions. The attorney must "advocate" and present a reasonable, persuasive explanation. Summation supplements the presentation of the facts and law. Cases are won by what happens during the entire trial or hearing.

B. PURPOSES

The purposes of summation are to:

- Summarize the story of the case.

- Explain the significance of the evidence presented.

- Comment on the credibility of witnesses.

- Highlight real and demonstrative exhibits.

- Draw reasonable inferences, argue conclusions, refer to common sense, and explain implications the fact finder may not perceive.

- Explain why a party deserves to win.

- Describe the law, elements of the claims and defenses, and jury instructions in jury trials.

- Answer questions from a judge or arbitrator in bench trials and arbitrations.

- Highlight the rational, emotional, and humanistic issues.
- Integrate the case theories, evidence, and law into a cohesive and comprehensive presentation.

C. THE FINAL STORY

A case begins with the story told during the opening statement and concludes with the story summarized in the closing argument. The factual story of the case recreates what happened and should move the fact finders to *want* to render a favorable decision. An effective summation provides the decision makers with reasonable explanations, appropriately evokes the human dimensions of the events that occurred, and provides a motivation to return a favorable decision.

All cases involve reasons and emotions and have facts that support the telling of a compelling story. Criminal cases involve matters of freedom and liberty. Personal injury cases involve pain and suffering. Commercial litigation cases involve the economic livelihood of people. Antitrust cases involve public interest issues. The advocate must bring to life the factual, legal, and human dimensions underlying the case.

D. HUMAN DIMENSIONS

Decision makers base their conclusions not only on the logic and rational reasons supporting a position but also on the human dimensions of the case. An intellectual argument that reaches only the minds of the fact finders may not be sufficient. The advocate must present an argument that touches the emotions and feelings of the decision makers as well as their intellects and thoughts. Decision makers want to do what is right, and they also want to be fair. They want to do what is reasonable, and they also want to feel good about their decision.

The advocate must consider using these psychological and emotional influences. Every advocate has this ability. Every attorney, outside the courtroom and hearing room, has told a story to someone that touched the emotions of the listener and produced positive feelings. This same ability will be needed during summation when the advocate must present the argument in a way that favorably influences the fact finders.

This goal of presenting a humanistic story is the art of presenting a compelling summation. An advocate has goals that are similar to the goals of speakers in other professions. Take a moment and think about effective speakers and consider their approaches. They not only presented information and advanced reasonable positions but also said something that appropriately tapped emotions and feelings that affected decisions.

An improper or inappropriate argument that appeals only to emotions is ineffective and must be avoided. Fact finders who hear an inapt or unsuitable appeal to their feelings may conclude that the facts, law, and reason do not support the attorney's position. An appeal to emotion must be buttressed by compelling facts and persuasive law.

E. VALUES AND VIEWPOINTS

Summation has the same goals as other aspects of advocacy. The focus must be on what is likely to most help the decision maker decide the case favorably. The values, background, viewpoints, experiences, and life principles of each decision maker will have a strong influence on how the stories are heard and interpreted and what must be said in summation that successfully influences the decision maker.

In deciding a case, it is unlikely that the final decision will be based on factors that contradict the core values and guiding principles of the judge, jurors, or arbitrator. A summation that includes reasons, facts, opinions, and explanations that reflect the *beliefs and norms* of the decision maker will be more effective.

§ 11.2 WHAT CAN BE PRESENTED

A. FACTS AND OPINIONS

All facts and opinions that are a part of the case, even those in dispute, may be described during summation. The attorney should explain all the important evidence and selectively discuss other evidence.

B. INFERENCES

Inferences are conclusions drawn from the evidence. Generally, the attorney may make and explain all reasonable factual inferences.

C. THE STORY

The attorney should summarize the case story using the words and phrases presented throughout the trial or hearing. The closing argument provides an opportunity for the attorney to connect the themes and theories of the case with the evidence and applicable law.

D. EXHIBITS AND VISUAL AIDS

Advocates may use exhibits and visual aids in the final argument. These exhibits and aids may contain compelling images, depictions of events, descriptive diagrams, graphic reproductions, listings of issues or damages, or a summary of arguments. Computer generated presentations can further enhance the argument. The extent to which they should be used depends upon the nature of the facts, types of issues, and the ability of the advocate to use them effectively.

E. LAW AND LEGAL THEORIES

During closing argument, the attorney needs to explain how the law applies to the facts to support the decision sought and how the evidence supports the legal theories. While the advocate is not the source of the law, the advocate can apply the law to the facts and argue why the law supports the verdict that is sought. In jury trials, the judge has the responsibility to explain the law through jury instructions. Lawyers know what jury instructions and verdict form will be provided and can use the instructions and verdict form to explain how they support the verdict.

F. THEORY OF THE CASE

A focal point of closing argument is an explanation of the theory of the case. Opening was the first time the advocate introduced the theory of the case; summation is the last time the theory can be further developed and explained. See Section 2.5.

G. ANECDOTAL REFERENCES

Counsel has the opportunity during summation to present anecdotes, analogies, and metaphors involving common life experiences and to employ a variety of persuasive techniques, including the use of appropriate fictional stories, poems, and works of literature and art.

H. UNDERLYING VALUES AND NORMS

Explanations how a favorable decision supports and is consistent with the values and norms of the decision maker will increase the chance of success. Arguments based on positions contrary to the decision maker's principles and beliefs will not be persuasive.

I. NEW EXPLANATIONS

An important goal of summation is providing a decision maker with an explanation of the case that has not been thought of or considered. The advocate should strive to present relevant ideas and explanations and interpretations of the facts, law, and events. An effective advocate provides insights into a case that are not apparent from the evidence.

J. URGING A RESULT

The closing argument is the last opportunity the attorney has to ask for a specific result, and it should be stated clearly and persuasively.

K. NO REQUIREMENT TO DISCUSS EVERYTHING

The attorney is not required to summarize or comment upon all the facts, opinions, inferences, and law involved in a case. A failure to comment on and refute a credible position or defense developed by opposing counsel, however, may be a mistake. A decision not to address an issue, an opponent's theory, or a particular fact should be based on an analysis of the importance of that subject and the ability of the attorney and the opponent to persuasively explain the position to the fact finder.

L. USING CREATIVE ARGUMENTS

Summation provides advocates with an opportunity to use creative explanations to bolster a case. Examples:

Creative presentation. In an employment discrimination case, the plaintiff fashioned charts and diagrams based on groups of employees hired, retained, promoted, and fired to display how the defendant business committed discriminatory acts. These demonstrative evidence exhibits were based on the data and statistics entered into evidence and depicted overt discriminatory acts and conducts.

Creative events. Day in the life videos can display what parties go through in their daily existence after an accident. A video of plaintiff paraplegic seeking money damages for her care can portray the difficulties in leading an ordinary life involving events such as eating, exercising, working, driving, bathing, and sleeping. A video of a plaintiff offered by the defense showing plaintiff doing things the plaintiff testifies he can no longer do such as playing golf or tennis vividly impeaches the plaintiff's version of his injuries.

Creative anecdotes. An advocate can establish gross negligence by using history to portray an opponent who fails to heed clear warnings and take notice of obvious mistakes. The history of the Titanic and its captain who failed to take proper and careful steps to avoid icebergs can be used as an analogy in a business fraud case against the manager of the business. An advocate used this technique to contrast scenes from the film *Titanic* with actual events that occurred in a case to graphically depict purported misfeasance and malfeasance.

Creative metaphors. Literature may provide a source of stories that parallel the circumstances of a case and that bring to life the human dimensions inherent in a case. The lyrics of the song poem *O Danny Boy*, which has been interpreted as an ode by a parent to a son leaving the family, was effectively used in a case involving the death of a young boy who died because of the negligence of the defendant.

Creative use of evidence. Cases involving documents present opportunities to craft a descriptive summary of events. A case that involves many, and sometimes conflicting, emails can be explained by a comparison summary of the highlighted portions of the supportive emails. This use of evidence can be very effective in contrasting what the real evidence shows compared to the oral testimony of witnesses.

Creative demonstrative evidence. Events can be re-created to show that an event could not have occurred or did occur according to the way a party claims it happened. A computer generated graphic display of the cause of a fire claimed to have been started by the defendant can demonstrate it could not have started that way based on explanatory and compelling expert testimony.

§ 11.3 PREPARATION

A. EARLY AND CONTINUING PREPARATION

The planning of a case begins with the preparation of the closing argument. See Section 2.4. Summation provides the focus for the entire case. Throughout the case, the attorney should be preparing the fact finder for what will be heard during the final argument. Summation should reemphasize the theory of the case previously presented. The factual summary and legal theories of a case that were selected prior to the trial or hearing provide a framework of ideas for the final argument. While a closing argument is developed in advance, it must be refined and revised depending on how the evidence develops during the case.

1. Jury Selection

In a jury trial, the first opportunity to explain a case is during jury selection. The attorney is prohibited from directly arguing the case in this initial stage of the trial, but may inform the potential jurors about the theories of the case. Through questions, the attorney prepares the jurors for what they will hear and see during the trial. During summation, references may be made to jury selection responses. The attorney may attempt to persuade jurors to render a favorable verdict by asking a question during jury selection and later, during closing argument, refer back to the answer, promise or commitment the jurors gave.

For example, in a civil case involving damages, plaintiff's counsel during jury selection can ask questions regarding the jury's ability to return a verdict for a substantial amount of money if substantial damages are proven. During summation, counsel may refer to the jury's "agreement" or "promise" to award substantial damages based on the evidence proven during the trial.

2. Opening Statement

Opening statement provides an opportunity to begin to lay a foundation for the closing argument. During an opening, the attorney explains the evidence that will be discussed during final argument. What is presented during the opening should be consistent with the summation, otherwise counsel will appear to have failed to prove part of the case.

3.　Presenting the Evidence

Direct and cross-examination testimony and exhibits develop the facts that were initially explained during the opening statement. The comprehensive and credible presentation of evidence is essential to complete the factual and legal foundation for summation.

B.　JURY TRIAL INSTRUCTIONS

Prior to the closing argument in a jury trial, the judge informs the attorneys of the precise instructions of law to be provided to the jury. In most jurisdictions, the judge's instructions to the jury take place after summation. In some jurisdictions, the judge instructs the jury before summation. The attorney must review these final instructions and make certain the evidence explained in the final argument supports the law that will be explained by the judge. See Section 12.2.

All statements of law made by the attorney must be accurate. The judge will tell the jury that if the attorney has explained the law differently than the judge, the jury must rely on the judge's description. If the attorney misstates the law, the attorney loses credibility and diminishes the impact of summation. If the attorney states the law correctly, even using the same words as the judge, the result can raise the credibility of the attorney and positively reinforce the summation.

C.　IDENTIFYING PIVOTAL ISSUES

The advocate must simplify the issues for the decision makers. A review of the factual summaries and legal theories will determine which facts and what legal elements are undisputed and which important, controversial issues remain disputed. Evidence that has been stipulated or uncontradicted may resolve some issues.

The following presents a closing argument framework:

1.　Believable Story

- Identify reasons why the story ought to be believed.

- Use analogies or common sense explanations.

- Rely on favorable legal principles.

2.　Credibility of a Witness

- Summarize the testimony of the witness.

- Describe the favorable demeanor of the witness.

- Rely on exhibits introduced through the witness.

- Draw on corroborating testimony or exhibits.

- Use reasons that support the credibility of the witness.
- Attack opposing witnesses with contradictory testimony.
- Describe the unfavorable demeanor of opposing witnesses.

3. Reasonable Inferences

- Summarize favorable testimony.
- Identify supportive facts and lay and expert opinions.
- Rely upon favorable law.
- Employ a supporting analogy or anecdote.

4. Application of Law to Facts

- Reasonably interpret the law.
- Specifically apply the legal standards to the evidence.

5. Available Exhibits and Visual Aids

- Select and show real evidence exhibits.
- Plan to display demonstrative exhibits.
- Re-use visual aids that were used in the opening statement.
- Create visual aids to be used during closing.

6. Consider the Perspective and Views of Decision Makers

- Make sure all the crucial issues have been addressed.
- Discern what values and beliefs influence them.
- Consider what final questions they need answered.

D. ANTICIPATING OPPONENT'S POSITION

In preparing summation, counsel needs to anticipate and predict the various arguments and positions of the opposing case. By the close of the evidence, an advocate should know what the opposing attorney will argue in summation and can analyze how to best address those arguments and how to effectively counter or reduce the adverse impact of the closing.

E. SELECTING EXHIBITS AND VISUAL AIDS

Considerations regarding what exhibits and visual aids should be used during summation include: the impact they may have on the decision maker, the importance of the exhibits in the case, and how effectively the visual aids can be employed. Real evidence, demonstrative evidence, deposition transcripts, witness statements, discovery responses, and any other exhibit that has been introduced during the case may be used during closing argument. Visual aids may also be created that highlight summation, such as: a summary of evidence or argument on a poster, a board, or monitor screen; handwritten notes by the attorney on a whiteboard or easel page; a printed timeline on a chart; a descriptive outline of damages; a power point presentation; a summary listing of the issues to be decided; a computer generated depiction of events; and an enlarged copy of the verdict form in a jury trial.

F. MEETING EXPECTATIONS

The same considerations about the expectations of judges, jurors, and arbitrators regarding opening statements apply to final arguments. See Section 6.2(F). As described previously, modern fact finders/decision makers are influenced by what they see and hear on television, in the movies, on websites, and by attending video and live presentations such as TED talks. They may expect lawyers to meet and exceed these performances. Advocates need to craft closings that highlight the favorable facts and the supportive law and which also reasonably meet the expectations of their legal audience.

G. LENGTH

Summation should be long enough to cover the essential arguments of the case, yet short enough to maintain the attention of the decision maker. The reasonable, optimum length for a closing argument varies depending upon the circumstances and complexity of the case and the speaking ability of the attorney. Effective closing arguments often last between thirty and sixty minutes. Simple cases may require shorter summations. Final arguments in complex and lengthy cases will take longer. The longer a closing argument is, the more difficult it is to maintain the attention of the decision maker. The use of visual aids and exhibits can enhance the presentation and make a lengthy summation easier to follow. If rebuttal is permitted, the attorney may need to reserve time for rebuttal by requesting permission from the judge or arbitrator.

Judges and arbitrators ordinarily ask the attorneys how long they anticipate the closing argument will take and usually allow advocates a sufficient amount of time for summation. Judges and arbitrators usually have broad discretion in allowing or restricting the time available. They will limit the time if the requested amount is unnecessarily long or out of proportion to the length of the trial or hearing or the issues to be resolved. They may also allow additional time if counsel provides legitimate reasons for needing more time.

H. ORDER AND SEQUENCE

The general rule is that the party who has the burden of proof closes last. Because the plaintiff/claimant/prosecutor has such a burden, they argue last. However, in a very few jurisdictions the order is different and defense will have the last opportunity to present.

In those jurisdictions that permit rebuttal argument, there are three summations: the first argument by the party with the burden, the opposing argument, and a rebuttal argument. In those jurisdictions that do not permit rebuttal, there are two summations: the defense argues first followed by the plaintiff/claimant/prosecutor. In civil cases, in which both parties carry the burden of proof, usually the plaintiff/claimant has the opportunity to have the final argument. If the burden of proof in a civil case rests with the defendant/respondent, the defense is permitted the last closing argument.

The attorney who argues last usually has an advantage because the attorney can rebut any argument the opposing lawyer makes. The lawyer who argues first and has no rebuttal needs to anticipate what the opposing counsel will present and counter those points. Counsel who has rebuttal can divide the argument and save some persuasive parts for rebuttal.

I. "OPENING" ARGUMENT

In jurisdictions that permit rebuttal, the advocate must decide what to include in the initial closing and what to save for rebuttal. Usually, the scope of rebuttal is limited to the points made during the opponent's argument that were not explained during the initial summation. Practically, however, the scope of rebuttal is broad because the closing argument by the opposing lawyer generally covers all important issues in the case. A rebuttal lawyer may prefer to save some important points for rebuttal to reduce the chance opposing counsel can counter them.

J. REBUTTAL ARGUMENT

Rebuttal summation should emphasize the pivotal issues not covered during the initial closing and counter points made by the opponent. A rebuttal is more effective if begun by advancing positive reasons in support of a favorable decision, instead of beginning with defensive explanations. The points made by the opponent can be countered during or after presenting this affirmative rebuttal argument.

Rebuttal summation can be prepared in advance by predicting what the other attorney will argue. The preparation should include a persuasive and perhaps dramatic conclusion appropriate for the case.

K. PREPARED OUTLINE AND DETAILED SCRIPT

The final argument outline that was prepared during case preparation will need to be revised. The final outline should include all parts of the closing argument to make certain that every matter is addressed. Form 11.1 provides an outline of summation factors that can be included.

Some lawyers prefer to prepare a complete closing argument. This approach helps the attorney finalize the contents of the closing argument and helps determine whether some matter has been omitted. However, reading a prepared script of a closing argument bores the listeners and significantly diminishes the persuasive power of the attorney because the presentation may appear dry and impersonal.

A summation outline should be sufficient and permit the advocate to be more persuasive. It should be as detailed as necessary to assist counsel in presenting a complete closing. Portions of this outline can be displayed with a visual aid that permits the decision maker to follow along. The visual aid can be displayed on a computer monitor, or printed on a poster board, or written on a white board or easel paper.

L. REHEARSAL

The final argument must be rehearsed. Practice permits the attorney to improve both the content and the style of delivery. The attorney may rehearse the closing argument before colleagues, in front of a mirror, or on a video recording for review and critique. The use of visual aids and exhibits also needs to be rehearsed.

Thorough preparation and repeated practice enhances the ability of the advocate to be effective. When presenting the closing argument, the attorney should not necessarily attempt to recall all the exact words used during the practice sessions, but express the important concepts. A flowing and persuasive argument can be sincerely presented when the attorney is comfortable with the material and the delivery.

FORM 11.1
CLOSING ARGUMENT WORKSHEET

Case _____ File _____

Case Theories/Themes

Structure

Introduction

Argument

Inferences

Explanations

Evidence

Witnesses

Credibility of Witnesses

Circumstantial Evidence

Law/Jury Instructions

Special Interrogatories/Verdict Form

Analogies/Metaphors/Anecdotes

Exhibits/Visual Aids

Emotional Aspects

Case Weaknesses

Burden of Proof

Opposing Argument

Facts Not Proved/Promises Not Kept

Request for Order/Award/Decision/Verdict

Conclusion

Rebuttal

M. SPECIFIC REQUIREMENTS

The attorney needs to determine before summation whether the judge or arbitrator has any special requirements or time limitations or whether applicable rules regulate the final argument. Knowing the requirements avoids having the closing argument interrupted by objections from opposing counsel. Prevailing practice and procedures may limit what can be done during summation, including prohibitions on the use of distorted visual aids or unfairly prejudicial exhibits.

§ 11.4 ORGANIZATION

A. STRUCTURE

Summation, like all parts of the case, must be presented in a structured manner to be effective. The selection of a structure depends upon the theories, facts, law, circumstances, and strategies of the case. The following are examples of different structures:

1. Chronology

The closing argument can follow the story chronology.

2. Flashback

Summation can begin with the conclusion of the story, which the fact finder has already heard, and flashback to earlier events.

3. Undisputed and Disputed Facts

The evidence can be explained first by describing the undisputed facts and then highlighting the disputed facts, with an explanation that the facts supporting the advocate's case are what actually happened.

4. Order of Key Witnesses

If key witnesses testified in a logical or reasonable order, closing argument can be structured based on their testimony.

5. Issues, Positions, Topics

Summation can be structured based on the order the issues, positions, or topics were presented in a case.

6. Exhibits

A case dependent on exhibits may be structured around the most relevant and persuasive exhibits.

7.   Claims or Defenses

The structure of a closing can be based on the claims or defenses asserted. For example, claimant's counsel in a contract case can present an argument based on the factors that prove the existence of a breach of warranty, and defense counsel may organize an argument based on the number of defenses supported by the facts. For another example, a criminal defense attorney can structure a closing based on the number of reasonable doubts.

8.   Liability and Damages

In civil cases, the closing argument could begin with an explanation of the liability issues followed by the damage issues, or vice versa.

9.   The Law, Jury Instructions, Verdict Form

Summation can be based on the elements of the applicable law or order of the substantive jury instructions and verdict form. For example, in a criminal case, the prosecutor can structure a final argument by following the elements to be proved in a burglary case. In a contract dispute, respondent's counsel can structure a final argument that rebuts the elements of law covering the creation of a contract, its breach, and damages. In a jury trial, a verdict form that contains special interrogatories provides an organized way of reviewing the evidence. The jurors will sequentially answer these questions as they appear in the form, and counsel can use the same format during closing argument.

10. Multiple Substructures

Most closing arguments employ a number of these alternative structures. For example, a closing argument may contain a description of undisputed facts, followed by a narrative chronology of the disputed facts, followed by an explanation of legal elements. Section 2.6 explained the various issues that can be decided in a case. Each of these issues may be described during summation by employing different structures.

B.   THE INTRODUCTION

Final argument should begin with an introduction that draws the attention and interest of the decision makers to the content of the argument. The attention level will usually be high at the beginning of summation as the case is drawing to a close. The introduction can initially set the scope and focus of the presentation. The best approach depends upon the facts and circumstances, themes and theories, and the primary goals established in the opening statement.

1. Case Theory

An effective way to begin the closing argument is to summarize in a few sentences the factual summaries and legal theories of the case. This approach reinforces what the decision maker has heard during the case.

Example (Civil Plaintiff):

This case is about a job that was arbitrarily taken from a hardworking woman. This case is about Libby Joyce and her right to be treated fairly and decently. This case is not about some abstract facts. What you heard from this witness stand and what you read from these documents really happened. It happened to this woman. It happened because of the poor judgment and mismanagement by this corporate employer. For the past two days you heard this story unfold in this arbitration.

Example (Civil Plaintiff):

This lawsuit is about safety. Thomas Harvick had a right to the safe functioning of the product he bought from the defendant. He had a right to expect he would not be electrocuted by a defectively designed product—a tragedy that could have been prevented by inexpensive insulation. Insulation protects people against shock and could have and would have prevented his unnecessary death. A small expense of $65 for a ceramic insulator on the chain of this window washer's harness—would have prevented the electrocution of Tom Harvick.

---

2. Memorable Introduction

A memorable introductory statement attempts to establish an atmosphere, set a tone, and grab the jury's attention. A dramatic statement appropriate to the case and presented in a sincere way can be effective.

Example (Civil Plaintiff):

What is more precious than the birth of a child? A child who is healthy and who has a full life to live. To love, to cry, to laugh, to fail, to succeed. What is more tragic than the birth of a child who is born without the ability to take care of herself, to ever tell her parents how much she loves them, to ever talk, to ever fail or succeed at school or work? This is the fate of Lateefah.

Example (Criminal Prosecution):

Members of the Jury, that man (pointing to the defendant) on the morning of August 16 walked into his garage, opened up his toolbox, and pulled out a claw hammer. That man (looking at the defendant), grasping the claw hammer in his right hand, walked from his garage, through his kitchen, up the stairway, into the bedroom of his home, and deliberately stood over his wife, who was peacefully asleep. That man, the defendant Hajim Bey, intentionally raised that claw hammer in the air and with all his might smashed that claw hammer into the face of the woman who loved him and lived with him until he ruthlessly killed her.

3.   Outline of Argument

Summation may begin with an explanation of the outline of the presentation. The decision maker may find it easier to follow the argument if they know how it is organized and what structure the attorney will use.

Example (Plaintiff Contract):

This presentation consists of three parts—the same three parts I discussed during opening statement. First, I will show how the evidence establishes the existence of a valid and enforceable contract. Second, I'll explain that the evidence clearly establishes why and how the respondent breached its contract with my client. Third, I will review with you all the damages my client, Tuskegee Institute, incurred that defendant is obligated to pay.

4.   Explanation of Summation for Jurors

In jury trials, final argument can begin with an explanation of the purpose of summation. The advantage of these preliminary remarks is that the jurors may better understand the reasons for closing argument. The disadvantage of these remarks is that they may not be the most effective and persuasive way to begin summation.

Example (General):

We are now about to come to the end of this trial. Soon you will deliberate together and reach a verdict on behalf of Lewis and Clark. This part of the trial—summation—provides me with an opportunity to speak to you for the last time. What I will say to you will be consistent with what I have said to you before and with what you have heard and seen during this trial.

Example (General):

Over the past three weeks you have heard the testimony of many witnesses and have seen Facebook entries, Instagram postings, and YouTube videos. On the first day, I presented to you an opening statement—a story of what you would hear and see. Today, I'll summarize that evidence and explain how the facts and law lead you to the conclusion that my client, Milo Hoffman, is entitled to a verdict in this case against Gary Winston.

These introductory remarks are sometimes used because attorneys need something easy to say to reduce their nervousness, or because they have heard another attorney make similar statements, or because they have not considered alternative introductory remarks. Many attorneys prefer not to begin summation with these explanatory remarks but may delay making such comments until after they explain their case theory or use an alternative attention-grabbing statement.

5. Expressing Gratitude

It is customary for many advocates during summation to thank the decision makers for their attention and time. A statement of appreciation should be sincere, brief, and not patronizing. Whether the beginning of summation should include this statement or whether it should be mentioned later, if it all, depends on the preference of the attorney . Some lawyers believe there is no need to thank them because they are doing their job or duty; other attorneys always thank them, especially the jury.

Example (General):

We have now come to the stage of the trial called closing argument. The witnesses have all testified. The documents have all been introduced. We, the attorneys, are almost done. You will shortly begin your deliberations to reach a just and fair verdict. My client, Elsa Arendelelle, and I, and all of us here, thank you for the time and attention you have devoted to this case.

---

6. Defense Introductions

Defense counsel can begin summation with any one of these suggested openings in jurisdictions where there is no rebuttal. In jurisdictions with rebuttal, defense follows the plaintiff/claimant/

prosecutor. An alternative introductory statement may include a reference to a statement made by opposing counsel.

Example (Civil Defense):

You have just heard part of the story of what happened on August 1. You didn't hear an explanation of the entire story. You will now, and when you do, you'll understand how the evidence supports the story told by the defendant Will Grimm and does not support the partial story told by the plaintiff Jacob Grimm.

Example (Defense Multiparty Case):

In some cases there are two sides to a story. In this case, there are three parties and three sides, but only one compelling story told very movingly by Goldilocks. During the trial, you heard and saw evidence introduced in bits and pieces supporting different versions of what happened four years ago. I'll help piece together the third story and show how the evidence leads you to only one conclusion: that Goldilocks told the only true story.

Example (Criminal Defense):

The prosecutor used this chart to explain to you the legal elements of the crime the government had to prove beyond a reasonable doubt for you to conclude that my client is guilty of burglary. I will explain to you how the prosecutor failed to prove each of these elements, and then I will present to you six additional reasonable doubts why Inspector Closeau did not commit the crime that happened on June 15.

---

7.   Rebuttal Introductions

An advocate with a rebuttal argument can begin with introductory comments or with remarks contradicting the opposing argument.

Example (Plaintiff):

Defense counsel wants you to think there are six reasons which show there is reasonable doubt in this case that her client did not steal over one million dollars worth of jewelry. There are no such six reasons. The evidence clearly establishes the guilt of the defendant. I told you during opening statement we would present evidence to you of the guilt of the defendant, and we did. I now want to clarify some remarks counsel made during her closing argument and answer a few questions you may have in your mind about how Closeau committed the crime of burglary.

---

8. Alternative Introductions

The attorney should prepare introductory remarks that most effectively meet the primary goal the attorney wants to achieve during the beginning of summation. Other approaches in addition to the previous examples may be considered. Attorneys may obtain ideas about other introductory statements from the world of art and literature, including plays, movies, books, and websites, or from arguments given by other attorneys.

An attorney may prepare a number of alternative introductory statements and, after selecting the most effective statement, modify the other statements and use them during some other stage of the closing argument. For example, an attorney may prefer to begin with an explanation of the case theory followed by an explanation of the purposes for summation. Or, an attorney may prefer to begin with a dramatic statement followed by an explanation of the outline of the final argument.

C. BODY OF FINAL ARGUMENT

Section 11.5 provides numerous illustrations of the content of the main body of summation, which needs to be presented in an orderly manner. An example of such a structure is:

- The introductory statement,
- Explanation of pivotal issues in the case,
- Summary of important facts, opinions, and inferences,
- Description of who, what, when, where, how, and why,
- Application of facts to support legal elements,
- Explanation of legal elements or jury instructions and verdict form,
- Description of important exhibits,
- Summary of strengths of the case,
- Explanation of weaknesses of opponent's case,
- Reference to burden of proof,
- Explanation of reasons supporting favorable decision,
- Description of the remedy sought,
- Responses to questions from judge or arbitrator in bench trials, administrative hearings or arbitrations,
- Conclusion.

D. THE CONCLUSION

Summation should conclude with a strong ending emphasizing persuasive points. The attorney should review the facts, the theories, and the law to create a conclusion that leaves the decision maker wanting to find in the favor of the client.

Example (Criminal Defense):

Chuck's liberty and future are in your hands. Years from now when you look back at this trial, you must be able to conclude that your verdict was the right one, that it was fair and just. The prosecutor may not remember this case, nor may the public. But you not forget, and neither will Chuck. He must live all his life with your decision, which can only be not guilty.

Soon you will go and deliberate. Let me tell you a story to help direct you. There was an old man and a young boy.

The old man was known to be very wise. The young boy was scheming of a way to prove that the old man was not wise about everything. And so the young boy trapped a little bird, and he took it in his hands and went up to the old man. He said, "Old man, old man, what do I have in my hands?" And the old man being wise, said, "You have a little bird." And the clever little boy said, "Tell me, old man, is the bird alive or dead?" (And the young boy gleefully thought to himself: Now I have him. If the old man says the bird is alive, I'll crush it and show him it was dead. And if he says it's dead, I'll open my hands and turn the little bird free, proving him wrong.) And the old man, being very wise, looked at the clever little boy straight in the eyes and said, "The answer is in your hands." And the liberty and future of Charles Aspen is now in your hands.

Example (Criminal Prosecution):

Defense counsel has asked you to find his client not guilty and send him home to live his life. Defense counsel was here to speak on behalf of his client who sits here in the courtroom. But there is someone who is not here and who no longer has a life. Her precious life came to a brutal end by the hands of the man who now asks you for mercy, who now asks to go home. Where is the mercy he showed for Marni Winona? She will never go home. She will never see her six-year-old child, Olivia. Who will speak for Marni? Members of the Jury, you will speak for her when you return the only verdict supported by the facts and law in the case: a verdict of guilty of murder in the first degree.

Example (Civil Plaintiff):

I'm going to close now. Defense counsel for Dan Hamline told you a number of times that you were not to decide this case based on sympathy you might have in this case for Marci Mitchell. Indeed, the judge will instruct you that you are to base your decision upon the facts of this case and not upon passion or prejudice. It would be natural for you to feel sympathy for Ms. Mitchell, who told you in this courtroom how she is struggling to maintain the operation of her neighborhood service station and food store she has worked hard to maintain for 10 years.

Members of the Jury, Marci Mitchell does not want your sympathy. Her family and friends can empathize with her. You should not and need not decide this case based upon sympathy. Ms. Mitchell wants only what she is legally entitled to. She has a right to her money from the defendant, the money he owes her under the franchise agreement. Marci Mitchell deserves a verdict in the amount of $975,000, an amount supported by the facts, the law, and your wise judgment.

E. FINAL ARGUMENT CRITIQUE

After constructing the closing argument, the attorney can review the following factors to determine if the argument is effective:

- Does it explain why the decision maker should find for the client?

- Does it make the decision maker want to find for the client?

- Does it tell to the decision maker how to find for the client?

- Does it satisfy the questions the decision maker likely has?

- Does summation cover all issues the decision maker has to decide in favor of the client?

Advocates have difficulty constructing a closing argument that covers everything that needs to be said. Several barriers must be overcome to construct a comprehensive closing. First, the attorney who knows the case very well may have some trouble deciding what the decision maker, who does not know the case as well, needs to be told. Second, every case has some gaps, caused by missing evidence or natural omissions, which need to be covered during closing. If gaps or missing evidence are not explained, the fact finder will create conclusions and inferences, which may not support the decision requested by the attorney. Third, the natural curiosity of the decision maker needs to be satisfied. Information that is not legally relevant to the case may need to be discussed to make a more complete story and to satisfy the fact finder's curiosity.

Conversations with decision makers after a decision (where permitted) sometimes reveal they deliberated over matters counsel did not consider important or were not covered in detail during the case. These discussions provide an opportunity to learn from hindsight what should have been presented during the trial or hearing. The attorney should consider in advance what the decision maker may want to know, fill in these gaps, and answer potential questions during summation.

One way of determining this information is to rehearse in front of colleagues or friends and ask them what is missing, what prompts their curiosity, and what questions they have. Focus groups and mock juries can also be very helpful in testing the effectiveness of the argument.

Using all available information, the attorney can then present an argument that not only contains legally relevant evidence but also provides the information that satisfies their curiosity. For example, the evidence in a theft case may include testimony by a victim that the defendant stole her purse as she walked home after work and that she called the police immediately after the theft when she arrived at her apartment. The prosecutor would have the victim describe how she got in her apartment if her stolen purse contained her apartment key. This answer prevents the jurors from incorrectly speculating how she got in her apartment, information that is legally irrelevant.

§ 11.5 CONTENT

One of the primary goals of closing argument is for the advocate to provide reasons that support a favorable decision. The attorney has broad latitude in explaining these reasons that are based on the theories of the case, facts, opinions, inferences, conclusions, and the law.

Summation should attempt to involve decision makers, whom already may have decided some factual and legal issues. An attorney needs to recognize this and employ techniques that take advantage of it. One approach is to suggest that some or much of what will be said during final argument will only reaffirm what the decision maker is already thinking. Another technique is to acknowledge that the decision maker may have some unanswered questions and that the closing will summarize the evidence and resolve these concerns in the client's favor. In bench trials, administrative hearings, and arbitrations, the attorney may suggest the judge or arbitrator ask unresolved questions.

Factors to consider for inclusion in summation include:

A. ARGUMENT

1. Types of Arguments

The closing argument allows an attorney to say almost anything that falls within the broad definition of argument. An attorney may:

a. *Draw Reasonable Inferences from Direct or Circumstantial Evidence*

Example (Civil Defense):

My clients, Blake and Brady, the defendants, received a hand-delivered note at their home from the plaintiff at about 6 p.m. on July 20—the very day the plaintiff claims her life was threatened by them. I'm sure you'll agree that someone supposedly in fear for her life is not going to hand-deliver a note to her enemies' home after a supposed threat was made. What can we infer from this fact? That the plaintiff's alleged claim of civil assault by my clients is not supported by the facts. She made it up.

---

b. *Suggest That Certain Evidence Implies a Reasonable Conclusion*

Example (Civil Plaintiff):

The fact that Lake Minnetonka Bank hired five part-time computer clerks, that the manager took Jeffrey Michael off his computer duties once the temporary clerks were trained and put Jeffrey to work cleaning the office—a task degrading and not related to his job—and that Jeffrey was laid off during the same week two additional part-timers were hired all suggest one conclusion: The Bank unfairly wanted to get rid of Jeffrey Michael because he was a full time employee.

---

c. *Present Conclusions Based upon the Circumstances of the Case*

Example (Civil Defense):

The plaintiff, Emma Elamein, drank a fifth of bourbon before the snowstorm ended. She had a cigarette in her mouth when she poured gasoline from a 2 gallon canister into the fuel tank of the Blizzard Snowblower. She acted irresponsibly and failed to take reasonable steps for her own safety when she tragically caused her own death.

d. Suggest the Decision Maker Apply Common Sense in Deciding a Case

Example (Civil Defense):

You are to use your common sense when deciding this case. You are to rely upon your sense of how reasonable people act in deciding how probable and likely is Chase's story. You are to use your common sense in concluding how unlikely and untrue his story is in this case. And when you do, you will reject the coincidences they want you to believe.

e. Recommend the Jurors Apply Life Experiences in Determining a Fact

Example (Civil Plaintiff):

You know what it means in this society to be attractive. You know you cannot tell Rita Riley that her grotesque scars don't matter. Everything Rita deals with in life will remind her she is scarred—that she is ugly and not attractive. You know what value our society places on physical beauty. Rita will never meet another human being face-to-face without that other person's face reflecting the horror of her disfigurement.

2. The Story

The explanation of the facts may be told in a story form that includes descriptions of the scene, the characters, and the event. The goal of the attorney should be to summarize facts in a way that is reasonable and consistent with the recollection of the fact finder.

Example (Civil Plaintiff):

Elaine Santaluz began working part-time for Spearfish Bank when she was 59 years old in order to supplement her husband's income. Roger Santaluz's income was severely cut back because of his retirement due to a partial knee replacement. Elaine's work was praised; she received annual salary merit raises; she was promoted to a full time position. But then Spearfish Bank was taken over by Grant Park State Bank. Suddenly Elaine was pressured into working nearly ten hours a day. Next she was given demeaning tasks to do that had nothing to do with her skills as a financial analyst. Finally, Elaine was ordered to train two new employees, both under 30 years of age. After these two were trained, the Bank laid Elaine off. Why? Because she's 65 years old and was paid more than the replacement workers. Grant Park State Bank has never recalled Elaine to work.

3. Explaining Why Something Happened

The evidence presented may tell the decision maker what happened and how something happened. The attorney may, during closing argument, need to explain why something happened.

Example (Civil Plaintiff):

You have heard the evidence in this case and you know what happened during the surgery and how Dr. Isobel Stevens conducted that surgery in error. You must decide why she performed the surgery the way she did. The evidence leads you to only one conclusion: She was negligent and made a tragic mistake. Even though she's a surgeon, she is still human, and she committed malpractice. Dr. Stevens did not intend to hurt my client, Kelsey Lauren. The Doctor didn't plan to puncture Kelsey's internal organs. But she did. She was irresponsible and must be held accountable for the severe injuries Kelsey suffered.

B. EVIDENCE

1. Explanation of the Evidence

A substantial part of a closing argument consists of the attorney summarizing and explaining the evidence. This description should be consistent both with the facts described in the opening statement and with the evidence produced during the case. Some attorneys take closing argument to an extreme and argue that certain evidence has more value than it deserves. The attorney should be careful not to exaggerate the evidence presented because decision makers easily recognize such overstatements and lose faith in the credibility of the attorney.

Example (Civil Defendant):

The judge and the lawyers refer to this part of the case as closing argument. I do not intend to argue but rather to explain the evidence to you. Time does not allow me to cover every bit of testimony or every piece of evidence. I may not mention some things that you recall, but I am sure you will remember those matters and discuss them during your deliberation. Now I would like to summarize the evidence you have heard and seen which supports a verdict on behalf of Will Brooks.

2.   Witnesses

The attorney may summarize the evidence by connecting the witnesses with the facts and opinions. Witnesses who were especially effective, persuasive, or credible should be referred to by name. If a large number of witnesses who testify over a lengthy period of time are involved, the decision maker may have some difficulty remembering who testified about what. The attorney should not only identify the witnesses by name but also establish when they testified and what they said.

Example (Civil Defendant):

We brought before you the testimony of the two people who talked to each other in the cell phone conversation on October 15. First, there was Louis Armstrong. Mr. Armstrong was the manager of the Cosmos Band. He took the stand and told you he had been managing the band for two years and during that October 15 phone conversation he told Ms. Tatooine the band was available to play on New Year's Eve. After he testified, Ms. Tatooine testified. She was the manager of the Mos Eisley Cantina. Ms. Tatooine told you it was her job to contract with bands to play at the Cantina. She also told you Louis Armstrong told her in that same cell phone conversation on October 15 that the Cosmos Band was available to play on New Year's Eve.

3.   Credibility of Witnesses

An attorney may comment on the credibility of a witness, may demonstrate how an observation or statement is inaccurate, may attempt to show a witness is biased or prejudiced, or may comment on the witness' demeanor. Impeachment techniques may be used during the case to establish facts to reduce that witness' credibility. The attorney can restate the facts developed on cross-examination, which establishes why a witness should not be believed or that a witness' perceptions are improbable or implausible. In a jury trial, the attorney may also refer to the instruction on credibility that the judge will provide the jury and explain how those factors reduce the credibility of opposing witnesses.

Example (Lie):

You heard the plaintiff's boss, Alberta Dowlin, testify that she fired the plaintiff because the plaintiff lied on his employment application. The plaintiff had lied on that application not once but on every page. Page one, the plaintiff was not honorably discharged from the Marines, he was never a Marine. Page two, the plaintiff was not laid off from Rapid City Community College, he was fired for sexually harassing students. Page three, the plaintiff did not receive a PhD in linguistics from Black Hills University, the plaintiff's last degree was a B.A. in speech and communication from Sturgis College. Plaintiff is not an honest or honorable person in his professional or personal life.

Example (Mistake):

The judge will tell you that you decide whether a witness is credible or not, whether a witness is to be believed or not. There are two key witnesses who testified for the plaintiff. You have to determine whether they saw what they say they saw. The judge will give you an instruction regarding the credibility of witnesses that will help you in making your decision.

There are several factors that influence the ability of an eyewitness to see what actually happened. One factor is how close they were to the scene of the accident. Another factor is what they were doing immediately before the accident. Another is how clear a line of vision they had of the accident Let's apply these three factors to the testimony of the plaintiff's two key witnesses: Lloyd Christmas and Harry Dunne. They were half a block away playing Frisbee in a park that was surrounded by large, leafy trees. Now let's go over their testimony in detail.

Example (Demeanor):

One of the factors you can consider in determining the credibility of a witness is the demeanor of the witness—the way they testify on direct and cross-examination. Do they appear to be telling the truth? Did they seem sure? Did they seem uncertain? Were they evasive? Did they hesitate? You will need to apply those standards to the testimony of Gordon Gekko.

You will recall that he was the stockbroker who works for the defendant, and that he testified in this witness stand two days ago. During his direct examination, he appeared to be uncertain about the time of the day he met with the defendant in his office. Counsel for defendant had to suggest the answer to him. If he was uncertain about that key piece of evidence, perhaps he was uncertain about other matters. During his cross-examination, when I asked him questions, his attitude changed, and his memory became worse. He was not as cooperative in answering my questions and giving you information the way he was when he answered questions asked by opposing counsel. He remembered fewer details about conversations he had with his supervisor, the person for whom he's still working.

Example (Relationship):

We all heard the testimony of the defendant's wife. We all heard her testify in direct examination that her husband was with her the entire evening when the crime was committed. We all heard her testify in cross-examination that she loved her husband very much and continues to love him very much. There is nothing more beautiful than the bond that exists between a loving wife and husband. There is no doubt that Lorraine Bracco loved her husband, Ray, before the murder, and that she loves him after the murder. She loves him because he is her husband. She loves him even though he is a murderer. And she naturally wants to give him an alibi and tell you he was with her when he committed the murder. She would rather violate her oath to tell the truth than have you find him guilty.

---

4.   Circumstantial Evidence

Evidence consists of both direct and circumstantial evidence. In a jury trial, the judge will give a jury instruction describing the types of evidence to the jurors, which often requires further explanation by the advocate including how the legal descriptions apply to the facts.

Example (General): Power

Circumstantial evidence can have the same persuasive power as direct evidence. An example of circumstantial evidence that demonstrates its strength and value is the story of Robinson Crusoe. You recall that Crusoe was on an island and he thought he was all alone. One morning he went down to the beach and he saw a footprint on the sand. Knowing that someone else was on the island, he became so overcome with emotion that he fainted.

He didn't see anyone, but he knew because of the footprint there was someone else on the island. He woke to find Friday, the person who made the footprint, standing beside him, who was to be his friend on the island. The footprint—the marks on the sand made by a human foot—was circumstantial evidence. His seeing Friday was direct evidence. Both were true and compelling. Let's look for the footprints that tell what happened in this case.

Example (Criminal Defense):

There is no direct evidence in this case linking my client to the crime. There's no DNA, no fingerprints, no laser ablation inductively coupled plasma mass spectrometry that you might expect there to be based on modern forensic science. The prosecution relies on unreliable circumstantial evidence in a feeble effort trying to prove the guilt of my client, but that evidence proves nothing.

You know how weak, inaccurate, and misleading this type of evidence is. Some of you may recall the story from the Bible regarding Joseph and his brothers. Joseph was the favorite son of his father, Jacob. His brothers were very envious of him and they beat him and sold him into slavery. They wanted their father to believe that Joseph was dead, and so they took Joseph's coat and some goat's blood, and they smeared the goat's blood on the coat, and showed the coat to their father who believed that Joseph had been killed by some evil beast. Of course, the truth was that Joseph was alive, but his father thought him dead. And so it is in this case. The truth is that my client is innocent. The prosecutor has no direct, compelling evidence proving guilt. You can't rely on uncorroborated circumstantial evidence. If you did, you'd be making the same tragic mistake Joseph's father did.

5. Detail and Corroboration

An accurately detailed factual explanation has the advantage of refreshing the recollection of the decision maker and explaining the relationship between various types of evidence that may not have been obvious or made clear during the case. A detailed presentation has the disadvantage of increasing the risk that the decision maker's memory of the evidence differs from that of the attorney's explanation. A long and overly detailed presentation is tedious and boring. Summation provides an opportunity to identify the primary sources of compelling evidence, to describe specific sources of circumstantial and corroborating evidence, and to explain the connecting facts the fact finder may have missed.

Example (Civil Defendant):

My client is not liable for the tragic death of Ms. Magdalen because the facts show Mr. Oxford was not using reasonable care for his own safety. You heard testimony from Mr. Hampshire, a friend of Mr. Oxford, that Mr. Oxford didn't know how to use the all-terrain vehicle, and that Mr. Oxford put the owner's manual—still in its unbroken plastic seal—on the shelf of the garage. Mr. Oxford's wife, Catherine, testified that Exhibit No. 6, the owner's manual, taken from the Oxford's garage, remains unopened, just as Mr. Oxford had left it. You also heard Ms. Cambridge, Mr. Oxford's neighbor, testify that after Mr. Oxford started the ATV, he said to Ms. Cambridge: "Well, here goes. I want to see how fast this thing can go."

6.   Reference to Evidence

The factual explanation should employ words used by the witnesses or words that appear in documents. The attorney should neither overstate nor understate the facts. Quoting the testimony of a witness and mixing the quote with a factual summary can be an effective approach. Reading testimony quotes from a transcript of the case is permissible and may also be very persuasive. Reading from an exhibit or showing highlighted portions of the exhibit can be equally effective.

Example (Criminal Prosecution):

Yesterday you heard Sylvia Plath testify about meeting Ted Hughes after the Mateus poetry reading. She testified that Ted admitted his part in the crime. This transcript—which you heard yesterday—of what Ted said proves what he did:

Q: When did you next see Ted?

A: He picked me up right after my English lit class, about 3:30.

Q: What did you do when you were driving?

A: I talked about my day. I mentioned that I was in Newnham Auditorium waiting for Mateus to arrive for a poetry reading, when all of a sudden three police officers came in and told us to go down to the lobby.

Q: After you told him what happened, what was his reaction?

A: He laughed so hard he had to pull over to the side of the road. He said at 12:45, just before the 1:00 reading was scheduled, he called Yeats, the secretary, and threatened that a bomb would go off in Newnham Auditorium if Mateus went ahead with the reading.

Now, ladies and gentlemen, no reasonable person makes an admission like that unless he actually did what he admitted. Ted wanted to impress Sylvia. He wanted her to share in his secret.

C.　SUMMATION TO JURORS

1.　Explanation of Law

The judge will explain the law during final jury instructions. An attorney should summarize and explain pivotal instructions, and must accurately state the content of the instructions. The attorney can read from or quote the exact jury instructions. Some instructions will not adequately or clearly explain the law because they contain abstract legal concepts. In these situations, the attorney may comment on the instructions and provide an expanded (and correct) description of the instruction and its meaning in simple, easy-to-understand language.

An accurate explanation of jury instructions can be very persuasive. The final instructions come from the judge, whom the jurors usually respect and understand to be impartial and the source of the law. Jurors are likely to be persuaded by an explanation by counsel that is supported by the instructions. A copy of the jury instructions is typically given to the jurors for use during deliberations, and an argument based upon these instructions will more likely be remembered and discussed by the jurors.

Example (Civil Defendant):

The law provides you with legal explanations to guide and assist you in reaching a verdict. These explanations are called instructions on the law. The judge has explained some of them to you already. The judge will explain more of them to you after we have completed our summation. Now I would like to discuss with you how those instructions apply to this case.

This is an accident case. The judge will tell you about the law of negligence. I am quoting what the court will tell you:

"Negligence is lack of ordinary care. It is the failure to exercise that degree of care which a reasonably prudent or careful person would have exercised under the same circumstance." That is the standard. That is the law: A person must do what a reasonable person would do under the circumstances of the case. And that is what the defendant, Sacagawea, did in this case. She acted reasonably and prudently.

2.   Special Interrogatories

A case may involve special interrogatories that require the jury to make specific findings of fact. These interrogatories may accompany a general or special verdict. The attorney may read the questions to the jury and urge the jurors to answer in a favorable, specific way. Rules and case law determine whether an attorney can inform the jury that the answers may determine the outcome of the case. In most cases, but not all, the attorney can comment upon the effect of special interrogatories.

Example (Civil Defendant):

There are several things the plaintiff Hanna Horvath has to prove to you before you can hold my client, Adam Sackler, responsible for the alleged mistakes in her life. To help you decide who is responsible for what happened, you will be given a list of questions you must answer in the jury room. The judge will provide you those questions. I've had them enlarged so that we can go through them to discuss how they should be answered.

The first question is: "Did the plaintiff and the defendant enter into a binding relationship contract on May 1? _____ Yes, _____ No." The judge will explain the legal factors that make up a contract. Those elements appear on this monitor. Let's apply the facts introduced in this case to each of these legal elements to discover that the answer to that question is: No.

3.   Explaining the Jury System

In jury trials, it is common for counsel to explain the purpose the jury serves in our system of justice and the importance of the jury's decision. These descriptions, if done sincerely and concisely, can be effective.

Example (Power of the Jury):

As jurors you are part of a tradition that is hundreds of years old. You are members of our local Rhenish township, and you have come together to decide the outcome of this case. Individually you are each a citizen. Collectively sitting here as jurors you are part of our system of justice. You hold in your hands the power to judge the difference between right and wrong. Today you will exercise that power to set right what the defendant has done wrong.

Example (Conscience of the Community):

Jurors, you are the conscience of our Plymouth community. When you speak, the community speaks. You represent this community and its principles and attitudes. You shape and form the conscience of our community through your decision.

---

4.   Request for Verdict

A closing argument must include an explanation of the specific verdict the attorney wants for the client. This explanation should be clear so the jurors understand what conclusion they must reach to find for a party. In most cases, the request will be a specific request for a verdict of guilty or not guilty or for a verdict for the plaintiff or defendant.

Example (General):

Verdict is a Latin word meaning to speak the truth, so by your verdict you are going to speak the truth here today.

Once you reach your verdict, no one can change it. You can't be called back and told, "That's not right. You didn't do it right. Do it again." What you do here today is done forever.

It is also important that you reach your verdict for the right reason. Not only should the result be right—it is just as important that the reasons for it are the right reasons.

When you decide that the defendant Wile E. Coyote was negligent and caused the accident, your decision will be the correct verdict because it will be supported by the facts and law.

D.   TECHNIQUES

1.   Analogies, Metaphors, Anecdotes

The attorney may wish to refer to similar situations, or use metaphors or tell an anecdotal story to make a point during summation. The images described by an attorney through an analogy, a metaphor, or anecdote may assist the decision maker in understanding the point of law or application of fact to law. An effective story will command the attention of the fact finders and will provide them with a comparison to determine the appropriateness of a point made during argument. An example of an anecdote to bolster circumstantial evidence is the story of Robinson Crusoe described in Section 11.5(B)(4).

Example (Civil Plaintiff):

They left a time bomb ticking at Bearpath Estates. It was just a matter of time before Seneca would use his master key to get into Phaedre's apartment. It was just a matter of time before he would renew his acts of terror. That time struck on May 15 when Seneca, hiding in Phaedre's kitchen, surprised her, held a knife to her throat, and brutally assaulted her. Bearpath Estates lit that fuse and started that time bomb ticking when Bearpath negligently hired Seneca on the basis of his resume with no references and no prior places of employment. Even when the secretary of the Bearpath Board of Directors found him in a drunken and disorderly state and reported this to the Board, the Board did nothing. The Board could have defused the situation and spared Phaedre, but the Board didn't make the one phone call to the authorities that would have stopped the disaster. One phone call would have informed Bearpath Estates that Seneca was on parole for another assault. But the Board didn't take the time to investigate and fire him, and that was all the time he needed. They are responsible for Seneca exploding and viciously attacking and assaulting Phaedre.

While a carefully drawn, common sense metaphor or analogy may assist the decision maker in understanding a concept, careful consideration should be given before one is used. If the analogy or metaphor is confusing or does not make sense, the point will be missed. If opposing counsel has an opportunity to argue following the use of an analogy or metaphor, the opponent could make this technique appear simplistic or foolish.

Example:

Plaintiff's Attorney:

The agreement between Dolores Saki and Health Center, Incorporated was like a web. Doctor Saki completed her residency and wanted to begin her pediatric practice. Health Center required her to sign an employment contract according to its terms: if she ever wanted to leave Health Center, she could not practice in a 100 mile radius of Santa Fe for two years. She knew she wanted to begin a practice in Santa Fe. What she didn't know was that Health Center was not the kind of professional practice she wanted. They had entrapped her.

After three months, Dr. Saki had to resign. She was caught in a web and she couldn't pull away. The more she struggled and tried to reason with Health Center's administration, the more menacingly loomed the corporate spider.

When Dr. Saki ventured from Health Center Incorporated, she started her own office in Santa Fe. And it cruelly flung out its web again. An injunction closed her office and stopped her from earning a livelihood to support herself and her six-year-old son in their modest home. She is unable to practice; her medical school loans are in default; her mortgage payments are overdue. Health Center, like a spider that stores up victims for later consumption, wrapped Dr. Saki in its web as an example for the rest of its employees.

Defendant's Lawyer:

Members of the Jury, counsel has spent a lot of time talking about spiders and webs. However, this case is not about bugs; it's about facts and the law. Let's consider the reality. Doctor Dolores Saki is a competent, well-educated adult. She knew what she was doing when she signed her employment contract. She certainly could have sought advice from another professional—a doctor friend or even a lawyer. She choose not to. Society, and you, must hold her responsible for her commitments. She just changed her mind for no good legal reason. There is nothing menacing about Health Center. The Center provides a vital service to the Santa Fe community.

2.　Creativity

One of the primary tasks of the attorney in summation is to be creative and innovative and explain the significance of inferences. While the evidence may lead decision makers to clear and evident conclusions, the advocate's task is to explain the less obvious conclusions. The advocate needs to highlight the subtle nuances of direct and circumstantial facts.

Example (Criminal Defendant):

Presume that the defendant is accused of assaulting the victim in an alley one block away from a bar where the defendant and victim had a fight.

My client, Claire Stenwick, has been accused of hiding in an alley, waiting for the victim to pass so that she could jump out and attack the victim with a big stick because of something that happened in the bar. My client did not hide in that alley, didn't jump out, did not attack the victim. It was somebody else.

You recall that the victim, Ray Koval, said that he had never met my client before that night, did not know where my client lived, and didn't tell my client where he lived. And you recall that Mr. Koval said he and my client never talked before or after their argument in the bar.

You may also recall during my cross-examination of Mr. Koval, he told us that when he left the bar he could have left through the rear door on Mason Street, or he could have gone out through the front door and turned left and walked west toward Dixie Street, or could have gone through the front door and crossed over toward First Avenue. Instead, he testified that he went out through the front door and turned right toward Madison Avenue.

You may have wondered why I asked those questions. His answers tell us that my client is innocent and didn't assault him. My client, Ms. Stenwick, did not know where Mr. Koval lived. My client didn't know which way he would leave when he left the bar that night. My client wouldn't know to hide in a dark alley one block east on Madison Avenue. There was no way my client would have known whether Mr. Koval would have left the bar through the front or rear doors or which way the victim would have walked home—because my client didn't know where he lived. Some stranger was waiting in that alley, ready to attack anyone who passed. Mr. Koval was that unfortunate person who happened to walk by. He was tragically attacked by that stranger while my client was on her way home on a bus.

---

3. Use of Exhibits

Section 11.3(E) described how to select visual aids and exhibits to be used in closing argument. The design, placement, and use in the argument can be as important as the visual aid or exhibit itself. The importance of the exhibit, the impact words and colors on the visual aids, the size and number of monitors, the location in the room for easy access and clear viewing, the placement in the closing, and the use of and reference to the exhibit are important considerations in determining whether the exhibit will aid or interfere with summation.

The use of exhibits and visual aids allows the attorney to approach a judge or arbitrator or walk over to the jury box and stand in front of the decision maker and point to, quote from, or use the exhibit there. This technique can enhance the summation impact of a point and add interest.

Example (Defense Exhibit):

The most critical piece of evidence in this case did not come from the testimony of witnesses. The most important evidence is contained in Exhibit No. 1, the diagram created by the defendant Feng Shui and sent to plaintiff's employer. This diagram was introduced during the trial. I had it highlighted so we can focus on the meaning of how it was designed.

Example (Defense Visual Aid):

Over the past two weeks of trial, you have heard from many witnesses and reviewed many documents. The judge will tell you that you must find my client not guilty if, based on all that evidence, you have a reasonable doubt that he committed a crime. In this case, the evidence reveals there are eight reasonable doubts. We prepared a chart listing those eight reasonable doubts and the supporting evidence. Please look at the monitor as we go over the reasons why Gamal is not guilty.

---

4. Parallel Experiences

Decision makers will more likely accept an explanation of an event if something similar has happened to others. It can be helpful during summation to mention situations that other people might have experienced that resemble what happened in the case. For example, if the issue is the eyewitness identification of the defendant and the defense is that the witness misidentified the defendant, the defense attorney can suggest this happens to people in other parallel life situations.

Example (General):

Often people at a party see someone from a distance across the room and recognize the person as a friend, only to approach that person and find out they were wrong.

At a restaurant, people call for their server only to be embarrassed because the person they called was not their server, even though they had seen and talked with him several times.

The witness in this case picked out the wrong person. And that is perfectly understandable. She was scared and frightened and didn't expect to confront a stranger. At a party or restaurant, reasonable people make mistakes identifying friends or persons they meet even when they are relaxed. In this case, Frankie Heck was afraid and unexpected events happened quickly. She made the same wrong identification mistake as others do.

---

5. Reason and Emotion

Summation may include appeals both to reason and to emotion. An explanation of the facts and law can support a logical reason why a party is entitled to win. An appeal to emotion may create a motivating force to support a decision based on reason and logic. Appeals to emotion create an atmosphere in the room and feelings within the decision maker to render a favorable decision. An appeal made only to logic and reason may diminish the humanistic elements of the case. Appeals to compassion and empathy are as vital to an argument as other appeals. Judges, arbitrators, and jurors do not leave their humanity at home but bring it with them to deliberations.

The extent to which an attorney relies upon both emotion and reason to support an argument depends upon the circumstances of a case. With some cases it will be more effective for the attorney to emphasize a rational, logical explanation of the evidence and the law. In other cases, it will be more effective for the attorney to rely on the emotions and feelings created by the facts. An attorney must carefully balance the use of sentiment in a case. An attorney may make the presentation of an argument more dramatic by relying upon its emotional aspects, but the attorney must be cautious not to play to the passion and prejudice of the decision makers.

Example (Defense):

We all have feelings for what happened. Those emotions are natural and appropriate. You should use those reactions in your evaluation of the facts of this case. This is why you will never be replaced by a computer decision maker. Only a person can understand and appreciate the facts of this case. You are not a robot. And you are not required to act like a robot. You are to use your feelings just as you are to use your reasoning in deciding this case. That does not mean that you should decide this case on emotions. Neither party is entitled to a decision based purely on sympathy. But, you may and you should have empathy for the parties in this case including Shodan.

Two common basic emotions are like and dislike. Appeals to emotions during summation can be based on these two feelings. Generating a feeling of dislike or hate toward a party sufficient to support a decision against that party is difficult, unless the facts justify such an attack. The positive emotion is easier to establish to persuade the decision maker that a party is entitled to win. The more effective position is to show that a party is entitled to the benefit of a favorable decision, rather than trying to show that a person ought to be punished by losing a case.

Example (Civil Plaintiff):

Counsel for defendant has told you that there are some expenses Mr. and Mrs. Gallagher will not incur as a result of Liam's death, that there is some money they will not have to spend on their dead son. That is true. There are also some things they will never have to put up with because Liam is no longer with them. They will never have to sit in the heat of the sun on a hot, July afternoon, watching Liam play Little League baseball. They will never have to wait in long lines in some crowded toy store before the hectic days of Christmas buying Liam some toy that will break the day after Christmas. They will never have to lay awake at night, worrying about where their teenage son is and why he isn't home. They will not have to live through all that.

6.   Rhetorical Questions

A rhetorical question can be an effective tool of persuasion because it directly involves the decision maker in the presentation. The essential aspect of a rhetorical question is that the answer should be obvious.

Example (Civil Plaintiff):

(*Counsel holding photograph.*) Quasimodo is severely disfigured. His back will require significant grafting and plastic surgery. Can anyone look at this picture and fail to see years of anguish— emotional and physical—that will haunt him?

To avoid the possibility that the decision maker may not answer the rhetorical question correctly the attorney should provide the answer.

Example (Civil Defendant):

Was Garfield House Apartments negligent in inspecting and maintaining the Ruud water heater? There is only one answer: No. Garfield House Apartments not only had a maintenance manager periodically check the system but also had a service contract to cover any repairs.

7.   Questions from Judges and Arbitrators

A judge or arbitrator may ask questions during summation. This is usually very helpful to the advocate because the questions reveal the issues the judge or arbitrator needs help in assessing. Indeed, having questions asked can make summation more focused and relevant. The advocate wants and needs to address the issues and answer the questions that judge or arbitrator think are important. Even if the lawyer disagrees with the issues raised or believes the questions are the wrong questions to ask, it is vital to understand the perspective and position of the decision maker. Questions reveal what it is that concerns the judge or arbitrator, and the advocate can directly address those concerns.

An advocate should answer questions promptly and effectively. If a question is asked and the lawyer does not know or have an answer, the lawyer should say so and not try to avoid the answer, evade the issue or make a misstatement. The lawyer can move on to a related area and use the question as a transition to an effective part of the final argument. In general, advocates should welcome and encourage the judge or arbitrator to ask questions, however difficult the questions may be.

E. TACTICAL CONSIDERATIONS

1. Contradictions

It may well be obvious to the decision maker that a dispute exists between the parties. What will not always be obvious, however, are the specific factual contradictions in the case. Some cases do not involve apparent factual differences but involve subtle contrary inferences and conclusions. The attorney should highlight the inconsistencies between witnesses, point out the contradictions in testimony, and make certain the decision maker understands the factual disputes.

Example (Civil Defendant):

The issue in this case you must decide is whether a face-to-face conversation took place on May 2. The plaintiff, Harry Houdini, has raised another issue—a side issue that is not relevant to the merits of this case. That side issue might misdirect you from focusing on the real issue in this case. That misdirection is a magician's tool, a magic trick. And like a magic trick, that side issue is an illusion. It's not the real issue in this case.

---

2. Case Weaknesses

Every case will have some weak points that the attorney must address in closing argument. If an attorney can think of a reasonable interpretation that reduces the obvious weakness of a point, that explanation should be provided. If the attorney cannot think of any mitigating explanation, then the weakness can be conceded in a candid and forthright manner. This disclosure may enhance the credibility of the attorney and reduce the impact of the opposition's focus on such weakness. Or, the advocate, rather than raise it and emphasize the problem, may ignore the matter and not address it at all.

Example (Civil Plaintiff):

It may not have been a good idea to let a 6 year-old child ride a full-sized, new bicycle. But Nicolas was ecstatic with his birthday present. Nothing could have kept that child from trying out that bike. His parents—preoccupied with their 3 week-old baby, Mary Jane, and Nicolas' birthday guests—couldn't have known Nicolas was taking that bike onto the county road instead of the farm driveway where he always rode his old bicycle. They couldn't have known the defendant would drive his speeding truck negligently over the center-line severely injuring Nicolas.

---

3.   Attacking Opposition's Positions

An effective technique may be to attack the logic and reasonableness of the opponent's contentions. An attorney may select a specific argument of the opponent, demonstrate its inconsistencies and contradictions, and explain how this must be reconciled in favor of the attorney's client.

A significant portion of the closing argument should not be spent defensively responding to the opponent's issues, positions, and argument. The decision maker may perceive a lawyer who does this as an advocate without any substantial positions. Arguments that attack the opponent's case must be balanced with arguments supporting the attorney's case.

Example (Civil Defendant):

Counsel has tried to tell you how reasonable the substantial restrictions were in Dr. Saki's contract with Health Center, Incorporated. Let's review how unreasonable those restrictions really are. Two years of no practice within a 100 mile radius of Santa Fe means that Dr. Saki would have to terminate her credentials with Linda Vista Hospital, would have to end the more than 500 doctor/patient relationships she has developed with people in this community who looked to her for aid and comfort, would lose the goodwill from her medical practice that she has developed over the past four years, and would leave this community short of a highly capable, very experienced general practitioner. Those restrictions are unfair and illegal.

---

4. Mentioning Negative Suggestions

The opposition's case may have some minor weaknesses or inconsistencies that ought not to be used as a reason why the opponent should lose. These weaknesses may not be sufficiently relevant or material to be a significant point, or it may not be tactful to rely on a weakness because the decision maker may perceive the reliance to be a "cheap shot." For example, if an opponent in a real estate case is a recovering alcoholic, it would be folly to use that former lifestyle as a reason why the opponent should lose. However, there are some weaknesses that can be mentioned during summation that tactfully remind the fact finder of some problems.

Example (Civil Defendant):

You don't need to rely on other problems with the testimony of the plaintiff's major witness, Ricky Vaughn, to disbelieve his story. You needn't consider the fact that he drove away immediately after the accident to get to the major league baseball game on time and didn't stop to leave his name as a witness. You can disregard the fact he didn't call the police until one week after the accident to tell what he says he saw. And you can ignore the fact he refused to talk to our investigator when she called and asked him some questions about the accident and that he willingly talked to counsel for the plaintiff. But, you can't ignore the fact that Mr. Vaughn could not have seen in his wildest imagination what he said he saw.

This approach can work effectively if the comments are presented in a way the fact finder does not view as unfair or sarcastic.

5. Absent Evidence/Witnesses

During closing argument an attorney may comment on facts that were described by opposing counsel during the opening statement but not proven during the case. If the opposition has failed to offer evidence or introduce exhibits, an attorney may comment on the significance of that non-evidence. If a party could have called a witness, if that witness could have been subpoenaed, and if that witness was a material witness, an attorney may comment on the failure of the party to call such a witness. The non-appearance of a witness may create an inference that the witness would have testified adversely to that party.

Some situations may prohibit comments about the lack of certain evidence. For example, it is unconstitutional for a prosecutor to comment on the criminal defendant's failure to testify. It may also be improper for a party to comment on the lack of certain evidence if that information is protected by a privilege.

Example (Civil Defendant):

Counsel for plaintiff told you they would prove to you the defendant committed discriminatory acts against the plaintiff. Counsel for plaintiff told you they would prove the defendant made racist statements. How did they try to prove that to you? Did they call one single witness to come to this courtroom and say they heard the defendant make racist statements? No. Did they bring before you any piece of evidence containing any racist statement written or posted by the defendant Frederick Douglass directed to the plaintiff? No. It's not enough in our system of justice for somebody to claim something happened. It's not enough in our system for someone to say they will prove to you that something happened. Our system requires the facts be brought before you so you can determine what happened. But those facts don't exist. The only reasonable conclusion you can reach is: what the plaintiff says happened did not happen.

---

6. Lie vs. Mistake

Every trial involves contradictory evidence pitting the testimony of one witness against another. Although some witnesses deserve to be called a liar, a better tactic is to describe a witness as being mistaken about a fact. It may be sufficient to point out that everyone sees an event from different perspectives and how the witness has perceived an event may be a mistaken observation based on an incorrect perspective.

When claiming that a witness has lied or is mistaken, an attorney should provide a reason why that person is lying or is mistaken. Merely asserting that a witness has made an intentional or negligent mistake is not enough. The facts established on cross-examination of that witness must be summarized to demonstrate that witness' lack of credibility.

Example (General):

Mary Kay Ash told you under oath the salesperson said the warranty would cover all major mechanical problems with the car. You then heard from the salesperson, Don Draper, who denied making that statement to Ms. Ash. You have to decide whether that statement was made. Mary Kay remembers it was made because it was a very important factor in her decision to buy that car. Does Mr. Draper really remember what he said? You can easily conclude he's mistaken about what he remembers. He told you he has sold hundreds of cars and has talked to many hundreds of customers. He has no reason to remember what he told Ms. Ash when she asked him specific questions that were important to her about the warranty. He is confused and mistaken.

7. Jury Selection Commitment

In a jury trial, the attorney may refer to promises the jurors made during jury selection to remind the jurors of their commitments.

Example (General):

Several days ago during jury selection, we asked you questions. And to some of those questions you answered "yes." You said you would decide this case based upon the testimony of the witnesses you heard from this witness stand. You said you would decide this case based upon additional evidence contained in the websites and blogs that you have seen introduced in this case. All of us must rely on those promises that you have made, that you will not base your decision on other facts or other evidence or other matters unrelated to this case involving Emojis.

8. Broken Promises

During opening statement, the opposing attorney may have made some promise to the jury that has not been met. An attorney before closing argument should review the statements made during the opening and argue that the opposing counsel failed to do what was promised.

Example (Civil Defendant):

During this trial, counsel for Nicolas Michaux promised to prove the Whizzer bicycle was unreasonably dangerous. All counsel has shown you is that it was unreasonable and irresponsible for Nicolas' parents to let a small child ride a full-sized bicycle, unsupervised on a road where vehicles traveled at 55 miles an hour—and more—in both lanes. And that is part of the tragedy.

9. Anticipating Rebuttal Argument

In a jurisdiction where the party with the burden has an opportunity for rebuttal, opposing counsel may need to explain that there will be no opportunity to counter what the opposing party will say during the rebuttal closing argument.

Example (Civil Defendant):

Because the plaintiff has the burden of proof in this case, the plaintiff has the opportunity to again present an argument after I have finished. I anticipate plaintiff will question the ability of Afshar Navistar to identify the truck involved in the accident. As you listen to plaintiff's counsel you should ask yourself whether what the plaintiff says about the identification is supported by the evidence you heard in this case or whether it is clear Ms. Navistar saw that truck. I will not have another opportunity to talk to you after plaintiff, but I am confident you will believe her and not counsel's argument.

F.　CRIMINAL CASES

1.　Burden of Proof

Both the prosecution and the defense may explain "beyond a reasonable doubt" burden of proof. The explanation should be understandable to help the decision maker properly apply the standard.

Example (Prosecution):

The term "beyond a reasonable doubt" does not mean proof beyond a shadow of a doubt or beyond all doubt. For if that were the standard, criminal convictions would be impossible. The term "reasonable doubt" only applies to the elements of the crime that must be proved. If you have a doubt that is unreasonable, the defendant must be found guilty. If you have a doubt about something that is not part of any element of proof, the defendant must also be found guilty. In this case, there is no reasonable doubt that Carson Wells committed the crime of robbery.

Example (Defense):

The judge will tell you that a reasonable doubt is a doubt that would cause a person to pause in making an important decision or transaction in life. For example, an important decision is the purchase of a house. Imagine that the three witnesses for the prosecution are real estate agents selling a home and that the buyer of the home learns that one of the salespersons has never seen the home, another salesperson lied both to the police and under oath to a judge, and the third salesperson is a convicted felon. A reasonable buyer would pause in entering into that transaction, reasonably doubt the accuracy of the statements made by those salespeople, and decide not to buy the house. Similarly, you should reasonably doubt and reject the testimony of the three witnesses for the prosecution and decide the defendant, Ms. Trump, is not guilty.

2.   Lesser Included Offenses

Lesser included offenses are difficult to explain without diminishing the strength of the argument in support of the most serious offense or of an acquittal on all charges. A prosecutor may have to decide how to deliver an argument seeking a premeditated murder conviction and, in the same argument, explain the elements of manslaughter. The defense must consider how to reduce the chances the decision maker will find a defendant guilty of premeditated murder and at the same time not concede a conviction based on manslaughter. These and related issues need to be carefully explained during summation.

Example (Prosecution):

We have proved the defendant Raylan Givens committed the crime of murder in the first degree. He shot and killed his business partner with premeditation and with the intent to murder him. In this case, just like many others, there are other crimes involved. When we established the facts that proved murder in the first degree, we also proved the crime of kidnapping and the crime of assault with a deadly weapon.

G.   CIVIL CASES

1.   Burden of Proof

Counsel for both plaintiff and defendant must decide whether to discuss or describe the burden of proof. When making this decision the attorneys must consider the importance of the decision maker understanding and applying the correct standard of proof. Section 2.12 discussed whether the burden should be explained or relied on. In a jury trial, if an attorney decides the burden of proof should be explained during summation, consideration must be given to whether the judge's instructions defining the preponderance of evidence are clear and sufficient, whether they should be emphasized and related to the facts, or whether an example and a more detailed definition should be given.

Many jurors may confuse the burden of proof in a civil case with the burden of proof in criminal cases and think that the phrase "beyond a reasonable doubt" (which they have heard countless times in movies, websites, and television) should apply. The plaintiff's attorney should make certain the jury does not confuse the applicable burden of proof. In some civil cases, the burden of proof is the "clear and convincing" standard. See Section 2.12(C).

Example (Plaintiff):

In this case, we have the burden of proof—the burden of proving our case to you. We have met that burden of proof. The judge will tell you—and now I am quoting from what the judge will read to you later in this case: "The party that has the burden of proof must persuade you by the evidence that the claim is more probably true than not true and that it outweighs the evidence opposed to it." Now that is the law.

As the plaintiff, our proof must outweigh the defendant's proof. The phrase, "preponderance of the evidence," means nothing more than the greater weight of the evidence, the greater likelihood of the truth. To prove our case all we have to do is to tip the scales in our favor. It may help you to visualize in your mind the scales of justice. One side of the scale holds the evidence of my injured client, Nicolas Michaux; the other scale holds the evidence of the defendant bicycle manufacturer, Whizzer. Little Nicolas doesn't have to topple the scales. He just has to tip them in his favor. All we have to do is tip those scales by the weight of the evidence, slightly in our favor, and we have carried our burden of proof. We have proved by a preponderance of the evidence that the defendant, the Whizzer company, was negligent when they designed, manufactured and sold a defective bicycle.

In jury trials, the use of the "scales of justice" is usually effective because the description provides a visual explanation of an abstract concept and because the jurors may not have previously heard this description. Jurors may want to impose a greater than a probability burden because they want to be fair and make the right decision. The party with the burden will try to reduce its effect; and the party opposing the burden will want to maximize its impact.

In bench trials and arbitrations, the judge or arbitrator will understand the applicable burden. They understand the probability percentage and that the plaintiff wins if the evidence more likely than not supports the claims. In close cases, these professional decision makers also understand that the defendant wins if the plaintiff fails to meet that burden. It can be effective in these cases for the advocate to remind the judge or arbitrator of the impact of the burden of proof.

2. Liability and Damages

A plaintiff in a civil case may prefer to argue damages after explaining the elements of liability. This tactic may leave the decision maker with a memorable impression of the damages the plaintiff has suffered.

A defense attorney may prefer to argue against the amount of damages initially in summation and then argue the lack of liability. This approach reduces the awkwardness of having to explain the possibility of damages after arguing the plaintiff has no right to recovery.

Example (Defendant):

Nicolas Michaux is a brain-damaged child who will need constant medical care and supervision. His condition is irreparable. This is a tragedy. The cost of medical care must be reasonable and not exaggerated. The lawyers for the plaintiff have exaggerated that cost just as they have exaggerated the fault of the men and women from Whizzer who made the bicycle and who are not responsible for this accident. Nicolas was too small for the bike his grandparents bought him. His own parents never took the time to have the seat or bars adjusted. Nicolas' bike did not malfunction. He was way too small to control that bike. And his parents knew that. Their heartbreak is that they are at fault.

---

3. Award of Damages

The plaintiff's attorney may need to explain why damages should be awarded to reimburse the plaintiff for the injuries suffered, income lost, or expenses incurred.

Example (Plaintiff):

A long time ago people were guided by the law of retribution in these matters. The law was to do to another what was done to you and your family. You may have heard it expressed as: "an eye for an eye, a tooth for a tooth, blow for blow." But with the development of our system of justice, we have become more civilized. All we ask is that Sister Mary Clarence fairly compensate the plaintiff for the wrong done with money damages. Why money? Because it is the only remedy the law provides. It is the only way you have to make sure that justice is done in this case.

4.   Amount of Damages

The argument may contain a request for a specific amount of damages to be awarded with an explanation for the amount of money sought. Asking for a specified amount is usually much more effective than leaving the assessment to the jurors. There are some cases where a request for a general amount of damages may be effective, but usually the better strategy is to request a specific amount or provide the decision maker with a range of adequate, reasonable, and proportionate awards.

Example (Actual Damages):

And now, (pointing to monitor screen listing damages), here is a list of the damages Princess Odette has suffered. Your responsibility is to determine the amount of damages the defendant must rightfully pay to Ms. Odette because she lost her leg. It is up to you to determine the amount of damages she is rightfully entitled to as a result of the negligence of the defendant. The defendant's negligence prevents her from leading a full and complete life, and prevents her from continuing her lifelong dream of being a professional dancer. I will go through each of these types of damages and suggest a reasonable amount of money the Princess has a right to receive:

The nature and extent of the injury and physical disability	$150,000.
Loss of past earnings	$35,000.
Loss of future earnings	$1,500,000.
Past medical expenses	$275,000.
Future medical expenses	$135,000.
Disfigurement and inability to walk	$2,000,000.
Past pain and suffering	$500,000.
Future pain and suffering	$1,000,000.
TOTAL	$5,595,000.

This total of $5,595,000 is a substantial amount of money, but just think of the substantial pain endured by Ms. Odette, the substantial loss of her professional career, and her substantial personal loss. This is a reasonable amount of compensation.

Example (Intangible Damages):

The tragedy in this case is that Megan and Mallory will never see their mom again. She died under the wheels of the defendant's truck. The further tragedy is that there is no way that Ms. Jasmine can be brought back to life to live with her children. As I mentioned before, the only thing our society allows to compensate Megan and Mallory for the loss of their mother is money damages. In this jurisdiction, the judge will tell you they are entitled to receive an award of damages for the loss of the love and affection of their mother, for the loss of never being able to love, hug, be held by, laugh with, cry with, and just be with, their mother. You have to decide how much to award Megan and Mallory. How does one assess the loss of the love and affection of a mother? How does one put a dollar amount on such a terrible loss? Sometimes, stories help determine the value of life. This story might help you decide the worth of a lost mother.

The story requires us to go back in time, before this tragedy. Imagine that Megan and Mallory are on vacation with their mom along the ocean. Mom relaxes on the beach, and they tell her they are going for a walk down the beach looking for shells. They walk about a block down the beach, and Megan stumbles over something in the sand. She looks down and sees something silver gleaming. Mallory says "What's that?" Megan says "Let's find out." And they begin to dig around this gleaming silver object. When they finish digging, Megan says "You know what this looks like? This looks like one of those magic genie lamps." And Mallory says "You mean one of those lamps you rub and a genie appears and grants your wishes?" And Megan says "I'm going to find out. I'm going to rub it." And so she rubs it, and magically a genie appears and says to them, "Today, Megan and Mallory, this is your lucky day. You have released me from the magic lamp and I am going to reward you by giving you ten million dollars." You can imagine how excited they are. They hug each other and Mallory says to Megan, "Mom will be so thrilled!". . . . "Aaaahhh," the genie interrupts, "There is one condition. I will give you ten million dollars, but you see your mother over there lying on the beach—you will never, ever see her again." Now, I ask you, members of the Jury, do you think Megan and Mallory would consider for one moment taking the millions of dollars, or any amount of money, and never see, hug, and love their mom ever again?

Example (Punitive Damages):

Judge Scott is going to tell you that you may award punitive damages in this case if you find the conduct of the defendant wanton and willful and in gross disregard for the safety of others. The law allows you to award punitive damages in this case to punish the defendant. An award of punitive damages allows you to take away some money from the defendant to make the defendant and other future defendants realize this should not happen ever again. An award of punitive damages is not made to give the plaintiff something that is undeserved, but rather it's a deterrent, that is, it sends the message to the defendant and other defendants never to do this in the future.

To send this message, the amount of punitive damages must be significant. The amount must be enough so the defendant feels it is being punished. How do you set that amount of damages? It depends on the amount of actual damages, who the defendant is, how much of a profit it makes, and how much it is worth.

The defendant Dunder Mifflin Corporation is worth 120 million dollars and has average profits of 12 million dollars a year. Those are staggering amounts of money. But only a substantially large amount of punitive damages will affect the defendant and have an impact on its future conduct. If you took away from it 12 million dollars—which is four times actual damages and only one year's profit—the defendant would be properly punished under the law. And when you consider how wanton, how willful, and how grossly indifferent it was to the safety of the plaintiff and others, you may conclude that even 12 million dollars is not enough money to fairly punish the defendant corporation.

---

5.   Per Diem Argument

A plaintiff's attorney may use a "per diem" argument, which divides a period of time into small units and assesses a dollar value for each of these units. For example, if a party will suffer permanent injuries for the remaining thirty years of life, the plaintiff's attorney might argue the plaintiff is entitled to receive $100 a day for thirty years because of this continuing injury, for a total of $1,095,000.

Many jurisdictions prohibit per diem arguments. Some jurisdictions permit the argument when coupled with a mitigating jury instruction. Other jurisdictions permit the argument to be used by the plaintiff's attorney as an alternative way to determine certain damages. For example, the plaintiff's attorney could suggest that the decision maker may decide upon a value of $100 per day, or $200 a day, or more in determining recovery for pain and suffering. This attorney could not, however, in these jurisdictions suggest an amount of damages based on a specific formula.

Example (Plaintiff):

How do you arrive at dollar amounts for the intangible things— for pain and suffering? You have heard the testimony about the pain the plaintiff has suffered in this case. How do you determine how much to compensate the plaintiff for that pain? If a person goes to a dentist to have a cavity filled, the dentist might say, "I can drill your tooth without any Novocain or any painkiller, but for an additional $60 I can give you Novocain, and you will be free from pain for one hour." $60 for freedom from pain for 60 minutes. Who would refuse to pay $60 for freedom for one hour from such excruciating pain? Here, Stu Price has lived with intense, agonizing pain every single hour for over a year.

---

6.   Collateral Source Rule

An injured party may have received partial recovery from sources other than a favorable verdict or judgment, including workers' compensation, health insurance, or government benefits. Many jurisdictions require the judge or arbitrator to subtract damages obtained from collateral sources from a damage award. Other jurisdictions have statutes or rules that require collateral source payments to be deducted from a verdict. The specific rules of a jurisdiction determine whether and how collateral source payments affect what is said in closing arguments.

7.   Financial Status of Party

The general rule is that the financial status of a party is irrelevant and cannot be referred to during summation, unless the financial status is an issue in a case. For example, if punitive damages are sought, the financial status of a defendant is relevant because the assessment of punitive damages depends upon the financial status of that party.

8.   Impact of Tax Laws

If the amount of the verdict or award is not taxable income, then the general rule is that tax law cannot be relied on during summation nor considered by the decision maker. In some cases, tax laws will have an effect upon the award or verdict. In these cases it might be appropriate for the decision maker to consider the impact of these tax laws, proper for a counsel to refer to the tax laws during summation, and proper, in a jury trial, for the judge to explain the tax laws during jury instructions.

9.   Existence of Insurance

The general rule is that neither party may refer to the existence or non-existence of insurance during a case, and this rule covers summation. Insurance may only be mentioned if it is an issue in the case. Evidence rules prohibit references to liability insurance. See Fed.R.Evid. 412.

§ 11.6   PRESENTATION AND DELIVERY

The more effective and persuasive an attorney is in presenting a closing argument, the greater the chance a favorable determination will be reached by the judge, arbitrator, or jury. If the evidence presented in a case is weak, the attorney will have little chance of convincing the decision maker in final argument to return a decision for the client. If the evidence presented during the case is strong, statements made by the attorney during summation will most likely match the conclusions the decision maker has already reached. If, however, the evidence presented by both sides is balanced, the closing argument becomes vitally important and may have a significant influence in the outcome of the case.

Many of the factors that influence the presentation of an opening statement also affect summation. The following factors supplement factors of persuasive advocacy discussed in Sections 1.8 and 6.6, including confidence, sincerity, interest, honesty, dress, demeanor, voice, tone, understandable language, selection of impact words, and use of visual aids and exhibits.

A.   LOCATION

The attorney needs to present the summation from a position that enhances its presentation. In general, the more effective location for an attorney is to stand or sit in front of the decision maker and avoid being hidden by a lectern or table. In administrative and arbitration forums, it may be common for the attorney to sit, but permission may be obtained to stand. In other tribunals, rules require the attorney to stand behind a lectern when presenting the closing argument. In these situations, the attorney can ask permission to stand away from the lectern in order to make a more effective presentation. If this request is denied, the attorney may use visual aids and exhibits allowing movement away from the lectern and closer to the decision maker.

If a lectern must be used, it may be used as a tool, and all the effective communication techniques can be applied with the restrictions that a lectern places on such things as movement and gestures. A lectern may also provide a safe refuge for those attorneys who are uncomfortable with or have not had the time to practice speaking away from a table or lectern. It is too easy, however, to overuse notes while at a lectern or to use no gestures and remain frozen in one spot which may make both the attorney and argument appear boring. Displaying a summation outline or portions of exhibits on a monitor can focus the attention of the fact finder on the arguments and evidence.

B. MOVEMENT

Movement, if appropriate, can be effective during summation. The attorney may need to move to provide the decision maker with a different view, particularly if the summation is lengthy. Location and stance should be orchestrated to avoid appearing random, purposeless or distracting. Movement can be used as a transition or to make a point more emphatically.

C. APPROPRIATE DISTANCE

The attorney must maintain an appropriate distance from the decision maker. This distance should neither be so far away that personal contact is lost, nor so close that the decision maker feels uncomfortable. During summation, the attorney should maintain a reasonable distance from the decision maker. The appropriate distance will depend upon the size of the room, the location of everyone, the placement of visual aid devices and equipment, and the preferences of the judge or arbitrator.

In a jury trial, the attorney can move closer to the jurors and stand by the rail of the jury box. For example, it is possible to make part of the presentation right at the jury box. The attorney must avoid making a juror uncomfortable by standing too close or for a long period of time. When close to the jury the attorney will need to speak quietly and must avoid making prolonged eye contact with any one juror, particularly those near the attorney. One way to avoid this is to stand at the jury rail between two jurors and make eye contact with the jurors in the back row, saving eye contact with the front row for the approach to and movement away from this close presentation. The distance that an attorney maintains should be flexible and vary in different circumstances. Closeness should be used for emphasis. An attorney should observe the jurors' reactions and move closer when appropriate and stand further away when necessary to avoid making jurors feel uncomfortable.

D. GESTURES

An attorney needs to use appropriate gestures during summation to make the presentation more interesting. A lack of gestures or use of awkward hand movements or wild gesticulations needs to be avoided. Purposeful, firm, and natural gestures should be used.

E. EYE CONTACT

One of the most effective ways to be persuasive and compelling is to look the decision makers in the eyes during summation. This also helps hold their attention and allows the attorney to observe their reactions. In jury trials, eye contact should be made with all jurors and not just a few selected jurors. Often an attorney can identify those jurors who appear to be dominant, one of whom is likely to be selected the foreperson. Eye contact should be directed towards these jurors when presenting important points during summation. Eye contact does not mean staring at or looking at jurors so intensely that they become uneasy.

F. TRANSITIONS

Summation is more effective if the attorney uses transitions during the presentation. Preparatory remarks, silence, a louder voice, a softer voice, exhibits, movement, and gestures can act as transitions.

G. DEVELOPING OWN STYLE

An attorney must deliver the final argument in a style that reflects the advocate's abilities. A lawyer should avoid copying and mimicking another lawyer's style but should be open to adapting and reworking what someone else has done if this style appears effective. Parts of summation may be taken from previous arguments made by other attorneys because of the similarity of the cases, the issues, or the quality of the ideas. This form of mimicking is appropriate and can be most effective if the advocate appears to be presenting it in a spontaneous, fresh manner.

H. OBSERVING DECISION MAKER'S REACTION

The attorney must observe the reactions of the decision maker during the closing argument and consider these reactions during the argument. A lawyer who remains conscious of the observed reactions will more easily maintain interest and attention. The facial expressions, body language, and eye contact displayed by the decision maker communicate some information about attitude or position. What the jurors, judge, or arbitrator write down as notes, or do not write down, also needs to be observed. These perceptions may not always be accurate and an advocate must be cautious when attempting to read the mind of the decision maker. Because it is difficult to determine accurately what someone is thinking, care must be taken not to overreact or completely change an approach because of a perceived reaction.

I.   NOTES AND OUTLINES

It will be necessary for an attorney to rely upon notes or an outline during closing argument to ensure all important points have been covered. The longer the closing argument the more likely it is for an advocate to rely on extensive notes. A lawyer should never read a prepared argument or follow the notes so closely that eye contact is not established and maintained with the decision maker. Reading the argument will lead to a very boring and uninteresting presentation.

References to notes are appropriate as long as such references do not unreasonably interfere with or detract from the presentation. A persuasive, flowing argument usually is more effective, even if minor points are omitted. The continuous use of notes to cover every detail can lead to a monotonous and ineffective presentation.

Prepared outlines can be effectively used in summation if combined with the use of visual aids. A prepared diagram, a whiteboard, easel paper, or a monitor screen may contain an outline of part or all of the closing which highlights important matters and assists the attorney in explaining the argument. Portions of real and demonstrative exhibits may also be used as part of the overall summation outline.

§ 11.7 OBJECTIONS

The lawyer is generally allowed wide latitude in discussing the evidence and presenting explanations during summation. All the tools of effective oratory are at the lawyer's disposal, and tactics calculated to convince or persuade the decision maker should be used. Objections may be asserted to prevent improper closing arguments.

If an attorney has an opportunity for a final argument or rebuttal after the opposition, the attorney may prefer not to object but later comment on the inappropriate statement made by the opposing lawyer. If an attorney has no further summation, then an objection may be necessary to repair any damage and to preserve a matter for appeal. Many attorneys do not object during summation unless the opponent is saying or doing something that is clearly improper and unfairly prejudicial.

An objection to improper summation must be made in a timely fashion. Usually, the objection must be made immediately during or at the end of the final argument. In a jury trial, the objecting attorney should also request a curative instruction. The trial judge may then attempt to reduce the prejudicial impact of the improper comments by instructing the jurors to disregard the comments. Some jurisdictions require the attorney to make the objection as well as request a curative instruction. The reason for the curative instruction is to provide an opportunity for the judge to rectify the error. The damage done by some improper comments may not be correctable by a curative instruction.

Appellate courts have reversed verdicts and granted new trials even where the trial judge gave curative instructions because the comments were so prejudicial as to deny the objecting party a fair trial. For example, comments made by an attorney regarding the existence of insurance in a civil case may be impossible to correct. Improper comments made in a case in which the issues are evenly balanced may be sufficient to support a motion for a mistrial. See Section 3.8(C)(9).

Usually, a judge in a jury trial will not interrupt a summation unless there is an objection interposed or unless some fundamental rights are being violated. In bench trials and administrative and arbitration hearings, the judge or arbitrator may interrupt if they believe some comments are improper or if they do not want to listen to the arguments.

The circumstances of each case determine whether the impropriety of the remarks is incurable. Appellate courts may reverse a verdict without objections being made to the final argument where the substantial interests of justice require a reversal. See Section 12.9. The advocate should not rely on such results because the granting of a new trial or an appellate court reversal for improper closing argument seldom occurs.

The following paragraphs describe objections to improper comments made during summation.

A.　ARGUING NEW MATTERS

An attorney may not introduce or argue new matters during closing argument beyond the scope of admitted evidence, including testimony and exhibits. Section 11.2 described what can be presented in final argument. References to facts or to the law which go beyond the evidence or legal issues are objectionable. References to evidence deemed inadmissible or to facts that were not introduced during the case are also improper.

Objection:

Counsel is improperly referring to matters not part of this case.

Response to Objection:

- Explain the evidence or law that supports the comments made.

- Avoid referring to inadmissible or unproven evidence.

B. MISSTATING THE EVIDENCE

Misstating or mischaracterizing evidence is improper. In a jury trial, the judge may not recall the exact evidence or may permit the attorney broad latitude in characterizing the evidence because the judge has given or will give an instruction that what the attorneys say during summation is not evidence. The jurors will be instructed that they are to rely upon their own recollection of the evidence. In some cases, the judge may give a curative instruction during summation advising the jury to ignore an improper statement made by the attorney.

Misstatements or mischaracterizations may also occur regarding evidence that was not introduced, or received, or admitted only for a limited purpose. The attorney, during argument, might use evidence admitted for one purpose to prove something else, which is objectionable.

Objection:

Counsel misstated the evidence presented during the case.

Response to Objection:

- Explain the source of evidence supporting the comment.

- Explain the comment is a permissible inference that may be drawn from the facts presented.

- Argue the statement is a good faith belief by the attorney of what the evidence was.

- Remind the judge an instruction will be given to the jurors that what the lawyers say is not evidence.

C. IMPROPER LEGAL ARGUMENT

The lawyer may not argue a personal interpretation of the law applicable to the case. An advocate may and should correctly explain the applicable law and apply it to the facts. It is improper for the attorney to misstate or misinterpret the law or ask that the law be disregarded.

Objection:

Counsel is incorrectly stating the law.

Response to Objection:

- Identify the legal elements of the claim or defense.

- Assert the explanation is a fair interpretation of the law.

D. IMPROPER PERSONAL ARGUMENT

An attorney may not state a personal viewpoint or make personal remarks about the facts, credibility of witnesses, expert opinions, or other evidence. The decision maker is to decide the case upon the evidence and not be influenced by the personal opinion of counsel. For example, the advocate may not state: "There is no question in my mind that the plaintiff lied to you. I heard what you heard, and I saw what you saw. I am convinced the plaintiff lied." A prosecutor may not state: "I have prosecuted over 20 drug dealers over the years. I have never been as sure as I am in this case about the guilt of the defendant. I not only think he is guilty, but I firmly believe as an officer of the court that he's guilty as charged." While an inadvertent, occasional use of a statement prefaced by "I believe" may not call for an objection, any prejudicial effort to influence the decision maker with a personal opinion calls for an objection.

Objection:

Counsel is stating improper personal opinions.

Response to Objection:

- Avoid making personal opinions.

- Avoid using "I" in a statement referring to an opinion.

- Preface such remarks with:

    "It is clear from the evidence. . . ."

    "The only conclusion that can be reached is. . . ."

E. IMPROPER "GOLDEN RULE" ARGUMENT

The "Golden Rule" argument is a statement by an attorney asking decision makers to put themselves in the place of a party or witness. An example is "What if you were the defendant in this case. How would you want yourself to be treated?" Decision makers are to decide the case based on the facts, not based upon how they personally want to be treated as a party or believed as a witness.

Objection:

Counsel is improperly asking the decision makers to put themselves in the place of a party.

Response to Objection:

- Avoid making this statement.

- Do not use the word "you" (referring to the decision maker).

- Ask the decision makers to rely upon their common sense or how a reasonable person would respond and not how they would respond.

F. APPEALS TO PASSION

Statements are improper if they unfairly inflame the passions of the decision maker. Attorneys may legitimately invoke emotions in a case, but may not rely on improper sympathy. The drama inherent in many cases will naturally result in appropriate emotional closing arguments. Empathy, sadness, and tears may naturally result from the atmosphere of the courtroom or hearing room. The nature of the issues and the degree of the appropriate emotional comments determine propriety.

Objection:

Counsel is unfairly inflaming passions.

Response to Objection:

- Explain that emotions are a natural part of the case.

- Present the argument in a less emotional manner.

G. MISUSE OF VISUAL AIDS AND EXHIBITS

Advocates may inadvertently or intentionally prepare visual aids that distort the actual evidence or refer to portions of exhibits taken out of context. Some visual aids prepared for summation will not be easily reviewed by opposing counsel before the argument because they are not visible or apparent. Many jurisdictions require a lawyer using visual aids to make them available to the other side a reasonable time before they are to be used. Or a lawyer can ask permission of the judge to timely review the exhibits to be used by the opponent.

Objection:

Counsel is using a visual aid that distorts the evidence or is improperly referring to exhibits taken out of context.

Response to Objection:

- Explain that the visual aid accurately presents one side of the story and is based on the evidence.

- Explain that the exhibits are relevant to the point being made or that opposing counsel will have—or had—an opportunity to introduce other portions of the exhibits during summation.

H. BEYOND THE PROPER SCOPE

Section 11.3(I) explained that the scope of rebuttal may be limited in some jurisdictions. During rebuttal, the attorney may improperly make statements that exceed the scope of the rebuttal.

Objection:

The argument by counsel exceeds the proper scope of rebuttal.

Response to Objection:

- Explain that the topic raised by opposing counsel relates to the rebuttal argument.

- Include the arguments during the initial summation and do not save them for rebuttal.

- Ask the judge or arbitrator to exercise discretion and permit a broader rebuttal.

I. IMPROPER INFERENCES

All jurisdictions recognize evidentiary privileges that prevent the introduction of relevant information. These jurisdictions differ regarding whether opposing counsel may suggest that the fact finders draw adverse inferences from the invocation of such a privilege. For example, in jurisdictions that recognize marital privileges and prevent spouses from testifying to confidential marital communications, opposing counsel usually may not refer to the excluded marital conversation and may not draw the inference that what was discussed must be harmful to the case.

In some cases, a party may not be able to introduce relevant evidence for legitimate reasons. The evidence may have been inadvertently lost by a third party. A key witness may not be able to be located after substantial efforts. Some evidence may be outside the subpoena power of the court, arbitrator, or agency. In many jurisdictions, it is improper for opposing counsel to ask that adverse inferences be drawn from the failure of the other attorney to introduce such evidence.

Objection:

Counsel is improperly asking that adverse inferences be drawn from the lawful invocation of a privilege.

Response to Objection:

- Check the laws of the jurisdiction to determine whether this is permissible. If so, provide a cite to the authority.

- Make a reference to the missing evidence without asking for any adverse inference.

J. PROSECUTORIAL MISCONDUCT

In criminal cases, the prosecutor must be careful not to overstep the bounds of fair argument. Prosecutors may be bound by a higher standard than defense counsel. Defense counsel may rely on the constitutional rights of the defendant that protect against an overzealous prosecutor. For example, it is a constitutional violation for a prosecutor to comment negatively on a defendant's presumption of innocence. And it is improper for a prosecutor to say that the defendant would not have been arrested if he was innocent or that, unless a conviction occurs, a lot of taxpayer money will have been wasted.

Objection:

Prosecutor has made unfair prejudicial comments.

Response to Objection:

- Do not make such statements.

- Avoid sounding vindictive.

K. APPEALS TO PREJUDICE

It is a gross violation of the fundamental precepts of our system to appeal to the prejudices or biases of the decision maker regarding racial, sexist, economic, religious, political, or similar arguments. These comments are unethical and unconscionable.

Example:

Plaintiff's Lawyer:

Whatever doubts you may have about the defendant's liability in this case can be resolved by considering the wealth of the defendant. This very rich and well-off defendant can clearly afford to pay the plaintiff a lot of money and should be made to do so, even if you aren't sure the defendant is negligent.

Defendant's Attorney:

Objection. Counsel is making unfairly prejudicial comments.

Judge:

Sustained. And the lawyer is reprimanded for such unprofessional conduct.

L. IMPROPER REFERENCES

Attorneys may not cite or quote the results of similar cases when arguing to a decision maker. The case is to be decided based on the facts of the present case and not on what other decision makers have done in other cases, unless it is controlling precedent.

Example:

Plaintiff's Lawyer:

This is not the first case where the defendant's product injured someone. There have been other trials, where the defendant lost. You should do what those other jurors did.

Defendant's Attorney:

Objection. Counsel's remarks about previous verdicts are improper and unfair.

Judge:

Sustained. And I will admonish counsel for this malfeasance.

M. IMPROPER COMMENTS

The following statements represent examples of improper comments in civil cases: mentioning liability insurance; implying that the jurors as taxpayers would ultimately be responsible for a damage award to a plaintiff who sued a governmental agency; telling the decision maker that the present case is not the first time litigants have asked for excessive damages; comments that denounce or degrade opposing counsel or the adverse party; comparisons made between the massive resources of the opposing counsel's law firm and the limited resources of the advocate's firm; and any other unprofessional or unfair statements.

N. IMPROPER INTERRUPTIONS

Objections may not be made merely to interrupt the attorney. If an opposing lawyer makes inappropriate or harassing objections, counsel should object to the unfounded and improper objections.

O. ADMONISHING COUNSEL

If opposing attorney makes improper comments or continues to make inappropriate comments after an objection has been sustained, objecting counsel can ask the judge or arbitrator to admonish counsel and instruct the attorney to stop such behavior. See Section 3.13(B).

CHAPTER 12

VERDICT AND APPEAL

■ ■ ■

Trial Advocacy Supplement
Verdict and Appeal

An example of jury instructions and a deliberation in a civil jury trial appears in the *Supplement to Trial Advocacy Before Judges, Jurors, and Arbitrators*. The transcript of the *Rita Riley v. Garfield House Apartments* jury trial demonstrates approaches that are explained in this Chapter. Commentary with the transcript explains the jury trial procedures. The *Supplement* also contains applicable Federal Rules of Civil Procedure explained in this Chapter.

REFLECTING ON ADVOCACY

Whereof you are a well deserving pillar, Proceed to judgment.

—SHAKESPEARE

MERCHANT OF VENICE, ACT IV,
SCENE I

There are four sides to every answer: Right and wrong, yours and mine.

—BO HAMILTON

§ 12.1 INTRODUCTION

This Chapter covers the procedures that occur after all evidence has been introduced and the parties rest. For jury trials, these include final jury instructions, jury deliberations, and the announcement of the verdict. For all trials, these include post-trial motions, stays of proceedings, and the appellate process. For other cases, these include post-arbitration matters and post-administrative case proceedings.

§ 12.2 JURY INSTRUCTIONS AND VERDICT FORMS

A. JURY INSTRUCTION CONFERENCE

After the attorneys have submitted their proposed instructions and verdict form to the judge, the judge selects the instructions to be given and the verdict form to be used. The instructions and verdict form the judge ultimately decides to use constitute the "charge" to the jury.

The judge's decision is based on whether evidence has been introduced requiring or supporting an instruction and what applicable law must be contained in the charge, all of which must be accurate, fair, and understandable. Section 2.9 explained the need for the attorneys to prepare proposed jury instructions early in the case and the procedures involved in submitting these instructions and verdict forms to the judge.

The judge must inform counsel before summation and before the charge to the jury what final instructions and verdict form will be given to the jury. Typically, the judge holds a jury instruction conference in chambers. During this conference, the judge advises counsel what revisions, additions, or deletions the judge made to the instructions proposed by counsel. Following this conference, the judge issues an order on the record specifying the instructions and verdict form the court plans to give to the jury. The order also notes the proposed instructions and verdict form the court has refused to give. Frequently, when there are reasonable disagreements over instructions, the judge will work with the lawyers in an effort to reach a compromise agreement.

Some judges provide each attorney with a copy of the final instructions and verdict form. Also, some judges note on the proposed instruction which points were granted, denied, modified, or granted or denied in part. The attorneys should know what exact charge will be given to determine what references or explanations they can make regarding the instructions and verdict form during summation. The proposed and the final jury instructions become part of the court file, in order to ensure their availability for possible appellate court review. In some jurisdictions proposed instructions are not part of the record, and advocates need to make certain they are included in the record.

During this jury instruction conference additional matters may be reviewed, including whether any anticipated problems may arise during closing argument, the time limits or restrictions regarding summation, the making or renewal of motions outside the hearing of the jury, which exhibits will be provided to the jurors during deliberations, and whether it is still not too late for settlement or mediation in civil cases.

B. THE JUDGE'S CHARGE

The judge instructs the jury in open court before or after closing arguments. Most commonly, the judge instructs after summation. Many jurisdictions permit the judge to explain instructions before summation, particularly in cases involving factually or legally complex issues. An attorney may request that the judge instruct the jury periodically before trial, during trial, or both, as well as after summation if such instructions will help the jurors better understand the law. The trial judge has broad discretion in determining how best to instruct the jury. See Section 2.9.

Most judges attempt to read the instructions and verdict form to the jury in such a way as to make the charge informative and understandable. The jurors may also be provided with a copy of the charge they can use to follow along and to have available during their deliberations. Some judges explain the instructions to the jury by paraphrasing or summarizing the instructions. While this approach may make the explanation more conversational, it runs the risk an instruction will be misstated or an important word or phrase omitted.

In addition to instructing the jury regarding the law, federal judges and state court judges in some jurisdictions may comment on the evidence. These judges, instead of merely explaining the law, can refer to issues in the case and suggest interpretations for the jury. In these jurisdictions, the jury still makes factual determinations, not the judge. The scope of proper comments varies among judges and jurisdictions.

At the end of the charge, the judge may ask if the jurors understood the instructions and verdict form or if they have any questions. Some jurors may occasionally ask for a re-reading or an explanation, which the judge has discretion to do.

The verdict form is given to the jury to take into the jury room to complete. Judges typically give the jurors a printed copy of all of the instructions for their use during deliberations. This submission increases the chances the jurors will properly apply the law and reduces the chance the jury will need the judge to repeat certain instructions.

C. OBJECTING TO INSTRUCTIONS AND VERDICT FORM

Errors made in jury instructions are a ground for the trial judge or appellate court to grant a new trial. The standard for a new trial and appellate reversal is whether an instruction was legally accurate and whether evidence supported the instruction. An attorney must make a timely and proper objection to preserve errors based on the jury instructions or verdict form. A party waives all errors unless the attorney objects and provides the court with an opportunity to correct the mistake.

Objections to instructions and the verdict form may be made at the time the judge informs the attorneys of the charge to be given, or, alternatively, objections may be made right after the jury has been charged, before they begin deliberations. In some jurisdictions, the objections must be made at both times. In most jurisdictions, objecting before the charge has been given is sufficient. If an error is first noted during the charge, the objection must be made after the instructions and before the jury retires to deliberate. This prevents an attorney from remaining silent and objecting later only if the verdict is not favorable. Whenever made, the objection must be made on the record and outside the hearing of the jury. Usually, this is done verbally in the presence of the court reporter, either in chambers or in the courtroom.

The trial lawyer must specifically state the objectionable matter and the grounds for the objection. A general objection is usually insufficient. Examples of objections to proposed instructions include:

The proposed instruction:

- Misstates the law,
- Fails to follow the approved instruction,
- Is cumulative,
- Is argumentative,
- Will confuse the jurors, or
- No factual support in the record exists for the instruction.

The preferred practice is to identify the instruction that is faulty and provide controlling authority. The objection is made to allow the judge an opportunity to correct the mistake. For example, the written instructions given by the judge to the attorneys may be proper, but during the oral charge the judge may misstate or omit an instruction. The attorney must call the error to the court's attention to preserve a ground for a new trial or appeal. An exception to this rule may involve errors of fundamental law or mistakes that could not have been corrected by the judge.

After the attorneys have objected to the instructions given by the judge, the judge has an opportunity to modify or add to the instructions given. Explanations given by the judge that may have misled or confused the jury should be clarified.

D. BENCH TRIAL

In a civil bench trial, the judge usually decides the case by making findings of fact and conclusions of law in writing or orally on the record. The drafting of proposed findings and conclusions by the counsel parallels the considerations involved in drafting proposed jury instructions. See Section 2.10. The attorneys typically submit proposed findings of fact and conclusions of law that are consistent with the relief sought. See Fed.R.Civ.Proc. 52 and Section 3.11(E).

To withstand a challenge at the trial or appellate court level, findings and conclusions should accurately reflect the supporting evidence and the law. They should also be clear and concise, balanced and not biased. A comprehensive draft of proposed factual findings should follow the evidence introduced and assist in persuading the judge the facts have been proved. A draft of proposed conclusions of law similarly assists the judge in determining the legal elements have been proved.

In a criminal bench trial, the judge will declare the defendant either guilty or not guilty. In some jurisdictions, the judge may have to prepare written findings. In some cases, the judge may explain the decision on the record or in writing, without making specific findings.

E. ADMINISTRATIVE DECISIONS

An administrative law judge issues a decision, often called an order, with an accompanying explanation of supporting reasons or findings of fact and conclusions of law. The applicable statutes or rules determine the type of decision made.

F. ARBITRATION AWARDS

An arbitrator issues an award after an arbitration hearing. The award describes the relief awarded to the prevailing party which typically is money damages and may be any form of relief, including injunctive relief. The arbitrator generally has the same power a judge has and can issue an award within the scope of the agreement, the rules, and the law. The award may be a short, summary statement or may include findings, conclusions, and explanations.

If the losing party fails to abide by the award, the prevailing party can seek to enforce the award in court. Awards can be confirmed as a judgment in any court with jurisdiction, including state or federal, by following the statutory and court processes. See Section 12.8(D).

G. JURY TRIAL STIPULATIONS

Trial counsel may stipulate to certain procedures. Before a case is submitted to the jury, the judge may request, or the attorneys may suggest, the following stipulations be agreed upon:

- *The court, in the absence of counsel and the parties, may re-read and explain to the jury any instructions previously given or answer any relevant questions, if the jurors request such information while they are deliberating.* This stipulation speeds up jury deliberations and allows the judge to meet with the jury without requiring counsel to be present. It may be difficult for the attorneys to be located and advised of the jury request because of their schedules.

- *The parties waive the right to have the clerk or court reporter present when the jury returns a verdict.* The jury may deliberate outside of normal court hours when some court personnel are not present, and this stipulation allows such personnel to be absent. A judge must be present to accept a verdict from the jury. If the judge who presides at the trial is not available, a substitute judge accepts the verdict.

- *A sealed verdict may be returned.* The judge who accepts the verdict may review it and place it in a sealed envelope. Some jurisdictions permit the parties to stipulate that a court employee (a clerk or bailiff) may accept and seal a verdict instead of the judge. The verdict will be opened in court later when the judge, attorneys, and parties are available. This stipulation permits jurors to be discharged and a verdict announced when court is in session.

- *The parties waive their right to be present when the jury returns the verdict and allow the judge to announce the verdict in open court on the record.* If the parties would have difficulty in arranging their schedules to attend, they may consent to this procedure.

- *The parties waive their right to poll the jury.* This allows the judge to discharge the jury immediately after receiving the verdict from the jury. Many lawyers prefer to have the jury polled especially if there may be some concern regarding the decision reached by the jurors.

- *A stay of entry of judgment for an agreed upon number of days shall be granted after a verdict.* This provision allows the losing party to serve post-trial motions without having to seek a stay of entry of judgment or a stay of execution on a judgment that has been entered. See Section 12.6(A).

While these stipulations are routine in some jurisdictions, they are uncommon or not even allowed in other jurisdictions. The parties in civil cases are usually free to waive any of their rights regarding the verdict return procedures. Defendants in criminal cases have the constitutional right to be present for all procedures and may or may not waive any of their rights depending upon the nature of the proceeding.

Ordinarily, nothing goes wrong with these procedures. If something unusual should happen, such an occurrence would rarely present grounds for a new trial. Because of this, many lawyers willingly enter into these stipulations. Many other attorneys, however, reasonably believe that it is wise or necessary to be in court in case something does go wrong. Further, after all the excitement and emotion of a trial, the attorneys and parties may be eager to be present for the reading of the verdict.

§ 12.3 JURY DELIBERATION PROCEDURES

After the judge has instructed the jury, the jurors are sworn by the clerk to render a true verdict and are taken to the deliberation room by the bailiff. The jury room is typically adjacent to the courtroom. While deliberating, the jury is in the bailiff's custody.

A. DELIBERATIONS

Jurors typically deliberate during normal court hours on weekdays until they reach a verdict. If they deliberate more than one day, they usually go home and return for continued deliberations the following day. The judge instructs them not to discuss the case with anyone not a juror, nor to use their cell phone except perhaps to contact family for a ride home, nor to search the web for information relevant to the case, and not to read any newspapers or articles about the trial nor watch television or listen to the radio if the trial has engendered some publicity. Some jurors will be tempted to use a smart phone, tablet, or laptop to seek information about issues or questions they have; and judges need to communicate clearly that such actions are prohibited. Verdicts have been overturned and new trials granted when such improper conduct has occurred.

Many juries deliberate during evening hours or over the weekend, especially if they are close to a verdict, or if there is some reason to accelerate the reaching of a verdict, for example, an upcoming holiday. Jurors are usually free to set their own pace and establish their own hours for deliberation, as long as the schedule is reasonable.

B. SEQUESTERING THE JURY

In major criminal cases and in well-publicized civil cases, the jury may be sequestered during deliberations and stay at a hotel or motel instead of going home. This does not happen often because of the expense involved and because most trials do not warrant such an additional safeguard. The bailiff, assisted by marshals or other court personnel, is responsible for the jurors and arranges for transportation, lodging, food, edited reading materials, restricted use of cell phones and other devices including internet, and selected television or video programs.

C. COPY OF JURY INSTRUCTIONS

As explained previously, a judge may order, or an attorney may request, that a copy of the jury instructions be provided for use by the jurors during deliberations. Some portions of the original instructions, which are not needed by the jurors, may be removed, such as the number, caption, citations to authority, and other comments.

D. EXHIBITS

The trial judge has discretion to decide which exhibits received into evidence will be allowed in the jury room during deliberations. In some jurisdictions, all exhibits are provided to the jurors, unless the attorneys object and present a substantial reason for changing this practice. In other jurisdictions, only real evidence exhibits go to the jury. Demonstrative evidence such as diagrams may or may not be allowed to go with the jury.

Usually, visual aids presented during the opening and summation are not provided to the jurors for their use during deliberations. The jurors can make notes about these presentations when they listen to them, and these notes may be available during deliberations if permitted by the judge. Trial attorneys should review all exhibits to determine which, if any, should be provided to the jurors.

Favorable exhibits provide jurors with an available and visual statement as well as a reminder of the evidence and may have a useful impact on the jurors. Attorneys should request the court to have these exhibits provided to the jurors by arguing that the exhibits provide the jurors with an accurate and complete set of relevant facts that will expedite their deliberation process. On the other hand, if unfavorable exhibits will be provided to the jurors, trial counsel may argue against their submission by claiming that the jurors will give the exhibit undue weight and fail to consider oral testimony equally.

A judge may decide not to submit an exhibit to the jury because the jury might place undue emphasis on the exhibit, the exhibit may be dangerous, or because the exhibit would not help the jury to arrive at a verdict. The judge has broad discretion in making these decisions.

E. JURORS' NOTES

The judge has broad discretion in deciding whether to allow jurors to take notes and whether the notes are allowed in the jury room. Many judges allow jurors to take notes during the trial and to use notes during deliberations. Some judges do not allow the jurors to bring these notes to the deliberation room. The exclusion of jurors' notes avoids the problems of notes being considered evidence and prevents note-taking jurors from exercising more power in deliberations than other jurors. Usually, jurors are instructed to rely on their own recollection of testimony, and if their notes are inconsistent with their recollection, to disregard their notes.

F. QUESTIONS BY JURORS

A jury may have questions regarding the case or want to have some instructions re-read or explained by the judge. In these situations, the foreperson can write a note to the judge asking to meet or may reduce the questions to writing and submit them through the bailiff to the judge.

The judge has discretion to reinstruct, explain, re-read instructions, answer questions or decline to do anything. The proper way for the judge to meet with the jury is in the courtroom and on the record. Usually, the judge contacts counsel or their offices, advises them of the jury's request, and asks whether they wish to attend. In civil cases, some judges may meet with the jurors without notice to the attorneys. In criminal cases, the defendant and the attorneys have a right to be present.

Many juries never have any questions for the judge. Some judges are reluctant to respond to jury requests because they do not want to interfere with the decision making of the jurors. Some judges, perceiving that a jury is having major disagreements, will attempt to assist the jurors in an effort to avoid a hung jury. See Section 12.3(H).

The judge may not be able to resolve some problems the jurors may have. The jurors may want help on factual issues that are exclusively within their domain, or they may ask the judge to assist in the application of jury instructions to the facts, something only the jurors themselves may do. For example, if the jurors ask the judge to explain the meaning of a word or phrase in a jury instruction, the judge may do so. If the jurors ask the judge to resolve a factual dispute, the judge must refuse this request. Resolving the facts of the case is the exclusive duty of the jury, and the judge may not infringe on that responsibility.

After the judge responds to the questions or problems, the jurors return to deliberate.

G. UNANIMOUS JURY VERDICT

In criminal cases, a jury verdict must be unanimous. In civil cases, verdicts are typically unanimous, but many jurisdictions allow non-unanimous verdicts in some situations. These jurisdictions, including federal courts, allow civil parties to stipulate to less than unanimous verdicts. Some jurisdictions, by statute or rule, allow a less than unanimous civil verdict to be returned after the jurors have deliberated for a certain period of time without reaching a unanimous verdict. For example, a jurisdiction may permit a civil verdict to be returned by five out of six jurors after the jurors have deliberated more than four hours.

H. HUNG JURY

If the required minimum number of jurors cannot agree on a verdict after a significant amount of time, the jury is said to be "hung," and the judge may discharge them and declare a mistrial. What is a significant amount of time depends upon the facts and circumstances of each case. Usually, the judge will not declare the jury hung unless a lengthy period of time has passed and it is clear that the jurors are deadlocked.

The time period may be several days or several weeks depending upon the number and complexity of the issues, how far from agreement the jurors are, how the deliberations are proceeding, and how fruitless further deliberations are likely to be. In a simple case, a judge may declare a jury to be hung after several days of unsuccessful deliberations. In a complex case, several weeks of daily deliberations may pass before a judge will declare a jury hung.

Because the remedy for a trial resulting in a hung jury is a new trial with a new jury, courts are reluctant to declare a jury is hung. Judges will do what they can to explain jury instructions, answer appropriate questions from jurors, and encourage the jurors to reach a verdict to avoid having to go through another trial of the same case.

Many jurisdictions allow a judge to give the jurors a "dynamite" charge (also known as an *Allen* charge). This occurs when the judge brings the jurors in open court and firmly and assertively reminds them of their responsibilities and their need to reach a verdict in the case. Some jurisdictions prohibit this type of charge because of the undue pressure the judge may exert on the jurors' decision.

§ 12.4 RETURN OF THE VERDICT

The foreperson of the jury advises the bailiff when the jurors have reached a verdict. The bailiff advises the clerk or the judge a verdict has been reached, and they, in turn, contact trial counsel, who may want to attend with their client parties. When the jury returns a verdict during regular court hours, the presiding trial judge or a substitute judge brings the jurors into the courtroom for the return of the verdict.

If the jurors return a verdict outside of normal court hours, the bailiff will contact the judge who will then accept the verdict. Counsel may, however, stipulate neither they nor the judge need be present when the verdict is returned. In that case, the verdict is usually sealed and opened by the judge during working hours, with or without the lawyers being present, depending upon the stipulation.

When the jurors return to the courtroom, the foreperson typically hands the completed verdict form to the bailiff or clerk who in turn hands it to the judge who reviews it. If the verdict form is incomplete or inconsistent, the judge usually orders the jurors to return and properly complete the verdict form. If the verdict form is properly completed, the judge, or clerk, or foreperson reads the verdict in open court; and the judge or clerk may then ask the jurors if the verdict is true and accurate.

A. POLLING OF THE JURY

After the verdict has been read, and before the jurors have been dismissed, the attorney who has lost may request that the jury be individually polled. The trial judge or clerk usually polls the jury by asking each individual juror whether the verdict is her or his true and correct verdict. If all the jurors agree, the judge dismisses them. If, and this rarely occurs, a juror dissents from the verdict, the judge usually orders the jurors to continue deliberations to reach a unanimous verdict. In civil cases where a less than unanimous verdict is permitted, only those jurors that supported the verdict need to affirm their position.

In some jurisdictions, polling the jurors is a routine procedure. In other jurisdictions polling is uncommon. Some lawyers do not do so unless they believe there were problems among the jurors during deliberations. There is no disadvantage for a losing trial attorney to ask the jurors be individually polled, except the hurt of being repeatedly rejected by each juror in open court.

B. DISCHARGING THE JURY

After the verdict has been read and after polling, the judge discharges the jurors, thanking them for their participation, and advising them they may, but need not, speak to anyone about the case.

C. CONTACTING JURORS

A trial attorney may talk to or with the jurors after they have been discharged. The topics the attorney may discuss with the jurors vary among jurisdictions. Some jurisdictions prohibit the attorneys from talking with the jurors except to thank them for their time. It is common courtesy for the winning and losing attorneys to thank the jurors before they leave the courtroom. Other courts allow the attorneys to ask the jurors to comment on trial strategies or to critique the trial skills of the attorney. Many jurors will be candid and the attorneys can learn much from these conversations. Some lawyers retain a professional to contact the jurors and ask them prepared questions seeking information on what went right with the trial presentation, or what went wrong.

Most jurisdictions prohibit attorneys from contacting jurors after they leave the courthouse if the purpose is to discover what happened during deliberations or to obtain information in support of a motion for a new trial. These jurisdictions typically enforce these restrictions by declaring these contacts by the attorneys improper and unethical and by refusing to consider any information obtained in this manner.

Some jurisdictions allow contacts. If an impropriety involving the jury may have occurred, these jurisdictions permit attorneys to contact jurors after the trial and ask whether any prejudicial or extraneous matters affected the deliberations. Other jurisdictions only permit these inquiries by the lawyers to occur during a post-trial hearing granted by and presided over by the trial judge. Relevant information that is established may be a ground for a new trial.

All jurisdictions prohibit attorneys and parties from pressuring or harassing the jurors and prohibit inquiries into the confidential jury deliberations.

D. MISCONDUCT OF THE JURY

Misconduct occurs if the jurors allow their verdict to be influenced by factors other than the evidence admitted in the case or if the jurors fail to follow the law. If a nonjuror contacts a juror about the case before a verdict is reached, the juror must immediately inform the judge. If the contact prejudicially affects the juror's ability to be fair and impartial, the juror will be dismissed and replaced with an alternate. If there is no alternate juror in a civil case, the judge may declare a mistrial unless the parties agree to or the law allows a verdict reached by fewer jurors.

Jurors may not decide the verdict on the basis of personal knowledge of the case. Any personal knowledge should be disclosed during jury selection, and the juror excused. Likewise, jurors may not base their decision on personal experiences as if those experiences were evidence to consider. Further, jurors cannot base their decision on information improperly obtained from prohibited sources such as internet web sites.

Jury misconduct is a ground for a motion for a new trial or a reason for appellate reversal of a verdict. The misconduct must be of such a nature that a party has been unfairly and prejudicially affected. The mere occurrence of misconduct is usually not enough. The mistake must result in substantial prejudicial error. Misconduct may occur when jurors obtain prohibited information because it is impossible for the jurors to forget the information or not be unfairly influenced by it. See Section 12.9(D).

E. IMPEACHING A VERDICT

Jury deliberations are confidential and protected by the law. Deliberations will not be interrupted, and a verdict will not be discarded, unless some extraneous prejudicial information or improper influence has improperly affected the process or verdict. Examples of such improprieties include bribing the jurors or improper comments by a court official, such as the bailiff, telling the jurors how they should decide. Jury misconduct that occurs during deliberations is very difficult to discover. A juror who observes prohibited conduct by other jurors, such as searching web sites, has an obligation to reveal such misconduct to the judge.

Most jurisdictions follow the federal rule that prohibits a juror from testifying to any statement made during the course of jury deliberations, or to the effect of anything that may have influenced the juror's minds or emotions, or to any matter concerning the juror's mental processes. See Fed.R.Evid. 606(b). The federal rule and similar state rules permit jurors to testify only in unusual situations where some extraneous prejudicial information was improperly brought to the jury's attention or where some outside influence was improperly brought to bear upon any juror. These restrictions severely limit the ability to impeach a jury verdict and insure that verdicts will be final and stable. These limitations also reduce the chances that jurors, after a trial, will change their minds about their verdict because of pressures placed on them by participants or outsiders.

F. MOTION TO QUESTION THE JURORS

A trial attorney who learns that prejudicial matter may have adversely affected jury deliberations may move the court for a hearing regarding such matter. The moving attorney must first establish that such information is reliable. Many jurisdictions accept hearsay information as sufficiently reliable if the information shows the existence of improper and extraneous information that may have prejudiced the verdict. If a judge agrees a hearing is warranted, the judge usually calls the jurors back to be questioned individually about the extraneous, prejudicial matter. The judge typically conducts the questioning, with the attorneys submitting proposed questions to be asked by the judge. The attorneys may also be able to ask questions of the jurors after the judge has completed questioning. These hearings are infrequently granted because of the difficulty in learning about extraneous matter and the high burden of proving it had a prejudicial effect on the verdict.

§ 12.5   POST-TRIAL AND POST-HEARING MOTIONS

After a final order, award, or verdict, one or all parties may submit post-trial or post-hearing motions requesting the judge to review the decision. These motions are almost always required to preserve the right to appeal based on trial or hearing errors allowing the judge or arbitrator to correct any mistakes.

A.   MOTION TO DISMISS

A defending party may bring a motion to dismiss during a trial or hearing to seek the dismissal of a bench trial, administrative hearing, or arbitration. Section 3.8(C)(7) explained motions to dismiss. It would be unusual and usually unnecessary to bring a motion to dismiss after a trial or hearing before a judge or after an arbitration because there is no advantage in so doing. All the parties have already completed presenting their evidence, and they prefer a final decision be made by the judge or arbitrator, not a ruling on a motion.

B.   MOTION FOR JUDGMENT AS A MATTER OF LAW (JML)

A party may bring a motion for a judgment as a matter of law during a jury trial at the close of the opponent's evidence, at the close of all the evidence, or on both occasions. Or a party may bring a motion after the jury has returned a verdict. These motions request the judge to review the evidence in a light most favorable to the nonmoving party and rule that the evidence is insufficient to sustain a verdict for the opponent.

In federal courts and in some state courts, these motions are known as motions for judgment as a matter of law (JML), whenever they are brought. In most state courts, a motion brought during the trial or at the end of all the evidence is known as a motion for a directed verdict; and a motion brought after the jury has returned a verdict is known as a motion for judgment notwithstanding the verdict (judgment n.o.v. or j.n.o.v. from the Latin "non obstante verdicto"). In all courts, the grounds for these motions, however named, are the same as described above.

C.   MOTION DURING TRIAL

The basis for determining whether a motion for judgment as a matter of law or directed verdict motion should be granted is whether any reasonable person could find on behalf of the respective party. There is no reason for the jury to decide a case if no reasonable juror could so find. That party should lose, and the judge can and should make that decision.

If a motion brought by the defendant after the plaintiff has rested is granted, the defendant need not introduce any evidence and judgment is granted for the defendant. If the motion brought by either party after both sides have rested is granted, there is no need for closing argument or jury deliberations, and a judgment is entered for the prevailing party.

Judges are not inclined to grant pre-verdict motions but prefer to allow cases to go to the jury and then perhaps grant post-trial motions to remedy any problem. Judges will grant a motion in part and dismiss some claims in a multiple count lawsuit if the evidence supports some but not all the causes of actions.

D. MOTION AFTER THE JURY VERDICT

The same reasonable person standard for determining whether to grant or deny a JML or j.n.o.v. motion is identical to the standard explained in the previous Section 12.5(C). The judge must find that, as a matter of law, the only reasonable conclusion that could be reached from the evidence is that the moving party is entitled to judgment and the jury's determination of the evidence was unreasonable.

There usually is some reasonable evidence to support the verdict and judges cannot merely substitute their judgment for that of the jury, and these motions are seldom granted. If the JML or j.n.o.v. is overturned on appeal, the jury's verdict is reinstated and becomes the final verdict.

In many jurisdictions a motion for a verdict before the jury deliberates must be made before a judge will consider a post-verdict motion after the jury has returned the verdict. In other jurisdictions, either or both motions can be timely made.

E. MOTIONS IN BENCH AND CRIMINAL TRIALS

In civil bench trials, a motion to amend findings, conclusions, and the order is brought, not a verdict motion, because there is no verdict. In criminal cases, the defense brings a motion for judgment of acquittal to challenge the verdict. A prosecutor cannot bring such a motion because the government cannot challenge the insufficiency of the evidence, and a judge cannot reverse a verdict rendered in favor of the defendant.

F. MOTION FOR NEW TRIAL

A party may seek a second trial if some serious error or misconduct regarding the law, facts, rules or procedure occurred during the first trial. Ordinarily a losing party brings a new trial motion, but a prevailing party might also seek a new trial on all or some of the issues if the verdict did not provide the winning party with complete or sufficient relief. Parties are entitled to a fair trial, but not a perfect one or even a very good one. Before a verdict will be overturned and a new trial granted, the party must have been denied a fair trial.

A new trial motion may raise questions of law and fact. See Fed.R.Civ.Proc. 59 and Fed.R.Crim.Proc. 33. The exact grounds vary from jurisdiction to jurisdiction, but, generally, a new trial may be granted if:

- A party was deprived of a fair trial because of significant procedural irregularities caused by the judge, jury, or prevailing party.

- The jury, judge, or prevailing party committed misconduct.

- The trial result was prejudiced by a surprise situation that could not have been anticipated or prevented by using ordinary care.

- Material evidence has been newly discovered which, with reasonable diligence, could not have been found and produced at the trial.

- Excessive or insufficient damages were awarded by the jury based on passion or prejudice.

- Errors of law occurred at the trial, including wrong evidentiary rulings and incorrect jury instructions that resulted in an unfair verdict.

- The verdict is not justified by the evidence or is contrary to the law.

- A verdict is otherwise fatally defective.

Commonly, a motion for a new trial is brought at the same time as a motion for JML or j.n.o.v. or a motion to amend. In some jurisdictions, when a motion for a new trial is not made to the trial court, the appellate court will only review the case to determine if the evidence and law support the verdict. Other issues, including errors of law and fact, may not be reviewed unless the attorney has made a motion for a new trial. A party may also bring a new trial motion before a judge in a bench trial based upon some of the above applicable grounds.

G. RULINGS ON POST-TRIAL MOTIONS

A losing party may bring a motion for a judgment as a matter of law and a motion for a new trial. In ruling on these motions, the trial court has four options:

- The court may grant the JML and also the new trial,

- The court may grant the JML and deny the new trial,

- The court may deny the JML and grant the new trial, or

- The court may deny both motions.

The alternative motions present separate and distinct questions to the trial court as described in the preceding sections. The most common ruling is the fourth option listed; the others are not often granted.

H. MOTIONS TO REDUCE OR INCREASE JURY AWARD

In some civil cases, the losing party or unhappy prevailing party may not want a new trial on the merits but may want a different dollar award. A losing party may seek a reduction in the award by bringing a motion for a new trial requesting a remittitur. This motion requests that the court determine the verdict amount is unreasonable or is based on errors and that the court conditionally grant a new trial, unless the opposing party accepts a reduced judgment.

For example, if a jury returns a $1,000,000 verdict in favor of the plaintiff, defense counsel may request the court to order a remittitur to $400,000 or grant a new trial. If the court grants this motion, the plaintiff, faced with this remittitur, must either accept the reduced $400,000 judgment or proceed with a new trial.

Some state courts, but not the federal courts, permit a post-trial motion to increase the dollar award of a jury verdict for an unhappy prevailing party. This procedure, known as additur, has the opposite effect of a remittitur. The verdict winner requests that the court order an additur or grant a new trial. For example, a plaintiff who received a verdict of $250,000 may have a court upon request by the plaintiff order an additur of $100,000. Faced with this additur, defense counsel must either accept the increased judgment of $350,000 or proceed with a new trial.

I.   MOTION TO AMEND COURT FINDINGS AND CONCLUSIONS

In a bench trial and in some administrative hearings, a party may move to amend the findings of fact, conclusions of law or order a judge has entered. The motion must explain which findings are not supported by the evidence, which conclusions are not supported by the law, and why the order is improper. The motion should also suggest revised findings and conclusions. Some jurisdictions require this motion be made to preserve issues for appeal. Section 3.11(E) explained the procedure for submitting proposed findings, conclusions, and orders to the judge. Motions to amend ask for a change of mind and heart, which is a very unlikely event. A judge is not likely to do so unless the advocate accurately shows the record does not support a factual finding or the law is clearly contrary to the conclusion reached and the order entered.

J. MOTION TO MODIFY AN ARBITRATION AWARD

In arbitration, a party may bring a motion to reopen an award under very limited circumstances. These alternative situations include:

- The award is not final.

- The award is ambiguous or contains evident material mistakes.

- A party was not served with the proper documents.

- A party was denied a fair opportunity to present evidence.

- The arbitrator did not decide a submitted issue.

K. TIMING

When a post-trial or post-hearing motion must be made depends upon rules of the court or arbitration or administrative agency that vary among jurisdictions. The time available for these motions is ordinarily limited to no more than 10 or 30 days after a verdict or after a party has been notified of the filing of the decision. See, e.g., Fed.R.Civ.Proc. 59; Fed.R.Crim.Proc. 29, 33, 34, & 45. These time limits are usually strictly enforced. If an untimely motion is made, the motion will not be considered. The reason for such short, strict time limits is that these motions need to be considered while the events are fresh and recent and because there is a need to timely close cases.

L. SUPPORTIVE MEMORANDUM

The submission of a supportive memorandum explaining the factual and legal grounds for the motion may be required and, if done well, will increase the chances of obtaining a favorable ruling. In some cases, supportive affidavits will be necessary to establish the grounds for a motion. See Section 3.8(A)(2).

§ 12.6 ENFORCEMENT OF JUDGMENT

A. STAY OF ENTRY OF JUDGMENT

A losing party ordinarily needs to obtain an order from the judge staying entry of the order or judgment or the enforcement of a judgment, award, or decision until the post-trial or post-hearing motions have been decided and an appeal taken. Judges commonly grant stays to preserve the status quo until they rule on the post-trial or post-hearing motions or an appeal is taken. See Fed.R.Civ.Proc. 62 and Fed.R.Crim.Proc. 34. Without a stay, an entered judgment can be immediately enforced.

After a verdict has been reached by the jury or a decision made by the judge, the losing party should bring a motion to stay entry of the judgment or decision based on the verdict or order. A stay will prevent the winning party from obtaining and enforcing a judgment. If the judge denies a motion for stay of entry of judgment or judgment has already been entered, the losing party should bring a motion to stay enforcement of the judgment. If that motion fails, the losing party may be able to bring these motions before an appellate court.

B. ENFORCING CIVIL JUDICIAL DECISIONS

The winning party will seek voluntary compliance with the judgment by the losing party after it has been entered, unless a stay has been granted, or the judgment has been upheld on appeal. Otherwise, the winning party may seek to enforce the judgment. See Section 12.8(A).

C. ENFORCING ADMINISTRATIVE DECISIONS

The nature of the administrative decision and the law determine how it is to be enforced. Some administrative decisions are self-enforcing, others may be enforced by the administrative agency, and others may be enforced by a court in the same way a judicial order is enforced.

D. ENFORCING ARBITRATION AWARDS

An arbitration award may be enforced by having it confirmed into a judgment. If the losing party refuses to abide by the award, the prevailing party can bring a motion or petition in court to confirm the award into a civil judgment and enforce the judgment. See Section 12.8(D).

§ 12.7 COSTS, INTEREST, AND ATTORNEY'S FEES

A. COSTS AND EXPENSES

A prevailing party in a civil case or arbitration is entitled to receive reimbursement for the costs incurred during the case unless the court orders otherwise. Recoverable expenses typically include witness fees, reasonable expert witness fees, service fees, filing fees, expenses for depositions used during the trial, the cost of transcripts used during the case, and related expenses. An arbitrator can include costs in an award. Administrative judges and arbitrators can assess costs allowed by law.

Courts commonly have forms available from the clerk or administrator that the prevailing attorney may complete to obtain reimbursement for costs. The clerk will automatically add (tax) these costs to the judgment unless the losing party, within a limited period of time, challenges the costs, or the clerk believes the costs are not recoverable. A party may request a hearing before the trial judge to determine whether the expenses are recoverable.

B. INTEREST

A victorious party is usually able to recover interest in a case. There are two major forms of interest: prejudgment or prehearing interest and post-judgment or post-hearing interest.

Prejudgment/prehearing interest usually covers the period of time between the date the cause of action arises and the entry of order, award or judgment. This period of time covers the trial or hearing procedures and may cover several years.

Jurisdictions commonly also permit interest to be earned during subsequent periods of time. Post-verdict or post-order interest covers the time period between the rendering of a verdict by a jury or the decision made by a judge and the date judgment is entered. This period of time covers the post-trial motion proceedings and may cover a few weeks or a few months. Post-judgment/post-hearing interest covers a period of time from the date of entry of judgment, order or award until it is paid. This time period covers the appellate process and may cover a year or more.

Prejudgment/prehearing interest is recoverable if a contract between the parties provides for interest or if the law allows such interest. The general rule in most jurisdictions is that prejudgment/prehearing interest is recoverable for liquidated damages (i.e., contract cases) and not for unliquidated damages (i.e., tort cases). Many jurisdictions have enacted statutes that modify this general rule and permit interest to be recovered in many different types of cases.

Some statutes establish the amount of this interest by setting a fixed percentage of four percent, eight percent, or more. Other statutes, which are more common, call for courts to adopt a floating method of calculating interest, based upon treasury bills or some other financial instrument. Attorneys may contact an administrator or clerk or review the court's website or applicable statutes to determine the rate of interest.

Post-judgment/post-hearing interest is available for all federal court money judgments and is usually also available for state court judgments, arbitration awards, and some administrative monetary orders. The amount of the interest is usually set by statute or rule similar to the way the percentage is set in prejudgment/prehearing situations.

C. ATTORNEY'S FEES

The prevailing party is usually not entitled to recover attorney's fees. This rule, known as the American rule, prevents the winning party from recovering attorney's fees unless a statute, contractual agreement, or judicially created exception permits the recovery of attorney's fees.

There are many situations when attorney's fees are recoverable. Cases involving consumer law issues, securities law matters, antitrust problems, and civil rights violations may permit the recovery of attorney's fees based upon specific federal and state statutes. Civil cases involving contractual agreements may include contract terms that permit the prevailing party to collect attorney's fees from the losing party. Judicially created doctrines that permit the recovery of attorney's fees are few and limited. A prevailing party may be able to recover attorney's fees in cases brought or defended in bad faith by the opposing party or if a party has been declared in contempt of court. Some jurisdictions also permit fee recovery if a common fund exists in case, such as a class action, or if the winning party has won a common benefit for a group of injured persons.

When available, the prevailing party may ask to recover attorney's fees from a judge or arbitrator, who have the power to determine the reasonable amount recoverable and to add that amount to the judgment or award. The party seeking attorney's fees usually must bring a motion requesting an award of the fees. In determining the proper recoverable fee, judges and arbitrators may use a formula which multiplies the number of reasonable, compensable hours worked times the normal hourly billing rate of the attorney or a reasonable attorney (called the "lodestar" formula), or a variation of these methods. This formula may be adjusted upward or downward depending upon several factors including: the complexity of the case, the quality of legal services rendered, the issues litigated, the likelihood of success, the opportunities foregone by counsel, and related factors. Judges and arbitrators have reasonable discretion in establishing the amount of attorney's fee awards.

§ 12.8 CIVIL AND CRIMINAL JUDGMENTS

A. ENTRY OF CIVIL JUDGMENT

A judgment is not effective or enforceable until entered by the clerk or administrator. See, e.g., Fed.R.Civ.Proc. 58. In a jury trial, if a general verdict form is used, the clerk automatically enters the judgment unless the court orders otherwise. If a special verdict form or general verdict form with interrogatories is used, the judge must issue an order entering judgment. In a bench trial, the judge must direct that judgment be entered based upon the order of judgment decided by the court.

Entry of judgment is critical in order to permit the filing of a notice of appeal or to permit a party to execute on the judgment. In many jurisdictions, unless judgment is entered, no appeal may be taken from that judgment. In all jurisdictions, a prevailing party cannot execute on a judgment until the judgment is entered. As previously explained, a losing party who plans to appeal or prevent the opposing party from enforcing a judgment pending appeal must obtain a stay from the trial judge that stops enforcement of the judgment. In some jurisdictions, after an appeal has been filed, this stay must be obtained from the appellate court because the trial judge no longer has jurisdiction over the case.

B. ENTRY OF ADMINISTRATIVE DECISION

An administrative decision becomes final when it is issued by the administrative law judge or when it is filed or entered with an administrative agency. The applicable statute or rule determines how it becomes final and how it is enforceable as a judgment.

C. ENTRY OF ARBITRATION AWARD

An arbitration award becomes final when it is issued by the arbitrator or when it is entered by the administrative organization. An arbitration award can readily be converted into a civil judgment by a court with jurisdiction through a confirmation proceeding.

D. CONFIRMATION OF ARBITRATION AWARD

The prevailing party may bring a motion or petition to confirm the arbitration award in a jurisdiction where the losing party resides, does business, or has property. Federal and state arbitration acts govern the procedures. See Federal Arbitration Act, 9 U.S.C. Section 15. The confirmation process is a simple process with the court reviewing the written documents and entering judgment on the award at a hearing on the request. After the court confirms the award, it becomes a judgment and is enforceable like any civil judgment.

E. SATISFACTION OF CIVIL JUDGMENT

A judgment is satisfied when it is paid by the losing party. A judgment may be satisfied upon partial payment. A winning party may accept partial payment on a judgment to avoid an appeal or to obtain immediate recovery on a judgment that may not be collectible.

F. EXECUTION OF CIVIL JUDGMENT

If the losing party fails or refuses to voluntarily pay a money judgment, the winning party may need to enforce the judgment to collect the money. A variety of remedies and methods to enforce a judgment exist in every jurisdiction by statute and rule. Common remedies include execution, garnishment, liens, attachment, replevin, and other forms of statutory or judicially enforced collection. If a trial results in an injunctive decree, the order may be monitored and the remedy for failure to abide by the decree is for the defendant to be held in contempt.

G. ENTRY OF CRIMINAL JUDGMENT

A verdict of not guilty will be entered as a final judgment. A verdict of guilty does not necessarily mean a judgment of guilty will be entered and reflected on a defendant's record. The method of entry of judgment depends upon local law and practice.

A judge may:

- Stay entry of judgment until the completion of the appeal,
- Enter judgment and stay sentencing until after the appeal,
- Stay entry of a judgment and continue a matter for later dismissal if the defendant complies with probation terms,
- Enter judgment of guilty and stay imposition of a sentence, and place the defendant on probation,
- Enter judgment, impose a sentence, and stay execution of sentence with probation, or
- Enter judgment, impose and execute a sentence.

Sentencing options available are based on statutory sentencing limits, judicial or legislative guidelines, and constitutional provisions.

§ 12.9 APPEALS

A. JUDICIAL APPEALS

Advocates are involved directly or indirectly in appellate practice. All advocates must make certain that a record of appealable issues has been properly preserved. See Section 3.12(A). Many trial and hearing lawyers write the appellate brief and argue the appeal. Other lawyers have another member of their firm who specializes in appellate practice participate in the appeal. Still other lawyers refer the appeal to another law firm. It is the client, of course, who decides which attorney will handle the appeal. The winning party usually stays with the winning lawyer. The losing party, however, may decide that a change in expertise may be what is needed to improve the chances of succeeding on appeal.

Clients also decide, in consultation with their attorneys, whether an appeal should be taken or whether a cross-appeal should be filed if the opposing party appeals. An explanation of the appellate process and the decision of whether to appeal extends beyond the scope of this book. There are several appellate considerations that an advocate must understand, however, and the remainder of this chapter explains these matters.

B. ADMINISTRATIVE APPEALS

Administrative decisions are usually appealable. Some decisions are appealable to another level of the administrative agency and reviewed by an administrator or administrative judge. Other administrative decisions are appealable to a judicial judge.

C. ARBITRATION APPEALS: MODIFYING OR VACATING AN AWARD

Arbitration awards are final and binding and are reviewable by a judge in limited circumstances. A party may seek to modify or vacate an arbitration award on limited grounds. Federal and state arbitration acts specify the reasons supporting a motion to modify or vacate. The reasons are narrower in scope than appellate grounds and include:

- The award was procured or obtained by corruption or fraud.

- The arbitrator exceeded the power provided by the agreement, the rules, and the law.

- The losing party was denied a fair opportunity to present relevant, reliable evidence.

- The arbitrator did not follow the applicable substantive law.

- Manifest injustice under the law has occurred.

These limited grounds protect a party from being denied a fair arbitration proceeding. The judge who considers a motion to vacate or modify is limited to these grounds and cannot second guess the arbitrator or change the award because the judge disagrees with the arbitrator. Nor may a court review and reverse or alter the factual determinations of the arbitrator unless no evidence exists supporting a finding.

There is no direct appeal of an arbitration award to a judicial appellate panel. A losing motion to modify or vacate an award brought before a judge can be appealed to an appellate court. Alternatively, parties may agree in an arbitration agreement to appeal an award to an arbitration panel. A party cannot collaterally attack an award by bringing an action against the adverse party, arbitrator or arbitral organization.

D. WHETHER TO APPEAL

The major factors that influence the decision whether a verdict or order ought to be appealed include the following:

- Type and degree of the error,
- The economic resources of the client, and
- The chances of success on appeal.

1.   Type and Degree of Error

A party is not entitled to a perfect trial but is entitled to a fair trial, as stated previously. Mistakes and errors occur in every trial. Minor or inconsequential mistakes do not support the granting of a motion for a new trial or a reversal on appeal. The errors must be serious and substantial to obtain a new trial and to win on appeal. There are three types of errors most jurisdictions recognize:

a.   Unfair Prejudicial Error

Prejudicial error occurs when the substantial rights of a party have been adversely affected. Any error short of depriving a party of substantial justice is not prejudicial error and is insufficient to overturn the result. An example of prejudicial error is the failure of the trial judge to allow a key witness to testify who has highly relevant and credible testimony. Another example is the refusal of the judge to give a requested jury instruction that explains the law on a pivotal issue in the case.

b.   Harmless Error

An error that the appellate court does not deem to be prejudicial error is harmless error. This type of error is a mistake that occurred at the trial level but did not deprive a party of a substantial right. This error is not sufficiently harmful to warrant a new trial. Incorrect rulings by the trial judge regarding the use of leading questions on direct examination would be an example of harmless error. Another example is the refusal by the judge to allow exhibits to be seen by the jury during deliberations.

c.   Plain Error

The "plain error" doctrine allows an appellate court to review an error even though the error was not properly preserved on the record. This type of error must severely prejudice a party and deny the losing party a fundamental right. An example of plain error is a prosecutor commenting in summation on the refusal of the defendant to testify, and the error is not objected to by the defense or corrected by the judge.

2.   Economic Resources

A client who has expended substantial resources for the trial may decide it is not economically worthwhile to take an appeal. A losing party may be able to negotiate the payment of an amount less than the judgment by agreeing not to appeal. The winning party may accept less than the judgment to avoid the risks of an appeal.

3.   Chances of Success

The chances of success depend upon the nature of the issues to be appealed and the prior decisions of the appellate court. There may be little precedent to support reversal. Statistics from each appellate court reveal that certain types of appeals have a greater chance of being successful. For example, issues of law may be reversed a substantial percentage of the time by some courts of appeal or less often in other jurisdictions. Trial lawyers need to consider specific precedents in the appellate jurisdiction and the prior decisions of the appellate judges.

E.   FINALITY OF JUDGMENT AND ORDER

The general rule is that a case is not appealable until a final judgment has been entered. This requirement prevents piecemeal appeals from rulings the trial judge makes as the trial progress. Exceptions authorizing intermediate appeals are explained in the following sections.

The entry of a final judgment permits an appeal to be taken from the judgment and from any order entered by the judge during the trial prior to the entry of judgment. The final judgment incorporates all previous orders, rendering all pretrial and trial rulings by the judge appealable. Rulings on post-trial motions may precede or follow the entry of final judgment, depending upon whether the judge delays entering judgment until after ruling on the post-trial motions. The normal appeal procedure is to appeal from the entry of final judgment and the orders denying the post-trial motions. The appeal from the judgment makes appealable all pretrial and trial rulings. The appeal from the post-trial order preserves all errors raised in the post-trial motions.

F.   INTERMEDIATE APPEALS

Pretrial and trial orders entered by a judge are generally not appealable during the trial. They are appealable as of right after a final judgment has been entered. Some pretrial orders and a rare trial order may be appealable prior to the final judgment if one of the exceptions permitting an intermediate appeal is met. These exceptions are:

1.   An Order That Determines Some of the Claims

An appeal may be taken from a judgment entered in a multiple party or multiple claim case if the judge declares there is no reason to delay entry of judgment on fewer than all of the parties or claims and enters a judgment. Federal Civil Procedure Rule 54(b) and similar state rules codify this procedure and recognize that a judge may make a final decision in a complex case that ought to be appealed before completion.

2. Immediate Appeal Designated by Federal or State Statute

Other orders immediately appealable vary among jurisdictions but generally include interlocutory orders involving preliminary injunctive remedies. These statutes recognize that in order for the status quo to be preserved, an order may need to be immediately appealable.

3. Collateral Order Doctrine

Many jurisdictions permit a limited number of collateral orders to be appealable. Collateral orders are final determinations of claims collateral to and severable from the main claims in the lawsuit, but which are too important to be denied review and too independent of the case to require that appellate review be deferred until the entire case is adjudicated. The scope of these appealable orders varies among jurisdictions. In federal courts, appealable interlocutory orders include rulings granting or denying significant motions in limine and orders denying joinder of claims for essential parties. In state courts, appealable orders may include privilege disclosure orders and procedural orders affecting substantive matters.

4. Writs of Mandamus or Prohibition

All jurisdictions permit a losing party to request the appellate court to order a trial judge to do something (mandamus) or to restrain a judge from doing something (prohibition). These writs are available in extraordinary situations where substantial rights of the parties are being adversely affected, or substantial injustice occurs, or if the judge makes a bizarre ruling. For example, these writs may be available to review a motion granting or denying a change of venue or pretrial rulings excluding or denying evidence or establishing trial procedures.

5. Petitions for Discretionary Review

Some jurisdictions, by court rule or statute, permit a party to bring a petition for discretionary review requesting the appellate court to immediately review an order of the trial judge. The rules in each of these jurisdictions describe the scope of appealable orders, which typically include orders appealable under the collateral order doctrine.

6. Intermediate Appeals in Criminal Cases

A defendant's constitutional right to a speedy trial and the procedural rules of a jurisdiction determine whether an intermediate appeal is available. The government or the defendant may appeal pretrial rulings if the they have a substantially prejudicial effect on the case.

G. STANDARD OF REVIEW

The standard of review is the standard employed by the appellate court in determining whether to affirm or reverse the decision of the trial court. The party losing on an issue carries the burden of establishing that the applicable standard, justifying a reversal, has been met. Most jurisdictions apply three standards of review depending upon the type of error that judge has purportedly made:

1.   If the issue is a legal issue and involves an error of law, the appellate court will review the conclusion of the trial judge "de novo." Under this standard, the appellate court substitutes its judgment for the trial judge and determines the law.

2.   If the issue is a factual issue and involves a factual error, the appellate court will review the finding of the trial judge to determine if the factual finding is "clearly erroneous," that is, if it is against the manifest weight of the evidence.

3.   If the issue is a mixed question of law and fact, and involves a discretionary decision, the appellate court will reverse the trial judge only if the trial court "abused its discretion," that is, if there was no reasonable basis to support the judge's decision.

§ 12.10   APPEAL PROCEDURES

A. INITIATING THE APPEAL

An appeal is usually initiated by filing a "notice of appeal" in the trial court and with the appellate court within a prescribed period of time, for example, 30 days in a civil appeal or 10 days in a criminal appeal. Many appellate courts also require the submission of a statement of the appeal or a docketing statement or the completion of an information form. These documents provide the appellate court with information about the judgment and orders appealed from and the issues raised in the case.

B. APPEAL BONDS

In civil appeals, the appellant may need to post a cost bond or a supersedeas bond, or both, with the notice of appeal. A cost bond ensures payment to the appellee if the appellee prevails on appeal and ordinarily covers the costs of printing and submitting the briefs. An appellant typically has to file a cost bond, or provide other security, to ensure payment of these costs incurred by the appellee on appeal. The specific amount of this cost bond is established by statute or rule or by motion brought by the prevailing party before the trial judge.

An appellant may also have to file a supersedeas bond, or provide other security, to ensure that the judgment, enforcement of which is suspended during appeal, will be paid or enforced if the appellant loses the appeal. A supersedeas bond makes whole the prevailing party if the appeal is unsuccessful. See Fed.R.Civ.Proc. 62 and Fed.R.App.Proc. 7 & 8. The amount of the bond is often equal to the amount of the money judgment and is fixed by the trial court in determining the risk to the prevailing party during the appeal process. The supersedeas bond is usually secured by one or more sureties that submit to the jurisdiction of the court and will pay the judgment amount if the appellant loses and fails to pay.

Some jurisdictions do not require cost or supersedeas bonds unless the prevailing party brings a motion for these bonds. The parties to the appeal may stipulate to alternative methods of security instead of the posting of a bond. An appellee may not be concerned with either bond if the appellant has substantial financial assets or will remain solvent during the pendency of the appeal.

C. STAYS

The filing of an appeal notice does not stay enforcement of a judgment or order. If the appellant has not obtained a stay of execution from the trial court, the appellant will need to obtain a stay from the appellate court during the pendency of the appeal. See Section 12.6(A).

D. RECORD

The appellant usually must order the record for the appeal from the court reporter. The record typically consists of the pleadings, rulings, and orders appealed from, relevant portions of the trial transcript, and trial exhibits. The appellee may also designate other parts of the record to be included in the record for appeal. The mechanics of gathering and transmitting the record to the appellate court varies among jurisdictions, and usually requires a cooperative effort among the appealing parties, the trial court clerk, and the appellate court clerk.

The appellant also must make arrangements with the trial court reporter to transcribe those portions of the trial record needed for appellate review. Not all of the trial transcripts need be included in the appellate record. Only those portions of the transcript that contain the issues raised on appeal are included in the appellate record. The appellant ordinarily provides a list of the designated portions of the record that need to be transcribed, and the appellee may designate other portions of the transcript that need to be transcribed. The appellant must make satisfactory financial arrangements with the reporter for this work.

E. BRIEFING AND ARGUMENT SCHEDULE

After the completion of these procedural steps, the appellate court provides the attorneys with a briefing schedule indicating the deadlines for submission of the briefs and oral argument. And, with that, the advocates and parties are on their way to an intermediate appellate or a supreme court. And that is a grand adventure beyond this book.

INDEX

References are to Sections